The Elizabethan Journals

VOLUME I

G. B. HARRISON was born in 1894 and educated at the University of Cambridge. He was for many years on the faculty of the University of London, whence (after a period in Canada) he came to the University of Michigan in 1949. He has written many books on Shakespeare and the Elizabethan period, of which the most important are the five volumes of *Elizabethan* and *Jacobean Journals, Elizabethan Plays and Players, Shakespeare at Work,* and *The Life and Death of Robert Devereux, Earl of Essex.* He has also edited *Shakespeare: the Complete Works.* In 1962 he set forth his notions on the teaching of English literature in *Profession of English.* In 1964 he edited *The Bible for Students of Literature and Art* (Anchor A394).

THE
Elizabethan Journals

VOLUME I

*Being a Record of Those Things
Most Talked of During the Years*
1591 – 1597

By G. B. Harrison

EDITED AND ABRIDGED
BY THE AUTHOR

Anchor Books
Doubleday & Company, Inc.
Garden City, New York

1965

Foreword to the Anchor Edition

The Elizabethan Journals were first conceived in the summer of 1921. I was then preparing the texts for the series known as the Bodley Head Quartos which included Nashe's *Pierce Penniless* and Kemp's *Nine Days' Wonder*—the record of Will Kemp's famous dance from London to Norwich which caused universal excitement and was talked of for years. It so happened that about this time another famous clown— Charles Chaplin—was visiting England where he was most royally received. His triumphal progress was top news in every newspaper (except, of course, the London *Times*). Neither Chaplin nor Kemp was of interest to professional historians, yet each had a far larger place in the hearts of his countrymen and was more talked about than the august personages who are usually regarded as of historic importance.

A reading of *Pierce Penniless* also stressed another truth: that to understand what an author is saying, his reader must know what was being talked about when the book was first written. On every page Nashe was commenting in his own fruity style on events and persons who were familiar to his readers but had passed beyond the understanding even of his most learned editor. If only there had been a record of gossip for the years when Shakespeare's plays were first performed, we should become sensitive to so many nuances and new meanings, for we should read them as contemporaries. For later periods such records existed. The diary of Mr. Pepys, for instance, is a marvellous companion for the first decade of the Restoration; for the last years of Elizabeth I and the first of James I there was nothing comparable. Accounts of life in Shakespeare's England are useful for the social historian and often illuminate details in this or that play, but something more intimate was needed.

Thus was conceived the idea of compiling a chronicle of gossip, of those things, serious and frivolous, which excite the common man and are summed up in the words of Democritus Junior:

> I hear new news every day, and those ordinary rumours of war, plagues, fires, inundations, thefts, murders, massacres, meteors, comets, spectrums, prodigies, apparitions, of towns taken, cities besieged in *France, Germany, Turkey, Persia, Poland,* &c. daily musters and preparations, and such like, which these tempestuous times afford, battles fought, so many men slain, monomachies, shipwrecks, piracies, and sea-fights, peace, leagues, stratagems, and fresh alarms. A vast confusion of vows, wishes, actions, edicts, petitions, lawsuits, pleas, laws, proclamations, complaints, grievances, are daily brought to our ears. New books every day, pamphlets, currantoes, stories, whole catalogues of volumes of all sorts, new paradoxes, opinions, schisms, heresies, controversies in philosophy, religion, &c. Now come tidings of weddings, maskings, mummeries, entertainments, jubilees, embassies, tilts and tournaments, trophies, triumphs, revels, sports, plays: then again, as in a new shifted scene, treasons, cheating tricks, robberies, enormous villanies in all kinds, funerals, burials, deaths of Princes, new discoveries, expeditions; now comical then tragical matters. To-day we hear of new Lords and officers created, to-morrow of some great men deposed, and then again of fresh honours conferred; one is let loose, another imprisoned; one purchaseth, another breaketh; he thrives, his neighbour turns bankrupt; now plenty, then again dearth and famine; one runs, another rides, wrangles, laughs, weeps, &c. Thus I daily hear, and such like, both private and publick news.

Such were to be the topics for my companion to Elizabethan literature, but it was not easy to decide on the form. It should be more coherent than a source book, less personal than a diary. Chronology, as exact as possible, was essential; it should, so far as might be, record the day to day fluctuations of opinion. Further, each entry should be directly based on a contemporary source, faithfully recorded, and without interpretation or comment in the text. These sources, as the list of authorities consulted shows, were considerable.

Moreover it was essential that the work be well planned: too detailed a record would be unending; too brief, as unreadable as an entry in *Who's Who*. I decided therefore to give about thirty thousand words to each year with about three entries to each week. Naturally it did not work out quite so mechanically but the scheme gave some guide for the amount of space that could be given to any one event. Then I began to collect the material.

A work of this kind needed daily access to a great library which was impossible so long as I was a schoolmaster in a small English Public School in the country, but in 1924 I was appointed assistant lecturer ("instructor" in an American college) at King's College in the University of London. Now I could start on the book. Unfortunately the net salary of an assistant lecturer in the University of London was £285 per annum. Though he had time, opportunity, and encouragement for scholarly labours, he had also a family to be fed. Before I could venture on so ambitious an undertaking, I needed a publisher who would print the book and even pay something for the support of its author.

By 1926 I had acquired a literary agent, David Higham, then with Curtis Brown. We talked about the idea and he encouraged me to set down the plan of the book, then called *Elizabethan Gossip,* for submission to a publisher. At that time the publishing trade was optimistically expanding. Young men with more enthusiasm than experience thought to revolutionize the making of books; finely printed books in limited editions were bought up by hopeful collectors; and many new firms appeared overnight and disappeared six months later.

Among these hopeful venturers was the firm of Robert Holden and Company which had as its patron a Yorkshire manufacturer who had made vast profits in the War of 1914–18 and who guaranteed the overdraft with the bank. Robert Holden and Company proposed to buy their way into the publishing world by offering better royalties and advances on royalty than older and more cautious members of the trade.

The scheme for *Elizabethan Gossip* attracted Robert Holden who offered a royalty of 20 per cent and an advance of £300 —equivalent to a year's salary—on delivery of the manuscript. He proposed a lavish volume full of finely reproduced illustrations. When the contract had been signed, I started work with eager enthusiasm and drew up a kind of rule of life. Three days a week I would work at the British Museum or the Public Record Office, three days at home. Each day the allotment was a minimum of one thousand words or seven entries; and on the whole I did keep to this schedule. By the summer of 1927 the Gossip Book was nearly complete and the reward was almost in the bag. I was on my way to deliver the manuscript when David advised me to hold back: a strange misfortune had happened to Robert Holden and Company.

One of the most successful theatrical ventures in London during the 1920s was a revue called *Black-Birds,* presented by a company of coloured performers from America, whose particular star was a most attractive little lady called Florence Mills. By this time Holden's original patron had died, leaving his fortune to a son whose main interests were far from literary. This young man was persuaded to invest his fortune in a rival revue called *Whitebirds,* a lavish vulgarity which lasted less than a week. Robert Holden and Company were thus starved of their resources and perished.

David and I consulted anxiously. Experienced authors seldom start to write a book until it has been commissioned by a publisher; and *Elizabethan Gossip* was rather specialized fare which would not appeal to many publishers. However, I knew that Helen Waddell (newly famous for *The Wandering Scholars*) was literary adviser for Constable, and this book might interest her. Thither the manuscript was despatched and the report soon came back, for (unlike American publishers who will cheerfully sit on a manuscript for six or even twelve months) English publishers are usually quick in their decisions. Constable would publish the book (but not with an advance of £300) if I would rewrite it in a manner they would suggest. My reply was an indignant *No.*

Two days later I encountered Helen Waddell on the steps of the British Museum, and straightway she marched me off to Molly's teashop, in those days a gossip place for Museum workers. For two hours she held forth on the book: the idea was fine but the writing too scholarly—for in its original form the Gossip Book was written deliberately after the manner of a Calendar of State Papers. My book, said Miss Waddell, was a reference book for scholars; it should be a book to give pleasure to readers; and the way to do it was to write it in Elizabethan language as if it were an Elizabethan journal. But, I protested, if I did that, then the scholarly reader would not be able to tell which was direct quotation from the source and which was mine. To which she retorted that scholars could look after themselves, and if one was so dishonest as not to go to the original he deserved to be deceived.

So we agreed that she would spend a day with our family and go over the manuscript, and we could see how it would work out.

When we came to our meeting, I was soon convinced that she was right. The few exact scholars would have little use for such a book anyway but the general reader might enjoy it. Moreover she convinced me that the Journal must be as much a work of art as of scholarship, for often it would be trying to convey moods as well as to state facts; and moods depend on style. And I had the good fortune to come upon a passage in Anatole France's *Life of Joan of Arc* which exactly expressed this attitude:

> I believe that unless it possesses a certain unity of language a book is unreadable, and I want to be read. It is neither affectation of style nor artistic taste that has led me to adhere as far as possible to the tone of the period and to prefer archaic forms of language whenever I thought they would be intelligible, it is because one cannot substitute modern for ancient expressions without altering sentiments and characters.*

Elizabethan Gossip was therefore rewritten as *An Elizabethan Journal, being a record of those things most talked of during the years 1591 to 1594.* Each entry was recorded as it might have been noted down by a contemporary in his journal of events. But it was not intended to be a personal diary; and the criticism made by one reviewer that no one man could have known all this seems to me to be just silly. Actually, I was at some pains to verify the publicity of my news items; and in the later years I have at times noted evidence that some Top Secret matters were being publicly discussed. It is clear that even the private letters which passed between Essex and his enemies at Court were widely known.

The first volume appeared in 1928 and was so well received that Constable ventured on a second, and a third. As the *Journal* progressed, the problems changed. In the early 1590s there were months when it was difficult to find any news at all. As the years went on the records were multiplied fivefold. In the *Salisbury Papers*, for instance, the Calendar for the years 1591–94 occupies 622 pages; over 4000 pages are needed for 1595–1602. Moreover many new sources, rich and intimate, began to appear. So much material remains

* *Life of Joan of Arc,* translated by Winifred Stephens, 1925, vol. i, lxv.

for the last years of Queen Elizabeth's reign that it would be possible to compile a daily newspaper! The problem now was rather one of what to select or to compress.

My original hope was twofold: to recreate a feeling of life as it was in the days of Shakespeare and his contemporaries, and to provide a background which would make more vivid a reading of Elizabethan literature and particularly of Shakespeare's plays. How far these hopes have been realized is a matter for the individual reader; but if he passes direct from a reading of the events of 1596 and 1597 to the two parts of *Henry the Fourth,* or of 1599 and 1600 to *Troilus and Cressida,* or of 1600 and 1601 to *Hamlet* and *Twelfth Night,* he may find that these plays take on some new meanings.

The three original *Journals* came out in 1928, 1931, and 1933; all three were photographically reproduced in one volume in 1938, and again in 1955.

For the present reprint in Anchor Books some changes have been made. The text has been somewhat abridged, a few entries have been omitted or pruned, and the notes are now given at the foot of the page and not at the back of the book. I have also omitted the periodical lists of new plays as these have since been far more elaborately recorded in Alfred Harbage's *Annals of English Drama, 975–1700* (1940, revised 1963).

Ann Arbor, Michigan   G. B. HARRISON
1965

Table of Contents

VOLUME I

"The hand of the Lord was upon me, and carried me out in the Spirit of the Lord, and set me down in the midst of the valley, which was full of bones, and caused me to pass by them round about: and, behold, there were very many in the open valley: and, lo, they were very dry.

"And He said unto me, 'Son of man, can these bones live?'

"And I answered, 'O Lord God, Thou knowest.'"

Abbreviations

The following abbreviations have been used for sources frequently cited. The footnotes to the day entries are numbered consecutively, starting anew with [1] each succeeding month.

APC. *Acts of the Privy Council*. Edited by J. R. Dasent, 1900, etc.

BIRCH'S HISTORICAL VIEW. *An Historical View of the Negotiations between the Courts of England, France and Brussels, 1592–1617*. By Thomas Birch, 1749.

BIRCH'S MEMOIRS. *Memoirs of the Reign of Queen Elizabeth from the year 1581 till her Death . . . from the original papers of his [the Earl of Essex's] intimate friend, Anthony Bacon, Esquire, and other manuscripts never before published*. By Thomas Birch, D.D., 2 vols., 1754.

CAMDEN'S ELIZABETH. *The History of the Most Renowned and Victorious Princess Elizabeth, late Queen of England . . . composed by way of annals*. By William Camden. Translated into English, 1630, etc.

CAREW MSS. *Calendar of the Carew Manuscripts in the Archiepiscopal Library at Lambeth*. Edited by J. S. Bullen and W. Bullen, 1869.

CATH. REC. SOC. Catholic Record Society.

CHAMBERLAIN'S LETTERS. *The Letters of John Chamberlain*. Edited by N. E. McClure, vol. i, 1939.

CORRESPONDENCE OF KING JAMES VI. *Correspondence of King James VI of Scotland with Sir Robert Cecil and others in England during the reign of Queen Elizabeth*. Edited by J. Bruce. Camden Society, 1861.

DE MAISSE. *De Maisse: A Journal of all that was accomplished by Monsieur de Maisse Ambassador in England from King Henri IV to Queen Elizabeth Anno Domini 1597.* Translated and edited by G. B. Harrison and R. A. Jones, 1931.

DEVEREUX. *Lives and Letters of the Devereux, Earls of Essex . . . 1540–1646.* By the Hon. W. B. Devereux, 2 vols., 1853.

D'EWES' JOURNALS. *A Compleat Journal of the Votes, Speeches and Debates both of the House of Lords and House of Commons throughout the whole Reign of Queen Elizabeth.* Collected by . . . Sir Simonds D'Ewes, Baronet. Published by Paul Bowes, of the Middle Temple, Esq., 1693.

EDWARDS' RALEGH. *The Life of Sir Walter Ralegh.* By Edward Edwards, 2 vols., 1868.

ELIZ. STAGE. *The Elizabethan Stage.* By E. K. Chambers, 4 vols., 1923.

FOLEY. *Records of the English Province of the Society of Jesus.* By Henry Foley, S.J., 1877, etc.

FUGGER NEWS-LETTERS (2nd Series). *Fugger News-Letters, being a further selection from the Fugger papers especially referring to Queen Elizabeth.* Edited by Victor von Klarwill. Translated by L. S. R. Byrne, 1926.

GAWDY LETTERS. *Letters of Philip Gawdy.* Edited by I. H. Jeayes, 1906.

HAKLUYT. *The Principal Navigations, Voyages, Traffiques and Discoveries of the English Nation.* By Richard Hakluyt. References to the edition in 8 vols. in The Everyman Library, 1907, etc.

HAWARDE. *Les Reportes del Cases in Camera Stellata, 1593–1609.* By William Hawarde. Edited by W. P. Baildon, 1894.

HENS. DIARY. *Henslowe's Diary,* Vol. i, The Text; vol. ii The Commentary. Edited by W. W. Greg, 1904–7.

LAW. *The Archpriest Controversy.* By T. G. Law, 1896.

m.e. Modern edition.

MSC. Malone Society Collection.

MSR. Malone Society Reprint.

MIDDLESEX SESSIONS ROLLS. *Middlesex County Records.* Vol. i, *Indictments, Coroner's Inquests post mortem, and recognizances from 3 Edward VI. to the end of the reign of Queen Elizabeth.* Edited by John Cordy Jeaffreson, 1886.

MURDIN'S STATE PAPERS. *A Collection of State Papers relating to foreign affairs . . . 1571 to 1596.* By William Murdin, 1759.

NUGAE ANTIQUAE. *Nugae Antiquae: being a miscellaneous collection of original papers . . . by Sir John Harington, etc.* Edited by T. Park, 2 vols., 1804.

PEARSON. *Thomas Cartwright and Elizabethan Puritanism.* By A. F. Scott Pearson, 1925.

PENSHURST PAPERS. *Papers of Lord D'Isle and Dudley at Penshurst Place.* Historical Manuscripts Commission.

PROCLAMATIONS. *A Book containing all such Proclamations as were published during the Reign of the late Queen Elizabeth. Collected together by the industry of Humphrey Dyson, of the City of London, Publique Notary,* 1618. This is an actual collection, not a printed book: references are to the manuscript pagination of the volume in the British Museum (G. 6463).

PURCHAS. *Hakluytus Posthumus, or Purchas his pilgrims,* 1625. References to the edition published by MacLehose and Co., 1905.

RYMER. *Foedera, conventiones, literae, et cuiuscumque generis Acta Publica inter Reges Angliae et alios quosuis . . . ex schedis Thomas Rymer potissimum edidit Robertus Sanderson,* 2nd edition, 1727.

SP DOM. *State Papers Domestic.* Abstracted in the *Calendar of State Papers Domestic.*

SP FOR. *State Papers Foreign.* There is as yet no Calendar or abstract of this collection in the Record Office.

SP IRELAND. *State Papers Ireland* preserved in the Public Record Office. Abstracted in the *Calendar of State*

Papers relating to Ireland in the reign of Queen Elizabeth. Edited by E. G. Atkinson, 1893.

SR. *A Transcript of the Registers of the Company of Stationers of London; 1554–1640 A.D.* Edited by Edward Arber, 5 vols., 1875–94.

STC. *A Short Title Catalogue of Books printed in England, Scotland and Ireland, and of English Books printed abroad.* Compiled by A. W. Pollard and G. R. Redgrave, 1926.

SALISBURY PAPERS. *Historical Manuscripts Commission. Calendar of the Manuscripts of the Marquis of Salisbury preserved at Hatfield House,* 1892.

SECRET CORRESPONDENCE. *The Secret Correspondence of Sir Robert Cecil with James VI, King of Scotland.* Edited by David Dalrymple, 1766.

SIDNEY PAPERS. *Letters and Memorials of State . . . from the originals at Penshurst Place,* etc. By Arthur Collins, 2 vols., 1746.

SIEGE OF ROUEN. *Journal of the Siege of Rouen, 1591. By Sir Thomas Coningsby.* Edited by J. G. Nichols. Camden Miscellany, vol. i, 1847.

SMITH. Ricardi Smith Abendoniensis, *Rerum vulgatorum nota,* a manuscript in the British Museum (*Sloan,* 414, ff. 50–61).

SPEDDING. *The Life and Letters of Francis Bacon.* By James Spedding. 7 vols., 1861 [numbered vols. viii–xiv in the Spedding-Ellis edition of Bacon's *Works*].

STOW'S ANNALS. *Annales or a General Chronicle of England.* By John Stow, 1592, etc. As there are several editions both of Stow and Camden and references are quite easy to find, I have not specified particular editions or pages.

STRYPE'S ANNALS. *Annals of the Reformation . . . during Queen Elizabeth's happy reign.* By John Strype, 4 vols., 1731, and 7 vols., 1824. [The later edition marks the pagination of the earlier; my references are therefore to the earlier.]

TOWNSHEND. *Historical Collections, or, An exact account of the Four Last Parliaments of Queen Elizabeth . . .* Faithfully and laboriously collected by Heywood Townshend, Esq., a Member in those Parliaments, 1680.

Apart from a few details, there is nothing in Townshend which is not more fully reported in D'Ewes, but I have thought it best to give references to both.

UNTON CORRESPONDENCE. *Correspondence of Sir Henry Unton, Knt, Ambassador from Queen Elizabeth to Henry IV., King of France, in the years 1591 and 1592.* Edited by Rev. Joseph Stevenson, Roxburgh Club, 1847.

WILBRAHAM'S JOURNAL. *The Journal of Sir Roger Wilbraham . . .* Edited by H. S. Scott. Camden Miscellany, vol. x, 1902.

The Elizabethan Journals

VOLUME I

(1591–1597)

A Brief Survey of the Year 1590*

In the beginning of spring, the Queen, lest she should be taken unawares by the Spaniard, made levies of men in England and the south part of Ireland, fortifying Duncannon in the mouth of the river and also Milford Haven in Wales; and for the safeguard of the Navy assigning £8970 yearly. She was at great charges against the attempts of the Pope and the Spaniard in Scotland, also in lending money for the Army in Germany; and for the pay of the garrisons in Flushing and Brille she paid every two months 125,000 florins, and to the 3000 horse and foot serving in the Netherlands 260,000 more.

Nevertheless she repaid beyond expectation the money borrowed not long since of her subjects, so that many wondered whence this money came, seeing she was in no man's debt. But the truth was that, being providently frugal, she scarcely spent anything but for the maintenance of her royal honour, the defence of the Kingdom or the relieving of her neighbours; and Burleigh, the Lord Treasurer, looked narrowly into those that had the charge of customs and imports, by whose avarice much was underhand embezzled, and through negligence much not exacted. Not long before this the Queen being informed by one Carmarden of the mysteries of her farmers of Customs had caused Sir Thomas Smith, the customer, as he was called, who farmed the Customs for £14,000 a year, to pay from thenceforth £42,000 and afterwards £50,000.

Abroad the Zealanders were reconciled with the Hollanders. The ships of the Venetians and Florentines taken by the English were restored and strict proclamation made that

* CAMDEN'S ELIZABETH. The Catholic League had been formed by 1589 when, on the death of the Duke of Anjou, Henry of Navarre (a Protestant) became heir to Henry III. Civil war followed between Henry III and the League, whose leaders were the Dukes of Guise and Mayne. Shortly afterwards Henry III was assassinated, leaving his throne to Henry of Navarre. With the aid of Queen Elizabeth (£22,000 in gold and 4000 men) he defeated the Leaguers at Arques and invested Paris, but being unable to draw De Mayne to a pitched battle, he withdrew. The English army having done notable service was disbanded, and a way thereby left open for the Spaniards.

no violence should be offered to the Italians, Venetians, French, Danes, Netherlanders or those of the Hanse Towns. Yet the Spaniards were grievously afflicted, many prizes being taken near the Azores, and the castle in the isle of Fayal razed to the ground by the Earl of Cumberland.

Between the Turks and Moldavia peace was established and the Poles saved from the threat of a difficult war.

In Scotland, to confirm amity with the Scottish King, the Earl of Worcester was sent to congratulate him on his marriage and safe return from Denmark, and to signify to him that he and the French King had been chosen Knights of the Garter, and withal to put him in mind to suppress in time the Popish faction growing strong in Scotland. The King received him very graciously, and to show his amity to England sent Colonel Stewart into Germany that some course might be taken with the King of Denmark and the Ambassadors of the Princes for renewing the peace between England, Spain and France.

In France, the rebellion of the Leaguers aided by the Spaniards held many dangers, and in England there was much deliberation whether the old soldiers in the Low Countries should join with the Germans, or whether a strong army should be sent to the Netherlands to stay the Duke of Parma, who was now proposing to come through France, but especially to keep the coast of France from the Spaniard, who was said to be practising to reduce Newhaven by corruption, and send a fleet into lesser Brittany.

In the midst of these consultations, the Duke of Parma entered France with a strong army, after the French King had won a notable victory at Ivry, overran Picardy, victualled Paris, then miserably famished, won Carboil and Laigny, that victuals might be carried into Paris, and led back his forces. On the other side, in the autumn, other companies of Spaniards arrived at Blavet in Brittany under the conduct of Don John D'Aquila, besieged Henebon, a little town on the sea, and took it with the aid of Philip Emanuel, Duke of Mercure, of the House of Lorraine. Against these Spaniards, Henry Bourbon, Prince de Dombes, who was Governor of Brittany with La Noue, craved aid from England, which the Queen and the Council thought not fit to send on the request of a subject, as the King himself did not then request it. Yet the danger was well understood that the Spaniard might bring under subjection a country so convenient for annoying or invading England, Holland or Zealand.

Some urged that the Queen should spare her money and put no trust in the French, alleging that they had been lately treacherous to their own kings, murdering the one who had been a most devout Catholic, and another, professing the reformed religion, they now pursued with popish curses and arms; that within remembrance of their fathers they had unjustly withdrawn from the German Empire Metz, Toul and Verdun; and that they had so often deceived the English in money matters that those creditors whom they meant to deceive they called by a by-word 'les anglais.' But the Queen rejected these counsels, and when others put her in mind of that saying of Charles of Burgundy, 'that the neighbouring nations would be in happy case when France should be subject not to one sceptre but to twenty petty kings,' she rejected it with much stomach, saying, 'whensoever the last day of the Kingdom of France cometh, it will undoubtedly be the eve of the destruction of England.'

During this year died Ambrose Dudley, Earl of Warwick, and not long after Sir Francis Walsingham, the Queen's secretary.

In Ireland, Hugh Gairlock accused the Earl of Tyrone of secret conference with some Spaniards, shipwrecked in 1588. To prevent this charge the Earl took him and caused him to be strangled, then being summoned to England, upon submission obtained the pardon of the Queen; undertaking most religiously to keep the peace with his neighbours, not to put any man to death but by law, and to reduce Tyrone into more civility. Being sent back to Ireland, he confirmed these things before Sir William FitzWilliams, the Lord Deputy. Shortly before the Lord Deputy had taken Hugh Roe MacMahon, a great lord in the territory of Monaghan, and hanged him for that he had with banners displayed exacted contributions of his people. His lands were divided between the English and certain of the MacMahons, so that the family might be weakened, being strong and powerful through many tenants and adherents, and the tyranny of MacMahon blotted out together with the title.

Whereupon Brian O'Rourke, a great lord in the neighbouring County of Bren, fearing lest the same might happen to him, took arms against the Queen; but being hunted and put to flight by Sir Richard Brougham, Governor of Connaught, fled into Scotland, and was by the Scottish King delivered into the Queen's hands when she required it, he protesting that he accounted all the Queen's enemies as his own.

1st January. THE PRIVY COUNCIL.[1] At the beginning of this
year the Lords and others of the Queen's most Honourable
Privy Council are Dr. John Whitgift, Archbishop of Canterbury; Sir Christopher Hatton, Lord Chancellor of England;
Sir William Cecil, Lord Burleigh, Lord Treasurer of England; Charles Howard, Baron of Effingham, Lord Admiral
of England; Henry Carey, Lord of Hunsdon, Lord Chamberlain; Thomas, Lord Buckhurst, Lord High Butler of England; Sir Francis Knollys, Treasurer of the Queen's Household; Sir Thomas Heneage, Vice Chamberlain to the Queen,
Chancellor of the Duchy Lancaster; Mr. John Wolley, Esquire, Secretary for the Latin Tongue, Chancellor of the most
Honourable Order of the Garter; Mr. John Fortescue, Esquire, Master of the Great Wardrobe, and Under Treasurer
of the Exchequer.

A 'TREATISE OF ECCLESIASTICAL DISCIPLINE.'[2] Dr. Matthew
Sutcliffe dedicateth to the Earl of Bath his *Treatise of Ecclesiastical Discipline,* which is sent to the press, wherein is
confuted article by article the doctrine and practice of those
who attack the Church of England, either preferring the
Presbyterial Government or disliking the disorders of the
Church. Of these, some have consumed their own goods
and devoured the late lands of Abbeys and are now so eager
that they would digest not only tithes but also glebe and
parish churches. Others are moved by violent ambition, that
although they talk much of equality, yet hope to be chosen
presidents of the consistory, willing to hazard all and have
a part in the government, for they disdain to be governed

---

[1] APC 22:3, under date 1st Oct,
where the name of Sir Robert Cecil
(sworn 2nd Aug) is added.
[2] SR 2:587; STC 23471. A good state-
ment of the case of the Church of
England against the Presbyterian
Discipline.

by others. Added thereunto are the stirring minds of men malcontent who however they fare always deem their present condition most burdensome, and so that they may see an innovation and change care not whether church or commonwealth be changed.

13th January. STEPNEY'S 'SPANISH SCHOOLMASTER.'[3] *The Spanish Schoolmaster,* by William Stepney, professor of the Spanish tongue in the city of London, is entered, containing seven dialogues, wherein is plainly shown the true and perfect pronunciation of the Spanish tongue, together with proverbs, sentences, the Lord's Prayer, the Articles of belief, the ten commandments and other necessary things. Giveth many pithy and useful examples, meet for travellers on a great variety of occasions both at home and abroad. Noteth it as a new custom that divers dames in London do break their fast in their beds, and when they have broken it, they will lie down again, and sleep on it.

14th January. THE MURDER OF THE LORD BURKE.[4] Arnold Cosby, better known as Captain Cosby, a professional soldier, well known about the Court, hath stabbed to death the Lord Burke in a field near Wandsworth.

23rd January. WRIGHT'S 'PILGRIMAGE TO PARADISE.'[5] *The Pilgrimage to Paradise,* a book written by Leonard Wright, is entered, compiled for the direction, comfort and resolution of God's poor distressed children, in passing through this irksome wilderness of temptation and trial, and giving consolation to Christians in the warfare of their passage to Paradise.

25th January. COSBY CONDEMNED.[6] Arnold Cosby was this day brought from Newgate and taken over London Bridge to the Sessions on St. Margaret's Hill, where he was immediately put into the docket. He was wearing a yellow frieze doublet over which a loose nightgown had been thrown. A great pair of bolts was put on his feet and his arms were pinioned, though

³ SR 2:573; STC 23256. A racy little book, giving the Spanish equivalent of those intimate inquiries which the provident traveller makes on arriving at his inn; also the necessary dialogue for a brief wooing of the chambermaid.

⁴ STC 5813. See *25th Jan.*
⁵ SR 2:573; STC 26032.
⁶ STC 5813; SR 573. Entered on the day of the trial. This sensational case inspired two ballads and three pamphlets.

his hands were free. Soon after there came to the Court, the Lord Chamberlain, the Earl of Wormwood, Sir George Carey, Knight Marshal of England, and Mr. Popham, the Queen's Attorney General. For the Queen the chief witness was Mr. Powell of Wandsworth, who declared that the Lord Burke's footman coming to him had told him that his master and Cosby had gone out to fight. Thereon he immediately took horse and spurred as fast as he could until he came to a place where the Lord Burke lay wounded and on point of death. There he found a woman giving such help as she could; she had laid her frieze safeguard over him and was trying to stop the bleeding with cloths. The Lord Burke, being asked how he came by his hurts, replied, 'Cosby hath villainously wounded me to death, I striking never a blow, nor giving thrust, but whilst I was striving to unbuckle one of my spurs, having unbuckled the other before through his persuasions, saying they would be some trouble, he most cowardly thrust me in at the top of the shoulder which ran far into the body; yet if I had striven but two blows with him, it would never have grieved me, had he manfully slain me in fight.' Then procuring a cart, Mr. Powell took the Lord Burke to his own house, where he died about two hours after, twenty-one wounds being found on his body.

In his defence, Cosby declared that the cause of the quarrel was that the Lord Burke the night before pulled his nose. When they met in the field, having the Lord Burke at his mercy, he offered him his life if he would break the point of his sword, return to the Court and acknowledge that he had wronged him, fought with him, and been spared by him.

While the jury were away, the Lord Chamberlain spoke to those present, showing how manifestly God had wrought in this case. When Cosby tried to escape on the Lord Burke's gelding, it broke from him; even his own nag could scarcely be forced to take him to the wood at Wimbledon. Finally, when he passed behind the house where the body lay, the wounds began to bleed afresh. The jury, after a short deliberation, gave in a verdict of guilty, and Cosby is condemned to be hanged.

27th January. COSBY HANGED.[7] Arnold Cosby was hanged at Wandsworth for the murder of the Lord Burke near to the place where his crime was committed.

7 STC 5813.

30th January. SIR EDMUND YORKE SENT TO THE FRENCH KING.[8] Sir Edmund Yorke is to be sent to the French King to treat for the sending of English forces to Brittany. He is instructed when he shall have audience with the King to say her Majesty thinks it strange that in the four months since the Spaniards have invaded Brittany, she has not received any knowledge from him of what he means to do for the repelling of these forces, nor that he has sent any aid to the Prince de Dombes, who is unable with his present power to encounter the enemy though at this time reduced to 1800 men. But it appears from sundry sources that the King of Spain makes ready a greater number of ships, men and victuals to possess himself of all Brittany; whereof her Majesty is very mindful, first for the loss of so rich a dominion as Brittany, and by consequence of the evil neighbourhood of so mighty a Prince possessing so great enmity towards her.

Whilst she was in this doubtful state, there came a gentleman from the Prince de Dombes moving the French ambassador to be a means to her to help him with 2000 footmen to be sent into Brittany, whose charge should be answered by the King. To this she had answered the ambassador that it was a strange thing for her to be required of a subject to send forces into the King's country and more strange would it be for her to send them without the King's knowledge, or even request. Nevertheless having now heard that the succours coming in to the King are but few, and that the enemy prosper in possessing all the ports, saving Brest, where they have their galliasses and ships, and intend to fortify the mouths of the ports, the Queen hath told the French ambassador that she is content, if the King so wishes it, to prepare some 2000 or 3000 men or more to be sent into Brittany. For the ambassador's better information certain articles were delivered to him to be sent to the King, but no answer has been received. Sir Edmund Yorke is now to procure answer to every point in these articles and especially to procure for our shipping and people the use of the haven of Brest, the commodity of the roads for the ships, and the town and lodgings for the men; without this assurance neither ship nor men can be in any safety.

1st February. DRAYTON'S 'HARMONY OF THE CHURCH.'[1] The Harmony of the Church, containing The Spiritual Songs and

Holy Hymns of Godly Men, patriarchs and prophecy; meet to be read or sung, for the solace and comfort of the godly, written by Michael Drayton, (a gentleman of the household of Sir Henry Goodere), is entered, being dedicated to the Lady Jane Devereux of Merivale. In this book are gathered nineteen songs and prayers from the Old Testament and Apocrypha rendered in English verse.

3rd February. FLESH PROHIBITED DURING LENT.[2] As in years past the killing and eating of flesh during the season of Lent is restrained. Six butchers only may be licensed to kill flesh for the City and liberties, to be bound by bonds of £200 to sell no flesh in Lent but to such sick persons as should show a special warrant from the Lord Mayor. Moreover they shall truly keep books of their daily sales and the names of those to whom they sell, with the quantities and the times. The Lord Mayor will also cause to appear before him or his deputy before Lent all innkeepers, table keepers, victuallers, ale house keepers, and taverners and to take bonds of every one of them in good sums of money, not under £100 a piece to her Majesty, not to dress any flesh in their houses this Lent time for any respect except for some person lying in their house that had licence through sickness or any other necessary cause.

A PROCLAMATION AGAINST PIRACY.[3] A proclamation is published to inhibit the offending on the seas of any persons in their ships or goods being subjects of any Prince, Potentate or State in amity with her Majesty. Certain complaints of late are made against some of the Queen's subjects, who have been this last summer under colour of recovering recompense on the Spaniard for the notable injuries by arrests and barbarous cruelties practised in Spain and Portugal, and have taken the ships and goods of the subjects of other princes and states. Lately one ship belonging to the Venetians and another claimed to belong to subjects of the Grand Duke of Tuscany were taken into some of the western ports but are certainly in safety.

Whosoever hereafter shall break any bulk of the goods of any prize (though the prize be lawful) before the title thereto is allowed in the Court of the Admiralty shall be imprisoned, and his ship with the prize forfeited. Likewise any person whatsoever that shall knowingly take any ship belonging to any subjects of her friends and allies, and doth not forbear to keep them, or takes out of them any goods, shall be reputed and tried as a pirate, and receive the due punishment for piracy.

9th February. JOB HORTOP'S 'TRAVELS.'[4] A book written by Job Hortop is entered called *The Travels of an Englishman. Containing his sundry calamities endured by the space of twenty and odd years in his absence from his native country; wherein is truly deciphered the sundry shapes of wild beasts, birds, fishes, fowls, roots, plants, etc.*

This Hortop being born at Bourne in Lincolnshire became servant to a gunpowder maker of Redriffe, in whose service he was pressed to serve in Sir John Hawkins' Guinea Voyage in 1567, and appointed to be gunner in the *Jesus of Lubec.* After many sufferings he returned to England in December last. Relateth many strange stories of things seen in his travels. In Guinea two of the company were slain by a sea horse who ate them; this sea horse being a beast in form like a horse in all proportions, saving that his feet are very short, and his teeth very great, long, and crooked like to the tusks of a wild boar. In this place also be many elephants which the negroes take by policy, for in the day time they search out the haunt of the beast which is every night against a great tree. Then they sever the tree almost in sunder, whereby the elephant coming at night, leaneth against it and falleth on his belly, whereby he cannot rise, being of a huge bigness; whereupon he roareth and the negroes come and kill him. The elephant hath a great trunk in his nose wherein he draws the negroes to him and kills them.

In the island of Corasa called the River de Latch, they took a monstrous aligarta; a beast which hath a head like a hog, bodied like a serpent and full of scales on the back, every one as broad as a saucer, his tail long and full of knots, of which one was taken by seven men in the pinnace, using a dog as bait; and as soon as the aligarta had swallowed the dog they rowed hard until it was choked. This beast was four and twenty feet long by the carpenter's rule; and his skin after being flayed was stuffed with straw to have been brought to England, but the ship perished by the way.

The General and the other ships soon after came into the port of San Juan de Ullva through stress of weather, where hostages were exchanged with the Spaniards that no occasion

---

[4] STC 13828. Another version (not in STC) came out in 1591. Both were printed for William Wright, but without his printer's device.

for breach of the league might be given; on our side six of
the gentlemen, on the Spaniards' six arrayed in rich habits
in the apparel of gentlemen but indeed the basest slaves in
their company. But in a few days the Spaniards treacherously
set upon the English ships and sunk four, Sir John Hawkins
scarcely withdrawing with the Admiral, and Hortop himself escaping from the *Jesus of Lubec* to the General's ship.
Hence in great distress through lack of victuals, they sought
the river Pannico for water where the mariners mutinied,
saying that they would rather be on shore to shift for themselves amongst their enemies than starve on ship board, so
that ninety-six wishing to depart were set on shore, amongst
whom was Hortop.

In Mexico they stayed two years until they were sent to
Spain. On their voyage thither, they discovered a monster in
the sea who showed himself three times from the middle upwards, in which part he was proportioned like a man, of the
complexion of a mulatto or tawny Indian. When they came
near the island called the Serres, Hortop and some others
essayed to escape in the pinnace, but being discovered were
like to have been hanged had not one of the Admirals of the
Spanish ships declared that if he were a prisoner he would
have done the like himself. When they came to Spain they
were sent to the Contratation House at Seville. A year after
Hortop and six others tried to escape but they were brought
back, and condemned by the Inquisition. Two were burnt, but
Hortop with one other was sent to the galleys, there to row at
the oars for ten years, and then to be brought again to the Inquisition House, to have the coat with St. Andrew's cross put
on their backs, and from thence to go to the everlasting prison
remediless.

Thereafter Hortop served twelve years at the galleys, being thence returned to Seville where he wore the coat four
years, but at great risk had it taken off for 50 ducats which
Hornanda de Soria, treasurer of the King's mint, lent him;
with whom he served as a drudge for seven years until in
October 1590 he came away in a fly boat laden with Flemish
goods, which was taken by an English ship, and Hortop set on
shore the 2nd day of December 1590.

FRAUNCE'S HEXAMETERS.[5] *The Countess of Pembroke's Ivychurch*, together with *The Countess of Pembroke's Emanuel*,

[5] SR 2:575; STC 11339. For Fraunce,
see DNB. Jonson said to Drummond
'that Abram Francis in his English
hexameters was a fool'; certainly a
persevering enthusiast.

by Abraham Fraunce, one of her gentlemen, is entered; *The Ivychurch* being a translation in English hexameters founded on Tasso's Italian and Mr. Thomas Watson's Latin. In his dedication to the Countess of Pembroke, Mr. Fraunce defendeth himself against those who mislike the reformed kind of verse, saying that as there is no penalty appointed for him that would not read, so if any begin to read, when he beginneth to take no delight, let him leave off and go no further. The first part of the *Ivychurch* is in form of a pastoral dialogue wherein Amyntas lamenting of the hardness of his Phillis is at last comforted by her love; the whole being written in such hexameters as these:

Once on a time when Nymphs and Pastors chanc'd to be
    sporting,
Standing all in a round, and each one whispered a secret,
Into another's ear, poor fool I began to be buzzing,
'Phillis, I burn with love. O take compassion on me;
Help, or I die, Phillis.' But Phillis straight with a lowring
Look and frowning face, and downcast eyes to the ground-
    ward,
Blush'd for spite and shame, and gave not a word for an
    answer,
But conveyed her away, and flew from the place in a fury.

Phillis having died after their betrothal, Amyntas laments her in twelve days of Eclogues.

In the *Countess of Pembroke's Emanuel* are related the Nativity, Passion, and Resurrection of Christ, together with certain psalms of David, all in rhymed hexameters.

20th February. THE SCOTTISH KING'S POOR ESTATE.[6] From Scotland it is reported that the King is in some peril of surprise by the Earls of Arroll, Moray and Athol which will not be prevented because the King is of such a disposition that he will not believe such matters until they are too evident; nor will he be restrained from the fields or in his pastime, for any respect. Such dangers might be avoided if the King had a guard, but this he is not by any means able to maintain, for his table and the Queen's are almost unserved through want. The Queen and her house are more costly to him than his own, all the servants of great place abuse him, serving one another's turn; and the King, being over

frank and somewhat negligent, endureth this want and shame,
for he hath nothing that he accounteth certain to come into
his purse but what he receiveth from her Majesty.

26th February. HARINGTON'S 'ORLANDO FURIOSO.'[7] The
English translation of *Orlando Furioso* upon which Mr. John
Harington hath been long employed is this day entered for
the press by Richard Field, the printer. It is said that Mr. Harington first translated that story of Giacondo in the 28th
book, in which are told the adventures of Jocundo and
Faustus who discovered their wives to be false, and ranged
over Europe to see if anywhere was to be found a faithful
dame. But after their wanderings, having tried many ladies,
and being at length beguiled even in their own bed by their
maid Fiametta, they concluded that fidelity was no part of
woman's nature. The translation of this story being handed
about among the ladies of the Court at length reached the
hands of the Queen, who thereupon sent for her godson
and severely censured him for endangering the manners of
her ladies with so bawdy a tale, laying on him a punishment
to translate the whole of the work before he should again be
allowed to come into the presence.

11th March. PURITAN DISCONTENTS.[1] There is much discontent at this time amongst those that favour the Puritan principles; for the labouring and striving to bring in a uniformity
causes, and seems likely to cause, nothing but desolation.
The best and faithfullest preachers, say they, are cast into
prison, sometimes being closely shut up from the speech and
company of their dearest friends, degraded and deprived of
their livings, some even having six or seven children, who
are sent begging, for all the pillars of the church would do
for them. Cartwright has lain in the Fleet since September;
Fenne of Coventry with many more is in the Clink; Udall, a
profitable preacher of Kingston-on-Thames, lies sentenced to
be hanged for a book called *Demonstration of Discipline;* and
having been condemned before as its author, they now try
to make him acknowledge it as his doing. His life is spared
hitherto by the intercession of Sir Walter Ralegh. All these
things seem but a way to bring in popery, for atheism is here
already, and soon will overflow the land. It is rumoured

[7] SR. 2:576. The editor of *Nugae
Antiquae* received this well-known
story from a Mr. Walker, who had
it from the Earl of Charlemont. It is
clear from prefatory stanzas in Book
28 of the translation that the story
is not without foundation.
[1] BIRCH'S MEMOIRS 1:62.

that a general demand is proposed not only of the ministry but of all who bear public office throughout the land to subscribe that the authority of the bishops is lawful by God's Word. When the Lord Treasurer was asked to subscribe to it, he answered, 'It is lawfully the positive law; but to say it is lawful by the Word of God, that is another matter.' There the matter stayed for the time.

12th March. RUMOURS.[2] The loans that are being levied are to meet the triple charge for the companies in Brittany, the ships at sea, and the army coming from Germany. Men are willing to pay because they see the necessity for helping the King of Navarre, and are angry that the Council did not help him more roundly. The not naming of a Secretary to succeed Sir Francis Walsingham proceedeth from quietness at home, and the Queen's slowness in bestowing places of importance; the great ones about her would each have his friend. The Earl of Essex labours for Mr. Davidson's restitution; the Lord Treasurer for his son, Robert Cecil, and is like to prevail, and the Chancellor concurs, but either there is secret opposition or else the Queen is unwilling. The Lord Treasurer meanwhile executeth the office, as almost all other places of the realm, to the discontent of many. There is a jar between the Lord Treasurer and the Archbishop of Canterbury because the Treasurer said the Spiritual Courts would fall into the *praemunire* for taking oaths of men against law. The Archbishop answered stoutly, as if the other affected patronage of the Puritans. The Treasurer was sick for a few days upon it. The Earl of Essex and Sir Walter Ralegh are still rivals, but Essex is like enough, if he have a few more years, to carry Leicester's credit and sway.

22nd March. TOWN GOSSIP.[3] It is said that the Attorney and Solicitor General are busied with proofs against Sir John Perrot, the same who was Lord Deputy in Ireland in '88, and now a prisoner in the Tower. There is much diversity of opinion about him, according as men incline to the Chancellor or the Lord Treasurer, who was said to be sick when Perrot was committed to the Tower and has not since left his chamber. The Vice-Chamberlain and the Earl of Essex (whose sister is married to Sir Thomas Perrot) favour him; but the

[2] SP DOM *Addenda* 32:7.
[3] SP DOM 238:82. From a newsletter by Thomas Phellippes. Phellippes held a post in the Customs, but was employed by Burleigh as an expert decipherer of captured papers. He used also to send newsletters to spies abroad.

Chancellor has a great dependence, and, if his proofs be as evident as his accusations odious, they will weigh all down. He is said to have dealt with the King of Spain to be received into the Church of Rome, and to have practised with the Northern Lords of Scotland; but all the proofs rest on one priest, and he defamed. Advantages are now being taken from his insolent government in Ireland and his irreverent speeches against the Queen, which now come to light, as is usual when men are called in question, and being better proved, make the rest more probable.

The Earl of Cumberland is expected daily to depart with his fleet, but is detained by the lack of money, as the most part of his preparation is at his own charges. His design is upon the King of Spain's treasure. Some of the Low Country's forces are arrived; the rest to make up 2000 were expected daily with Sir John Norris.

The pique between the Archbishop and Lord Treasurer about Ecclesiastical proceedings is thought likely to cause a great quarrel between them. The Puritans are the weaker party but they hope well of the Earl of Essex, who makes Ralegh join him as an instrument from them to the Queen.

25th March. A 'TREATISE OF HUNTING.'[4] Sir Thomas Cockaine hath written *A Short Treatise of Hunting: compiled for the delight of noblemen and gentlemen*. Sir Tristram, saith he, one of King Arthur's knights, was the first writer of the exact knowledge of hunting, whose terms in hunting, hawking and measures of blowing he holds to be best and fittest to be used. These first principles of Sir Tristram, joined with his long experience of hunting these forty-two years past, have moved him to write more at large concerning the breeding and training of hounds, terriers, and whelps for hunting the fox, the hare, the roe, the stag, the buck and the otter; together with a note of Sir Tristram's rules for blowing the horn in hunting.

31st March. CAPTAIN GLEMHAM'S EXPLOITS.[5] News is come to London of the safety and exploits of Captain Edward Glemham who had been reported lost at sea in a fight with the Spaniards.

[4] STC 5457.
[5] SR 2:579; STC 11921. After refitting in Algiers, Glemham returned to England in 1592, having captured a ship laden with spices on the way.

The cargo on arrival was claimed by Philippo Corsini, representing the Venetian traders, and a lawsuit followed. See *17th May* 1592 and *19th Aug* 1594.

Edward Glemham, Esquire, of Benhall in Suffolk, set sail in August last in the *Edward and Constance* of the burden of 240 tons, and one pinnace, the *Falcon*, which alone at his own cost, he had equipped, furnished, and victualled in such sort and with such plenty as had seldom been known before. From Dover he shaped his course for the Islands of the Suryes and Canaries, leaving his pinnace at Dover for the repairing of some small fault which had appeared, but through the negligence of her master he never saw her again. Contrary winds drove them out of their course for two months, till, at the end of November, he returned to the Islands, having done little good, but being loath to return home without achieving some notable exploit for the honour of his country and the profit of his men, he resolved to land on St. George's Island.

Calling his company together and taking counsel with them he found them willing to follow him. So the long boat and the carvel were hauled up alongside, into which entered eighty-five men, sixty being musketeers, the rest armed with pikes or brown bills. The watch of the island, seeing so large a company draw near, gave warning and the whole force of the island was ready to receive them when they should attempt a landing. But the gunner letting fly on them from the ship from a sacer charged with a chain, slew or dismembered ten or twelve of them, and continued to play upon them so that, after two hours' fight, the Spaniards sounded a retreat and fled with all speed into the high country, leaving our men to land with the loss of but two killed. Thence they marched inland about a mile and made a camp, posting a strong watch for the night.

Day being come, the company divided into two parts, the General leading one, Mr. Edward Florecourt the other, at some distance so that their numbers might appear greater. So with colours displayed and drums and trumpets, they marched with easy pace, yelling terrible cries which might have terrified a great company. When they had proceeded about half a league, the scouts brought word that a mounted man was approaching as if to speak with them; but the General sent forward a guard of musketeers to stay him from coming nearer to view his forces. He was a gentleman sent by the Governor to know what they were and what they required. The General answered that he was a gentleman of England, but would not say what he intended to any private man; but if the Governor himself should come, he promised, by the faith of an English gentleman, that he should pass and repass in safety.

After a time, the Governor with twelve of his gentlemen approached the camp and halted about half a mile from the court of guard, where hostages were sent forward as pledges for his safety. The General having conferred for a while with the Governor declared that if the island should be surrendered to the Queen of England's use, the Spaniards might depart with their possessions; but if not, he would commit all to the hazard of the sword, for what advantage he had won and what spoil he could make he would keep or die for it. To this the Governor flat refused, but said that provided they neither spoiled the King of Spain's subjects nor their goods, he would give them what they wished from the island.

Hearing this the General went apart with his company and conferred with them, whether to accept the offer or to venture on force. They answered that they would ratify whatsoever he decided. But he, seeing the smallness of his own forces in the enemy's country, thought it best not to refuse what the Governor offered. So he returned to the Governor, and demanded victuals of all sorts for his ship and 1000 crowns as recompense for the loss of the two men slain at landing. To these conditions the Governor agreed and departed.

The next day the General feasted the Governor and his company in a brave manner to the honour of his country and his own worthy commendation, and, on the day following, wind and tide being favourable, they set sail and so ranged about the islands seeking their fortune.

The day after they had left St. George's Island two tall ships were discovered which they chased until the following noon when they came up with them, and commanded to strike for the Queen of England. Whereon as they showed the Leaguers' flag and refused to strike, the gunner shot one of them through, being the Admiral, so that she was forced to lie by the lee to stop her leak. Then the Vice-Admiral bare up to rescue her consort, whom the General commanded also to strike, but they answered despitefully they would not, but would sink in the seas ere they would yield or strike. So the company demanded who they were. They answered that they were the *Dolphins,* the *Great Dolphin* and the *Little Dolphin* of St. Malo, stout ships and well appointed, the least of them having two and twenty cast pieces.

Then began a hot fight in which they suffered loss, for some of our men who entered the Admiral saw seven or eight men slain and hauled up in their forecastle. At the third encounter our men grappled with the Admiral so that she was not able to sheer away, and the General with twenty more boarded her; but the Vice-Admiral coming up on the other side entered her men so that ours were forced to retire and break away, having given the enemy great damage but received little hurt themselves. For four hours longer the fight continued until night came on, when the General called his company together, first gave thanks to God for their preservation and then caroused with them, binding them all by their faith to fight it out with the enemy or die for it; but when day dawned, no Frenchmen were to be seen. Their hurts being repaired, they made thence for the Northern Cape but were chased by six Spanish galligoes whom they shook off after a hot fight of three hours.

The General, having thus sustained great hurt and accomplished but small good for himself, being still unwilling to return to England, determined to make for the Straits of Gibraltar, whither they framed their course, but meeting with tempests by the way the main mast, which had been damaged by shot during the last fight, was lost. So they harboured in Algiers to repair the ship. Here they remained for nearly two months waiting for the company of the English Fleet; but then refusing to stay any longer, the General resolved to sail by himself with no other company than the *Flower de Luce,* a ship of Dieppe. But as they came near the mouth of the Straits, they met with four of the King of Spain's gallies which engaged the *Edward and Constance* alone, for the French ship was unwilling to put herself into any danger until the General had fought with all four and sunk one, when she came up and at her approach the rest of the Spaniards withdrew. The rigging was so much damaged by shot in this encounter that the General was forced to put back again to Algiers, leaving the *Flower de Luce* to go on to Dieppe alone.

3rd April. INSTRUCTIONS FOR SIR R. WILLIAMS.[1] On his leaving for Dieppe in command of 600 soldiers for service in Normandy, Sir Roger Williams is instructed to confer with the Governor of Dieppe in what sort his services shall be required, especially in defending the town, but unless some special and manifest cause for some good attempt against the enemy appears he may not hazard the Queen's people out of

[1] RYMER 16:94.

the town. If, however, other forces be joined to those of the Governor's, and opportunity of doing some good service should appear, he may join with him provided that he and his men be not further burdened with any action than the Governor himself should be.

14th April.   A QUARREL IN THE PRESENCE CHAMBER.[2] The Earl of Essex and the Earl of Kildare, who had fallen out in the Presence chamber and used towards each other words very unfit to be uttered in that place and by persons of their quality, are summoned before the Council. Finding that the quarrel arose upon a very small matter the Council consider that the honour of the Queen may be greatly prejudiced by a fray begun so near her person and that great inconvenience would ensue if these noblemen pursue the cause in the heat of revenge. Therefore they enjoin them on their allegiance to keep the peace, binding each in securities of £10,000 not to assault, challenge or provoke the other.

24th April.   TRADING WITH THE FRENCH REBELS FORBIDDEN.[3] A Proclamation by the Queen is published declaring that Henry the Fourth, King of France and Navarre, is justly entitled the King of France, being recommended to the realm by the last king before his death, in presence of all the Princes of the blood and of the rest of the nobility, to be his most lawful successor. It now manifestly appears that this unnatural rebellion is favoured by none of the ancient nobility of France but by a very few of a strange blood, lately brought in and planted by marriages in France, and only branches depending of the House of Lorraine. Her Majesty therefore is moved to yield to the King, her brother and confederate, her favour, both in approbation of his right and wishing to him prosperity against his rebels, as she thinks there is no Monarch nor Sovereign Potentate in Christendom but does the like, save only one, who not contented with all the kingdoms and dominions which his noble father left him, by reason of his abundant riches brought out of the Indies, attempts to augment his estate by encroaching to himself the Dominions of his neighbours.

This rebellion against the French King is fed and maintained in sundry port towns of France and especially in Normandy and Brittany, where the people live by exchange of merchandise and by receiving succours of victuals and munitions of war from foreign countries, without which the rebels in their ports could neither continue their rebellions nor yet relieve their fellow rebels in the land. Her Majesty therefore expressly commands all her natural subjects and all other persons resorting to her realm to forbear to trade with any of the King's rebels, either in France or fraudulently here in England, upon pain of being punished as traitors, and relievers and succourers of the Queen's enemies.

26th April. A PROCLAMATION AGAINST UNAUTHORISED POSTS.[4] A Proclamation is published forbidding any to carry packets or letters to the countries beyond the seas except such as are ordinarily nominated to this service by the Master of Posts or otherwise show good warrant for their voyages and despatches under the hands of one of the principal Secretaries, an Ambassador, or others sufficiently authorised. All in authority, and especially the searchers, customers and controllers of the ports, shall make diligent search of all mails, budgets, and other carriages of such disavowed carriers, messengers and suspected persons coming or going out of the realm with packets of letters; all such discovered to be apprehended and kept in custody until by the view of their writings, sent up to the Privy Council, it is seen and advised what further should be done with them.

29th April. 'THE SHEPHERD'S STAR.'[5] *The Shepherd's Star* being a paraphrase dialoguewise upon the third of the Canticles of Theocritus, in prose, part with songs interspersed, is entered. It is written by Mr. Thomas Bradshaw, lately a gentleman of the company and retinue of the Lord Burgh at Brille.

30th April. FLORIO'S 'SECOND FRUITS.'[6] Signor John Florio, that wrote the *First Fruits,* being an induction to the Italian tongue, thirteen years since, now perfecteth his *Second Fruits* in twelve chapters, both in the Italian tongue and the English. In these witty and familiar discourses many subjects are treated of, such as the set at tennis, games of cards or chess, fencing, the thirty bodily parts of beauty in a woman; ending with a pleasant discourse of love and women. To this book is

[4] PROCLAMATIONS 293.
[5] SR 2:579; STC 3508.
[6] STC 11097. Florio is more interested in wit than utility in his phrases, but the book is a good example of the conversation of bright young men.

added *The Gardine of Recreation,* yielding six thousand Italian proverbs.

2nd May.   LODGE'S 'ROBERT, DUKE OF NORMANDY.'[1] *The famous, true and historical life of Robert, second Duke of Normandy, surnamed for his monstrous birth and behaviour, Robert the Devil,* is sent to the press, being dedicated to Mr. Thomas Smith, and penned by Mr. Thomas Lodge, that last year wrote *Rosalynde, Euphues' Golden Legacy.*

3rd May.   BRETON'S 'BOWER OF DELIGHTS.'[2] A book of Mr. Nicholas Breton's poems called *The Bower of Delights* is to be printed, containing his *Amoris lachrimae,* a discourse of the life, death and funeral of Sir Philip Sidney, with other poems to his memory, and pastorals and sonnets.

A POEM ON SIR P. S.

P   Perfection peerless, Vertue without pride,
H   Honour and Learning, linked with highest Love,
I   Joy of the thought in true discretion tied,
L   Love of the life that highest honours prove.
I   In Angels' arms with heavenly hands embraced,
P   Paradise pleased, and all the world disgraced.

S   Seek all the world, oh seek and never find,
I   In earthly mould, the mount of such a mind:
D   Divinest gifts that God or man bestoweth,
N   No glory such as of such glory groweth.
E   End of the joys that hath all grief begun,
Y   Yet let one weep when all the world is done.

8th May.   CARTWRIGHT THE PURITAN BEFORE THE HIGH COMMISSION.[3] Mr. Thomas Cartwright, formerly master of the Hospital at Warwick, one of the chiefest of the English Presbyterians who has lain in prison since October, was brought before the High Commissioners in Causes Ecclesiastical, the Bishop of London, the Attorney General, and four doctors. As it is now become a custom with the Puritans to refuse to take the oath before examination, the Bishop began in a long speech by demanding that he should take it.

Cartwright opening his mouth to speak, Mr. Attorney took the speech from him and also showed at length how dan-

[1] STC 16657.
[2] SR 2:581; STC 3635.   [3] PEARSON, p. 458.

gerous a thing it is that men should upon the conceits of their own heads and yet under colour of conscience refuse the things that had been received for laws of a long time. This oath that was tendered was according to the laws of the land, which he commended above the laws of all other lands, yet because they were the laws of men, they carried always some stain of imperfection.

After much controversy, Cartwright still resolutely refusing to take the oath, the Bishop commanded an act thereof to be entered. Then Cartwright put the Bishop in mind that he promised him leave to answer the charge which had been given against him; the Bishop replied that he had no leisure to hear his answer, and if he would answer it should be by private letter.

12th May. RIPLEY'S 'COMPOUND OF ALCHEMY.'[4] *The Compound of Alchemy* is entered, showing the ancient hidden art of Alchemy, the perfectest means to make the philosopher's stone, *aurum potabile,* and other excellent experiments. George Ripley, sometime Canon of Bridlington in Yorkshire, first wrote this book, which he dedicated to King Edward IV; but Mr. Ralph Rabbards, student and expert in alchemical arts, now sets it forth for the first time for the press. It is penned in twelve gates or books, each in verse, showing severally the properties of calcination, dissolution, separation, conjunction, putrefaction, congelation, separation, cibation, sublimation, fermentation, exhalation, multiplication, and projection. There is added also an Epistle to King Edward briefly summarising the whole. Wishing by all means possible to profit the Kingdom and State, Mr. Rabbards hath dedicated this work to her Majesty.

15th May. THE 'CENTURION'S' FIGHT WITH FIVE SPANISH SHIPS.[5] There has returned to London the *Centurion,* commanded by Mr. Robert Bradshawe, a very tall ship of burden yet weakly manned, that in November took a cargo to Marseilles. Here the master waited for about five weeks, and being about to sail, some ships of smaller burden entreated him to stay a day or two longer so that for their better safety they might sail in company, vowing together that they would not fly from each other if they should happen to meet with the Spanish galleys, but rather than be taken by the Spaniards to endure their accustomed cruelty, would fight it out to the end.

These small ships sailing along the Straits of Gibraltar upon Easterday, were suddenly becalmed, and immediately five galleys made towards them in very valiant sort, the chief leaders and soldiers bravely apparelled in silk coats, with great plumes of feathers in their hats and silver whistles round their necks. By ten o'clock they came up alongside the *Centurion* and grappled with her, two on either side and the Admiral at the stern which with her shot so sorely galled and battered the *Centurion* that the mainmast was greatly weakened, the sails filled with many holes, and the mizzen and stern almost unserviceable. In each of the galleys were about five or six hundred Spaniards, on the *Centurion* but forty-eight in all, men and boys.

For five and a half hours the fight continued, during which the trumpet of the *Centurion* sounded forth the deadly points of war and encouraged them to fight against their adversaries, but on the Spaniards' galleys there was no music, only the sound of the silver whistles. Many a Spaniard was turned into the sea, as they came crawling in multitudes and hung upon the sides of the ship intending to have entered into the ship. Five times was the *Centurion* fired with wild fire which the Spaniards threw in, yet by the diligent foresight of the master no harm was done at all. Four of her men were slain, one being the master's mate, and ten others hurt by splinters which the Spaniards shot; until, when their shot was almost spent and they were now constrained to shoot at them with hammers and the chains from their staves, by spoiling and overwearying the Spaniards our men at last constrained them to ungrapple themselves and get going.

Whilst the two other small ships had fled away, the *Dolphin* lay aloof and durst not approach near, so that one of the galleys went from the *Centurion* and set upon the *Dolphin*, which immediately caught fire through her powder so that both ships and men perished. The next day six other galleys came and looked at the *Centurion* but durst not approach her.

16th May. INVASION EXPECTED.[6] The Lords-Lieutenant and others, charged with the defence of the places on the coasts, are warned to have all things prepared to resist any attempt that the enemy may make. Forces are to be put in readiness

[6] APC 21:133.

and reviewed, and immediate order taken to watch and guard the beacons as has been done before in time of danger.

21st May. THE QUEEN AT THEOBALD'S.[7] On the 10th May the Queen came to Theobald's to stay with the Lord Treasurer, and there finding him very melancholy she caused to be delivered to him a charter addressed to 'the disconsolate and retired sprite, the eremite of Theobald's,' giving him leave to retire to his old cave, and abjuring desolations and mourning to the frozen seas and deserts of Arabia Petrosa. Amongst the shows there presented was a conference between a gentleman usher and a post, pretending to deliver letters from the Emperor of China. At her departure yesterday she knighted Mr. Robert Cecil, the Treasurer's younger son, whom some expected to be advanced to the Secretaryship; but in the Court it is said that the knighthood must serve for both.

RUMOURS.[8] It is rumoured that Sir John Norris has entered Brittany, taking an island near St. Malo, and has joined with the Prince de Dombes' forces; and that 20 Spanish ships are off Cornwall. The Earl of Cumberland has sailed out from Plymouth to meet them with his ships. 1500 men are to go to Ireland, whither these ships are suspected of going, and 1500 more to be taken from Brittany; Sir Walter Ralegh posts down to Cornwall. The Queen is much moved with this news, and was very melancholy at the Lord Treasurer's. In Scotland witches are discovered that, with the privity of Bothwell, have practised the King's death.

24th May. DR. BABINGTON'S SERMON.[9] Dr. Gervase Babington, Bishop of Llandaff, preached before the Court at Greenwich on II Kings, the 5th chapter; he compared the Lords of Council to the servants of Naaman, advising him for the best though it were to their own hurt. And speaking of the present discontents in religion, 'Woe is me to speak it,' quoth he, 'some of us cry, and too many of us cry instead of this, "No church, no sacraments, no ministers, no discipline at all"; and therefore we must leave all open assemblies in this land, and combine ourselves together to erect a form according to our wills, in woods, in fields, in holes and corners where we can. Yea, with more woe I speak it, some fear

---

[7] Nicoll's *Progresses*, vol. ii; STRYPE'S ANNALS 4:77.

[8] SP Dom 238:159 (Phellippes). See 29th Feb 1592.

[9] STC 1094.

not to write, "Pharaoh of Egypt gave the Israelites leave to worship God truly, but our magistrates, IF they should give us leave, yet could we not be suffered for such and such." Making an IF after these infinite mercies poured upon us by God, in the gracious government we live under, and casting the governors in merit towards us, beneath Pharaoh of Egypt. O sinful IF! O damnable and undutiful IF!'

26th May. SIR R. WILLIAMS COMMENDED.[10] The Council have sent a special letter to Sir Roger Williams, Colonel of the English companies at Dieppe, commending him for the good service performed by him and those who served with him in the late encounter with the forces of the Governor of Rouen.

In the beginning of May provisions being scarce in Rouen, two regiments of the enemy had been despatched to the village of Cingcens, to secure such supplies as they could. This village, which is nine leagues from Dieppe, they fortified with trenches and barricades, and lest they should be molested from Dieppe a troop of horse was sent out to a wood, two leagues off, covering the highway, so that if any force should come out from Dieppe they might either retire back to give intelligence or by making resistance should give those at Cingcens time to prepare themselves and to procure help from Rouen.

When news of this force was brought to the Governor, the Lord Chartres, formerly governor for the King in Malta, and Sir Roger Williams, who had lately arrived, they resolved to set out from Dieppe in the evening of 19th May with 400 Frenchmen and 300 English. After marching all night they came to the wood early the next morning, where they found the troop of horse waiting to stop their passage. On these they made so fierce an assault that all were slain and not one escaped. Accordingly, leaving the bodies in the wood and taking some of their horses, the Lord Chartres and Sir Roger Williams marched on, reaching Cinqsens somewhile before noon; and there they descried the enemy with their ensigns displayed within the fort.

The Lord Chartres, seeing that the fortification was so strong, declared that it was impossible to enter it, and tried to persuade Sir Roger to go back again, considering that the enemy was two to their one. But Sir Roger answered that it were a great dishonour to him to so do, and declared that he would set on them with his own three hundred, though it should cost him and them their lives. The Lord Chartres, being much encouraged with this bold resolution of Sir Roger, protested that he too would take part with his four hundred, whatever should chance. Thereupon he displayed his ensign, and together with Sir Roger, he vowed, with God's assistance, to enter the barricades and charge the enemy. So he spoke to his soldiers, exhorting them to fight for their lawful king whose right they were bound to defend.

Sir Roger likewise encouraged his men, showing them that though they were few and had to fight a great multitude, skilful, stout, hardy and trained in martial discipline, yet their enemy was but a multitude of traitors, opposing themselves to God's ordinance, and therefore condemned of God to a shameful death both here and in the world to come. He assured them that in putting their confidence in God not one of their hairs should fall, and finishing his speech, he prayed to the Lord with great confidence. Having ended his prayer, he made them promise to die every man rather than that they would fly one foot.

Then they marched forward with great courage, displayed their ensigns, struck up their drums and with their trumpets sounded defiance. In this spirit of resolution they assaulted the enemy as freshly as if they had not marched all night. The fight continued for two hours until at length they entered the barricades; Sir Roger himself being one of the foremost fought hand to hand with the chief officers of the enemy; and from the other side, the Lord Chartres also behaved valiantly. At length the enemy began to give back, and being enclosed in their barricades like a flock of sheep in a sheepcote they were all put to the sword, not one man being suffered to escape alive.

Having obtained this victory, on their knees they gave thanks to God, who had subdued their enemies under foot, and praised Him with psalms.

The losses of the Lord Chartres and Sir Roger are eleven men killed and a few slightly wounded. The Generals then immediately took order to return speedily to Dieppe lest some fresh force from Rouen should come upon them, or by casting about should meet them on the way. They gave order also that the soldiers should leave all spoil behind them, except that which could easily be carried. Thus they returned safely to Dieppe. The enemy, as was afterwards learned, did indeed come with a large force to meet them, but they had passed that place four hours before.

31st May. RUMOURS.[11] Six ships are being victualled to be sent to Lord Thomas Howard who has sailed for the islands with charge to do somewhat upon the coast of Spain as he goes. The talk of the slaughter of the men of Rouen by Sir Roger Williams is in everyone's mouth.

1st June. SIDNEY'S 'ASTROPHEL AND STELLA.'[1] Sir Philip Sidney's *Astrophel and Stella* that hitherto is known but in private copies is now printed and set forth before the world with a preface by young Nashe. 'Put out your rush candles,' quoth he, 'you poets and rimers, and bequeath your crazed quatorzains to the chandlers; for lo, here he cometh that hath broken your legs. Apollo hath resigned his ivory harp unto Astrophel, and he, like Mercury, must lull you asleep with his music. Sleep Argus, sleep Ignorance, sleep Impudence, for Mercury hath Io, and only Io Paean belongeth to Astrophel. Dear Astrophel, that in the ashes of thy love livest again like the Phoenix; O might thy body, as thy name, live again likewise here amongst us: but the earth, the mother of mortality, hath snatched thee too soon into her chilled, cold arms and will not let thee by any means be drawn from her deadly embrace; and thy divine soul, carried on an angel's wings to heaven, is installed in Hermes' place, sole prolocutor to the Gods.'

THE FIRST SONNET OF ASTROPHEL

Loving in truth, and fain my love in verse to show,
That the dear *She,* might take some pleasure of my pain:
Pleasure might cause her read, reading might make her know,
Knowledge might pity win, and pity grace obtain.
    I sought fit words to paint the blackest face of woe,
Studying inventions fine, her wits to entertain,
Oft turning others' leaves, to see if thence would flow,
Some fresh and fruitful shower, upon my sunburnt brain.

[11] SP DOM 238:188 (Phellippes).
[1] STC 22534. See *The Works of Thomas Nashe,* ed. R. B. McKerrow, 1905, vol. iii. A second edition of *Astrophel* was issued in 1591 but without Nashe's effusion. *Astrophel and Stella* is the most important volume of poetry of the year. Hereafter for the next five years most of the kept poets litter sonnets in Paul's Churchyard.

But words came halting out, wanting Invention's stay,
Invention, Nature's child, fled Stepdame Study's blows:
And others' feet still seemed but strangers in my way,
Thus great with child to speak, and helpless in my throes,
   Biting my tongue and pen, beating myself for spite:
'Fool,' said my Muse to me, 'look in thy heart and write.'

Tempus adest plausus, aurea pompa venit, so ends the scene
of idiots, and enter Astrophel in pomp.

5th June. THE TAKING OF GUINGCAMP.[2] In Brittany Sir John
Norris hath taken Guingcamp, a town very strongly fortified,
with ditches and walls, and protected on one side with marshes.

The General having found that part of the town which was
fittest for a breach, made a show on the contrary part, causing trenches to be dug at the south side, and passages to be
made through the old houses, even up to the counterscarp
itself. A long trench was likewise made on the east side of the
town, with a platform of earth in the middle as if the cannon
should have been placed there. In the meantime great labour
was used in making a mine near to the intended breach, and
in preparing passages and emplacements for the cannon.
This was performed with such zeal that on the 20th May the
artillery was brought down to the Jacopins' cloister, and there
set up within less than a hundred paces of the wall. In this
action the General exposed himself unceasingly.

On 21st May the battery began, and though it continued
all day, yet by reason of the few pieces of artillery not able
to make sufficient battery, the day's work brought no further
effect than the crushing of two flankers and the beating down
of the parapet so that but a very small breach was made,
which was repaired continually by the soldiers and inhabitants
within the town, who maintained the rampart with feather-
beds, horse dung, and bags of earth almost to the lowest
part of their parapet.

Very early the next day the battery began again, and continued until two or three in the afternoon, by which time the
breach seemed very fair. Whereupon the French urged hotly
to an assault and so importuned the Prince de Dombes that
he consented. Sir John was not in favour of an immediate assault, as he learned from a sergeant, whom he had sent forward to examine the breach, that the approach was very
steep, sliding, and difficult, but especially because his mine

had not yet been pushed far enough forward. Nevertheless, seeing that if the Frenchmen offered to attempt the place themselves, it would be a disgrace to us, he instantly demanded the point and honour of the assault for the English. Such was the emulation of the English captains that to avoid contention the General caused the dice to be cast and it fell to Captain Jackson and Captain Heron to lead the first two hundred to the assault, which, after devout prayers recommending themselves to God, they performed very valiantly, scrambling up the slope, and standing for half an hour at the push of the pike in the face of a whole storm of small shot, but through the steepness of the place the soldiers were unable to get up, and in the end withdrew in as good order as they had assaulted. Captain Heron was killed by a shot in the throat, and about twelve others, Captain Jackson dangerously hurt, and some thirty were wounded.

The second attempt was made by the Baron de Molac, Colonel General of the French infantry in those parts, who attacked bravely with some few of the French gentlemen, the common soldiers advancing to the breach but coldly received greater hurt, and many were slain. Some others then presented themselves for a third assault, but it was considered best to stay until the next day when the battery should have made the breach larger. In these assaults, Captain Dennis, being sent to another part of the town with some forces to make a feint of scaling, advanced too near and received a musket shot in his stomach, whereof he died at midnight.

During the night those within the town demanded a parley, and when this was granted some deputies from the town came next morning to the Prince de Dombes. Terms of capitulation being agreed on, on Whitsunday the town was surrendered and on the 24th May the garrison marched out, being 120 horse, and about 260 foot. Great store of victuals was taken, 2000 weight of powder and some cannon.

The capture of this town of Guingcamp is of great import to the French king, for all lower Brittany depends on it, and the Courts of Parliament ordinarily held at Rennes have by the Leaguers been transferred thither.

6th June.   UNLAWFUL GAMES.[3]   Unlawful games are again to be put down, since the Queen is informed that archery, though an exercise not only of good recreation but also of great use in the defence of the realm, is now greatly decayed; she knows that many at great charge furnish themselves with the muskets and harquebusses now come into use and that it will seem hard to lay on them the burden which the law imposes; yet, with very good reason, she requires those games and pastimes prohibited by law, that is, bowls, dicing, cards and such like, to be forthwith forbidden, and instead archery revived and practised; for by this ancient weapon hath our nation won great honour in times past. Moreover by this means those poor men whose living chiefly depends thereon, as bowyers, fletchers, stringers and arrowhead makers, will be maintained and set to work in their vocations.

25th June. TERMS OF AGREEMENT FOR TROOPS FOR NORMANDY.[4] At Greenwich this day articles of agreement were signed for the despatch of a further force of 3400 to be added to the 600 men under Sir Roger Williams at Dieppe in Normandy; by M. de Beauvoir and M. de Reau for the French King, and by the Lord Treasurer and the Lord Admiral for the Queen. The King to pay all the costs of the levying, furniture, transportation and wages of these soldiers, with a General Captain to govern them, and all accustomed officers; and to discharge this and the charges due for the men in Brittany with Sir John Norris, he grants the Queen all profit of the tolls, customs and taxes to be received from the towns of Rouen and Newhaven, which her Majesty shall begin to receive so soon as either town be restored in its obedience to the King.

There are in Brittany at this time 1675 men; with Sir John Norris 722, and with Sir Henry Norris 540, and Captain Anthony Shirley 413.

1st July. RUMOURS.[1] Sir John Norris was reported to have received a blow and his brother to be slain; but later letters show that there have been several skirmishes but no fight. The Earl of Essex is now to go to France, although the Queen was long unwilling, and his friends in England advised him to the contrary, wishing him rather to seek a domestical greatness like his father-in-law, but the Earl is impatient of the slow process he must needs have during the life and greatness of the Chancellor and the Lord Treasurer.

4 RYMER 16:102, 127. Newhaven was the Elizabethan name for Le Havre.

1 SP DOM 239:70 (Phelippes).

5th July. THE WAR IN BRITTANY.[2] After winning the town of Guingcamp, the purpose of the Prince de Dombes was to have assailed the town of Morlaix and to bring the rest of lower Brittany to the King's obedience; but, learning that the Duke Mercury, commanding the French rebels in those parts, had joined with 4000 Spanish, and was marching towards Morlaix by way of Corlay, he considered that it would be most dangerous to engage his army before the town until he had made himself master of the field, especially as the enemy were of greater strength, and he was in an unfriendly country where there were many peasants, armed and hostile. Accordingly he stayed at Guingcamp to repair the fortifications and the breach made by our artillery, and also to await the coming of two cannon and two culverin.

On 7th June the Duke Mercury arrived at Corlay, within three leagues of Guingcamp, where the castle was treacherously yielded to him, and thence the Duke sent a trumpeter to the Prince de Dombes about some prisoners, who signified that he had in charge to entreat the Prince to appoint some day and place of battle. To this the Prince answered that it was the most acceptable news that could be brought, for it was a thing he had long sought and desired. He refused therefore to send an answer by word of mouth through the trumpeter lest it should afterwards be denied, but wrote a letter, signed with his own hand.

Next day the Duke removed from Corlay to St. Gilles, less than two leagues from Chateau Laudran, whither the Prince de Dombes moved with his army and encamped. There the trumpeter of the Duke met the trumpeter of the Prince and delivered the Duke's answer, signed with his own hand, which was that he would be ready with his army on the Thursday following at ten o'clock in the morning in the fittest place for action between Corlay and Guingcamp; and if the Prince should refuse this offer, he should show the world that his actions were not answerable to his brags.

Whereupon the Prince sent this reply, couched in such terms as to give the Duke all provocation possible to force him to give battle. The cartel was sent by a trumpeter and de-

[2] SR 2:588; STC 13156. *A Journal or brief report of the late service in Britaigne. . . . Published to answer the slanderous bruits raised of late by some evil affected to that and other good actions undertaken against the enemy of God's true Religion.* 1591. The book was entered in the *Stationers' Register* 'by order of the Council under Master Wilks his hand, one of the clerks to the Council.' The 'slanderous bruits' seem to have been caused by a feeling that the English casualties were not justified by the results obtained.

livered to the Duke in the presence of many of the principal men of his army.

The Duke, being greatly moved, openly vowed a solemn oath to offer battle to the Prince within three days. On the 9th June (which was Wednesday) he moved his camp to Quenelac, a village about a league and a half from Chateau Laudran, situated at the foot of a high hill which by deep hedges, ditches, and inclosures, confronted a little heath of two miles' compass. As soon as he heard of the enemy's approach the Prince mounted on horseback to make choice of a place for battle between the enemy and the hill, and found about three-quarters of a league off the village, a large plain or heath, skirted on the side of the enemy with a coppice and a little hill, and the ground crossed by ditches, of great advantage for the enemy, who without any difficulty could enter the heath by three large passages.

The next day the enemy within a quarter of a league of the heath showed his whole army in order of battle on the top of a hill, and the Prince also set his troops within the heath, disposing of them, by the advice of Sir John Norris, into three battalions, of which the English infantry made two, the lance-knights the third. The day was spent in slight skirmishes.

On 11th June the enemy drawing his army to the foot of the hill, placed his artillery upon the side of the heath where it commanded the whole place, and bordered all the hedges with shot. By this time our army was marched into the heath, and immediately 200 infantry were sent out to view the countenance of the enemy. These advanced and charged the enemy, and, driving them back to their main body, cleared the hedges and barricades, and slew several; but on our men withdrawing, the Duke sent out 500 French and 200 Spanish to repossess these places, following them with main body of his army.

When the Prince, who remained in the plain with the advanced guard, perceived this, order was given for 300 infantry, commanded by Captain Anthony Wingfield, Sergeant Major, and Captain Morton, and the English horse under Captain Anthony Shirley, to be sent forward. Meanwhile, under cover of the hedges the enemy despatched a number of musketeers, thinking to lodge them on our left and to take some two or three houses and a small wood on the edge of the heath. Against this the Prince sent 100 men, musketeers and pikemen, and 150 French musketeers, led by the Baron de Molac, and supported by 40 light horse, under Monsieur de Tremblay.

The action was so gallantly performed, especially by our English, that the enemy's horse and foot in the plain were forced to fly, many being slain and the rest driven to save themselves within the artillery, where the whole strength of the Spaniards and the rest of the army was placed. In this charge, M. de Guebrian, Colonel of the foot, was taken by M. de Tremblay; Don Roderigo, chief Marshal of the Spaniards, was killed, together with a Spanish Captain, 200 French and 60 Spanish. The attack so amazed the enemy that our men were allowed within ten paces of the cannon to disarm the dead, and lead away the prisoners, none ever offering to follow. The rest of the day was spent in slight skirmishes and cannonades.

Next day, the enemy made a great show but at last sent out some shot to skirmish, whom Captain Anthony Shirley, with 15 horse and a few foot, speedily put to their heels, pursuing them to their barricades, where his horse was shot. In the skirmish, Mr. Kempe, a gentleman of the cornet, was killed, and Mr. Charles Blunt had his horse killed under him with a cannon shot.

On 13th June, the enemy made some light skirmishes but would not abide a charge either of horse or foot. The day following, being St. John's day with the Spaniards, it was expected that the enemy would give battle, but nothing was done. In the night the Duke prepared to remove, and withdrawing his cannon, the next day he repassed the hill on which he had first appeared, and retired to Quenelac. The Prince, having now waited with his army on the heath from Friday the 11th June to the 15th, in readiness to give battle, also withdrew his artillery and returned his troops to quarters.

16th July.   A CONSPIRACY FOR PRETENDED REFORMATION.[3] There is much disquiet in the City by reason of three fanatical preachers, Hacket, Arthington and Coppinger. About ten o'clock this morning, these men, having met in a house in Broken Wharf, set out, and began to proclaim to passers-by that Christ was come again from heaven. Thence Coppinger led the way by Watling Street and Old Change towards Cheapside, all the time crying out, 'Repent, England, repent.'

Moved by the unwonted sight of these new prophets arisen in London, the people soon crowded about them until by the

[3] STC 5823. A detailed account of the affair. See also STOW'S ANNALS, CAMDEN'S ELIZABETH, APC.

time that the Cross in Cheapside was reached, the throng
was so dense that they could go no further. Whereupon they
got up into a cart from which Coppinger and Arthington
spoke to the people, declaring that Hacket was Christ's representative on earth by partaking of His glorified Body, by
His Spirit, and by the office, which had been conferred upon
him, of separating the good from the bad. They themselves
were two prophets, the one of Mercy, the other of Judgment,
sent and extraordinarily called of God to assist Hacket in his
great work. Then one pronounced mercy, comfort, and joy
unspeakable to those that should repent; the other denounced
terrible judgments on those who refused to hear them.

They declared that Hacket was King of Europe and that
all other kings must obey him. The Queen of England had
forfeited her crown and was worthy to be deprived. Finally
they prayed God, in very unmannerly and saucy terms, to
confound especially the Archbishop of Canterbury and the
Lord Chancellor, cursing them even to the pit of hell.

At first they hoped to repeat this declaration at different
parts of the City, but as the people still increased, they were
forced to go into the Mermaid Tavern in Cheapside. Here
they rested for some time and then returned to the place
whence they had set out, Arthington all the way repeating his
cry of 'Repent, England, repent.'

When rumours of these happenings reached the Queen at
Greenwich, two of the Council, Mr. Wolley and Mr. Fortescue, were sent post haste to the City to find out the truth
and to take action. About one o'clock in the afternoon,
Hacket and Arthington were arrested and taken to the Lord
Mayor's house, where they were examined by the two councillors. Here they refuse to show any signs of respect to those
present, even remaining covered until their hats are plucked
off, though all the time Arthington treateth Hacket with the
utmost reverence, even kneeling before him.

They say that this Hacket, in former time an evil-liver,
who was converted to Presbyterianism, hath wrought himself
into the belief that he is Christ's representative on earth. He
has been the servant of a gentleman at Oundle, where his
loose life and violent temper are notorious. Once his master,
a certain Mr. Hussey, had quarrelled with one Freckington,
an artificer of the town, whose son was the schoolmaster.
Hacket taking up the quarrel and one day meeting with this
schoolmaster at an inn, pretended to be exceedingly sorry that
there should be bitterness between him and his master. The

schoolmaster deluded thus into thinking that he meant friendship, was taken unawares and thrown on the ground, where
Hacket having him now at his mercy, with great savagery,
bit off his nose. Yet though both Freckington and a surgeon
who chanced to be present, begged him to restore the nose
so that it might be stitched on again while the wound was still
green, he not only refused to part with it, but showed it ex-
ultingly to all who cared to look; some even say that he ate
it up.

19*th July*.   RUMOURS.[4] The Queen herself is said to be going
down to Portsmouth with the Earl of Essex, but his friends
mislike the voyage, and wish that he had left it to some other
in respect of the great charge it is to him to put himself forward according to his dignity; but he and his think the cost
well bestowed, conceiving that the coming of the Duke of
Parma maketh worthy the adventure. The Queen allows
him only 100 lances and 50 harquebusiers; but there are 100
more of his own cost, and his friends have sent him bountifully, both horse and money. There are great expectations for
him, and if he should return with honour from his voyage,
he is like to be a great man in the state; both soldiers and
Puritans wholly rely on him.

   Hacket's conspiracy is in everyone's mouths, some liking
him to John of Leyden who took on himself the kingdom of
the Anabaptists, and thinking that Hacket plotted some
such kingdom as these prophets might have assembled; others
take them to be mere fanatics; but the enemies to the Puritans take great advantage against them, as these prophets
have been great followers of their preachers and have solicited
with their books and letters all those that they knew affected
to their sect, especially the Lord Treasurer, the Earl of Essex,
the Countess of Warwick and Mr. Davidson. Meanwhile the
Queen is more troubled with them than it is worth.

24*th July*.   SIR HENRY UNTON MADE AMBASSADOR TO THE
FRENCH KING.[5] Sir Henry Unton is appointed ambassador to
the French King, being furnished with certain instructions
signed by the Queen's own hand. He is commanded in all his
behaviour to preserve the reputation and royal dignity of her
Majesty, and especially by observing the rites of religion and
following the form of Daily Prayer both himself and his

---

[4] SP DOM 239:93 (Phellippes).   [5] UNTON CORRESPONDENCE, p. 1.

household according to the Church of England as established by law. To acquaint himself with the ambassadors of Venice and of the Duke of Florence, and through them to learn of the affairs of Italy, as well as of the Pope and the King of Spain; and if any should come from the King of Scots or the King of Denmark or any other of the Protestant Princes of the Empire, to let them understand how friendly the Queen is to them. With regard to the money which is owing from the French King, not to press for it by any expostulation or to move any unkindness, but to put him in remembrance of the benefits he hath received.

He shall have especial regard to the actions of the Earl of Essex, giving him understanding from time to time what is thought of them, approving to him what are considered to be good, informing of such things as are to the contrary, and giving him good advice to reform them. He is charged on his allegiance not to fear to deal plainly with the Earl.

25th July. PLAYING RESTRAINED.[6] Notwithstanding former orders to restrain the playing of interludes and plays on the Sabbath day, these orders are being neglected to the profanation of this day, and by reciting their plays on all other days of the week, the players cause great hurt to the game of bear baiting and like pastimes maintained for the Queen's pleasure. The Lord Mayor and the Justices of Middlesex and Surrey are required to take order that no plays be shown openly either on Sunday or on Thursday when the games are usually practised.

26th July. THE CONDEMNATION OF WILLIAM HACKET.[7] This day Hacket was brought up from Bridewell to the Sessions house near Newgate for trial before the Commissioners, amongst them the Lord Mayor, Lord Wentworth, Sir Gilbert Garrard, Master of the Rolls, Sir Wolfstone Dixie, Sir Richard Martin, Mr. Sergeant Fleetwood (the Recorder), and Mr. Daniel.

He was arraigned on two indictments. Being asked to plead to the first, he answered, 'All must be as you will'; which was taken as a plea of guilty. To the second, he answered, 'You have wit enough to judge for me and yourselves too.' The question being put to him again, he replied, 'Few words are best; it is good to know much and say little.' It was shown that this answer would of itself condemn him of treason if he

still refused to answer to the point, and being once more asked
if he pleaded guilty or not guilty, he said, 'ambo.' At last
he was persuaded to plead not guilty to the second indictment.
He was next asked by whom he would be tried, but refused
to give answer according to the form of the law, 'By God and
my country.' Instead he replied, 'By the jury.' But realising
that he now stood in very great danger, he began to blaspheme
violently. At last, seeing that Hacket obstinately refused to
plead according to the form of the law, the Attorney General
rose and demanded judgment. As Hacket had pleaded guilty
to one indictment and refused to plead to the second, there
was no need to call witnesses or to enlarge on the case. Nevertheless for the better satisfaction of those present, both the
Attorney General and the Solicitor General spoke at length.
This done, the Recorder sentenced Hacket to death as a
traitor, and he was taken away to Newgate.

28*th July.*   HACKET EXECUTED.[8]   In the morning William
Hacket was brought from Newgate to execution for treason.
All the way as he was dragged on the hurdle, he cried out
continually, 'Jehovah Messias, Jehovah Messias,' and at another time, 'Look, look, how the heavens open wide and the
Son of God cometh down to deliver me.' The crowd was so
vast that it was a long time before the officers could bring
him to the gibbet which had been set up by the Cross in
Cheapside. There, when silence had been called for, Hacket
was exhorted to ask God and the Queen for pardon, and to
fall to his prayers, but he began to rail and curse her Majesty.
Being the more vehemently urged to remember his present
state, he began to pray thus:

'O God of Heaven, mighty Jehovah, Alpha and Omega,
Lord of Lords, King of Kings and God Everlasting, that
knowest me to be the true Jehovah whom Thou has sent, send
some miracle out of a cloud to convert these infidels and deliver me from mine enemies. If not, I will fire the heavens
and tear Thee from Thy throne with my hands.' Then turning
towards the executioner, he said, 'Ah, thou bastard's child,
wilt thou hang William Hacket, thy king?'

The magistrates and people were much angered by these
speeches and called out to the officers to have him despatched;

[8] STC 5823. There was a recognized
etiquette in quartering. Prisoners
who annoyed the crowd or the
authorities were quartered living;
those who behaved in a markedly
courageous and seemly manner (e.g.,
by praying for the Queen or expressing repentance) were allowed
to hang until they were dead or at
least insensible.

so with much ado they got him up the ladder, where he struggled with his head, to and fro, to avoid the noose. Then he cried out very fearfully, 'O what do you, what do you? Have I this for my kingdom bestowed on me? I come to revenge thee, and plague thee——' and so was turned off. But the people, unwilling in their fury that any mercy should be shown him, cried out that he should be cut down at once, being very angry with the officers for not showing more haste. As soon as he was taken down, almost in a trice, his heart was cut out and shown openly to the people.

29th July. COPPINGER DIES IN PRISON.[9] Coppinger, who had been Hacket's companion in the 'Conspiracy for pretended Reformation,' has died in Bridewell prison, having refused all food for more than a week.

Now that Hacket is dead there is much discontented murmuring. Some that seem moderate men, yet favour his opinions in Church government, think that he and his fellows intended good though they mislike the manner of the action. Others, extenuating the fault, believe that they were stark mad, and knew not what they said or did. Some even are heard to mutter that matters were made out to be worse and of greater peril and consequence than they were in fact, and that they were persecuted with greater sharpness than the offence deserved.

2nd August. SIR ROBERT CECIL A PRIVY COUNCILLOR.[1] Sir Robert Cecil, second son to the Lord Burleigh, Lord High Treasurer of England, was this day sworn of her Majesty's Privy Council.

3rd August. A SUSPECTED PORTUGUESE.[2] Mr. Mills, Signor Botello and Dr. Lopez, the Portuguese physician, are instructed to go to Rye to examine certain prisoners lately sent over from Dieppe. First, Emanuel Andrada, a gentleman of Don Antonio, who previously offered to do the Queen some secret service but is suspected of designs against her. He is to be dealt with civilly at first, and then threatened with fear of his life to induce him to declare the truth; his papers are to be examined through Dr. Lopez. The second, John

[9] STC 5823. For the connection of Hacket and his companions with the Puritan leaders, see PEARSON.

[1] APC 21:358.
[2] SP DOM 224:123. See also 23 *Jan* 1594.

Semple, a Scot, to be examined about rebels and fugitives and his connexions in England and Scotland. The other two are Portuguese.

7th August. AN ASSAULT IN WESTMINSTER.[3] At the special Session of Oyer and Terminer, William Dethick, Garter King of English Arms, was indicted for assaulting Henry Brown in the Church of St. Peter's at Westminster, drawing his dagger and striking him on the head. He pleaded not guilty and was acquitted.

13th August. ANDRADA'S DECLARATIONS.[4] Andrada, the Portuguese prisoner, has declared to Mr. Mills that he is sent by King Philip to treat in his name with the Queen for a false peace, and to take her answer to the Duke of Parma who will write to the Council of Spain, the King replying by way of Italy. This is to while away time that by coming and going he may thoroughly understand what is happening in England. He was ordered by Don Christophoro Moro and Idiaques, the present rulers in Spain, to try by all means to kill Don Antonio, and there should be no lack of money or honour. To sound them he asked what should be done if any were willing to kill the Queen; they replied that King Philip had often been desired to do it, but he hoped before her death to see the ruin of her kingdom, and to have her in his hands, and would not therefore treat of her death.

Andrada further reporteth that in many ports of Spain and Portugal forty galleons are building, stronger than the King ever had. He has contracted with the Genoese at Madrid for forty Flemish ships, armed and victualled for six months, to be prepared at Antwerp and other free cities. From Germany and Biscay are coming this winter quantities of gunpowder, cordage, masts, munitions, and victuals to Brittany, where the King forms a magazine of ships, artillery and so forth; that province will furnish mariners, and then they will assault England. Don Juan, a captain of St. Malo, intends to assault Jersey in September.

[3] MIDDLESEX SESSIONS ROLLS 1:194.
[4] SP DOM 239:135. See *24 Jan 1594*: the Lopez case. Don Antonio was the pretender to the throne of Portugal. In 1589, to carry the war into the enemy's country, Drake and Norris, joined by the young Earl of Essex, had led an expedition to Portugal; but though the English soldiers showed great valour, the voyage was a disaster. The Portuguese lacked enthusiasm for Don Antonio, and out of 11,500 men, 6000 died, mostly from disease. Since then Don Antonio had remained an unwelcome pensioner in England. See also *9th Mar 1592* and *15th Jan 1594*.

21st August. THE QUEEN ON PROGRESS.[5] On Saturday the 14th the Queen in her progress came from Farnham to Cowdray in Sussex, where she was royally entertained by the Lord Montague.

As the Queen and her train came into sight about eight o'clock in the evening, they were greeted with loud music which ceased suddenly as soon as she came to the bridge. Here a person in armour, standing between two porters carved out of wood, with a club in one hand and a golden key in the other, made a speech, after which he delivered the key to the Queen, who alighted from her horse and embraced the Lady Montague and her daughter, the Lady Dormir.

The next day being Sunday, the Queen rested and was most royally feasted, the portion for breakfast being three oxen and one hundred and forty geese. On Monday, about eight o'clock in the morning, the Queen and her train rode out into the park to a delicate bower which had been prepared for her. Here while the musicians played, a nymph delivered her a cross-bow with which to shoot at the deer, some thirty in number, enclosed in a paddock. The Queen killed some three or four, and the Countess of Kildare one.

The rest of the week was spent in feasting and entertainment, and on Friday the 20th, the Queen moved from Cowdray to Chichester.

22nd August. THE BORDEAUX WINE FLEET STAYED.[6] An open placard is sent by the Council to all officers of the Port of London, the Cinque Ports and other ports on the south and west to stay all vessels about to trade with Bordeaux at the vintage time. It is credibly reported that certain merchants intend to set out in a very disorderly manner, and not in one or more fleets, forgetting that the state is interested in their private loss and that those ships which went unprotected last year have not yet returned.

28th August. MR. THOMAS CAVENDISH'S EXPEDITION.[7] Mr. Thomas Cavendish departed two days since from Plymouth with his fleet of three tall ships and two barks, *The Galleon,* wherein Mr. Cavendish himself sails, being the Admiral, *The Roebuck,* vice-admiral, whereof Mr. Corke is Captain, *The Desire,* with Mr. John Davis as Captain, *The Black Pinnace,* and a bark of Adrian Gilbert, commanded by Mr. Randolph Cotton.

5 STC 7583.   7 HAKLUYT 8:289.
6 APC 21:413.

31st August. RUMOURS.[8] The Queen is said to be at Portsmouth, having been at Chichester, whither she came from Lord Montague's at Cowdray, where she and the whole Court were magnificently entertained. Nothing is heard from Normandy from the Earl of Essex. From Brittany it is reported that there hath been some quarrelling with the French, who laid in wait for the English and slew eight of Sir John Norris's horsemen; whereupon he marched into the Prince de Dombes' camp, and slew a great number of his, and told the Prince that he would not serve under such rash heads. It is also said that 110 Spanish ships are at sea, to waft home the Indian fleet; the Earl of Cumberland and the rest of the venturers are wished home again safe.

3rd September. ILLEGAL BUILDING IN LONDON.[1] The Justices of the Peace for Middlesex are sharply rebuked for allowing the Queen's express commandment to be broken, in that during this vacation when the Queen was on progress divers disobedient persons not only finish those buildings lately begun about the City of London but also begin new. The Council warn them how little the Queen will like this negligence, for not only did the magistrates refrain from removing the tenants of these cottages, according to the order given in the Star Chamber, but allow them still to be inhabited and others to be built.

4th September. THE EARL OF ESSEX IN FRANCE.[2] The news from France is that the Lord General (the Earl of Essex) leaving his army hath been to see the King and is at Pont de l'Arch, some three leagues from Rouen. On their way to the King not above ten people were seen; the villages and houses were utterly abandoned, yet milk, cider, fresh water and bread were set ready to relieve our soldiers almost in every house, which the grooms and footboys brought their masters, for there was no straggling because the enemy followed from hill to hill, but only, as it seemed, to view and discover the size of the company.

At the gates of Noyon the Marshal Biron awaited him to conduct him to the King, who was in a garden attended by the Duc de Longueville, the Count St. Pol and many more. The King received my Lord most kindly, and after a long discourse led him into the castle where he banqueted him.

[8] SP DOM 239:159.   [2] SIEGE OF ROUEN, p. 13 *et seq.*
[1] APC 21:422.

Afterwards, escorted by the Marquis Pisana and many other nobles, the Lord General was conducted out of the town and taken into a village a mile off; but before the troops reached this place the King, accompanied by two or three, overtook them and said to all the train in English, 'You are welcome.' Having brought the Earl to his lodging, he remained half an hour and after was escorted back to his own quarters by the Earl and his company.

Next morning my Lord went to the King and attended a preaching in his house, being afterwards entertained to dinner. In the afternoon, the Earl accompanied only with a dozen gentlemen attended the King to Noyon (which he had recently besieged and taken), to consult with the Marshal Biron who lay there sick of the gout. Here the pitiful tokens of these lamentable wars were very manifest, the country being all spoiled, the bridges broken, all the suburbs of the town burned, orchards and gardens utterly destroyed, churches beaten down, the walls rent and the town within very filthy.

The Lord General came to the Pont de l'Arch on the 30th, where he held a council and determined to send for his army to Arques. He was advertised by letter that in his return from the King he was in great danger of being taken by Villiers, Governor of Rouen, who pursued him at the trot with at least 700 horses.

6th September. THE QUEEN DISCONTENTED.[3] The lack of all news from the ambassador in France breeds much disquietness, for though many rumours were noised abroad there hath been no certainty until the coming of M. de Reauloc, which causeth the Queen to hold much offence both towards the King for not holding to his purpose to besiege Rouen, and the Earl of Essex for departing from his camp so long a journey without her licence. The Queen is therefore much discontented, saying that she wishes with all her heart, that she had never consented to it, though she had lost double the sum of money spent in the expedition.

12th September. MR. WALTER DEVEREUX SLAIN.[4] Mr. Walter Devereux, the only brother of the Earl of Essex, was slain with a small shot in the head four days since. The Lord General being then at a village called Pavilly with his horse and foot marched, in a bravado, to see whether Villiers or

3 UNTON CORRESPONDENCE, p. 59.
4 *Memoirs of Robert Cary,* King's
Classics, 1905, p. 14.

any of his troops in Rouen durst come out and skirmish; and in that skirmish Mr. Devereux was slain.

THE WINE SHIPS TO SAIL IN CONSORT.[5] The Council order all who purpose to trade in wine or salt with Rochelle or Bordeaux to be ready with their ships, furnished with men and munitions, by the 25th of the month, either at the Downs or Dover, where there shall be a company of good ships with which they may pass safely. Those that cannot be ready by this time to forbear their voyage until they can go with a company of at least fourteen or fifteen good ships.

13th September.   ESSEX REBUKED.[6] The Council very sharply rebuke the Earl of Essex, for the Queen greatly dislikes that he left his army without any head except a Sergeant-Major and, not without danger, journeyed to the King, especially since she understands by letters from the French King that this journey was made voluntarily without any request from him. She therefore condemns him of rashness, reminding him that the purpose of his voyage was the recovery of Rouen and Newhaven. Moreover, she has contracted to pay the force but for two months from the time of their arrival, which was the 2nd August. She much misliketh that he came so near the town of Rouen to make a bravado upon the enemy in sight of the town, whereby to his own great loss and as a reward for his unadvisedness he hath lost his only brother.

Accordingly, considering how untowardly this action falls out under his government, the Queen is resolved that he shall return at the end of the two months. Moreover, she is determined to recall the force as well; nevertheless if it appear probable that in one or two months more the King will retake either Rouen or Newhaven, and furnishes good assurance for the payment of the English forces, then is she content for some to stay, but not all.

16th September.   PROCLAMATION AGAINST SUPPLYING THE KING OF SPAIN WITH CORN.[7] 'For as much as it is manifestly seen to all the world how it hath pleased Almighty God of His most singular favour to have taken this Our Realm into his special protection these many years, even from the beginning of Our reign, in the midst of the troubled estate of all other kingdoms next adjoining, with a special preservation

[5] APC 21:442.
[6] UNTON CORRESPONDENCE, p. 72.
[7] PROCLAMATIONS 296. The opening words of the proclamation are a good example of the doctrine of 'God's own Englishmen.'

of Our own person, as next under his Almightiness, supreme Governor of the same, against any malicious and violent attempts:—'

It is commanded that no corn or grain nor any ordnance of brass or iron be carried to any foreign countries without special licence upon pain that the owner and master of the vessel so offending be committed to close prison for a year and further until they have answered fines to the quadruple value of the goods carried.

This proclamation is very necessary because though the King of Spain hath abundance of treasure by his Indian mines yet his own country is greatly wanting in victual, especially of corn and of munitions of war, and of mariners, and other furniture for his navy. He hath attempted to corrupt some of the Queen's subjects and some strangers inhabiting the realm to satisfy his wants either directly by stealth to his own country, or indirectly and colourably first to some other countries next adjacent to his.

21st September.   A SECRET MARRIAGE.[8] The Queen hath for some time been highly displeased with Mr. Thomas Shirley, son of Sir Thomas Shirley, her Majesty's Treasurer for the wars in the Low Countries, for that he secretly married Mistress Frances Vavasour, one of the Ladies in Waiting. When this became known Mr. Shirley was committed to the Marshalsea. She hath now somewhat abated her wrath, but Sir Robert Cecil is to write to Sir Thomas that her pleasure is that he shall make it publicly known that he cannot digest such an act of contempt to her Court, as well as wilful perjury and disobedience to himself, nor do for a son that has so highly offended her who always furthers any honourable marriage or preferment for any of hers, when broken to her without infamy and scandal. Should Sir Thomas come to Court, she will tell him her mind.

24th September.   THE QUEEN VISITS ELVETHAM.[9] On Monday, 20th September, the Queen came to Elvetham to stay with the Earl of Hertford, where great preparations were made for her worthy reception. As the house is small and unable to accommodate so large a company, there were built especially the following: A room of estate for the nobles,

---

[8] SP DOM 240:17. This Thomas Shirley was one of the three famous Shirley brothers, and father of the dramatist. The more notorious Anthony (see Index) was another.
[9] STC 7583.

with a withdrawing place for her Majesty; the outsides all covered with boughs, and clusters of ripe hazel nuts, and inside with arras, the roof with works of ivy leaves, the floor with sweet herbs and green rushes. Near to this were the special offices: the spicery, lardery, chandery, wine-cellar, ewery, and pantry, all of which were tiled. There were also a large hall for the entertainment of knights, ladies and gentlemen of account; a separate place for the Queen's footmen and their friends; a long bower for the Queen's Guard; another for the Officers of the Household; another to entertain all comers, suitors and others; another for the Earl's steward; another for his gentlemen that waited on him.

There were also made a great common buttery; a pitcher house; a large pastery, with five new ovens, some of them fourteen feet deep; a great kitchen, with four ranges and a boiling place; another great kitchen for all comers; a boiling house for the great boiler; a room for the scullery; and another for the cooks' lodgings.

Between the house and the hill, where these buildings were set up, was made in the valley a pond, cut to the perfect figure of a half moon. In this pond were three isles; the first the Ship Isle, a hundred feet long and forty broad, with three trees for masts; the second the Fort, twenty feet square and overgrown with willows; the third the Snail Mount, rising to four circles of green privy hedges, twenty feet high, and forty feet broad at the bottom. In the water were boats prepared for musicians and a pinnace fully furnished.

Everything being in readiness, the Lord Hertford, calling his retinue apart, in a few words put them in mind of the quietness and diligence they must use so that their services might bring her Majesty content and thereby his honour and their credit, with the increase of his love and favour to them. This done, the Earl with his train, amounting to the number of three hundred, most of them with chains of gold about their necks, and in their hats yellow and black feathers, rode out to meet the Queen, who entered the park between five and six in the evening. Proceeding towards the house, a poet met them and saluted them with a Latin oration. This poet was clad in green to signify the joy of his thoughts at her entrance, a laurel wreath on his head to express that Apollo was the patron of his studies, an olive branch in his hand to declare what continual peace and plenty he wished her Majesty, and booted to betoken that he was *vates cothurnatus*, and not a loose and creeping poet. His speech being ended, the poet presented the scroll to the Queen, who graciously received it with her own hands, and all moved on toward the house, being preceded by six maidens who strewed flowers, singing a song. After supper, a consort of six musicians was admitted to the presence and played before the Queen, who was so pleased with their music that she gave a new name to one of their pavans, made by Thomas Morley, formerly organist of St. Paul's.

The next day broke stormy and the rain continued until after dinner so that no devices could be shown in the morning. But the afternoon and evening were fine and the pageant was able to proceed. Immediately after dinner, a large canopy of estate was set up at the head of the pond for the Queen to sit under and view the sports. This canopy, which was held by four of Lord Hertford's chief gentlemen, was of green satin, lined with green taffeta sarcenet, every seam covered with broad silver lace; valanced about and fringed with green silk and silver, more than a hand's-breadth in depth; it was supported with four silver pillars, and decked above with four white plumes spangled with silver. All about the head of the pond was tapestry spread. The Queen came down to the pond about four o'clock and sat under the canopy, when a pageant of Nereus and the Tritons and Sylvanus was enacted in the water.

On Wednesday morning, as the Queen looked out of her casement window about nine in the morning, three musicians, disguised in the ancient country attire, greeted her with a country song of Coridon and Phillida. This song was so acceptable to the Queen that she commanded it to be sung again.

The same day after dinner, about three o'clock, ten of the Lord Hertford's servants, all Somersetshire men, hung up lines in a green court in the form of a tennis court, making a cross line in the middle. In this square they played, five against five, with the hand ball at 'board and cord' to the great liking of her Majesty, who sat watching them for more than an hour and a half.

After supper, the two delights prepared were curious fireworks and a sumptuous banquet. During the time of these fireworks from the pond, two hundred of the Earl's gentlemen served the banquet, all in glass and silver, every one carrying so many dishes that the whole number amounted to a thousand; and there were to light them in their way a hundred torches. The dishes in the banquet were:—The Queen's arms and the arms of all the Nobility in sugar work; men,

women, castles, forts, ordnance, drummers, trumpeters, soldiers of all sorts, lions, unicorns, bears, horses, camels, bulls,
rams, dogs, tigers, elephants, antelopes, dromedaries, apes, and
all other beasts; eagles, falcons, cranes, bustards, heronshaws,
bitterns, pheasants, partridges, quails, larks, sparrows, pigeons,
cocks, owls and all birds; snakes, adders, vipers, frogs, toads,
and all kinds of worms; mermaids, whales, dolphins, congers,
sturgeons, pikes, carps, breams, and all sorts of fishes. All
these were in sugar work, some in standing dishes, some in
flat work. There were also in flat sugar work and marchpanes,
grapes, oysters, mussels, cockles, periwinkles, crabs, lobsters,
as well as apples, pears and plums of all kinds, preserves,
suckets, jellies, leaches, marmalades, pastes, and comfits.

On Thursday the day began with a song by the Fairy Queen,
dancing round a garland with her maids, which so pleased
the Queen that she caused it to be repeated twice over, graciously dismissing the singers with largess. An hour later,
the Queen and her nobles took their departure from Elvetham.
On all sides as they went, the actors in the entertainment
were grouped in melancholy postures, wringing their hands
in dumb show at her going away. Last of all, as the Queen
passed under the park gate, a consort of musicians, hidden
in a bower, played while two sang.

So highly was the Queen pleased with her reception at
Elvetham, that she declared to the Lord Hertford that the
beginning, process and end of his entertainment was so honourable that hereafter he should find reward in her especial
favour.

29th September.   BEACON WATCHES.[10] To those asking that
the watches at the beacons be discontinued, the Council answer that they would be very willing but that they have been
advertised of the arrival of certain galleys of the King of Spain
in the Narrow Seas, and some attempt may be made on the
coast, especially on those parts that lay towards France.
Nevertheless, that the charges may be diminished, the beacons
need only be kept when there are land winds blowing and
at spring tides, and at such times three or four only need be
appointed to each beacon, provided they be vigilant.

30th September.   DR. COSIN'S 'THE CONSPIRACY FOR PRE-
TENDED REFORMATION.'[11] Dr. Richard Cosin hath written an

---

[10] APC 21:470.   [11] STC 5823.

account of the conspiracy and death of William Hacket that was executed on 28th July, called *Conspiracy for Pretended Reformation: Also, an answer to the caluminations of such as affirm they were mad men: and a remembrance of their action with the like, happened heretofore in Germany*. The book is now at the press to be printed by Christopher Barker, the Queen's printer.

2nd October. THE CAPTURE OF GOURNAY.[1] The town of Gournay having been besieged for some days by the troops of the Marshal and the Lord General is now taken. Those within at first refused to yield, defending themselves in hope of relief until the cannon played and two fair breaches were made. When the English were ready to go to the assault, the town was yielded with very hard conditions; the composition being that the governor, captains, leaders, officers and gentlemen of quality should become prisoners, but not *de guerre*, for want of these words being at the King's mercy; the soldiers were to depart with white sticks only in their hands and the burgesses to be used as others of the King's subjects. It was agreed also that any of the Queen's subjects taken therein should be delivered, but only one was found, an Irishman who had run away from Sir Edward Norris.

4th October. THREE OF LYLY'S PLAYS TO BE PRINTED.[2] Three of Mr. John Lyly's plays are to be printed, being *Endimion*, *Galathea*, and *Midas*, that were formerly played before the Court at Greenwich by the Children of Paul's.

10th October. THE BORDEAUX WINE FLEET.[3] Sir John Hawkins, Sir George Barnes, Sir George Bond and William Burrows, Esquire, are to call in two of the Masters of the Trinity House and with them to view the fleet about to set sail for Bordeaux and to set down such orders for their strengthening as they thought necessary. Further to imprest two suitable merchant ships of those lying in the Thames to be furnished in warlike manner at the charges of the merchants who trade for wines.

[1] UNTON CORRESPONDENCE, p. 96. Gournay was captured on 26th Sept.
[2] STC 17050, 17082, 17083. An important publication. Lyly's plays were written for a courtly audience and not acted on the public stages, and might not be expected to appeal to the usual play-going public. The printer realised this and appealed for support—'And if this may pass with thy good liking, I will then go forward to publish the rest.' The printed drama now becomes literature, and not merely the book of words of a stage play.
[3] APC 22:17.

16th October. ESSEX TAKES LEAVE OF HIS ARMY.[4] The gentlemen in the army in Normandy were much distressed on learning that they were to return to England. It was hoped at this time to attempt some enterprise against Rouen, and on the 6th of the month every man was ordered to put himself in readiness to march by two o'clock in the morning. Very early next day, the Lord General with his voluntary gentlemen went to the Marshal Biron's quarters, where he found the Marshal ready and accompanied with many of the nobility.

The Lord General being very glistering with a great plume of feathers in his hat, the Marshal began to say to him merrily, 'What, you young gallant, are you come hither to brave me with your white feathers? I think I have white feathers too'; and with that called for a hat set with a mighty plume, and a horseman's coat of tawny velvet frill of silver lace; and thereupon put on the hat which caused him to look like an old cutting ruffian of Smithfield. This pleasant humour grew out of a confident hope of the good success of some intelligence received from Rouen, which was that one of the Colonels of the Governor of Rouen had promised, on account of some injury he had received from the Governor, to deliver a gate of the town to Monsieur Rollett, Governor of Pont de l'Arch.

An hour before day, Monsieur Rollett with the Lord General came to the rendezvous at Martinville. With him were about 2000 Gascons, harquebusiers on foot, two regiments of Swiss, Hallard Mountmorency with five troops of mounted cuirassiers; and the English under Sir Roger Williams, 2500 men with 140 horses. The troops that before were dull with sickness and discontent now grew into wonderful hope of what the French promised, and after a short breakfast marched towards Rouen three leagues, but here, having reached a wood in sight of the town not half a league off, a messenger came from the Marshal to the Earl of Essex who was with the foremost troop that he should halt because there was treason in the intelligence; which much amated the soldiers.

After resting a while the Marshal came up and directed that they should march to a place called Direntoun, about as near from Rouen as Mile End is to London, which was reached so suddenly that many of the inhabitants were surprised in their homes. There much booty was taken, and in

4 SIEGE OF ROUEN, p. 23.

the morning great store of wine was found under the ground, of which the soldiers took as much as they could carry and let the rest run.

The next day (8th) the Earl of Essex took his horse very early and went to a hill near the town, not far from St. Katherine's Castle, bemoaning his fortune that he was recalled before he was master of the market place; and there on a fair green in sight of the town (where there were 3000 soldiers besides the inhabitants), commanding all the gentlemen to dismount, he told them he was very sorry that no opportunity was offered him to have led them into a place where they might have gained honour; but the fault was not his neither was it theirs, for he had received great good will in all, and thereof was determined to give notes of honour to some. And there he made twenty-four knights.

The Lord General then took his leave of the army and attended with all his gentlemen went to the Marshal's quarters, where he stayed an hour in consultation. Then the Marshal rode with him for a league on his way until they came to a windmill, where they halted for a while. They reached Dieppe about ten o'clock at night, and the Lord General scarcely stayed to eat, but went on board, leaving behind him a great many mourning but hoping for his return. The next day Mr. Robert Carey came from England with good news, but the Earl was gone before him.

18*th October*. THE BORDEAUX WINE FLEET.[5] The Council having received Sir John Hawkins' report on the state and strength of the fleet about to sail for Bordeaux, order the ships to be stayed until further information is received of the disposition of M. Lucon.

20*th October*. THE LOSS OF THE 'REVENGE.'[6] News is received in London of a great fight about the Azores, in which the Queen's ship, the *Revenge,* was lost. This report is confirmed by certain Spanish prisoners who fought in that action.

On 31st August, Lord Thomas Howard, with six of the Queen's ships (the *Defiance,* being the admiral, the *Revenge,* commanded by Sir Richard Grenville, vice-admiral, the *Bonaventure,* commanded by Captain Cross, the *Lion* by George Fenner, the *Foresight* by Mr. Thomas Vavasour, and the

---

[5] APC 22:30.
[6] SR 2:599; STC 20651. Approximate date, but Phellippes writing on 31st Oct says the news is now stale.

Crane by Duffield, these two last being small ships), were riding at anchor near Flores, one of the westerly islands of the Azores, when news was brought of the approach of the Spanish fleet, and the report no sooner made than the enemy was in sight.

The English ships were all in confusion, many of the ships' companies being on shore, everything out of order, and in every ship half of the company sick and unserviceable. From the *Revenge* there were ninety men sick ashore; in the *Bonaventure* not enough left to handle the mainsail, and, had not twenty men been taken out of a bark of Sir George Carey's, which was then burnt, she would never have reached England. In this plight the Spanish fleet, having shrouded its approach by the island, came upon them so swiftly that the English ships had scarcely time to weigh their anchors, some even being forced to slip their cables and set sail.

Sir Richard Grenville, having stayed to recover his sick men from the shore, was the last to weigh, and had by now delayed too long to recover the wind before the enemy was upon him. The master of the ship and others urged him to cut his mainsail and cast about, but Sir Richard refused to turn from the enemy and persuaded his company that he would pass through their two squadrons and force them to give way before him. This he did with the first ships, but the *San Philip,* a great ship of 1500 tons, coming towards him took the wind out of his sails so that the *Revenge* could neither keep way nor feel the helm. The *Revenge* being entangled with the *San Philip,* four other ships boarded her; two on the starboard and two on her larboard.

The fight thus beginning at three o'clock of the afternoon continued very terrible all that evening. But the great *San Philip,* having received the lower tier of the *Revenge,* discharged with crossbar-shot, shifted herself with all diligence from her sides, utterly misliking her first entertainment. The Spanish ships were filled with companies of soldiers, in some two hundred, in some five, in others eight hundred, besides the mariners. In the *Revenge* there were none at all besides the mariners but the servants of the commander and some few voluntary gentlemen only. After many vollies had been interchanged from the great ordnance and small shot the Spaniards essayed to enter the *Revenge* by boarding, hoping to force her by the multitudes of their armed soldiers and musketeers, but were repulsed again and again, and at all times beaten back either into their own ships or into the sea.

In the beginning of the fight, the *George Noble* of London, having received some shot through her by the armados, fell under the lee of the *Revenge* and asked Sir Richard what he would command him; Sir Richard bad him save himself and leave him to his fortune.

After the fight had thus without intermission continued while day lasted and some hours of the night, many of our men were slain and hurt, and one of the great galleons of the armada, and the *Admiral of the Hulks* both sunk and in many other of the Spanish ships great slaughter was made.

The Spanish ships which attempted to board the *Revenge* as they were wounded and beaten off so always others came in their places, and having never less than two mighty galleons by her sides and aboard her. So that ere morning, from three of the clock the day before, there had been fifteen several armados assailed her; and all so ill approved their entertainment that they were by break of day far more willing to hearken to a composition than hastily to make any more assaults or entries. But as day increased, so our men decreased; and as light grew more and more, by so much the more grew our discomforts. For none appeared in sight but enemies, saving one small ship called the *Pilgrim* commanded by Jacob Whiddon, who hovered all night to see the success; but in the morning bearing with the *Revenge,* was hunted like a hare among many ravenous hounds.

All the powder of the *Revenge* to the last barrel was now spent, all her pikes broken, forty of her best men slain, and the most part of the rest hurt. In the beginning of the fight she had but one hundred free from sickness, and fourscore and ten sick, laid in hold upon the ballast; a small troop to man such a ship and a weak garrison to resist so mighty an army. By those hundred all was sustained; the volleys, boardings, and enterings of fifteen ships of war, besides those which beat her at large. On the contrary, the Spanish were always supplied with soldiers brought from every squadron; all manner of arms and powder at will. Unto ours there remained no comfort at all, no hope, no supply either of ships, men or weapons; the masts all beaten overboard, all her tackle cut asunder, her upper work altogether razed, and in effect evened she was with the water, but the very foundation or bottom of the ship nothing being left over either for flight or defence.

Sir Richard finding himself in this distress, and unable any longer to make resistance, having endured in this fifteen hours' fight the assault of fifteen several armados, all by turns aboard him, and by estimation 800 shot of great artillery, besides many assaults and entries; and seeing that he himself and his ship must needs be possessed by the enemy, who were now all cast in a ring about him, for the *Revenge* was not able to move one way or other but as she was moved with the waves and billows of the sea, commanded the master gunner to split and sink the ship that thereby nothing might remain of glory or victory to the Spaniards, and persuaded the company to yield themselves unto God and to the mercy of none else; but as they had like valiant and resolute men repulsed so many enemies, they should not shorten the honour of their nation by prolonging their own lives for a few hours or a few days. The master gunner readily condescended and a divers few others; but the Captain and the Master were of another opinion and besought Sir Richard to have a care of them, alleging that the Spaniard would be as ready to entertain a composition as they were willing to offer the same; and that there being yet divers sufficient and valiant men still living, and whose wounds were not mortal, they might do their country and Prince acceptable service hereafter; and that where Sir Richard had alleged that the Spaniards should never glory to have taken one ship of Her Majesty's, seeing that they had so long and so notably defended themselves, they answered that the ship had six foot of water in hold, three shot under water which were so weakly stopped as with the first working of the sea she must needs sink, and was besides so crushed and bruised as she could never be removed out of place.

The matter being thus in dispute and Sir Richard refusing to hearken to any of those reasons, the master of the *Revenge* (while the Captain won unto him the greater party) was conveyed aboard to the General, Don Alfonso Bassan. Who finding none over hasty to enter the *Revenge* again, doubting lest Sir Richard would have blown them up and himself, and perceiving by the report of the master his dangerous disposition, yielded that all their lives should be saved, the company sent to England, and the better sort to pay such reasonable ransom as their estate would bear, and in the mean season to be free of the galley or imprisonment.

When this answer was returned and safety of life was promised, the common sort being now at the end of their peril, the most drew back from Sir Richard and the master gunner, it being no hard matter to dissuade men from death to life. The master gunner, finding himself and Sir Richard thus prevented and mastered by the great number, would have slain himself with a sword had he not been by force withheld and locked in his cabin. Then the General sent many boats aboard the *Revenge* and divers of our men fearing Sir Richard's disposition, stole away aboard the General and other ships. Sir Richard thus overmatched was sent unto by Don Alfonso Bassan to remove out of the *Revenge,* the ship being marvellous unsavoury, filled with blood and bodies of dead and wounded men, like a slaughter house. Sir Richard answered that he might do what he list, for he esteemed it not, and as he was carried out of the ship, he swooned, and reviving again desired the company to pray for him. The General used Sir Richard with all humanity and left nothing unattempted that tended to his recovery, highly commending his valour and worthiness.

The *Admiral of the Hulks* and the *Ascension of Seville* were both sunk by the side of the *Revenge;* one other recovered the road of St. Michael's and sunk there also; a fourth ran herself on the shore to save her men. Sir Richard died, as it was said, the second or third day aboard the General and was by them greatly bewailed; what became of his body, whether it were buried at sea or on land, is not known.

A few days after the fight was ended and the English prisoners dispersed into the Spanish and Indy ships, there arose so great a storm from the West and Northwest that all the fleet was dispersed, as well as the Indian fleet which were then come unto them as the rest of the Armada that attended their arrival, of which fourteen sail, together with the *Revenge,* were cast away upon the Isle of St. Michael. On the rest of the islands there were lost in this storm fifteen or sixteen more of the ships of war; and of a hundred and odd sail of the Indian fleet, expected this year in Spain, what in this tempest and what before in the Bay of Mexico and about the Bermudas there were seventy and odd consumed and lost with those taken by our ships of London, besides one very rich Indian ship which set herself on fire being boarded by the *Pilgrim,* and five other taken by Master Watts and his ships of London between the Havanna and Cape St. Antonio.

25th October. PRECAUTIONS AGAINST DISORDER AT THE PORTS.[7] News is received that the Lord Thomas Howard's ships have taken prizes from the Indian and Mexican fleet, laden with treasure and things of great value. Sir Thomas

[7] APC 22:37.

Gorges and Mr. Carmarden are to be sent down to take order
that no mariners be permitted to come on shore until the
ships have been visited and the goods inventoried lest the
sailors embezzle or take away short ends and such things as
they may come by.

27th October. DISORDERS AT DARTMOUTH.[8] The mariners
and other loose and dissolute persons have committed foul
outrages and disorderly embezzlements of the goods brought
in to Dartmouth by the two prizes newly arrived. Sir Francis
Drake is required with all speed and circumspection to restrain these contempts and to recover from any party such
parcels or portions as he can find by proof, suspicion or examination; and to this end to use the assistance there of any
gentleman of quality.

28th October. THE TRIAL OF BRIAN O'ROURKE.[9] Brian
O'Rourke was brought to trial and arraigned at Westminster.
As he spoke no English, Mr. John Ly of Rathbride, a gentleman from Ireland, interpreted between him and the Judge.
He was charged on several counts of having sought the deprivation of her Majesty from her royal seat, the destruction
of her person and the overthrow of her realm of Ireland.

Amongst other accusations it is declared that at Dromaher
he caused a picture of a woman to be made, setting to it Her
Majesty's name, and causing it to be tied to a horse's tail
and drawn through the mud in derision; and after he caused
the galliglasses to hew it in pieces with their axes, uttering
divers traitorous and rebellious words against Her Majesty;

That after the Spanish fleet sent by the King of Spain and
Pope Sixtus V. had been dispersed by the English fleet till
they came round Scotland and so into Ireland, O'Rourke
entertained and succoured divers of the Spaniards who had
been employed in the invasion; and that after proclamation
was made by the Lord Deputy that upon pain of death no
man should keep any of the Spaniards but send them to him
by an appointed day, O'Rourke kept the prisoners and afterwards despatched them safe to Spain with a Spanish friar and
an Irish friar;

That he violently entered and burned Ballingaffe and other
villages in Roscommon, and the town of Knockmallen, murdering Her Majesty's subjects, and continuing these outrages
until he was forced by the Queen's forces to fly to Scotland;

[8] APC 22:44.
[9] STOW'S ANNALS. See *A Brief Survey
. . . 1590* and *3rd Nov.*

That at Glasgow he offered the King of Scots that if he would maintain him and suffer his subjects to join him he would bring the realm of Ireland to his subjection.

After many speeches had passed between O'Rourke and his judges, he declared that he would not consent to be tried by the jury unless he might have a week's respite to allow of papers from Ireland being sent to him, and a good man of law to be assigned to him who should swear to deal as truly for him as for the Queen's heir apparent if he were in his place; and besides he would have the Queen herself to be one of the jury. Upon this it was shown through Mr. Ly, that the law was that if he refused to be tried by twelve men he should be judged guilty forthwith and so be guilty of his own death. Yet for all this as he still refused trial he was condemned to death as a traitor. When the sentence was explained to him, he said nothing but if that were their will, let it be so.

31st October. RUMOURS.[10] Now that the loss of the *Revenge* is generally known, some condemn the Lord Thomas Howard for a coward, saying that he is for the King of Spain. The Lord Admiral and Sir Walter Ralegh have quarrelled and offered combat. Seven prizes have recently been brought in by the merchants who went to second Lord Thomas Howard. The war in Normandy and Brittany is greatly liked, and 1000 pioneers are to be sent over to the siege of Rouen and 1000 new soldiers to the Earl of Essex, who has obtained leave to remain there till he has done something to revenge his brother's death; but his making of twenty-four knights is greatly mocked. General musters were assembled on a rumour being received that the traitor Sir William Stanley would attempt an invasion. The Lord Chancellor is very sick with a strangury and not expected to recover. A proclamation against the Jesuits is being printed but is not yet published.

1st November. JENNINGS, A NOTABLE JESUIT, TAKEN.[1] Edmund Jennings, a Jesuit, hath been taken prisoner by Topcliffe at the house of Mr. Swithin Wells in Holborn where he had been saying Mass. Topcliffe came on him while he

[10] SP Dom 240:53 (Phellippes). In 1587, Sir William Stanley, being governor of Deventer, had betrayed it to the Spaniards. They pensioned him with the intention of using his services in the proposed invasion of England.

[1] CATH. REC. SOC. 5:206. Topcliffe was in charge of the counter-recusant spy service; he greatly distinguished himself by his success in rounding up the Jesuits who came over with Campion in 1580, and since then had enjoyed considerable extra-legal power. He was expert in the methods of the 'third degree' and had certain special tortures of his own. See 22nd June 1592.

was still in his vestments, and he, with some ten others who were present, was taken to prison. During the fray Topcliffe was thrown down the stairs by Mr. Brian Lacy's man.

3rd November. THE EARL OF ESSEX IN NORMANDY.[2] On 17th October the Earl of Essex, Lord General, returned to the army from England to the surprise and delight of most: that day he took counsel and resolved to send off to tell both the King and the Marshal of the success of his journey into England. The next morning Sir Roger Williams was sent to the King. News was now brought of the rendering up of Caudebec, by composition that all the men of war should depart to Rouen with a convoy for their security, the drums beating, ensigns flying, matches lighted and the horsemen with pistols in their hands.

On the 21st the Earl held a martial court where many grievances were heard and determined; some being condemned to die for going without passport to England and for other offences. On the 24th the Earl and his gentlemen were invited to dine with M. D'O, where they were most sumptuously entertained, and so far from meaner things that they feasted on musk and amber in tarts; and the day following the Earl brought M. D'O to see the army which was drawn up, over 2000 strong, besides 300 sick. On this day the English army began to draw their pay from the French King, but not to their content.

On the 28th the army marched towards Rouen and was well lodged in certain villages. That night Sir Roger Williams returned with letters from the King to the Earl showing his full determination to besiege Rouen with might and main and that he was marching thither with all expedition. Sir Roger was then despatched to England with the news, and the army moved to a village called Ophin, and the next evening marched towards Rouen which was about six miles off.

Next morning (29th) the point of the English army entered the village of Mount de Mallades about a quarter of a mile from the walls of Rouen, and looking down from thence they saw a great skirmish between the enemy from Rouen and the Marshal Biron's companies, the enemy holding on to a house and the hill until five in the evening when about 250 men issued out of the town to a place of advantage and assaulted the quarters of Hallard Mountmorency, which were next to the English, so sorely that he was forced to quit some

[2] SIEGE OF ROUEN, p. 29.

part of them. The enemy so pursued him that they burned
half his quarters, his troops offering no resistance, and would
have burnt the rest if the Lord General had not sent certain
harquebusiers to draw them into a skirmish, and offering
to cut in between them and the town; which was so well performed that they were forced by our horse to wheel about,
and by some pikes led by Sir John Wingfield to give ground.
In this skirmish Captain Barton's lieutenant was slain, and
two knights and one captain besides others wounded. Several
horses were hurt and the Earl's was shot dead under him.
Towards night the fight was broken off and our men returned
to their lodging.

THE EXECUTION OF O'ROURKE.[3] Brian O'Rourke was to-day
drawn to Tyburn for execution. As they came to the gallows,
while he was still standing in the cart, Mr. John Ly, with
many good exhortations, bade him to remember the many
odious treasons he had committed, and to ask Her Majesty
and the world for forgiveness. But he obstinately refused,
saying that if she would have given him time, and the writings which had been sent from Ireland against him so that
he might answer them, and also if she would give him his
life, then he would ask her forgiveness and henceforth serve
her truly; adding further that he little thought the King of
Scots would have sent him to the Queen without good assurance of his life and pardon for his offences.

Still Mr. Ly urged O'Rourke to repent and ask forgiveness,
and likewise to forgive for that was the only way for him
to come to the Heavenly Kingdom, and the standers by also
urged him to repent. To all this he replied that they should
make means for themselves to come to God, and he would
look after himself; and with that fell to his prayers. The
standers by then asked Meylerns, Lord Archbishop of
Cashell, who was present, to counsel O'Rourke to call to God;
but O'Rourke turning on him answered that he had more
need to look to himself and that he was neither here nor
there. So the cart went from him. His body was taken down,
his members and bowels cut out and burned in the fire, and
his heart taken out by the hangman, who showed it to the
people as an archtraitor's heart; then his head was cut off
and his body quartered.

4th November. 'MEDIUS' PRINTED.[4] *Medius,* being the sec-

---

[3] STOW'S ANNALS.   [4] STC 4248.

ond book of sacred songs, some made for five, some for six voices, by William Byrd, the Queen's Organist, hath been printed with the music.

5th November. PROCLAMATION AGAINST VAGRANT SOLDIERS.[5] A Proclamation is published against vagrant soldiers, declaring that there is a common wandering abroad of a great multitude, of whom the most part pretend that they have served in the wars on the other side of the seas, though it is known that very many of them neither served at all, or else ran away from their service and are justly to be punished and not relieved; some indeed have served, and, falling with sickness, are licensed to depart; these deserve relief.

Her Majesty therefore commands that discretion be used between unlawful vagrant persons and the soldiers now lawfully dismissed from their service. The vagrants, who have neither been brought to sickness or lameness in their service and are not able to show sufficient passport for their dismission, to be taken as vagabonds and so punished. And if any allege that they have been in the Queen's pay on the other side the seas and cannot show sufficient passport from the Lord General, he shall be indited and suffer as a felon, as a soldier that hath run away and left the service traitorously.

The Treasurer of Wars will make payment of sums of money to those who lawfully return to conduct them to the places where they were levied. Furthermore for the repressing of the great number of mighty and able vagrants now wandering abroad under pretence of begging as soldiers, by whom open robberies are committed, the Lieutenants of every county, who have sufficient warrant by their commissions to execute martial law upon such offenders, are charged to appoint Provost Marshals for the apprehension of such notable offenders, and to commit them to prison thereupon to be executed.

MEASURES OF RELIEF FOR RETURNED SOLDIERS.[6] Every soldier on landing, having the passport of the Lieutenant General or any special officer of commandment, to be paid 5s. for his conduct to the place where he was levied. Where there is no person of the Treasurer, the principal officer of the place to pay this sum immediately, which will be duly repaid by the Treasurer of Wars or the Council. On payment of the conduct money, the passports of the soldier shall be retained and a new passport given for his travel allowing sufficient time by convenient journeys from the place of landing to the place of his first levy. To be warned at the same time that if he lingers by the way in roguish manner or does not reach his former abode within the time limited, he shall be taken as a vagabond and punished according to the law.

8th November. 'MARY MAGDALEN'S FUNERAL TEARS.'[7] *Mary Magdalen's Funeral Tears*, written as it is said by Robert Southwell the Jesuit, though without his name on the title-page, has been entered, wherein is expressed the sorrowful thoughts and lamentations of Mary Magdalen at the Sepulchre of Christ, in the manner of the writers of romantic tales. The author seeing how the finest wits are now given to write passionate discourses hopeth by his book to woo them to make choice of such passions as it were neither shame to utter nor sin to feel.

15th November. SPANISH LOSSES.[8] By examination of various Spaniards and Portuguese it appears that the King of Spain sustained very heavy losses this last summer. Of the Nova Spania fleet of 52 ships but 33 returned to Havannah, there being 2600 lost in 19 sail; of the Terra Firma fleet only 23 ships came to Havannah, having lost some 3000 men. As well as these 55, there met at Havannah 12 ships from S. Domingo and 9 from Funduras, 77 in all, and set sail on 17th July, keeping company till the 10th August, when they were scattered by tempests so that by the end of August all but 48 had been lost, 5000 men being thought to have perished in the ships cast away. The King of Spain's treasure is all landed at Havannah to be sent home in frigates in January.

20th November. DEATH OF SIR CHRISTOPHER HATTON.[9] This day Sir Christopher Hatton, the Lord Chancellor, died at Ely House in Holborn of a flux of his urine, aggravated with grief of mind because the Queen somewhat vigorously exacted of him a great sum of money collected of tenths and first fruits, whereof he had charge, and which he had hoped, in regard of the favour he was in with her, that she would have forgiven him. Neither could she once having cast him down with a harsh word raise him up again, though she visited and endeavoured to comfort him. He was re-

[7] SR 2:598; STC 22950.   [9] CAMDEN'S ELIZABETH; STOW'S AN-
[8] STRYPE'S ANNALS 4:77.   NALS. See *15th Aug* 1592.

puted to be a man of pious nature, a great reliever of the poor, of singular bounty and munificence to students and learned men (for which reason those of Oxford chose him as their Chancellor of their University), and one who in the execution of the office of Lord Chancellor could satisfy his conscience in the constant integrity of his endeavours to do all with right and equity.

21st November. THE PROCLAMATION AGAINST JESUITS.[10] The Proclamation declaring the great troubles intended against the realm of seminary priests and Jesuits is now published though dated 18th October and printed some time since. The dangers and preparations made against the realm by the Pope and the King of Spain, and by English fugitives beyond the seas, are set forth and severer measures to be taken.

'And before all things, We do first require of the Ecclesiastical State, that the like diligence be used by the godly ministers of the Church, by their diligent teaching and example of life to retain Our People steadfastly in the profession of the Gospel and their duty to Almighty God and Us; as it is seen a few capital heads of treason are continually occupied within their Seminaries in withdrawing a multitude of ignorants to their inchantments.

'And secondly, for having sufficient forces in readiness by Sea, We hope by God's goodness and with the help of our subjects to have as great or greater strength on the seas as at any time we have had to withstand these puffed vaunts from Spain. And for Our forces by land, Our trust is that seeing We have distributed Our whole realm into several charges of Lieutenancies, that they by themselves when they may be personally present, and otherwise by their deputies and assistants of other Our ministers, will now after the general musters which have been by Our special order taken, consider of all things requisite to perform, and make perfect all defects that shall appear necessary, to make the bands both of horsemen and footmen fully furnished with armour, weapons and munition and with all other things requisite for their conduction to the place of service; and there also to continue as time shall require to defend their country. And so We do most earnestly require and charge all manner of Our subjects, with their hands, purses and advices; yea, all and every person of every estate, with their prayers to God, to move Him to assist this so natural, honourable and profitable a service, being only for the defence of their natural country, their wives, families, children, lands, goods, liberties and their posterities against ravening strangers, wilful destroyers of their native country, and monstrous traitors.

'And lastly, to withstand and provide speedy remedy against the other fraudulent attempts of the seminaries, jesuits, and traitors, without which as it appeareth his forces should not now be used, the same being only wrought by falsehood, by hypocrisy, and by undermining of Our good subjects under a false colour and face of holiness, to make breaches in men's and women's consciences, and to train them to their treasons: and that with such a secrecy, by the harbouring of the said treacherous messengers in obscure places, as without very diligent and continual search to be made, and severe orders executed, the same will remain and spread itself as a secret infection of treasons in the bowels of Our Realm; most dangerous, yea, most reproachful to be suffered in a well ordered Commonwealth.

'Therefore we have determined by advice of Our Council to have speedily certain commissioners, men of honesty, fidelity and good reputation, to be appointed in every shire, city, and port-town within Our realms to enquire by all good means what persons by their behaviours or otherwise worthy to be suspected to be any such persons, or have been sent, or that are employed in any such persuading of Our people, or of any residing within Our realm to treason, or to move any to relinquish their allegiance with Us, or to acknowledge any kind of obedience to the Pope or to the King of Spain; and also of all other persons that have been thereto induced, and that have thereto yielded: And further to proceed in the execution of such their commission, as they shall be more particularly directed by instructions annexed to their commission.

'And furthermore, because it is known and proved by common experience upon the apprehension of sundry of the said traitorous persons sent into the realm, that they do come into the same by secret creeks, and landing places, disguised both in names and persons; some in apparel as soldiers, mariners, or merchants, pretending that they have heretofore been taken prisoners, and put into galleys, and delivered. Some come in as gentlemen, with contrary names, in comely apparel, as though they had travelled into foreign countries for knowledge: and generally all, for the most part, are clothed like gentlemen in apparel, and many as gallants; yea in all colours, and with feathers and such like, disguising themselves; and many of them in their behaviours as ruffians, far off to be thought or suspected to be friars, priests, jesuits, or popish scholars. . . .

'And finally, We admonish and strictly charge and command all persons that have any intelligence with any such so sent, or come from beyond the seas to such purpose, to detect them to the commissioners, in that behalf to be assigned as aforesaid, within twenty days after the publication hereof, in the shire town, or city or port, within the precincts of the said commission: upon pain that the offenders herein shall be punished as abettors and maintainers of traitors: wherein We are resolutely determined to suffer no favour to be used for any respect of any persons, qualities or degrees: nor shall allow nor suffer to be allowed any excuse of negligence for not detection, or for not due examination of the qualities of such dangerous persons, according to the order hereafter prescribed, being no wise contrary, but agreeable to the most ancient laws and good usages of Our realm, devised for the good order of all manner of subjects in every precinct of every leet, to be forthcoming, to answer for their behaviours towards the Dignity of Our Crown, and the common peace of Our realm.

'Given at Our Manor of Richmond, the 18th of October, 1591, in the 33rd year of Our reign.'

Instructions set forth for the guidance of the commissioners show the form of questions to be put to those suspected of being recusants. The commissioners shall obtain from the *custos rotulorum*, the clerk of the peace, or the clerk of assizes, the names of those suspected, but their names not to be published unless some probable cause appear why they should be examined or apprehended. Nor shall suspected persons be pressed to answer any matter touching the conscience in religion, other than whether they usually come to Church or not; if they appear wilful recusants, then are they to be examined concerning their allegiance to the Queen, and of their devotion to the Pope or to the King of Spain, and whether they maintain any Jesuits, Seminaries, priests or other persons sent from beyond the seas to dissuade the Queen's subjects from their allegiance. In every town or large parish where the parsons or vicars are faithful and careful of their cures, they are to be urged to observe all such as refuse obstinately to come to Church. Those called before the commissioners, but not punished by the law, to be warned that their recusancy causeth them to be suspected of being disloyal in the duties towards the Queen and State or of favoring the common enemies.

25th November. THE SIEGE OF ROUEN.[11] The Earl of Essex hath returned from Rouen, which is now besieged. There have been skirmishes but nothing of great moment. On the 4th November in the night there sallied out of the Castle against the quarter of Monsieur Flavencourt 400 soldiers, burnt it over his head and slew as many as stood the defence, took his baggage, his horses and mules; but were at last forced to retire by certain Gascons and a regiment of French, leaving on the ground 26 dead and 8 prisoners, of whom two were English and one Spanish.

The next day one of the enemy's horse issued forth, a brave fellow all in crimson velvet, and called out one of ours to the sword on horseback, which he bravely answered and wounded his enemy in two places, and would have brought him in prisoner, had he not been rescued by his fellows. The Lord General the same day invited the three Colonels of the Switzers and there was general drinking of healths till some of them were sick and asleep. After dinner the General's party went out and came near a gate of the town where Villiers, the Governor of Dieppe, was quartered, and it happened that he was there with some twenty horse. Seeing the General's party he drew out certain shot and so began to come up the hill; but the General knowing who he was called to him and said he would speak with him at a blow with a sword or pistol, but he answered nothing except the shot of four or five harquebus. On the 7th our horsemen brought in some sixty kine, as well as sheep and swine. There came too a soldier from the Governor of Dieppe, sent from his master to the General, who reported that they had great desire to force the English quarter. There was a hot skirmish both of horse and foot near the castle of St. Katherine, where the people of the town stood on the bulwarks of the town, beholding as if it had been a triumph or a sport. On the 9th a trumpet of one Jerpenville being sent into the town, Villiers the Governor desired him to signify to the Lord General that whereas he had sent unto Chevalier Pickard to break a

[11] SIEGE OF ROUEN, pp. 33–47. Gabrielle d'Etrées was Henry's mistress.

pike with him, he would the next day bring him into the field, either armed or in his doublet, to answer his challenge; and if he listed he would bring sixteen of his gentlemen against sixteen of the General's.

To this the Earl of Essex answered in writing, that at his first coming into France he was occasioned to send his drums thither, understanding that the Chevalier Pickard was in the town, to tell him that he was sorry for old acquaintance that he should persist in so bad an action and against so brave a King. But since it were so, he would be glad to find him at the head of his troop with a pike. And he was to know that he was a General of an army from an absolute Prince in which there were many chevaliers, Pickard's equal at least. Besides, that if he or any others had desire to find him, all those of his could justify that the first day of his sitting down here he was twice at the head of his troop and offered to charge; and he refused and wheeled about. But for that he himself was in some respect of his government, he challenged him that he would make it good upon him either armed or in his doublet; that the King's cause was more just and honest than that he upheld of the League, that he himself was a better man than he, and his mistress fairer than his. And if he would have help and parley, he would bring twenty of like quality to Chevalier Pickard, or sixty, that the meanest of them should be a Captain in Chief.

The answer of Villiers was received on the 11th to the effect that, in saying the cause of the King was juster cause than that of the League's and that the General was a better man than he was, he did lie; and would fight thereon when the Duc de Mayne should come. To this the Earl answered by trumpet that his lie was very frivolous and did no way concern him considering it was not given him upon a good ground; yet eftsoons he did call him to the maintenance of that he had denied, and if he did not answer now, he had no excuse; then shame and infamy must light upon him, which was generally spoken of him by all the French themselves. The Governor also sent a challenge to any foot captain, man to man with shot and with rapier, which was accepted; and Captain Acton, desirous of that combat, had his name sent to the Governor. But in the end they made excuses and nothing came of it.

On the 13th after breakfast, the General went to the Marshal's quarters accompanied by sundry gentlemen in their best attire to meet the King, when all dismounted to kiss his hand, and he alighted to embrace the Marshal and the General; after which they brought him to his quarter and went to council.

The 16th it was rumoured, as it had been ever since he came, that the King was going to Dieppe to hasten provisions and necessaries; but some of his servants said that his journey was to meet a Saint (for he owed devotion to more than one Gabrielle only) to whom he had long been devout, whose body was transported thither from Caen, that his devotion and his vows might be performed with more ease.

On the 19th about twelve o'clock at night some of the King's nobility and eight gentlemen approached the castle of St. Katherine, and there the pioneers began to build a fort, and, because it could not be finished in one night, the King's nobles and twenty-five of the Lord General's principal gentlemen, armed with pikes, came thither to guard against any sally that should be made out of the town or castle; and about an hour after day, the King himself came to cheer the pioneers to work and the rest to a resolute defence. The King seemed very desirous of some sport, and turning to Mr. Thomas Coningsby asked him whether the enemy would sally or no; who answered that if they were honest men they should, but if they were Englishmen they would; to which the King replied, 'By my faith, I believe it.' In the evening came news that the Lord General was to return to England in the morning.

On the 20th the Lord General rose very early and went towards the King's quarters, having first despatched and ordered many things for the army, and so accompanied with Sir Henry Unton and many others he alighted on a fair plain, and there he knighted Sir Henry Killigrew. After despatching his business in the King's quarters he took his journey towards Dieppe.

26th November. THE QUEEN'S LETTERS TO THE EMPEROR OF RUSSIA.[12] Sir George Barnes, who tradeth much with Russia, understanding that the Queen, at the request of the King of Scotland, is about to write to the Emperor of Russia for the enlargement of a Scottish Captain, a prisoner in Moscow, writes to the Lord Treasurer that since the Queen hath sent several letters for particular men and causes of little moment, it is said in the Emperor's Court that the Queen of England's letters are very cheap.

[12] SP DOM 240:70.

THE CHARGES OF THE BORDEAUX FLEET.[13] A charge of 3s. on the tun is to be levied on all wines and other merchandise arriving from the ports of Rochelle and Bordeaux at any port in England to cover the cost of waftage for the fleet. These charges fell formerly on the merchants of London, but as the ships of other ports take advantage of the convoy they shall be borne by all.

4th December. A PETITION OF THE PURITAN PRISONERS.[1] Cartwright and eight other Puritan prisoners have petitioned the Lord Treasurer praying that they may be allowed bail until the Council is pleased to call them for further trial of their innocency. His lordship, say they, will easily discern that over a year's imprisonment strikes deep into their healths. It is well known that divers papists, who not only deny the Queen's lawful authority but give it to a stranger, a sworn enemy of theirs and all other Christians, yet receive favour of freedom from their imprisonment. Never a one of them but has been sworn to the Queen's supremacy and is ready to take the oath again.

ORDERS FOR REFORMING THE ARMY IN NORMANDY.[2] Orders are sent by the Council for the better ordering and reforming of the army in Normandy under the Earl of Essex. He shall cause all captains of the foot bands to deliver on oath perfect rolls of all their officers and soldiers showing those now serviceable and any others remaining there sick and unable to serve; and in another roll the names of all that first came over with them but are not now present, making a distinction of those sent away by passport, those dead, and those that have run away; further they shall deliver in the roll a certain note of all the armour and weapons of those no longer in service, and where it is.

Having received these rolls the Lieutenant General shall consider how many bands of 150 (allowing 15 dead pays) or how many bands of 100 (allowing 10 dead pays) can be made of the whole number. And because this cannot be done without cassing some of the bands, he shall, for an example, cass his own band of 200, and also the bands of those receiving special allowance as officers of the army or colonels of regiments; also the bands which are weakest.

He shall take special care to preserve the ordnance and munition from water, and to recover, if he can, such as have fled away from the Queen's service. If they are apprehended in France they should be hanged as they deserve, and proclamation made that any who presume to come over to England will be hanged up whensoever he shall be apprehended.

5th December.   AN UNSUCCESSFUL AMBUSCADE AT ROUEN.[3] From Rouen it is reported that the commanders taking at heart the ill success of a recent skirmish in which two brave soldiers had been killed and their bodies lost, planned to lay an ambuscade on the 30th November. Captain Barton with 24 shot hid in the cellar of a house pulled down near the ditch and town port; Captain Henry Power in another place with 16 pikes; and some shot of M. Hallard Mountmorency on the other side of the port. This ambush being laid before day, about 8 o'clock the enemy opened the ports and came to the usual place of the court of guard, which was some six or eight score paces from the port.

After they had been there a while and set out their sentinels, Sir Roger Williams and the choicest of the gentlemen being in the trenches, caused some musketeers to shoot at their sentinels and sent other shot to beat them in. As the skirmish grew warm, our men according to directions retreated to bring the enemy more within danger of the ambuscade; then the sign was given, which was the throwing up of a hat with feathers of Sir Thomas Baskerville. But this was not observed by Captain Barton, who should first have discovered himself, so that our men were fain to call and cry, which caused the enemy to suspect and to retreat as fast as their legs could carry them to the port. Captain Barton, for want of better speed than they fell short of them, but some four or six were said to have fallen, and our men had the spoil of the court of guard, some cloaks and weapons. As our men retreated some artillery were shot, one of which lighted upon M. Hallard Mountmorency, slaying his horse and breaking his leg below the knee.

6th December.   GREENE'S 'A MAIDEN'S DREAM.'[4] *A Maiden's Dream; upon the death of the Right Honourable Sir Christopher Hatton,* written by Robert Greene, is entered, being dedicated to the Lady Elizabeth Hatton, to whom he noteth that, having long wished to gratify the father with something worthy of himself, he now takes opportunity to show his duty to him in his daughter. In this funeral elegy is

[3] SIEGE OF ROUEN, p. 52.   [4] SR 2:600; STC 12271.

shown the complaint of Justice, of Prudence, of Fortitude, Temperance, Beauty, Hospitality, and Religion; and of primates, soldiers, and people for the loss of the Lord Chancellor, ending with the maiden's vision of the soul of Sir Christopher carried by Astraea among the hierarchies.

10th December. SEVEN CATHOLICS EXECUTED.[5] White, Plassden and Lacy, Jesuit priests, with two lay Catholics, taken by Topcliffe at the beginning of November, were executed at Tyburn. Edmund Jennings, the Jesuit, and Mr. Swithin Wells were dragged on hurdles to Holborn, over against Mr. Wells' house, where Jennings was discovered saying Mass. When Jennings arrived at the gallows he began to say, *'O Crux diu desiderata et iam concupiscenti animo praeparata.'* Being bade to confess his treason, for so the Queen would doubtless pardon him, he answered, 'I know not ever to have offended her. If to say Mass be treason, I confess I have done it and glory in it.' These words so enraged Topcliffe that he refused him leave to say any more, scarcely even to recite the *Pater noster,* but caused him to be turned off the ladder and the rope immediately cut. Jennings was thus thrown on his feet, but the hangman tripped up his heels, cut off his members and disembowelled him. In this agony Jennings began to call on St. Gregory to the great astonishment of the hangman, who cried out with a loud voice, 'God's wounds! his heart is in my hand and yet Gregory is in his mouth.'

13th December. GREENE'S BOOKS OF CONNY-CATCHING.[6] Robert Greene that was wont to write for the pleasure of our gentlemen and ladies hath penned a *Notable Discovery of Cosnage* and *The Second Part of Conny-Catching* now that riper days call him to repentance. These books are for the commodity of his countrymen, to warn them, and especially merchants, farmers, and honest-minded yeomen, against the practisers of the Art of Conny-Catching and the Art of Cross-biting.

[5] STC 11728; CATH. REC. SOC. 5:206. See *1st Nov*.

[6] SR 2:600. Both pamphlets went into second editions in 1592. There were two important results of Greene's conny-catching pamphlets; they turned the attention of the gentleman reader, now beginning to grow weary of *Arcadia* and *Euphues,* to new interests, and they attracted a new kind of reader. Greene's previous works, *The Mourning Garment* and *Never Too Late,* were dedicated to the gentlemen scholars of both Universities; now he successfully appeals to merchants, apprentices, farmers, and plain countrymen. The conny-catching pamphlets are a symptom of the reaction to realism which was the first stage towards the satires and the humour plays at the end of the century. STC 12279, 12281.

For the Art of Conny-Catching, or cosening at card play, there be needed three parties, the setter to draw in the conny (that is to be cheated) familiarly to drink with him, the verser to join them in the tavern and to offer to play with them, and the barnacle appearing to be but a stranger that is invited to join them. The barnacle and the verser begin to cut the cards, and the verser, asking the conny secretly by signs if he will help him to cheat the barnacle, begins his game, and at the first winneth the stakes until the conny is also drawn in and venturing a high stake, by some sleight the cut falls against him and he is cheated of all.

The art of crossbiting is the practice of harlots and their mates that entice a young man into their houses and there either pick his pockets or else, on the woman sending for her husband or friend, the crossbiters fall upon him and threaten him with Bridewell and the law so that for fear he gives up his purse or makes them out a bill to pay a sum of money by a certain day.

In the *Second Part of Conny-Catching* are displayed the villainies of the nip and the foist, the priggar, the Vincent's law, the lifting law, the courber, and the black art. The nip and the foist, though their subject, a well-lined purse, is the same, yet is their manner different; the nip using a knife to cut the purse, the foist his hand to draw the pocket. These foists holding themselves to be of the highest degree term themselves Gentlemen foists, and so much disdain to be called cutpurses that the foist refuseth even to wear a knife about him lest he be suspected to be a nip. The priggar is the stealer of horses. The courber worketh with a hook or curb, made with joints (like an angle rod that he might hide it beneath his cloak), which he thrusteth through at a window to draw out what he shall find. The black art is the picking of locks, and Vincent's law the cheating at bowls.

It was objected by some that read the first book that Greene used no eloquent phrases as in his former works, and to this he answereth that it were an odious thing to apply a fine style to so base a subject.

15th December. A NEGLIGENT COMMISSARY DISMISSED.[7] Thomas Wyatt, commissary for the companies in the Low Countries dispersed under Sir Francis Vere, is dismissed from his post, having neglected to send over certificates or muster rolls of the companies whereby their strength might

[7] APC 22:125.

be discerned. By reason of his omission the strength of the companies lately sent into France was not known, so that instead of 1000 complete with the dead pays but 638 arrived, which numbers might have been redressed, if it had appeared before by his timely certificate.

16th December. SIR CHRISTOPHER HATTON'S FUNERAL.[8] Sir Christopher Hatton was this day honourably buried in St. Paul's; one hundred poor people having gowns and caps given them going before; of gentlemen, and yeomen, in gowns, cloaks and coats, more than three hundred, with the Lords of the Council and others, besides fourscore of the Guard which followed.

17th December. MASTERLESS MEN TO BE TAKEN UP.[9] The Lord Mayor and Aldermen are required to take up within the City and liberties of London 100 loose and masterless men, there being at this time a great many, especially of those returned from service in France. These men are to be sent forthwith to Ostend in Flanders to complete the companies serving there under Sir Edward Norris. The men are to be bestowed in Leadenhall or some other fit place where they can be kept together and not allowed to slip away until the whole number is complete; and thence to be safely conveyed to their shipping near about St. Katherine's. The manner employed, either by privy search in the night or otherwise, is referred to their discretion. Orders have already been taken by Sir Edward for their victualling until they be embarked so that the City shall not be charged with them.

18th December. TWO SUSPECTED RECUSANTS.[10] The Attorney General and the Solicitor General are to examine two Englishmen, Anthony Skinner and Richard Acliffe, who were apprehended at Gravesend coming up the river in a small boat of Calais. These men are both recusants and had been absent from the realm for eight years, remaining for the most part at Rome, the one as servant to Cardinal Allen, the other with the Bishop of Cassano.

A NOTABLE INSTANCE OF THE CORRUPTION OF THESE WARS.[11] A gentleman that had a fair house in a village not far from Rouen was desirous to have protection from the Lord Gen-

8 STOW'S ANNALS.   10 APC 22:131.
9 APC 22:129.   11 SIEGE OF ROUEN, p. 60.

eral, who promised to provide him with a certain quantity of oats and hay weekly. Two Englishmen were sent to guard his house, but certain of M. Hallard Mountmorency's lackeys coming for forage to the village roughly intreated them and took away their horses. Whereupon, returning to their master, the following night at midnight, forty cuirassiers entered the house, with force took the two Englishmen prisoners, wounded the master to death, spoiled his house, took the Englishmen's horses and all his; and the next news heard was that the Englishmen were prisoners in Rouen, having been sold to the enemy.

19th December. FURTHER MEASURES AGAINST RECUSANTS.[12] The Commissioners specially chosen to inquire into the secret repair into the realm of Jesuits and seminary priests are warned that as the special commission will be renewed when necessary, they shall privately inform the Council whether any in the commission are suspected to be unsound in religion or have wives, children or any of their families known recusants or harbour persons suspected to be backward in religion. Moreover if they find the number not sufficient or not so placed for their habitations that they may divide the service, or that others meet to be employed in this service are omitted, they are likewise to certify their names and dwelling places, with their opinions of the men.

21st December. MASTERLESS MEN IN KENT.[13] The Lord Mayor hath not been able to find above eighty masterless men in the City for service in the Low Countries. The Lord Cobham is now to give order to his Deputy Lieutenants in the County of Kent to take up loose and vagrant persons to make up the total number to one hundred.

24th December. A HIGHHANDED ARREST.[14] The Recorder of the City of London is summoned to appear before the Council on St. Stephen's Day to declare upon what foundation he subscribed a warrant whereby one Paine was taken out of his lodging in the night by a constable and a servant of his and a dozen persons, servants and friends of Sir Francis Willoughby, and conveyed to the Counter in Wood Street, there to be forthcoming to answer divers points touching high treason. They think it strange for him to be committed to prison upon treason that should hereafter be laid to his charge, as though a man should be made prisoner before his offence was known.

26th December. THE TRIPOLI MERCHANTS RECOMMENDED TO CHARITY.[15] There be six Turks lately arrived from France in an English vessel, of whom three are said to be of the guard of the Grand Signior. They allege that they have been retained more than twenty years as slaves in the galleys of the Spanish King before they found means to escape. These men have made humble suit to the merchants trading in Tripoli to be relieved by the loan of some hundred crowns, offering to be bound to repay the money when they come to the first place of Turkish dominion, before they set foot on shore. The Council recommend their request to the merchants, praying and requiring them to furnish this aid, which would be gratefully accepted by the Grand Signior and the other people in general of that country.

BEACON WATCHES.[16] Beacon watches are now to be discontinued until 15th March; but nevertheless the beacons to be kept in good order and furnished with sufficient fuel to be used if cause should require.

29th December. GOODS RIFLED FROM PRIZES TO BE RESTORED.[17] The captains of the London ships in the Lord Thomas Howard's fleet are reported to have carried their prizes into remote ports and havens and there enriched themselves by rifling the prizes and selling divers parcels to persons dwelling in the port towns, to the great slander and prejudice of sea discipline and wrong to the merchant adventurers of London. Her Majesty not willing to suffer so great a disorder now causeth proclamation to be made in Cornwall, Devonshire, Dorsetshire and Hampshire straightly charging all that in any ways have received any foreign coin, bullion of gold or silver, jewels, pearls, stones, musk, wrought or raw silk, cochenilia, indigo or other merchandise, within ten days to bring in a note of it in writing showing the prices they paid and the names of those off whom they bought, declaring also the day, time, and place. Those not obeying this order shall be held as felons and abettors to pirates.

31st December. THE SIEGE OF ROUEN.[18] From Rouen there

15 APC 22:158.
16 APC 22:160.
17 PROCLAMATIONS 302.
18 SIEGE OF ROUEN, p. 56.

is news of a sally made by the enemy on the 6th of the month, who came on with such speed that the sentinels had no leisure to give the court of guard any warning but by coming away without resistance. They quitted three of Hallard Mountmorency's courts of guard, not without the loss of their lives. The fourth court of guard, where the greatest strength lay, was a large house without a roof, the walls being a pike length high, with many loopholes to shoot out at. The enemy, with men for the purpose excellently well armed, by the advantage of the walls got to the top and leaped in amongst them most resolutely, putting to the sword all within, and those that escaped there fell upon the horsemen who had the like mercy. The horsemen advanced so far that our sentinels and the rest quitted the trenches, but Sir Thomas Gerrard at the instant drew out the guard of the day into the field to make stand, and gave alarm to all our army which came out full fast.

When the enemy perceived the fast stand of our pikes, they had no will to come nearer, but after some discharge of pistols towards our forward gallants, when Captain Barton was dangerously hurt in the face, seeing 150 of our pioneers coming out with their pikes, they retired and our men repossessed the trenches. After the fight nearly fifty dead were counted in the court of guard. Two captains in chief were slain, and two gentlemen of especial mark, both whose bodies the enemy took away. Soon after there grew a new alarm, and our men began to run in panic but were stopped by Sir Roger Williams, Sir Thomas Baskerville, Sir Thomas Gerrard and other gentlemen. On the 7th Sir Richard Acton died of the disease of the camp, a pestilent ague, now very prevalent. On the 12th, a sergeant of the pioneers was discovered to be conspiring to lead away fifty or sixty of the principalest into Rouen. Whereupon a Council of War was held, and all brought to the tree but the sergeant only executed for example in presence of them all.

On the 14th the Lord General returned to the army from England, and notwithstanding his long and great journey, he would needs before alighting go down to the trenches, and, hearing of the great threatenings which were expected, must call to a sentinel of the enemy and bid him tell M. Villiers that he was come with some twenty gentlemen with him; and that if he would enterprise anything against the English quarter he must do it that night or never, for the next day we should be too strong for him, there being 2000 English of the old bands of the Low Countries coming this night.

On the 17th and 18th muster was taken, and it was found that there were less than 200 horse. The 25 old companies were reduced to 8, and those short of their number. On the 19th the bands of the Low Countries were mustered, and five of them sent to another quarter where they watched every third night, and the Lord General himself with many other principal gentlemen also watching every third night within three pikes' length of the enemy's guard, where they had continual shooting. The Lord General had great speech with Monsieur Pickard, who asked for his mistress that he had in England, and promised to come and dine with him one day.

On the 24th the Lord General went to the trenches with many, where they forced the enemy from the counterscarp and slew many, taking cloaks, weapons and the like. Marshal Biron took upon him to defend the ground that was won, which was of great importance, but the enemy sallying out in great numbers the next day about eleven o'clock forced the guard there. Our men fought bravely for about half an hour, never seconded of the French; the soldiers spending all their powder and shot, and the enemy with great fury driving down the barrels of earth. Sir Thomas Baskerville saw no remedy, but to sally out, and beat them with the pike and halbert, but he was slenderly followed, and forced to retire, abandoned of too many of our common soldiers; but seventeen gentlemen and officers rallied and made a stand.

Other Books Printed in *1591*

i. *Narcissus, siue Amoris iuuenilis et praecipue Philautiae breuis atque moralis descriptio*, written in Latin hexameter verses, and dedicated to Henry, Earl of Southampton, by John Clapham. Herein Narcissus, being smitten by the arrow of love came to the fountain Philautia, and there falling in love with his own image, cried out to it; but was answered back in mockery by Echo. Night coming on, the image vanished, and the infatuate youth unable anywhere to find his love, fell from the bank into the river and so perished.

ii. *An Apology: of and for sundry proceedings by jurisdiction Ecclesiastical, of later times by some challenged, and also diversly impugned by them*, written by Dr. Richard Cosin, though without name either of author or printer on its title. Noteth that of late certain disturbers of Her Majesty's happy reformation had rested themselves most in advancing a new-found discipline and in discrediting the present government Ecclesiastical by their speeches and writings, as well by impugning the callings and form of Ecclesiastical government as by defaming the persons of the governors with unchristian gibes, contumelies and other indignities. But when these had not succeeded according to their wish, they pursue a more politic course; for by themselves, and others more simple excited cunningly by them, they challenge divers received proceedings in Courts Ecclesiastical as not justifiable by law; and by their frequent clamours, some very grave, wise and learned (no way affected to their other fancies), either not being well informed of proceedings Ecclesiastical, or not weighing for want of leisure certain points doubtfully reported in the book of common law as their learning doth afford. In a kind of commiseration toward some of those who

i. STC 5359. One of several poems of this period which glorify the physical attractions of male youth. See also *Cephalus and Procris* (*22nd Oct 1593*), *Arisbas* (*14th Nov 1593*), *The Affectionate Shepherd* (*1609*), Shakespeare's *Sonnets*, Marlowe's *Edward II* and *Hero and Leander* (*26 Feb 1598*); and E. K. Chambers' gloss on Hobbinol in the first month of *The Shepherd's Calendar*.

seem distressed and to be otherwise well meaning men divers proceedings Ecclesiastical have lately been called in question, both for matter and for circumstance and manner, that they are contrary to the laws of this realm. Therefore he taketh in hand to show the reasons for the contrary based on the law and the Scriptures.

iii. A new edition of *A Geometrical practical treatise named Pantometria*, revised by the author, Mr. Thomas Digges and his son, Mr. Leonard Digges. This book besides giving the theories of Geometry, addeth many engravings showing the practical use of measuring distances and heights with such instruments as the quadrant geometrical, the geometrical square, the theodolitus, the measuring of plane surfaces, the contents of solids, and so forth.

iv. *The Art of War,* written by William Garrard, gentleman, who had served the King of Spain in his wars of 14 years and died in 1587, corrected and finished by Captain Hitchcock, dedicated to the Earl of Essex. Herein are five books, of which the first treateth of the behaviour of a good soldier, disnier or corporal, together with the martial laws of the field; the second, adorned with many figures, the office of a sergeant, ensign bearer, lieutenant, and gentlemen of a band; the third of the governing of bands, squadrons and battles, of captains, colonels, and sergeant-majors-general; the fourth of the general of horsemen, the scout-master, and the office of the marshal of the field; the fifth of the great master of the artillery, of the master gunner, and of general notes of fortification; of the besieging, expugning and defending of a fortress.

v. *A Work worth the Reading,* by Charles Gibbon, of Bury St. Edmunds, dedicated to Sir Nicholas Bacon, wherein is contained five profitable and pithy questions, *videlicet:* 1st, whether the election of the parents is to be preferred before the affection of their children in marriages; 2nd, whether the father may lawfully disinherit his first born; 3rd, whether a

ii. STC 5820. This was Whitgift's reply to Burleigh's criticism of his persecution of the Puritans. See 22 *Mar*.
iii. STC 6861. A learned and finely printed folio, first published in 1571.
iv. STC 11625. An important military manual with many diagrams. Anyone who has studied the elaborate numerical diagrams, illustrating the formation of troops in close order, will realize why Iago called Cassio a 'great arithmetician.'

reasonable allowance may be taken for lending of money; 4th, whether the rich or the poor are to be accounted most blessed; 5th, whether there be degrees of glory in Heaven or differences of pains in Hell. These questions are argued by Philogus and Tychicus, two lovers of learning, the latter supporting his arguments more from the Scriptures, the former rather from common experience.

Of the rights of parents in marriage Tychicus saith that if a man may bestow his goods to whom he will, he may as well bestow his children where he thinketh best, for children are the goods of the parents. To which Philogus answereth that if parents impose upon their children a match more to content their desire for more than their children's godly choice for love then they should not be obeyed, for what greater occasion of incontinency could be given than to match a young and lusty maid against her own mind with an infirm and decrepit person to satisfy another's pleasure? To this Tychicus replieth that to match a young maid and an old man is indeed most miserable.

vi. *The Book of the Russe Commonwealth*, by Mr. Giles Fletcher (that was employed in the Queen's service to the Emperor of Russia in 1588), being dedicated to the Queen. Herein is described the cosmography of the country; the ordering of the state, with the condition of the commonality or vulgar sort; the judicial procedure; their warlike provisions and martial discipline; the ecclesiastical state; ending with a chapter upon the œconomy or private behaviour of the people of that nation.

The Emperor of the country is a person of mean stature, somewhat low and gross, of a sallow complexion, and inclining to the dropsy, hawk nosed, unsteady in his pace by reason of some weakness of his limbs, heavy and inactive, yet commonly smiling, almost to a laughter. For quality otherwise simple or slow witted, but very gentle and of an easy nature, quiet, merciful, of no martial disposition, nor greatly apt for matter of policy, very superstitious, and infinite that way.

The Russe because he is used to extremities both of heat

v. STC 11821. The question of the right of parents to enforce a marriage on their child was much discussed at this time, and especially after the sensational murder of old Mr. Page of Plymouth by his girl-wife Ulalia in 1590, recorded in ballads, a pamphlet, and a lost play by Dekker and Jonson. Deloney in writing a suitable dying speech for Ulalia lays the ultimate responsibility on her parents. See, too, *16th June 1593*.

and cold beareth both very patiently. They can be seen coming out of their bath stoves, all on a froth, and fuming as hot almost as a pig at a spit, and straightway to leap into the river stark naked, and that in the coldest of winter time. The women to mend the bad hue of their skins, use to paint their faces with white and red colours so visibly that any man can perceive it. But this is no matter, because it is common and liked well by their husbands, who make them an ordinary allowance to buy colours to paint their faces, delighting themselves much to see their foul women become fair images. This practice parcheth the skin, and helpeth to deform them when their painting is off.

Of the vulgar sort he noteth that they are much oppressed by the nobility so that though otherwise hardened to bear any toil, they give themselves to idleness and drinking, as passing no more than from hand to mouth.

vii. *The true and perfect spageric preparation of minerals, animals and vegetables,* originally written by Dr. Josephus Quercetanus of Armenia, now set forth with divers rare secrets not heretofore known of many, by John Hester, a practitioner in the spagerical art; and dedicated to Sir Robert Carey.

Amongst those remedies especially recommended for the plague is a preparation of mummy (in former times prepared of bodies embalmed with pitch, frankincense, myrrh or aloes, but now made only of dried flesh), either in liquid, balm or tincture; also *balsamum urinae,* which Mr. Hester regardeth almost as *catholicum* in its uses. This tincture to be made thus: 'Take the urine of young children about the age of twelve years, that hath drunk wine for certain months if it be possible; the same putrefy *in balneo* or dung a philosopher's year; then distil it with a gentle fire in sand, being also luted, the which ye shall note diligently. The flame ye shall put upon the feces four times; then the last water keep close shut, the which is white and stinking, and therefore ye may give it both taste and smell with cinnamon and sugar. The feces that remained in the bottom being black ye shall sublime by degrees of fire, and you shall have a most precious salt, the which some affirm will dissolve gold, silver and other metals; some philosophers call it their *menstrua.*'

viii. The two parts of *The Troublesome Reign of King John*, a play that hath been sundry times acted by the Queen's players in the City of London. In the first part is shown the discovery of King Richard Cordelion's base son (called the Bastard Faulconbridge), the wars in France and the supposed death of Arthur. In the second part is portrayed the death of Arthur Plantagenet, the landing of Lewis, and the poisoning of King John at Swinstead Abbey.

ix. *The Tragedy of Tancred and Gismund,* compiled and acted by Robert Wilmot and other gentlemen of the Inner Temple before the Queen more than twenty years before, being newly revised and polished according to the decorum of these days, on the importunity of some of Mr. Wilmot's friends. This tragedy, whereof the story is taken from Boccaccio, is written after the pattern of the ancients, the action being related and not shown upon the stage.

viii. STC 14644–45.   ix. STC 25764.

1st January. SPENSER'S 'DAPHNAIDA.'[1] Mr. Edmund Spenser hath sent his *Daphnaida, an Elegy upon the death of the noble and virtuous Douglas Howard, daughter and heir of Henry Howard, Viscount Bindon, and wife of Arthur Gorges, Esquire,* to the Lady Helena, Marquess of Northampton, wherein in the form of a pastoral Alcyon complains of the death of his Daphne.

7th January. THE LEVANT COMPANY.[2] The Levant Company are granted a patent allowing them with other privileges the sole right of trading to the Levant Seas, Turkey and Venice, and of importing the small fruits called 'currants,' being the raisins of Corinth.

THE COMMISSION AGAINST JESUITS.[3] The Commission for enquiry of Jesuits and Seminaries is renewed for the counties of Kent, Buckingham, Middlesex, Surrey and Durham.

MR. HENRY CAESAR RELEASED.[4] Mr. Henry Caesar that was committed to the charge and custody of Sir Richard Martin for his recusancy is now to be released, since the Council learn that through conference of learned preachers he now conforms himself in religion, professing that he is indeed resolved in his conscience according to the truth.

9th January. A PROTEST ON BEHALF OF THE PURITANS.[5] Sir Francis Knollys hath written to the Lord Treasurer on behalf of the Puritans still in prison that he marvels how the Queen can be persuaded that she is in as much danger of the Puritans as of the Papists; for she cannot be ignorant that the Puritans are not able to change the government of

[1] STC 23079.
[2] SP DOM 241:11.
[3] APC 22:174.
[4] APC 22:174.
[5] Thomas Wright, *Queen Elizabeth and Her Times*, 1838, 2:417.

the clergy but by petition; and even then the Queen could not do it but she must call a parliament for it, and no act could pass unless she give her royal assent thereto. As for their seditious conduct, if the bishops or the Lord Chancellor or any of them could have proved *de facto* that Cartwright and his fellow prisoners had gone about any such matter seditiously, then they had been hanged before this. But the Queen must keep a form of justice as well against Puritans as any other subjects, and they tried in convenient time, whether suspected for sedition or treason or Puritanism or by whatever name it is called.

16th January.   CERTAIN GOODS PROHIBITED TO BE CARRIED TO SPAIN.[6] Notwithstanding former warnings to the citizens of the Hanze Towns and Stade that they should forbear to send into Spain or Portugal any kind of provision fit for the wars upon pain of confiscation, the enemy is daily being furnished with corn, munition, and other things. To the list of prohibited wares are added iron, steel, all sorts of weapons, planks, deal boards, wainscot, pipe staves, flax, tow, hemp and resin.

19th January.   THE EARL OF ESSEX RETURNS TO COURT.[7] The Earl of Essex on his return from France hath come to the Court, and being received very graciously by the Queen is able to allay her anger with Sir Henry Unton, the ambassador, for that he had allowed the Earl to see a certain letter of hers. This letter was sent to Sir Henry by Sir Robert Cecil, written in Her Majesty's own hand, and to be shown to the Earl only if he refused to return to England. When the packet of letters reached the ambassador, being brought by one of my Lord's servants and delivered in his presence, he required the packet to be opened forthwith, saying that he hoped there were letters for him. Upon Sir Henry opening the packet, my Lord seeing a letter addressed to himself, snatched it out of his hands before he had time to read that letter of Sir Robert Cecil's which accompanied it. The Queen hath hitherto been much displeased that her letter should have reached the Earl's hands thus, and by the hands of the Lord Treasurer had severely censured the ambassador. Moreover the Earl speaketh very highly of the ambassador's good services to the Queen, who is thus appeased. It is be-

[6] APC 22:183.
[7] UNTON CORRESPONDENCE, pp. 251, 265, 276, 294.

lieved that his return to Court will make the Queen more favourable to helping the French King.

22nd January. ABUSES IN THE CLOTH TRADE.[8] A proclamation is published for the reformation of sundry abuses about making of cloths, called Devonshire kersies or dozens, ordering that from the Feast of the Annunciation of Our Lady these cloths as they come raw from the weaver's beam shall weigh fifteen pounds at the least and contain between fifteen and sixteen yards in length.

28th January. A COMMISSION FOR IMPRISONED RECUSANTS.[9] Owning to matters of greater weight and importance, to which the members of the Council are bound to attend, some prisoners suspected of being Jesuits or Seminaries from over seas remain for a long time without being thoroughly heard or examined. A special commission of twelve gentlemen, amongst them Sir Richard Martin, Mr. Sergeant Fleetwood, the Recorder of London, Richard Topcliffe and Richard Young, is now appointed. On any special cause three or more of them shall summon such persons before them, and for their better proceeding the keepers of the prisons shall deliver weekly the names of such prisoners as they have received. They meet once a week in some convenient place, either at the prison or some place near, to examine them on such information as they receive. Moreover as some are prisoners at large, and some may be bestowed in prisons not fit for them to remain by reason of favour shown to them, the commissioners will take order, as they think fit, for their more straight keeping or removing to other prisons.

30th January. FLESH PROHIBITED DURING LENT.[10] The Lords-Lieutenant of the counties near London are charged that the orders restraining the use of flesh during the time of Lent shall be put in execution and not as in former years so neglected that at this time of the year wherein young cattle should most be spared for increase a greater quantity is killed than in any other season. The money received from the butchers for their licences is reserved for the use of poor soldiers, lame, impotent or maimed in the wars.

4th February. DANIEL'S 'DELIA.'[1] *Delia, containing certain sonnets,* by Samuel Daniel, is entered. In the Epistle Dedica-

---

[8] PROCLAMATIONS 304.   [10] APC 22:217.
[9] APC 22:214.   [1] SR 2:603; STC 6253.

tory to the Lady Mary, Countess of Pembroke, Mr. Daniel writeth that although he rather desired to keep in the private passions of his youth from the multitude, as things uttered to himself and consecrated to silence, yet seeing that he was betrayed by the indiscretion of a greedy printer and had some of his secrets betrayed to the world uncorrected, doubting the like of the rest, he is thus forced to publish that which he never meant.

6th February.   NEWS FROM FRANCE.[2] The news from France is that the Duke of Parma is likely to give battle, and if he doth not besiege some town by the way will reach Rouen within a week. Sir Henry Unton, the ambassador, is not only out of favour with the Queen over the matter of her letter to Essex, but with the King, who is advertised that he hath done ill offices for him with the Queen.

7th February.   GREENE'S 'THIRD PART OF CONNY-CATCH-ING.'[3] Greene hath written a *Third and last part of Conny-Catching, with the newly devised knavish art of fool-taking.* Herein are set forth notes of the devices of the conny-catchers delivered to him by a certain justice of the peace, and showing how divers had been beguiled.

12th February.   THE QUEEN REFUSES FURTHER AID TO THE FRENCH KING.[4] Notwithstanding the letters of the King, and the solicitations of the French ambassador to yield more succour, the Queen will in no wise be induced to consent, though no more than 1500 men are required, 3000 having been asked for at first. Some fourteen days since the Lord Treasurer made ready letters and warrants for the Queen to have sent over one or two thousand pikemen; but when they came to the signing, she changed her mind, and ever since denies it, putting forward these reasons:

Firstly, her former offence against the King for that the last summer he neglected the taking of Rouen and wasted his own people and her treasure to no purpose. Secondly, she thinketh so hardly of the King's fortune and success that she is loath to adventure any more of her people with him. Thirdly, she thinketh it impossible to levy and send any power out of the country to be able to join with the King's forces before the Duke of Parma should force the King to battle. Lastly, she

[2] UNTON CORRESPONDENCE, p. 301.   [4] UNTON CORRESPONDENCE, p. 319.
[3] SR 2:603; STC 12283.

is loath to send 2000 of her men out of the Low Country, and
to hazard and waste her disciplined soldiers; for if need be to
have their service in England she will be greatly disappointed
by the loss of them.

But in truth the Queen and her realm are become very
weary with the great expense both in loans of money, and
in waging of men both by land and sea.

14th February.   NEWS FROM FRANCE.[5] From France it is reported that the Duke of Parma hath captured Neuchâtel upon
honourable composition, a place of great advantage to the
enemy.

On the 7th the King was engaged with the enemy, and in
the fight the Count Challigny (the Duke Mercury's brother)
who commanded them was taken prisoner by Chicott, the
King's fool, and very sore hurt. Many were slain and some
captured; the rest escaping gave the alarum to the Duke of
Guise's quarter, who barricaded their lodgings, and armed
themselves. Most of their horse and foot sallied out, but by
this time many shot had come up to the Baron de Biron and
the enemy were forced back into Bures, where the King's
men entering pell-mell with them slew two hundred in the
village and took divers prisoners. The rest were forced to
retire to the other side of the river. All the Duke of Guise's
baggage was taken, his plate and money, and all he had there.
In this engagement Sir William Sackville is either taken or
slain, having been separated from the rest. For himself the
ambassador declareth that he is in great straits; all his horses
are dead or harried out, for they never rest, being on horseback almost day and night; his servants die daily, and many
of them are very weak and sick and cannot live long. The
King meanwhile anxiously expects succour from England.

15th February.   FLESH PROHIBITED IN LONDON DURING
LENT.[6] As in former years, killing and eating flesh in London
during Lent is restrained.

19th February.   PLAYING RESUMED.[7] The Lord Strange's
Players now begin to play at the Rose Theatre on the Bankside, and act this day *Friar Bacon.*

SOLDIERS FOR FRANCE.[8] The Queen having now resolved that
1600 soldiers shall be sent with diligence to Dieppe to the aid

[5] UNTON CORRESPONDENCE, p. 303.   [7] HENS. DIARY 1:13, 2:151.
[6] PROCLAMATIONS 306.   [8] APC 22:256.

of the French King, the Council have ordered 300 to be levied in Sussex, which in heads are to be only 270, deducting the dead pays after the usual rate of 10 in the hundred, to be coated and armed forthwith and embarked at Rye; similarly another 300 from Kent to be embarked at Dover on the 28th of the month.

20th February. NEWS OF ROUEN.[9] Two lackeys of M. Villiers, Governor of Rouen, taken returning from the Duke of Parma, who has now advanced to Cinqsens, declare that he would succour Rouen or force the levying of the siege.

21st February. A JESUIT EXECUTED.[10] Thomas Pormort, a seminary priest, was executed for high treason. This Pormort, being lodged in the house of Topcliffe after his arrest in October 1591, had been pressed very straightly to give information. He declared that in the course of these examinations Topcliffe, hoping to persuade him to recant, used very lewd and familiar speeches to him to show his favour with the Queen. Topcliffe said that all the Stanleys in England were to be suspected as traitors; he himself was so familiar with Her Majesty that he hath very secret dealing with her, having not only seen her legs and knees but felt her belly, saying to her that it was the softest belly of any womankind. She had said unto him, 'Be not these the arms, legs and body of King Henry?' to which he answered 'Yea.' She gave him for a favour a white linen hose wrought with white silk. He said that he was so familiar with her that when he pleased to speak with her he might take her away from any company; and that she was as pleasant with anyone that she loved. The Archbishop of Canterbury, he declared, was a fitter councillor in the kitchen among wenches than in a Prince's Court; as for Justice Young, he would hang the Archbishop and three hundred more if they were in his hands.

At the execution Pormort was forced to stand in his shirt almost two hours on a very cold day while Topcliffe pressed him to deny these words; but he would not.

23rd February. SIR R. WILLIAMS IN COMMAND IN NORMANDY.[11] On the return of the Lord General from Normandy Sir Robert Williams succeedeth to the command.

9 UNTON CORRESPONDENCE, p. 331.   11 APC 22:248.
10 CATH. REC. SOC. 5:209.

24th February. VICTUALS SENT TO NORMANDY.[12] It is said that some hard measure was offered to the Vice-Treasurer by the captains of bands in Normandy for refusing to satisfy them in their undue demands of pay for soldiers under them. Sir Roger Williams is instructed to cause this matter to be reformed and to require the captains to forbear to demand their pay till a muster can be made; and also to let them know that the matter is very offensively taken.

As there hath been so great waste and spoil made in Normandy that victual will be scant and dear, a supply to the value of £1000 is being sent over with the 1600 men under Sir Edmund Yorke, to remain in magazine at Dieppe for the relief of the forces when needful but not otherwise. The price of this victual is to be defalked accordingly from the captains' weekly payments.

The rates to be charged for victual:

Beer, 3 pints—2d; biscuit, 1 lb.—1½d; butter, 1 lb.—5d; cheese, 1 lb.—3d; beef, 1 lb.—3d; bacon and pork, 1 lb.—5d.

25th February. A PETITION AGAINST PLAYS.[13] The Lord Mayor hath complained to the Archbishop of the daily and disorderly exercise of players and playing houses erected in the City whereby, saith he, the youth is greatly corrupted and their manners infected by the wanton and profane devices represented on the stages, prentices and servants withdrawn from their work; and all sorts in general from their daily resort to sermons and other godly exercise, to the great hindrance of the trades and traders of the City and the profanation of religion. To the playing houses resort great numbers of light and lewd persons, harlots, cutpurses, coseners, pilferers, and such like. The Lord Mayor understandeth that the Queen must be served by this sort of people, and for this purpose did licence Mr. Tilney, the Master of the Revels, to reform, exercise and suppress all manner of players, by which he first licensed the playing houses within the City, for the Queen's service. But the Aldermen conclude that the Queen's players might as conveniently exercise in some private place, the City be freed from these continual disorders, and the great offence to the Church removed which would be to the contentment of all good Christians, especially the preachers and ministers who have long time made complaint for the redress of these abuses.

---

[12] APC 22:273, 279; UNTON CORRESPONDENCE, p. 341.

[13] *Remembrancia* 1:635, quoted in MSR 1:68.

26th February.   PARMA RETREATS.[14] The ambassador now reporteth that on the 18th the King dislodged his whole army from Claire, fully resolved to give the Duke of Parma battle rather than to suffer his siege to be raised, for he had heard that the night before the Duke had marched from his camp near Cinqsens, with the greatest part of his vanguard to Cinqsens and Bellencombre with intent to raise the siege or thrust succours into Rouen. But the enemy, having received news of this intent, and being advertised of the effect of the last sally, retired with all possible diligence to Aumale, intending to go along the river to Abbeville. The next day the enemy lodged at Sinarpoint; and the next day still continued his way to Abbeville. This sudden retreat and the diligence used therein cannot be understood, neither is the siege raised nor the town succoured, except that a few men are sent in by stealth, 15 or 20 in a company at several times.

28th February.   MAIMED SOLDIERS TO BE EXAMINED.[15] A proclamation by the Council is published ordering all soldiers who allege that they have served in the wars and still remain in London to be brought before those appointed at the Sessions Hall in the Old Bailey on Saturday next at one o'clock. They are to be examined and viewed so that some good order may be taken for the maimed in service, and for the punishment of the others, common beggars, rogues and able persons, counterfeiting the name of soldiers.

29th February.   THE SCOTTISH WITCHES.[16] There is a book called *News from Scotland* of the damnable life and death of Doctor Fian, a noted sorcerer who was executed at Edinburgh in January last, together with the examination of the witches, as they were uttered in the presence of the Scottish King.

The conspiracy of these witches was first brought to light by one David Seaton, deputy bailiff of the town of Trewent. This Seaton had a maid servant called Geillis Duncan that used secretly to be absent from her master's house every other night when she took in hand almost miraculously to help all that were troubled with any kind of sickness or infirmity, which caused such wonder that her master began to suspect these things to be done by some unnatural or extraordinary means. Whereupon he began to be very inquisitive, and when

[14] UNTON CORRESPONDENCE, p. 341.
[15] PROCLAMATIONS 307.
[16] STC 10841. Some of the evidence brought out in these trials was afterwards incorporated into *Daemonology*, 1597.

she gave him no answer, that he might the better learn the truth, with the help of others he tormented her with the torture of the pilliwinks upon her fingers and by binding a rope round her head. Still she would not confess anything, which made them suspect that she had been marked by the devil, and making diligent search about her they found the enemy's mark in her throat, whereon she confessed that all her doings were done by witchcraft through the wicked allurement of the devil.

After her confession she was committed to prison, where through her accusations she caused certain other notorious witches to be apprehended, notably Agnes Sampson of Haddington, and Dr. Fian, *alias* John Cunningham, master of the school at Saltpans in Lowthian. This Agnes was brought to Holyrood House before the King and others of the nobility of Scotland, but stiffly denied all that was alleged against her, whereon they caused her to be taken back to prison, there to receive the tortures lately provided for witches. Moreover it has been found by careful examination of witches and witchcraft, and by the confession of the witches themselves, that the devil marketh them with some secret mark; for when he receives them as his servants he licketh them with his tongue in some privy part of the body, which is commonly covered with hair, so this mark may not easily be seen, and so long as the devil's mark is not seen by the searchers the witch will not confess to anything.

For over an hour Agnes Sampson was grievously tortured with a rope thrawen round her head, according to the Scottish custom, but would confess nothing until the devil's mark was found upon her privities, when immediately she confessed all that was demanded of her. And now being again brought before the King she confessed that on All Hallowe'en last she with a great company of other witches, to the number of two hundred, had gone to sea, each one in a riddle or sieve, drinking and making merry as they sailed until they came to the kirk of North Berwick in Lowthian, where they landed and danced a reel; Geillis Duncan going before them playing on a small trumpet, called a 'Jews' trump,' until they entered the kirk. This declaration so astonished the King that he sent for Geillis Duncan, who played this dance upon the trumpet before him, much delighted to be present at such strange examinations.

Agnes Sampson said further that the devil in likeness of a man had waited for their coming at North Berwick kirk, and being vexed that they tarried over long in the journey had enjoined on them a penance, which was to kiss his buttocks in sign of duty to him. Then he made an ungodly exhortation, greatly inveighing against the King of Scotland; and took their oaths for their good and true service. So they returned to sea and home again. At this time the witches asked the devil why he so hated the King of Scotland, and he replied that the King was his greatest enemy in all the world.

Sundry other things Agnes Sampson confessed before the King so strange and miraculous that he said they were all extreme liars. Whereupon she answered that she would discover a matter whereby he should not doubt. So taking him a little aside, she declared the very words which had passed between him and his Queen at Upslo in Norway the first night of their marriage, with their answers one to the other; whereat the King wondered greatly and swore by the living God that he believed all the devils in hell could not have discovered the same, acknowledging that her words were most true. Thereafter he gave more credit to what she confessed.

The examination of Dr. Fian also showed the great subtlety of the devil; for being apprehended at the accusation of Geillis Duncan, when he was tortured with the accustomed torments his tongue would not serve him to speak until the rest of the witches bad them search under his tongue, where two pins were found thrust up to the head. At this the witches cried, 'Now is the charm stinted.' Then he was immediately released and brought before the King; his confession was taken, and he willingly set his hand to it. Amongst other things, he declared that he had sought the love of a gentlewoman by witchcraft and sorcery. This gentlewoman being unmarried had a brother who went to his school. Calling the boy to him he asked if he slept with his sister; he answered that he did. Therefore Dr. Fian secretly promised the boy that if he would bring three hairs of his sister's body he would teach him without stripes, giving him a piece of conjured paper to wrap them in.

The gentlewoman being asleep with the boy suddenly cried out to her mother that her brother would not let her sleep; whereon her mother, having a quick understanding, for she was a witch herself, rose immediately and asked the boy very closely what he meant, and the better to extort the truth she beat him. The mother recognising the doctor's purpose thought it best to answer him in his own art, so she took from the boy the paper in which he should have wrapped his sister's hair and went to a young heifer which had never gone to the bull and clipping off three hairs from the udder she told the boy to deliver them to his master, which he immediately did.

As soon as the schoolmaster had received them, he wrought his art upon them, thinking that they were the maiden's hairs; but no sooner had he conjured than the heifer whose hairs they indeed were came to the door of the church where he was, and made towards him, leaping and dancing upon him, and following him out of the church and wherever he went, to the great astonishment of all the townsmen of Saltpans.

Having signed this confession Dr. Fian was taken back to prison, where for a time he appeared very penitent, but in the night he found means to steal the key of the prison door, which he opened and fled away to Saltpans. Hot pursuit was made after him, and he was taken and brought back to prison. There being called before the King he was again examined concerning his flight and what had happened before. But notwithstanding his former confession, he utterly denied all. The King therefore thinking that he had made a fresh league with the devil, commanded a new and most strange torment to be applied to him. The nails on his fingers were split and pulled off with a pair of pincers and under every nail were thrust two needles up to the heads. But for all this, and for the torments of the boots which followed, he would not confess, but said that what he had said and done before was for fear of the pains which he had endured. After great consideration by the King and his Council, Dr. Fian was arraigned and condemned to be burned according to the law of the land. Whereupon he was put in a cart, and being first strangled was cast into a fire made ready and so burned on the Castlehill in Edinburgh on a Saturday at the end of January last past.

1st March. MEN TO BE IMPRESTED FOR SERVICE IN FRANCE.[1] As well as the 330 already imprested, the Lord Mayor is to cause 200 able and sufficient men to be taken up and delivered to Sir Matthew Morgan; and because there are but 400 men musketeers in the whole 1600 soldiers and it is thought that more shots in proportion to the number of the pikes are needful, so these 200 serve as shot.

ANOTHER PETITION OF THE PURITAN PRISONERS.[2] Cartwright and the other Puritan prisoners have again written to the Lord Treasurer asking for release from imprisonment on bail. If, say they, they have transgressed some of the laws of the land, whereof their consciences set in the presence of God do not accuse them, yet seeing it plainly appears by their own answers on oath and by the depositions of witnesses that they have special care in their meetings to keep within obedience of the laws, their transgression, being of ignorance, may find the easier pardon.

Since their coming to prison, divers papists, known enemies of the state, of the Church and commonwealth, have been delivered without renovation of any error; and it is universally granted to any, either papist or schismatic, that upon promise of coming into the Church, they enjoy the same freedom as other subjects. Their hope therefore is that they who not only come to church but labour to the utmost to entertain men in the fellowship of the Church and to reduce others estranged from it, should not be more hardly dealt with in being forced to any confessions or submissions against the testimony of their consciences. Moreover by reason of their long imprisonment and lack of convenient air some five or six of them are sore and dangerously sick.

2nd March.   Sir Walter Ralegh's Expedition.[3] A proclamation is published ordering all mariners, who are pressed to serve with Sir Walter Ralegh, Captain of her Majesty's Guard, to repair to their ships immediately, upon pain of death, so that the service be in no way delayed.

3rd March.   The Fishmongers Rebuked.[4] The Wardens of the Fishmongers' Company are rebuked for their negligence in carrying out the restraint of the killing and uttering of flesh in Lent, for where they were authorised to appoint some trusty and discreet persons to search the houses and shops of victuallers, they did appoint but some mean men for that purpose who negligently execute it. Though but one butcher is licensed for the County of Middlesex and six for the City, there are twenty about the City and suburbs that licentiously and contemptuously kill and utter flesh.

5th March.   Rumours of Peace.[5] The ambassador in France reporteth that the French King is resolved to conclude a peace with his subjects upon any reasonable conditions, to which they are now as much inclined as himself, being weary of the Spanish yoke, and that it is likely to take effect.

3 Proclamations 308.   5 Unton Correspondence, p. 352.
4 APC 22:305.

7th March. THE STATE OF FRANCE.[6] Sir John Norris, who has been called home from Brittany to report on the state of affairs in France, saith that the retreat of the Duke of Parma is not because he intendeth to desert those of his party besieged in Rouen but to join certain troops that come to him under conduct of the Duke of Brunswick and the Count Mansfield, nor is it because of some fear of confusion in the Low Countries, nor of dislike or disagreement with the French. Had this been so he would have hastened to his own Government, and not have taken care to fortify the Bridge of St. Remy where he passed. Seeing his obstinacy in continuing enterprises and his jealousy for reputation, it is likely that he will venture the extremity of his fortune rather than that Rouen be taken.

He doubteth whether the King's army can hope for any good event of the siege. His French disband very fast, all those of Normandy being already retired, his rutters are diminished and will shortly want pay, his lance-knights so decayed with want and sickness that not above 3000 are left, his Switzers ready every day to mutiny. The greatest ground of the siege lies upon the English and Dutch, and whether they are strong enough to take the town when Parma shall seek to succour it must be advised on; or whether the King, leaving the siege if the Duke of Parma should approach, should be able to compel him to fight.

Brittany is in worse case, for the King of Spain has continual care to see his party strengthened; they are possessed of the best towns, and have but weak enemies; only the Queen's assistance kept them well the last year, and as that decayed, so they prevailed; and if it be not now increased, the whole province will be lost, for it is a vain hope to attend any succour from the King. Its maintenance must proceed from her Majesty, and the longer it is deferred, the more difficult will it be; and if much time passes before it is looked into it will be irrecoverable.

ORDERS AGAINST THOSE WHO AIDED DESERTERS.[7] The Lord Mayor is required to cause verbal proclamation to be made throughout the City and suburbs that all victuallers, innkeepers, alehouse keepers and others having in their houses any soldier that has been levied shall upon severe penalties bring him forth to receive punishment according to the laws. Like-

---

[6] RYMER 16:174.   [7] APC 22:318.

wise if any soldier hath run away from his captain and sold or pawned his armour and furniture, it shall be seized and the party with whom it is found committed to prison.

8th March. UNDUTIFUL GENTLEMEN.[8] Some of the inhabitants of Middlesex, divers of them gentlemen of good calling, and some being her Majesty's servants, very wilfully refuse to bear their contribution in the levy of sums of money for the setting forth of soldiers and other public services, so that oftentimes for the expedition of the service the Justices are themselves constrained to disburse money for armour, weapons, and other provisions, whereof some are not yet satisfied for money disbursed three years since. The Council have instructed the Justices to will and require these persons, of what quality and sort soever, to contribute the sums demanded of them (excepting only the ordinary yeomen and grooms of her Majesty's Chambers).

9th March. A SPANISH PRISONER'S ACCOUNT OF THE STATE OF ENGLAND.[9] A certain Spanish prisoner that was released about a month since hath declared that many of all conditions, men and women, assured him of their good wishes for the success of the Spanish in England, and their zeal for the Catholic faith. If they do not openly avow their sympathy it is that they may not lose homes and possessions; others confess themselves Catholics, and, though they have suffered many punishments, yet openly say that they will remain firm and die in the faith. Many complaints, saith he, are made of the large number of declared Catholics, and the Queen is petitioned to have them punished, but she hath ordered that such complaints should not be made against them, and that they shall be allowed to live freely as they wished. There is great fear of the galleys and their commander. Sir Francis Drake is very unpopular, the people of quality saying that he is but of mean origin to have risen so high, the common people regarding him as the cause of the wars; but the Queen esteemeth him highly. They cannot bear the name of Don Antonio, who is called 'The King of Portugal,' as he is considered the cause of all the wars in Portugal. They threaten to stone him, and it is said that the Queen keeps him in a castle which he does not leave. He is miserably poor, lacking both money and servants.

[8] APC 22:312.
[9] *Spanish State Papers* 4:593. For

Don Antonio see note on *13th Aug* 1591.

12th March. BOTHWELL AND THE BORDER.[10] The Wardens
of Border are bidden to keep watch for Bothwell and his com-
plices in the late treasonable attempt on the Scottish King
at Holyrood House, since they are reported to have been received into the northern parts of the kingdom. Thus is the
Queen's government maliciously slandered as though her
realm by her permission or offer were a refuge to the rebels
of the Scottish King, with whom she is in good amity. Special search is to be made at the races and running of horses
in the wardenry of the Lord Scroop, and knowledge of this
order to be given to the opposite Wardens or their deputies,
requiring them to advertise if they know or suspect any of
the rebels to be in this realm.

21st March. HOPEFUL NEWS FROM FRANCE.[11] The Ambassador in France reporteth that the King and his Council resolve to batter Rouen, though everything is done by the
Catholics in his army to hinder that resolution. The King now
awaiteth the coming of the English, and then will immediately begin his approaches. The Governor of Rouen hath
lately much angered the burgesses by a stratagem to enrich
himself by a trick. Some days since a part of the wall of the
town fell down, leaving a breach of forty paces. Thereupon
Monsieur Villiers assembled the people, using feigned persuasions to them to make a composition with the King and alleging that the late succours were not sufficient for their defence, the Duke of Parma had retired and that the King was
resolved to batter the town. On this speech sixty of the burgesses, best inclined to the King's service, answered that they
would very willingly agree to his motion; then these men,
well noted by the Governor, were sent for from their houses,
and made prisoners, being forced to pay great ransoms at his
pleasure for their release. The late offer of a peace is likely to
come to nothing, for the first part of the Leaguers' demand
will be for the King to become a Catholic. They have
proffered it but to confuse the King, distaste his Catholics,
and to better their condition with Spain.

24th March. VOLUNTEERS TO BE LEVIED IN LONDON.[12] The
Lord Mayor and the Justices of Peace for the County of Middlesex now begin to imprest and take up 200 voluntary men

10 APC 22:331.   12 APC 22:361.
11 UNTON CORRESPONDENCE, pp. 361,
379, 384.

to fill up the companies of the bands remaining in Brittany under Sir John Norris.

25th March. DISTRESS IN ROUEN.[13] The garrison of Rouen are reported to be daily thrusting out forty or fifty women and many prentices; they want wine and have forbidden the making of beer because they would spend no corn in drink. They cannot hold out longer than two months if the King do not force them otherwise to yield. Two thousand French that had disbanded have rejoined the army and more return daily in hope of spoil at Rouen. Sir Edmund Yorke with twelve companies arrived at Dieppe on the 18th.

COMPLAINTS AGAINST THE GOVERNOR OF OSTEND.[14] Complaints against Sir Edward Norris, Governor of Ostend, have been renewed by the Council of the States of the United Provinces. The Council now give orders that he shall repair to them when they should send for him to satisfy their demands and yield account of how the contributions of the country have been expended, and to clear himself of the imputations preferred against him; but they in requiring his presence should make choice of a fit time so that the enemy may have no advantage by his absence. When they have viewed his accounts and heard what he can say in his own defence and excuse, they shall not give any sentence or decree against him until the Queen hath been duly informed. She hath given order in respect of the dislike which they conceive of him, that, if they be not satisfied with his answers, he shall be recalled home as soon as he is dismissed by them to be charged with those matters wherein they find fault with him.

RECUSANCY IN THE NORTH.[15] The Earl of Derby is much commended for his zeal in the reformation of his tenants from their sinfulness in not resorting to their parish churches. He hath also joined with the Commissioners to reduce the recusants throughout Lancashire, now almost overflown with a multitude of obstinate persons, offending publicly in the sight of the world, as it seemeth without any fear of punishment. Her Majesty greatly allows of their honourable, wise and politic proceedings; and the Council pray him not to stay the good cause begun in restraining the principal obstinate recusants either by imprisonment or by committing them to the custody of such as be sound in religion.

[13] UNTON CORRESPONDENCE, p. 391.   [15] APC 22:369.
[14] APC 22:363.

This course is a most necessary to be taken in the present dangerous state of the country; nor should the reformation be delayed by following a long course in answering strictly all the statutes, howsoever any of the Justices may have delivered their opinions upon the strict point of law, not respecting what is most necessary at this time and in that county. If any should repine against his former proceedings upon conceit that any Justice or learned man showeth opinions to the contrary, he is to be forthcoming and caused to declare the name of the Justice who shall be charged therewith, as a matter not any wise allowable.

27th March.   GLEMHAM'S SHIPS TO BE STAYED.[16] It appeareth that certain goods and merchandise have lately been taken out of a Venetian argosy at sea by Captain Glemham and his consorts. The Council order that any of his ships that be found shall be stayed and the goods in them sequestered, and six of his chiefest ships stayed.

31st March.   PURITAN PRISONERS RELEASED.[17] The Puritan prisoners are now released from prison, the Council being pleased that the charges against them should no further be proceeded with.

2nd April.   MERCY TO BE SHOWN TO DEBTORS.[1] Some time since Commissioners were appointed to inquire into the causes of poor prisoners detained a long time in prison for debt. They report that the adverse parties will not be reduced to conformity or commiseration. Now are the Council moved by the pitiful complaints of the prisoners, and by reports that of late very many of them are dead in prison, whereby their creditors lose all their debts, whereof in time they might have received a good part if not the whole sum. But if no persuasion or intreaty shall move the creditors to compassion, then shall they be plainly let to understand, that, if at any time information be brought against them upon a penal statute, or other advantage taken against them in any matter by the strictness of the law, let them look for no favour but all extremity that may be used.

7th April.   TWO PRISONERS' RANSOM.[2] Some time since John Dipford and Walter Horsey, merchants of Exeter, sent

---

[16] APC 22:373. See also *31st Mar*   [1] APC 22:384.
1591, 17th May 1592, 19th Aug 1594.   [2] APC 22:392.
[17] PEARSON, pp. 357, 479.

their servants John Gupwell and Thomas Dipford to the town of Lanyon in Brittany with lawful merchandise. Not only did the Leaguers take their goods but committed the men to prison to the Castle of Callett near Morlaix, whence Dipford was released on ransom, but Gupwell is held to ransom by the first of May or else is threatened with execution. For the relief of their losses and the discharge of their servants' ransoms, the Council instruct the customers of Dartmouth and Opsam to permit these merchants to transport 20 packs of kerseys, 4 packs of broad cloths, 3 packs of bays, and 3 packs of coarse cloth stockings, after paying the customs due, in a bark of twenty or thirty tons.

DISTRESS IN ROUEN.[3] It appeareth that Rouen is in some distress for victual by the disbanding of many soldiers of the garrison who daily leave the town and submit themselves to the King's mercy, whereby the King and his Council have great hope of the timely rendering of the town if it be not relieved by the return of the Duke of Parma.

12th April.   BRETON'S 'PILGRIMAGE TO PARADISE.'[4] *The Pilgrimage to Paradise*, joined with *The Countess of Pembroke's Love*, compiled in verse by Nicholas Breton, gentleman, is sent to the press. The first telleth of the journeyings of the Soul, with his five servants the senses, past the snaring temptations of the flesh until he reaches an angel by whom he is forewarned against the beast with seven heads which are ambition, avarice, gluttony, sloth, lechery, malice, and murder, and protected with seven books by which, after long debate, the monster is slain. At length the pilgrim comes to a fisherman with whom he sails and who tells him his story. And continuing their way they meet a world of people making piteous moan.

In *The Countess of Pembroke's Love* he likeneth her to a phœnix in rarity, aspiring to the Heavenly Love and despising all earthly gifts which men of all kinds and degrees brought in to her.

17th April.   THE SIEGE OF ROUEN RAISED.[5] It is reported from France that the siege of Rouen is raised, the King having been suddenly advertised that the Duke of Parma was marching towards his camp with 12,000 foot and 4000 horse.

[3] UNTON CORRESPONDENCE, p. 408.
[4] STC 3683. Dated 12th April in the Epistle.
[5] UNTON CORRESPONDENCE, p. 413.

He was within four leagues of Rouen before the army rose, using all possible diligence in his march to surprise the King and defeat his army of rutters in their lodgings and the English troops in their quarters. This was only prevented by the discovery and advertisement of the Duke of Boullion, who made his retreat with the rutters in view of the Duke of Parma's army with great hazard and no loss. Thus the King's army was forced to march away with all haste, and at its rising had very hot skirmishes but without loss. Sir Roger Williams' horse was shot, and his hat in two places; he served very honourably with great courage and discretion in the view of the King, greatly to his commendation, as did many of the English who were the last to retreat. That night the army encamped within a league of Pont de L'Arch, expecting the coming of the Duke of Parma to give battle whereunto the Duke of Mayne and Villiers earnestly pressed him. Whereupon the King was immediately advertised and made choice of the place of battle, fortifying and trenching the place. The Duke of Parma lodged at Croissett, and his army along the river. He sent to all castles and gentlemen's houses where was great store of corn to cause them to bring it to Rouen.

21st April. 'THE DEFENCE OF CONNY-CATCHING.'[6] The conny-catchers have one 'Cuthbert Connycatcher' that answers Greene in a book called *The Defence of Conny-Catching, or a Confession of those two injurious pamphlets published by R. G. against the practitioners of many nimble witted and mystical sciences.* Herein Greene is attacked for having touched small scapes but let gross faults pass without any reprehension, and himself accused of conny-catching; 'ask the Queen's players if you sold them not *Orlando Furioso* for 20 nobles, and when they were in the country sold the same play to the Lord Admiral's men for as much more?' And to show the nature of more gross abuses examples are given of the villainy of an usurer; a miller; a serving man, counterfeiting to be gentlemen to make a good match; a man that was married to sixteen wives but well cured by the last; and a tailor.

27th April. THE FRENCH KING ATTACKS PARMA.[7] The Ambassador reporteth that on the 17th Caudebec surrendered by composition to the Duke of Parma, who had encamped his army within a league of Ivetot in open field where he was strongly entrenched; the Dukes of Mayne and Guise with 2000 horse and 1200 foot, lodging at Ivetot. Hereupon the King marched towards them with all his army in order of battle, and ten pieces of artillery, until he was within a mile and a half. There he made a stand, and himself with 500 horse advanced further to discover the enemy. The Duke of Mayne showed himself with 1000 horse, whom the King charged with two troops of horse and pursued to their quarter, in which charge M. Coutenan, a special commander of horse, was taken prisoner, who assured the King that the Duke of Parma had but then taken the alarm of his coming and would not believe that the King durst look upon him; if he did, he was resolved to give battle.

This news much contented the King, who retired in time to lodge his army in the villages, preparing the next day to give the Duke of Parma battle, if he would accept it, near Ivetot in a fair champaign field.

Early in the morning (18th) the King drew all his forces together waiting for the enemy; but finding no likelihood of their preparation to fight, he resolved to force their lodging of Ivetot, and to lodge there himself in despite of them or else to force them to accept the battle. He therefore marched with his whole army, advancing certain cuirassiers and harquebusiers on horseback to observe the enemy's countenance who were now marching towards him with horse and foot. On perceiving the King with his forces to come on so resolutely, they retired most dishonourably, quitting their quarter and setting it on fire, and fled in disorder until they came to Parma's camp. The King with his horse had them in chase, himself conducting them, killing many and taking some gentlemen prisoners, amongst them the Baron of Chastre, son of M. Chastre. The Duke of Mayne hardly escaped, for he fled so fast that his horse was like to have failed him for want of breath.

That night the King lodged at Ivetot, and the rest of the army in the villages a league beyond it, within three-quarters of a mile of Parma's intrenchment, who was much amated with this dishonour, imagining that he was betrayed by his French.

The 19th the King's army stayed at Ivetot, offering many skirmishes to the enemy, which they coldly entertained. The 20th the King dislodged with his army and marched to Varqueville, a mile and a half from Ivetot towards Newhaven, which way the Duke of Parma's army most lodged, in order to cut off his victuals from Newhaven and for want thereof to force him to a battle. After the King's army was quartered and lodged, the enemy's horse made towards them; whereupon the King sent for Sir Roger Williams to come to him with 200 muskets and 150 pikes of his best, who were no sooner come to the King but five cornets of Spanish and Italian horse charged them before any horse could succour them. The English encountered them with so great resolution and courage that they took two or three cornets; whereof one the King sent to the Queen, another was torn by the soldiers. Divers of the chief leaders of the horse were slain, and many other of the enemy. 600 Spanish foot, with muskets and pikes, came to second their horse and entered a very hot skirmish with the English; in the meantime other English companies came to their succour. In the end they forced the enemy's horse and foot to retire into their quarters with very great dishonour and loss. Of the English, 40 were hurt and 8 slain; Captain Rush was hurt in the thigh, no other men of quality hurt or slain.

Sir Roger Williams unarmed served most honourably and unhorsed their best leader, and, encountering besides with George Basta, did, as it was thought, hurt him in the neck, giving him a very great blow with his sword. The King commended him highly and did more than wonder at the valour of our nation. Sir Matthew Morgan and his brother also served very valiantly, and Captain Henry Poore. This action greatly encouraged our men, who had very good spoils of the enemy. The King gave great honour to Sir Roger Williams and his men, whom he had held as lost, and caused public thanks to be given to God.

A letter of the Duke of Parma to the King of Spain was intercepted wherein he represented his misery for want of sufficient forces to encounter the King, and his want of victuals and means to return. He complained greatly of the Duke de Mayne and the French, concluding that he must hazard the loss of his army, for without fighting he could not return.

The Duke of Parma had been wounded some days before, being shot in the arm between the bones; the hurt is not dangerous of itself, yet his sickly body and the accidents that usually follow such hurts give some cause of doubt to physicians. Many troops are now daily coming to the French King, and more daily expected.

THE TRIAL OF SIR JOHN PERROT.[8] Sir John Perrot, who hath lain a prisoner in the Tower for more than a year past, was brought to his trial before the King's Bench Bar, before the commissioners being the Lord Chamberlain, the Lord Buckhurst, Sir Robert Cecil, the Lord Chief Justice and other judges. He was charged on two indictments; the first that in 1587 he went about to depose and raise rebellion against the Queen, that he had promised help to the King of Spain, and that he had procured and moved Sir Brian O'Rourke to rebellion. The second that he conferred with Sir William Stanley in 1586 about his treasonable practices.

To these indictments he pleaded not guilty very vehemently. The jury was then sworn, and the indictments having been read, Sergeant Puckering for the Queen rehearsed the principal points of the indictment. But before he came to the particular offences, he told them that the origin of these treasons proceeded from the imagination of the heart; which imagination was of itself high treason, albeit the same proceeded not to any overt fact; and the heart being possessed with the abundance of his traitorous imagination and not being able so to contain itself, burst forth in vile and traitorous speeches and from thence to horrible and heinous actions.

At this Sir John prayed Sergeant Puckering to lay aside words and proceed to the matter of the indictment; to which he answered that he would proceed by degrees, but would first begin with his contemptuous words which in themselves contained the high treason.

Amongst other speeches, it was reported that when Sir Nicholas Bagnol, Marshal of Ireland, was with Sir John in his house, hot words had broken out and Sir John cried, 'If it were not for yonder pilled and paltry sword that lieth in the window I would not brook these comparisons,' meaning her Majesty's Sword of Justice which was carried before him.

Sir John answered that he had called the sword 'pilled and paltry' because the scabbard was old and worn; and within a week after he had caused a new scabbard to be made. Then falling into other idle discourse, the Lord Buckhurst begged him not to speak from the purpose for it would but hurt his cause.

Then it was shown that Sir John, having called a parliament in Dublin, moved, amongst other matters, to suppress the Cathedral Church of St. Patrick; and her Majesty then sending letters to the contrary he said, with a stern countenance, 'Nay,

[8] Cobbett's *State Trials* 1:1315.

God's wounds, I think it strange she should use me thus.' With these words the Bishop of Meath was moved to find fault with his undutiful demeanour, for he spoke as though the kingdom were his own and not the Queen's. Sir John answered that the Archbishop of Dublin was his mortal enemy, and the reason why he was moved to suppress the Cathedral was to have a University created thereon, but he was withstood by the Archbishop because he and his children received 800 marks a year from the Cathedral, and further the Archbishop bore him great malice because when the Queen had sent him letters to discharge idle and unnecessary pensioners he had discharged among the rest one of the Archbishop's sons.

Then it was shown that when the office of the Clerk of the Exchequer was empty and letters were sent from the Queen that Mr. Errington should be admitted to this office, Sir John said, 'This fiddling woman troubles me out of measure: God's wounds, he shall not have the office, I will give it to Sir Thomas Williams.' This was proved by the oath of Philip Williams. Sir John declared that this Williams was his mortal enemy, a naughty, lewd man of no credit who had abused the Lord Treasurer in a letter, for which he had beaten him in his chambers.

It was also shown that when the Queen had written him a letter about the time that the Spaniards should come, to look well to his charge, he said, 'Ah, silly woman, now she shall not curb me, she shall not rule me; now, God's lady dear, I shall be her white boy now again: doth she think to rule me now?' Shortly after John Garland brought Sir John a letter, which so greatly displeased him that he broke forth into these terms: 'God's wounds, this it is to serve a base bastard pissing kitchen woman; if I had served any prince in Christendom, I had not been so dealt withal.'

All these speeches Sir John denied very vigorously with oaths.

Next Mr. Attorney proceeded to open the treasons which were alleged against Sir John. He declared that when Dr. Craugh, a known traitor and papist, should have been arrested, Sir John sent out warrants that he should be sought in all places except the White Knight's country, where he knew Craugh to be. To this Sir John answered that there was a God above all, and he marvelled that he who had known religion these forty-six years should be charged with favouring of papists and mass-mongers.

Other witnesses showed that he had favoured traitors,

amongst them Sir Brian O'Rourke, lately executed at Tyburn, whom he might have arrested had he wished.

Then Sir Dennis O'Roughan was called to testify against Sir John, and the book being offered him to swear, Sir John said it was no matter whether he swore or not, for his word and his oath were all one; for there was neither truth nor honesty in him. Sir Dennis testified amongst other things that Sir John had used extreme malice towards the Cavener, and the better to execute his purpose, he had found means that the Cavener should offend the law by making an escape out of prison, and, being afterwards taken, he was hanged for having escaped.

Sir John now began to discredit the evidence of Sir Dennis, declaring he had changed his religion five times in six years; was a common drunkard, a common liar, and had been forsworn a thousand times. Sir Dennis, being again called, swore that Sir John Perrot and Sir Brian O'Rourke had been confederates together in the last Parliament and that each had sworn to the other to help the King of Spain. Here Sir John grew very angry with O'Roughan and declared that he was a lousy villain, a rogue, and had the pox on him.

Other witnesses declared that Sir John had exchanged letters with Sir William Stanley, and that when he came to England he went about to get a pardon, wherein he showed his guilty conscience.

After the Queen's Counsel and Sir John had addressed the jury, they departed from the bar and within three-quarters of an hour they returned with a verdict of guilty. Then Sergeant Puckering in the Queen's name began to pray judgment; but Sir John desired most humbly that he might speak with some of their honours before sentence should be pronounced.

To this after some conference they agreed, and judgment was deferred until the Queen's pleasure should be known. Then the Court was adjourned until the 2nd May.

4th May. AN ACCIDENT AT GREENWICH.[1] A tiltboat of Gravesend carrying some forty persons was run down by a hoy near Greenwich, where the Court now remains. Most of the passengers were drowned in sight of the Queen, who hath been much frightened.

7th May. PARMA'S CAMP PILLAGED.[2] From France the ambassador reporteth that the Duke of Parma, who intended by stealth to regain Rouen and to pass from thence to Neuchâtel, was pursued with such diligence by the King that he was forced to retire towards Caudebec, where for want of a bridge he resolved to cross over in boats, having gathered together all the boats of Rouen. But the weather is so tempestuous that they cannot as yet pass many over.

On 30th April, the King assembled early in the morning 1000 English, as many Scots and Netherlands, 800 lance-knights, 1500 Switzers, 2000 French shot, 1500 French cui-rassiers and as many rutters, causing three small pieces of artillery to march with them. The rest were left at their quar-ter. The King gave the leading of 200 cuirassiers and as many rutters and 300 shot to the Baron of Biron, and 1500 French shot to Grilion. Sir Roger Williams was appointed to second him with 200 English and 400 Scottish and Netherlands; the Marshal D'Aumont with 300 cuirassiers; the rest of the force remained with the King for their retreat. The Baron Biron and the others were commanded to give in to the quarter where the Duke of Parma's horse were lodged, to defeat them, to take spoil of their baggage and burn their quarter; which they accordingly performed. But the Baron's overhastiness, enter-ing the quarter with the troops before the rest could come to second him, and the greediness of the soldiers to spoil, hin-dered the performance of the enterprise and was the occasion that the enemy escaped and that few were killed; and had not Sir Roger Williams with his 200 English withstood the enemy better, the Baron with his companies and the Marshal D'Au-mont had been overthrown. But God gave them very good success, for the enemy wanted courage, and our men, forcing the quarter, killed 150, taking the spoils of 500 waggons, and all the baggage, and brought away 1000 horse of all sorts, and as much spoil as is worth 50,000 crowns at least. The rest of the quarter and spoils our men set on fire and then retired without loss. The attempt was most desperate and resolved by the King to force the enemy to fight, which nothing could work.

The English soldiers in these days are much harried and many disband daily for want of money and victuals.

8th May. FURTHER REINFORCEMENTS FOR FRANCE.[3] The Queen upon the present great and urgent occasion determines to have 2000 footmen complete, and 100 horsemen from the

[3] APC 22:431.

troops in her pay in the Lowlands to be speedily transported by sea into France.

13th May. AN UNLUCKY GAOLER.[4] Richard Mudford, Keeper of the Counter in Southampton, had in his custody one Edmund Mellish, imprisoned for debt. This Mellish escaped some two years since, and, notwithstanding the Council's warrant for help and assistance in the speedy recovery and apprehension of the prisoner, and Mudford's diligent travail in search of him, yet is he still at large; and the keeper, unless some charitable course be taken, liable to pay his debt of two hundred crowns and £14 in costs, besides the loss of his great expenses and travail, amounting to no less sum. The Council therefore write to Mellish's mother, the Lady Allot, moving her charitably to consider the poor keeper's distress by discharging him of the whole payment of her son's debt.

DESERTERS AT DOVER.[5] It is credibly reported that, notwithstanding the Council's orders for the restraint of such soldiers as without passport draw themselves from the service of the French King in Normandy, above two hundred men of strong and able bodies are landed at Dover and the places near without passport, in the company of some few sick men, and without stay. These men are allowed to beg in the county with the passport of the Mayor, using most slanderous speeches of the Queen's service and entertainment, tending to the great discouragement of such as be willing to serve.

17th May. A CLAIM AGAINST GLEMHAM.[6] In the Admiralty Court was heard the cause between John de Riviera, a merchant stranger residing in London, acting on behalf of certain Venetians, and Captain Edward Glemham of the *Edward and Constance,* touching sugars and other goods taken in the Levant Seas, which Riviera claims, though without proof, as belonging to Venetians. The judges order that the goods shall be appraised by six experienced men chosen by de Riviera and Glemham, and the inventory lodged in the Admiralty Court; Glemham to have possession and to dispose of them at his pleasure in a bond in double their value to pay their first value within two months after proof has been made or for so much as can be proved to belong to Venetians or others not the subjects of the King of Spain.

[4] APC 22:443.
[5] APC 22:448.
[6] SP DOM 242:19. See *31st Mar 1591.*

21st May. WEAKNESS OF THE NORMANDY COMPANIES.[7] It appears from the certificates sent by Sir Edmund Yorke before his death that on the first of the month the companies in Normandy are so decayed that there are not above 1500 men, and since then these are much more weakened by sickness, famine, escaping and other indirect means. By good estimation the numbers remaining there, though in the name of nineteen captains, will not make above eight companies, whereby her Majesty is much abused both in her opinion of the strength of the forces there and in the greatness of her charge, as much by weekly pays and lendings as if the companies were full and complete. Sir Roger Williams is ordered to take a general muster and to reduce all unto eight companies or according to the numbers of able men, appointing 100 men to serve under such captains of the old bands from the Low Countries as by their valour and by careful preserving their companies together best deserve. The captains of every band to be caused to be paid and discharged without unnecessary delay.

25th May. RUMOURS.[8] This morning it is said that the Queen is out of quiet with her foreign foes and home broils. It is expected that the new Lord Chancellor will be nominated to-day, and the choice believed to be between the Solicitor-General and Sergeant Puckering; but the Queen is not yet determined.

PUCKERING MADE LORD KEEPER.[9] John Puckering, Esquire, one of her Majesty's Sergeants at Law, about three o'clock in the afternoon was by the Queen made a Knight in the Privy Chamber, and straightway going into the Council Chamber he took the oath of supremacy and of a privy councillor at the Council Board. Thereupon being placed in the lowest place of the Council according to his calling, and having signed a letter as Councillor, he returned to the Queen, in company with the rest of the Council, into the Privy Chamber, where, after some grave speeches and admonitions how to use such a great office to the pleasing of God and the content of all people having any causes afore him, she delivered into his hands the Great Seal, to have and keep the same as Lord Keeper of the Great Seal of England. And so he came down again into the Council Chamber, took his place as Lord Keeper and signed letters accordingly.

[7] APC 22:478.   [9] APC 22:500.
[8] SP DOM 242:25.

28th May. SEDITIOUS BOOKS FROM ABROAD.[10] Divers traitorous and seditious books have recently been brought into the country by most lewd persons, who the better to colour their vile doings wrap them up in merchandise and after disperse them to evil disposed persons, infecting them and others with their poisoned libels. All ships arriving in the realm are to be searched, as well as any houses or places where it is suspected that such slanderous books may be hidden.

31st May. A DISASTER IN BRITTANY RUMOURED.[11] Sundry rumours are abroad of a great success of the enemy under the Duke Mercury against the Princes of Conde and Dombes, who were besieging the town of Craon in Brittany. The Princes have been compelled by the Duke's Bretons and Spaniards to leave their siege and forced to fly with the loss of the most part of their footmen, amongst them many English, about whom there is no certain news how many be lost, taken or escaped. Sir Henry Norris, that is lieutenant to his brother, the General in that part, is to repair thither with all speed to understand the true estate of the Queen's people. To take with him a quantity of arms and powder, and order from Sir Thomas Shirley, the Treasurer for Wars, for a proportion of money so that the English who want weapons may be furnished, and those saved may have money to relieve them for their victualling and other necessaries. He carries a special letter from her Majesty to M. Hallard Mountmorency, Governor of Caen, requesting his advice and assistance. Also he shall resort to both the Princes (if he finds it convenient), declaring to them how much her Majesty is discomfited with this great loss, and requiring them to show all favour to her people that be saved.

MR. HARINGTON AND THE PRINTER.[12] Mr. John Harington, High Sheriff of the County of Somerset, some time since did withdraw one Thomas Wells, a prentice, from his master Augustine Rither, printer and graver of London, to serve him in his profession. The Council rebuke Mr. Harington for so uncharitable an action, not fitting a gentleman of his quality. He is strictly charged to redeliver Wells to his master or to make personal appearance without delay to answer his default.

1st June. RALEGH DISGRACED.[1] It is rumoured that Sir

10 APC 22:486.
11 APC 22:502.
12 APC 22:504.
1 W. Stebbing, *Sir Walter Ralegh*,

1899, p. 88. There is no direct contemporary evidence of Ralegh's offence though Camden briefly records it. It caused considerable scandal.

Walter Ralegh hath been recalled from the fleet which is now at sea and hath been cast into the Tower. He hath offended with Mistress Elizabeth Throckmorton, one of her Majesty's Ladies-in-Waiting.

2nd June. FOREIGN ARTISANS IN ENGLAND.[2] Monsieur Caron, Agent for the States, hath lately made suit to the Queen and the Council on behalf of divers poor men of those countries living in London, some of them candlemakers or exercising like manual trades. He petitioned that certain proceedings under penal statutes made against them might be stayed, and these poor men permitted to continue their accustomed trades whereby they maintain themselves and their families. Hereupon those that laid the informations, being called before the Council, brought in their defence some requests from the Lord Mayor showing that of late years the numbers of handicraftsmen of strangers are so much increased within the City and suburbs that the freemen of the City are supplanted and their living taken from them. These strangers who came hither in these times of trouble abroad the better to enjoy the free exercise of their consciences are so extraordinarily favoured that some are grown to great wealth. Some of them convey beyond the seas the commodities of this realm, whereby the prices of divers things are increased and the Queen deceived in her custom.

The Council now instruct Sir Henry Killigrew and other gentlemen to make inquisition how many strangers of every nation use handicrafts that are not allowable in the City and suburbs, where they inhabit, what occupations they use, how many both men and women they keep in their houses, how long they have been in the realm, to what churches they resort, and whether they keep any English born in their houses.

This inquisition is to be made with as much secrecy as may be whereby neither the English artisans and apprentices take any comfort or boldness to contemn the strangers, or the poor strangers be made afraid to be hardly used.

5th June. THE DISASTER IN BRITTANY.[3] Sir Henry Unton hath now reported at length upon the disaster in Brittany. It appeareth that on the 13th May, the Princes of Conde and Dombes raised their siege from Craon, understanding of the approach of the Duke Mercury towards them with all his

[2] APC 22:506.
[3] UNTON CORRESPONDENCE, p. 460. News of the disaster in general terms had reached London by 29th May. Burleigh answered Unton's letter of the 24th on 6th June.

forces; and intending to retire (for they were too weak to encounter their enemies) they were suddenly surprised through
want of advertisements, of counsel and good resistance, being
charged by the enemy both before and behind, they having
taken an unfit, straight passage to retire with their cannon and
their forces. The English and lance-knights only came to
blows, who served with great courage and paid for it accordingly, being most of them slain. The rest of the French ran
away at the first and saved themselves until the Duke Mercury
coasted them, and then overtaking some of them in rout killed
many but took the most part prisoners. Of the artillery they
saved not one piece, having seven cannon and four demi-
culverin, without ever making shot with them.

The Princes' forces were about 3500 foot and 400 horse,
and the enemy between 5 and 6000 foot and 800 horse. The
Duke Mercury hath since pursued his victory and taken Chateau Goutyer and Le Val, which surrendered voluntarily, both
being passages of the Mayne and therefore of very great importance. He is now before Mayne, the chief town.

This unhappy accident hath struck a great fear and terror
into all the hearts of the King's subjects in Brittany, and therefore will hazard the loss of the towns and places there if they
be not relieved immediately and better assured. The King's
designs of blocking Rouen and Newhaven and clearing Normandy are frustrated, he is diverted from following the Duke
of Parma, as before he intended, and hath now been forced to
return to Vernon to take counsel for his best course to succour
Brittany. The Leaguers are animated and the Parisians receive
1200 Spaniards, Italians and Walloons into garrison, and in
a manner become less willing for peace.

Immediately after the receipt of these news the King sent
for Sir Henry Unton and imparted them to him at length with
great passion and discontent, discoursing at large of his miserable estate, of the factions of his servants, and of their ill dispositions. Then he required the ambassador's opinions touching his course for Brittany, and also what further aid he might
expect from the Queen, alleging that unless he were immediately strengthened from England, it was impossible for him to
resist the greatness of Spain who assailed the country by Brittany, Languedoc, by the Low Countries, by the Duke of Savoy
and the Duke of Lorraine.

The ambassador replied mildly, humbly craving pardon
from the delivery of any opinion as a public minister, but not
refusing as a private person to deliver his conceit by way of

discourse, not of advice. On this being granted by the King he began to set out the importance of Brittany; the King's want of providence therein; his breach of promise in not sending forces thither; the King of Spain's great desire to have that country and how much his honour, profit, and safety might be specially impeached and endangered. He then delivered such reasons as might urge the necessity of his defence of that country; and lastly peremptorily pressed his going in person with an army into Brittany to resist the enemies' pursuit of victory, concluding by giving him neither any manner of comfort nor discomfort of the Queen's resolution.

To this the King gave a willing ear, and replied with many thanks, yielding many excuses of his want of means, not of disposition to provide a remedy. In the mean season, he said he would take counsel and then acquaint the ambassador with his resolution.

Soon after this, the Queen's letters for the ambassador's revocation (for which he hath long petitioned) came to hand; whereupon he took occasion to repair to the King and to crave his leave to depart, which the King very willingly granted, requesting him, partly for his better safety, but chiefly for the better understanding of his further resolution concerning his affairs, to attend him to Vernon, where within six days he should meet his Council.

12th June. RIOTS IN SOUTHWARK.[4] There was great disorder in Southwark last evening, until about 8 o'clock at night, when the Lord Mayor, taking with him one of the Sheriffs, came down upon the rioters, finding great multitudes of the people assembled, especially some apprentices of the feltmakers, out of Barmsey Street and the Blackfriars, together with a number of loose and masterless men. Whereupon proclamation was made and, the multitude having been dismissed, the Lord Mayor apprehended the doers of the disorder and committed them to prison. This morning, examinations being taken, it is found that the disorder began upon the serving of a warrant from the Lord Chamberlain by one of the Knight Marshal's men upon a feltmonger's servant who was committed to the Marshalsea without any cause of offence. Whereupon the apprentices, under pretence of meeting at a play, assembled themselves to make a rescue. The inhabitants of Southwark of best reputation complain that the Knight Marshal's men in serving their warrants use not themselves with good discretion

[4] *Remembrancia* 1:662, in MSC 1:71.

and moderate usage, but by their most rough and violent manner provoke them whom they have to arrest by their rough and violent manner. In this case they entered a house where a warrant was to be served with a dagger drawn, affrighting the good wife of the house who sat by the fire with a young child in her arms; and afterwards taking the party and several others committed him to prison where they lay five days without making their answer. When therefore the apprentices' men assembled themselves before the Marshalsea, the Knight Marshal's men issued forth with their daggers drawn and bastinadoes in their hands, beating the people, of whom some came, as their manner was, merely to gaze; and afterwards drew their swords, whereby the tumult was incensed and they themselves endangered but that help came to prevent further mischief.

15th June.   SOME ENGLISH SAILORS ILL-TREATED.[5] Sir Henry Unton is to make complaint to the King of the hard treatment offered to certain English sailors. It seemeth that in August last a ship called the *Mary of Waterford,* laden with salt, pepper, suckats, marmalade, and other commodities, about 60 leagues from Cape Finisterre was taken by one Govant, Captain of the *Salamander* of Dieppe, and other subjects of the French King. This man spoiled them of all their goods, worth £800, beside the hindrance and damage to the extent of £200, and so left the company of the ship, being sixteen persons, only with a basket of broken bread and a small roundlet of cider mixed with water. In this state they continued at sea twenty-five days before they could recover any land, so that two died with hunger and the rest were brought in so weak that they were greatly endangered.

17th June.   UNTON RETURNS.[6] Sir Henry Unton hath come to London, having received his despatch on the 10th.

19th June.   RECUSANCY IN WALES.[7] The Council write to the Earl of Pembroke to certify the names of those gentlemen in the Principality of Wales, that be sound in religion and well affected, to be appointed commissioners for the inquiry of Jesuits, Seminaries and other suspected persons. Since no commission is appointed for Wales numbers of recusants flee

5 APC 22:532.   7 APC 22:543.
6 UNTON CORRESPONDENCE, pp. 470, 471.

thither so that there is daily infection and falling away from religion in those parts.

In Carmarthen many, both men and women, in the night season and by day repair to certain places where in times past were pilgrimages, images or offerings; they assemble sometimes in great numbers, a thing intolerable to be permitted after so long a time of the preaching of the Gospel. These superstitious monuments are to be pulled down, broken, and quite defaced so that no remnant, token or memory may remain. Should any hereafter repair to those places they shall be apprehended and severely punished for their lewd behaviour that others may be warned by their examples to take heed of such intolerable abuses.

22nd June. FATHER SOUTHWELL THE JESUIT.[8] Topcliffe hath written to the Queen concerning Father Southwell the Jesuit that he took prisoner a few days since, saying that he keeps him very straitly in his strong chamber at Westminster; and if her Majesty wishes to know anything in his heart, then shall he be made to stand against the wall, his feet standing upon the ground and his hands put as high as he can reach against the wall—like a trick at trenchmore—shall enforce him to tell all.

23rd June. PLAYING CEASES AT THE ROSE THEATRE.[9] The Lord Strange's men have ceased from playing at the Rose Theatre, their plays during the five days past being *The Spanish Tragedy, Harry the Sixth, The Comedy of Jeronimo, Tamar Cam, The Knack to Know a Knave.*

RUMOURS OF PEACE IN FRANCE.[10] It is reported that peace in France is expected and the King has sent M. de Saucy to acquaint her Majesty therewith or else to see how he may be helped at her hands to stand the war. The Duke de Mayne is at St. Denis with the King on safe conduct, the terms offered by the League being liberty of religion on both sides where it is, and, where it is not, no inquisition; the Protestants to have churches in the fauxbourgs, and the Leaguers to have in every province certain towns of caution for certain years.

ABUSES IN THE NORTH.[11] In the north those evilly disposed towards religion hold May games, Morris dances, plays, bear baitings, ales and other pastimes on Sundays and holy days at

[8] STRYPE'S ANNALS 4:132.   [10] SP DOM 242:58.
[9] HENS. DIARY 1:15.   [11] APC 22:547; SP DOM 240:138.

the time of divine service to draw away the people when men assemble together for the hearing of God's Word and to join in common prayers. The Council have prayed the Earl of Derby to give special direction to all Justices to forbid these pastimes on Sunday or holy days at the time of divine service, sermons, or other godly exercises; and to cause the chief offenders to be sent up to answer their contentious and lewd behaviour.

Small reformation has been made in those parts by the Ecclesiastical Commissioners as appeareth by the emptiness of churches on Sundays and holy days, and the multitude of bastards and drunkards; great sums have been levied under pretence of the commission, but the counties are in worse case than before and the number of those that do not resort to divine service greater. The people lack instruction, for the preachers are few, most of the parsons unlearned, many of those learned not resident, and divers unlearned daily admitted into very good benefices by the Bishop. The youth are for the most part being trained up by such as possess papistry; and no examination made of schools and schoolmasters. The proclamation for the apprehension of seminaries and Jesuits, and for calling home children from parts beyond the sea is not being executed. Some of the coroners and justices and their families do not frequent church, and many of them have not communicated at the Lord's Supper since the beginning of the Queen's reign. In many places the seminaries have lately offered disputations against the settled religion, but nothing is said to them.

They that resort to church are so few that preachers who were determined to preach on Sundays and holy days refrain from lack of auditors; the people so swarm in the streets and alehouses during service time, that open markets are kept and in many churches only the curate and the clerk are present. Marriages and christenings are celebrated by seminary and other priests in corners, and in some parts children baptized according to law have afterwards been rebaptized by priests. Divers mass priests, being apprehended, refuse to be examined upon oath as to where they frequent. Alehouses are innumerable, and the law for suppressing and keeping them in order not executed, whereby toleration of drunkenness, unlawful games and other abuses follow. Small or no reformation has followed the letters of the Council. The recusants have spies about the Council to give intelligence when anything is intended against them so that they may shift out of the way and avoid being apprehended.

RIOTING EXPECTED IN LONDON.[12] The magistrates of the City and the suburbs are warned that certain apprentices and other idle people their adherents, the same that were the authors and partakers of the late disorder in Southwark, have a further purpose on Midsummer evening or night to renew their lewd assembly by colour of the time and to commit a breach of the peace or other foul outrage. To prevent this mischief, a strong and substantial watch, sufficient to suppress any tumult, is to be kept both on Midsummer evening, Midsummer night and Sunday night of householders and masters of families, to continue from the beginning of evening to the morning. All masters of servants to be straightly charged, as they shall answer to their perils, to keep their servants in their houses for these two nights, and not to let them have any weapons if they be disposed to execute any evil purpose. If, notwithstanding this strait charge, any servants, apprentices or suspected persons be found in the streets they shall immediately be committed to prison. No plays may be used at the Theatre, Curtain or other usual places, nor any other sort of unlawful or forbidden pastime that draws together the baser sort of people from henceforth until the Feast of St. Michael.

26th June.   PERROT CONDEMNED.[13] Sir John Perrot appeared to-day before the Commissioners for judgment. He was brought in a coach from the Tower to the Old Swan, thence by water to Westminster Bridge where he landed and so into Westminster Hall between 8 and 9 in the morning. He was accompanied by Mr. Blunt and Mr. Cooke, son and son-in-law to the Lieutenant of the Tower, and strongly guarded by divers of the yeomen of the guard with halberds and the Lieutenant's men all round him. In this fashion he was brought to the Queen's Bench bar where he stood for a quarter of an hour waiting for the Commissioners. He was clothed in a doublet and hose of plain black satin and a gown of wrought velvet furred, with a plain white ruff and wearing a square, or flat crowned, black felt hat with a small band; and he carried a carnation in his hand.

The Commissioners having taken their places, Sergeant Snagg for the Queen prayed that judgment might be given.

[12] APC 22:549. For the Midsummer   [13] Cobbett 1:1327.
Watch see Stow's *Survey of London*,
ed. C. L. Kingsford, 1:101–3.

Then the Clerk of the Court asked Sir John whether he had anything to say why judgment to die should not be given.

Sir John made protestation of his innocence in a speech of about a quarter of an hour in which he complained very bitterly of the hard and false dealings of the witnesses against him. He said that he knew of her Majesty's mercy which proceeded from the providence of God, who knew his innocence and so stayed him so long from judgment. Whereupon the Lord Chamberlain, conceiving his meaning to be that the Queen had deferred judgment being persuaded of his innocency, interrupted his speech and declared that he had received more favour than any traitor ever saw. But Sir John prayed the Lord Chamberlain not to misconstrue his meaning.

Both the Lord Buckhurst and the Lord Chamberlain spoke to Sir John declaring that he had been most manifestly proved guilty of treason by a number of witnesses. Sir John answered that the matter had been set forward by his enemies in Ireland, and that he was condemned by Irish witnesses all; and further, that the Irish witnesses had no respect of an oath, and for a small value, a man might procure a number to swear anything.

After further talk with the Commissioners, Anderson, the Lord Chief Justice of the Common Pleas, asked him whether he had anything to say in arrest of judgment. Sir John answered that seeing it had pleased God and the Queen to bring him to that pass he had nothing to say, but humbly submitted himself to the law and their lordships.

Then the Lord Chief Justice began with a long discourse, showing how God from time to time had revealed the treasons that had been practised at home and abroad. He said that he agreed with the others that Sir John was justly condemned of treason, and so proceeded to judgment: that he should be carried to the Tower which was the place from which he came, and thence to be drawn upon a hurdle through the City of London to the place of execution, and there to be hanged, and to be cut down alive, and his bowels and privy members to be cut off and cast into the fire in his sight, his head to be cut off and his body to be cut in four quarters, to be disposed at the Queen's pleasure, and God have mercy upon him.

Sir John then again declared his innocency very fervently and concluded by asking that certain petitions might be granted. He asked that, if it would please the Queen to grant him his life, he might have a better room, for his lodging was a small chamber, room only for his chair and table. To this the

Lord Chamberlain answered that the room was fit for such a man as he was. He begged that if he should suffer death he might die a gentleman's death and be spared from drawing through the streets and the rest of the judgment. He also asked, amongst other petitions, that their Lordships would enlist the Queen to be good to his son and his wife, and, as he heard, to a little son which they had who might hereafter do her Majesty service.

Then Sir John was taken away from the bar in the same manner as he had been brought thither, and so back to the Tower. The Commissioners having sat a little longer after his departure caused proclamation to be made that the present commission of Oyer and Terminer was ended, and on the stroke of ten o'clock at night, the court broke up.

28th June. THE MURDER OF JOHN BREWEN.[14] This day Anne Brewen and John Parker were executed in Smithfield for the murder of John Brewen.

Two and a half years before Anne Welles (as she then was) by divers young men was beloved, but especially by John Brewen and John Parker, both goldsmiths, being bachelors and good friends. Brewen had the favour of her friends and kinsfolk, but notwithstanding his long suit and the gifts of gold and jewels that he gave her he was disdained in favour of Parker, who enjoyed her love in secret. At length seeing his suit despised and having no hope of her favour, Brewen determined to demand again his gold and jewels, and coming to her he requested that his gifts might be given back; to this she answered contemptuously that he should stay for it. Without more ado the young man had her arrested for the jewels.

The damsel was so dismayed that she promised if he would let his action fall nor ever think the worse of her, she would marry him and make him her husband by a certain day; and this before witnesses she vowed to perform. Brewen therefore was not a little joyful and made preparation for his marriage; but when Parker heard of it he was grievously vexed and taunted her so bitterly that she repented of the promise made to Brewen, and began to hate him; and after this Parker would never let her rest but continually urged her to make away with him.

She had not been married above three days to Brewen when

14 STC 15094. Attributed by F. S. Boas to Thomas Kyd on the strength of a signature at the end of the only surviving copy (in Lambeth Palace Library). The affair inspired four ballads.

she put in practice to poison him. Although her husband loved her dearly she would not stay with him after the first night of their wedding, saying she had vowed not to lie with him until he had got her a better house, and the more to cover her treachery and to show her discontent with him she provided a lodging near to the place where Parker lived, so that he had free access to her.

Two days after her marriage Parker brought her a deadly poison that would work speedily on the heart without any swelling on the body or outward sign of infection. This poison she carried secretly to her husband's house, and, coming in the next morning with a pleasant countenance, she asked him if he would have a mess of sugar sops that cold morning. 'Ay, marry, with all my heart,' said he, 'and I take it very kindly that you will do so much for me.' Then she prepared a mess for him with the poison, but in rising from setting the pot back on the fire her coat spilled the mess, and she began to lament that so good a mess of sugar sops should be wasted. But her husband said, 'What, woman, vex not at the matter, your ill luck go with them.' 'Marry, amen,' answered she. Then she asked him to fetch her a pennyworth of red herrings.

When he came back, he found that she had made ready a fresh mess of sugar sops for him, one for herself and another for a little boy that she brought with her. In a little while Brewen began to wax very ill about the stomach, with a grievous inward griping; and immediately after to vomit exceedingly so that he requested her to help him to bed. When it grew somewhat late, she told her husband that she must return to her lodging, and though he begged her to stay with him, she said she could not and would not; and so left the poisoned man all alone for the whole night without comfort or company. All that night he was extremely sick, worse and worse, never ceasing to vomit until (as was afterwards supposed) his entrails were all shrunk and broken within him. The next morning she came to him again but made little show of sorrow. When he rebuked her for her unkindness, she asked him if he would have her forsworn. 'Well, Anne,' said he, 'stay with me now, for I am not long to continue in this world.' 'Now God forbid,' she replied, affecting a great show of sorrow. Then she made a caudle with sugar and spices which she gave him, and immediately after he had eaten it, he died. The next day he was buried, none of the neighbours suspecting that any evil had been done to him.

Parker now became very bold with the widow so that ere

long she durst deny him nothing or he would threaten to stab
her with his dagger. In this state he kept her unmarried for
two years after her husband's death until at length she was
with child. And now, to save her credit, she begged him to
marry her, but he reviled her most shamefully, taunting her
with Brewen's murder. While they were thus quarrelling very
vehemently, some of the neighbours overheard their words
and revealed them to the magistrate. Whereupon the woman
was carried before Alderman Howard to be examined, and
the man before Justice Young; but both denied the deed very
stoutly until the woman was made to believe that Parker had
confessed, when she revealed all. She was therefore taken into
the country to be delivered of her child and then brought
back to prison. Both were arraigned and condemned at Newgate; the woman to be burnt in Smithfield, the man to be
hanged before her eyes.

10th July. RALEGH'S COMPLAINTS AGAINST THE DEPUTY OF
IRELAND.[1] Sir Walter Ralegh hath written from the Tower
to Sir Robert Cecil complaining that when his disgrace was
known in Ireland, the Deputy, Sir William FitzWilliams, an
enemy of his, dealt very despitefully with him. Pretending a
debt to the Queen of £400, he sent a sheriff to take away all
the cattle of Sir Walter's tenants in Munster and unless the
money were paid the same day to sell them on the next. The
debt was but for 50 marks, and paid; but the sheriff did as he
was commanded, and took away five hundred milch kine from
the poor people; of whom some had but two, and some three,
to relieve their poor wives and children, and in a new country
set down to milch and plant. He had forcibly thrust Sir Walter
out of possession of a castle because it was in law between him
and his cousin, and would not hear his attorney speak. He had
admitted a ward (and given it to his man) of a castle which
was the Queen's, which Sir Walter had built and planted with
English these five years; and to profit his man with a wardship,
lost the Queen's inheritance; and would plant the cousin of a
rebel in the place of an Englishman, the castle standing in the
most dangerous place in all Munster.

21st July. 'A QUIP FOR AN UPSTART COURTIER.'[2] Greene's
Quip for an Upstart Courtier, or *A Quaint Dispute between*

[1] EDWARDS' RALEGH 2:48.
[2] STC 12300-05. This is the beginning of the quarrel between Gabriel
Harvey and the Greene-Nashe set.

See R. B. McKerrow, *Works of
Thomas Nashe,* 5:65. Three editions
came out in 1592.

Velvet Breeches and Cloth Breeches is entered, being dedicated to Mr. Thomas Barnaby, Esquire, wherein in the form of a dream are set down the disorders in all estates and trades. In some copies of this book is printed a very bitter satire on ropemakers, aimed at the father of Dr. Gabriel Harvey, who hath caused offence to Greene and his friends; but in others this leaf is cancelled either because Greene thinketh better of it or in fear lest that he bring himself within the law.

23rd July. A MONOPOLY IN STARCH.[3] The Council have granted to Mr. Richard Young an open letter preventing all persons from buying or bringing starch into the country contrary to the special grant giving him sole licence and authority for the making, bringing in and selling of starch in the realm.

28th July. SOUTHWELL SENT TO THE TOWER.[4] Southwell, the Jesuit, is now committed to the Tower by order of the Council to be kept a close prisoner, and to see none but the keeper that Mr. Topcliffe shall appoint.

31st July. RALEGH'S LAMENTABLE COMPLAINT.[5] Sir Walter Ralegh, writing to Sir Robert Cecil from the Tower, complaineth in very extravagant terms of the departure of the Court and of the Queen from London. 'My heart was never broken,' saith he, 'till this day that I hear the Queen goes so far off; whom I have followed so many years with so great love and desire, in so many journeys, and am now left behind her, in a dark prison all alone. While she was yet near at hand that I might hear of her once in two or three days my sorrows were the less; but even now my heart is cast into the depth of all misery. I that was wont to behold her riding like Alexander, hunting like Diana, walking like Venus, the gentle wind blowing her fair hair about her pure cheeks, like a nymph; sometimes sitting in the shade like a goddess; sometimes singing like an angel; sometimes playing like Orpheus.' He concludeth, 'Do with me now, therefore, what you list. I am more weary of life than they are desirous I should perish, which if it had been for her, as it is by her, I have been too happily born.'

6th August. DESERTERS IN HERTFORDSHIRE.[1] Many soldiers of a company levied in Hertfordshire have deserted their cap-

[3] APC 23:45.
[4] APC 23:70.
[5] EDWARDS' RALEGH 2:51.
[1] APC 23:94.

tain without leave, both before embarking and after landing.
These men now lurk in very riotous and disordered sort in the
remote places in the county, not only to the harm and prejudice of peaceful subjects but also showing a dangerous example. The magistrates from whose divisions the men come
are ordered to apprehend the ringleaders and commit them
to the common jail.

7th August. IRISHMEN TO BE DEPORTED.[2] Certain able-
bodied Irishmen, masterless men, that now for a long time frequent the City and the suburbs begging, are to be despatched
to Ireland and set to work by Mr. William English, that complains that by reason of his long imprisonment in England
his tenants and followers have left his lands and possessions
waste and unpeopled.

8th August. NASHE'S 'PIERCE PENNILESS.'[3] Nashe hath written a book called *Pierce Penniless; his Supplication to the
Devil*, being a satirical pamphlet on the abuses of the times.

Seeing that now gentle Sir Philip Sidney is dead and no one
left to care for poor scholars, Pierce Penniless in despair pens
his supplication to the devil, wherein he writeth invectively of
usurers, the deadly sins of greediness, nigardize, and pride
(attacking by the way the antiquaries for their rusty wits in
so doting upon worm-eaten eld), envy, murder, wrath, and
railery, and especially those that rail upon playing. For the
policy of playing, saith he, is very necessary for a state, since
those that are their own masters (as gentlemen of the Court,
the Inns of Court, captains and soldiers) needs must spend
their afternoons upon pleasure, either gaming, following of
harlots, drinking, or seeing a play, of which the last is the
least evil. Nor are plays evil, though some petitioners of the
Council dislike them; for no play encourages any man to tumults or rebellion but lays before him the halter and the
gallows; or praises or approves pride, lust, whoredom or
prodigality but beats it down utterly; and besides they bring
upon the stage our forefathers' valiant acts. Thence Pierce
passeth to gluttony, drunkenness, sloth and lechery, and so to

[2] APC 23:99.
[3] SR 2:619; STC 18371. A most popular book, and an epitome of the gossip of these years. It went into three
editions immediately and was again
reprinted in 1595. Its popularity was
due to the slashing vituperation of
well-known personages. In answer to
their protests, Nashe took refuge in
the conventional defence of the satirist that he was not attacking in-
dividuals, and if antiquaries, for instance, took offence it was not his
fault or intention. For an official answer to the defence of plays see *3rd
Nov* 1594, A PETITION. . . .

a discourse on the nature of Hell and the Devil. Amongst many others attacked in this book are Dr. Gabriel Harvey and his brother Richard.

11th August. COUNT MOMPELGARD IN LONDON.[4] This day Frederick, Count Mompelgard, is come to London, having set out from Mompelgard with his train of servants to travel and see the world. They reached Dover two days since, being much frightened at sea through their unfamiliarity with the waves, and distressed through their frequent horrible vomitings. Having landed, noting on the way the wrecks of the Spanish Armada still lying on the beach, they took post horses for Gravesend. The journey hath been very wearisome to them by reason of our English saddles, which being covered only with bare hide are painful to strangers and hard to ride upon, especially for the Count who is corpulent and heavy.

They are much amazed with the throngs of people in London, and their magnificent apparel, but they complain that the inhabitants are extremely proud and overbearing; and because the greater part, especially the tradespeople, seldom journey into other countries but always remain in their houses in the City attending to their business, they care little for strangers, but scoff and laugh at them. Moreover, say they, no one dare oppose our citizens else the street boys and apprentices collect together in great crowds, and strike right and left unmercifully without regard to person.

13th August. THE COUNT MOMPELGARD FEASTS WITH THE FRENCH AMBASSADOR.[5] Being Sunday the Count Mompelgard attended the French service and afterwards at midday partook of a magnificent banquet provided by the French Ambassador. The French wine did not agree with the Count, though he relished the beer exceedingly.

15th August. A SCURRILOUS JESUIT PAMPHLET.[6] Some copies have been found in England of a book written in Latin by Father Parsons, the Jesuit, under the name of 'Andreas Philopater,' answering the proclamation made against the Jesuits and seminary priests dated 18th October, 1591. There is also a digest in English, pretended to be put forth by an English Intelligencer in a letter to the Lord Treasurer's sec-

[4] W. B. Rye, *England as seen by Foreigners in the days of Elizabeth and James the First*, 1865.   [5] Rye, p. 9.   [6] STC 19398, 19885.

retary. The Latin book hath been translated into French and circulated amongst the Queen's enemies. In this book the proclamation is answered point by point in a preface and six sections, and some of the Council and principal men of the state very slanderously described.

Of Sir Christopher Hatton, Philopater saith that he departed very unwillingly from this life on the very day before this edict was published, which he was said to have resisted so long as he lived and would never have assented to, partly because, being a more moderate man, he would not have approved such cruelty, partly because he differed so heartily from Cecil and the Puritans, to whom Cecil showed patronage. Hence arose that suspicion of poison for his removal which was written in divers letters from England. Being born of a family honest rather than famous, he had come to London to study the municipal laws of the kingdom; but when the labours of study seemed to him too heavy to be borne of an equal mind, he did, what now a great part of the youth of England are wont to do who come to London to study, but frequent the Presence Chamber rather than the school. It happened not long after the accession of the Queen, when there was much rejoicing, with merriment, shows, mummings and other childish exercises, that on the very birthday of Our Lord a comedy with the utmost show was presented in the Queen's hall in the name of the University by the students themselves. On this occasion when many acquitted themselves very fairly, Christopher Hatton was thought to have excelled them all in beauty of person and grace of action, by which he so pleased the Queen that henceforward she always had him in the Presence Chamber, and promoted him through all the grades of honour to the very top, which is the Chancellorship; for first he was Captain of the Queen's Bodyguard, then of the Bed-chamber, finally Chancellor.

Of Cecil it is written that though he is Treasurer, guardian of the wards of nobles, and controls almost all things in England by his own judgment, yet he came of humble and obscure origin. His father, whose name was David Cecil, served almost in the meanest rank in King's Wardrobe. His grandfather was one of the Guard of the King's Person, and kept a public tavern in the town of Stamford. After spending some time at the University of Cambridge, where for a time he sought part of his living by tolling the bell in St. John's College, at the beginning of the reign of King Edward VI Cecil insinuated himself into the household of the Duke of Somerset, the Protector.

After thus running through the Lord Treasurer's life from his youth, this Philopater declareth though he would not deny that the Queen assented to the Proclamation (for which she would render her account to God), yet it was not of her own accord, but extorted from her by the importunity of others and especially by the fraud of Cecil, who is believed to be not only the instigator of the proclamation but even the writer, because as well as other offices which he has ambitiously grasped, he alone has usurped the office of Secretary after the death of Walsingham. From him proceeded the framing of the whole affair; from him the odious names and phrases newly applied to the Catholics, and not taken over from previous proclamations; from him the insults and lies against Catholic Princes which in the judgments of all are manifestly false and impudent.

Of Ralegh it is written that he keeps a school of Atheism much frequented, with a certain necromantic astronomer as schoolmaster, where no small number of young men of noble birth learn to deride the Old Law of Moses as well as the New Law of Christ with ingenious quips and jests; and among other things to spell the name of God backwards.

He compareth the seminaries, which the proclamation denounced, with the colleges in the two Universities of England, declaring that the students come out of England neither for lack of living nor for crimes committed, for they are commonly gentlemen, or wealthy peoples' children, and might easily have had preferment if they would apply themselves to the protestants' proceedings. Showeth moreover that a great multitude of gentlemen's sons leaving their inheritances and other hopes of worldly possibilities at home come over daily to study and to be made priests with infinite desire to return again quickly to England. There are more gentlemen at this time in the English seminaries of France, Rome and Spain than in all the clergy of England twice told, to which no gentleman will afford his son to be a minister and much less his daughter to be a minister's wife.

With the order and studies observed in the seminaries are compared the loose proceedings of the English Universities and Colleges where Cecil, Leicester and such like, cancellers of virtue rather than Chancellors of Universities, have overthrown all. The porters are taken away from College gates which used to keep students in awe, whence come confusion and immodesty in apparel, every man wearing either as his pride or his fancy serve, or his purse and ability permit. Hence the filling up and pestering all colleges with harlots to be baits for the young men, headships given to light and wanton companions, fencing and dancing schools crowded, taverns filled with scholars, statutes of founders condemned and broken, leases embezzled, the goods made away, and the places of fellows and scholars publicly sold.

18th August. COUNT MOMPELGARD AT COURT.[7] The Count Mompelgard being summoned to the Court which is now at Reading, arrived there yesterday about noon and lodged with the Mayor. Hardly had he changed his apparel when the Earl of Essex visited him in his lodging, welcoming him in the Queen's name and inviting him to take dinner in his apartments, whither the Count was conveyed in a coach. After being most sumptuously feasted, he was entertained with sweet and enchanting music. The repast being ended, he was again accompanied by the Earl of Essex to his lodging, but shortly afterwards he was summoned by the Queen and conducted to her own apartments. This afternoon the Count had another audience with the Queen, when she herself made and delivered an appropriate speech in the French language in the presence of M. de Beauvoir, whom she holds in especial favour. After he had been conversing with her in a very lively and good-humoured manner he so far prevailed on her that she played very sweetly and skilfully on her instrument, the strings of which are of gold and silver.

20th August. THE COUNT AT WINDSOR.[8] The Count was conducted to Windsor, and the day being Sunday, he visited the Chapel where he listened for more than an hour to the music, the usual ceremonies and the English sermon. He noted especially the beauty of the playing of the organ and the singing of a little boy, finding the ceremonies very similar to the papists'. Dinner being ended the Count with the English and French deputies went to view the Castle of Windsor, and on the lead of the highest tower of all he hath cut his name. After this, he was shown the beautiful royal bed-hangings and tapestries of gold and fine silk, also a unicorn's horn and other costly things.

21st August. 'THE BLACK BOOK'S MESSENGER.'[9] Greene's

[7] Rye, pp. 11–12.   [9] SR 2:619; STC 12223.
[8] Rye, p. 16.

Black Book's Messenger is entered, wherein is laid open the life and death of Ned Browne, one of the most notable cutpurses and crossbiters that ever lived in England. This is the messenger to that Black Book, giving a beadroll of all the notable conny-catchers about London which Greene promised in his *Disputation*. Telleth the merry tales of Ned Browne's villanies until he went over to France, where being condemned for robbing a church near Aix he was hanged at a window, in default of a gallows; and his body being buried without the town was in the night torn out of his grave by a company of wolves and devoured.

24th August. CONDEMNED CRIMINALS AS SOLDIERS.[10] Some of the prisoners remaining in the common jails in Oxford and Berkshire on criminal charges and in danger of capital sentences have promised that if they be sent abroad as soldiers they will not return without special leave. Since some of these men are able and strong, and may prove good subjects to the State, the Council have ordered that means be taken in the discretion of the Lord Chief Baron to deliver them to Sir John Norris after examination of their charges.

27th August. A PRIEST'S INFORMATIONS.[11] James Young, *alias* Dingley, an arrested priest, hath declared to the Lord Treasurer that he heard from Father Parsons that the King of Spain had promised Sir William Stanley to invade England, but not till 1593, because of the hindrances in France. By which time he hoped to have brought in Brittany and have thence 16 great ships and 10,000 men, and more commodity to come to the Irish kerns; thence Sir William Stanley could go to his own country, where the Earl of Derby would be ready to assist him. He hoped that the young Lord Strange would also help; but now he discloses every one that moved in the matter. The King of Spain said that he remembered the Earl very well, as he was one of the last noblemen married in his time, and that if Lord Strange had been unmarried, none would have been more fit to have been proclaimed King at their first arrival.

A certain Captain Cripps, that came to the Jesuits' College at Seville, spoke to Father Parsons on an embassy wherein Lord Derby was sent, and of a minister that came there from whom a soldier stole a portmanteau; whereupon Parsons replied, he would rather he had stolen my Lord's golden

breeches with which he had been known these thirty years
at least.

The assault of Stanley is to be attempted next April, and
as soon as his arrival is reported, the whole Spanish fleet is
to be ready; Parsons is to be present, and Cardinal Allen to
come from Rome, but not to England until the event of
the navy is seen.

ANXIETY FOR OSTEND.[12] Great anxiety is felt that the enemy
will attempt to surprise the town of Ostend. The companies
in Ostend which were to have proceeded to Brittany to re-
inforce Sir John Norris are to be retained. Further, that Sir
Francis Vere and Sir Thomas Morgan who are in command
of the companies in Holland shall have everything in readiness at Flushing by the 6th September to embark for Brittany.

29th August. SIR ROGER WILLIAMS' COMPLAINTS.[13] Sir
Roger Williams writeth to the Lord Treasurer from France
that the estate of the poor King is now very desperate and
our own far from any hope of peace, for in time the greater
purses will eat and consume the lesser. The Spaniard will
not greatly feel the matter unless the war is made in his own
country, or his Indian navy (the armadas and not the merchant ships) defeated, or the Duke of Parma defeated in
battle. It seems strange to him to see how we entered into
war for the Netherlanders' defence, who traffick freely with
the Spanish, whilst we ourselves are barred; by which means
Holland and Zealand grow rich, and England greatly im-
poverished, and will be far greater if it continue any time.
Holland and Zealand are rich and invincible, France ruined
and poor, ready to be conquered; wherefore the Queen's
forces in the Low Countries, saving strong garrisons in Flushing and Brille, should be transported for service in France.

1st September. INVASION EXPECTED.[1] It is credibly reported
that a large fleet of ships with a great store of men and munitions have been sent out by the King of Spain and the
Leaguers and are now in the Sleeve, which forces are believed to be intended against the Isle of Wight or one of the
seaports of Sussex. All armour, furniture, munitions and
weapons in those parts are forthwith to be put in readiness,
and upon the first notice or discovery of their arrival the

forces shall immediately assemble to repulse the enemy; beacon watches also to be renewed and diligently kept.

3rd September. THE DEATH OF ROBERT GREENE.[2] Robert Greene, author of plays, poems and pamphlets, is dead, having lain sick for a month of a surfeit which he had taken with drinking, and though he continually scoured, yet his body continued to swell upward until it swelled him at the heart and in his face. All this time he continued most patient and penitent, with tears forsaking the world, renouncing oaths and desiring forgiveness of God and men for all his offences, so that throughout his sickness he was never heard to swear, rave or blaspheme the name of God as he was accustomed to do before, but he was continuously calling on God even until he gave up the ghost, to the great comfort of his well willers to see how mightily the grace of God worked in him. It is noted that his sickness did not so greatly weaken him, for he walked to his chair and back again the night before he died.

About nine o'clock last night as he lay in bed a friend of his told him that his wife sent her commendations, whereat he greatly rejoiced, and, confessing that he had mightily wronged her, wished that he could see her before he died. But, feeling that his time was short, he took pen and ink and wrote her this letter:

'SWEET WIFE,
As ever there was any good will or friendship between me and thee, see this bearer (my host) satisfied of his debt. I owe him ten pound, and but for him I had perished in the streets. Forget and forgive my wrongs done unto thee, and Almighty God have mercy on my soul. Farewell, till we meet in heaven, for on earth thou shalt never see me more. This 2nd of September, 1592.
Written by thy dying husband,
ROBERT GREENE.'

4th September. COUNT MOMPELGARD DEPARTS.[3] The Count Mompelgard after visiting the Universities of Oxford and Cambridge hath received his passports and is embarked at Gravesend for Flushing.

5th September. DR. HARVEY AND GREENE.[4] Dr. Gabriel

Harvey is at this time in London, intending to prosecute Greene at law for what he wrote of his father and brothers in *The Quip for an Upstart Courtier*. But learning that Greene was lying dangerously sick in a shoemaker's house in Dowgate he was speaking of the matter with some friends when he heard that Greene was dead.

Accordingly he went down yesterday to Dowgate to speak with Mrs. Isam, the shoemaker's wife, who told him of Greene's poverty and miserable end: how in his extremity he would beg a penny pot of malmsey, and how none of his old acquaintances came to comfort him except a certain Mistress Appleby and the mother of his bastard son, Fortunatus. Even Nashe, his fellow writer, that was his companion at the fatal banquet of rhenish and pickled herring never after came near him. Mrs. Isam also told Dr. Harvey, with tears in her eyes, how he was fain, poor soul, to borrow her husband's shirt whilst his own was a-washing; and how his doublet and hose and sword were sold for three shillings; and besides the charges of his winding sheet, which was four shillings; and the charge of his burial in the new churchyard near Bedlam, which was six shillings and fourpence; how deeply he was indebted to her poor husband as appeared by his bond for ten pounds, and how, for a tender farewell, she herself crowned his head with a garland of bays. All these things Harvey spreads about to his friends.

Greene's lamentable end is much talked of, for he was notorious in London for his dissolute and licentious living, his unseemly apparel and his loose companions, his monstrous swearing and impious profanation of sacred texts, his outrageous surfeiting. He had in employment one 'cutting' Ball, till he was hanged at Tyburn, to levy a crew of his trusted companions to guard him from arresting, and kept this Ball's sister as his mistress, of whom was born his bastard son, Fortunatus Greene, having forsaken his own wife a few months after marriage.

6th September. GREAT WINDS.[5] To-day the wind blowing west and by south as it hath for two days past, very boisterous, the Thames is so void of water by forcing out the fresh and keeping back the salt, that in divers places men have gone over two hundred paces and then flung a stone to land. A certain collier on a mare rode from the north side to the

[5] STOW'S ANNALS; BIRCH'S MEMOIRS 1:86.

south and back again on either side of London Bridge; but
not without great danger of drowning. This unusual event
causeth much wonder especially among the Dutch, who fear
lest the sea by some violent inundation has broken the banks
in some of the Low Countries.

THE RETURN OF SIR MARTIN FROBISHER'S FLEET EXPECTED.[6]
Sir Martin Frobisher's fleet is expected to return soon, and
it is likely that on news of his coming merchants from the
city of London will resort to Plymouth and Portsmouth to
buy up the goods, and thereby carry the plague from London
to those parts still free from infection. No one may be allowed to go to these towns unless licensed by the Council
or the Lord Admiral; and as some of them may come in
disguise, sufficient guards are to be set at the gates to examine
all who repair thither.

7th September. THE PLAGUE IN LONDON.[7] The soldiers levied
in Nottinghamshire, Leicester and the neighbouring counties
are not to enter the City because of the infection, but to march
by land to Southampton.

10th September. THE TAKING OF THE GREAT CARRACK.[8] The
Madre de Dios, the great carrack, that was taken at the Islands of the Azores, was brought into Dartmouth the 7th,
and the manner of her taking reported.

The season being so far advanced before the expedition
set sail, Sir Walter Ralegh abandoned his enterprise upon
Panama, and before leaving the fleet, gave directions to Sir
John Burgh and Sir Martin Frobisher to divide the ships
into two parts; Sir Martin, with the *Garland,* Captain George
Gifford, Captain Henry Thin, Captain Grenville and others
to lie off the South Cape and thereby to amaze the Spaniards
and keep them on their own coasts; while Sir John Burgh,
Captain Robert Cross, Captain Thompson and others should
attend at the Islands for the carracks or other Spanish ships
coming from Mexico or other parts of the West Indies. This
direction took good effect; for the King of Spain's Admiral
receiving intelligence that the English Fleet was come on
the coast, attended to defend the south parts of Spain, and
to keep himself as near Sir Martin Frobisher as he could
to impeach him in all things that he might undertake, and
thereby neglected the safe conduct of the carracks.

6 APC 23:177.   8 HAKLUYT 5:57.
7 SP DOM 243:5.

Before the fleet severed themselves, they met with a great Biscayan on the Spanish coast, called the *Santa Clara,* a ship of 600 tons, which after a reasonable hot fight was entered and mastered, being found to be freighted with all sorts of small iron work as horse shoes, nails, plough shares, iron bars, spikes and the like, valued by our men at £6000 or £7000 but worth to them treble the value. This ship, which was sailing towards St. Lucar, there to take in further provision for the West Indies, was first rummaged and after sent for England.

The fleet now coasted along towards the south cape of St. Vincent, and on the way about the Rock near Lisbon, Sir John Burgh in the *Roebuck* spying a sail afar off gave her chase, which being a flyboat and of good sail drew him far southwards before he could fetch her. Not long after, sailing back toward the rest of his company he discovered the Spanish fleet to seaward of him, and they also having espied him between them and the shore spread themselves before him; but trusting to God's help only he thrust out from among them; and knowing that it was but folly to expect a meeting there with Sir Martin Frobisher (who when he understood of this armada as well as himself would be sure not to come that way) he began to shape his course towards the Azores.

Arriving before Flores upon Thursday, the 21st of June, towards evening, accompanied only with Captain Caulfield and the master of his ship, for the rest were not yet arrived, he made towards the shore with his boat, finding all the people of Santa Cruz in arms to bar their landing and ready to defend their town from spoil. Sir John contrariwise made signs to them by advancing a white flag which was answered with the like. Whereupon ensued intercourses of friendship, and pledges were taken on both sides, the Captain of the town for them, Captain Caulfield for ours; so that whatsoever our men wanted which the place would supply either in fresh water, victuals or the like, was very willingly granted by the inhabitants; and good leave given to refresh themselves on shore as much and as oft as they would without restraint.

At this Santa Cruz Sir John was informed that there was indeed no expectation of any fleet to come from the west but from the east, three days before his arrival a carrack had passed by for Lisbon, and that there were four carracks behind of one consort. Sir John being very glad of this news, stayed no longer on shore but at once embarked himself and quickly discovered one of the carracks. Meanwhile, part of the rest of the English fleet drew also towards the Azores, so that the same evening Sir John descried two or three of the Earl of Cumberland's ships (whereof one Mr. Norton was captain), which having in like sort perceived the carrack pursued her by that course which they saw her run towards the Islands. But on no side was there any way made by reason of a great calm, so that to discover what she was Sir John took his boat and rowed the space of three miles to make her out more exactly: and being returned he consulted with the better sort of the company upon boarding her in the morning.

But a very mighty storm arose in the night, the extremity whereof forced them all to weigh anchors; yet their care not to lose the carrack in wrestling with the weather was such that in the morning the tempest being now qualified, and our men bearing in again with the shore, they perceived the carrack very near the land and the Portugals confusedly carrying on shore such things as they could in any manner convey out of her. Seeing the haste our men made to come upon them, they forsook her, but first set fire to that which they could not carry away, intending wholly to consume her that neither glory of victory nor benefit of ship might remain to our men, and, lest the English should extinguish the flames, they entrenched themselves on the land, being four hundred men, to protect the carrack and keep our men aloof so that the carrack might be utterly destroyed. When Sir John Burgh noted this, he landed one hundred of his men, whereof many did swim and wade more than breast high to shore easily scattering those that guarded the coast, and he no sooner drew towards their new trenches but they fled immediately, leaving as much as the fire had spared to be the reward of our men's pains.

Here was taken among others one Vincent Fouseen, a Portugal, purser of the carrack, with two others, one an Almain, the other a Low-Dutchman, both cannoneers, who refused to make any voluntary report of those things which were demanded of them till the torture was threatened; the fear whereof at last wrested from them the intelligence that within fifteen days three other greater carracks would arrive at the same island. Five carracks had set out from Goa, being specially commanded by the King of Spain not to touch at the island of St. Helena, where the Portugal carracks were always wont to refresh themselves, because of the English men-of-war who (as he was informed) lay there in wait to intercept them. The last rendezvous for them all was the Island of Flores, where the King assured them not to miss his armada sent thither to waft them to Lisbon.

Upon this information Sir John drew to counsel, meeting there Captain Norton, Captain Bownton, Captain Abraham Cock, Captains of three ships of the Earl of Cumberland, Mr. Thompson of Harwich, the Captain of the *Dainty* of Sir John Hawkins, one of Sir Walter Ralegh's fleet, and Mr. Christopher Newport, Captain of the *Golden Dragon*, newly returned from the West Indies, and others. These being assembled, he communicated with them what he had learned and what great presumption of truth the relation did carry, wishing that forasmuch as God and good fortune had brought them together in so good a season, they would show the uttermost of their endeavours to bring these Easterlings under the lee of the English obedience. Hereupon a present accord on all sides followed not to part company or leave of those seas till time should present cause to put their consultations in execution. The next day, the Queen's good ship, the *Foresight*, commanded by Sir Robert Cross, came in to the rest, and he, being likewise informed of the matter, was soon drawn into the service.

Thus Sir John with all these ships departing thence six or seven leagues to the west of Flores, they spread themselves abroad from north to south, each ship two leagues at least distant from another, by which order of extension they were able to discover the space of two whole degrees at sea.

In this sort they lay from 29th June to 3rd August, what time Captain Thompson in the *Dainty* had first sight of the huge carrack called the *Madre de Dios*. The *Dainty* being of excellent sail got the start of the rest of the fleet, and began the conflict, somewhat to her cost, with slaughter and hurt of divers of her men. Within a while after Sir John Burgh in the *Roebuck* of Sir Walter Ralegh's was at hand to second her, who saluted her with shot of great ordnance and continued the fight within musket shot, assisted by Captain Thompson and Captain Newport, till Sir Robert Cross, Vice-Admiral of the fleet, came up, being to leeward. At his arrival Sir John demanded of him what was best to be done, who answered that if the carrack were not boarded she would recover the shore and fire herself as the other had done.

Whereupon Sir John concluded to entangle her and Sir Robert promised also to fasten himself at the same instant; which was accomplished. But after a while Sir John Burgh receiving a shot with a cannon perrier under water and being ready to sink desired Sir Robert to fall off that he might also clear himself and save his ship from sinking, which with much difficulty he did; for both the *Roebuck* and the *Foresight* were so entangled that they had much ado to clear themselves.

The same evening Sir Robert Cross finding the carrack then sure and drawing near the island persuaded his company to board her again, or else there was no hope to recover her. And they after many excuses and fears were by him encouraged and so fell athwart her foreships all alone and so hindered her sailing that the rest had time to come up to his succour. Toward the evening after he had fought with her for three hours alone, the Earl of Cumberland's two ships came up and with very little loss entered with Sir Robert Cross, who had in that time broken their courages and made the assault easy for the rest.

The General having disarmed the Portugals and stowed them for better security on all sides, now saw the true proportion of the great carrack which did then and may still justly provoke the admiration of all men; yet the sight of so many bodies slain and dismembered drew each man's eye to lament and hands to help. No man could step but upon a dead carcase or a bloody floor, especially about the helm; for the greatness of the steerage required the labour of twelve or fourteen men at once, and some of our ships beating her in at the stern with their ordnance, oftentimes with one shot slew four or five labouring on either side the helm. Whereupon our General moved with singular commiseration of their misery sent them his own surgeons, denying them no possible help that he or any of his company could afford.

The carrack is in burden estimated at 1600 tons, of which 900 tons are stowed with merchandise. Her length from the beak head to the stern (whereon is erected a lantern) is 165 feet; her breadth at the widest in the second close deck (whereof she hath three) is 46 feet 10 inches. She drew in water 31 feet at her departure from Cochin in India but not above 26 at her arrival in Dartmouth. She carries in height seven several stories, one main orlop, three close decks, one forecastle, and a spar deck of two floors apiece. The length of the keel is about 100 feet, of the main mast 121 feet, and the circuit about at the partners 10 feet 7 inches; the main yard is 106 feet long. There were between 600 and 700 persons on board.

THE PLAGUE IN LONDON.[9] The plague is greatly increased, and it is feared that the infection may grow with the prisons pestered with the great numbers committed for debt or on small charges. The Lord Mayor is required in common charity to cause speedy inquiry to be made, and, having summoned debtors and creditors, to persuade them to come to some composition; for if the imprisoned die, the creditors will lose their whole debt.

TWO RICH SPANISH PRIZES BROUGHT IN.[10] Mr. Thomas White in the *Amity* is returned to London with two Spanish prizes which he reporteth to have taken on the 26th July off the coast of Barbary.

At four in the morning, having sighted two ships about three or four leagues distant, that proved to be a Biscayan and a flyboat, they came within gunshot by seven, supposing by their boldness in having the King of Spain's arms displayed that they were ships of war.

The enemy having placed themselves in warlike order, one a cable's length from the other, the *Amity* began the fight, in which our men continued as fast as they were able to charge and discharge for the space of five hours, being never a cable's length distant from either.

In this time they received divers shot both in the hull of the ship, masts and sails to the number of 32 great, besides 500 musket shot, and harquebuses a crock at least. And because they perceived the enemy to be stout, our men thought good to board the Biscayan which was head on to the other, where lying aboard about an hour and playing their ordnance, in the end they stowed all the enemy's men. Then the other in the flyboat, thinking our men had entered into their fellow, bare room with the *Amity* meaning to have laid her aboard and so entrapped her between them both. But the *Amity,* quitting herself of her enemy, hoisted top sails and weathered them both. Then coming hard aboard the flyboat with her ordnance prepared, gave her whole broadside and slew several so that our men saw the blood running out at the scupper holes. After that they cast about, new charged all the ordnance, and, coming upon them again, willed them to yield or else they would sink them: whereupon the one would have yielded, which was shot between and water, but the other called him traitor. To whom our men made answer that if he would not also yield immediately, they would sink him first.

Thereupon, understanding their determination, he put out a white flag and yielded, yet they refused to strike their own sails because they were sworn never to strike to any Englishman. The captains and masters were then commanded to come aboard, which they did; and after examination and stowing some, certain of our men were sent aboard who struck their sails and manned their ships, finding in them 126 persons living and 8 dead, besides those whom they themselves had cast overboard. Our men were but 42 and a boy. These two ships are rich prizes, laden with 1400 chests of quicksilver with the arms of Castile and Leon fastened upon them, and a great quantity of bulls or indulgences, and gilded missals or service books, besides a hundred tuns of excellent wines, so that what with his silver which should have delivered from the quicksilver and his taxes on the bulls at 2 reals the piece, the King of Spain's loss amounts to £707,700.

14th September. SPANISH HOPES.[11] The priest, George Dingley, is again examined before the Lord Keeper, Lord Buckhurst and Mr. John Fortescue about the things he had heard in Spain. He declareth that many of our nobility were believed to be discontented at not being advanced and would easily be moved to follow the Spaniard, who would promise to put them in places of authority if he should possess England. The Earls of Oxford and Cumberland, and the Lords Strange and Percy are much talked of as alienated by discontent. Their chief hope is the Queen's death; wherefore the Spaniard lingers in his attempt at again assaulting England because time will call her away, when they have certain hope of a debate between the two houses of Hertford and Derby, who will seek the throne, each for himself; during which contention the Spaniard thinketh entry into England would be without danger.

They greatly rejoiced in the mutterings of the Martinists, translating the book into Spanish and presenting it to the King, judging from its hot words that some uproar would shortly be moved by that faction which would find favour amongst the noblemen in hopes of enjoying the bishops' and other spiritual revenues. They think Lancashire and the north will soonest favour them, and Sir William Stanley would have the Spanish navy come to Milford Haven rather than to the narrow seas.

[11] SP DOM 243:11.

Though there are many beyond sea who wish this new assault attempted, yet Father Parsons is the only man England need fear; he by his travail and credit with the Spaniard, solicits the King and his councillors by all means possible, and maintains Cardinal Allen and Stanley with accounts. There is not a man executed in England for religion who is not known there, and sermons openly preached in his praise, with bitter inveighing against the cruelty of our present governors.

16th September. THE GREAT CARRACK.[12] The sailors are making great pillagings of the spoil of the Great Carrack. Sir Robert Cecil and Mr. Thomas Middleton are sent down in haste to take charge of the matter, being instructed to inquire into the proceedings of Sir Ferdinand Gorges and the other Commissioners; to cause all lading to be viewed and entered in registers and especially to search out all precious things; and also to hire sufficient ships to bring the goods into the Thames. Sir Walter Ralegh, in the charge of Mr. Blunt, is also despatched from the Tower to join them on the Commission.

17th September. THAME FAIR PUT OFF.[13] Thame fair that is usually held on Michaelmas day is postponed for 15 days lest the Londoners resorting thither should spread the plague, to the danger of the Queen who proposes at that time to visit Lord Norris at Ricott on her progress.

19th September. THE SPREAD OF THE PLAGUE.[14] The plague is now reported at East Greenwich. Sir John Hawkins is to take special measures to prevent it from spreading to Deptford and Lewisham, lest the Queen's service should be hindered; also to cause the making of starch at a house in Deptford Strand to cease because of the number of dogs used therein which, being a noisome kind of cattle, especially at this contagious time, are very apt to draw on the infection.

20th September. GREENE'S 'GROAT'S-WORTH OF WIT.'[15] Chettle hath sent to the press *Greene's Groat's-worth of Wit, bought with a million of repentance,* collected out of certain papers that Greene left at his death. In the forepart of the book are displayed the adventures of one Roberto, a scholar,

[12] SP DOM 243:14.
[13] APC 23:195.
[14] APC 23:203.
[15] SR 2:620; STC 12245. The 'famous

gracer of tragedians' is Marlowe, 'young Juvenal' Nashe, and 'the only Shake-scene' Shakespeare.

that despising the wealth heaped by his dying father, a miser and an usurer, was left but a groat. The money thus passing to his younger brother Lucanio, Roberto practised to fleece him with the help of Mistress Lamilia, a courtesan, and found small difficulty in bringing the two together. But no sooner had Lamilia enticed Lucanio into her power than she betrayed Roberto to his brother, who cast him out of doors. Then Roberto, being in extremities, began to lament his woes in verse when a player, chancing to come, offered him employment, which, seeing no other remedy, he accepted; and thereafter falling into bad company, mingled with thieves and harlots, until by immeasurable drinking and the scourge of lust he now lay comfortlessly languishing. Here, noting that Roberto's story agreed in most parts with his own, Greene broke off his tale, adding certain rules for young gentlemen that are delighted with the like fantasies, warning them of God's judgment on those who follow their own lusts.

To his fellow scholars in the City that also made plays he wrote a very invective letter, especially warning two of them, the one termed a 'famous gracer of tragedians' to beware of atheism, the other, a 'young Juvenal that biting satirist,' that with him lately wrote a comedy, to avoid getting enemies by bitter words. To these is joined a third, that also dependeth on the making of plays, to shun the ingratitude of the players, for, saith he, 'there is an upstart crow, beautified with our feathers, that with his *Tiger's heart wrapped in a player's hide*, supposes he is as well able to bombast out a blank verse as the best of you; and being an absolute *Johannes factotum*, is in his own conceit the only Shake-scene in a country.' These words are very offensively taken by those intended.

22nd September. THE GREAT CARRACK.[16] Sir Robert Cecil writeth from Exeter that he has brought back everyone he met within seven miles of Exeter that had anything in a cloak, bag or mail, which did but smell of the prizes (for he could smell them almost, such had been the spoils of amber and musk). He stays anyone, who might carry news to Dartmouth or Plymouth, at the gates of the town; he compels them also to tell him where any trunks or mails are, and finding the people stubborn, has committed two innkeepers to prison; had this been done a week ago, it would have saved the Queen £20,000. In a Londoner's shop, he found a bag of seed pearls, pieces of damask, cypresses and calicos, a very great port of musk, and certain tassels of pearl.

He hath left an impression by his rough dealing with the Mayor and orders a search of every bag coming from the west. There never was such spoil; letters have been intercepted to friends in London to come down, all which he keeps to charge the parties at Dartmouth, and over two thousand buyers are assembling; them he will suppress. In his search he hath found an armlet of gold, and a fork and spoon of crystal with rubies, which he reserves for the Queen. Sir Walter Ralegh came after him, but having outridden him will be at Dartmouth first.

THE QUEEN AT OXFORD.[17] The Queen, on her progress, leaving Woodstock is gone to Oxford. She entered the bounds of the University at Godstow Bridge about three o'clock in the afternoon, where she was waited for by the Vice-Chancellor of the University, the Heads of Colleges in their scarlet gowns, and the proctors and beadles. As soon as the Queen learned that the Vice-Chancellor and the rest were ready to present their duties to her, she caused her coach to be stayed, notwithstanding the foulness of the weather, and signified her pleasure to hear a speech, provided it were not too long. Whereupon Mr. Saville, the Senior Proctor, being then on his knees with the rest of the company, entered into a short speech signifying the great joy of the University. This done, the Queen with the nobility and the rest of her royal train went towards the City, being met by the Mayor, with the Aldermen and Bailiffs, the Recorder and the townsmen, who received her in a short speech, offering in the name of the city a cup of silver gilt containing sixty angels. As she entered the City, she was received with great applause from the crowds of scholars that thronged the streets from the North Gate to Christchurch, signifying their joy by speeches and singing. Then as she passed by St. John's College she was presented with a private speech on behalf of the College and so to the Carfax, where the Reader in Greek offered a short speech in Greek, being thanked by her Majesty in the same tongue. Thence they moved to the great quadrangle of Christchurch where the Public Orator declared the abundant joy of the University. After a short time the Queen entered the Cathedral Church under a canopy borne by four doctors, where the *Te Deum* was sung and thanksgiving offered for her safe arrival.

[17] Nicoll's *Progresses*.

CONSTABLE'S 'DIANA.'[18] Mr. Henry Constable hath sent to the press his *Diana,* eight decads of sonnets, dedicated in a sonnet by Mr. Richard Smyth to 'Her Sacred Majesty's honourable Maids.'

23rd September. THE QUEEN AT OXFORD.[19] Between two and three o'clock in the afternoon the Queen went to the Church of St. Mary, riding in a rich carriage and attended by the nobility on horseback with foot cloths. The Queen being placed under her cloth of estate upon a very fair stage, purposely erected for her in the east end of the church, a philosophy act was provided for her, which was begun on the word '*incipiatis*' being uttered by her. Whereupon the proctors called on the first replier, who after three congés to the Queen propounded the questions unto the answerer. Hereupon the answerer, Mr. Thomas Smith, Orator of the University, repeated the questions, which were: i. Whether the soul of one man be more excellent than the soul of another. ii. Whether, on account of the age of the world, men be less heroic now than formerly. And so entered into his position, which continued for almost half an hour, which the Queen thought somewhat long, for when the Proctors said to the replier, in the accustomed words, '*procede magister,*' she supposing that they spoke to Mr. Smith said that he had been too long already.

Upon these words Mr. Gwynne first addressing himself to her Majesty to excuse his disability to speak in that honourable presence, spoke discreetly and wittily for about a quarter of an hour, and was then cut off by the Proctors. After the others had spoken the argument was ended by Mr. Saville, who determined the questions in a very good speech though somewhat long, ending with thanks to her Majesty for her great patience in hearing. This done the Queen returned to her lodging attended as she had come.

A PROCLAMATION ABOUT THE GREAT CARRACK.[20] A proclamation is published charging all who have taken or received goods of any value out of the Spanish carrack lately brought to Dartmouth, either while she was on the seas or since her coming into the haven, that within ten days they discover to the principal officer of the place where they reside what they have received or sold.

Likewise all innkeepers, householders, or owners of any

[18] SR 2:620; STC 5657.   [20] PROCLAMATIONS 311.
[19] Nicoll's *Progresses.*

vessels, where any person shall come with any carriage wherein they may suspect any portion of the commodities from the carrack to be bestowed, shall cause the same to be stayed.

Further, that if anyone who claims any portion of the goods by reason of his consort or adventure in the late service be proved to have taken or bought anything from the carrack without revealing it to the Commissioners, he shall lose all the benefit he might claim from the adventure.

24th September. THE QUEEN AT OXFORD.[21] Being Sunday the sermon was preached before the Queen by the Dean of Christchurch, Dr. James; and at night a comedy, called *Bellum Grammaticale,* was acted in the hall of the College which was most graciously and patiently heard by the Queen, though but meanly performed.

SIR ROBERT CECIL AT DARTMOUTH.[22] Sir Robert Cecil now writeth from Dartmouth of his dealings with the Great Carrack. As soon as he came on board the carrack with the rest of the Commissioners, Sir Walter Ralegh arrived with his keeper, Mr. Blunt. His poor servants to the number of 140, and all the mariners came to him with such shouts of joy that he was much troubled to quiet them. But his heart is broken, and he is extremely pensive unless he is busied, in which he can toil terribly. The meeting between him and Sir John Gilbert, his half-brother, was with tears on Sir John's part; but Ralegh finding that it is known that he hath a keeper, whenever he is saluted with congratulation for his liberty answers, 'No, I am still the Queen of England's poor captive.' Sir Robert wished him to conceal it, because it diminished his credit, which was greater among the mariners than he had thought; therefore he graces him as much as possible, finding Ralegh very greedy to anything to recover the conceit of his brutish offence.

They have found a thing worth looking on: rats, white and black, and a drink like smoke in taste.

25th September. THE COURT AT OXFORD.[23] At nine in the morning a divinity lecture was read by Mr. Holland, her Majesty's Reader in Divinity, at which many scholars were present but few of the nobility. The Lords of the Council dined with Mr. Saville at Martin College in the common hall, where,

21 Nicoll's *Progresses.*   23 Nicoll's *Progresses.*
22 SP DOM 243:17.

after dinner, they heard a disputation in philosophy which was determined by Mr. Saville, who because one of the questions had been *'An dissensiones ciuium sint respublicae utiles?'* (Whether the disagreements of citizens are useful for the state) took occasion to commend by name the Lord Treasurer, who was present, the Lord Chamberlain, the Lord Admiral and the Earl of Essex. This done the Lords went to sit in Council.

27th September. THE QUEEN AT OXFORD.[24] In the afternoon the Queen came again to St. Mary's and listened to questions in Law and Divinity, the last act being determined by the Bishop of Hereford, who argued against the question, Whether it be lawful in a Christian commonwealth to feign in the cause of religion. Upon which he made so copious and eloquent an oration that the Queen twice sent to him to cut short his words because she meant herself to make a speech that night. But he either would not, or else could not, put himself out of a set methodical speech for fear lest he should have marred it all and perhaps confounded his memory. The Queen was so tired that she forbore her speech that day.

28th September. THE QUEEN LEAVES OXFORD.[25] About 10 in the forenoon the Queen sending for the Vice-Chancellor and the Heads of Houses made them a speech in Latin in which she thanked them for their entertainment; but in the middle of her oration casting her eye aside and seeing the Lord Treasurer standing for want of a stool, she called in all haste for a stool for him, and would not proceed in her speech till she saw he was provided with one. Then she fell to it again as if there had been no interruption, whereupon one, who might be so bold with her, afterwards told her that she did it of purpose to show that she could interrupt her speech and not be put out although the Bishop of Hereford durst not do so for a less matter the day before. Shortly afterward, about 11 in the forenoon, the Queen and her train left the University, and heard, lastly, a long tedious oration made by the Junior Proctor of the University, at the very edge of their boundaries near Shotover.

1st October. THE INCREASE OF THE PLAGUE.[1] The plague

24 Nicoll's *Progresses.*
25 Nicoll's *Progresses.*
1 APC 23:220.

still grows in the City. The Lord Mayor and Aldermen are straightly warned that if the infection do not abate the Queen will remove the Term to some other place, to the great hindrance of the City. Moreover, by the Queen's special direction, the Council demand what means are being taken to keep the sick from the sound, and to relieve those whose houses were shut up; and why the Lord Mayor and Aldermen refuse to allow fires to be lit in the streets which has been found by good experience very effective in purging the air in places infected.

REINFORCEMENTS FOR BRITTANY.[2] A further reinforcement of 1000 men is to be enrolled for Sir John Norris in Brittany; of whom one-third to be armed with pikes and halberds, the remainder furnished with harquebusses and calivers, of which one-fourth were to be muskets. In choosing men especial care is to be taken that they be of able body and fit for service and not, as is too common, so light or so fearful that, after they have marched to the seaside or to their destination, they either run away from their captains, or offer them money to be discharged and suffered to return.

6th October. 'THE REPENTANCE OF ROBERT GREENE.'[3] *The Repentance of Robert Greene* is entered, being written by himself as he lay dying, in which he relates the story of his life and the misery of his end brought on himself by loose company, drunkenness, swearing, contempt of the Word, and other gross and grievous sins.

KYD'S 'SPANISH TRAGEDY.'[4] *The Spanish Tragedy,* written by Thomas Kyd some years before, that was lately played at the Rose Theatre, is to be printed.

11th October. CITY FEASTS TO BE FORBORNE.[5] Because of the infection the feasts at the Guildhall and in other Halls of the City Companies are to be omitted and the money so saved given to relieve those whose houses are infected. For this end the preacher at Paul's Cross shall notify to the people why the feasts are for this time to be forborne, and let them understand that it is not to spare charge but because of the inconvenience that might come from drawing together assemblies; and also that the money is being put to a use more ac-

[2] APC 23:223.
[3] SR 2:621; STC 12036.
[4] SR 2:621; STC 15086.
[5] APC 23:232.

ceptable to God and for the good of the City. Moreover those poor men who are thereby relieved will be more willing to keep within their houses.

12*th October*. PRECAUTIONS AGAINST THE PLAGUE.[6] That the Court may be the better preserved from the infection, no one, except those who have cause to come thither for their ordinary attendance on the Queen's person, may repair to the Court or within two miles of it. Nor shall anyone attending on the Queen repair to London or the suburbs or places within two miles of the city without special licence in writing, upon pain to be imprisoned by attachment of the Knight Marshal. He is to cause search to be made for all vagabonds, commonly called rogues, that haunt about the Court or within the verge.

18*th October*. PLAGUE DEATHS.[7] This last week 198 persons died of the plague in London.

19*th October*. SIR JOHN NORRIS DELAYED.[8] The weather at Southampton remains so contrary that the soldiers with Sir John Norris are unable to sail. Upwards of one hundred men have run away, and though Sir John has written to the justices thereabout to apprehend them, yet such is the slender care found in them and in the constables and other officers charged to follow the hue and cry that not a man has been returned. They are received into houses in the country, and helped to convey themselves and their furniture away. Sir John hath asked the Council that one hundred men may be pressed in Hampshire to fill up their places and to give the county better minds than to hinder the soldiers and assist them to escape.

Not finding sufficient shipping at Southampton, Sir John wrote to the Mayor of Poole, who showed himself very willing, charging the masters and owners of some suitable shipping in the road to put themselves in readiness; but they disobediently and contemptuously took down their masts and rigging, using very bad language and threatening revenge. For this the Mayor has committed them.

20*th October*. THE DEATH OF COUNT MONTAIGNE.[9] News is received in London of the death of Count Michael de

6 PROCLAMATIONS 312.   8 SP DOM 243:43.
7 FUGGER NEWS-LETTERS, p. 243.   9 BIRCH'S MEMOIRS 1:87.

Montaigne, which occurred on the 13th September from a quinsy.

THE GREAT CARRACK.[10] Certain persons from Antwerp and other towns of the Low Countries, subjects of the King of Spain, are lately arrived in London to buy part of the goods taken in the Carrack. As they have come without licence or safe conduct, the Lord Mayor is to make immediate search within the City that it may be known who they were; and, when any are found, their hosts to be made chargeable that they be forthcoming to obey such directions as shall be given them. Also they are to be searched for jewels, and if any be found in their possession these are to be taken away and kept in safe custody.

21st October.   A PROCLAMATION CONCERNING THE PLAGUE.[11] As the infection in London and Westminster is but little abated, the remainder of the term is adjourned to Hertford, and all with causes or suits in the Courts of Chancery, Star-chamber, Exchequer, Wards and Liveries, the Duchy of Lancaster or Court of Requests to proceed thither.

Further if there should be any access at the Castle or Town of Hertford of those that have the plague in their houses or have been infected with it, there may ensue great evil and damage to the rest of the realm. It is commanded that no persons who have had the plague in their houses or have been infected themselves since the 1st of July shall repair to the town of Hertford unless summoned by special process for their personal appearance. Any one so summoned shall openly notify by some message his state to those appointed by the Lord Keeper of the Great Seal to keep the gates. If the party then be ordered to come into the town or castle, to bear in his hand, upright to be seen, one red rod of the length of a yard or more.

22nd October.   ALLEYN THE PLAYER MARRIED.[12] Edward Alleyn, the tragedian, hath married Joan Woodward, step-daughter to Philip Henslowe that built the Rose Theatre.

23rd October.   BEACON WATCHES.[13] Now that the nights grow very long and cold with the approach of winter, the

[10] APC 23:246.   [12] ELIZ. STAGE 2:296.
[11] PROCLAMATIONS 313.   [13] APC 23:264.

watching of beacons is become very tedious and troublesome, and no longer necessary. The Council have ordered it to be discontinued until the spring.

27th October. THE NORMANDY FORCES TO BE SENT TO BRITTANY.[14] The companies in Normandy go to Brittany in the conduct of Sir Roger Williams to serve under Sir John Norris in Brittany. On arrival Sir Roger shall be appointed a Marshal of the Field in place of Sir Henry Norris, and Colonel of one of the regiments of 400.

30th October. ABUSES AT HERTFORD.[15] Now that the Michaelmas Term is adjourned to Hertford excessive prices the inhabitants there demand for chambers and lodgings. The Clerk of the Musket is to repair thither to set reasonable prices on all manner of victuals, as dear at least as in London, and likewise on the houses, lodging, stables, shops and other rooms; and for the convenience of those that repair thither, a harbinger of the Queen's to inform them of these prices. Moreover divers Londoners have already hired houses and lodgings, intending to offer victuals for sale, retail wares, and let out chambers for their own private gains. The magistrates shall suffer no one from the City of London, Westminster, the suburbs, or Southwark to hire any houses or chambers or other rooms that is not a professed Counsellor, Attorney or Solicitor of the law.

THE LORD MAYOR REBUFFED.[16] The Lord Mayor and Aldermen petitioning that the term might be held in London, the Council reply that they wish with all their hearts that the Lord Mayor had observed the orders prescribed for preventing the spread of infection, and then the Queen would have had no cause to remove the Term. Had their suit been made earlier it might have been considered, but she is now fully resolved on it and the preparations are too far forward for them to be recalled without great inconvenience.

4th November. THE DEATH OF SIR JOHN PERROT.[1] Sir John Perrot died last night in the Tower, where he has remained under sentence of death since June.

14 APC 23:268.
15 APC 23:274.
16 APC 23:276.
1 Richard Rawlinson, *The History*

of . . . *Sir John Perrot*, 1728; Robert Naunton, *Fragmenta Regalia*, 1649; DNB.

THE CHARACTER OF SIR JOHN PERROT

Sir John Perrot was exceedingly tall and big in stature, yet his body was very compact and well proportioned, and as he exceeded most men in stature so did he in strength of body. His countenance was full of majesty, his eye marvellously piercing and carrying a commanding aspect, insomuch that when he was angry he had a very terrible visage, but when he was pleased or willing to show kindness, he had then as amiable a countenance as any man. His mind was answerable to his body, for he was of an undaunted spirit, never regarding his adversaries were they never so many or so great. In time of danger he showed himself always resolute and valiant; he had a very sharp wit and was naturally wise. But he had also some defects; for he was by nature choleric and could not brook any crosses or dissemble the least injuries although offered by the greatest personages, and thereby he procured to himself many and mighty adversaries who in the end wrought his overthrow. In anger he would sometimes deal roughly, and so long as any man did oppose him he would contend with him by sword or by law: but if submission were offered by an inferior or reconciliation by his equal he would receive it readily. When moved by wrath he would swear excessively, partly from custom, partly from choler. He was also addicted to incontinence, leaving children by several ventures, as well as his lawful son, who succeeds him.

Many declare that his fall was brought about through the malice of Sir Christopher Hatton, the Lord Chancellor, whom Sir John had taunted because, as he said, he danced himself into favour. But the Chancellor hath a greater injury against Sir John, in that he seduced his daughter. On his return from his trial he cried with oaths and fury to Sir Owen Hopton, the Lieutenant of the Tower, 'What, will the Queen suffer her brother to be offered up as a sacrifice to the envy of my flattering adversaries?' These words being carried to the Queen, she refused to sign the order for his execution, and swore that he should not die, for he was an honest and faithful man. His mother was a lady of great honour in the Court of King Henry VIII who was married to Sir Thomas Perrot, a gentleman of the Privy Chamber, but Sir John in his person, qualities, gesture and voice so much resembled the late King that it is very generally believed that he was indeed a surreptitious child of the blood royal.

'SOLACE FOR THE SOLDIER AND THE SAILOR.'[2] *The Solace for the Soldier and the Sailor,* written by Simon Harward, that was a Chaplain in the Earl of Cumberland's fleet, is to be printed, being dedicated to the Archbishop of Canterbury. He saith that he hath written this pamphlet for three causes; first because he is thereunto requested by certain godly and valiant captains and shipmasters amongst whom he laboured on the Spanish seas; second, to answer the obloquies and reproachful speeches of many that affirm that his voyages are a blot and discredit to the doctrine which he delivereth on land; and thirdly because of the many seditious malcontents who by their unthankful grudgings will not afford a good word to those that are willing to undergo so many dangers abroad to procure peace and quietness at home. Justifieth from Scripture the lawfulness of the profession of arms, and especially of the war against the Spaniard.

13th November. MR. HERRICK'S GOODS.[3] Mr. Nicholas Herrick, a goldsmith, who lately fell from an upper window in his house in the City is dead. Hereupon some credibly think that he cast himself out wilfully, whereby his goods and chattels are forfeited to the Queen's Almoner, though by others the matter is endeavoured to be found casual. The coroners of the City of London are straightly charged that they receive no verdict until the evidence which the Almoner shall bring is thoroughly known and examined.

14th November. NORRIS'S COMPLAINTS.[4] Sir John Norris writeth that fresh Spaniards to the number of 2500 have appeared in Brittany, but his own men run away infinitely, so that when all shall come together there will not be 3000, wherewith he will not spare himself, but he can make them no more worth than they are, for he never saw men more fearful. The King has sent for these troops to assist him to the recovery of the Castle of Pont de l'Arch, and Sir John awaiteth the Queen's instructions thereon.

17th November. CORONATION DAY.[5] Upon the Coronation Day, at night, there came into the Privy Chamber two armed knights (being the Earl of Essex and the Earl of Cumberland) and there made a challenge that upon the 26th February next

[2] SR 2:622; STC.
[3] APC 23:289; F. W. Moorman, *Robert Herrick*, 1910, p. 19. This was the father of Robert Herrick the poet, then aged 14 months.
[4] SP FOR 29:f.296.
[5] GAWDY LETTERS, p. 67.

they will run all comers to maintain that their mistress is the worthiest and fairest Amadis of Gaul.

20th November. A FAVOURITE LADY-IN-WAITING.[6] Her Majesty is so pleased with the behaviour of the Lady Bridget Manners, one of her Ladies-in-Waiting, and daughter of the Countess of Rutland, that she hath caused Sir Thomas Heneage, her Vice-Chamberlain, to write to the lady's mother in high commendation of her daughter.

'SOLIMAN AND PERSEDA.'[7] *The Tragedy of Soliman and Perseda* is entered for printing.

7th December. UNWILLING CAPTAINS TO BE PUNISHED.[1] Certain captains and soldiers of the forces ordered to pass from the Low Countries to Brittany excuse themselves for frivolous reasons. The Deputy-Treasurer in the place shall withhold the pay and imprest money of any who refused to embark, and also inform the Governor, requiring him to commit the offender to prison, not to be released until he hath certified the Council and received direction.

8th December. CHETTLE'S 'KINDHEART'S DREAM.'[2] Chettle hath entered his *Kindheart's Dream,* wherein he taketh occasion to clear himself of the charges made against him for allowing that letter in Greene's *Groat's-worth of Wit* to be printed. 'With neither of them,' saith he, 'that take offence was I acquainted, and with one of them I care not if I never be. The other, whom at that time I did not so much spare as since I wish I had, for that as I have moderated the heat of living writers, and might have used my own discretion, especially in such a case (the author being dead); that I did not, I am as sorry as if the original fault had been my fault, because myself have seen his demeanour no less civil than he excellent in the quality he professes; besides, divers of worship have reported his uprightness of dealing, which argues his honesty and his facetious grace in writing that approves his art. For the first, whose learning I reverence, and at the perusing of Greene's book stroke out what then in conscience I thought he in some displeasure writ; him I would wish to use me no worse than I deserve. I had only in the copy this share: it was ill written, as sometimes Greene's hand was none of the best;

---

[6] *Rutland MSS* 1:305. See *20th Aug*   [1] APC 23:348.
1594.   [2] SR 2:623; STC 5123.
[7] SR 2:622; STC 22894.

licensed it must be, ere it could be printed, which could be never if it might not be read. To be brief, I writ it over, and, as near as I could, followed the copy, only in that letter I put something out, but in the whole book not a word in; for I protest it was all Greene's; not mine nor Master Nashe's as some unjustly have affirmed.'

16*th December.* THE FUNERAL OF THE DUKE OF PARMA.[3] The Duke of Parma died of his wound on the 3rd of this month and on the 10th his body was brought with great pomp and solemnity from Arras to Brussels. The soldiers and fraternities, all the clergy, the Counts Von Mansfield, Arenburg, Barlaimont, and de Fuentes, with all the rest of the nobility, and the members of the Council came out to meet the corpse with lighted lanterns in their hands, and escorted it to the Castle Chapel.

18*th December.* 'ELIOT'S FRUITS FOR THE FRENCH.'[4] Mr. John Eliot hath written *Orthœpia Gallica or Eliot's Fruits for the French,* being penned for the practice, pleasure, and profit of all English gentlemen, who will endeavour by their own pain, study and diligence, to attain the natural accent, the true pronunciation, the swift and glib grace of this noble, famous and courtly language. In the first part of the book are three dialogues, showing the words and sentences used by the scholar and traveller, followed by the two books of *The Parliament of Prattlers,* giving the words and sentences needed by gentlemen on two and thirty kinds of occasion. In the former of these books the French words are shown in the first column; in the second the way of pronouncing them; and in the third the English.

30*th December.* PLAYING RESUMED.[5] Yesterday the Lord Strange's players began again to play at the Rose Theatre after their inhibition in the summer, and played *Muly Mullocco;* and to-day *The Spanish Tragedy.*

31*st December.* THE BILLS OF MORTALITY FOR THE YEAR.[6] This year first beginneth a custom of keeping weekly bills of mortality for the City of London and the parishes immediately adjoining. When anyone dies either the tolling and ringing of

[3] FUGGER NEWS-LETTERS, p. 244.
[4] SR 2:624; STC 7574.
[5] HENS. DIARY 1:15.
[6] John Graunt, *Reflections on the*

Weekly Bills of Mortality, 1665, p. 3, and *Observations on the Bills of Mortality,* 1662, p. 33.

the bell or the bespeaking of a grave intimateth it to the searchers (who keep a strict correspondence with the sextons); and thereupon the ancient matrons sworn to that office repair to the place where the corpse lies, and upon their own view and others' examination, make a judgment of what disease or casualty the corpse died, which judgment they report to the parish clerk. He on every Tuesday night bringeth to the clerk of the Hall an account of every christening and burial that week; whence on Wednesday the general account is made up, and printed. During this year 1592, there have died in London from March to December 25,886 persons, whereof of the plague 11,503.

Other Books Printed in 1592

i. *Hypnerotomachia: the Strife of Love in a Dream.* Written in Italian by Francisco Colonna, and translated into English by Richard Dallington, being dedicated to the thrice honourable and ever living virtues of Sir Philip Sidney, Knight, and to the right honourable and others whatsoever, who living loved him, and being dead gave him his due, and the epistle written to the Earl of Essex. The story telleth of the amorous visions of the monk Potiphilus, and the first Italian copy is much noted for the beauty of its cuts.

ii. *A Disputation between A He Conny-catcher and a She Conny-catcher,* written by Robert Greene, in which Lawrence, a foist, and Nan, a traffic, dispute for a supper whether a thief or a whore is more prejudicial to a commonwealth, both alleging instances out of their experience until Lawrence confesseth that he is beaten.

In writing these two discourses Greene declared that he was acting for the good of his countrymen at the peril of his own life, for the conny-catchers had protested his death, and one evening had beleaguered him being at supper in the Saint John's Head within Ludgate, and thought to have slain him, but that the citizens and apprentices took his part, so that two or three of them were carried to the Counter, although a gentleman in his company was sore hurt. Greene also promiseth that he will print a bead-roll of all the foists and conny-catchers about the City.

iii. *The Groundwork of Conny-catching,* purporting to be a new book, but in fact Thomas Harman's *Caveat for Common Cursetors* (first printed in 1567).

iv. *The Nine Worthies of London: explaining the honourable exercise of arms, the virtues of the valiant, and the memorable*

i. STC 5577.   iii. STC 12789.
ii. STC 12234.

attempts of magnanimous minds; pleasant for gentlemen, not unseemly for magistrates, and most profitable for prentices: compiled by Richard Johnson, being dedicated to Sir William Webb, the Lord Mayor. Herein Fame and Clio, meeting together, cause the ancient worthies of the city to rise from the ground and declare their own fortunes in verse, namely Sir William Wallworth, fishmonger, who slew Wat Tyler; Sir Henry Pritchard, vintner; Sir William Sevenoake, grocer; Sir William White, merchant tailor; Sir John Bonham, mercer; Sir Christopher Croker, vintner; Sir John Hawkwood, merchant tailor; Sir Hugh Caverley, silk weaver; and Sir Henry Maleveret, grocer, surnamed Henry of Cornhill, which last having fought in the Holy Land, to rescue the oppressed Jews, was by envious tongues defamed.

iv. STC 14636.

1593

3rd January. RUMOURS.[1] There is great disagreement about the goods of the Great Carrack. The Earl of Cumberland would claim them, having taken her when she was like to have carried away the Queen's ship, and had beaten Sir John Burgh's; but for the Queen's part it is alleged that by her prerogative she may challenge the services of all her subjects' ships, that are bound to help her at sea, and recompense them according to her princely bounty, which she would do liberally enough to the Earl, but for some that would make a profit by buying it at her hands. All the others, that served the Queen, and Sir Walter Ralegh, receive only their pay, and are discontented at receiving so little out of so rich a prize, worth £150,000, though indeed much of the richest is purloined and embezzled.

The Lord Treasurer is much offended with the libels printed against him and lately brought over; it is thought that they will do no good to the Catholics, against whom a book is being written.

8th January. THE WAR IN FRANCE.[2] Fresh levies are demanded of the Lord Mayor and the Lords Lieutenant of ten counties for Normandy to the number of 1200, of which 450 are from the City, to be ready to embark on the 12th February. Special care is to be taken in the choice of the men and their appointments.

From Brittany it is reported that the English Captains are still prisoners, being held at extreme ransoms, especially the Sergeant-Major, for whom they demand 10,000 crowns. If they be not relieved, others will be discouraged from undergoing the like dangers.

[1] SP DOM 244:1. The libels presumably were the books summarised under *15th Aug 1592.*

[2] APC 24:14; SP FOR 30:f7.

12th January. NASHE'S 'STRANGE NEWS.'[3] Nashe hath replied to Dr. Gabriel Harvey in a book called *Strange News of the intercepting of certain letters and a convoy of verses as they were going privily to victual the Low Counties,* where, in the form of a commentary paragraph by paragraph upon the *Four Letters,* Harvey is very abusively handled.

In Greene's defence Nashe noteth that he inherited more virtues than vices; a jolly long red peak like the spire of a steeple, he cherished continually without cutting, whereat a man might hang a jewel, it was so sharp and pendant. Why should art answer for infirmities of manners? 'He had his faults, and thou follies. Debt and deadly sin who is not subject to? With any notorious crime I never knew him tainted (and yet tainting is no infamous surgery for him that hath been in so many hot skirmishes). In a night and day would he have yarked up a pamphlet as well as in seven year, and glad was that printer that might be so blessed to pay him dear for the very dregs of his wit.'

To Harvey's praise of the English hexameter Nashe answereth that the hexameter verse is a gentleman of an ancient house (so is many an English beggar), yet this clime of ours he cannot thrive in: our speech is too craggy for him to set his plough in, he goes twitching and hopping in our language like a man running up quagmires, up the hill in one syllable and down the dale in another, retaining no part of that stately smooth gait which he vaunts himself with amongst the Greeks and Latins.

18th January. RUMOURS.[4] The Parliament that is summoned for 19th February is said to be only for money to maintain the troops in Brittany and elsewhere, the last payment of the last Parliament's subsidy being now due, and almost all spent already if the soldiers' debts were paid.

The Lord Treasurer is now well recovered of his dangerous sickness, at which there is much satisfaction, for on him the whole state of the realm dependeth; and if he were to go there is no one about the Queen able to wield the State.

21st January. PLAGUE INCREASING.[5] Weekly returns of the plague which for some weeks past were diminishing now show an increase, so that the Lord Mayor and Aldermen of the City are sharply rebuked for their neglect, because either they do

[3] SR 2:624; STC 18377. Went into five printings.   [4] SP Dom 244:18.
[5] APC 24:21.

not observe good order for preventing the plague or else the orders themselves are insufficient. They are commanded by the Council at their utmost peril to cause immediate note to be taken of all houses infected or suspected to be infected and themselves to see them shut up either by locks hanging outwardly in the doors or by a special watch on every house. Thus the infected shall be prevented from resorting abroad to mix with the sound. Those so shut up shall be provided with sufficient food and other provision, to be paid for by those of ability; but the poorer sort, artificers or those who live by handiwork or by alms, to be relieved with the charity of the parish and of the City, especially to be collected for that purpose. The Lord Mayor and the Aldermen are further warned that if they continue to be careless, the Queen, in addition to the punishment she meaneth to inflict on them, will remove the Parliament away from the City.

28th January.   EVASION OF SERVICE IN PRIVILEGED PLACES.[6] Many of late resort to St. Martin's, Blackfriars, Whitefriars, and other places privileged and exempt from the authority of the Lord Mayor to avoid the imprest for service.

SIR HENRY KNIVETT'S SUBMISSION.[7] Sir Henry Knivett was this day called before the Council and after he had confessed his fault in showing contempt for the authority of the Lord Keeper was admonished to beware of such presumption hereafter and given leave to depart. He had been committed to the Fleet by the Lord Keeper for having allowed his servants to commit an outrage upon a person coming to serve a process on a gentlewoman then residing in his house. Being released he wrote a letter to some of the Privy Council in which he slandered the proceedings of the Lord Keeper, alleging them to have been unjust; which letter being read at the Council Board in his presence, the Lord Keeper, although not liable to render account for his sentences given in the Queen's Court to any but the Queen, was nevertheless willing that their Lordships should hear the proofs of the accusation. Accordingly Sir Henry was called to the Council Board and required to show proofs of his allegations; which being carefully heard, it appeared that he had unjustly, undutifully and indiscreetly slandered the Lord Keeper, and for this offence he was committed to the Fleet; whence after some days he wrote a letter of submission, acknowledging his offence, beseeching the pardon of their Lordships and their favourable mediation with the Lord Keeper.

2nd February.   PLAYS AND GAMES PROHIBITED.[1] As the plague increaseth continually all manner of concourse and public meetings of the people (preaching and Divine service at churches excepted) at plays, bearbaiting, bowling and other assemblies for sport are inhibited. At the Rose Theatre *The Jew of Malta* was played, and on the days before *Friar Bacon* and *Harry the Sixth*. Owing to the increase of plague the theatre is now shut up.

3rd February.   'GREENE'S NEWS FROM HEAVEN AND HELL.'[2] *Greene's News both from Heaven and Hell,* commended to the press by B. R., is to be printed, being dedicated to Gregory Coolle, chief burgomaster of the Castle of Clonars. In this collection of merry tales B. R. saith that he met the ghost of Robert Greene which popped into his hands his papers to be committed to the press.

7th February.   LAWLESSNESS ON THE SCOTTISH BORDER.[3] The Bishop of Carlisle and others complain of the spoils and robberies made not only by the Scottish borderers but the English also, especially since Michaelmas. Divers gentlemen have been invaded in their dwelling-houses, their goods and chattels taken by violence and carried into Scotland, and themselves put to ransom. Most of the gentry dwelling within twenty miles of Carlisle go in fear of their lives and goods, so that not only they but justices of the peace even are forced to keep their cattle within their houses nightly, and dare not suffer them to pasture on their grounds. The justices and sheriffs are unable to give any relief, nor can the Warden help them.

8th February.   INVASION EXPECTED.[4] It is said that the Spaniard will attempt an invasion of the realm by means of some dangerous conspiracy with some of the nobility of Scotland. As they will pass the seas between Ireland and England, it is thought likely that they will try to surprise the Isle of Man, and fortify it as a place very convenient for their victualling and watering. The Earl of Derby is therefore to send trustworthy persons straightway to put the island in a state of defence, but especially to take care of any trusted with the charge of any

[1] APC 24:31; HENS. DIARY 1:16.   [3] SP DOM *Addenda* 32:66.
[2] SR 2:626; STC 12259.   [4] APC 24:53.

place because some be suspected. Good heed especially to be taken of one Dudley that hath of late been in Scotland to some evil purpose.

11th February. CONTRIBUTIONS EVADED.[5] Many persons of quality, having houses in the City, and especially most of the Doctors of the law, now refuse to contribute to the charges of the Lord Mayor in the present public services. The Council order that anyone refusing to contribute to the defence of the realm be informed of their wish; and if he still refuse, bonds shall be taken of him to appear before them. Further, if he refuse to enter into a bond, it is necessary that the Queen be acquainted with his unwillingness and to this end the Lord Mayor shall commit him to prison.

12th February. THE GREAT CARRACK.[6] The goods taken in the Great Carrack are said to have amounted to £150,000, whereof the Earl of Cumberland receiveth £37,000 by way of reward, Sir Walter Ralegh for his adventure £24,000, the City of London £12,000, some others £7000 or £8000, and the rest to be the Queen's. £10,000 worth of goods are already sold at Dartmouth to pay the mariners' wages, besides other booty plundered at sea. The Queen's share is £80,000 with all the pepper.

14th February. INSUFFICIENT MEN IMPRESTED AS SOLDIERS.[7] Of 50 men sent by the County of Bedford 14 were unable and insufficient, and most of them very evilly apparelled, their coats of very bad cloth and unlined. Of the 50 men levied in the County of Cambridge but 49 had arrived in London, one having run away, and of the rest 10 were insufficient; most of them are ill and nakedly apparelled, wanting doublets, hose, stockings, shirts and shoes, their cassocks also of very bad cloth and unlined. Yet from Buckinghamshire, Essex and Middlesex come men able and sufficient, well furnished with armour and weapons.

18th February. REGULATIONS FOR BUTCHERS DURING LENT.[8] The Lord Mayor is advised to take strict charge that the orders concerning the eating of flesh in Lent be duly en-

---

[5] APC 24:44.
[6] SP DOM 244:35. The signed award of the Commissioners (*Lansdowne MSS* 73:f40) gives the following figures: Earl of Cumberland, £18,000; Ralegh, £15,900; Hawkins, £2,400; City of London, £12,000 in goods.
[7] APC 24:62, 65, 66.
[8] APC 24:71.

forced and the disorders of last year avoided, wherein over
12,000 lbs. of the meat of calves, sheep and lambs were sold in
the space of five weeks to the great prejudice of the State by
the spoil of the breed of young cattle.

19th February.   PARLIAMENT ASSEMBLES.[9] Parliament having been summoned for this day, in the morning the knights
and burgesses came to Westminster, where each one, after
declaring his name to the Clerk of the Crown who entered it
in his book, went into the House.

The House being set, the Earl of Derby, Lord High Steward
for this Parliament, came in to take their oaths, being instructed by Sir Thomas Heneage as to what order he should
use. First, all removed into the Court of Requests where the
Lord High Steward, sitting at the door, called the knights and
burgesses of every county according to the letters of their
names in the alphabet. Each one, having answered as he was
called, went next to the Parliament House door and there took
the Oath of Supremacy given to him by one of the Privy Councillors; this done he entered again and took his place as a member of the House.

There was no further proceeding until two o'clock in the
afternoon, about which time the Queen, having come privately
by water, entered the House of Lords, accompanied by Sir
John Puckering, Lord Keeper of the Great Seal, and many of
her lords spiritual and temporal. The members of the Lower
House, having received intelligence that the Lords had taken
their places, went to attend in the Upper House before the
Bar, and, when as many had been admitted as conveniently
could be, the door was shut, and the Lord Keeper, by command of the Queen, began to speak to the effect that the assembling of Parliament hath anciently been, and still was, for
the enacting of laws and reforming of grievances and abuses
of the subjects of the Realm; yet at this time the Queen was
chiefly desirous to have the advice of her loving people concerning the defence and preservation of herself, her realms
and subjects from the power and oppression of a foreign
enemy.

At this point the Lord Keeper's speech was interrupted by
the murmuring outside. It appeared that the place of the
Lower House in the chamber had been filled by those who
came in privately before the Commons had been summoned,

so that when the rest came up they found the door shut, contrary to custom, and were so discontented that the noise reached the Queen's ears. When she understood the cause of the discontent, she immediately commanded the doors to be set open, and the Lord Keeper continued his speech.

This enemy, he said, was the King of Spain, and his malice was increased by his loss and shame received in '88. That his resolution still was to invade this kingdom did plainly appear by his building and getting together many ships of less bulk, which would be fitter for service in our seas, than those greater galliasses and galleons had been in '88. He desired some nearer place from whence to invade England, and therefore at that time he was labouring to plant himself in Brittany. He had also raised factions in Scotland and conspiracies against the King there, finding him an enemy to his ambitious designs.

'And therefore,' quoth the Lord Keeper, 'we, her Majesty's subjects, must with all dutiful consideration think what is fit for us to do; and with all willingness yield part of our own for the defence of others, and assistance of her Majesty in such an unsupportable charge. Were the cause between friend and friend, how much would we do for the relief of one another? But the cause is now between our Sovereign and ourselves; seeing there is so much difference in the parties, how much more forward ought we to be?

'The aid formerly granted to her Majesty in these like cases is so ill answered, and with such slackness performed, as that the third of that which was granted cometh not to her Majesty. A great show, a rich grant, and a long sum seems to be made; but little it is, hard to be gotten, and the sum not great which is paid. Her Majesty thinks this to be for that the wealthier sort of men turn this charge upon the weaker and upon those of worst ability; so that one dischargeth himself, and the other is not able to satisfy that he is charged withal. These things should be reformed by such as are commissioners in this service.

'Wherefore it is her Majesty's pleasure that the time be not spent in devising and enacting new laws, the number of which is so great already as it rather burdeneth than easeth the subject; but the principal cause of this Parliament is that her Majesty might consult with her subjects for the better withstanding those intended invasions, which are now greater than ever before were heard of. And where heretofore it hath been used that many have delighted themselves in long orations, full of verbosity and vain ostentations, more than in speaking things of substance; the time that is precious would not thus be spent. This session cannot be long; the spring time is fit that gentlemen should repair to their counties; the Justices of Assize also to go their circuits; so the good hours should not be lost in idle speeches, but the little time we have should be bestowed wholly on such business as is needful to be considered of; and Thursday next is appointed as the day to present the Speaker.'

As soon as the Lord Keeper's speech was ended, the Clerk of Parliament read the names of receivers of petitions, and, after the other business was ended, the Parliament was adjourned by the Lord Keeper in these words: *'Dominus Custos Magni Sigilli ex mandato Dominae Reginae continuat praesens Parliamentum usque in diem Jovis proximam futuram.'*

20th February.   PRECAUTIONS AGAINST DESERTION.[10] The officers of ports on the south and east are ordered to search any ship from beyond seas in which deserters might be carried, and all suspected to have come from Normandy or Brittany without sufficient passport from Sir John Norris or Sir Roger Williams to be committed to prison.

21st February. THE FRENCH AMBASSADOR ALLOWED MEAT.[11] The French ambassador with his family is specially allowed by the Council to be served with meat by his own butcher during Lent, but bonds are put in that the butcher do not sell meat to others under colour of this order.

22nd February. THE SPEAKER PRESENTED.[12] The Queen herself came to Westminster about three o'clock this afternoon accompanied by the Lords spiritual and temporal; there being present the Archbishop of Canterbury, Sir John Puckering, Lord Keeper of the Great Seal, William, Lord Burleigh, Lord Treasurer of England, the Marquis of Winchester, twelve Earls, two Viscounts, fifteen bishops and twenty-three barons.

The Queen and the Lords having taken their places, the members of the House of Commons were summoned, and immediately came up with their Speaker, Edward Coke, Esquire, the Queen's Solicitor, into the Upper House. The Speaker being led up to the Bar at the lower end of the House between two of the most eminent personages of the Lower House, as soon as silence was made and the rest of the House

10 APC 24:72.
11 APC 24:75.

12 D'EWES' JOURNALS, p. 458; TOWNSHEND, p. 34.

of Commons had placed themselves below the bar, made a humble speech, declaring his own unfitness, and concluding:

'But howsoever I know myself the meanest and inferior unto all that ever were before me in this place, yet in faithfulness of service and dutifulness of love, I think not myself inferior to any that ever were before me: and amidst my many imperfections, yet this is my comfort; I never knew any in this place but if your Majesty gave him favour, God, Who also called them to this place, gave them also a blessing to discharge it.'

The Lord Keeper having received instructions from the Queen made answer, commending the Lower House for their choice and bidding him proceed:

Then began the Speaker a new speech wherein, after expressing his loyalty to the Queen for the great and wonderful blessings which had been enjoyed under her rule, he related the great attempts of the Queen's enemies against us, especially the Pope and the King of Spain, from whom we were wonderfully delivered in '88. Then having touched on the supremacy which the Kings of England since Henry III's time had maintained, he went on to speak of the laws that are so many and great that they are fitly to be termed *elephantinae leges;* wherefore it might seem superfluous to make more laws, yet the malice of the devil, though it is always great, was never so great as now; and, *dolus* and *malum* being crept in so far amongst men, it was necessary that sharp ordinances should be provided to prevent them, and all care used for her Majesty's preservation.

'Now,' quoth he, 'am I to make unto your Majesty three petitions, in the names of your Commons. First, that liberty of speech and freedom from arrests, according to the ancient custom of Parliament, be granted to your subjects: that we may have access to your Royal Person to present those things which shall be considered of amongst us: and lastly, that your Majesty will give us your Royal Assent to the things that we agreed upon. And, for myself, I humbly beseech your Majesty, if any speech shall fall from me, or behaviour be found in me not decent and unfit, that it may not be imputed blame upon the House but laid upon me, and pardoned in me.'

To this speech the Lord Keeper, having received new instruction from the Queen, replied that he commended the Speaker greatly for his speech; and he added some examples for the King's Supremacy in Henry II's time, and Kings before the Conquest. As for the deliverance we received from our enemies, and the peace we enjoyed, he said the Queen would have the praise of all those to be attributed to God only. To the commendations given to herself, she said well might they have a wiser Prince, but never should they have one that more regarded them, and in justice would carry an evener stroke without acceptation of persons; and such a Princess she wished they might always have.

'To your three demands,' he concluded, 'the Queen answereth, liberty of speech is granted you, but how far, this is to be thought on. There be two things of most necessity, and those two do most harm; which are, wit and speech: the one exercised in invention, the other in uttering things invented. Privilege of speech is granted, but you must know what privilege you have, not to speak everyone what he listeth, or what cometh in his brain to utter; but your privilege is to say, "Yea or no."

'Wherefore, Mr. Speaker, her Majesty's pleasure is that if you perceive any idle heads which will not stick to hazard their own estates, which will meddle with reforming of the Church and transforming of the Commonwealth, and do exhibit any Bills to such purpose, that you receive them not until they be viewed and considered of by those whom it is fitter should consider of such things and can better judge of them.

'To your persons all privilege is granted with this *caveat*, that under colour of this privilege no man's ill doings or not performing of duties be covered and protected.

'The last, free access is also granted to her Majesty's person, so that it be upon urgent and weighty causes, and at times convenient, and when her Majesty may be at leisure from other important causes of the Realm.'

The Parliament was then adjourned to the Saturday following.

24th February. WENTWORTH'S PETITION.[13] Mr. Peter Wentworth and Sir Henry Bromley delivered a petition to the Lord Keeper, desiring the Lords to join with the Lower House as suppliants to the Queen that she would entail the succession to the Crown; and for this purpose they have a bill already drawn. When the Queen heard of it, she was so highly displeased, for this is a matter directly opposite to her commands, that she charged the Council to call the parties before them. They are sent for, and are commanded to forbear coming to Parliament and not to go out of their lodgings.

[13] D'EWES' JOURNALS, p. 470; TOWNSHEND, p. 54.

THE SPEAKER SICK.[14] This day the House being set and Mr. Speaker not coming to the House, some said that they had heard that he was sick, whereon it was moved that the Clerk should in the meantime proceed to the saying of the Litany and prayers. Which done, the Sergeant of the House brought word that the Speaker had been this last night and also the present forenoon extremely pained with a wind in his stomach and looseness of the body so that he could not as yet without great peril adventure into the air. Whereupon all the members of the House being very sorry for Mr. Speaker arose and departed away.

SIR ROGER WILLIAMS' COUNSEL.[15] Sir Roger Williams writeth his opinion that the greatest danger to England may proceed by the Scots or the Irish, especially by Ireland, where it stands her Majesty upon to make sure of those people by cutting off the principal instruments and persuading the rest of the faction by fair means; if not, immediately with good squadrons of horsemen and footmen, for there is such meanings in them that if 8000 strangers, with the treasure they would carry with them, join them, there will be great mischief. The state of France is not too desperate so long as the King keeps the field, and the Spanish do not possess the rest of the parts of Brittany and Normandy; if this were to happen, then will there be wars in England.

25th February. MR. WENTWORTH BEFORE THE COUNCIL.[16] Mr. Wentworth, Sir Henry Bromley and two others have been called before some of the Council, who treated them favourably and with good speeches. But so highly is the Queen offended that they said they had no choice but to commit them. Whereupon Mr. Wentworth is sent to the Tower, Sir Henry Bromley and the others to the Fleet.

THE EARL OF ESSEX ADMITTED TO THE COUNCIL.[17] This day the Earl of Essex, Master of the Horse, having taken the Oath of Supremacy, and of a Privy Councillor, took his place at the Council Board.

DESERTERS IN GLOUCESTERSHIRE.[18] Of 150 soldiers that were imprested in Gloucestershire and await a favourable wind at Southampton, 40 have escaped or been released by the indirect means of the officers that have the conducting of them.

[14] D'EWES' JOURNALS, p. 470.
[15] SP FOR 30:f118.
[16] D'EWES' JOURNALS, p. 470; TOWNSHEND, p. 54.
[17] APC 24:76.
[18] APC 24:81.

26th February.   A COMMITTEE OF THE HOUSE APPOINTED.[19]
In the House it was proposed that a grave Committee should
be elected to consult about the provision of treasure in this
present time of danger.

Sir Robert Cecil spoke first, showing that when the King of
Spain sent his Navy against us, it was almost upon our banks
ere we were aware of it; yea, and we were so slack in provision that it was too late to make resistance, had not God preserved us. Now he hath gone about to win France, wherein
he hath greatly prevailed, and specially in Brittany, having
most part of the port towns in his possession, whither he
sendeth supply daily, and reinforces them every four or five
months. This province he specially desireth, for it lieth most
fit to annoy us, whither he may send his forces continually and
there have his Navy in readiness; and besides may keep us
from traffic to Rochelle and Bordeaux; as he hath done in the
Straits from Tripoli and St. Jean de Luce. And so he hindereth
us from carrying forth and bringing into this land any commodities from those parts, where the realm might be inriched
and her Majesty's impost ever eased, being one of the great
revenues of the Crown. In Scotland also the King of Spain's
malice daily increaseth against us, and at home the number of
papists, or at leastwise becomes more manifest.

After him Sir John Wolley exhorted the House to a speedy
agreeing of a subsidy, and then Sir John Fortescue spake
showing the great charges that the Queen had been at, insomuch that the burden of four Kingdoms rests upon her, which
she maintained with her purse, England, France, Ireland and
Scotland. She had assisted the French King with men and
money which hath cost her about £100,000; and as for the
Low Countries, they stood her in yearly, since she undertook
the defence of them, £150,000.

'All which,' quoth he, 'her Majesty bestowed for the good
of the Realm, to free us from war at home. Besides when her
Majesty came to the Crown, she found it £4,000,000 indebted; her Navy, when she came to view it, greatly decayed:
yet all this hath discharged, and (thanks be to God) is nothing
indebted, and now she is able to match any Prince in Europe,
which the Spaniards found when they came to invade us. Yea,
she hath with her ships encompassed the whole world whereby
this land is famous throughout all places. She did find in her
Navy all iron pieces, but she hath furnished it with artillery of
brass, so that one of her ships is not a subject's but a petty

King's. As for her own private expenses, they have been little in building; she hath consumed little or nothing in her pleasures. As for her apparel it is royal and princely, beseeming her calling, but not sumptuous or excessive. The charges of her house small, yea, never less in any King's time.'

After Sir Edward Stafford and Mr. Francis Bacon had spoken, the whole House agreed to the committee.

27th February. UNREASONABLE DEMANDS FROM PRISONERS.[20] Some that receive grants for the keeping of gaols lease them out at exceeding great rents or other profits. Thus their assigns are constrained to exact excessive prices for victual, bedding, fire, fees of irons and other things from poor prisoners, who for want of means to satisfy these unreasonable demands, so perish through famine: for they remain in prison a long time after they are discharged of the principal cause of their commitment only for lack of ability to defray the great sums exacted of them. The Justices of the Assizes at every place of gaol delivery in the next circuit shall inform themselves thereof; and because they will not have leisure themselves they shall appoint certain of the discreetest Justices of the Peace, and such as be not interested with the granters of the goods, to examine strictly the prisoners in every place and bolt out what hath been laid on them for their meat, drink, bedding and so forth. These being recorded in writing, a reasonable rate and prices shall be set down to be paid by the prisoners from time to time.

A BILL AGAINST THE BISHOPS.[21] Mr. Morris, Attorney of the Court of Wards, delivered a Bill to the Speaker which touches on the abuses of the Bishops in the matter of lawless inquisition, injurious subscription and binding absolution, asking that, if the House thought well of it, they might petition the Queen to have it allowed. Thereupon Mr. Dalton and Sir John Wolley spoke against the Bill, but Sir Francis Knollys was for reading it. Sir Robert Cecil, putting the House in mind that her Majesty had strictly forbidden them to meddle in such cases, the Speaker, perusing the Bill, answered that it was so weighty and long that he needed time to consider it, and to this end asked the leave of the House to keep it for a while. It was therefore put to the House whether the Bill should be committed to the Speaker only, or to the Privy Council and to him; but as it was held to be against the Order of the House that a Bill should be committed before it was read, it was agreed that the Speaker should keep it. About two o'clock in the afternoon the Speaker was summoned to the Court, where the Queen herself gave him commandment what to deliver to the House.

THE SUBSIDIES.[22] The committee of the House have agreed that, should the House assent thereto, the treasure to be provided for her Majesty be two entire subsidies and four fifteenths and tenths. After consultation the House agreed that the Bill to this effect should be drawn, with a preamble signifying that so great and extraordinary supply is at this time given for resisting the power and preventing the malice of the King of Spain.

ROGER RIPPON'S CORPSE.[23] Roger Rippon, a Barrowist, having died in Newgate, his body was taken by his friends and enclosed in a coffin which they laid at the door of Justice Young, bearing this inscription: 'This is the corpse of Roger Rippon, a servant of Christ and her Majesty's faithful subject, who is the last of sixteen or seventeen which that great enemy of God, the Archbishop of Canterbury, with his High Commissioners, have murthered in Newgate within these five years, manifestly for the testimony of Jesus Christ. His soul is now with the Lord; and his blood crieth for speedy vengeance against that great enemy of the saints and against Mr. Richard Young, who in this, and many the like points, hath abused his power, for the upholding of the Romish Antichrist, Prelacy and priesthood.' Many copies of this libel are spread about the City.

28th February. THE BILL AGAINST THE BISHOPS.[24] Mr. Morris hath been sent for to Court and committed into Sir John Fortescue's keeping.

In the Lower House the Speaker showed that he had kept the Bills delivered him the day before by himself and no one else had seen them. A little after he had perused them, he was sent for by special messenger from the Queen, who commanded him to deliver a message to the House.

'I protest,' he declared, 'a greater comfort never befell me than that this my integrity and faithful promise to this House is not violated; for her Majesty, in her gracious wisdom, before my coming determined not to press me in this, neither

22 D'EWES' JOURNALS, p. 474; TOWN-   24 D'EWES' JOURNALS, p. 478; TOWN-
SHEND, p. 61.   SHEND, p. 61.
23 STRYPE'S ANNALS 4:133.

indeed did she require the Bill of me; for this only she required of me: what were the things spoken of by the House? Which points I only delivered as they that heard me can tell.

'The message delivered me from her Majesty consisteth of three things: First, the end for which Parliament was called. Secondly, the speech which her Majesty used by my Lord Keeper. Thirdly, what her pleasure and commandment now is.

'For the first it is in me and my power (I speak now in her Majesty's person) to call Parliaments, and it is in my power to end and determine the same; it is in my power to assent or dissent to anything done in Parliament. The calling of this Parliament was only that the Majesty of God might be more religiously served, and those that neglect this service might be compelled by some sharper means to a due obedience and more true service of God than there hath been hitherto used. And, further, that the safety of her Majesty's person, and of this realm, might be by all means provided for against our great enemies, the Pope and the King of Spain.

'Her Majesty's most excellent pleasure being then delivered unto us by the Lord Keeper, it was not meant that we should meddle with matters of State, or in causes ecclesiastical, for so her Majesty termed them. She wondered that any should be of so high commandment to attempt (I use her own words) a thing contrary to that which she had so expressly forbidden; wherefore with this she was highly displeased. And because the words then spoken by my Lord Keeper are not now perhaps well remembered, or some be now here that were not there, her Majesty's present charge and express commandment is *That no Bills touching matters of State, or Reformation in Causes Ecclesiastical, be exhibited.* And upon my allegiance, I am commanded if any such Bill be exhibited not to read it.'

FLESH IN LENT.[25] The Lord Mayor is rebuked for his forwardness in giving leave to certain butchers to kill and utter flesh during this season of Lent. The Council ask that a butcher may be admitted to provide flesh for the use of Don Antonio, who hath never used to eat fish.

A PLOT TO KILL THE QUEEN.[26] Gilbert Layton, a recusant, that was taken, hath voluntarily confessed that he was sent over to England by Parsons, Sir Francis Englefield, and Don Juan de Idiaques to kill the Queen. It was to be performed

[25] APC 24:84, 87.　　　　　　　[26] SP DOM 244:55.

while she was still on progress, with a wire made with jemos or with a poniard.

1st March. ROGER RIPPON'S CORPSE.[1] Christopher Bowman, goldsmith, being examined before Justice Young concerning the corpse of Roger Rippon, declareth that his whole congregation consented to the making of the coffin, for which they paid 4s. 8d. He will not disclose who the congregation are, nor their secrets, nor the place of meeting. He will not be persuaded to go to his parish church, nor to Paul's Cross to hear a sermon, seeing that any man, however wicked he might be, is admitted to receive the communion; and he would not join with the minister who gave holy things to dogs. Moreover, he refuseth to sign his examination.

EXTREME TENETS OF THE PURITANS.[2] Amongst the more extreme opinions of the Puritans, shown either in their writings or examinations, it appeareth that in Church matters they would take away all gifts of bishoprics and deaneries from the Queen by dissolving them, and all patronages; for they hold that all ecclesiastical functions should be elective by the people or their elders. When supremacy was restored to the crown, one chief supereminency was that the final appeal in all ecclesiastical causes should be made to the King in chancery; this they would take away, making the appeal from an Eldership Consistory to a Conference, thence to a Provincial Synod, lastly to a National Synod which should be final.

They would have the Queen, being a child of the Church, subject to the censures of examination by their elderships as well as any other person, and that all, great or small, must willingly be ruled and governed, and must obey those whom God had set over them. If the Prince without God's warrant intermeddle with the Church, he must think it none injury to be disobeyed; for we are not bound to obey the Prince's law for conscience' sake, because only God's laws bind men's consciences. The Prince must take heed that he pass no weighty matter of the Commonwealth without the assembly of all the estates of the realm, whereby he is debarred from treating or capitulating, either for war, peace or league with any other prince without the Parliament being privy to it. In all matters of the Church the highest ecclesiastical authority belongeth to the eldership.

[1] SP Dom 244:62.
[2] STRYPE'S ANNALS 4:140. Strype notes 'This paper seems to have been drawn up by the Lord Keeper Puckering, to be produced against them in the Star Chamber, after their examinations before him.'

They would administer baptism to no known papist's children, to none excommunicate person's children and to none but to their children that be within the Church, that is, to those who submit themselves to their order of discipline, all others being accounted out of God's covenant and so no true Christians.

They would have the judicial law of Moses for punishing divers sins with death to be in force, so that no prince nor law could save the lives of those who offend wilfully as blasphemers of God's Name, conjurers, soothsayers, persons possessed with an evil spirit, heretics, perjurers, breakers of the Sabbath day, neglecters of the sacraments without just reason, any that disobeys or curses his parents, incestuous persons, daughters who commit fornication in their fathers' houses, adulterers, and all incontinent persons, save single fornicators, and any who conspire against any man's life. The *lex talionis*, that is an eye for an eye, ought to be observed in every commonwealth.

They would cut off the state ecclesiastical, being one of the three in Parliament, and have all laws made by the lords temporal and the commons only. It is unlawful, say they, for any State to tolerate the present Government Ecclesiastical, for it is false, unlawful, bastardly and unchristian, and can be defended by no good or sound subject; those that do so are traitors to God and His Word, enemies to the Queen and the land, and shall answer for the blood which the Spaniard or other enemies might spill, for they bring in hazard the Queen's life and the prosperity of the kingdom, being its greatest enemies.

The sect called the Barrowists hold all these positions and besides, that it is not lawful to use the Lord's Prayer publickly in church for a set form; for all set prayers are a mere babbling in the sight of the Lord. The Church of England in its public prayers and worship is false and superstitious, and, as now established, antichristian and popish.

If the Prince or Magistrate should refuse or defer to reform the faults in the Church, the people may take the reforming of them into their own hands before or without his authority. The Presbytery and Eldership may for some causes, after admonition, excommunicate the Queen if there ensue no reformation. They will not communicate with those in the Church of England, neither in prayer nor in sacraments, nor come to church because they hold that the Church of England as by law es-

tablished possesses neither a true Christ nor a true religion
nor has it indeed ministers nor sacraments.

3rd March.   UDALL'S PETITION.[3] Dr. John Udall, the Puritan
preacher, hath petitioned the Lord Treasurer for release from
prison, where he hath lain these three years. He hath consented with the Turkey merchants to go to Syria and remain
there two years with their factors if his liberty may be obtained. The Archbishop hath consented and the Lord Keeper
promised his furtherance; the Earl of Essex hath the draft of
a pardon ready when the Queen would sign it; but unless he
have liberty out of hand the ships will be gone.

THE SUBSIDY.[4] This morning in the House of Commons
was received a message from the Lords to the effect that they
did look to have heard something from the Commons before this concerning the provision of treasure; and desiring that according to former usage a committee of some
grave and settled members of the House be appointed to have
conference with a committee of the Lords. It was agreed accordingly that a committee should be appointed to meet with
the Lords at two in the afternoon.

A STRANGER IN THE HOUSE.[5] In the House of Commons it
was found that a certain man, being no member, had sat there
during the greater part of the forenoon. He was brought to
the Bar and examined by Mr. Speaker of his name and place
of abode. He answered that his name was John Legg, a servant to the Earl of Northumberland; and pleading simplicity
and ignorance for his excuse, alleged that he had some business from his master to Mr. Dr. Herbert, the Master of Requests; and therefore he entered the House, not thinking any
harm nor knowing the danger thereof. After humbly praying
pardon he is committed to the custody of the Sergeant of the
House till the House shall upon further examination take other
order.

4th March.   PENRY TO BE ARRESTED.[6] A warrant directed
to all public officers is issued by the Council for the arrest of
John Penry, that is said to have written *Martin Marprelate*.

THE SUBSIDY.[7] In the House of Commons Sir Robert Cecil
showed that at the conference had yesterday between the com-

[3] SP DOM 244:64. Udall died in prison   [5] D'EWES' JOURNALS, p. 486.
a few days later.   [6] APC 24:94.
[4] D'EWES' JOURNALS, p. 480.   [7] D'EWES' JOURNALS, p. 483.

mittees of the two Houses their Lordships signified that they would by no means assent to pass any Act for less than for three entire subsidies to be paid in the next three years. Sir Robert urged therefore that further conference should be held with their Lordships. Whereupon arose a question on the matter of privilege, Mr. Francis Bacon showing that the custom and privilege of the House was to make offer of a subsidy or else to assent to a Bill presented to the House, but not to pair with them in this motion. After much debate it was agreed that the committee should have further conference with their Lordships.

5th March. 'THE GARLAND OF GOODWILL.'[8] A collection of ballads and songs is to be printed, entitled *The Garland of Goodwill,* amongst them *A Mournful Ditty on the Death of Rosamond; The Lamentation of Shore's wife; How Coventry was made free by Godiva, Countess of Chester; Locrine; A Song of Queen Isabel, wife to King Edward the Second; A Song of the Banishment of the two Dukes, Hereford and Norfolk; Patient Grissel.* Also *A Dialogue between plain Truth and blind Ignorance,* wherein Ignorance lamenteth the passing of the old religion.

6th March. LEGG RELEASED.[9] Legg, that has remained prisoner at the bar of the House these three days, after good exhortation given him by the Speaker, and the Oath of Supremacy pronounced by him, is upon his humble submission and craving of pardon, set at liberty by the order of the House, on paying his fees.

THE SUBSIDY.[10] After further debate yesterday, it was today agreed that the committee of the House of Commons confer with the committee of the Lords, but not in anywise to conclude or resolve of anything in particular without the privity and consent of the House.

7th March. MUSTERS TO BE HELD IN THE NORTH.[11] The Earl of Huntingdon, President of the Council of the North, is to muster and view the strength of the counties towards Scotland as well for men and horses as for castles and houses of strength, and to cause all wants to be supplied.

THE SUBSIDY.[12] In the House of Commons to-day there was

[8] SR 2:627; STC 6554.
[9] D'EWES' JOURNALS, p. 491.
[10] D'EWES' JOURNALS, p. 489.
[11] APC 24:105.
[12] D'EWES' JOURNALS, p. 491.

further debate concerning the subsidy and of the poverty of the country. Sir Henry Knivett affirmed that the principal reason of our poverty was because we bring in more foreign wares than we vent commodities, and so by this means our money is carried out of the country. He made two motions; first, that the Queen should be helped by a survey taken of all men's lands and goods in England, and so much to be levied yearly as to serve the Queen to maintain wars, the proportion being set £100,000 yearly; secondly, if this were misliked, every man upon his word and power to deliver what were the profits of his lands and worth of his goods, and so a proportion to be had accordingly.

Sir Walter Ralegh, answering those who argued the poverty of the realm by the multitude of beggars, said that those who came back maimed from the wars in Normandy and the Low Countries never went back to the towns whence they came. For a multitude of clothiers now have their own looms and spin wool for themselves, and unless these men could spin for them cheaper than they could for themselves, they will never give them work to do. This engrossing of so many trades into their hands beggareth many that usually live by trade. He thought it inconvenient to have men's lands surveyed because many are now esteemed richer than they are, and if their land and goods were surveyed they would be found beggars; and so their credit, which is now their wealth, would be bound nothing. But he agreed to three subsidies, for the longer we defer aid, the less shall we be able to yield aid, and in the end the greater aid will be required of us.

Sir Francis Drake described the King of Spain's strength and cruelty where he came, and wished a frank aid to be yielded to withstand him; and he agreed to three subsidies.

In the afternoon the House considered of the subsidies in committee and after long debate it was agreed for three subsidies payable in four years.

9th March. BARROWISTS ARRESTED.[13] Many of the sect called Barrowists have been taken at one of their meetings at Islington. One, Daniel Buck, a scrivener, was to-day examined before Justice Young. Concerning the bishops he thinketh that they have no spiritual authority over the rest of the Church. Being demanded who was their pastor, he said one Mr. Francis Johnson; and about six months since this Johnson delivered

13 STRYPE'S ANNALS 4:174.

the sacrament of baptism to seven persons; but they had neither godfathers nor godmothers. He took water and washed the faces of them that were baptised, saying only in the administration of the sacrament, 'I do baptise thee in the name of the Father, of the Son, and of the Holy Ghost,' without using any other ceremony therein, as is usually observed according to the Book of Common Prayer.

Being further demanded the manner of the Lord's Supper administered among them, he saith that five white loaves or more were set upon the table. The pastor did then break the bread, and delivered it to some of them, and the deacons delivered to the rest; some of the congregation sitting and some standing about the table. And the pastor delivered the cup unto one, and he to another, till all had drunken, using the words at the delivery thereof as it is set down in the eleventh of I Corinthians, the 24th verse.

10*th March.* THE SUBSIDY AGREED.[14] After further deliberations of the committee of the House of Commons, it was resolved that a triple subsidy and six fifteenths and tenths to be paid in four years should be yielded to her Majesty towards the provision against the great and imminent perils of this Realm.

11*th March.* DEFIANT BUTCHERS.[15] Many butchers, apart from those six specially licensed, do kill and make open sale of flesh. The Warden of the Fishmongers is ordered to call them before him and to examine them by what authority they do the same, certifying their names and dwelling-places, and from whence they received their licence. He shall also examine the six licensed upon their oath what money they have paid to the Lord Mayor for their licences.

12*th March.* A BILL AGAINST RECUSANTS.[16] A Bill against recusants was read in the Lower House for the first time. When this Bill had been presented to the committee of the House, divers hard penalties in goods and lands were set down; but many of these were altered before the Bill came before the House. Among the penalties proposed are that a recusant shall be disenabled to be Justice of Peace, Mayor, Sheriff, etc. He shall forfeit for keeping a recusant in his house, either servant or stranger, £10 every month. His children being

10 years old shall be taken from him till they be 16 to be disposed of at the appointment of four Councillors, the Justices of Assize, the Bishop of the diocese or the Justices of the Peace. He shall be disenabled to make any bargain or sale of his goods or chattels.

MR. DARCY'S UNSEEMLY CONDUCT.[17] There have of late been complaints made of Mr. Edward Darcy's patent for sealing of leather. Yesterday he went to the house of the Lord Mayor to confer with him and with Sir George Barnes and Dr. Fletcher, who usually attend the Lord Mayor in such cases. They having said that in some things Mr. Darcy's fees were hard and excessive, he in a very unseemly and unreverent manner 'thou'd' Sir George Barnes (who had used him with very moderate and friendly terms), preferring himself above the knight in birth and degree, which in good discretion and modesty he might have forborn. Not content withal he suddenly strake Sir George with his fist on the face in most violent manner, wherewith the blood gushing out and embruing his face, his eye also was in great danger by the force of the stroke. Moreover Mr. Darcy would hardly have escaped without great hurt and peril of his life, especially if his abuse and outrage had been known to the apprentices and those dwelling thereabout; but the Lord Mayor thought good to dismiss him with all present speed and to be conducted part of his way before the fact was rumoured abroad.

To-day the Lord Mayor maketh complaint to the Council of this injury towards an ancient Alderman of the City of London, begging them to take notice of it, and showing what great mischiefs and tumults might have arisen, especially seeing the original cause of Mr. Darcy's negotiation was a thing not very grateful to the common sort of the City, nor, as he supposeth, to any other subject.

13th March. A SPANISH NOBLEMAN SENT HOME.[18] Don Pedro Valdes, a Spanish nobleman, that was taken prisoner at sea during the fighting in 1588, is given leave to depart. A few days ago he was taken to Court by orders of the Queen and treated very handsomely, being visited by the Council, the nobles and the captains of ships. All request, saith he, that when he shall reach the Spanish King's Court he will use his best offices in favour of peace. He was then taken to the City and entertained to a banquet by the Lord Mayor and the

[17] *Remembrancia* 1:651.   [18] *Spanish State Papers* 4:596.

Aldermen. Next day he visited the Lord Treasurer, who also pressed him to use his influence for peace. The Lord Treasurer is now very ill, and the doctors give up hope of saving him.

16th March. MEASURES AGAINST THE BUTCHERS.[19] When the Wardens of the Fishmongers' Company called on the butchers to appear before them, they withdrew themselves and would not be found when they were sent for, to the contempt of the Council's orders. The butchers' shops are to be shut up.

19th March. 'TRUTH AND FALSEHOOD.'[20] There is entered a book by Mr. Francis Bunny, Fellow of Magdalen College in Oxford, called *Truth and Falsehood, or A Comparison between the truth now taught in England, and the Doctrine of the Romish Church,* to which is added *A Short Answer* to reasons which commonly the popish recusants in the north parts allege why they will not come to our churches. At the head of each chapter is set the doctrine of the protestants and beside it the answer of the papists, upon which is argued the position, thus running through the chief points of variance between the reformed and the Catholic doctrine. The magistrates are exhorted not to show lenity to recusants, seeing that God commands idolaters to be stoned, nor to atheists, though nothing so dangerous as papists.

21st March. KELLWAY'S 'DEFENSATIVE AGAINST THE PLAGUE.'[21] Mr. Simon Kellway hath written *A Defensative against the Plague,* containing two parts, the first how to preserve from the plague, the second how to cure those that are infected, with a short treatise of the smallpox, which is entered, being dedicated to the Earl of Essex.

The causes of the plague are great and unnatural heat and dry or great rain and inundations of waters; great store of rotten and stinking bodies lying unburied which corrupt the air so that corn, fruit, herbs and waters are infected; dunghills, filthy and standing pools of water; by thrusting a great number of people into a close room, as in ships, common gaols, and in narrow lanes and streets where many dwell together. But for the most part it cometh from clothes and such

19 APC 24:118.   21 SR 2:629; STC 14917.
20 STC 4102.

like that have been used about some infected body. It may also come by dogs, cats, pigs and weasels.

Certain signs foreshow the plague, as when the spring time is cold, cloudy and dry, the harvest stormy and tempestuous with mornings and evenings very cold, and at noon extreme heat; fiery impressions in the firmament, especially in the end of summer, such as comets; great store of little frogs in the beginning of harvest, or of toads creeping on the earth having long tails, or when there is abundance of gnats, caterpillars, spiders and moths, showing the air to be corrupt. Also when young children flock together in companies, and feigning one of their members to be dead, solemnise the burying in mournful sort.

Our magistrates are advised to observe certain rules:

To command that no stinking dunghills be allowed near the City. Every evening and morning in hot weather to cause cold water to be cast in the streets, especially where there is infection, and every day to cause the streets to be kept clean and sweet, and cleansed from all filthy things. Where the infection is entered to cause fires to be made in the streets every morning and evening, wherein should be burnt frankincense, pitch or some other sweet thing. Not to suffer any dogs, cats or pigs to run about the streets. To command that all excrements and filthy things voided from the infected places be not cast into streets or into sewers that are daily used to make drink or dress meat. No surgeons or barbers that use to let blood should cast it into the streets or rivers. Nor should vaults or privies be emptied therein, for it is a most dangerous thing. All innholders should make clean their stables every day and cause the filth and dung therein to be carried out of the City, for by suffering it in their houses as some use to do a whole week or a fortnight, it putrefies so that when it is removed there is such a stink as is able to infect the whole street. To command that no hemp or flax be kept in water near the City or town, for that will cause a very dangerous and infectious savour. To have special care that good and wholesome victuals and corn be sold in the markets, and to provide that no want thereof shall be in the City, for there is nothing that more increases the plague than want and scarcity of necessary food.

In the remainder of the book are given receipts for perfumes, pomanders, preservatives, purges, cataplasms, powders, unguents and so forth for the various occasions of the plague, with directions for its prevention and cure.

22nd March. BARROW, GREENWOOD AND OTHER PURITANS CONDEMNED.[22] Yesterday at the Session Hall without Newgate, Henry Barrow, John Greenwood and three others were indicted of felony before the Lord Mayor, the two Lord Chief Justices of both benches and others of the commission. To-day they are arraigned and condemned, Barrow and Greenwood for writing sundry seditious books, the others for publishing and setting them forth.

23rd March. A DISHONEST CAPTAIN.[23] Sir John Norris is to call before him one Captain Joshua Hilliard, and to command him to appear before the Council. This Hilliard, when the 150 men levied in Gloucestershire were sent to Southampton under their proper officers, took upon himself to be their captain received £10 for the discharge of certain of the company.

24th March. 'THE ENGLISH PHLEBOTOMY.'[24] *The English Phlebotomy* or method and way of healing by letting of blood, written by Nicholas Gyer, minister of the Word, is published, being dedicated to Mr. Reginald Scott that wrote the *Discovery of Witchcraft*. This book is directed against those that for want of skill in blood-letting either straightway kill or leastwise accelerate the immature deaths of divers faithful Christians. Giveth the reasons for phlebotomy; the method of practice; the proper astrological observation, showing what members and parts of the body are to be opened according to the several seasons of the year; the observation of the blood with the signs of the excess or deficiency shown therein.

27th March. A RECUSANT EXECUTED AT WINCHESTER.[25] Two days since James Bird, a young layman, was executed at Winchester for recusancy, having been condemned some time before, after enduring ten years in prison. When he was arraigned at the General Assizes, the Lord Chief Justice Anderson addressing the jury said, 'Here you have James Bird, a recusant. You know what a recusant means. A recusant is one that refuseth to go to church; this no one refuseth unless he hath been reconciled to the Church of Rome. The man that hath been reconciled to the Church of Rome is a rebel and a traitor. Now you know your evident duty.' After a short retirement, they pronounced Bird to be a traitor.

22 STOW'S ANNALS.   24 STC 12561.
23 APC 24:137.   25 CATH. REC. SOC. 5:228–32.

The execution having been long delayed, at length the men arrived to lead Bird to the gallows, and he went down to meet them with joy and gaiety, when a messenger came to say that the execution was again put off; at which he showed evident signs of grief.

When at length the day arrived, as he was on the ladder, he said to the Sheriff, 'I beg you, Mr. Sheriff, seeing that I am a native of this city, that you would grant me one favour before I die.' 'What favour?' said he. 'Tell me what I die for,' answered Bird. 'I know not,' quoth the Sheriff; 'you received the sentence of death in the presence of the Judge; who can know better than you the reason for which you were condemned?' 'Nay,' said he, 'I do not understand it at all.' Then said the Sheriff, 'Come now, confess your crime, promise to go to church, and the Queen's pardon will be begged for you.' 'Right heartily do I thank thee,' then answered Bird; 'if by going to church I can save my life, surely all the world will see this, that I am executed solely for faith and religion, and nothing else. It was just this that I wished to elicit from you. Now I gladly die.' And with these words he was thrown from the ladder.

31st March.   BARROW AND GREENWOOD RESPITED.[26] Barrow and Greenwood, that were condemned on the 22nd March, were brought in a cart to Tyburn, but respited as they were about to be trussed up.

1st April.   A COUNTERFEIT CAPTAIN.[1] From Rutland it is reported that one calling himself Captain Bayton hath been in that county, and by colour of a counterfeit commission to levy men and horse for the Queen's service taken sums of money from sundry of the inhabitants.

2nd April.   MAIMED SOLDIERS TO BE EXAMINED.[2] A Commission is appointed to meet in two days' time to view and examine a number of captains and soldiers that claim to have been maimed or sore hurt within the last four years' war in France, the Low Countries or on the seas. The names of the men are to be enrolled, showing their names and surnames, the counties where they were born, and where they were levied, with the times and places, and under what captain or leader they were hurt.

[26] STOW'S ANNALS.   [2] APC 24:159.
[1] APC 24:149.

4th April. A BILL AGAINST THE BROWNISTS.[3] The question of the Brownists again arose in Parliament on the Bill for the explanation of a branch of a Statute made in the 23rd year of the Queen's reign, entitled *'An Act to retain Her Majesty's subjects in their due obedience.'* After divers members had spoken, Sir Walter Ralegh said that in his conceit the Brownists are worthy to be rooted out of a Commonwealth; but what danger may grow to ourselves, if this law passed, it were fit to be considered. 'For it is to be feared,' said he, 'that men not guilty will be included in it; and that law is hard that taketh life, or sendeth into banishment, where men's intentions shall be judged by a jury, and they shall be judges what another man meant. But that law that is against a fact is just, and punish the fact as severely as you will.

'If two or three thousand Brownists meet at the seaside at whose charge shall they be transported? or whither will you send them? I am sorry for it; I am afraid there is nearly twenty thousand of them in England; and when they are gone, who shall maintain their wives and children?'

5th April. CHARITABLE CONTRIBUTIONS FOR MAIMED SOLDIERS.[4] It is agreed in the House of Lords that there shall be a charitable contribution made towards the relief and help of soldiers maimed and hurt in the wars of France, the Low Countries and on the seas. To this end every Archbishop, Marquis, Earl and Viscount shall pay 40s., every Bishop 30s., and every Baron 20s. The Queen's Almoner, the Bishop of Worcester, is appointed to collect the money of the Bishops, and the Lord Norris of the Lords Temporal. These sums are willingly being paid by all who attend the Parliament. Further, it is agreed that those who have saved their charges by not attending the Parliament shall pay double, that is, the Archbishop of York and every Earl £4, Bishops £3, and Barons 40s.; and those who have been present but seldom shall pay a third part more than those who have attended regularly. And if any Lord Spiritual or Temporal should refuse or forbear to pay (which it is hoped in honour none will) the ordinary means to be used to levy the money.

PRECAUTIONS AGAINST PLAGUE.[5] The Lord Mayor is bidden take extraordinary care to prevent the increase of the infection in the City, and to keep the streets clean and sweet, es-

[3] D'EWES' JOURNALS, p. 516; TOWNSHEND, p. 76.
[4] D'EWES' JOURNALS, p. 463; TOWNSHEND, p. 42.
[5] APC 24:163.

pecially because the Queen proposes to stay longer at St. James's, being near the City. All infected houses are to be shut up and watched, the other orders which have been devised to be obeyed.

The Justices of Middlesex shall do the like, giving strict charge that such as have grounds where there are laystalls have them removed at once; and that they allow no dung or filth to be laid in any of the highways, being a great annoyance both to breed infection and to the Queen riding sometimes in the fields to take the air.

6th April.   BARROW AND GREENWOOD HANGED.[6] Barrow and Greenwood, that were respited last week, were hanged early this morning. It is said that the execution proceeded through the malice of the Bishops towards the Lower House because of the dislike shown yesterday to the Bishops' Bill against the Puritans. The reprieve was through a supplication to the Lord Treasurer that in a land where no papist was ever put to death for religion theirs should not be the first blood shed who concurred about faith with what was professed in the country and desired conference to be convinced of their errors. The Lord Treasurer spoke sharply to the Archbishop of Canterbury, who was very peremptory, also to the Bishop of Worcester, and wished to speak to the Queen, but none seconded him.

7th April.   SPECIAL WATCH TO BE KEPT FOR TRAITORS.[7] Now that the King of Spain dischargeth English, Irish and Scotch fugitives and rebels of the pensions given by him, many of them are likely to come into the realm in secret and covert manner. The officers of the Cinque Ports are ordered to make diligent search and enquiry upon the arrival of any shipping, causing all suspicious persons to be stayed and examined.

8th April.   THE DISORDERLY BUTCHERS.[8] The Justices of the Peace of Middlesex are to call before them the butchers who have killed and uttered flesh contrary to the proclamation and to the wrong of those poor men that paid good sums of money for licences for the use of maimed soldiers. They shall be indicted by a jury and for their contempt fined in good round sums of money to be converted to the use of maimed soldiers.

The Lord Mayor is forthwith to send the sum of £90, be-

[6] STOW'S ANNALS; SP DOM 245:124   [7] *Hist. MSS* Com. *Rye MSS*, p. 105.
(Phellippes).   [8] APC 24:166, 170.

ing the balance of £120 collected for maimed soldiers from the butchers' licences to the Council, that it may be distributed; otherwise the Council will send a number of the maimed soldiers with tickets to receive money from him, and to be relieved until they be satisfied of the sum. Further, seeing that the Lords of the Upper House, and the Bishops and Clergy of the Convocation House have made a charitable contribution for this purpose, the Lord Mayor and the rest of the Aldermen are required to show the same forwardness amongst themselves and the City Companies. Hereby the poor men may have some reasonable relief, and the City be eased of the clamour and trouble of these lame, maimed and poor creatures, going up and down the streets begging.

9th April. 'CHURCHYARD'S CHALLENGE.'[9] *Churchyard's Challenge,* being a collection of twenty pieces of prose and verse written at divers times by Thomas Churchyard, and by him presented to different gentlemen and ladies at Court, is to be printed, the whole being dedicated to Sir John Wolley, secretary of the Latin Tongue and one of her Majesty's privy councillors. Among these discourses are 'The Tragedy of Shore's Wife,' much augmented; 'A commendation to them that can make gold'; 'A warning to the wanderers abroad, that seek to sow dissension at home'; 'The man is but his mind,' a prose discourse of the different kinds of mind; 'A discourse of true manhood'; 'The honour of a soldier.'

THE WITCHES OF WARBOYS.[10] On the 7th April Alice Samuel and her husband, John, and her daughter, Agnes, were executed at Huntingdon for having bewitched to death the Lady Cromwell, wife of Sir Henry Cromwell, and for bewitching the daughters of Robert Throckmorton, Esquire.

It appears that for many months past, beginning at the end of the year 1589, the daughters of Mr. Throckmorton have been thrown repeatedly into strange fits, wherein they accused Mother Samuel of bewitching them, and of having a spirit in the form of a chicken which snatched at her chin. Soon after the beginning of this time, the Lady Cromwell, who then lay at Ramsey, a town two miles distant from Warboys, came with her daughter-in-law, Mrs. Cromwell, to visit the children

9 SR 2:629; STC 5220.
10 SR 2:633; STC 25019. From a detailed eye-witness account (probably Dr. Dorrington). Lady Cromwell was the second wife of Oliver Cromwell's grandfather. SR notes that the book was 'recommended for matter of truthe by master Judge Ffenner vnder his handwrytinge.' Moreover 'the note vnder master Justice Ffenners hand is Layd vp in the Wardens cupbord.' This was the most famous witch trial of the generation.

and to comfort the parents. She had not been long in the house before the children all fell into their fits, to the great distress of the lady, who could not abstain from tears. She therefore caused the old woman Samuel to be sent for, who, because her husband was a tenant of Sir Henry Cromwell, durst not refuse; but so soon as she was come the children grew much worse. Then the Lady Cromwell took her aside and charged her deeply with the witchcraft, using hard speeches to her, which she stiffly denied, declaring that Mr. Throckmorton and his wife did her great wrong to blame her without cause.

The lady answered that neither Mr. Throckmorton nor his wife accused her, but the children in their fits did it, or rather the spirit of them. One of the children, by name Joan, being then in her fit, when she heard the old woman clearing herself (though by reason of her fit she heard neither the Lady nor any other), said that it was she who caused all this, 'and something there is,' said she, 'doth now tell me so,' asking if nobody heard it but she, affirming that it squealed very loud in her ears.

Mother Samuel still continuing in her denial, the Lady Cromwell would have taken her into a chamber where Dr. Hall, a doctor of Divinity, was present, to examine her more closely, but she refused to go with them. At length, when the Lady perceived that she could not prevail with her, she suddenly pulled off Mother Samuel's kercher and taking a pair of shears clipped off a lock of her hair and gave it privily to Mrs. Throckmorton together with her hairlace, willing her to burn them. Mother Samuel seeing herself thus dealt with spake to the Lady, 'Madam, why do you use me thus? I never did you any harm as yet.'

Towards night the Lady departed, leaving the children much as she had found them. That night the Lady Cromwell suffered many things in her dreams concerning Mother Samuel and was very strangely tormented by a cat (as she imagined) which Mother Samuel had sent to her which offered to pluck off all the skin and flesh from her arms and body. Such was the struggling and striving of the Lady in her bed and the mournful noise which she made, speaking to the cat and to Mother Samuel, that she awakened her bedfellow, who was Mrs. Cromwell, wife of Mr. Oliver Cromwell. Not long after, the Lady fell strangely sick and so continued until her death which occurred in about a year and a quarter. The manner of her sickness, except that she always had her perfect senses, was much like the children's, the pains taking her sometime in one part of the body, sometime in another, but always the grieved part shook as if in a palsy. But the saying of Mother Samuel would never go out of her mind: 'Madam, I never hurt you *as yet.*'

Some time after Mother Samuel, who was then staying at Mr. Throckmorton's house, became very sick, and being very penitent in her sickness she confessed her witchcraft. Mr. Throckmorton sent to Dr. Dorrington, the minister of the town, relating the whole circumstance and desiring him to console her. The next day being Sunday, and Christmas Eve, Dr. Dorrington to comfort her chose his text of repentance out of the Psalms, and there declared in the whole assembly all the matter of Mother Samuel's confession, applying himself especially to the consolation of a penitent heart. All through this sermon Mother Samuel did nothing but weep and lament, and was so loud in her passion, that she caused all in church to look at her. That night she returned to her husband and daughter, who thereon set upon her for having confessed, so that the next day she denied all.

Then Dr. Dorrington and Mr. Throckmorton went to her house to learn the truth, and there found the husband and daughter talking of the matter. Being asked whether she had not confessed, she now answered, 'I confessed so indeed, but it is nothing so.' This so angered Mr. Throckmorton that the next morning early he went to Dr. Dorrington and told him he would not let the matter rest there lest the worser sort of people should imagine that it was some device of theirs against the old woman. Therefore they sent for the constables, and giving both mother and daughter in their charge ordered them to provide for the journey, for they should go before the Bishop of Lincoln at Buckden. They were therefore taken before him the same day (26th December) and there examined.

She was then asked whether a dun chicken did ever suck on her chin and whether it was a natural chicken. She answered that it had sucked twice, and no more, since Christmas Eve. She declared that it was a natural chicken, for when it came to her chin she scarce felt it, and when she wiped it off with her hand, her chin bled, and further she declared that all the trouble that had come to Mr. Throckmorton's children had come by means of this dun chicken.

Mother Samuel was again examined three days afterwards before the Bishop of Lincoln, and Francis Cromwell and Richard Fryce, Justices of the Peace. At this examination she

declared that she knew the dun chicken had now gone from
the children because it had returned to her with the rest and
was now at the bottom of her belly with the others, which
made her so full that she could scarce lace up her coat, and
that the way as she came they weighed so heavy that the horse
fell down. She said also that she had five spirits given her by
an upright man in the shape of dun chickens, three she called
to her by the names of Pluck, Catch and White; the others
by smacking her lips. She was then committed, with her
daughter, to the jail at Huntingdon till the Assizes; but Mr.
Throckmorton, hoping to get something out of the daughter,
persuaded the Justices to let her out on bail to come home
with him.

The fits continued very grievous with the children all the
while she was in prison. On Wednesday, 4th April, Mistress
Joan Throckmorton went to Huntingdon, and was very well
on her way, but half an hour after they had entered the Crown
Inn, she fell again in her fit, and neither saw nor heeded any.
In the evening after the Court had broken up, Mr. Justice
Fenner, the Judge, who was lodging at the same inn, went
into the garden to see the girl, still grievously tormented by
her fit. Mr. Throckmorton told the Judge that if he would
command Agnes Samuel, who was standing by, to say certain
words his daughter would immediately be well. The words
were these: 'As I am a witch and a worse witch than my
mother, and did consent to the death of the Lady Cromwell, so
I charge the devil to let Mistress Joan come out of her fit at
present.' But first, the Judge himself and others to make trial of
these words repeated them themselves without avail.

Then the Judge bade Agnes Samuel pray for the girl, and
whenever she named God or Jesus Christ in her prayer, Mistress Joan was more troubled than before. Then she was commanded to say, 'As I am no witch, neither did consent to the
death of the Lady Cromwell, so I charge the devil to let Mistress Joan come out of her fit at this present'; but all was to no
purpose until Agnes Samuel repeated the first words, when
Mistress Throckmorton immediately wiped her eyes and
came out of her fit, and made a low reverence to the Judge.
But a short while after she fell into another fit, first shaking
one leg, then another, with many other extraordinary passions. When the Judge and others had prayed without avail,
Agnes Samuel was ordered to speak these words: 'As I am
a witch and would have bewitched to death Mistress Joan
Throckmorton in her last week of her great sickness, so I

charge the devil to let Mistress Joan to come out of her fit at this present.' This said, Mistress Joan was immediately well again.

The next day Mother Samuel, her husband, and her daughter were indicted with having bewitched to death the Lady Cromwell, and having bewitched Mistress Joan Throckmorton and others, contrary to God's Laws and the Statute made in the 15th year of the Queen's reign. These things and many others were sworn in testimony against them, and the jury brought in a verdict of guilty.

Then the Judge, passing sentence, asked old Father Samuel what he had to say for himself; he answered that he had nothing to say but the Lord have mercy on him. Then he asked Mother Samuel what she had to say to stay judgment; she answered that she was with child, which set all the company laughing, for she was nearly eighty years old, and she herself more than any, because she thought that for this reason no judgment should be given. The Judge moved her to leave that answer; but she would not be driven from it till at length a jury of women was empanelled, who gave up their verdict that she was not with child, unless, as some believed, by the devil. All three were therefore condemned to be hanged.

10th April. THE PARLIAMENT DISSOLVED.[11] Between five and six this afternoon, the Queen accompanied by her Officers came to the Upper House, and as soon as she was seated with the Lords Spiritual and Temporal, the knights, citizens and burgesses of the Lower House were summoned, and came up with their Speaker, bringing the Bill of Subsidy. The Speaker being placed at the Bar of the Upper House with as many of the Commons as could be admitted, after humble reverence to the Queen, made an oration in which he spoke of the antiquities of the Parliament, first holden in the time of Ina, Queen of the West Saxons. Then he compared the Parliament to the sweet Commonwealth of the little bees, and concluded by asking pardon for every offence he might have committed through ignorance or insufficiency.

The Lord Keeper then received instructions from the Queen and afterwards replied to the Speaker that her Majesty did most graciously accept of these services and devotions of this Parliament, commending them that they had employed their time so well, and spent it on necessary affairs; save only that in some things they had spent more time than was needed; but she perceived some men did it more for their own satisfaction than the necessity of the thing deserved. She misliked also that such irreverence was shown towards Privy Councillors (who were not to be accounted as common knights and burgesses of the House that were but councillors during the Parliament); whereas the others were standing councillors, and for their wisdom and great service were called the Council of State.

Then he said that the Queen's Majesty had heard that some men in the case of great necessity and grant of aid had seemed not to regard their country and made their necessity more than it was, forgetting the urgent necessity of the time and dangers that were now eminent. She would not have the people feared with reports of great dangers but rather to be encouraged with boldness against the enemies of the State. And therefore she charged and commanded that the mustered companies in every county should be supplied if they were decayed and that their provisions of armour and ammunition should be better than heretofore it had been used.

For this offer of three subsidies she most graciously in all kindness thanketh her subjects; but except it were freely and willingly given she did not accept it; for her Majesty never accepteth anything that is not freely given. If the coffers of her treasure were not empty or if the revenues of the Crown and other Princely ornaments could suffice to supply her wants and the charges of the Realm, in the word of a Prince she did pronounce it, she would not now have charged her subjects nor accepted of this they gave her.

The Lord Keeper's Speech being ended, after some intermission, the Queen herself, sitting in her chair of State, spoke to the two Houses:

'This Kingdom hath had many wise, noble and victorious Princes. I will not compare with any of them in wisdom, fortitude or any other virtues, but saving the duty of a child that is not to compare with his father, in love, care, sincerity and justice, I will compare with any Prince that ever you had or should have.

'It may be thought simplicity in me, but all this time of my reign I have not sought to advance my territories and enlarge my dominions; for opportunity hath served me to do it. I acknowledge my womanhood and weakness in that respect, but though it had not been hard to obtain yet I doubted how to keep the things so obtained; that hath only held me from such attempts, and I must say my mind was never to invade my neighbours or to usurp over any.

'I am contented to reign over mine own and to rule as a just Prince. Yet the King of Spain doth challenge me to be the quarreller and the beginner of all these wars, in which he doth me the greatest wrong that can be; for my conscience doth not accuse my thoughts wherein I have done him the least injury; but I am persuaded in my conscience, if he knew what I know, he himself would be sorry for the wrong that he hath done me.

'I fear not all his threatenings; his great preparations and mighty forces do not stir me, for though he come against me with a greater power than ever was his *Invincible Navy,* I doubt not (God assisting me, upon Whom I always trust) but that I shall be able to defeat and overthrow him. I have great advantage against him; for my cause is just.

'I heard say, when he attempted his last invasion, some upon the sea coast forsook their towns and flew up higher into the country and left all naked and exposed to his entrance. But I swear unto you by God if I knew those persons, or of any that shall do so hereafter, I will make them know and feel what it is to be fearful in so urgent a cause.

'The subsidies you give me I accept thankfully, if you give me your goodwills with them; but if the necessity of the time and your preservations did not require it I would refuse them. But let me tell you that the sum is not so much but that it is needful for a Prince to have so much always lying in her coffers for your defence in time of need, and not be driven to get it when we should use it.

'You that be Lieutenants and gentlemen of command in your counties, I require you to take care that the people be well armed and in readiness in all occasions. You that be judges and justices of the peace, I command and straightly charge that you should see the laws to be duly executed and that you make them living laws when we have put life with them.'

And so with most gracious thanks to both Houses, her Majesty ended her speech.

Then the titles of all the Acts were read in order, beginning with the Bill of Subsidies, to which the Clerk of the Parliament, standing up, did read the Queen's answer: *La Royne remercie ses loyaule Subjects, accept leur benevolence, et ainsi le veult.*

Next the Clerk pronounced the thanks of the Lords and

Commons in these words: *Les Prelates, Seigneurs et Communes en ce present Parliament assembles, au nomes de touts vous autres subjects, remercient tres humblement vostre Majesty, et prient Dieu que vout il done en sante bonne vie et longue.*

At each Public Act, to everyone allowed by the Queen the Clerk said, *Le Royne le veult;* to every Private Act, he said, *Soit fait come il est desiré;* and to such Acts as the Queen forbore to allow, *Le Royne se advisera.*

After which the Parliament was dissolved by the Lord Keeper of the Great Seal in Latin with these words: *Dominus Custos Magni Sigilli, ex mandato Dominae Reginae tunc praesentis dissoluit praesens Parliamentum.*

11th April. RELIEF FOR MAIMED SOLDIERS.[12] Until the Act of Parliament made for the relief of maimed soldiers can be put into execution the Lords Lieutenant of counties shall give every man weekly the sum of two shillings. For the convenience of those too impotent to come themselves to fetch the money, some trusty person residing near is to be appointed to receive and pay the money. All these maimed soldiers having received conduct money at the rate of 1d. a mile, and to the most lame 2d. a mile, are ordered to return to their own counties where they shall receive relief.

14th April. FALSE REPORTS CONCERNING THE QUEEN'S DEALINGS WITH THE TURKS.[13] There have of late been set forth in Germany many scandalous libels about her Majesty as if she had invited the Turk to make war against Christendom; and the letters which she sent the Turk published, but falsified and corrupted many things being added. A letter is now sent to the Emperor very strongly denying these calumnies and showing how by the Turk's own confession her Majesty did make peace between him and the King of Poland. This letter also setteth forth the insatiable desire for conquest of the King of Spain, and the troubles which he stirreth up in France and in Scotland.

15th April. DIRECTIONS FOR SIR JOHN NORRIS.[14] Some days since Sir John Norris wrote showing what inconveniences would follow if his troops were withdrawn and to ask for absolute directions whether to stay or return. The Queen now answereth that his doubts appear strange, for she could not

[12] APC 24:178.

[13] STRYPE'S ANNALS 4:154.

[14] SP FOR 30:f272.

have written more plainly or directly to him; for she had first assured him that not one man would be sent if the King had not in those parts such settled troops as might make head against the enemy; she had also commanded him to take special care not to be so engaged by any siege as to be driven either dishonourably to quit the place, or else to plunge her into the necessity of relieving him; being an action of more charge and hazard than for the town of Pempole or Brehat she meant to be put. Yet if he were not likely to be pressed by the forces of the enemy he might remain a short time; but in referring anything to his judgment as General, it ought not to be used as a reason to complain of want of plain direction; unless he preferred her either to judge certainly of things there which time and distance must make uncertain, or else to leave him no more reputation of his opinion than as a cipher that could judge of nothing.

However understanding his apprehension of the dangers the country will take from his sudden return, she is now content that he shall stay for a short time if he find the enemy retired from him, or can have such intelligence of his approach as not to be overtaken with a siege. If not, he is commanded to retreat to the Islands with the ships already provided.

16th April. THE LIBELS AGAINST STRANGERS.[15] A certain man hath been arrested on suspicion of being the author of a libel against strangers. He is to be very strictly examined by the Lord Mayor of his meaning and purpose in making that writing and who are in any way privy of that fact; if there be any pregnant matter to argue him to be guilty of writing the placard and he will not by fair means be brought to utter his knowledge, he shall be punished by torture and compelled to reveal it.

17th April. MEASURES AGAINST VAGABONDS.[16] An order is to be printed and set up in the City that all poor, aged and impotent persons repair to the place where they were born or where they were most conversant during the space of three years, there to be maintained; likewise all others wandering about as beggars, being whole and strong in body and able to get work, having no lands or other means to get their living, shall be taken as rogues and vagabonds. And if any impotent person so provided for wander abroad out of his parish without licence he shall be whipped and returned, but if eft-

soons he offend again then to be punished as a rogue. To this
end the officers of the City and of Westminster shall make
inquisition of all beggars to compel them to depart to the
places where they were born.

18th April.   'VENUS AND ADONIS.'[17] *Venus and Adonis,* a
poem written by William Shakespeare, is entered, being dedicated to Henry Wriothesley, Earl of Southampton. In this
poem is described the hot love of Venus for the youth Adonis
who scorneth her love, and leaving her to pursue the boar is
by it slain.

22nd April.   THE LIBELS AGAINST STRANGERS.[18] Dr. Julius
Caesar, one of the Masters of Requests, Sir Henry Killigrew,
and others are appointed commissioners to examine by secret
means the authors of the libels against the strangers, and their
favourers and abettors, and to discover their intentions.

THE LIBEL

'Doth not the world see that you, beastly brutes, the Bel-
gians or rather drunken drones, and faint-hearted Flemings;
and you, fraudulent fathers, Frenchmen, by your cowardly
flight from your own natural countries, have abandoned the
same into the hands of your proud, cowardly enemies, and
have by a feigned hypocrisy and counterfeit show of religion
placed yourselves here in a most fertile soil under a most
gracious and merciful Prince; who had been contented, to the
great prejudice of her own natural subjects, to suffer you to
live here in better case and more freedom than her own
people?

'Be it known to all Flemings and Frenchmen, that it is best
for them to depart out of the realm of England, between this
and 9th of July next. If not, then to take what follows. For
there shall be many a sore stripe. Apprentices will rise to the
number of 2336. And all prentices and journeymen will down
with Flemings and Strangers.'

23rd April.   DRAYTON'S 'IDEA.'[19] *The Shepherd's Garland,
fashioned in nine Eclogues, Rowland's Sacrifice to the nine
Muses,* by Michael Drayton, being dedicated to Mr. Robert
Dudley, is entered. In the first of these eclogues (founded

[17] SR 2:630; STC 22354. A very popular poem, 7 issues being known in 9
years.
[18] APC   24:200; STRYPE'S ANNALS
4:167.

[19] SR 2:630; STC 7202. An interesting imitation of Spenser, and useful
for the philologist for its archaic
and rare words.

after the pastoral mode of *The Shepherd's Kalendar*), Rowland malcontent bewaileth the winter of his grief; in the second old Wynken reproveth Motto's unbridled youth, giving him Rowland's example; in the third Perkin rouseth Rowland to song, who praises Beta the Queen of Virgins. Wynklyn in the fourth bewaileth the loss of Elphin (Sir Philip Sidney). In the fifth, Rowland singeth the praises of Idea, his lady; and of Pandora (the Countess of Pembroke) in the sixth; in the seventh eclogue Dorrill, an aged shepherd swain, rebukes Batto for falling in love; in the eighth, Gorbo sings of the age of the golden world, ending with a tale of Dowsabel and her shepherd lover.

The book ends with the lament of Rowland that his Idea is unkind to him.

24th April. PLAGUE DEATHS.[20] The plague is not yet died out of London, 34 persons being reported dead of it during the past week.

29th April. A CHARITABLE GENTLEMAN.[21] Some years since Mr. Edward Cotton of his charity disbursed the sum of £444 for the redemption of four captives from the Turks, yet hath he hitherto received but £40, though letters were then sent to the Lord Mayor that his charges should be satisfied from the collections ordinarily made about Easter for this charitable purpose. The Council have again written to the Lord Mayor that the money specially collected for the redemption of captives since Maundy Thursday or before at Spittle sermons or other places be now paid to him, that others may be encouraged to the like good and charitable deed upon like occasions.

4th May. THE NUMBERS OF STRANGERS IN LONDON.[1] The certificates giving the numbers of strangers in London show the total of all strangers living in London with their children and servants born out of the realm to be 4300; 267 being denizens. This scrutiny hath been taken in every ward because of the complaints of English shopkeepers that the strangers are not content with manufactures and warehouses but would keep shops and retail all manner of goods.

[20] FUGGER NEWS-LETTERS, p. 248.   [1] STRYPE'S ANNALS 4:167.
[21] APC 24:209.

5th May. LIBELS AGAINST STRANGERS.[2] Between eleven and twelve o'clock at night a rhyme was found set up on the walls of the Dutch Churchyard beginning:

> 'You strangers that inhabit in this land,
>   Note this same writing, do it understand;
> Conceive it well for safeguard of your lives,
>   Your goods, your children and your dearest wives.'

This was taken down and brought to the constable.

10th May. 'PARTHENOPHIL AND PARTHENOPHE.'[3] *Parthenophil and Parthenophe,* by Barnabe Barnes, is entered. In this book are contained sonnets, madrigals, elegies and odes setting forth the passion and desire of Parthenophil for Parthenophe, his mistress, his distress at her refusing, and at the last his enjoyment of her love; with sonnets to the Earl of Northumberland, the Earl of Essex, the Earl of Southampton, the Countess of Pembroke, the Lady Strange and the Lady Bridget Manners. The wantonness of some few of the verses in this book much to be noted, especially of that sonnet wherein the poet wisheth himself the wine that his lady drinketh.

11th May. MORE LIBELS AGAINST STRANGERS.[4] Malicious libels against strangers continue to be set up and one especially upon the wall of the Dutch Churchyard that excels the rest in lewdness. The special Commissioners are ordered to take extraordinary pains to discover the author and publisher thereof; to make search and apprehend every person suspected, and for that purpose to enter into all houses where they may be staying; and upon their apprehension, to make search in chambers, studies, chests and the like for all manner of writings or papers that might give light for the discovery of the libellers. All that after due examination be suspected and refuse to confess the truth are to be put to the torture in Bridewell, that by its extremity (to be used as often as the Commissioners deem necessary) they be drawn to discover their knowledge.

12th May. THOMAS KYD ARRESTED.[5] Thomas Kyd, that wrote the *Spanish Tragedy* some years since, hath been ar-

[2] STRYPE'S ANNALS 4:168.
[3] SR 2:631; STC 1469.
[4] APC 24:222.

[5] F. S. Boas, *Works of Thomas Kyd,* pp. lxx–lxxiii.

rested and carried to Bridewell by the officers of the Lord Mayor searching for the authors of the libels against strangers. When they examined his papers some fragments of a disputation denying the divinity of Jesus Christ were found; these papers Kyd declareth to have been left in his study by Marlowe when they wrote together two years ago.

20th May. MARLOWE BEFORE THE COUNCIL.[6] This day Christopher Marlowe, who was sent for by the Council two days since, hath entered his appearance and is commanded to give his daily attendance until licensed the contrary.

21st May. A PRIEST'S DECLARATION OF HIS MOTIVES.[7] William Harrington, a priest, that was taken, being charged with treason, and examined, hath set forth his reasons for coming to England in a letter to the Lord Keeper.

He saith that he is a gentleman by birth, a Catholic, and a priest of the Seminary of Rheims. He first left his country, desiring to imitate others of innocent lives and glorious deaths, especially Edmund Campion (that was executed in 1580), whom he believed guilty of no treason to the Queen nor the country. He hath always abhorred treachery but is not amazed at being accused as a traitor, nor troubled at the popular outcry, 'Hang him, hang him.' If his cause is good, he suffereth for Justice's sake, and that law is too severe that maketh his function treason; if his cause be bad, death itself is too merciful a punishment. He is compelled by his conscience to discharge his priestly office, but hath refrained from other practices, which he detests. Having so determined, he would make his life of no account. He hath never been made privy to any plot against the Queen or the country or he would have been forced by his oath of allegiance to give notice of it. Since he will not serve his Prince or country by betraying his friends, he hopeth to be excused for not wishing to live with such a spot of infamy. He therefore beggeth life and liberty on such conditions as he may conscientiously observe; if not, he resigns himself to God's disposal.

23rd May. THE PLAGUE IN THE SAVOY.[8] The Master of the Hospital of the Savoy is to forbear for the time to receive any into the hospital because of the danger that the poor people repairing there daily may be infected with the plague, to the great danger of the inhabitants in general and especially

[6] APC 24:244.
[7] SP Dom 245:66.
[8] APC 24:252.

to some of the Council that dwell in those parts and are often occasioned to be at Court and near the Queen. This hospital was founded in former times for poor suitors from the country that are unable to defray the charge of lodging during their abode in the City on their necessary business, but the greater part of those now received are young boys, rogues and vagabonds.

24th May. PENRY CONDEMNED.[9] John Penry, the Puritan, was arraigned this day. At his trial many seditious and slanderous speeches were urged against him, collected from his papers and writings. He had said that the Queen stands against the Gospel and will not move a finger to help it, nor speak a word to reform it. The magistrates, ministers and people are conspirators against God, murder whole troops of souls, and are godless men. The Council are rebels against God and levy their force against the Gospel. Nor may the people serve God under the Queen but are bond slaves of the man of sin; nor would the Queen have embraced the Gospel if she could have received the crown without it, and only useth it to strengthen her sceptre. If Queen Mary had reigned to this day, the Gospel would have flourished more; without the Gospel, outward peace is nothing.

A REQUEST OF THE CITIZENS OF PARIS.[10] From Paris it is reported that 500 of the inhabitants went to the lodging of M. de Blyn, and signified to him that they would live and die in the maintenance of the Catholic religion, but if the King would render himself a Catholic they would make a peace with him that would not be in the power either of the Governor or of M. de Mayne to impeach. They prayed him signify so much to M. de Mayne; and if he would have it better confirmed, they would within an hour bring ten thousand persons who would affirm their resolution.

26th May. MARLOWE'S BLASPHEMIES.[11] Information hath been received by the Lord Keeper of the opinions of Christopher Marlowe, and by him laid before the Queen. This Marlowe is accused of many vile and horrible blasphemies concerning Christ and His Mother; affirmeth that Moses was but a juggler and that one Harriott, Sir Walter Ralegh's man, can do more than he. Into every company he cometh

[9] SP DOM 245:21.
[10] SP FOR 31:f60.
[11] *Harleian MSS* 6848:f185. Reprints   in *The Life of Marlowe* and *Dido*, ed. C. F. Tucker Brooke, 1930, pp. 98–100.

he would persuade men to atheism, willing them not to be afeared of bugbears and hobgoblins, and utterly scorning both God and His ministers.

28th May. PRECAUTIONS AGAINST PLAGUE.[12] Trinity Term is adjourned owing to the great increase of the plague in London, Westminster, and the parts adjoining. But seeing that great prejudice would grow to many in their causes and suits if the term be wholly adjourned, some few days at the beginning and ending of the term shall be held for the better expediting those causes that can be performed in the absence of the parties by their attorneys. No party, save in case of outlawry, is compelled to appear in person.

STRATFORD GOOSE FAIR FORBIDDEN.[13] At this time of the year there is usually held a 'Goose feast' at Stratford Bow, whither a disordered assembly of all the vagabond and idle persons come from the City; whereat through excess of drinking, divers quarrels and other great inconveniences have fallen out in that place. As an opportunity is offered thereby to the worst sort of apprentices and others ill disposed to resort thither to make their matches and appointments to sundry ill purposes, and also because the infection is more dispersed that way than towards any other villages, the Council have ordered the magistrates to take timely order to prevent this inconvenience. They shall charge the taverners, alehouse keepers and other victuallers to forbear to make extraordinary provision of victuals and to cause a straight watch to be set about the place for better intercepting all that pass to the town without good and lawful occasion.

MR. WENTWORTH IN THE TOWER.[14] Mr. Peter Wentworth, who is very old and subject to continual infirmities, is much impaired in health, by reason of his close imprisonment and especially owing to the great heat of the present season. The Council allow him the liberty of the Tower in company with some trusty servant and also to see his sons, friends, and physicians for his better comfort and recovery of health; but he shall not be permitted to have any conference with them except in the presence of the Governor or his servants.

30th May. MARLOWE SLAIN.[15] Christopher Marlowe is slain by one Ingram Frizer at the Bull Inn at Deptford.

[12] PROCLAMATIONS 319.
[13] APC 24:265.
[14] APC 24:269.

[15] J. L. Hotson, *The Death of Christopher Marlowe*, 1926, p. 31.

31st May. JOHN PENRY HANGED.[16] John Penry, suspected of being the author of the Martinist pamphlets, that was condemned at the King's Bench on the 24th May, was hanged at St. Thomas Watering, with little warning and few spectators, lest he should have raised some tumult, either in going to the gallows or upon the ladder.

1st June. THE INQUEST ON MARLOWE.[1] At the inquest on the body of Christopher Marlowe, it was testified by those present at the time that Marlowe with three gentlemen, Ingram Frizer, Robert Poley and Nicholas Skeres, met in the house of a certain Eleanor Bull, and there dined. After dinner they walked in the garden until 6 o'clock in the evening, when they returned and supped. Thereafter malicious words passed between Marlowe and Frizer about the payment of the reckoning, until Marlowe, who was lying on a bed, sprang on Frizer, then sitting at the table, and taking Frizer's dagger from his back wounded him twice in the head. Frizer being then put in fear of his life strove to get back his dagger, and in the struggle gave Marlowe a mortal wound over the right eye of which he instantly died.

Frizer is found to have acted in defence of his own life. But though this is the Coroner's verdict, there want not other stories making his end more fearful. He is reported to have been an atheist, a blasphemer, given to the vice of sodomy; which offences with many others of a like nature had been charged against him in a paper sent to the Lord Keeper but three days before his death. It is much noted that he was smitten in the brain where he conceived his blasphemies and by his own hand wherewith he wrote them, and that together with his last breath an oath fled out of his mouth. Some say that the quarrel first arose over a lewd love. He is buried in the churchyard at Deptford.

5th June. PRECAUTIONS AGAINST PLAGUE AT WINDSOR.[2] Since the Queen will make her residence at Windsor for most part of the summer, the Mayor of Windsor is to order that no citizen of London or other person coming from any place

[16] W. Pierce, *John Penry,* 1923, p. 480.
[1] Hotson, pp. 11–17, 24–34. Hotson's discovery of the coroner's report revealed the official account of Marlowe's death. As usual in these cases of fatal quarrels, the survivor is always the innocent party. The stories are retailed by Thomas Beard in *The Theatre of God's Judgments* (1597), Francis Meres in *Palladis Tamia* (1598), and others of which Hotson prints relevant extracts.
[2] APC 24:284.

where there is infection do resort to the town or make stay there.

7th June. MR. COTTON'S CLAIMS TO BE SATISFIED.[3] Mr. Edward Cotton complaining that the Lord Mayor not only refuseth to pay him any money but will not so much as vouchsafe an answer to the Council's letters, the Council have required the Lord Mayor either to make some reasonable satisfaction or else to send a true and perfect account of the collection for the release of captives of every year from the beginning of 1589 until the end of April last, showing what captives have been released and for what sums of money.

8th June. RELIEF OF MAIMED SOLDIERS.[4] The Sheriffs and Justices of the Peace throughout the realm are ordered to confer together and consider of the Statute passed this last Parliament for the relief of those hurt or maimed in the service of the Queen. Officers shall be ordained for receipt of the collections, that such as should come with warrant to demand their allowances may receive the benefit without any further trouble to them or occasion ministered to the Queen to think any slack in the performances of their duties.

10th June. CHARITY FOR A PRISONER.[5] The Lord Mayor and Aldermen are asked to bestow on Peter Brown, a captive in the hands of the Leaguers, so much money as will satisfy his ransom from the collections that have been made for this purpose. This Brown, one of the ordinary posts, coming towards England in a voyage from Sir R. Williams, was lately taken by the garrison of Rouen. There he remains, and will not be delivered without paying so great a ransom as far exceedeth his ability to pay.

12th June. RUMOURS OF CHANGES IN FRANCE.[6] There is much talk at this time of the likelihood that the King of France has turned Catholic, and of a peace between the King and the League. This detaineth all resolution with the Vidame of Chartres, his ambassador. The Queen stormed at first but it is believed that nothing will come of the matter.

16th June. 'BEAUTY DISHONOURED.'[7] *Beauty Dishonoured: written under the title of Shore's Wife,* by Mr. Anthony Chute, is entered, being dedicated to Sir Edward Wingfield.

[3] APC 24:295. See *29th April.*   [6] SP Dom 245:30.
[4] APC 24:298.   [7] SR 2:632; STC 3262.
[5] APC 24:305.

18*th June*. A PROCLAMATION TO RESTRAIN SUITORS AT COURT.[8] A Proclamation is published to restrain the access of so many suitors to the Court. No persons but such as have cause to come to the Court for their ordinary attendance on the Queen shall repair within two miles upon pain of contempt, and all that attend on the Queen, her Councillors and the Officers of her Chamber and Household, are straightly commanded to see these orders obeyed.

If for any extraordinary cause anyone do come to the Court with matter to be certified to the Queen or to any of the Privy Council, he may not enter within the gates until he be licensed by the Lord Chamberlain or some other of the Council.

20*th June*. CAPTAIN JOHN DAVIS RETURNS TO ENGLAND.[9] Captain John Davis hath returned with some few of his men to Cornwall on the 16th, being but the poor remainder of the company of seventy-six that had left Plymouth on 26th August, 1591, on board the *Desire* with Mr. Thomas Cavendish's fleet.

After losing sight of Mr. Cavendish, their General, on the night of the 20th May, 1592, they had returned to Port Desire, being now in very miserable case, the shrouds all rotten, without pitch, tar or nails, and living only upon seals and mussels. Here they remained hoping for sight of the General until 6th August, when they made for the Straits of Magellan, and there stayed, in the deep of winter, with but little victual and not enough clothing to defend the extremity of the winter's cold. In these seas they were lamentably driven by storms until on 25th October they came to an island named Penguin Island. There the boat was sent on shore, which returned laden with birds' eggs; and the men said that the penguins were so thick that the ships might be laden with them. The Captain therefore sent some of the men ashore whilst he sailed the ship up a river in the mainland, where she was run aground and made fast to the shore with running ropes moored to stakes. Here nine of their men were slain by savages, but the rest remained feeding on eggs, penguins, young seals, gulls, and other birds. In this place they found a herb called scurvy grass which so purged the blood that it took away all kinds of swelling, of which many had died, and restored them to perfect health of body.

In this harbour they stayed until 22nd December, in which

time they had dried 20,000 penquins on the island, of which 14,000 were taken on board, but not being able to fetch the rest by reason of the dangerous tides, they shaped course for Brazil. On 30th January, 1593, they landed at the Isle of Placencia, hoping to surprise the Portugals, but when they came to the houses they were all burnt, so that they thought no man remained on the island. Then the Captain went to the gardens and brought thence fruits and roots for the company, and all laboured to put the water casks in order.

The 5th February at night many of the men dreamed of murder and slaughter, and the Captain likewise having dreamed very strangely himself, gave straight charge that those who went on shore should take weapons with them. All the forenoon they laboured in quietness, but when it was ten o'clock, the heat being now extreme, they came to a rock near the woods' side (for all this country was nothing but thick woods) and there they boiled some cazavi roots and dined. After dinner some slept, some washed themselves in the sea, all being stripped to their shirts, and no man keeping a watch. Suddenly as they were thus sleeping and sporting, having gotten themselves into a corner out of sight of the ship, there came a multitude of Indians and Portugals upon them, and slew them sleeping; only two escaped, one very sorely hurt, one unharmed, who ran to the ship.

With all speed the boat was manned and landed to succour the men, but they found them all slain, and laid naked in a rank, with their faces upward and a cross set by them. Moreover, they saw in the river two very great pinnaces full of men. So the next day, choosing rather to fall into the hands of the Lord than into the hands of men, they cast off in great distress, having only eight tuns of water in bad casks.

And now as they came near to the sun the dried penquins began to corrupt and there bred in them a most loathsome and ugly worm of an inch long, which so mightily increased and devoured the victuals that there was in reason no hope of avoiding famine; for there was nothing they did not devour, only iron, cloths, boots, shoes, hats, shirts, stockings, and for the ship they did so eat the timbers that there was great fear lest they should gnaw through her side. In this woeful case after passing the equinoctial toward the north, the men began to fall sick of a monstrous disease so that their ankles and whole bodies began to swell, and some to grow raging mad, and perished thus in most loathsome and furious pain, so that all but sixteen died, and of these but five were able to move, and upon them only stood the labour of the ship.

Thus as lost wanderers upon the sea, it pleased God that they arrived at Bearhaven in Ireland the 11th of June, and there ran the ship on shore, where the Captain left the master and three or four of the company, and within five days after he and certain others passed in an English fishing boat to Padstow in Cornwall.

26th June. 'THE CONSPIRACY OF THE SCOTTISH PAPISTS.'[10] *A discovery of the unnatural and traitorous conspiracy of Scottish Papists against God, his Church, their native country, the King's Majesty's person and estate,* is entered, being extracted from the confessions and letters of Mr. George Ker, that is still in prison, and David Graham of Fintry, justly executed for his treason the 15th February, 1593, with other letters intercepted. This book was first printed and published in Scotland at the special commandment of the King, and is now again to be printed in London.

29th June. CITY FEASTS TO BE CURTAILED.[11] Owing to the plague, the customary great feasts made by the City Companies at this time are to be curtailed, and the choice of officers made with as small an assembly as conveniently may be. The charges so saved are to be converted to the relief of those infected; and that this contribution may be made without fraud, the Lord Mayor is required to find out what is usually spent by the heads of companies at their feasts.

There is great negligence in the City in suffering houses and shops to remain open or only to be shut up a few days in places where the plague is well known to have been. The Queen is so greatly offended therewith that, except the Lord Mayor and Aldermen take better regard, she will be moved to seize their liberties and commit the government of her City to some others.

1st July. MR. CAVENDISH'S VOYAGE.[1] From letters received from Mr. Thomas Cavendish, who sailed from England nearly two years since, it appeareth that he hath passed through the Straits of Magellan into the South Sea, where prizes of great value are sometimes taken. Sir Francis Drake and others are ordered that, if God should bless these ships with any such

[10] SR 2:633; STC 14936.   [1] APC 24:346.
[11] APC 24:342.

purchase, and if the ships or prizes taken by them should enter any port, they should immediately go on board and see the hatches nailed down. A just inventory shall be taken of all goods found in the cabins or above hatches lest any disorder be committed by the ship's company to the loss of the owners and adventurers and the prejudice of the Queen's customs.

FAIRS TO BE ABANDONED.[2] Owing to the dangerous increase of the plague, the fairs usually held in the months of July, August and September are to be abandoned. In London, St. Bartholomew's Fair in Smithfield upon 24th August and the Fair in Southwark on 8th September; and near London in July, Uxbridge the 20th, St. James's the 25th, and Brainford the 27th; in September, St. Giles in the Bush the 1st, Ware the 7th, Waltham Abbey the 13th, Croydon and St. Catherine Hill near Guildford the 21st.

6th July. MARLOWE'S 'EDWARD THE SECOND.'[3] The play of *The Troublesome Reign and Lamentable Death of Edward the Second, King of England, with the tragical fall of proud Mortimer,* written by Christopher Marlowe, and sundry times acted by the Earl of Pembroke's players, is entered for the printing.

9th July. THE PLAGUE.[4] The Lord Mayor hath written to the Council of the discommodity which will arise, especially to the clothiers, if Bartholomew Fair be not held. The proclamation forbidding the Fair may now be stayed for a while until it is seen how by God's goodness and the Lord Mayor's careful endeavour the increase of sickness be allayed.

Since the white crosses painted on those houses visited with the plague are wiped away in a short space, red crosses are to be nailed upon the doors and a watch kept to prevent those within from going abroad.

THE COLLECTION OF THE SUBSIDY.[5] The High Sheriffs are appointed commissioners for the collections of the fifteenths and tenths voted for the Queen's use. They are urged to choose men of sufficient worth for this work. As for the Justices of the Peace, since by the statute none should be admitted unless they hold lands to the value of £20 per annum, so is it expected that none of these shall be assessed at under this rate. The commissioners themselves shall give a notable example in

2 APC 24:347.   4 APC 24:373.
3 SR 2:634; STC 17437.   5 APC 24:376.

the taxation of themselves so that the rest which are able may be drawn the more willingly to assent to the larger taxation now laid on them.

SPANISH SHIPS OFF THE BRITTANY COAST.[6] From the Isle of Jersey comes news that 30 ships of the enemy and 5 galleys have been seen on the coast of Brittany about Conquett. Letters are therefore sent to Sir John Gilbert and Sir Francis Drake to warn the forces of the counties on the sea coast to be ready against any sudden incursion that might be made, and especially to take care for the defence of Plymouth now being begun to be fortified.

BLUNDEVILLE'S 'EXERCISES.'[7] *Master Blundeville, His Exercises,* is to be printed, being six treatises; the first, of Arithmetic; the second, of the first principles of Cosmography; the third, a plain and full description of the globes, both celestial and terrestrial, with certain tables for the better finding out of the true place of the sun and moon and of all the rest of the planets on the celestial globe; the fourth, a plain description of the universal map of Petrus Plancius set forth in 1592; the fifth, a plain description of Mr. Blagrave's Astrolabe; the sixth, the first and chiefest principles of navigation, showing how the navigator should use his proper instruments and presage the movements of the celestial bodies.

14th July. SIR THOMAS WILKES SENT TO THE FRENCH KING.[8] Because of the continual rumours that the French King is turned Catholic, Sir Thomas Wilkes is urgently despatched as a special ambassador to the King. He is instructed, after delivering his letters of credence, to say to the King that the Queen hath forborne hitherto to inquire what course he meaneth to hold in the present state of his affairs, but now she findeth occasion to delay no longer sending unto him. If either the King hath not fully yielded to his conversion to the Catholic religion, or hath not bound himself by promise to perform it, the ambassador shall say that she can in no wise allow or think it good before God that for any worldly respect or cunning persuasion he should yield to change his conscience and opinion in religion from the truth wherein he was brought up from his youth, and for the defence whereof he hath continued many years in arms. He shall require that the King not

[6] APC 24:406.
[7] STC 3146.
[8] SP FOR 31:f248.

only hear a number of reasons conceived by her Majesty to stay his resolution, but also to permit them to be communicated to his principal Catholic estates.

But if in coming thither Sir Thomas Wilkes shall find that the King is converted indeed, nevertheless he shall show the reasons conceived by the Queen to stay his resolution, that he may understand her mind and good will towards him. And though she would be grieved with his conversion, being contrary to her opinion and conscience, and indeed by good policy to be misliked, because he would become thereby subject to the Pope, (who is her mortal enemy, and who might enjoin him to keep no amity with her); yet she requireth him to advertise her what she may expect thereof.

First she wisheth to know how and by what means he will be stronger in his estate by his conversion than he was before as well against his rebels, that will not be content with his conversion, as also against the King of Spain. Then shall the ambassador ask how the King meaneth to proceed to acquit Brittany of the Spaniards, telling him that the Queen thinketh it the principal matter of weight after he shall be established in his crown; and is of such importance that she thinketh it more convenient for the King himself to take the same in hand, and in his own person, than to commit it to others, as hitherto.

Further, the King is to understand that until some port town in Brittany be allowed to her forces whither they may repair when sent, or to which they may retire for their relief, she cannot with any honour or the good respect of her natural subjects send any more forces thither to be wasted and spoiled as the former have been for the lack of such a place of retire.

The ambassador is also to know of the King what assurance she may have of him that he will continue jointly with her in offence and defence against the King of Spain. She doubteth not that he will give her this assurance under his hand and the great seal of France; for without it she will think all her kindness, favours and expenses of her treasure and wasting of her people to be as lost and of no effect. Then the ambassador is to require the King to call to his memory how long she hath aided him both before his title to the crown of France, and since, with money (as yet never repaid according to his bonds), and with her subjects with their lives, and in such number as England never yielded in any age to serve in foreign countries.

16th July. THE PLAGUE INCREASES.[9] The Council have written to the Lord Mayor and Aldermen saying that the Queen is greatly grieved at the increase of sickness, and although these plagues proceed from the hands of God as a due punishment of our wickedness, yet ought we to use all possible means to prevent their increase. If as good care were used in keeping the orders as had been taken for their making, and especially in restraining the infected from the sound, it would, with the help of God, do great good. In the town of Kingston, upon the first infection, they caused a house to be made in the fields distant from the town where the infected might be kept apart and provided for all things convenient for their sustenance and care; and the same should be done in London. There was also a little book set forth in the time of the great plague and the last year printed again which contained divers good precepts and orders; this might be recommended by the minister of every parish to all housekeepers. The Council require the suppression of all those that sell old apparel, a trade greatly used of late, and in no wise to be suffered in time of infection.

17th July. PLAGUE DEATHS.[10] In London this last week 149 persons are dead of the plague. The crops promise well, but notwithstanding corn is risen in price from £9 to £11 10s. owing to the shortage of corn in Spain and Portugal.

19th July. ASSIZES HELD IN ST. GEORGE'S FIELD.[11] This day the Court of Assize for Surrey was held in St. George's field, a tent being set up for the purpose. Many prisoners were there arraigned, condemned, and had judgment, nineteen being burnt in the hand but none executed. This assize is ended in one day which was thought would have needed three days' work, for the Justices (all duties being paid) make haste away for fear of being infected with the pestilence by the repair of people thither. The infection is much increased this past week, for out of 666 deaths in the City of London, 454 are from the plague.

29th July. THE COUNCIL'S LETTERS TO THE UNIVERSITIES OF OXFORD AND CAMBRIDGE.[12] The Council have written to the

[9] APC 24:400. The 'little book' is probably that summarised in *Other Books . . . 1594*, xii.
[10] FUGGER NEWS-LETTERS, p. 249.
[11] STOW'S ANNALS; FUGGER NEWS-LETTERS, p. 250.
[12] APC 24:427; STRYPE'S ANNALS 4:162.

Vice-Chancellor of the University of Cambridge showing how the Universities are nurseries to bring up youth in the knowledge of God and in all manner of good learning and virtuous living whereby they may serve their Prince and country in divers callings. For this respect a special care is to be had of these Universities that all means may be used to further the bringing up of the youths that are bestowed there in all good learning, education and honest manners; and like care used that all such things that may allure and entice them to lewdness, folly, and riotous manners, whereunto the nature of man is more inclined, in no wise be used. Understanding therefore that common players ordinarily resort to the University of Cambridge to recite interludes and plays, some of them being full of lewd example, and most of vanity, beside the gathering together of multitudes of people, the Council require the Vice-Chancellor to take special order that no plays or interludes of common players be set forth either in the University or any place within the compass of five miles, and especially in the town of Chesterton. Moreover, as Stourbridge Fair is at hand the Masters and Heads of the College should, because of the great infection, cause the gates of the College to be shut and no scholar permitted to repair thither. A like letter is to be sent to the Vice-Chancellor of Oxford.

30*th July*. RECRUITS TO BE STAYED.[13] Upon the new advertisements that are come out of France those soldiers that were to be levied in Hertford and Essex are stayed for a season that the county may not be charged with them. The men nevertheless are to be in readiness upon any new warning, and the armour and furniture provided by the county kept for use as occasion may serve.

3*rd August*. DR. HARVEY'S 'PIERCE'S SUPEREROGATION.'[1] Harvey hath answered Nashe's *Strange News* in a book entitled *Pierce's Supererogation or a new praise of the Old Ass*. He saith that if he is an ass, what asses are those courteous friends, excellent and learned men, worshipful and honourable personages that have written him letters of excellent commendation. As for Nashe, he is the son of a mule, a raw grammarian, a babbling sophister, a counterfeit crank, a stale rakehell, a piperly rhymer, a stump-worn railer, a dodkin author

whose gayest flourishes are Gascoigne's weeds, or Tarleton's
tricks, or Greene's cranks, or Marlowe's bravados; his jests
but the dregs of common scurrility, the shreds of the theatre,
or the off-scouring of new pamphlets; his freshest nippitaty
but the froth of stale inventions, long since loathsome to
quick tastes. His only art and the vengeable drift of his whole
cunning is to mangle the sentences of the *Four Letters,* hack
the arguments, chop and change the phrases, wrench the
words, and hale every syllable most extremely, even to the
disjoining and maiming of his whole meaning.

4th August. THE PLAGUE INCREASES.[2] The numbers of
plague deaths are reported to be much increased, but the Lord
Mayor is rebuked because no certificates of those dead or infected have been sent in these last two weeks.

5th August. A BOOK ON ASTRONOMY.[3] A translation of M.
Auger Ferrier's *Learned Astronomical Discourse* (first printed
in 1549) made by Thomas Kelway, gentleman, one of her
Majesty's Trumpets in Ordinary, is to be printed, being dedicated to the Lord Henry, Earl of Northumberland. In the ad-
dress to the courteous reader Mr. Kelway requesteth that
those who find this work of the judgment of nativities harsh
and unpleasant shall not wound it with injurious words,
thereby charging themselves with folly; for he that readeth
with derision, because he understandeth not, must blame his
own insufficiency, and not the book. The *Discourse* is divided
in three books, whereof the first treateth of the celestial figure
of a nativity, showing the fortunes and infortunes of the
planets; the second of the signification of the twelve signs and
the twelve houses; the third of revolutions and eclipses.

PLAGUE DEATHS.[4] The plague is worse than ever this last week
and whole households have died. Of 1603 deaths, 1130 are
from the plague.

6th August. THE TRUCE IN FRANCE.[5] The terms for a truce
general between the French King and the Leaguers were
agreed and by sound of the trumpet proclaimed on the 31st
July.

[2] APC 24:443.
[3] SR 2:635; STC 10833. Kelway's protest is significant of the growth of
incredulity in astrology.

[4] *Henslowe Papers,* ed. W. W. Greg,
1907, p. 37.
[5] SR 2:635; STC 11257.

The truce is for three months, during which all persons may return to their houses and estates, and enjoy them, except where garrisons are employed. Every man may freely travel through the realm without constraint of taking of passport. Prisoners of war that have not compounded for their ransom shall be delivered fifteen days after the truce; the common soldiers without ransom; the other men of war, having pay of either side, on procuring one quarter of their pay, except the leaders and chief of horsemen, who together with other gentlemen bearing charge shall be acquitted for the half year's worth of their revenue. All other persons shall be used, as touching their ransom, as courteously as may be, respecting their faculties and calling. Any woman or maid a prisoner to be set at liberty immediately without paying ransom, also children under the age of sixteen and men from sixty and upward not bearing arms. All men of war of either side are to be put in garrison, and not permitted to range and forage the country. No enterprises shall be made upon any foreign princes who hath assisted either side, but they shall withdraw their forces from the field and not make any re-enter of them during the truce. Those in Brittany to be sent back or separated, and put in garrison in such places as may not give matter of suspect.

BARTHOLOMEW FAIR.[6] In answer to the Lord Mayor's reasons against holding the fair on St. Bartholomew's Day in the fields towards Islington, the Queen hath hardly consented, though she were otherwise disposed to have no manner of fair or assembly at this time, to allow leather, butter, cheese and such like to be sold by gross in Smithfield but not by retail; but to avoid any access of the people no booths may be erected for victuallers. A proclamation is now published for the restraining of Smithfield Fair on Bartholomew's Day.

14th August. PLAGUE DEATHS.[7] No exact figures of the mortality were given out for this past week because there is commandment to the contrary, but it is rumoured that within the City and without the number is between 1700 and 1800 in one week.

16th August. RUMOURS CONCERNING FRANCE.[8] This proceeding of the French King in changing his religion is much wondered at and was not at first believed, but the news being now confirmed, the 1500 men levied for France are stayed

⁶ APC 24:448; PROCLAMATIONS 319.   ⁸ SP DOM 245:79.
⁷ *Henslowe Papers*, p. 39.

and determination taken to recall those in Normandy and Brittany. There is great expectation of the treaty of peace now in hand between the King and the Leaguers, being necessary and grateful to the towns, and their great hindrance being removed by the King's coming within the Catholic Church, so that it is likely that they will embrace the peace upon easier conditions.

19th August. SIR THOMAS WILKES' CONVERSATION WITH THE FRENCH KING.[9] From St. Denis near Paris, Sir Thomas Wilkes writeth that he arrived there on the 11th of the month, finding the King about to depart on the next morning for Fontainebleau; who granted him a brief audience. He presented the Queen's letters of credence, which the King opened but did not read at that time, alleging the difficulty of the hand. Then the King of his own accord fell into a slight discourse of the reasons of his conversion, promising at the next audience to detail it at large. To which Sir Thomas answered little more than to signify how strange it would appear to the Queen that of so resolute and long continued a Protestant he should so suddenly become a Catholic.

The ambassador saith that the King by his action hath assured his Catholics that were declining from him, and by breaking the neck of the third party hath doubtless gotten a strong party: the poverty of the Dukes of Mayne and Guise, the not performing of the promises of the Pope and the King of Spain, the uncertainty of the people of their faction, who all desire a peace, and the general misery of the country which is pitiful to behold, will drive them all to end their present dissensions.

DISBANDMENT OF THE SOLDIERS FROM FRANCE.[10] Sir John Hawkins prepareth seven hoys to bring 700 or 800 men from Dieppe. Sir Edward Brook and the muster master are to ascertain and record how many men there are in every company, how armed and weaponed, and from what counties they were sent. The treasurer's deputy shall give every soldier at his discharge some portion of what was due to him to pay his debts. If any so desire they may be suffered to tarry and serve the French King, and be paid their wages then due, but their armour to be detained and brought into England. Every captain shall see that the armour and weapons of all that return is brought to England and delivered to the Mayor at

Dover or Rye by indenture, and to give to each soldier of his band a billet of discharge and licence to pass to his county.

23rd August. WILKES' SECOND CONVERSATION WITH THE FRENCH KING.[11] The French King hath given Sir Thomas Wilkes a second private audience whereat he delivered at large the sum of his instructions, acquainting the King with her Majesty's care and desire to have prevented his conversion as tending the good of his soul, and giving a summary of the articles which he had received. These the King took in very grateful part, and did acknowledge that they were no small tokens of the Queen's love to him, but the necessity of his State was such that no verbal reasons could have prevented the mischief whereunto he had fallen if his conversion had not then been performed; which he confessed was precipitated by reason that the dangers came more suddenly on him than he expected, for that the day of his promised conversion was to have been two months after.

To the Ambassador's demand for a place of retreat in Brittany, he desired respite to confer with his Council, and promised that in case he might be so happy as to pacify his estate there, he would not fail with all the force he could make to repair in person to Brittany to remove the Spaniard.

26th August. COUNTERFEITERS SENT TO THE GALLEYS.[12] By order of the Lord Admiral, two men, Walter Pepper and George Ellis, very lewd and loose fellows that have beforetime been censured in the Star Chamber for counterfeiting the hands of some of the Lords of the Council and are now again apprehended and found culpable of the same offence, are committed to the new galleys to be employed as occasion should serve, and to be fast tied with chains that by no means they be allowed to escape.

8th September. NASHE'S 'CHRIST'S TEARS OVER JERUSALEM.'[1] Nashe hath written a godly book called *Christ's Tears over Jerusalem, whereunto is annexed a comparative admonition to London,* dedicated to the Lady Elizabeth Carey, wife of the Knight Marshal. Herein is shown how the Jews after God's great mercies to them refused to listen to Christ when

[11] SP FOR 32:f51.
[12] APC 24:486.
[1] SR 2:635; STC 18366. When Nashe found that Harvey was suspicious of his offers of friendship (see *1st Oct*) he retracted his apology in a violently abusive preface to the 1594 edition of *Christ's Tears.*

He pitifully reproached them; and how forty years after our
Lord's lifting up into Heaven, when the Jews pretended a
weariness of the Roman regiment, Jerusalem was sacked and
destroyed. So likewise is this London equally in danger of destruction by reason of the deadly sins committed within her
walls, being ambition, avarice, vainglory, atheism, discontent,
contention; disdain between courtier and citizen, merchant
and retailer, retailer and craftsman; gorgeous attire, wherein
England is become the ape of all nations' superfluities, the continual masquer in outlandish habitments; delicacy, gluttony,
lechery, and the great abundance of cunning bawds whose
trade is such that a great office is not so gainful as the prin-
cipalship of a College of Courtesans; sloth and security; the
whole ending with a prayer against the plague. In the Epistle
to the reader Nashe saith that he hath bidden farewell to fantastical satirism, desiring reconciliation even with Dr. Harvey,
whose fame and reputation he hath so rashly assailed.

10*th September*.   PLAGUE DEATHS.[2] There is still no sign of
an end to the mortality from plague. About a thousand deaths
of plague weekly are now being reported in the City, and outside some five hundred.

15*th September*.   RESTRAINT OF SUITORS AT WINDSOR.[3] A
Proclamation is published to reform the disorder in the great
number of persons who attend the Court at Windsor. In many
of the houses are lodged more than are allowed by the officers
of the town and the Queen's harbingers, and many of these
persons with their wives, children and servants. The Queen's
Knight Harbinger is now commanded to make a new search
with the assistance of the servants of the Knight Marshal and
the Mayor of the town. All owners of houses in Windsor,
Eton and the towns adjoining within five miles of the Court
are warned that within two days of the publication of the Proclamation from Windsor Cross they exclude all persons not
warranted by the harbingers' billets to have lodging, upon
pain of fine and having their houses shut up.

17*th September*.   NASHE'S 'UNFORTUNATE TRAVELLER.'[4] A
book called *The Unfortunate Traveller, or The Life of Jack
Wilton*, written by Nashe, is entered, dedicated to the Earl of
Southampton, wherein this Jack Wilton, that was a page at the

2 FUGGER NEWS-LETTERS, p. 251.   4 SR 2:636; STC 18380.
3 PROCLAMATIONS 320.

Court of King Henry VIII, telleth his own tale of what he did at the siege of Tournay, and afterward in his travels how he fared at Rotterdam and Wittenberg, and in Venice, Florence and Rome.

28th September. PLAGUE DEATHS.[5] It is reported that the plague deaths have abated during these last two weeks by 430; the last week between 1100 and 1200 in all died.

1st October. DR. HARVEY'S NEW LETTER OF NOTABLE CONTENTS.[1] *A New Letter of Notable Contents,* together with a *Strange Sonnet entitled Gorgon or the Wonderful Year,* being a letter of Dr. Gabriel Harvey's to John Wolfe, the printer, is printed. He noteth the strange conversion of Nashe from the *Strange News* to *Christ's Tears.* As for Nashe's protestations of repentance, great penmen and pamphlet merchants play much upon the advantage of the time and care not who be the enemy so long as Term be the friend. He loveth *osculum pacis,* but hateth *osculum Judae;* reverenceth the tears of Christ, but feareth the tears of the crocodile.

8th October. HIGH-HANDED DEALINGS.[2] The Lady Elizabeth Russell hath petitioned the Council for the punishment of her neighbour, Mr. Lovelace, to whom, saith she, she hath shown every friendship these twenty-six years, but who is guilty of foul riots against her. On Monday last he came to her house with sixteen or twenty men with halberds and long poles, broke open her porter's lodge and the lock of her stocks, and removed thence two of his men who had behaved very lewdly towards her. If she has offered him or his any wrong, the law is open, and it is not for him, a justice of the peace, to break his oath by so foul a riot.

On Thursday last, he sent a man for the key of the Tower at Windsor, where she had been all the year, having all her stuff there. She refused to leave upon such sudden warning, unless by order of the Lord Admiral, and offered him as much rent as it was worth, but it was refused. Two days since, being Saturday last, he and his men changed the lock of her lodging and commanded that none should undo it.

Now she petitioneth that this spite and injury be punished, and Mr. Lovelace put out of the commission of the peace,

⁵ *Henslowe Papers,* p. 40.   ² SP DOM 245:135.
¹ STC 12092.

otherwise it were better to be a mean justice of the peace than
a noble woman that dependeth upon God and her Majesty.

19th October. DANIEL'S 'DELIA AND ROSAMOND' AND 'THE
COMPLAINT OF ROSAMOND.'[3] Daniel hath augmented his *Delia
and Rosamond,* and added thereto *Cleopatra,* some few new
sonnets, and *The Complaint of Rosamond,* in which the Ghost
of Rosamond complaineth that though Shore's wife is graced,
her well-told tale finds no such compassion. She runneth
through the story of her sin with King Henry the Second, and
her death by poison at the hands of his wronged Queen.

The Tragedy of Cleopatra which is dedicated to the Lady
Mary, Countess of Pembroke, is not written for the English
stages, but after the manner of the ancients, preserving a unity
of the time, though not of place, and between each act a
chorus to point the moral of the action.

22nd October. EDWARDS' 'CEPHALUS AND PROCRIS.'[4] *Cephalus and Procris,* a poem written by Mr. Thomas Edwards
and dedicated to the Right Worshipful Master Thomas Argall,
Esquire, together with *Narcissus,* is to be printed. Herein is
described how Aurora wantonly loved the hunter Cephalus
and would have kept him; but he disdained her, being wan
with love for Procris. Aurora then taunting him, he went back
to Procris and by force and intreaty won his desire on her. But
Procris, thereafter overcome with shame at what she had allowed, fled away, and, hiding in a thicket, was by chance
struck with an arrow that Cephalus shot. In *Narcissus* the boy
betrayeth his effeminate love for his own reflection, supposing
it to be a maiden until he seeks it in the stream.

9th November. THE PLAGUE ABATING.[1] The plague deaths
reported in London this past week amount to 420.

14th November. DICKENSON'S 'ARISBAS.'[2] Mr. John Dickenson hath written a book called *Arisbas, Euphues amidst his
slumbers: or Cupid's journey to Hell. Deciphering a mirror of
constancy, a touchstone of tried affection, begun in chaste desire, ended in choice delights. And emblazoning Beauty's*

---

[3] SR 2:638; STC 6254. *Rosamond's
Complaint* is an acknowledged imitation of Chute's *Beauty Dishonoured.* These lamentations owe much
to the vogue of *The Mirror for Magistrates.*

[4] SR 2:658; STC 7525. Much influ-
enced by *Venus and Adonis.*
[1] FUGGER NEWS-LETTERS, p. 252.
[2] SR 2:589; STC 6817. A charming
tale in the best euphuistic vein; with
some pleasing poems.

Glory, adorned by Nature's bounty; with the triumph of true Love, in the foil of false Fortune.

17th November. CHURCHYARD'S VERSES.[3] The poet Thomas Churchyard, in resentment that the Lord Treasurer refused him what the Queen had granted, hath sent her these verses:

'Madam,
    You bid your treasurer on a time,
    To give me reason for my rhyme;
    But since that time and that season,
    He gave me neither rhyme nor reason.'

20th November. A CASE OF PLAGUE AT COURT.[4] There is much alarm in the Court because a page of the Lady Scroop, one of the ladies of the Queen's bedchamber, is dead of the plague in the keep at Windsor Castle. It is expected that the Queen will remove within a day or two.

28th November. THE ARRAIGNMENT OF RICHARD HESKETH.[5] This day Richard Hesketh, a Jesuit, was arraigned for having treasonably attempted to persuade Ferdinando Stanley, the new Earl of Derby, to revolt against the Queen.

This man had come from Sir William Stanley and the Catholics abroad, being authorised to offer the Crown of England to the Earl of Derby. He was instructed first to approach the Earl signifying to him in general that he had a message of importance to deliver from special friends of his, and to desire leave to utter it, and his promise of good security that he should incur no danger.

Having received this promise and given mutual promise of fidelity and secrecy, he should declare in general that the message concerned the common good of all Christendom, especially of England, and in particular of the Earl. If the Earl was content to hear, though drily and with small desire, he should name Sir William Stanley as having sent him, adding that there was another greater than he; and to know expressly whether the Earl would hear his message or no.

If he were willing, then Hesketh was to offer him all the endeavour, services and helps that the Catholics could employ if he would accept and agree to the Catholic faith; but to be capable he must be a Catholic, and bind himself to restore,

[3] BIRCH'S MEMOIRS 1:131.   [5] SALISBURY PAPERS 4:423, 461.
[4] BIRCH'S MEMOIRS 1:133.

advance and perpetually maintain the Catholic faith in England. Let the Earl signify what help he needed and when, and by God's help it would be provided: 4000 or 5000 men might be sent within seven or eight months. He was not to fear strangers; neither did the King of Spain now seek the Kingdom of England for himself; nor would the Pope or Cardinal Allen agree to it, if there was any other remedy; nor could the King of Spain hold it though he might invade and conquer the realm, for the people of England were most impatient of foreign government. The Pope himself held it better for Christendom to have many Christian Catholic kings than one too great and monarch of all, and the Cardinal was a true Englishman. It was better that he should obtain the crown now before the Queen's death, because he might prevent competition; besides, the Cardinal and Sir William Stanley were now able to assist, the Pope was willing (and perhaps another would not be); the state of France could not hinder but rather further, for now he could have some Spaniards, but not too many; it was like that some other was provided to challenge it after her death; and he had many enemies that were daily seeking his overthrow.

Hesketh delivered his message to the Earl, but was by him denounced and arrested. At his trial he acknowledged all his former confessions to be true so that there needed no further testimony against him. Nevertheless the Attorney General laid open all the plot and course of his treasons for the satisfaction of the standers-by, making collections from his confessions to note that the malice of those fugitive traitors and other enemies of the Queen proceeds from no other ground but that she preferreth the true worship of God and the peaceable government of her subjects above all other things. The Lord Chief Justice also, before passing judgment, used a very grave speech to the comfort of the Queen's subjects by these and the like graces which God hath showed.

29th November. A RECUSANT'S CONFESSION.[6] Edward Pemberton, a recusant, being examined by order of the Archbishop of Canterbury as to the coming and going of Catholic priests from overseas, declareth that those who leave England take shipping either at Portsmouth or Arundel, agree with the ship master to come at night and are away before morning. Those sent to England take shipping at Antwerp or any other place; if the ship is for London they take a boat between

Gravesend and London and so escape examining. When they come, if they are caught privily, any justice of the peace will take £10 and let them go, and the tithing men 20s.

30th November. THE QUEEN'S LETTER TO SIR JOHN NORRIS.[7] The Queen having been earnestly sued to grant Sir John Norris leave to return on his own affairs giveth him licence to repair home at his convenience. But he is put in mind what disaster happened in his last absence. If he is not assured of the troops being in safety and well guided he should not take the benefit of this favour; but if things are in such terms that he dare adventure he may choose his brother to command, who will have due care of her honour, of Sir John's, and of his own. In times past when the generals came away they brought with them captains and lieutenants, leaving the people without leaders. He is admonished not to commit any such error, as nothing can be more grievous to her than by negligence to suffer the poorest soldier in the company to perish.

7th December. GREENE'S 'ORLANDO FURIOSO.'[1] A play called *Orlando Furioso,* written by Robert Greene, is entered for printing, in which Alleyn played Orlando. This play was performed before the Queen.

11th December. HESTER'S 'PEARL OF PRACTISE.'[2] *The Pearl of Practise,* or practiser's pearl for physick and chirurgery, found out by John Hester (a spagerick or distiller), is entered, having since his death been gathered and brought into some method by James Fourestier. This book is dedicated to Sir George Carey and setteth out the methods, cures and prescriptions for many diseases, swellings, wounds, and injuries.

21st December. ANXIETY IN GUERNSEY.[3] From Sir Thomas Leighton, Governor of Guernsey, it is reported that five thousand or six thousand Spaniards are lately arrived at Blavet in Brittany. He beseecheth that the sum of £500, the remainder of the £1000 promised for the works to be done at the Castle, may be sent speedily.

22nd December. PEPPER FROM THE CARRACK.[4] The merchants that lately contracted with the Queen for the pepper

[7] SP DOM 246:22.   [3] SALISBURY PAPERS 4:440.
[1] SR 2:640; STC 12265.   [4] SP DOM 246:40.
[2] SR 2:641; STC 13253.

taken in the Great Carrack are unable to vend any quantity of it except at very mean prices because of the great quantities still remaining in the realm and being brought in. As they are bound to pay her great sums of money at Christmas and other short periods, the Queen in answer to their petition hath caused restraint to be put on the bringing in of all pepper into the realm from 25th December.

26th December.   PLAYING RESUMED.[5] As the plague is now abated, playing begins again at the Rose Theatre by the Earl of Sussex's men, who played *God Speed the Plough* this day.

31st December.   GENTLEMEN'S SONS OVERSEAS.[6] The Council issue a warrant for inquisition to be made in the counties of Lincoln, Hertford and Essex as to what gentlemen have sons relieved or maintained out of the realm that are sent over under colour to learn languages or for any other respects, and are not notoriously employed in the Queen's martial services or trade or merchandise as apprentices to known merchants. Bonds are to be taken of the fathers if any are known recusants or have been evil affected or are but feignedly reformed; and their houses to be searched for seminary priests, Jesuits and other suspected persons, books, letters and writings concerning matter against the State or established religion.

CHAPMAN'S Σκιὰ νυκτὸς.[7] Σκιὰ νυκτὸς, or *The Shadow of Night, containing two poetical hymns,* devised by Mr. George Chapman, is entered, being dedicated to Mr. Matthew Roydon, to whom he writeth that it is the exceeding rapture of delight in the deep search of knowledge that maketh men manfully endure the extremes incident to that Herculean labour. But what a supererogation in wit this is, to think Skill so mightily pierced with their loves who read but to curtail a tedious hour that she should prostitutely show them her secrets, when she will scarcely be looked upon by others but with invocation, fasting, watching, yea, not without having drops of their souls like a heavenly familiar. Yet are there those that most profitly entertain learning in themselves to the admirable lustre of their nobility, such as the most ingenious Derby, deep-searching Northumberland, and the skill embracing heir of Hunsdon. Of the two hymns, the first is dedicated to Night, which the poet calleth the day of deep students. The second hymn he dedicateth to Cynthia, under whom is figured the Queen.

PLAGUE DEATHS.[8] There have died in London and the suburbs this past year 17,893 persons, whereof 10,675 were from the plague.

[8] STOW'S ANNALS. Graunt (see *31st Dec* 1592 note) gives the figures 17,844 and 10,662.

Other Books Printed in *1593*

i. Dr. Richard Bancroft's *Dangerous positions and proceedings, published and practised within the Island of Britain, under pretence of a Reformation, and for the Presbyterial Discipline.* Herein is shown the history of the Consistorian Puritans from the first preaching of the Gospel by Farellus, Viretus and others at Geneva to the conspiracy of Hacket, Arthington and Coppinger in July 1591.

ii. *A Dialogue concerning Witches,* penned by George Gifford, wherein in form of a dialogue between Samuel, and his wife, Daniel, M.B. a schoolmaster, and the goodwife, is shown how craftily the devil deceiveth not only the witches but many others.

In the Epistle Dedicatory to Mr. Robert Clarke, one of the Barons of the Court of Exchequer, Mr. Gifford declareth that the devils are now let loose, and prevail more than ever he hath heard before, so that Satan is now heard speak and believed, speaking through conjurors, sorcerers and witches. But the devils do this by God's special providence, seeking by this means to punish the world. Yet are the witches themselves deceived when they believe that at their request or pleasure their spirits lame and kill men and beasts; and then to spread the opinion among the people, these subtle spirits betray them, and would have the witches openly confess that they do such things, which all the devils at man's request could never do; for if they could, they would not stay to be intreated. The devil worketh by his other sort of witches, whom the people called cunning men and women, to confirm all his matters, by them teaching many remedies that so he may be sought and honoured as a God.

These positions are demonstrated in the dialogue; Daniel holding that Satan can do nothing without God's leave, so that the witches are of themselves powerless to do much harm; and in the end convincing the others.

i. STC 1344. An important account of the Puritan movement.

Their talk being finished, there cometh to them the good wife R., being one of those upbraided as herself a witch for having thrust a hot poker into her cream when the butter would not come, burning a hen or a hog alive and other such devices. To their speeches she answereth, 'Is that witchcraft? Some Scripture men hath told you so. Did the devil teach it? Nay, the good woman at R.H. taught it my husband and she doeth more good in one year than all these Scripture men will do as long as they live.'

iii. Mr. Thomas Lodge's *Phillis*, being a collection of Sonnets and Eclogues wherein Damon declareth his love for Phillis and lamenteth her neglect, being followed by an Ode, bitterly complaining of her falseness; to which is annexed *The Complaint of Elstred*, who telleth the story of her life and death.

iv. Mr. Lodge's *The Life and Death of William Longbeard*, dedicated to Sir William Webb, the Lord Mayor.

There are also in this book divers pleasant histories of pirates and others.

v. *The first part of Speculum Britanniae*, an historical and chorographical description of Middlesex, compiled by the travel and view of John Norden, being consecrated to the Queen by the author, with an epistle of thanks to the Lord Treasurer. After a brief declaration of the titles, inhabitants, divisions and situation of England, the author describeth the history, the limits and bounds, the nature of the soil and fertility, the Ecclesiastical and Civil Government of the shire, its divisions, parks, and ancient highways; which are followed by an alphabet of the cities, towns, hamlets and villages, including the City of London, and concluding with the principal highways and a list of noblemen and gentlemen having houses within the shire.

vi. *The Practice, Proceedings and Laws of Arms,* described out of the doings of most valiant and expert Captains, and confirmed both by ancient and modern examples and precedents, written by Dr. Matthew Sutcliffe, printed by the Queen's printer, and dedicated to the Earl of Essex. In the Epistle Dedicatory Dr. Sutcliffe saith that all men's eyes are fixed upon

ii. STC 11850. There are some illuminating anecdotes in this treatise, and good patches of dialogue, especially when the women talk.

iii. STC 16682.
iv. STC 16659.
v. STC 18635.

the Earl of Essex, who hath already made his name honourable by his experience in the service of the Low Countries, of Portugal and France, so that the general hope of soldiers is that he who so well understandeth the common disorders of the wars, will one day be a means to correct them. It is not the courage of the Spaniard, nor force of the Dutch, nor bravery of the French that frustrated our late attempts; neither doth force so often overthrow armies in field, as dalliance, irresolution and delay; then, through niggardize and good husbandry, want of pay and necessary furniture; thirdly, presumption and want of strength and sufficient force; and lastly, those abuses which through want have crept into the armies of late times and cannot be corrected; for what conscience could punish those that spoil and wander abroad when otherwise they would starve. For all these things and for the abuses of imprests, false musters and accounts the only remedy is the true discipline of arms. In the Epistle to the Reader he saith that this discourse is framed because of the general lamentation that in those actions which have of late been attempted publicly the success hath been so slender, the loss of men so great, the charge so burdensome, and the proceedings and effects so contrary to antiquity.

vii. *God's Arrow against Atheists,* a sermon preached by Mr. Henry Smith, wherein in seven chapters he showeth the reasons for a belief in God; in the first touching on the absurdity of Atheism and irreligion; demanding who made the world, since it had a beginning and it must needs follow that it had an efficient cause or maker. In the second it is shown that the Christian religion is the only true religion in the world, and wherewith only God is pleased; in the third the Christian religion is defended against the Gentiles and all the infidels of the world; in the fourth that the religion of Mahomet is false and wicked; in the fifth that the Church of Rome is not the true Church of God nor observeth the right religion; and in the last he toucheth on schism and schismatical synagogues.

vi. STC 23468.   vii. STC 22666.

1st January. A PROGNOSTICATION.[1] It is prognosticated in the Almanack for this year that the spring shall be moist and windy but not very cold, the summer indifferent but with many unkind storms, sudden lightnings and thunder-claps; sicknesses not many but passing dangerous, with hot and fervent agues, great distemperature of men's brains, and immoderate heat, whereby many will run frantick. In the autumn there are like to be mighty storms to the great hindrance of those that shall be late in harvest, especially in the north; together with a great pestilence.

4th January. A MYSTERIOUS STRANGER.[2] Mr. Thomas Jeffreys, an English merchant at Calais, hath written to Lord Burleigh that a certain man named Emanuel Louis Tinoco is come to him with a private communication for the Council. He knoweth not the man but hath seen him divers times with Emanuel Andrada: he may do good, as he hath dealings with Count Fuentes and the King of Spain's principal secretary for war, whereby, as he saith, he hath discovered great matters pretended by the enemy which must be seen to with speed.

6th January. COURT REVELS.[3] Twelfth Night was celebrated at Court by dancing which continued till 1 o'clock after midnight, the Queen being seated in a high throne, and next to her chair the Earl of Essex with whom she often devised in sweet and favourable manner.

7th January. CATHOLIC STORIES FROM SCOTLAND.[4] About a month since (7th December) James Maxwell, Earl of Mor-

[1] STC 526.
[2] SP DOM 246:39.
[3] BIRCH'S MEMOIRS 1:146.
[4] *Spanish State Papers* 4:591.

ton, the Scottish King's Lieutenant General, was slain in pursuing the Lord Johnston to arrest him according to the King's warrant, and the Catholics make much note of his death.

Not many years since, the Earl of Morton, though he was a Catholic, had been persuaded to sign the articles expressing conformity and directed against the Catholic religion. But at 12 o'clock that day, being alone in his room, an angel appeared to him in the form of a youth who said, 'My Lord, do not as your kinsmen would persuade you; for if you do you shall lose the hand with which you sign, and your days shall end with shameful death.' Moved by this appeal, the Earl again put on the gold crucifix and an *agnus dei* which he used to wear round his neck, but had taken off when he abandoned his former professions. He then told the principal kinsmen who had persuaded him to sign how remorseful he was for his error, and what the angel had told him; and that God's mercy might for ever be remembered by his house, he added to his arms the figure of an angel. He refused also to sign the articles declaring himself an enemy of the ministers.

But after a time he was greatly moved by his kinsmen, and the King himself made him many offers, creating him his Lieutenant General, so that at last he gave way and signed the articles. But shortly afterwards going to arrest the Lord Johnston with 5000 soldiers he met with the end the angel foretold him.

For when he came up the Lord Johnston, taking advantage of the ground, had posted 600 horsemen in three squadrons in a triangle at some little distance from each other. The Earl of Morton's regiment entering into their midst, Lord Johnston and his men who were on one side threw themselves with such fury upon the Earl's men that they broke and fled; and the Lord Johnston, reaching the Earl, at the first blow smote off his right hand, and at the second cut off a leg. Then being thrown from his horse, the Earl was cut into a thousand pieces.

The Catholics also say that the Lord Claud Hamilton, against his conscience and at the persuasion of his wife and her brothers, had also subscribed to please the King and the ministers. At one time he was dining and, as was the custom in some Scottish houses, the gospel was being read at table during the repast. The reader came to the words, 'Whoso denieth me before men, him will I also deny before my Father'; and as he pronounced these words the Lord Claud rose from the table and attempted to cut his wife's throat, crying out that by her persuasion and that of her brothers, he had denied the faith and sacrificed his soul. For several days after this he remained in a state of frenzy so that it was necessary to bind him; nor is he yet entirely recovered.

ATTEMPTS AGAINST THE QUEEN.[5] The Portuguese that was sent over from Calais, by name Emanuel Louis Tinoco, being taken to the house of Sir Robert Cecil, hath delivered an advertisement of many things which should be made known to the Queen for the sake of her person. He declareth that he was the servant of Don Antonio from the day when he was proclaimed King until July last, serving him always with zeal, fidelity and love; but seeing him ungrateful, and poor of council and government, he consented with one Stephen Ferrara de Gama to seek liberty for their country, seeing that they had the Duke of Braganza, a young man and well beloved in the Kingdom. They therefore went to the Count Fuentes to seek the favour of the King of Spain, by means of Don Christofer de Moro, and to offer him service.

Upon this the King wrote to Count Fuentes that he should send Tinoco to England and that Ferrara should leave his wife there, feigning business in France, and thence go together to Don Antonio who would employ them. For less suspicion Ferrara was to go alone and bring Tinoco orders what to do; he was to try and win Dr. Lopez, the Portugal Jew that is her Majesty's physician, and endeavour to draw a letter from him, promising to do him service; he was to remind Lopez that he had daughters and that they should not want good marriages. They were to take knowledge of all affairs of England, especially of any secret preparations of an army, how many ships the Queen hath at home and abroad, the names of their captains, and to take a good view of the Isle of Wight and the Downs, and to note the forts and weak places.

16th January.   ANOTHER DECLARATION BY TINOCO.[6] Tinoco being very straightly examined by the Earl of Essex, and in some respects confused, hath again written to Sir Robert Cecil to clear himself. He will show the true intentions of his coming so as to clear all doubts, and that without reward, which shall be reserved until it should be lawful for him to demand recompense. He saith that he has come voluntarily to Court, and gives his word as a gentleman to serve the Queen with all possible diligence and fidelity by giving secret advertisements of all things. He hath served Don Antonio for thirteen years

[5] SP DOM 247:12.   [6] SP DOM 247:13.

and thereby lost all he had in Portugal, and the best part of
his life; for the remainder he would serve the Queen, but knew
of nothing that would do her service.

23rd January. LOPEZ DEEPLY IMPLICATED.[7] Tinoco the
Portuguese hath made further declaration, saying that Andrada
had offered him, on behalf of Dr. Lopez, service to the King
of Spain, and brought a jewel of great value from the King
of Spain to Lopez, which he now hath. Ferrara also wrote to
Count Fuentes that Dr. Lopez would do the King great service.

24th January. LOPEZ EXAMINED.[8] Dr. Lopez was called before the Lord Treasurer, Sir Robert Cecil, and the Earl of
Essex, who are appointed by the Queen to this end. The Earl
hath for a long time been sifting out matter against Dr. Lopez
but the other two opposed him. After the first hearing Sir
Robert Cecil posted to the Court before the Earl, and related
to the Queen that there was no matter of malice, for in the
poor man's home were found no kind of writings of intelligences of which he was accused, or otherwise that hold might
be taken of him. In the meantime he is committed to the custody of Mr. Gelly Meyrick, the Earl's Steward, at Essex
House. Upon my lord coming to the Queen, she, being pre-
possessed of the matter by the others, took him up, calling him
a rash and temerarious youth to enter into a matter against
the poor man, which he could not prove and whose innocence
she knew well enough; but malice against Dr. Lopez, and no
other, hatched all this matter, which displeaseth her much,
and more for that her honour is interested therein.

These words of the Queen's so angered the Earl of Essex
that he went back to his chamber, with great fury casting open
the chamber door before him, and so passed into his cabinet
where he kept himself shut in for an hour.

This enmity between the Earl of Essex and Lopez is of old
standing. Some time since, the Earl of Essex, having resolved
to make use of intelligencers to do him service, to this end
spoke to Dr. Lopez, telling that many did practise treason
against her Majesty. The Spaniard hated her; the Papists
would do her what hurt they could; she was ancient and child-
less; and the good of the Kingdom wholly depended on her
life. Now for preventing this design it would be best to find

[7] SP DOM 247:19.
[8] BIRCH'S MEMOIRS 1:149, 150; Bishop   Godfrey Goodman, *The Court of
                                                 James I,* 1839.

someone on whom the Spaniard might repose trust. After some talk with the Queen, Lopez undertook the business, and made offer of his service to some special friends in Spain or Portugal. They to whom he wrote gave him encouragement and promised a good reward.

Here began a mutual intercourse of letters between them; and as soon as ever Lopez received any intelligence, he went instantly to the Queen to acquaint her therewith; and afterwards he went to the Earl of Essex and acquainted him. Then did the Earl come to the Court and acquaint her with the same: and the Queen knowing it before did but laugh at him. And so it fell out several times, whereby the Earl saw himself utterly disappointed, for though he had gotten an intelligencer yet he proved not to be his but went in immediately to the Queen. This hath bred very ill blood between the Earl and Lopez.

In the last vacation, Dr. Lopez went to visit Don Antonio and Antonio Perez; and making merry with them, Lopez began to inveigh against the Earl of Essex, telling them some secrecies, how he had cured him, and of what diseases, with other things that did disparage his honour. But as soon as Lopez was gone, they went instantly to the Earl and, to ingratiate themselves into his favour, acquainted him with all. Whereupon the Earl was so much incensed that he resolved to be revenged.

25th January.   A NOTABLE JESUIT TAKEN IN THE NORTH.[9]
From York, Topcliffe reporteth that Fr. Walpole, a very notable priest and Jesuit, was taken on landing at Flamborough, together with his younger brother and one Lingen, both soldiers of Sir William Stanley. After the Lord President of the Council, with the aid of his chaplain, had toiled day and night with the prisoners, he so prevailed with the young Walpole to see his offence, that all the truth, secrets, and matter, even against himself, flowed from him as fast as the questions could be put. He confessed that his brother gave him six small pieces of parchment and twelve letters. When all had been examined, the Lord President sent the Jesuit and Lingen to rest; but to prove young Walpole's honesty, he despatched him to the sea side, well guarded, to see if he could find the place where he said that the letters were buried. The bundle was found, but all wet with rain, and brought to his Lordship who leapt for

[9] SP Dom 247:21. For Fr. Walpole, see CATH. REC. SOC., vol. 5.

joy, and after tenderly handling them before a fire twenty-two are unfolded without blemish.

31st January. RUMOURS AT COURT.[10] Since his rebuke by the Queen Essex hath kept to his chamber these two days, opening it to none but the Lord Admiral, who passeth to and fro about atonement which at last is made, and they two go off to London. It is rumoured that on further examination Lopez is deeply touched in the plot for working the Queen's destruction, and discovered to have been the King of Spain's pensioner these seven years, the ground of which treason is believed to have been discovered by Don Antonio before his recent going over to France. The Queen hath forbidden all access to her, except only of four persons, besides the Council and the ladies of nearest attendance, by which it appeareth that all is not yet discovered.

1st February. 'GREENE'S FUNERALS.'[1] Danter hath printed *Greene's Funerals,* by R. B., gentleman, contrary to the author's expectation and wish; wherein Greene's death and works are celebrated in fourteen sonnets of various metres. In the seventh, written in the English hexameter, R. B. protesteth against those that inveigh against the dead.

3rd February. BURGLARY AT WINDSOR.[2] Yesterday four of the gentlemen pensioners of the Court were robbed at Windsor. In their absence at six o'clock at night their chamber door, which is in one of the five towers of the tiltyard, was broken open, and all their trunks likewise, out of which the thieves took in jewels and ready money to the value of £400. Sir Robert Cecil is reported to be very busy coming and going very often between London and the Queen, so that he appeareth with his hands full of papers and his head full of matter, and so occupied passeth through the presence chamber like a blind man, not looking upon any.

PLAYING PROHIBITED.[3] Owing to the great multitudes of people who daily resort to the common plays, lately again set up in and about London, the Council fear that the sickness may gain very dangerous increase. The Lord Mayor is required to take straight order that no plays or interludes be exercised by any company within the compass of five miles of the City.

[10] BIRCH'S MEMOIRS 1:151.   [2] BIRCH'S MEMOIRS 1:155.
[1] SR 2:644; STC 1487.   [3] *Remembrancia* 2:6; MSR 1:73.

4th February. A PLOT TO KILL THE QUEEN.[4] A certain Polwhele that came over from Calais to give information to the Lord Treasurer hath declared that one Captain Jacques, a soldier from Sir William Stanley's company, hath a design to kill the Queen. This Jacques, saith he, several times urged him to come to England to murder the Queen, and on his refusing Jacques said that the end of a soldier was but beggary, to be killed with a bullet and thrown into a ditch, and to take such a matter in hand would be glorious before God, the Queen being a wicked creature, and likely to overthrow all Christendom. Jacques directed him how to get to England safely, and what speeches to use to the Lord Treasurer if intercepted, saying that if he himself could go to England, the killing of the Queen would be the first thing he would do. Polwhele also draweth in two men, John Annias and Patrick Collen, an Irish soldier, with having come to England to kill the Queen. Both are already taken and lodged separately in prison.

5th February. LOPEZ SENT TO THE TOWER.[5] Lopez, for all those that favour him, at noon was committed to the Tower, the Earl of Essex having so busied himself with the examinations for several days past that he scarce had leisure even to eat.

A CARTER'S WORDS.[6] The remove of the Court from Windsor is still constantly put off. The carter that three times came to Windsor with his cart to carry away some of the stuff of the Queen's wardrobe, when he repaired there for the third time and was told by those of the wardrobe that the remove held not, clapping his hand on his thigh cried out, 'Now I see that the Queen is a woman as well as my wife.' These words being overheard by her Majesty, who then stood at the window, she said, 'What a villain is this!' and so sends him three angels to stop his mouth.

6th February. A PLOT TO BURN THE TOWER.[7] John Daniel, an Irishman, hath given Mr. Justice Young to understand of a plot that is pretended for the firing of the Tower. He declareth that there is a vault where brimstone lies and over it gunpowder, and near to it a trapdoor that stands much open. It is purposed that two men like labourers shall come in as

---

[4] SP DOM 247:39. For an account of these plots, see Martin Hume, *Treason and Plot*, 1901.

[5] BIRCH'S MEMOIRS 1:152.
[6] BIRCH'S MEMOIRS 1:155.
[7] SALISBURY PAPERS 4:474.

though they were workmen in the Tower, and cast certain bales into the vault where the brimstone is so that in a short time it shall take fire and consume all. Further, that there is a device to set the ships at Billingsgate on fire, and the houses also; and then to set the inns and woodstacks on fire in London.

THE ROSE THEATRE CLOSED.[8] At the Rose this week the Earl of Sussex's men play *The Jew of Malta,* and *Titus Andronicus,* and now cease playing.

'TITUS ANDRONICUS.'[9] *The most lamentable Roman Tragedy of Titus Andronicus,* sometime played by the servants of the Earl of Derby, the Earl of Pembroke and the Earl of Sussex, is to be printed.

A CONVERSATION BETWEEN SIR ROBERT CECIL AND THE EARL OF ESSEX.[10] At seven in the morning Dr. Lopez was again examined before the Earl of Essex and Sir Robert Cecil, and confesseth more than enough.

The office of Attorney-General is still vacant, and canvassed by the Earl of Essex for Mr. Francis Bacon, though the Lord Treasurer and Sir Robert Cecil favour Sir Edward Coke. As the Earl of Essex and Sir Robert returned back in a coach together, Sir Robert began to broach the matter of the Attorney-General, saying, 'My lord, the Queen has resolved e'er five days pass without any further delay to make an Attorney-General. I pray your lordship to let me know whom you will favour.'

The Earl answered that he wondered Sir Robert should ask him that question seeing that it could not be unknown to him that he favoured Francis Bacon.

'Good lord,' replied Sir Robert, 'I wonder your Lordship should go about to spend your strength in so unlikely or impossible a manner.'

After further talk passed between them, Sir Robert said, 'If at least your Lordship had spoken of the Solicitorship, that might be of easier digestion to her Majesty.'

Upon this the Earl answereth, 'Digest me no digestions; for the Attorneyship for Francis is that I must have, and in that will I spend all my power, might, authority and annuity, and with tooth and nail defend and procure the same for him against whosoever; and that whosoever getteth this office out

8 HENS. DIARY 1:16.   10 BIRCH'S MEMOIRS 1:153.
9 SR 2:644; STC 22328.

of my hand for another, before he have it, it shall cost him
the coming by, and of this be you assured of, Sir Robert, for
now do I fully declare myself. And for your own part, Sir
Robert, I think it strange both of my Lord Treasurer and you
that can have the mind to seek the preference of a stranger
before so near a kinsman. For if you weigh in a balance the
parts every way of his competitor and him, only excepting five
poor years of admitting to a house of court before Francis,
you shall find in all other respects whatsoever, no comparison
between them.'

COLLEN'S CONFESSION.[11] Collen now declareth that Jacques
persuaded him to kill Antonio Perez, formerly the King of
Spain's Secretary, which he undertook, whereupon Jacques
gave him £30 in gold, for his voyage. He then departed immediately from Brussels for St. Omar, where he found an old
priest to whom he confessed. The priest dissuaded him, saying
that it was unlawful to commit murder; but next day Jacques
took him to Fr. Holt who said that he might lawfully enterprise anything for the King's service, and, advising him to prepare himself to God, gave him absolution.

8th February.   A RUMOUR OF THE QUEEN'S DEATH.[12] There
is a rumour in London that the Queen is dead and hath been
carried to Greenwich, but it is being kept very secret in Court.

11th February. 'THE TRIAL OF BASTARDY.'[13] William
Clerke's *The Trial of Bastardy* is entered, wherein are shown
the civil and ecclesiastical laws of matrimony and legitimate
issue, together with the statutes in marriage from the 25th
year of Henry VIII.

17th February. PRECAUTIONS AGAINST SUSPICIOUS PER-
SONS.[14] Because of the dangers threatened at this time to the
Queen's person, these special directions are proposed by the
Lord Treasurer. Officers are to be appointed in every port that
shall not suffer any person to land until examined as to the
cause of his coming, and if the cause do not appear clear, he
shall be committed to prison, or kept on board until his examinations have been taken and sent to the Council. It is
especially likely that such persons will land at Dover, Sandwich, Rye, Gravesend, Yarmouth and London. Every Irish-

[11] SP DOM 247:45.
[12] SP DOM 247:50.
[13] SR 2:653; STC 5411. Of interest

to anyone concerned with the marriage laws of the time.
[14] SP DOM 247:66.

man in London or about the Court that is neither a known householder, nor a resident in commons, in any house, court or chamber as a servant, nor in service with a householder for five years past, must present himself to one of the Council or to the Lord Mayor to be examined how he lives and why he remains in England.

To restrain the great resort of unnecessary persons lodging near or frequenting the Court, the Lord Chamberlain shall appoint an usher and a quarter-waiter, with one or two clerks of the household, to attend and daily view all persons that offer to come to Court; and the Knight Harbinger and Marshal, with some tipstaffs, and, if need be, with the aid of some of the Yeomen of the Guard, shall twice or thrice a week discover who are lodged within two miles of Court; and if any are found not allowed they shall be examined, and if they cannot give just cause be committed to prison.

18th February.   FERRARA'S CONFESSION.[15] Stephen Ferrara de Gama, being examined before the Earl of Essex, Sir Thomas Wilkes, and Mr. William Waad, declared that ten months since he received two letters from Lopez, written in his house in London to be delivered to Don Christophero de Moro. He wrote the letters from Lopez's lips wherein, though obscurely worded, he promised to do all the King required. He thinks that the Doctor would have poisoned the Queen had he been required. Andrada had said that Lopez was willing to poison both the Queen and Don Antonio; and afterwards Lopez said that Don Antonio should die the first illness that befel him.

21st February.   A PROCLAMATION AGAINST VAGABONDS.[16] A proclamation is published for the suppressing of the multitude of idle vagabonds. On certain days in the week, monthly watchers and privy searchers shall be appointed to attach and imprison these idle vagabonds and to send the lamed into their counties according to the statute.

In the City of London, and about her Majesty, a great multitude repair, whereof some are men of Ireland that of late years have unnaturally served as rebels against her Majesty's forces beyond the seas, and cannot have any good meaning towards her, as is manifestly proved in some already taken.

But seeing that the discovery of Irish traitors can hardly be made when so many other vagrants of that nation haunt about the Court, no person born in Ireland (except he be an householder known in some town, or a menial servant with some nobleman, gentleman or other honest householder, or resides, or is in commons, in any house of court or Chancery, as a student in the laws, or a student in any of the Universities, or sent out of Ireland by her Majesty's Deputy) may remain in this realm but shall repair without delay into the realm of Ireland to the place of his natural habitation, where he ought to live.

HUGH CAHILL'S CONFESSION.[17] Hugh Cahill, an Irishman, hath voluntarily confessed before Topcliffe that when at Brussels, Father Holt and others said it would be a most blessed thing to kill the Queen, as by it he would win Heaven, and become a saint if he should be killed; he that should do it would be chronicled for ever. He was advised to go to Court, and serve someone about the Queen's privy chamber, and then to waylay her in some progress and kill her with a sword and a dagger at a gate or narrow passage, or as she walked in one of her galleries. They promised him 100 crowns towards his charges, and 2000 more to be paid when he had killed her, and his pension augmented from 15 crowns a month to £30.

25th February. LOPEZ.[18] There hath been a great consultation at the Lord Treasurer's about the persons apprehended for Lopez's plot; at which all now appears manifest, as well by the confessions of those taken as by the letters found of the others beyond the seas, whereby it is evident that this practice hath long continued, and that Lopez is no new traitor. Great expedition is being made to bring the affair before the public, but it seemeth that this cannot be done so soon as the Court desire, since the indictment must have many branches and there are many Spanish and other foreign letters to be translated and abstracted.

28th February. LOPEZ ARRAIGNED.[19] This day Lopez was arraigned at the Guildhall before the Commission on which sit the Lord Mayor, the Earl of Essex, Lord Charles Howard, the Lord Admiral, Lord Buckhurst, Robert, Lord Rich, Sir Thomas Heneage, Vice-Chamberlain, Sir John Popham, Chief Justice of the Queen's Bench, Sir Robert Cecil, Sir John

---

[17] SP DOM 247:78.
[18] BIRCH'S MEMOIRS 1:158.
[19] SP DOM 247:97, 102; CAMDEN'S ELIZABETH.

Fortescue, Chancellor of the Exchequer, and other persons of worth.

The case against Lopez was conducted by the Solicitor-General, Sir Edward Coke, who opened by showing that the grounds of all the plots against the Queen and the realm are not for any offence on her part, but for her constant defence of Christ's cause and His Holy Word against the Pope, and for protecting her dominions against the ambitions of the King of Spain. These were the original causes of the cursed bull of Pius V., and from this root sprung all the rebellions, treasons and devilish practices since attempted. After the 'Invincible Navy,' as they termed it, had been defeated by God and her Majesty's princely care and providence, and by the valiantness of her nobles and true subjects, the King of Spain and his priests, despairing of prevailing by valour, turned to cowardly treachery, and what they could not do by cannon, they attempted by crowns. To achieve this, have they put in practice three devilish attempts: to burn the navy and ships with poisoned fireworks; to seduce some of the nobility to rebellion; and to take the blood of a virgin Queen. To this end many needy and desperate young men are seduced by Jesuits and seminary priests with great rewards and promises to kill the Queen, being persuaded that it is glorious and meritorious, and that if they die in the action, they will inherit Heaven and be canonised as saints.

This Lopez, a perjured murdering traitor and Jewish Doctor, worse than Judas himself, undertook the poisoning, which was a plot more wicked, dangerous, and detestable than all the former. He is her Majesty's sworn servant, graced and advanced with many princely favours, used in special places of credit, permitted often access to her person, and so not suspected, especially by her who never feareth her enemies nor suspecteth her servants. The bargain was made and the price agreed upon, and the fact only deferred until payment of the money was assured. The letters of credit for his assurance were sent, but before they came to his hands, God most wonderfully and miraculously revealed and prevented it. The manner of it is as follows:

Some followers of Don Antonio, hoping to raise themselves by his fortunes, and finding his success not answerable to their expectations, grew discontented, and so became instruments to betray their master to the King of Spain, and practise any treason that could be devised, either against Don Antonio or the Queen's person. Lopez, outwardly pretending to favour Don Antonio, was a secret instrument for the King of Spain, and carried his actions therein more covertly under pretext of service for Don Antonio. He continued his secret course of intelligence with the King of Spain for many years by means of Emanuel Andrada, Bernardino Mendoza and others. Andrada wrote to Mendoza that he had won Lopez, but the letter being intercepted, Andrada was apprehended and committed. Lopez practised to have secret speech with Andrada before he was examined, and directed him what answer he was to make, insomuch that Andrada was released. These services were so acceptable to the King of Spain that he sent Lopez a jewel.

After this Andrada dealt with Lopez for poisoning the Queen. They had many conferences when Lopez undertook to do it, and directed them to signify this to Count Fuentes and to Stephen de Ibarra, the King's secretary. Andrada then went to Calais to convey intelligence between Lopez and the King of Spain and his Ministers; he told Ferrara de Gama that he might commit all things to Lopez, who hoped to do one great service to the King, and a remedy for Christendom, which was to poison the Queen, the King paying for it. Lopez and Ferrara afterwards conferred together, and Lopez undertook the poisoning for 50,000 crowns, which Ferrara signified by letters to Count Fuentes and Stephen de Ibarra. Ferrara, with the privity of Lopez, wrote to Christofero de Moro, assuring him of Lopez's affection to the King of Spain. Lopez also sent two packets of letters to Count Fuentes, de Moro and de Ibarra, wherein he promised to do all the King of Spain should command, and, since the King knew the business, as he told Ferrara, he made him write in obscure and covert words.

Lopez often asked if the money and answer were come, and said he was ready to do the service. The money he was to receive at Antwerp, where he meant to go after the treason had been committed, and to this end he gave directions for a house to be prepared for him, intending afterwards to go and live at Constantinople.

Tinoco, who acted as go-between, was apprehended with the letters from the Count Fuentes and Ibarra, letters of credit for the money being found upon him, and, although Ferrara de Gama was then in prison, and examined long before and Tinoco since, without any conference with each other, both agreed in all things concerning the plotting of the treason. It is also to be observed that in handling of these treasons Lopez was so careful that he never wrote anything himself nor treated directly with Tinoco, but used Ferrara de Gama as a means between them. Nor did he ever discover any part of their proceedings or pretences to her Majesty or to any of the Council.

Being often charged with these treasons by his examiners, Lopez, with blasphemous oaths and horrible execrations, denied that he had ever had speech with any person or any understanding at all of any such matter, but then confessed that he had indeed spoken of it and promised it, but all to cozen the King of Spain. But when he saw that his intent and overt fact were apparent, the vile Jew said he had confessed talking of it, but belied himself only to save himself from racking.

At the bar Lopez said little in his own defence, but cried out that Ferrara and Emanuel were made up of nothing but fraud and lying. He had intended no hurt against the Queen, but abhorred the gifts of a tyrant; he had presented the jewel to the Queen that was sent by the Spaniard; and he had no other design in what he did but to deceive the Spaniard and wipe him of his money.

All these charges being plainly and fully proved by witnesses, by the intercepted letters, and by the confession of Lopez himself to the great satisfaction of the judge, jury and hearers, he is found guilty in the highest degree and judgment passed on him with universal applause.

5th March. '*A Looking Glass for London.*'[1] *A Looking Glass for London,* a play written by Thomas Lodge and Robert Greene some years since, and played by the Lord Strange's players, is to be printed, wherein is shown the story of the prophet Jonas and the repentance of the Ninevites.

6th March. The Coronation of the French King.[2] The account of the anointing and crowning of the French King is at hand. The King, having been advised by the Princes of his blood, the Lords of his Council and other notable persons to frame himself to his anointing as other Kings his predecessors always used, would have wished the ceremony to be performed at Rheims; but in as much as the city of Rheims was still in possession of the rebels it was determined to hold the Coronation at the Church of Our Lady at Chartres. From the 17th February when the King entered the town to

[1] SR 2:645; STC 16679.   [2] SR 2:647; STC 13138.

the day of the Coronation all the preparations were being finished.

Upon the 19th the Holy Vial, preciously preserved in the Abbey of Marmonster, near Tours, was brought to the City of Chartres, conducted by the Lord of Souure, the Governor and King's Lieutenant-General in the land and Duchy of Tourraine, accompanied by four friars of the Abbey. Being arrived at Chartres, the vial was carried with great ceremony to St. Peter's Abbey, attended on by the clergy and a great number of people, the streets being hanged all the way in honour and reverence of so precious a relic.

Thither was brought the Imperial Close Crown, the Middle Crown, the Royal Sceptre, the Hand of Justice, the Cloak Royal, the Shirt, the Sandals, the Spurs, the Sword, the Tunicle, and the Dalmatic, with all the other ornaments royal, as fair and rich as might be, but they had to be newly made because the rebels had molten and defaced the others which time out of mind had been preserved in the Church of St. Denis.

Upon Saturday the 26th, at eight o'clock at night, the King came to the Church of Our Lady there to do his devotions and to be shriven.

On the 27th, about six in the morning, the King sent four Barons to fetch the Holy Vial from the Abbey of St. Peter's. The King having been escorted to the Church, the different ceremonies of the anointing were performed, after which the Bishop of Chartres, then subrogated for the Archbishop Duke of Rheims, delivered to the King the garments he was to wear above his doublet, that is the tunicle, representing a subdeacon, the dalmatick representing a deacon, and the cloak royal a priest. The King being thus clothed, the Bishop took again the plate whereupon lay the Holy Ointment, and laid some upon the palm of the King's hands, which being thus hallowed he laid them close upon his breast. After this the Bishop put on the Ring wherewith the King married the realm; and then delivered him the Sceptre Royal and the Hand of Justice.

These things ended, the Lord Chancellor, standing against the Altar, and turning to the King, with a loud voice called the twelve peers according to their dignities, beginning first with the six lay peers. Then the Bishop rose from his chair, and turned to the High Altar from which he took the Close Crown and held it over the King's head, without touching it, whereto immediately all the peers temporal and spiritual set their hands to support it, the Bishop saying *'Coronet te Deus corona gloriae,'* etc. This prayer ended the Bishop set the crown upon the King's head. All the other ceremonies being ended, Mass was celebrated, after which the King came forth arrayed in his royal garments, to be received by the people with great acclamation and signs of joy.

13th March. LOPEZ'S HEALTH.[3] Lopez hath kept his bed for the most part since his trial, and it is suspected that he practises by slow poison to prevent his execution. The trial of the other conspirators is fixed for to-morrow but the Lord Chief Justice is ill. It is much feared that if the trial be longer deferred, Lopez may die before his execution, and great dishonour and scandal ensue thereby.

14th March. LOPEZ'S ACCOMPLICES ARRAIGNED.[4] This day Emanuel Louis Tinoco and Stephen Ferrara de Gama, the Portuguese conspirators with Lopez, were brought before the Commissioners at the Guildhall to their trial. Tinoco was arraigned upon an indictment from his own confession that he had sent secret messages and intelligences to the King of Spain and his ministers of things treated in this realm in order that they might prepare their forces and direct their actions against the Queen. Further, that Christoforo de Moro, one of the King's most secret counsellors, wrote letters to de Gama touching his service to the King and that Tinoco brought them to him in London; that he came from Brussels to London to deliver a message and an embrace from the Count Fuentes, as also a credence from Andrada to Lopez for himself; that he wrote word to Lopez that Count Fuentes had sent him a message and an embrace, and was glad that he was such a good servant to the King of Spain and that he should be liberally rewarded, requiring Lopez to procure the treaty of peace between the Queen and the King to be renewed as the King desired it; meaning by 'peace' her destruction by poison; which letters he delivered to Lopez; that under a false name he had written letters to de Gama in obscure words, such as 'the bearer will tell you the price in which your pearls are held,' by which was meant the poisoning of the Queen, and by 'musk and amber' the burning of the Queen's ships; that Count Fuentes told him on oath of secrecy that he had received order from the King of Spain to give Lopez whatever he required for poisoning the Queen, and that he delivered to de Gama in London several letters written by him in obscure words in the Spanish tongue concerning it, knowing their interests, which letters were found upon him when apprehended.

These matters being declared to him through a Portuguese interpreter he affirmed them from point to point, acknowledged his faults and called for mercy. Stephen Ferrara de Gama being also indicted pleaded not guilty; but his former confessions and other proofs being produced against him, confessed all to be true; whereupon he also was convicted by judgment of the Court for imagining and compassing the death of the Queen.

26th March. ATHEISTICAL SPEECHES OF SIR W. RALEGH.[5] At Cerne Abbas in Dorsetshire, on the 21st, was held an inquiry by the High Commissioners in Causes Ecclesiastical concerning blasphemous and atheistical speeches made by some in these parts. Several witnesses declared that Sir Walter Ralegh, his brother, Mr. Carew Ralegh, and Mr. Harriott of their household, are much subjected to atheism, also one Allen, Lieutenant of Portland Castle. This Allen tore two leaves out of a Bible to dry tobacco on, and spoke as if he denied the immortality of the soul, saying, on an occasion when he was like to die and one persuaded him to make himself ready to God for his soul, that he would carry his soul up to the top of a hill, and 'Run God, run Devil, fetch it that will have it.'

Of Sir Walter and his brother, the parson of Weeke Regis, declareth that some three years past on coming to Blandford his horse was stayed and taken for a post horse by Sir Walter and Mr. Carew Ralegh. When he entreated to have his horse released to ride home to his charge, from whence he had been some time absent, to preach there next day, being Sunday, Mr. Carew Ralegh replied that he might go home when he would but his horse should preach before him.

Some months before, at Sir George Trenchard's table, at which there were also present Sir Ralph Horsey, Lord Lieutenant of the County of Dorset, Sir Walter Ralegh, Mr. Carew Ralegh, Ralph Ironside, minister of Winterbottom, and others, Mr. Carew Ralegh uttered some loose speeches

[5] Harleian MSS 6849, pp. 183–89; reprinted in G. B. Harrison, Willobie His Avisa, pp. 255–71.

and was rebuked by Sir Ralph Horsey. Whereupon turning to the minister he demanded what danger he might incur by such speeches.

To which Mr. Ironside answered, 'The wages of sin is death.' Whereunto Mr. Ralegh making light of death as common to all, sinner and righteous, the minister inferred further that 'As life which is the gift of God through Jesus Christ is life eternal, so that death which is properly the wages of sin is death eternal, both of the body and of the soul also.' 'Soul,' quoth Mr. Ralegh, 'what is that?' 'Better it were,' answered Mr. Ironside, 'that we should be careful how the soul might be saved than to be curious in finding out its essence.'

Sir Walter then requested that the minister would answer the question that had been proposed by his brother; 'I have been,' quoth he, 'a scholar some time in Oxford, I have answered under a bachelor of art, and had talk with divines, yet hitherunto in this point (to wit, what the reasonable soul of man is) have I not by any been resolved.' The dispute was then continued until Sir Walter wished that grace might be said; 'for that,' said he, 'is better than this disputation.'

30th March. GREAT STORMS.[6] This month there have been great storms of wind, that overturn trees, steeples, barns and houses; in Beaulieu forest in Worcestershire, many oaks are uprooted, and on the Thursday before Palm Sunday, more than fifteen hundred in Horton Wood. In the town of Stafford the steeple is thrown down, and a thousand pounds' worth of damage done to the roof. In Cankewood more than three thousand trees overthrown, and some fifty other steeples in Staffordshire fallen.

31st March. DEATH OF SIR JOHN BURGH.[7] Sir John Burgh, that took the great carrack, hath been slain in a duel by Mr. John Gilbert, after various letters had passed between them. Sir John first challenged his adversary to meet him at five o'clock in the morning between Charing Cross and Hyde Park, with dagger and rapier, and accompanied only by one gentleman of good quality, or alone. No treachery would be used; let him not therefore use any boyish excuses or delays as he did the last time he sent to him, or else he would pick out a time to beat him like a boy. To this Mr. Gilbert replied

[6] STOW'S ANNALS.   [7] SP DOM 248:54; DNB.

that he would fight, but that the time, place, and manner of the meeting, and the weapons belonged to the challenged.

4th April. THE QUEEN'S BOUNTY TO MR. CAMDEN.[1] The Queen, having used the services of Mr. William Camden, schoolmaster, in things wherein he has attained skill and intending to employ him again, desireth him to be settled somewhere near her, and eased of the charge of living. She hath required the Dean of Westminster to admit Mr. Camden to the table of the Dean and prebends, and allow him diet for one service; this to be granted for life. The grant she will have sent to her that she may herself present it to Mr. Camden as a token of her gratitude.

11th April. A GREAT RAINSTORM.[2] The rain hath continued very sore for more than twenty-four hours long and withal such a wind from the north as pierces the walls of houses be they never so thick.

16th April. DEATH OF THE EARL OF DERBY.[3] Ferdinando Stanley, the young Earl of Derby, that hath been sick of some strange sickness these eleven days, is dead at Latham. Outwardly his diseases were vomiting of sour or rusty matter with blood, the yellow jaundice, melting of his fat, swelling and hardness of his spleen, a vehement hiccough, and, for four days before he died, stopping of his water. All these were caused in the opinion of his physicians partly by surfeit, partly by the excessive exercise that he took for four days together in Easter week. In all the time of his sickness, which began on the 5th April and continued until he died, he often took Beza's stone and Unicorn's horn; his pulse was always good but his strength indifferent, the number of his vomits being fifty-two and of his stools twenty-nine. His death is so unaccountable that many begin to suspect that he was bewitched. In the beginning of his sickness he had strange dreams. On the 10th April, Mr. Halsall, one of his gentlemen, found in my lord's chamber about midnight an image of wax with hair in colour like his hair twisted round the belly. This image was spotted and soon after spots appeared also upon the Earl's sides and belly. Mr. Halsall hastily cast the image in the fire before it was viewed by others, thinking that by burning it he should relieve his lord of the witchcraft and burn the witch who so much tormented him; but unhappily it fell out the contrary for after the melting of the image the Earl declined.

A homely woman about the age of fifty years was found mumbling in a corner of his chamber. She seemed often to ease his lordship both of vomiting and hiccough, but it was noted that whenever he was so eased she herself was much troubled in the same way, and the matter which she vomited was like that which passed from him. But at the last, one of the doctors, spying her tempering and blessing the juice of certain herbs tumbled her pot down and rated her from the chamber. The Earl himself cried out in all his sickness that the doctors laboured in vain because he was certainly bewitched. During this last illness the Bishop of Chester and his chaplain, Mr. Lee, were with him.

18th April.   LOPEZ EXECUTION POSTPONED.[4] The execution of Lopez, Ferrara, and Tinoco, that was fixed for to-morrow morning at 9 o'clock is by the Queen's orders stayed, to the great discontent of the commissioners and the people who much expect it.

23rd April.   ST. GEORGE'S DAY.[5] There is great press of the people at Court, though very few Knights of the Garter; the Lord Treasurer being unable to go in the procession because of his foot. The Queen is reported to be very angry with Sir Anthony Shirley and Sir Nicholas Clifford for having accepted the Order of St. Michael from the French King, first because they took it without her privity, and next for that they took the whole oath, one part whereof is to defend the Mass while they live.

'THE PRAISE OF A GOOD NAME.'[6] Mr. Charles Gibbon hath written *The Praise of a Good Name* in answer to certain slanders made against him, being a collection of apothegms, epigrams, and pithy sayings in praise of a good name, and of brief essays showing the reproach of an ill name.

29th April.   OLD LADY BRANCH BURIED.[7] The Lady Helen Branch, wife first of John Minors, citizen and grocer of London, secondly of Sir John Branch, was buried, having died on the 10th of the month in the ninetieth year of her life. Her funerals were very honourably furnished, and ac-

4 SALISBURY PAPERS 4:512, 513.   6 SR 2:647; STC 11819.
5 GAWDY LETTERS, p. 81.   7 STC 12731, 23579.

companied by the Lord Mayor, many mourners, doctors, gentlemen, and kinsfolk, honourable ladies, servants and poor men. In honour of these ceremonies, an *Epicedium* is printed, being a sequence of twelve sonnets describing her life, wherein the author invoketh our living poets. For her obsequies Joshua Sylvester also hath written *Monodia,* an Elegy in commemoration of her virtuous life and godly death.

THE GROWTH OF POPERY.[8] It is said that for all the dangers of Catholics and their narrow sifting, infinite numbers run daily into the Church and are reconciled to the Catholic faith. Good men, making no account of losing their lives, hazard themselves to save men's souls; and even in the Court there are as many Masses said daily as in any country abroad.

1st May. 'INSTRUCTIONS, OBSERVATIONS AND ORDERS MILITARY.'[1] A book called *Instructions, Observations and Orders Military,* written in 1591 by Sir John Smythe, is now printed. Herein is shown the reducing of single bands of horsemen or footmen into their simple or single order of ranks from point to point, and how to draw out many troops into squadrons and battles formed, as well to march into the field as to give battle with most advantages. As for those that allege new or old fashions used by such or such nations in matters military without reasons or allowable experience to fortify and confirm them, these Sir John holdeth for vain and frivolous. To those that think a far greater number of archers are not able to encounter a smaller number of musketeers, he answereth that their opinion proceedeth of nothing else but from their lack of understanding and knowing the wonderful imperfections and failings that belong to muskets and musketeers in the field by reason of the heaviness of their pieces; nor are harquebusiers of greater advantage, being more uncertain of their aim so that if they discharge at ten, eleven, or twelve score paces distant at the archers, it will be found that in ten thousand of their shot they would not hit so many as ten archers.

2nd May. 'THE TAMING OF A SHREW.'[2] The play of *The Taming of a Shrew,* that was sundry times acted by the Earl of Pembroke's players, is to be printed.

[8] SP DOM 248:83.   *Books . . . 1594,* iii and note thereon.
[1] SR 2:647; STC 22885. See *Other*   [2] SR 2:648; STC 23667.

3rd May. GREAT FLOODS.[3] Yesterday in Sussex and Surrey there came down great water floods by reason of sudden showers of hail and rain that have fallen, which bare down houses, iron-mills, the provision of coals prepared for the mills, and carried away cattle.

SIR NICHOLAS CLIFFORD AND THE ORDER OF ST. MICHAEL.[4] Sir Nicholas Clifford, that was imprisoned in the Tower for receiving the order of St. Michael from the French King, finding that his former letters to the Queen are received with displeasure hath now sent her the order to be disposed as she considereth best, and petitioneth for enlargement.

9th May. 'THE RAPE OF LUCRECE.'[5] *The Rape of Lucrece,* a poem written by William Shakespeare, is entered, and dedicated, as was his *Venus and Adonis,* to the Earl of Southampton. In the dedication the poet toucheth upon the favours which he hath received. 'The warrant I have of your honourable disposition, not the worth of my untutored lines makes it assured of acceptance. What I have done is yours; what I have to do is yours; being part in all I have devoted yours. Were my worth greater my duty would show greater.' This poem telleth of the ravishing of the chaste Lucrece by the tyrant Tarquin, and of his everlasting banishment therefor.

14th May. GREENE'S 'FRIAR BACON.'[6] The play of *The Honourable History of Friar Bacon and Friar Bungay,* written some years before by Robert Greene and played by the Queen's players, is to be printed, containing the story of the wooing of Margaret, the keeper's daughter of Fressingfield, by Lacy, Earl of Lincoln, and of Friar Bacon's Brazen Head.

16th May. PLAYING RESUMED.[7] The Admiral's men that were forced to travel through the inhibition on playing during the plague are returned to the Rose where they play *The Jew of Malta, The Ranger's Comedy* and *Cutlack.*

17th May. 'THE JEW OF MALTA.'[8] There is entered for the printing the famous *Tragedy of the rich Jew of Malta,* written some years since by Christopher Marlowe and now being played at the Rose Theatre.

3 STOW'S ANNALS.
4 SALISBURY PAPERS 4:523.
5 SR 2:648; STC 22345.
6 SR 2:649; STC 12267.

7 HENS. DIARY 1:17; 2:163.
8 SR 2:631; STC 17412. First surviving edition 1633.

30th May. 'IDEA'S MIRROR.'[9] Mr. Michael Drayton hath sent to the press his *Idea's Mirror,* containing fifty-one sonnets or amours, dedicated to the dear child of the Muses, and his ever kind Mecenas, Mr. Anthony Cooke, Esquire.

3rd June. THE DEATH OF THE BISHOP OF LONDON.[1] This day John Aylmer, Bishop of London, died at Fulham.

THE PLAYERS OF THE ADMIRAL AND THE CHAMBERLAIN UNITE.[2] The Lord Chamberlain's players have also returned to London and join with the Admiral's men to play together at the little theatre in Newington Butts.

7th June. LOPEZ, TINOCO AND FERRARA EXECUTED.[3] This day Roderick Lopez, with the two other Portuguese, was executed. They were conveyed from the Tower of London by the Lieutenant to the Old Swan, and thence by water to Westminster, where being brought before the King's Bench Bar, the Lieutenant was called to bring in his prisoners, which he then delivered and was discharged of them.

Then it was declared to them by the Court how they had been charged with high treason against the Queen, had been tried, found guilty, and had received judgment; wherefore it was demanded of them what they could say for themselves that they should not suffer death accordingly. One of the Portuguese began in his own language to tell a long tale, but was willed to be short, to which he answered that it could not be done without circumstances. Whereupon he was willed to hold his peace. The second answered by a writing in his own language, which being read by an interpreter, the Attorney General bade stay for it was not true. Lopez in English made his submission, affirming that he never thought harm to her Majesty.

Then the Marshal of the King's Bench was called and charged with the prisoners to convey them to the prison of the King's Bench and there to deliver them to the Sheriffs of London with a writ to see them executed. So they were conveyed by water from Westminster to the Bishop of Winchester's stairs in Southwark, from thence to the King's Bench, there laid upon hurdles and conveyed to the Sheriff of London over the bridge, up to Leadenhall, and so to Tyburn.

At the gallows Lopez declared that he loved the Queen as

9 SR 2:648; STC 7203.
1 STOW'S ANNALS.
2 HENS. DIARY 1:17.

3 STOW'S ANNALS; CAMDEN'S ELIZA-
BETH.

well as he loved Jesus Christ, which coming from a man of
the Jewish profession moved no small laughter in the
standers-by.

18th June. LYLY'S 'MOTHER BOMBY.'[4] *Mother Bomby,* a
play formerly written by Mr. John Lyly, and sundry times
played by the Children of Paul's, is entered for printing.

19th June. 'THE TRUE TRAGEDY OF RICHARD THE THIRD.'[5]
The play of *The True Tragedy of Richard the Third,* that
used to be played by the Queen's players, is to be printed;
wherein is shown the death of Edward the Fourth, with the
smothering of the two young Princes in the Tower; the
lamentable end of Shore's wife, an example for all wicked
women; and lastly the conjunction and joining of the two
noble houses of Lancaster and York.

21st June. THE SPANIARDS AT BREST.[6] From the west Sir
Walter Ralegh hath received trustworthy intelligence of the
strength of the Spanish Fleet and its readiness to sail. It
seemeth likely that some surprise is intended, for the carpenters and all others about the fleet work on the Sabbath
Day, which is confirmed by the hugeness of the ships, that
will carry many soldiers, since smaller vessels are far fitter
for the coast of Brittany. At Brest, the Spaniards, having
received no impediment, have finished the fortification of
Old Croyzon, within the port, and, the better to command
the haven, have also built a strong place at the very entrance.
Now that Blavet and Belle Isle are theirs, there will be no
entrance for the Queen's fleet. Their ships are huge, eight
being between 800 and 1000 tons, two others of good burden,
and divers galleys, full filled with soldiers.

22nd June. THE CHAMBERLAIN'S BREAK WITH THE AD-
MIRAL'S.[7] The Chamberlain's men have broken with the Ad-
miral's and go to play at James Burbage's house, the Theatre,
in Shoreditch. Their chief players now are Richard Burbage,
Will Kemp, the Clown, William Shakespeare, Thomas Pope,
John Heminges, Augustine Phillips and George Bryan. The
Admiral's, with Edward Alleyn, are returned to the Rose,
where they played this week *Bellendon* (twice), *Cutlack, The*

[4] SR 2:654; STC 17084.
[5] SR 2:655; STC 21009.
[6] SALISBURY PAPERS 4:552.

[7] HENS. DIARY 1:17; J. Tucker Mur-
ray, *English Dramatic Companies*
1:88 *et seq.*

Ranger's Comedy, The Massacre at Paris; with Alleyn go John Singer, Richard Jones, Thomas Towne, Martin Slaughter, Edward Juby, Thomas Dutton and James Dunstan.

26th June. THE FUNERAL OF THE BISHOP OF LONDON.[8] This day John Aylmer, Bishop of London, was solemnly interred in his cathedral church of St. Paul before St. Thomas' Chapel.

Bishop Aylmer was a man but mean of stature, yet in his youth very valiant, which he forgot not in his age. No bishop was more persecuted and taunted by the Puritans than he was by libels, by scoffs, by open railing and privy backbiting. The story is well known of what passed between him and one Mr. Madox, a Puritan; for when the bishop had reproved him about some matter and he answered somewhat untowardly and overthwartly, the bishop (as he was ingenious ever) said unto him, 'Thy very name expresseth thy nature, for *Madox* is thy name, and thou art as mad a beast as ever I talked with.' The other not long to seek of an answer, 'By your favour, sir,' said he, 'your deeds answer your name righter than mine; for your name is *Elmar,* and you have *marred* all the *elms* in Fulham by lopping them.' He used for recreation to bowl in a garden; and Martin Marprelate thence takes this taunting scoff, that the bishop would cry, 'Rub, rub, rub,' to his bowl, and when it was gone too far, say, 'the devil go with it'; and then, saith Martin, the bishop would follow.

When there was talk of dangers and rumours of war and invasion, then he was commonly chosen to preach in the Court, and he would do it in so cheerful a fashion as not only showed he had courage, but would put courage in others. And for this the Queen would much commend him; yet would she not remove him. It is noted as an ill fortune of his to have died Bishop of London, which eight before him in one hundred have not done, but been either preferred or deprived.

12th July. SIDNEY SUSSEX COLLEGE IN CAMBRIDGE FOUNDED.[1] A licence is granted to the Earl of Kent and Sir John Harington, the executors of Frances, Countess of Sussex, to erect a college, to be called Sidney Sussex College in Cambridge University, to consist of a master, ten fellows, and twenty scholars.

[8] STOW'S ANNALS; NUGAE ANTIQUAE.   [1] SP DOM 249:26.

15th July. CRUELTY IN PORTUGAL.[2] Certain merchants coming from Lisbon report that recently the chief Commander of the galleys invited three score and upwards of the chiefest of the city of Lisbon to a banquet aboard the galleys. After much feasting and triumph, having tricked them to sport down the river, he showed them a commandment he had received from the King to execute them all; which was immediately carried out. They were all beheaded; their bodies being taken back to Lisbon and their heads carried with speed to the King of Spain. The cause alleged for this murder is that letters were intercepted wherein they had intelligence with England.

16th July. SOLDIERS FOR BREST.[3] Three thousand soldiers and 50 pioneers are to be sent into Brittany to seize Brest, where the King of Spain is making fortifications. The pioneers are to be raised by Sir W. Ralegh in Cornwall and ready to embark at Plymouth on 5th August.

20th July. SPANISH PREPARATIONS.[4] Ralegh reporteth that the recent news of the Spanish preparations seem to be confirmed, for within the last week three great Spanish men-of-war have given chase to an English ship and her two prizes, driving them even to the very mouth of Dartmouth. All the Newfoundland men are like to be taken by them if they be not speedily driven from the coast, for the Newfoundland fleet is expected at the beginning of August, above 100 sail. If these are lost it will be the greatest blow ever given to England.

21st July. CAPTAIN DAWTRY'S OFFER TO LEAD AN IRISH REGIMENT.[5] A certain Captain Dawtry, one on whom an Irish pension has been conferred, hath written to Sir Robert Cecil asking to be entrusted to fetch a regiment of 1500 or 2000 trained soldiers of Irish birth out of Ireland to serve the Queen in the expedition to Brittany, which will bring commodity to her and her whole dominions. She will leave at home, saith he, many of her people of England to reserve their lives until further necessity. She will disarm her ill disposed subjects of Ireland whose unnatural mutinies and re-

[2] SALISBURY PAPERS 4:562.
[3] SP DOM 249:29.
[4] SALISBURY PAPERS 4:566.
[5] SALISBURY PAPERS 4:566. J. Dawtrey, *The Falstaff Saga*, 1927, claimed Dawtry as the original of Falstaff. The gallant Captain (who

also belonged to the same circles in Dublin as Edmund Spenser) had many of Falstaff's characteristics; he was moreover 'very large and unwieldy,' and a difficult object to move when wounded.

bellions are supported by these trained soldiers. They will win more spoil on the enemy than thrice as many soldiers of any other nation, for there are no better soldiers on earth than they, either for the use of their weapons or the strength of their bodies and minds, being such seasoned men of war that they can endure all fortunes, and keep their health when others with a little extremity will lie by the wall. Lastly, if they live, the Queen is like to be well served by them; if they die, she will be better served, for it is a pity they should ever go back again into their own country so long as she hath any employment for soldiers. If he may have this charge and lay down his opinion of the Captains, he will answer for their true and faithful behaviour.

25th July. THE EARL OF ESSEX NOT ALLOWED TO GO TO BREST.[6] The expedition to Brest being finally resolved, the Earl of Essex is eager to go, but the Queen using very gentle words to him says that his desire to be in action and give further proof of his valour and prowess is to be liked and highly commended; but she loveth him and her realm too much to hazard his person in any lesser action than that which shall import her crown and state, and therefore willeth him to be content, giving him a warrant for £4000 and saying, 'Look to thyself, good Essex, and be wise to help thyself, without giving thy enemies advantage; and my hand shall be readier to help thee than any other.'

26th July. A JESUIT EXECUTED AT DURHAM.[7] John Boste, a Jesuit, was executed for high treason at Durham on the 24th. When he was taken from prison towards the place of execution, more than three hundred ladies and women of good position, all with black hoods, set out to follow him, and being asked where they were going, they answered, 'To accompany that gentleman, that servant of God, to his death, as the Maries did Christ.' A minister offered to dispute with them by the way, but a horseman came up and pushed him away, crying, 'Begone, knave, Mr. Boste has shown himself a true gentleman and a true man.'

Having come to the scaffold, he kissed the ladder and mounting the first step, said, '*Angelus ad Mariam dixit: Ave gratia plena: Dominus tecum. Benedicta tu in mulieribus.*' On the second, '*Verbum caro factum est, et habitavit in nobis,*'

[6] BIRCH'S MEMOIRS 1:181.   [7] CATH. REC. SOC. 5:286.

at the third, *'Ecce ancilla Domini, fiat mihi secundum verbum tuum.'* Turning to the people, as he began to speak he was told that he came not to preach but to die. 'At least,' quoth he, 'you will allow me to thank these ladies and gentlemen who have done me the honour and kindness to accompany me to-day. Although I am now to be deprived of life, my blood withal and death and innocence shall preach in the hearts of those whom God will call and gather to His Holy Catholic Church. My head and quarters will preach every day on your gates and walls the truth of the Catholic Faith.'

Then he placed himself in prayer for a short while, and, as it were awakening, asked leave to recite the 114th Psalm, *'Dilexi quoniam,'* then returning thanks to God, he ended by saying that God had given him grace to die for the Catholic Roman Church, 'outside of which,' he declared, 'believe me, brethren (for this is not the time to dissemble nor to lie), it is impossible to enter unto the Kingdom of Heaven.'

1st August. A PROCLAMATION CONCERNING PRIZES.[1] A proclamation is issued against those that disorderly enter with ships brought as prizes into any haven, and secretly buy or convey away the goods before they can be customed and allowed as lawful prizes. For the reformation of this frequent abuse, all who go aboard any prizes, or buy, bargain, or receive any goods from the prizes, or from any of the company, shall not only forfeit his goods, but he and the seller be committed to prison, there to remain until order shall be given from the Lords of the Privy Council for their release. And for the better preventing of these disorders, it is commanded that immediately upon the coming in of any prizes from the seas, some of the officers of the Custom House of the port shall go aboard, and remain aboard quietly without any interruption or resistance of the captain, owner, master or mariners until the ship be discharged.

8th August. PLATT'S 'JEWEL HOUSE OF NATURE.'[2] *The Jewel House of Art and Nature,* brought together by Mr. Hugh Platt, of Lincoln's Inn, is to be printed. In the first book are set down more than a hundred new and conceited experiments, such as to write a letter secretly, to walk safely upon a high scaffold without any danger of falling, to fetch out any stain, the art of memory, one candle to make as great a light as two or three, to close the chops of green timber, to speak by signs only, to refresh the colours of old oil pictures, and many others. To prevent drunkenness, drink a good large draught of salad oil, for that will float upon the wine which you shall drink and suppress the spirits from ascending into the brain.

The second book entreateth of sundry new sorts of soil or marl for the better manuring of pasture or arable ground; the third divers chemical conclusions concerning the art of distillation; the fourth the art of casting and moulding; the last part is an offer of certain new inventions which the author will disclose upon reasonable consideration, being a new kind of fire in the form of balls made partly of seacoal; a vessel of wood to brew in; a bolting hutch; a portable pump; a wholesome, lasting and fresh victual for the navy; a speedy way for the inning of any breach; a light garment yet sufficient against all rainy weather; and a new conceit in peter works.

19th August. CAPTAIN GLEMHAM'S EXPLOITS IN THE LE-VANT SEAS.[3] News is published of all that befell Captain Edward Glemham since his departure from London in February 1593, whence he sailed with his ship the *Galleon Constance* to meet the rest of his company at Dartmouth. So many were the storms in the spring of last year that not until the 17th of April did he leave the English coast, being separated three days later from the others who believed him to have been cast away in the Gulf. Thence they made their way to Santa Cruz where, finding many other English ships, they refreshed themselves, and were joined by the *Tiger* and the *Elizabeth of Plymouth,* two of their company.

After meeting with several of the enemy it was concluded at length that they should make for Algiers. Here the King entertained them in the best manner, and to show the General what extraordinary favour he could, he came aboard to see the ship. Whereon the General prepared a sumptuous banquet, for which he would not stay, but taking a small repast of such confections as the General had brought for his store at sea he departed, being presented with a cup of silver, double gilt, a fair quilt of damask with his arms embroidered and a purse, richly wrought, with fifty double pistolets. All of which the King thankfully received, and at the General's departure gave him under his hand and seal free liberty to sell, exchange,

[3] SR 2:657; STC 20572. See *31 Mar* 1591 and *17 May* 1592.

carry over and recarry at his pleasure all such goods as he or any of his should bring for his port, without any manner of let or disturbance.

The company then set sail from Algiers to attempt some prize, but though they fought very valiantly with several of the enemy all escaped them, and at length for lack of victual they were obliged to put back to Algiers where they found that the King had seized the ship *Examiner* of their consort, imprisoning the Captain and owner and the company. Whereupon the General immediately went to the King demanding the cause of this vile dealing with his company; but he subtlely smiling on the General gave him good speeches and mused on his choler, saying that he wondered to hear him speak so rashly and unadvisedly to him being in so great authority. After some further parley, the General seeing he could have no answer of his business to his content, departed in fury without bidding farewell but leaving him to the devil whom they served. The next day the King sent to have the General's sails taken ashore. Upon hearing thereof the General commanded his companies that were ashore to repair on board, caused his ship to be provided, his nettings laced, and his ordnance all out, resolutely determined to sink there. But at length a composition was offered and the Englishmen and Flemings that were in prison were released.

But soon afterward other misfortune befell them. While the men were still in prison one of the chiefest men of the French leaguer who was consul in that place entered the prison where they were and began to abuse in most opprobrious terms the name of the Queen. Thereafter two of the Englishmen chanced to meet this Frenchman, and remembering his words, for lack of a weapon began to beat him with their fists, and the quarrel was taken up by others.

When the French Consul heard of it, he went immediately to the King with his complaint, who sent for the General. But he being advertised of the truth by one of his followers made answer that if the quarrel were such as was reported, he would kill him with his own hands that should not offer with his life to maintain the honour of his Mistress, whose match the world afforded not. After further talk the Consul offered his handkerchief to the General's face who was so moved thereat that he struck him over the face with his fist, and craved of the King to grant him the combat against the Consul. But the King, who had received abundance of gold from the Frenchman would not allow it and dismissed them for that night.

About eight o'clock the next morning the King sent for the General and the men who had begun the brawl, and caused the men to receive the bastinado and the General to be committed prisoner, threatening that if he did not become friends with the Consul, he should lose his hand. The General dreading naught his threats refused, but his company came to him and on their knees besought him to tender both his own estate and theirs, for on his welfare depended all their goods. So likewise his especial friend Mr. Benedick Winter pleaded with him, to whom he yielded. Then being sent for by the King he made friends with the Consul who ever afterward showed wonderful great kindness and pleasure to the General and all his company. And so, after many troubles, on the first of February, 1594 they departed the road towards the bottom of the Straits to seek their better fortunes: and from that time they engaged many times with enemy but without success until the 8th of May, when they met with the London fleet by whom news was brought of Captain Glemham's actions.

20*th August.* THE LADY BRIDGET MANNERS.[4] The Queen is much incensed at hearing of the marriage of the Lady Bridget Manners, one of her favourite ladies-in-waiting, that took place in the country without her consent. Two months since, the Countess of Rutland, the Lady's mother, concluded with the executors of Mr. Tyrwhitt for the wardship of his young son, and in July wrote asking that her Majesty would allow her daughter to visit her, whom she had not seen these five years. The Queen having given her consent, the Lady Bridget returned home to her mother and in a short while after is wedded to Mr. Tyrwhitt. Now that the marriage is known, the Queen is especially enraged with the Countess, refusing to believe that she could be ignorant of it, for the marriage was in her own house, and by her own chaplain, nor will she believe that the Lady Bridget is so undutiful a daughter to have adventured so great a breach of duty without her mother's acquaintance and consent had first been obtained. Mr. Tyrwhitt and his wife are sent to London, the former to be committed to prison, the latter, by the Queen's favour, not imprisoned but put in custody of some lady.

A PLOT TO KILL THE QUEEN.[5] Captain Edmund Yorke, a prisoner, son of Sir Edmund Yorke, under examination hath

4 *Rutland MSS* 1:322. See *20th Nov*   5 SP DOM 249:98.
1592.

confessed that he was persuaded by Father Holt to come over on the Queen's pardon, and to live in the Court, having the money due to his uncle sent for his maintenance and an assurance on oath of 40,000 crowns with present payment guaranteed by Stephen de Ibarra the Secretary of the King of Spain if he performed the required service of killing the Queen, by his own agents or by others. At the conference held thereon, Sir William Stanley and others were present; some spoke of a poisoned arrow or rapier, or a dagger as she walked in the garden. He was to serve the Earl of Essex; his fellows, Williams and Young, the Lord Chamberlain. They swore on the Sacrament to do it and were absolved by Father Holt.

He declares that one Moody has come, or soon will, to kill the Queen, when the crown will be offered to the Earl of Derby with the King of Spain's assistance. If their plot should fail they are to move some rebellion in the Earl of Derby's name, though he were not privy to it.

SUITORS AT COURT TO BE RESTRAINED.[6] The Council will restrain the inordinate repair of multitudes of suitors coming to the Court with petitions and complaints to the Queen or the Privy Council, which for the most part are either private, unmeet to be preferred to her or for a Council of State to deal in, or such as may be decided in some of the Courts of Justice. Any suitor, intending to exhibit complaint or petition, must first acquaint one of the Masters of Requests, if any be in Court; who, with one of the Clerks of the Council, upon view and consideration, shall indorse the substance of the matter with their opinions subscribed with their hands. All suitors whose causes are neither meet to be preferred to the Queen nor heard by the Privy Council nor of any other ordinary Court of Justice or Equity shall depart and not remain about the Court upon pain of imprisonment. The Master of Requests also to deliver the names of the parties that be rejected to the Porter that he may know whom to exclude.

21st August.   YORKE'S CONFESSION.[7] Yorke adds to his former confession that when he was first moved to perform the service he was promised 40,000 crowns, and told that many at Court would be glad and were looking for it. Having agreed that if they would give him a resolute man to execute the

6 PROCLAMATIONS 327.   7 SP DOM 249:103.

part, he was promised Richard Williams, cousin to that Throckmorton who was executed in 1585. He had then asked time to consider; they replied that they made him the offer as an honour and bade him not undertake it unless he were resolved. Williams has sworn to kill the Queen, he to aid him. Moody and two others are also coming over to kill her; and, if the English should fail, a Walloon and a Burgundian are to be employed.

24th August. FURTHER CONFESSIONS.[8] Captain Edmund Yorke adds to his former confessions that he and Williams had often wished the deed were done and they on their horses again, for they were to buy the best they could get. They resolved that when one drew sword, the other would do the same, to do the act if the other were hindered. It was plotted that Sir William Stanley should deny them a passport and that the governor of Burborow should stay them. Then Williams should seem to be in want and he would write for a pardon. Williams prevented his coming over without a passport lest he might damn himself, having taken the Sacrament to kill the Queen, by being taken and forced to confess it. Henry Young, one of the conspirators, examined at the same time declared that at Calais Yorke said he wondered at any man's wronging his friends for a little torture, and that he was armed for any torture. He said if they were secret they might soon ride in London streets with foot-cloths of cloth of silver. Williams declared that he would die rather than betray his friends, and if he said anything when on the rack would deny all again when freed from it.

27th August. WILLIAMS' CONFESSION.[9] Richard Williams being examined hath confessed that he was sent by Father Holt and Sir William Stanley to kill the Queen, with promise of great reward, and that he received the Sacrament thereon. Later he acknowledged his confession before the Earl of Essex, declaring that he will avow it to his death, even before Yorke's face.

28th August. YORKE AND WILLIAMS CONFRONTED.[10] Yorke and Williams being confronted together before the Commissioners in the Tower, Yorke swears that they took the Sacrament to kill the Queen and that Williams had wished

8 SP DOM 249:114.   10 SP DOM 249:125.
9 SP DOM 249:117.

his sword in her belly. Williams denying this, Yorke tells him he denies it on account of his oath, but it was unlawfully taken and therefore may be broken.

AN ORDER AT COURT.[11] A very strait commandment from the Queen is given by the Lord Chamberlain that no man shall come into her presence or attend upon her wearing any long cloak beneath the knee: which order comes in a good hour for tailors, mercers, and drapers, when all men are now wearing long cloaks.

THE RETURN OF THE EARL OF CUMBERLAND'S SHIPS.[12] The three ships sent out at the charges of the Earl of Cumberland and his friends, the *Royal Exchange* as Admiral wherein Mr. George Cave was Captain, the *Mayflower* under conduct of William Anthony, and the *Sampson* under Nicholas Downton, have returned to Portsmouth, having set out from Plymouth at the latter end of last year.

They report that on 13th June they met with a mighty carrack of the East Indies called *Las Cinque Llagas,* or *The Five Wounds.* The *Mayflower* was in fight with her before night, and soon after the *Sampson,* never ceasing to ply her with their great ordnance until midnight when the Admiral came up and Captain Cave wished them to stay till morning, when both should give three bouts with their great ordnance and then clap her aboard.

At ten o'clock the next morning the Admiral laid her aboard in the mid-ship, the *Mayflower* coming up in the quarter, as it should seem, to be at the stern of the Admiral on the larboard side; but her Captain was slain and the ship fell to the stern of the out-licar of the carrack which, being a piece of timber, so wounded her foresail that her men said they could come no more to fight. The *Sampson* went aboard on the bow, but not having room enough her quarter lay on the *Exchange's* bow, her bow on the carrack's bow. The *Exchange* also at her first coming up had her Captain shot through both legs, so that he was not able to do his office and in his absence had not any that would undertake to lead out her company to enter the carrack's side. Captain Downton also had been wounded the night before, but his men were led by Captain Grant; but his forces being small and not manfully backed by the *Exchange's* men, the enemy became bolder than he would have been,

[11] GAWDY LETTERS, p. 90.   [12] HAKLUYT 5:69. 'Benjamin is Gum.'

slew six and wounded many more, so that the rest returned on board and would not renew the assault.

The Portugals, thus encouraged by the slack working of our men, had barricades made where they might stand without any danger of our shot, and plied our men with fire so that most of them were burnt in some place or other, and while our men were putting out the fire, they kept on assailing them with small shot or darts. When the *Sampson's* men were not able to enter they plied their great ordnance, mounted as high as they could, and by shooting a piece out of the forecastle, they fired a mat on the carrack's keal, which ran from thence to the mat on the bowsprit, and from the mat up to the wood of the bowsprit, and thence to the top sail yard, which made the Portugals to stagger and to make show of parle. But they that had the charge encouraged them that it might easily be put out, so they stood again stiffly to the defence.

Anon the fire grew so strong that Captain Downton seeing it was beyond all help, desired to be off, but had little hope of saving his ship unlit, until by the burning asunder of the sprit sail yard with the ropes and sail, whereby they were fast entangled to the carrack, she fell apart. The *Exchange* also being further off from the fire was easier clear and fell off from abaft. Soon the fire crept into the forecastle of the carrack where was store of Benjamin and other combustible matter which flamed and ran all over the ship so that the Portugals leapt over in great numbers. Then Captain Downton sent Captain Grant with the boat with leave to use his own discretion in saving of them. So he brought aboard two gentlemen, one an old man called Nuno Velis Pereira, who had been governor of Mocambique and Cefala in 1582; three of the inferior sort were also saved in the boat. The rest which were taken by the other boats were set ashore in the Isles of Flores.

The carrack burnt all that day and the night, but next morning her powder which was lowest, being 60 barrels, blew her asunder. Some said she was bigger than the *Madre de Dios,* some that she was less; but though much undermasted and undersailed yet she went well.

On the 30th June after long traversing the seas another mighty carrack was sighted which some of the company took to be the *San Philip,* the Admiral of Spain, but next day fetching up with her they found her indeed to be a carrack, which after a few shot was summoned to yield, but they stood stoutly to their defence and utterly refused. Whereupon seeing that no good could be done without boarding her, Captain Downton consulted what course should be taken in her boarding, but partly because the chief captains had been slain or wounded in the former conflict, and because of the murmuring of some disordered and cowardly companions, his purpose was crossed, and the carrack escaped.

After waiting about Corvo and Flores for some West Indian purchase, but being disappointed of their expectation, and victuals growing short, they returned for England.

29th August.   SIR JOHN NORRIS DELAYED.[13] Sir John Norris who is not yet embarked for Brittany complaineth from Portsmouth that his men are continuing to run away. He desires that those counties which have so little care for the furtherance of the Queen's service, as a punishment may be commanded to send as many others in the place of those missing, especially Norfolk and Suffolk. He feareth that the seamen do not well intend the service for the fort by Brest, and asketh that any pinnaces sent after them may have special charge to have greater regard to that service than to anything else, otherwise they will seek the liberty of the sea; for he hath no authority but by bare advice to let them know what is fit for them to do, which is left to their discretion to follow.

3rd September.   'WILLOBIE HIS AVISA.'[1] A certain book entitled *Willobie His Avisa* is entered, setting out the triumphs of Avisa, a chaste British dame, over the many suitors who attempted her charity. It is believed that under guise of these suitors certain great ones are attacked, especially a young man, called 'Henrico Willobego,' with his familiar friend 'W. S.,' an old player.

'THE SEAMAN'S SECRETS.'[2] Captain John Davis hath written a book of navigation called *The Seaman's Secrets,* which he dedicates to the Lord Admiral, defending himself against the charges written by Mr. Richard Cavendish with his dying hand that he was the cause of his overthrow, and ran from him. He declares that his ship *The Desire,* separated by stress of weather and forced to seek a harbour to repair his most miserable wants, being without boats, oars, sails, cables, cordage, victuals, or health of the company sufficient for the attempt to find the North-West Passage, upon which he had set out.

[13] SP DOM 249:128.   [2] SR 2:659; STC 6369.
[1] SR 2:659; STC 25755.

In his searches for the North-West Passages where navigation must be executed in most exquisite sort, he has been enforced to search all possible means required in sailing which are here gathered in his treatise.

His book is divided into two parts; in the first are displayed the terms of the art of navigation, the movement of the moon, the tides, the use of the compass, the cross-staff and the chart; in the second are taught the nature and necessary use of the globe, with the circles, zones, climates and other distinctions, the perfect use of sailing, also the use of the cross-staff, the quadrant, and the astrolabe.

5th September. THE SCOTTISH KING'S SON BAPTISED.[3] The infant son of the King of Scotland was on 30th August baptised at Stirling, after some delays caused by the lateness of the English Ambassador in coming. The Earl of Cumberland was first chosen for this service, and prepared himself very richly with an honourable convoy of noblemen and gentlemen of renown, but falling sick, the Earl of Sussex was sent in his place; so it fell out that through the sickness of one nobleman and the hasty preparations of the other, the day for the baptism had constantly to be postponed.

During the time of their stay the King entertained the Ambassadors with banqueting and revelling, and, to make this occasion the more magnificent, he committed the charge of the revels to the Lord of Lendore and Mr. William Fowler, that by reason of their travels were much skilled in such things. Having consented together they concluded that the exercises should be divided into field pastimes, with martial and heroical exploits, and household with rare shows and singular inventions. At the first show, three Christians (presented by the King, the Earl of Mar, and Thomas Erskine, Esquire) were followed by three Turks and then by three Amazons, all having pages riding on their led horses, each bearing his master's *impresa* or device. The King's device was a lion's head with open eyes, which signified fortitude and vigilance. All having solemnly entered, they ran three courses at the ring and glove, and the prize was given to the Duke of Lennox.

When at last all the Ambassadors had reached Stirling the baptism was performed. The Chapel Royal was richly hung with a royal seat of state for the King, and at his right hand a fair wide chair over which was set the arms of the King of France; next to him sat the Ambassador of England, and after

him, and also on the King's left hand, the other Ambassadors.
The King having taken his seat, the Ambassadors were led into
the presence of the infant Prince who was carried with great
ceremony into the Chapel. All being seated, Mr. Patrick Gal-
loway, one of the King's preachers in ordinary, went up to
the pulpit, and entreated upon the text of the 21st of Genesis.
This done, the Bishop of Aberdeen stood up in his seat and
explained the Sacrament of baptism, first in the vulgar tongue,
next in Latin, that all might understand. Then the provost and
the prebends of the Chapel sang the 21st Psalm. Next the
Prince was baptised, being named 'Frederick Henry, Henry
Frederick.' When all were again seated the Bishop went up
into the pulpit where he delivered in verse a praise and commendation of the Prince, and then, turning the rest of his Latin
oration into prose, he addressed the Ambassadors, beginning
with the English Ambassador and so to the rest, making men-
tion of the chronology of each of their princes, and reciting
the proximity and nearness of blood they had with the King.
In conclusion, when the blessing had been given, Lyon King of
Arms cried with a loud voice, 'God save Frederick Henry,
Henry Frederick, by the Grace of God, Prince of Scotland.'

The Prince was then carried into the King's Hall where he
was dubbed Knight by his father, and proclaimed by Lyon
King of Arms, Knight and Baron of Renfrew, Lord of the
Isles, Earl of Garrick, Duke of Rosay, Prince and Great Steward of Scotland.

That night was held a very magnificent banquet, at which,
after the guests had refreshed themselves at the first service,
there entered a blackamoor, very richly attired, drawing as it
seemed, a triumphal chariot wherein stood Ceres, Fecundity,
Faith, Concord, Liberality, and Perseverance, set round a
table richly set out. This chariot should indeed have been
drawn by a lion, but because his presence might have brought
some fear to the nearest, or the sight of the lights and torches
might have moved his tameness, it was thought best to supply
the blackamoor in his place.

The chariot being withdrawn, a most sumptuous ship entered, her keel 18 ft. long, in breadth 8 foot, and to the top of
her highest flag 40 feet, and the motion so artificially devised
that none could perceive what brought her in. Neptune sat in
the forestern, with Thetis and Triton, and round about were all
kinds of marine people, such as the sirens, and within, mariners and musicians, besides Arion with his harp. By this device

was set forth the King's voyage into Norway to fetch his Queen when he was detained by the devices of witches; and as Neptune had then brought them safely home, so now he brought them such gifts as the sea affords to adorn this festival.

After these revels were ended the King and the Ambassadors went to another Hall where for the collation a most rare, sumptuous and prince-like dessert of sugar had been prepared, whence, after leave-taking and good-nights, the company departed about three o'clock in the morning.

8th September. GILES FLETCHER'S 'LICIA.'[4] *Licia or Poems of Love, in honour of the admirable and singular virtues of his Lady, to the imitation of the best Latin poets, and others,* by Mr. Giles Fletcher, is sent to the press, being dedicated to the Lady Mollineux, wife of Sir Richard Mollineux, to whom he writeth that though his thoughts and some reasons draw him rather to deal in causes of greater weight, yet the present jar of this disagreeing age drives him into a fit so melancholy that he has leisure only to grow passionate. There are fifty-two sonnets in honour of Licia, and other poems, one being *The Rising to the Crown of Richard the Third,* spoken with his own mouth, and imitated from *Shore's Wife* and *Rosamond.*

9th September. THE COUNTESS OF RUTLAND.[5] The Queen is not a little offended, thinking herself undutifully handled, because the Countess of Rutland neither answers nor obeys her command to send the Lady Bridget to London. The Lord Hunsdon hath therefore written in the Queen's name commanding the Lady to be sent up forthwith, and demanding why the order has not been obeyed hitherto.

10th September. NEWS FROM BREST.[6] Sir John Norris landed with new forces at Pempole on the 1st of the month, where he received letters from the Marshal D'Aumont and Sir Thomas Baskerville showing in what terms they lay outside Morlaix, expecting every day to be attacked by the Duke Mercury. But when the Duke Mercury heard of the coming of Sir John, he not only refrained from coming to the succour of Morlaix but withdrew his forces further away, so that those in the Castle yielded themselves when they heard of it.

4 STC 11055.   6 SR 2:665; STC 18654.
5 *Rutland MSS* 1:323. See *20th Aug.*

11th September. SIR THOMAS WILKES TO BE SENT TO THE ARCHDUKE.[7] The Queen wisheth to expostulate with the King of Spain for his barbarous action in contriving and furthering the foul and dangerous practices of Lopez and the others, and to force him either to avow it or else to cause him to correct those that were the instruments in these plots, such as Christofero de Moro, the Count Fuentes, and Ibarra. She is resolved therefore to send Sir Thomas Wilkes, her Secretary, to the Archduke Ernest, Governor in the Low Countries for the King of Spain, to open the matter and the proofs. A special messenger is now sent requiring safe conduct for the Secretary's coming and going.

18th September. THE WAR IN BRITTANY.[8] The news from Brittany is that after the taking of Morlaix Sir John Norris stayed ten days while the Marshal raised money to satisfy the men. Then Monsieur de Lyseot with some harquebusiers, aided by Sir Martin Frobisher and 400 men from the English ships, was sent forward to block up the fort of Croyzon by Brest.

The same night the Marshal with 400 French and Sir John with as many English marched to Quimpar-Corantin, and suddenly surprised the suburbs, entering them with small resistance. The town was willing to yield but the garrison would not allow them. So Sir John Norris, being still intent on some exploit against the Spaniards at the fort of Croyzon, left the town invested by the Marshal, and three English regiments; himself with one regiment and his own company of horse marched towards Croyzon and lodged there that night. He is now preparing approaches and platforms for the artillery, but much hindered by the badness of the weather.

A DUTCH MILL.[9] Two Dutchmen, Jacob Senoy and George Frise of Utrecht in Holland, have lately brought with them a certain mill which they have invented that will in very short time grind a greater quantity of corn than will be believed but by such as see the trial of it. These men are recommended to the Lord Mayor and Aldermen for albeit their mill most properly serveth for a camp or besieged city in time of distress yet it may serve the City of good purpose in times of frost when the mills go not. If the mill may be had at a reasonable rate it will be both a good monument to lay up in the Bridgehouse

[7] SALISBURY PAPERS 5:12, 13.   [9] *Remembrancia* 2:15.
[8] As for *10th Sept.*

against time of need and also for use as a pattern whereby to frame others by it.

30th September. THE BAD WEATHER AND THE PRICE OF GRAIN.[10] This summer, in May, there fell many great showers of rain, but much more in June and July; for it has commonly rained every day or night till St. James' Day. Notwithstanding there followed in August a fair harvest, but in September fell great rains, which raised high waters and bare down bridges at Cambridge, Ware, and other places. The price of grain grows to be such that a bushel of rye is sold for 5s., a bushel of wheat for six, seven and even eight shillings; this dearth according to common opinion, is caused more by means of over-much transporting by the merchants for their private gain than through the unseasonableness of the weather.

3rd October. INMATES TO BE REMOVED.[1] Great inconveniences grow daily more and more by the number of inmates, and by the erecting of new tenements within the City of London, Westminster and the suburbs, which are a great cause of infection by reason of the multitude of poor people that inhabit them, many dwelling together in one small house. There was a statute made in the last Parliament for the reformation of these inconveniences and especially for the avoiding of inmates. Now, seeing that the greatest number of those dead of the late infection are out of those houses that were pestered with inmates, no new persons shall be admitted to these tenements in the room of those deceased.

6th October. LE ROY'S 'OF THE INTERCHANGEABLE COURSE OF THINGS.'[2] Mr. Robert Ashley hath translated into English and dedicated to Sir John Puckering, the Lord Keeper, a book entitled *Of the Interchangeable Course or Variety of Things*, first written in French by Louis le Roy. Herein are surveyed the variety of tongues and arts, the state of arms, and learning, of religion in former ages compared with the present, concluding in the last chapter that the truth has not yet been thoroughly discovered, neither all knowledge forestalled by our forerunners. The learned therefore should add by their own inventions what is wanting in the sciences, doing for posterity that which Antiquity did for us, to the end that learning be not lost, but day by day receive some increase.

[10] STOW'S ANNALS.
[1] *Remembrancia* 2:17. 'Inmates' are lodgers. In the 'spacious days' men lived as close as in modern Oriental bazaars, and as squalidly.
[2] STC 15488.

15th October. THE LADY BRIDGET AT COURT.[3] The Countess of Rutland is come to London with the Lady Bridget. Mr. Tyrwhitt, who has been sick in prison, now begins to sue for liberty and the Lord Chamberlain promises to move the Queen on his behalf.

18th October. CAPTAIN ANTHONY WINGFIELD SLAIN.[4] From Brittany the news is that on the 6th October the enemy assaulted the trenches before Croyzon but were beaten back with the loss of 7 or 8 men, but on our side was killed Captain Anthony Wingfield, the Sergeant-Major General, who was shot by a cannon shot from the garrison, as he stood with his rapier drawn, which was by the shot beaten through his bowels. Captain Wingfield hath served the Queen with great reputation in the wars of the Low Countries, Portugal and France. It is noted at his last going into Brittany that he so disposed of his estate as if he were never to return, and on the day of his death he took such order for his debts as if he had a presage of his end.

The next day the Marshal D'Aumont and Sir Henry Norris with the rest of the English regiments came up from Quimpar that is now taken and were quartered at Croyzon. Four days were now spent in mounting the artillery and making platforms for them to play. On the 12th the enemy made a sally upon the trenches of the French who not having the leisure to arm themselves lost between 30 and 40 men, and as many wounded; from thence they advanced towards the English trenches but were repulsed with the loss of 10 or 12.

20th October. THE DISRESPECT OF THE ARCHDUKE ERNEST.[5] The messenger that was despatched to the Archduke Ernest to require a safe conduct for Sir Thomas Wilkes is returned with a passport in ample style, and a letter from the Archduke that greatly displeaseth the Queen, for on perusing it she found the style and form far inferior to that which she expected from the Duke, being barely addressed *Royne D'Angleterre*, and omitting all the honours formerly given her in all letters sent by Emperors and Kings. Moreover the Archduke expressed in his letter that he expected to have nothing propounded that might be to the disservice to the King of Spain. She is determined to deal no more in this way, but in a more

³ *Rutland MSS* 1:324. See *9th Sept.*   ⁵ SALISBURY PAPERS 5:12, 13.
⁴ As for *10th Sept.*

public manner to declare to the world how far the King was directly touched by these foul practices.

The messenger is now sent back with the passport and a bare and meagre letter to M. Richardot, one of the Duke's Council, signed by the Lord Treasurer, the Earl of Essex, the Lord Buckhurst, the Vice-Chamberlain and Sir Robert Cecil. In this letter it is written that at some other time the Queen might have overlooked the style and form but she is too tender of the greatness of her state, being by God an anointed Queen over Kingdoms and countries, to disregard so notorious an omission of her dignities whether made by error or of purpose. As for the Archduke's expectation to have nothing propounded to him that might be to the disservice to the King of Spain, the matters are in very truth such as, without some extraordinary course taken by the King for his clearing, there will be left upon him a most notorious and foul imputation in the judgment of the whole world. The Queen is resolved to trouble the Duke neither with letter or with message any more, being now rather through his cold and unrespectful manner towards her (which she little expected at his hands) induced to look for small indifference at his hands. She hath reserved to herself a further consideration how the same may be made known, even according to the naked truth confessed and sealed with the blood of the conspirators, without any addition or colouring of anything therein.

25th October. NASHE'S 'TERRORS OF THE NIGHT.'[6] Nashe's book *The Terrors of the Night, or a Discourse of Apparitions,* wherein he describeth the nature of dreams, spirits, prophecies and omens, is entered, being dedicated to Mistress Elizabeth Carey, daughter to the Knight Marshal. The spirits of fire are by nature ambitious, with a humour of monarchising that maketh them affect rare qualified studies; many atheists are with these spirits inhabited. The spirits of water be dull and phlegmatic; and all rheums, dropsies and gout of their engendering; seafaring men are their chief entertainers, and greedy vintners likewise, who having read no more Scripture than that miracle of Christ's turning water into wine at Canaan, think to do a far stranger miracle than ever He did

[6] SR 2:663, 633; STC 18379. An amusing skit, and an excellent gloss on contemporary gossip. Entered twice —30th June 1593 and 25th Oct 1594. Internal evidence shows that 1594 is the correct date.

by turning wine into water. Spirits of the earth do especially infect soldiers, for they delight in nothing but iron and gold. As for the spirits of the air, in truth they be all show and no substance, deluders of the imagination, and nothing else; carpet knights, politic statesmen, women and children they most converse with. Of conjurors and cunning men, Nashe saith that they ascend by degrees, first raking a dunghill from which to temper up a few ointments and syrups, until as their fame grows, at last they set up a conjuring school, and all malcontents intending evasive violence against their prince and country run headlong to this oracle. As for the interpretation of dreams and the arts of physiognomy and palmistry, this is the sum of all; some subtle humorist to feed fantastic heads with innovations and novelties first invented this childish gloss upon dreams and physiognomy, wherein he strove only to boast himself of a pregnant, probable conceit beyond philosophy or truth.

31st October. THE ATTACK ON THE FORT AT CROYZON.[7] From Brittany it is reported that an assault on the fort of Croyzon was begun on 23rd October. This place is very strongly defended by water on two parts, and the rest as strong as could be made by art or charge. On the south front of the fort are two exceedingly strong bastions, that on the west having frontage of 17 paces, that on the east 10 paces; the curtain between them 37 ft. thick at top, and within these they have a very large entrenchment. The bastions are well defended on the flanks by the water and great ordnance. Our trenches were within four paces of the counterscarp, the French being on the east side, the English on the west, with the battery between them.

On that day the artillery began to play and fired some 700 shot but did so little harm that scarcely any breach appeared; but as the cannon beat upon the parapet and some of the flankers, some 400 men, commanded by Captain Lister, were sent to view it, and to see if they could hold the counterscarp. Thereupon many of the men and the gallants, thirsty after honour and desirous to achieve something further, having possessed themselves of the enemy's counterscarp, undertook the breach as well, and, notwithstanding the inaccessibleness of the place and the great resistance of the enemy, most of them reached the very top and held it for a time, though afterwards

[7] As for *10th Sept.*

they were repulsed, so that six of the officers were killed and some 16 or 18 soldiers, and twelve other officers were hurt or burned with powder. This attempt was made by the Englishmen only on the bastion of the west side, for the Frenchmen never attempted anything against their bastion, alleging that it was not assailable. The next day the Marshal and Sir John seeing the little effect that the artillery wrought, devised to make a mine against the east bastion towards the French trenches.

3rd November. THE SERMON AT PAUL'S CROSS.[1] The sermon at Paul's Cross was this day preached by Dr. John Dove, on the Second Coming of Christ, and the disclosing of Antichrist, taking as his text I. John ii., verse 18. He spoke very strictly of those that buy patronages of Church livings to give them to base, ignorant, and beggarly men, who would easily accept of benefices upon unlawful conditions. In concluding he demonstrated at length that the Bishop of Rome was that Antichrist spoken of in the Revelations.

A PETITION AGAINST A NEW THEATRE.[2] Learning that some intend to erect a new theatre on the Bankside the Lord Mayor hath written to the Lord Treasurer begging him rather to suppress all stages than to erect any more. Nor will he allow the defence of these plays alleged by some that the people must have some kind of recreation and that policy requires idle and ill-disposed heads to be directed from worse practise by this kind of exercise. These plays, saith he, are so corrupt, profane, containing nothing else but unchaste fables, lascivious devices, shifts, cozenage, and matter of like sort that only the base and refuse sort of people, or such young gentlemen as have but small regard for credit or conscience, are drawn thither. Hence plays are become the ordinary place of meeting for all vagrant persons and masterless men, that hang about the City, thieves, horse stealers, whoremongers, cozeners, conny-catching persons, practisers of treason and such like; there they consort and make their matches. Nor can the City be cleansed of this ungodly sort (the very sink and contagion not only of the City but of the whole realm) so long as plays of resort are by authority permitted.

[1] STC 7086.
[2] *Remembrancia* 2:75; MSC 1:74. It is a considerable tribute to Nashe that the Lord Mayor should officially condemn the arguments in favour of plays made by Pierce Penilesse (see *8th Aug* 1592).

4th November. THE STATE OF IRELAND.[3] From Ulster Sir
Richard Bingham reports that the great ones are of late more
openly showing themselves in nature of a rebellion than at
first; and it seems that the Queen must take up the matter
by correcting the offenders, for her subjects there have been
promised peace, and by degrees much violence has been committed. But if the Queen and the Council wish the Lord
Deputy to do anything against the Ulster men let him be
given all due assistance and countenance that he might with
less strength and time go through with it. The province of
Connaught is generally first.

15th November. THE ASSAULT ON THE FORT AT CROYZON.[4]
It is reported from Brittany that Croyzon is taken. By the
7th November the mine being reasonably well perfected, it
was determined to begin the battery again with the resolution
that so soon as the mine (which was made against the bulwarks opposite the French trenches) should be blown up, the
French should attack that part, the English their bastion;
and others with scaling ladders should make attempts in every corner so that the defenders should be assailed on every
part. But the Marshal being that day sick sent in the morning
to our General, showing him that he had learned that Don
John d'Aquila, General of the Spaniards, was marching with
his Spaniards to rescue Croyzon and had already reached
La-coman, a village within five leagues. He therefore advised
our General to defloge to Croyzon, thinking it unfit to hazard
any more men with so strong an enemy at hand ready to join
battle.

But Sir John, nothing daunted, answered that it would be a
dishonour to abandon the siege and that if the fort were taken
the enemy would have little purpose in coming any nearer.
He so importuned the Marshal that he gave him the ordering of that day's service. The General immediately commanded the cannoneers to begin the battery; and every man
was assigned his charge, some to the assault, others with
scaling ladders to attempt to make entry. By 12 o'clock he
gave order for the mine to be fired which albeit it did not do
so much as was expected, yet it gave easy access to the French.
On the other bulwark our men led by Captain Lathom, Captain Smith, and Captain John Norris, with other gentlemen,
assailed the bulwark and continued the assault until at half

[3] Wright, *Queen Elizabeth and Her*   [4] As for *10th Sept.*
Times, 2:438.

past four they made entry, and seized upon three ensigns that were there, putting every man they found to the sword, except a certain Alferez. Some of the Spaniards leapt from the rocks into the water, but the mariners in their small boats met them and slew them. Three or four were taken and their lives spared, for no man was slain in cold blood.

In this fight there were slain four officers, eight gentlemen of the General's own company, besides other gentlemen and some 20 or 30 private soldiers. There are wounded Sir Thomas Baskerville who by his bravery won the admiration of all men, Sir Martin Frobisher, and Captains Norris, Brett and Smith.

Throughout the siege the enemy were worthy of all praise, especially their commander; they never showed themselves daunted, and made sundry sallies, mostly on the French, with great resolution. In the last assault, fifty of them were slain by the cannon, but they never quailed until their commander was killed shortly before the entry of our men. By that time the greater part were slain, the rest, overtired and hurt, were forced to give way before our gallants. There were killed of the Spaniards in this fort nearly 400.

The next day the fort was destroyed and the force moved from Croyzon to join the rest of the army and to wait for what the enemy should attempt; but two days afterwards he withdrew five leagues further off. The day after the fight Don John d'Aquila sent a trumpet to redeem his prisoners, to whom our General answered that their ransoms were already paid and that he was now ready and at leisure to fight with him. The three Spanish ensigns he hath sent into England to be presented to the Queen.

17th November. THE QUEEN'S ACCESSION DAY.[5] This day, on the anniversary of her accession thirty-six years, the Queen gave a great banquet. The three flags captured from the Spaniards in Brittany have been presented to her.

19th November. SPENSER'S 'AMORETTI' AND 'EPITHALA-MIUM.'[6] Mr. Edmund Spenser's *Amoretti* together with his *Epithalamium*, written in honour of his own wife that he married in July last, are sent to the press.

20th November. USE OF THE CITY GARNERS REFUSED.[7] When of late Sir Francis Drake and Sir John Hawkins de-

5 FUGGER NEWS-LETTERS, p. 262.   7 *Remembrancia* 2:79.
6 SR 2:655; STC 23076.

manded the use of the garners and bakehouses in the Bridgehouse to bake bread for the fleet about to be set forth, the
Lord Mayor refused the same. He allegeth that these garners
and bakehouses were built solely for the use of the poor in
times of scarcity who would be utterly disappointed if they
should be employed for any other use. At the same time he
hath petitioned the Lord Treasurer that the corn for the
fleet may be bought from Kent or other shires and not in
the City. Sir Francis and Sir John purpose to make their
provision out of the wheat brought from foreign parts for
the benefit of the City, and have already bought some, en-
forcing the same to a lower price than is usual or can be well
afforded; hereby the merchants shall be discouraged from
bringing in any more.

27th November.   THE LADY BRIDGET MANNERS.[8] The Queen
hath caused the Lady Bridget Manners to be set free; Mr.
Tyrwhitt was released some days since on the mediation of his
friends and in respect of his sickness. She now bids the Lord
Hunsdon to write to the Countess of Rutland in her name
that she imputes the fault more to her than to the young
couple, for though the Lady Bridget took the fault on herself to excuse her mother, yet the Queen is well assured that
the Lady Bridget would never have married without her
mother's consent. There now remains only that the Countess
should send for the Lady Bridget from the Countess of
Bedford, and the sooner the better, and her husband will
come down with her.

30th November.   A CONFERENCE ABOUT THE SUPPRESSING
OF ROGUES.[9] Since the Council approve the measures proposed against vagrants the Lord Mayor hath summoned the
Justices of Middlesex and Surrey to meet with him and with
the Lord Chief Justices touching the orders to be put in execution for the apprehending and suppressing of vagrant persons and the begging poor.

   Precise and strait charge shall be given to every several
ward that watch and ward be continued from 9 or 10 of the
clock at night till 6 in the morning, and the day watch to begin when the night watch giveth over, and to give over again
when the night watch beginneth. For the better executing
of these watches the constable shall be compelled to execute

8 *Rutland MSS* 1:324.   9 *Remembrancia* 2:75, 76.

his office not by deputy but in his own person, as the execution thereof by deputy constables is thought to be an occasion of great negligence and abuse in this service.

The watches to make continual searches at times convenient in all victualling houses, tippling cellars and other places likely to entertain idle and suspicious persons, men, women and children. Those unable to give an account of some dwelling-place and honest faculty to live by but shall appear to be vagabonds, rogues and idle beggars, having able bodies, them shall the watch commit to Bridewell, to be kept till the morning following; what time the constables with other honest persons of the same watch shall resort thither, there to charge them before those who are farther authorized to proceed against them for their lawful punishment.

For the better and more speedy avoiding of such vagabonds present consideration shall be had of some bodily labour to set them on work, as by beating of hemp, scouring the town ditches, abating the shelves in the river Thames, or such other, wherein no detriment can be done by them, in case they should demean themselves wilfully or negligently; which otherwise in matter of art they might and are likely to do. The young ones that can more easily be reclaimed and enforced shall be appointed to some occupation. Women walkers that be of the City or suburbs shall be forced to abide at their prescribed dwelling-places in some honest labour, making of flax, spinning, or such like.

2nd December. A PROCLAMATION AGAINST FIREARMS.[1] There is a proclamation now published reaffirming the former proclamations against the carrying of dags and longer pieces, such as calivers, in times and places not allowable for service, and against the carrying of small or pocket dags and the wearing of privy coats of armour. Yet is it to be allowed to those who come to the musters to serve as horsemen with dags, and also to any of the Queen's ministers or their servants for their more surety to carry her treasure or bring her revenue to places appointed, provided always that the dags be carried openly and manifestly seen.

'THE RESOLVED GENTLEMAN.'[2] *The Resolved Gentleman,* first written in French in 1483 by Oliver de la Marche who served Philip, and his son, Charles, Dukes of Burgundy; hence translated into Spanish verse by Don Hernando de Ancunia, and now with additions Englished by Mr. Lewis Lewkenor is entered, being dedicated to the Lady Hune, Countess of Warwick. In this allegorical fiction the author depicteth those qualities which sustain a man against the misfortunes of life, accident and old age; the evils of a courtly life; the blessings of memory, and the like, ending with a prophecy of the Destinies concerning Queen Elizabeth.

6th December. SIR W. RALEGH'S COMMISSION.[3] A commission is granted to Sir Walter Ralegh to prepare and arm two ships and two small pinnaces in which to do her Majesty service against the King of Spain and his subjects. As his own ability is not sufficient to furnish out such vessels, and he is driven to use the assistance of friends to adventure with him, the Queen for his satisfaction and their assurance further promises that he and they shall enjoy to their own use all goods and merchandise, treasure, gold, silver, and whatever else may be taken by him or his associates, either by sea or land, from the subjects of the King of Spain, after paying such customs and duties as appertain. He is given full power and authority over all captains, masters, mariners, and others, who are commanded to obey him. Whatever he shall do by virtue of his commission for the furtherance of the service and the enfeebling of the subjects and adherents of the King of Spain, he and all who serve under him shall be clearly acquitted and discharged.

8th December. THE DEATH OF CARDINAL ALLEN.[4] Cardinal Allen is dead at Rome, whereat the Catholics make great lamentation. He was in the 63rd year of his age and is buried in the English Church of the Holy Trinity.

William Allen, commonly called the Cardinal of England, was born in the county of Lancashire of honest parents and allied by kindred to some noble families. He was brought up at Oriel College in Oxford, where in Queen Mary's time he was proctor of the University, and afterwards a Canon in the Church of York. When religion changed in England, he departed the land, and professed divinity at the University of Douay in Flanders that was founded 32 years since. He

[3] SP DOM 250:46.
[4] SALISBURY PAPERS 5:27; CAMDEN'S ELIZABETH.

procured the seminary for the English to be founded at Douay, and the second seminary at Rheims, the third at Rome, and two others in Spain, for the conservation of the Romish religion in England, for the zeal whereof he cast off both his love for his country and his duty to his Prince, instigating both the King of Spain and the Pope of Rome to the conquest of England. Upon that account he engaged himself in dangerous counsels and designs for which Pope Sixtus V. honoured him with the title of Cardinal of St. Martin in the Mounts.

When the Invincible Armada threatened England he it was that brought into the Low Countries that Bull of Excommunication against the Queen, causing it to be printed in English; and withal he wrote an admonition to the English to adhere to the Pope and the Spaniard. But being disappointed of his hopes he returned to Rome, there greatly wearied by the dissensions and animosities of English fugitives, as well students as gentlemen.

14th December. REVELS AT GRAY'S INN.[5] The gentlemen at Gray's Inn, after many consultations, have now determined to hold revels this Christmastide, and more especially as these pastimes have been discontinued for three or four years. They make choice of Mr. Henry Helmes, a Norfolk gentleman, one accomplished with all good parts, a very proper man of personage, and very active in dancing and revelling, to be elected their 'Prince of Purpool' and to govern the state for the duration of the revels. Privy Councillors and all officers of state, of the Law and of the household are assigned to him, and an invitation in the form of a privy seal dispatched to the Gentlemen of the Inner Temple, bidding them appoint an Ambassador to be a minister of correspondence between the two houses or kingdoms.

20th December. THE REVELS AT GRAY'S INN.[6] The revels were begun this night. The Prince of Purpool with all his train marched from his lodging to the great Hall and there was installed on his Throne, under a rich cloth of State, with his councillors and great lords about him and before, the rest of his officers taking their places as belonged to their condition. Then the trumpeters were commanded to sound thrice, which being done, the King at Arms, in a rich sur-

[5] *Gesta Grayorum*, first printed in 1688; and in MSC 1914.   [6] *Gesta Grayorum*.

coat, stood forth before the Prince and proclaimed his style. After this entered the Prince's champion in complete armour, on horseback, and so came riding about the fire and in the midst of the Hall made his challenge and then departed.

King at Arms having next blazoned the Prince's Arms, the Attorney stood up and made a speech of gratulation, wherein he showed what happiness was like to ensue by the election of so noble and virtuous a Prince as then reigned over them. To whom the Prince answered that he did acknowledge himself to be deeply bound to their merits, and in that regard did promise that he would be a gracious and loving Prince to so well deserving subjects. Then the Solicitor, having certain great old books and records before him, made a speech to the Prince showing the names of such homagers or tributaries as held lordships, and the services belonging thereto, as that Bawdwine de Islington held the town of Islington by grand sergeantry, rendering at the Coronation, for every maid in Islington continuing a virgin after the age of fourteen years, one hundred thousand million sterling.

Then was a Parliament summoned, but certain necessary officers being absent, the purpose was frustrated, except that a subsidy was granted by the Commons, and the Prince gave his gracious and free pardon, which was read by the Solicitor, and after a further short speech the Prince called for his Master of Revels, and willed him to pass the time in dancing. So the gentlemen pensioners and attendants, very gallantly appointed, in thirty couples, danced the old measures, and their galliards and others kinds of dances, revelling until it was very late, when it pleased the Prince to take his way to his lodging, with the sound of trumpets and his attendants.

26th December. AN ATTEMPT TO MURDER THE FRENCH KING.[7] From France it is reported that on 17th December a young man, one John Chastel, seminary of the Jesuit College at Claremont, attempted to murder the French King, piercing his cheek with a poniard, and breaking some of his teeth. This Chastel has been tried and executed by the French Parliament, and their decree is now translated and published in English. He was condemned to go before the principal gate of the chief church in Paris, and there, naked to his shirt, with a burning torch of wax of the weight of two pounds, on his knees to acknowledge and confess that wretch-

[7] STC 5066.

edly and traitorously he had attempted the most inhuman and most abominable parricide, and that with a knife he wounded the King in the face. Also that being falsely instructed and persuaded he had affirmed that it was lawful to kill the King, and that King Henry IV, now reigning, was not in the Church until he had received approbation of the Pope; whereof, and every part whereof, he repented and asked forgiveness of God.

This done he was to be conveyed in a tumbril to the place called the Greve; there to have his arms and his thighs rent with burning pincers, and his right hand holding the knife wherewith he had endeavoured to have committed the parricide to be cut off. Then his body to be drawn in sunder and dismembered by four horses, and his carcase and quarters cast into the fire, and so consumed into ashes; and the said ashes to be scattered in the wind. Before the execution of this sentence he was to be put to the torture ordinary and extraordinary thereby to find out the truth of his confederates.

It was also ordained that all priests and scholars of the College of Claremont, and all others that entitled themselves to the Society of Jesus, as corrupters of youth, disturbers of common quietness, and enemies to the King and the State, should within three days after notice of this decree depart out of all towns and places where their colleges were situate, and within fifteen days more out of the whole realm.

28th December. THE CHAMBERLAIN'S PLAYERS AT COURT.[8] The Lord Chamberlain's players acted before the Court at Greenwich on St. Stephen's Day, among them being Richard Burbage, William Kemp, and William Shakespeare.

GRAY'S INN REVELS: A NIGHT OF ERRORS.[9] This night there was a great presence of Lords, Ladies and Worshipful personages, expecting some notable performance, especially after the common report of that which had gone before, but the multitude of beholders was so great that the inventions and conceits could not be performed. Against these performances the Emperor of the Inner Temple sent his Ambassador who was very graciously welcomed by the Prince. But when the shows were to begin there arose a disordered tumult and crowd upon the stage whither came so great a throng of worshipful personages that might not be displaced, and gentlewomen whose sex did privilege them from violence that when the Prince and his officers had in vain a good while endeavoured reformation at length there was no hope of redress. The Lord Ambassador and his train thought themselves not so kindly entertained as was before expected, and thereupon would not stay any longer but departed in a sort discontented and displeased.

After their departure the tumults somewhat ceased, though still so much as was able to confound any good inventions. In regard whereof, and especially since the sports were intended for the gracing of the Templarians, it was thought good not to offer anything of account saving dancing and revelling with the gentlewomen. After which a *Comedy of Errors* (much like to the *Menechmus of Plautus*) was played by the players. So the night was begun and continued to the end in nothing but confusion and errors, whereupon it was called 'The Night of Errors.'

30th December. THE NEW BISHOP OF LONDON.[10] Dr. Richard Fletcher, Bishop of Worcester, is elected Bishop of London.

[10] STOW'S ANNALS. He was the father of the dramatist, at this time aged 15.

Other Books Printed in 1594

i. *The Display of Folly,* by one O. B., in which under the form of a dialogue, Huddle and Dunstable, two old men, the one a retired gentleman, the other a middling or new upstart franklin, discourse upon the follies and vices of the time, especially amongst the wanton gentlemen of the City. The dedication is to the Earl of Essex.

ii. *The Affectionate Shepherd,* by Richard Barnfield, containing the very passionate complaints of Daphnis the shepherd for the boy Ganymede, that he would forsake Queen Gwendolen to be his love; and followed by 'The Shepherd's Content,' or the happiness of a harmless life, written upon occasion of the former subject.

iii. *A Brief Discourse concerning the force and effect of all manual weapons of fire,* by Humphrey Barwick, Gentleman, Soldier, Captain, in which he contesteth the opinions set forth by Sir John Smythe, and Sir Roger Williams; the former holding that the long bow of England is the only weapon in the world for the obtaining of battles and victories in these days, the latter accepting weapons of shot except the musket.

Captain Barwick showeth from his experiences of the wars (which began at the age of 18 in 1548) the greater worth of weapons of fire, being more certain and more deadly, and urging that there should be more men trained in their use. As for Sir John Smythe's saying that harquebusiers could give their volleys but at eight, ten or twelve yards while archers could wound and sometimes kill at nine, ten or eleven score, he would stand at six score yards distant from the best archer, armed but in pistol proof, and let him shoot ten arrows one after another at him, and if he stirred from his place let him be punished.

i. STC 1054.　　　　　　　iii. STC 1542.
ii. STC 1480.

iv. *The Death of Usury,* wherein are shown reasons against usurers from the jurists, divine and civil, and the statutes now in force concerning usury, being printed at Cambridge.

v. *Giacomo de Grassi His True Art of Defence,* being translated from the Italian by I. G., gentleman, and dedicated to the Lord Burgh, governor of the Brille, in an epistle by Thomas Churchyard. Herein is described the manner of single combat with the single rapier or single sword, the rapier and dagger, the sword and buckler, the sword and square target, the sword and round target, the case of rapiers; the two-hand sword, and the weapons of the staff as the bill, the partisan, the halberd, and javelin; together with a treatise of deceit or falsing; and a mean how a man may practise himself to get strength, judgment and activity.

vi. *Of the Laws of Ecclesiastical Polity,* by Richard Hooker, which he undertook because of the wonderful zeal and fervour wherewith the Puritans withstand the received orders of the Church of England; which led him to a consideration of their claiming that every Christian man standeth bound to enter in with them for the furtherance of the 'Lord's Discipline.' But after with travail and care he had examined the reasons he concluded to set down this, as his final persuasion is that the present form of Church government which the laws of the land have established is such as no law of God nor reason of man hath hitherto been alleged of force sufficient to prove that they do ill who to the uttermost of their power withstand the alteration thereof. Contrariwise, the other which men are required to accept is only by error and misconceit named the ordinance of Jesus Christ; no one proof is as yet brought forth whereby it might clearly appear so in very deed.

The work is four books, with a long preface to the Puritans wherein Dr. Hooker runneth through the history of the Puritan discipline from the time of Calvin, showing their doctrines which are based upon the Bible only (for they think no other writings in the world should be studied), and in rites and ceremonies professing their hatred of all conformity with Rome. The pretended end of their civil reformation is that Christ may have dominion over all, and the means whereby they allure and retain so great multitudes most effectual. They show a wonderful zeal towards God, a hatred of sin, and a singular love of integrity, which men think to be much more than ordinary in them by reason of the custom which they have to fill the ears of the people with invectives against their authorized guides. They bountifully relieve the broken estates of such needy creatures as are apt to be drawn away; and they show a tender compassion for the miseries of the poorer sort, over whose heads they use to pour down showers of tears in complaining that no respect is had unto them, that their goods are devoured by wicked cormorants, their persons had in contempt, all liberty both temporal and spiritual taken away from them, and that it is high time for God now to hear their groans and send them deliverance.

In the first of the four books that follow are considered laws and their several kinds in general; in the second is answered the position of those who urge reformation, in that Scripture is the only rule of all things which in this life may be done by men; in the third is answered the assertion of those who hold that in Scripture there must be of necessity contained a form of Church polity, the laws whereof may in no wise be altered. The fourth book answereth the assertion that the Church polity of the Established Church is corrupted with papist orders, rites and ceremonies.

vii. *The Tragedy of Dido, Queen of Carthage*, a play written by Christopher Marlowe and Thomas Nashe, and sometime played by the Children of Her Majesty's Chapel.

viii. *The Orchard and the Garden*, containing certain necessary, secret and ordinary knowledge in grafting and gardening. Herein the author giveth directions for the preparing of the soil and the divers fashions and ways of grafting. To make cherries grow without stones, pare a little cherry tree of one year old at the stump, and cleave it asunder from the top to the root, which do in May; and make an iron fit to draw the heart or marrow from both sides of the tree; then tie it fast together and anoint it with ox dung or loam; and within a year after, when it is grown and healed, another little tree of the same should be grafted upon it; so shall it bring forth fruit without stones.

vi. STC 13712. Entered 29 Jan 1593.   viii. STC 18838.
vii. STC 17441.

ix. *The Battle of Alcazar, fought in Barbary, between Sebastian, King of Portugal and Abdelmelec, King of Morocco; with the death of Captain Stukeley,* a play written by George Peele, and sundry times played by the Lord Admiral's men.

x. *Sonnets to the Fairest Coelia,* by William Percy, containing twenty sonnets in which he vainly begs his mistress's favour.

xi. *Present Remedies against the Plague.* In this little book the people are advised to keep their houses, streets, yards, backsides, sinks and kennels sweet and clean from all standing puddles, dunghills, and corrupt moistures; and not to let dogs, which be a most apt cattle to take infect of any sickness, to come running into the house. Rooms should be aired with charcoal fires, made in stone pans or chafing dishes, and not in chimneys. Of remedies against the plague a good preservative is to chew the root of angelica, setwall, gentian, valerian or cinnamon: to eat a toast of bread, sprinkled with red rose vinegar, buttered and powdered with cinnamon, and eat fasting; to drink rue, wormwood, and scabias, steeped in ale a whole night and drunk fasting every morning, or the water of *carduus benedictus,* or *angelica,* mixed with *mithridatum.*

xii. A little book entitled *A True Report of sundry Horrible Conspiracies of late time detected to have (by barbarous murders) taken away the life of the Queen's most excellent Majesty,* wherein it manifestly appeareth to the world how unjust and dishonourable the King of Spain and his ministers' actions are against the Queen of England; for contrary to all warlike, princely, manlike and Christian examples in any wars or other contentions he has attempted to take her life not by arms or other warlike actions but by secret murder, hateful to God and man from the beginning of the world. Bernardine Mendoza and other of the King of Spain's ministers are shown participant in the conspiracies of Lopez and his fellows, and Ibarra with Yorke and Williams.

ix. STC 19531.
x. STC 19618.
xi. STC 20867.

xii. STC 7603. Propaganda for neutrals. A French version was also issued.

3rd January. THE REVELS AT GRAY'S INN.[1] The revels at
Gray's Inn were this night continued and because of the
tumults on the 'Night of Errors' good watch was kept with
whifflers, so that all had good places to their liking and contentment. There were present many great and noble personages.

When all were placed, the Prince of Purpool came into the
Hall with his wonted state and ascended his throne at the high
end of the Hall, and after him the Ambassador of Templaria
with his train; who, after variety of music, were presented
with this device. At the side of the Hall within a curtain was
erected an altar to the Goddess of Amity, her arch-flamen
ready to attend the sacrifice that should be offered, and round
about nymphs and fairies with instruments of music. Then
issued forth of another room, the first pair of friends, being
Theseus and Perithous. They came arm in arm, and offered
incense upon the altar, which shined and burned very clear
without blemish, and so departed; and in like manner came
Achilles and Patroclus, Pilades and Orestes, then Scipio
and Lelius. But when Graius and Templarius came lovingly
to the altar and offered their incense, the Goddess did not
accept of their service, for the flame was choked by a troubled smoke and dark vapour. Hereat the arch-flamen, willing
to pacify the angry Goddess, preferred certain mystical ceremonies and commanded the nymphs to sing some hymns of
pacification, so that when the friends again proffered their
devotion the flame burnt more clear than at any time before:
and so they departed. Whereupon the arch-flamen pronounced
Graius and Templarius to be friends, and denounced a heavy

[1] *Gesta Grayorum.* SPEDDING claims
that the speeches of the Councillors
were written by Bacon, that on philosophy foreshadowing 'Solomon's
House' in the *New Atlantis.*

curse upon them that in any way go about to break the bond
and league of sincere amity.

Then the Prince, in token of their amity, offered the Ambassador of the Templarians and some of his retinue the
Knighthood of the Helmet, an order of his own institution.
So the King at Arms placed the Ambassador and some
of his followers, and also some of the Templarians, that they
might receive the dignity at his hands; which done, the Prince
came down from his chair of state, and put a Collar about
the Ambassador's neck, he kneeling on his left knee, and
said to him, *'Sois Chevalier';* and so was done to the rest,
to the number of twenty-four. Then the King at Arms stood
forth, and after a speech read out the Articles of the Order,
being of this nature:

Item, No knight shall be inquisitive towards any lady or
gentleman, whether her beauty be English or Italian; nor
to affirm that faces were better twenty years ago than they
are at this present time, except such knight have passed three
climacterical years.

Item, No knight shall put out any money upon strange
returns or performances to be made by his own person, as
to hop up the stairs to the top of St. Paul's without intermission.

Item, No knight, that hath licence to travel, be it by map,
card, sea or land, shall presume upon the warrant of a traveller to report any extraordinary varieties; as that he hath
ridden through Venice on horseback post.

Item, Every knight shall endeavour to be much in the
books of the worshipful citizens next adjoining to the territories of Purpool; and none shall unlearnedly, or without
looking, pay ready money for any wares, to the ill example
of others, and utter suppression of credit betwixt man and
man.

Item, Every knight shall endeavour to add conference and
experience by reading; and therefore shall not only read
and peruse Guizo, *The French Academy,* Galiatho, *The
Courtier,* Plutarch, the *Arcadia,* and the Neoterical writers
from time to time; but also frequent the Theatre, and such
like places of experience; and resort to the better sort of
ordinaries for conference, whereby they may not only become accomplished with civil conversations, and able to govern a table with discourse; but also sufficient, if need be, to
make epigrams, emblems, and other devices appertaining
to his Honour's learned revels.

Item, That no knight shall take upon him the person of a Malcontent, in going with a more private retinue than appertaineth to his degree, and using but certain special, obscure company, and commending none but men disgraced and out of office; and smiling at good news, as if he knew something that were not true, and making odd notes of his Highness's reign, and former governments, and the like.

When all these ceremonies were ended, there was variety of consort music; and in the meanwhile the Knights of the Order, brought into the Hall a running banquet, and gave it to the Prince, the Lords and other strangers. This done the Prince held a Council of six of his Privy Councillors, to whom he gave charge that they should advise him in general of the scope and end whereunto the government of the State might best be directed.

Then the first Councillor made a speech advising the exercise of war whereby in later years leave deep footsteps of his power in the world.

The second Councillor would have him study philosophy, commending four principal works: the collecting of a most perfect and general library; a spacious wonderful garden wherein whatsoever plant the earth bringeth forth may be set and cherished: with rooms to stake in all rare beasts, and to cage in all rare birds, with two lakes adjoining, the one of fresh water, the other of salt, for like variety of fishes; and so he might have in small compass a model of Universal Nature. The third, a goodly huge cabinet wherein shall be stored whatsoever the hand of man by exquisite art or engine hath made rare in stuff, form, or motion. The fourth, such a still house so furnished with mills, instruments, furnaces and vessels as may be a palace fit for a philosopher's stone. The third Councillor, confuting those that had gone before, would have the Prince's fame eternized by the magnificence of goodly buildings and foundations. The fourth Councillor advised absoluteness of state and treasure. The fifth Councillor advised virtue and gracious government, but the sixth would have him take counsel only of his five senses and follow his pleasures.

To all of which the Prince said he must take his time to consider. Then rising from his seat, he made choice of a lady to dance withal, and so likewise did the Ambassador and the courtiers attending on the Prince. So the rest of the night is spent in these pastimes, being so carefully and orderly handled that the former disgrace is now quite taken away.

4th January. GRAY'S INN REVELS.[2] To-day the Prince of
Purpool, accompanied with the Ambassador of Templaria
and attended by both trains, took a progress from Gray's
Inn to Crosby's Place, the Lord Mayor's house in Bishopsgate
Street, having before been invited to dine with him. This
show was very stately and orderly performed, and everyone
had his feather in his cap to distinguish of what state he was,
the Grayans using white and the Templarians ash-coloured.
Thus they rode very gallantly from Gray's Inn, through
Chancery Lane, Fleet Street, so through Cheapside, Cornhill
and to Crosby's Place, where there was a very sumptuous
dinner. Dinner being ended, the Prince and his company
returned the same way, the streets being thronged with people
who thought there had been some great prince in very deed
passing through the City.

10th January. A NOTABLE CASE OF COSENAGE.[3] A certain
widow, by name Mrs. Mascall, hath been notably cosened
by one Judith Phillips, otherwise known as Doll Pope. Two
men, the one called Peters, the other Vaughan, dealt with
this Judith to be a means to procure Peters' favour with the
widow. Thereupon Vaughan devised a letter in the name of
one Mr. Grace, a near friend of the widow's, to the effect
that she should make much of Judith, for she was one that
could do her great good. Peters and Vaughan also told Judith
what suitors the widow had and where they dwelt, also of
many accidents which they knew to be true, to the intent that
she might seem to be a wise woman.

Whereupon Judith going to the widow was well entertained
and had into her chamber. After some speeches past Judith
looked into her hand, and then began to tell her what suitors
she had. Also she asked of the widow whether she was not
troubled in the night with sights and noises in her house; to
which the widow answered yea.

'Yea,' said Judith, 'hath there not been lights seen in your
house?'

'How know you that?' said the widow.

'I know it well,' quoth Judith, 'and the cause too; for there
is money hid in your house.'

The widow therefore being more persuaded of Judith's
great skill began to speak of her suitors and prayed that she

[2] *Gesta Grayorum.*
[3] SALISBURY PAPERS 5:82. See *2nd Apr.*

would get the money. Judith told her that first she must have such gold as the widow had, which she would not carry away but leave in the house; and within two days the gold hid in the house should be found in the place which she appointed for this gold to be. So the widow brought forth certain gold, a chain of gold, seven rings and a whistle, all of which were put in a purse and delivered to Judith. Judith wrapped this purse up in yarn, and having before wound two stones in other yarn, closely conveyed the yarn with the two stones to the widow, which she took and laid up in the appointed place with charge from Judith not to look at it until three days were past. She also told the widow that she must have a turkey and a capon to give to the Queen of the Fairy, which the widow provided. Also she made the widow say certain prayers in sundry places of the house. Judith then departed with the gold and the chain, which she divided with Peters and Vaughan, but the rings she took out secretly and kept them to herself.

The next morning, intending to cosen the widow of her plate also, Judith brought the head and legs of the turkey in a basket to the window, and began to tell the widow that she must lay one leg under the bed and the rest in other places; but the widow having by this discovered the stones in the yarn knew herself to be cosened and caused Judith to be apprehended.

This Judith hath long used her trade of cosenage, wandering about the country in company with divers persons that call themselves Egyptians. For that kind of life she was condemned to die at Salisbury, but afterwards had her pardon.

13th January. GOSSON'S 'PLEASANT QUIPS.'[4] Mr. Stephen Gosson, parson of Great Wigborough in Essex, hath written very invectively against the fantastical foreign toys daily used in our women's apparel, which he entitleth *Pleasant Quips for Upstart New fangled Gentlewomen.*

Complaineth that masks were once to hide the face from wantons bold:

> But on each wight now are they seen,
>   The tallow-pale, the browning-bay,
> The swarthy-black, the grassy-green,
>   The pudding-red, the dapple-grey,

[4] SR 2:669; STC 12096. Anonymous but Gosson's name is written in a contemporary hand in the only surviving copy of the 1596 edition.

> So might we judge them toys aright
> To keep sweet beauty still in plight.

17th January. BARNFIELD'S 'CYNTHIA' AND 'CASSANDRA.'[5] Mr. Richard Barnfield hath written two poems, in praise of Cynthia, and of the life and death of Cassandra. Of Cynthia, he saith that the gods and goddesses all promised her wealth, wisdom and beauty, but that between the goddess and her Gracious Majesty there is this difference:

> She shines by night; but thou by day dost shine;
> She monthly changes; thou dost ne'er decline.

Of Cassandra, telleth the story of her lamentable life; how the god Apollo loved her so that, encouraging his love, she caused him solemnly to promise her the gift of prophecy, which promise being made she chastely counterchecked his approaches. Hereat the god, being greatly enraged, cursed her that she should indeed foretell truly of things to come, but for her falsehood no man should believe her; and moreover, for a penance on that sex, a constant woman should be hard to find; which prophecy (saith the author) hath proved true for that their sex are subject to inconstancy as other creatures are to destiny.

23rd January. COMPLAINTS AGAINST PATENTS.[6] The leather sellers in the City petition her Majesty concerning the enormities of Mr. Darcy's patent for stamping of leather which the Lord Mayor upholdeth; for, saith he, the exactions and other inconveniences of this patent cause great grief and murmur of the people throughout the land, and Mr. Darcy's violent manner of proceeding is very unmeet in this time of dearth when great numbers of poor people are exasperate enough by their own misery and great want of food. There are at this present time seven such patents: for leather to Mr. Darcy; for brushes, bottles and stone pots; for soap and barrel butter; for cards; for vinegar, alliger, *aqua vitae, aqua composita;* and for steel to a stranger.

'THE ESTATE OF THE ENGLISH FUGITIVES.'[7] There is entered a work entitled *The Estate of the English fugitives,* being the true copy of that book which, contrary to the author's intention, was lately printed in Paul's Churchyard, but corruptly

---

[5] SR 2:669; STC 1483.   [7] SR 2:670; STC 15562–65.
[6] *Remembrancia* 2:82, 83, 84.

intermixed with fictions of the publisher. Herein our unexperienced gentlemen and credulous Catholics are warned by many examples of the monstrous cruelty and treacheries of the Spaniard towards those who enter into his service.

Of the Jesuits it is written that there is not any man's business but they must have an oar in it; they never plant themselves in any places but in the midst of goodly cities where they wring themselves into the fairest palaces. Their churches are rich and sumptuous, their movables and household stuff magnificent, their gardens fine and comely, their fare plentiful and of the best; nor are they tied to any risings in the night, to which other religious houses are subjected. Their first mass doth never at any time begin before 8 of the clock. They are accounted the greatest intelligences and statesmen of the world. They may not receive any higher office or dignity, but they take the name of a Jesuit not to be any whit inferior to the title of a bishop; nor are they subject to any controlment, but only the Provincial of their order. But the best is to see how busy and diligent they are when they hear of a wealthy man that lieth sick and in danger of death.

As a proof of the affection of the subjects for the Queen, note the behaviour of the people when a traitor is carried to his execution; which though it should move the minds of men to commiserate of those unfortunate wretches, yet are the people, in jealousy of her safety and hatred of her enemies, many times hardly restrained by the officers from doing violence to the prisoners on the way. Then do they curse, ban and revile them with the most opprobrious speeches; and commonly applaud the instant of their deaths with a general shout of joy, and cries of 'God save the Queen and confound all traitors'; whereas they do usually accompany all other kinds to their deaths with sorrow and compassion.

24th January.   THE SCOTTISH AMBASSADOR GIVEN AUDIENCE.[8] To-day the Lord Wemyss was given audience by the Queen who taxed the King of Scots with unkindness in that he goes about to make a new league with the French King, to which he answereth that it is but the renewing of the old. When he had drawn to an end the Queen willed him to assure the King, his master, that when he had tried all his new friends, he should find that her kindness overweighted all theirs; to which he replied, 'As you have, madam, proved his love and fidelity

to have been above that which you can expect at the rest of
your kind friends' hands.' Coming forth from the Privy
Chamber he asked the Lord Chamberlain for Sir Robert
Cecil. 'Why, sir,' said he, 'he was within.' 'By my soul,' said
Lord Wemyss, 'I could not see him.' 'No marvel,' said Sir
George Carey, 'being so little.' Whereat the Lord Wemyss
burst out of laughing.

25th January. THE IRISH REBELLION.[9] Rebellion is now
broken out in Ireland and if forces be not sent both Enniskillen
and all the North will be lost. Such is the strong combination
of the Earl of Tyrone that there is not any dare show himself
a dutiful subject.

THE VACANT SOLICITORSHIP.[10] Mr. Francis Bacon's friends
at Court now deal with the Queen for his advancement to
the Solicitorship; for if he get not promotion, he declareth
that he will travel. But my Lord of Essex carrying the matter
somewhat too far, the Queen sweareth that if Mr. Bacon continue in this manner, she will seek all England for a Solicitor
rather than take him. She hath never, saith she, dealt so with
any as with him; she hath pulled him over the Bar and used
him in her greatest causes.

28th January. GRAY'S INN REVELS.[11] The revels at Gray's
Inn have been discontinued these three weeks past by reason
that the Prince of Purpool made a pretended voyage to Russia. But their purpose was frustrated by the Readers and Governors who caused the scaffolds to be taken away from the
Hall and would not have them built again by reason of the
term. This night there came into the Hall the King at Arms
to announce the Prince's return from Russia and summon
his subjects to meet him on the 1st February.

31st January. THE JESUITS AT WISBEACH CASTLE.[12] The
state of the seminary priests and Jesuits that are confined in
Wisbeach Castle is reported to be grown as dangerous as a
seminary college by liberty and favour of their keeper. There
are about twenty-eight of them who have compounded with
their keeper for their diet, provision and servants as if they
were in a free college. They send abroad their servants into

9 SP IRELAND 178:10.   12 STRYPE'S ANNALS 4:195. Wisbeach
10 SPEDDING 1:347–48.   Castle was used as a place of intern-
11 *Gesta Grayorum.*   ment for priests and recusants.

the town to the market where they buy up the best victuals. Great resort is daily made there of gentlemen and gentle-women and others who dine and sup with them, walk with them in the castle yard, and confer in their chambers, whereby they receive and send intelligence. They want no money, and by giving alms and devotions at the gate the poor esteem them for godly men. They keep eight poor townsborn children and two strangers of good wit and choice, beside their cooks, and those recusants. They are all young and lusty people, dis-posed to mirth and viciousness with women, and attempt them, as the keeper's maid and two daughters have been, in whorish manner. Most of these men were banished and have returned, some were men condemned for treason. Hereby scholars of the Universities and priests beyond the sea hold that if they be taken and so entertained the worst is but good cheer, and great hopes of bishoprics and preferments here-after.

3rd February. THE GRAY'S INN REVELS.[1] Yesterday the Prince of Purpool with his train came up the Thames in fif-teen barges, bravely furnished with flags and streamers from Blackwall, and so to Greenwich where a letter is despatched to Sir Thomas Heneage, praying that the Prince may pay his homage on Shrove Tuesday. To which the Queen returned answer that if he come at Shrovetide, he and his followers shall have entertainment according to his dignity. Then the Prince and his company continued their course to the Tower where, by the Queen's commandment, he was welcomed with a volley of great ordnance. At Tower Hill there waited for the Prince's landing men with horses, very bravely fur-nished, to the number of a hundred, whereon they rode very gallantly through Tower Street, Fenchurch Street, Grace Church Street, Cornhill, Cheapside, and so through St. Paul's Churchyard where at St. Paul's School his Highness was en-tertained with an oration made by one of the scholars, whom the Prince rewarded very bountifully before continuing on his way by Ludgate and Fleet Street to Gray's Inn.

This night the Prince of Purpool and some of his followers performed a masque of Proteus before the Queen at Court, who is much pleased by their good performance. She willeth the Lord Chamberlain that the gentlemen shall be invited to-morrow, and presented unto her.

[1] *Gesta Grayorum.*

4th February. SIR JOHN NORRIS'S RETURN.[2] Sir John Norris is now returned from Brittany having been delayed for want of shipping, and by ill weather. The soldiers that were employed in those parts are at Paimpol, waiting for their return.

THE GRAY'S INN REVELS ENDED.[3] The gentlemen of Gray's Inn were presented to the Queen this evening, and she gave them her hand to kiss with most gracious words of commendation. And afterwards there was fighting at the barriers, the Earl of Essex and others challengers, and the Earl of Cumberland and his company defenders; into which number the Prince of Purpool was taken and behaved so valiantly and skilfully that he had the prize adjudged due unto him, which it pleased the Queen to deliver with her own hands, telling him that it was not her gift, for if it had been it should have been better. The prize is a jewel set with seventeen diamonds and four rubies, in value accounted worth 100 marks. Thus are these sports and revels ended at the Court, and the principality of Purpool determined in the greater brightness of the royal presence of her Majesty.

7th February. AN ALARM AT OSTEND.[4] There is new alarm of an attack at Ostend for that a prisoner from the garrison, to save his life, is reported to have promised to show some places in the defences which would be easily battered and entered by reason of the new fortifications not half perfected. Wherefore the enemy sent men to discover the places, but nothing is yet come of it.

8th February. SIR WALTER RALEGH'S VOYAGE.[5] Sir Walter Ralegh set out with his fleet from Plymouth two days ago.

9th February. THE QUEEN'S LETTER TO THE GRAND SIGNIOR.[6] The Queen writeth to the Emperor of Turkey at the importunity of Sigismund, the Vayrod of Transylvania, that she should intercede on his behalf. Wherefore the Queen,

---

[2] SP DOM 251:16.
[3] *Gesta Grayorum.* The Revels at Gray's Inn are a revelation of the mentality of the bright young men of aristocratic and upper middle-class England. It seems extraordinary that this elaborate, and at times impudent, parody of State should not only have been tolerated but actively encouraged by the Council, the nobility, the City, and even by the Queen herself. *Gesta Grayorum* is a mirror of the mind of the younger generation—as brilliant as there has ever been in England—its wit, its tastes, amusements, and aspirations. See also note on Chapman's *Humorous Day's Mirth,* 11th May 1597.
[4] SALISBURY PAPERS 5:104.
[5] HAKLUYT 7:280. See 27th Sept.
[6] SALISBURY PAPERS 5:105.

by reason of her old friendship with Sigismund, and for that he followeth the same form of Christianity as we, (having rejected the superstition of the Pope of Rome and the worshipping of images), now urgeth the Grand Signor that the Vayrod's complaints may be heard and remedied according to law.

11th February.   BISHOP FLETCHER'S MARRIAGE.[7] Dr. Fletcher the new Bishop of London of late married a gallant lady and widow, sister to Sir George Gifford the pensioner, (the Bishop himself also being a widower), who if she be virtuous is the more unhappy in that the world believeth it not. Hereat the Queen is so greatly displeased that she sendeth the Lord Buckhurst to confer with the Archbishop about sequestrating him from his function of Bishop.

18th February.   MOSSE'S 'ARRAIGNMENT AND CONVICTION OF USURY.'[8] There is a book of sermons called *The Arraignment and conviction of usury,* by Miles Mosse, Minister of the Word, dedicated to the Archbishop of Canterbury, wherein are handled four principal points, namely: usury, what it is and what are the kinds and branches thereof; proof that it is manifestly forbidden by the Word of God, and sundry reasons alleged why it is justly and worthily condemned; the objections answered which are usually made out of the Scriptures for the defence of some kind of usury; divers causes why usury should not be practised of a Christian, especially not of an Englishman, though it is not simply forbidden in the Scriptures.

20th February.   THE TRIAL OF FR. SOUTHWELL.[9] Robert Southwell, the Jesuit, was arraigned at the King's Bench before Lord Chief Justice Popham, having been removed from the Tower to Newgate some days since. Being brought along with halberts and bills, and his arms tied with a cord, at length he came through the press to the bar, and there, having his hands loosed, he put off his hat and made obeisance. The Chief Justice, casting his eyes upon him, asked him his age, who answered that he was about the age of Christ when

---

[7] SALISBURY PAPERS 5:106; NUGAE ANTIQUAE 2:46; Fuller's *Worthies* (Kent).
[8] SR 2:571; STC 18207. Epistle Dedicatory is dated 1st Jan 1595; the Ep. to the Reader 6th Feb 1594 [-5]; the book was entered 18th Feb, i.e., after printing.
[9] CATH. REC. SOC. 5:333, from an account by Thomas Leake, an eyewitness.

he was brought before Pilate. 'Why then,' quoth he, 'you make yourself Christ, his companion?' 'No,' saith Southwell, 'but a poor worm created for to serve him.'

Then was the indictment read, to which Southwell after some pause answered, 'I confess I am a Catholic priest and, I thank God for it, no traitor: neither can any law make it treason to be a priest.' The Chief Justice importuned him to answer according to form of law, and his answer was 'Not guilty of treason.'

Then Mr. Coke, the Attorney-General, began to open the indictment. 'I had not thought,' quoth he, 'to have spoken anything this day; but that the prisoner let fall a word, *videlicet,* that no law could make his case treason. I have occupied this room but three years, and there have been divers high points of treason practised by Jebusites, I should say Jesuits'; and drawing upon recent examples, concluded that the statute upon which the prisoner was arraigned was not made but upon some urgent cause. 'They pretend conscience,' saith he, 'but you shall see how far they are from it.'

One Bellamy's daughter was then brought in that had betrayed Southwell to Topcliffe. Her deposition was that Southwell told them that if any should inquire for him and propose to them an oath whether they had seen him, they might deny it by oath though they had seen him that same day, reserving this intention—'not with a purpose to tell you.' Hereupon the Attorney exclaimed that the rotten Chair would down which maintained a doctrine by which all judgments, all giving of testimonies, should be perverted. Southwell answered that his words were not altogether as she reported; 'but I told them,' said he, 'that to an oath were required justice, judgment and truth.' Some few words he spake more; but his utterance was somewhat unready, and they always cut him off when he began to speak.

And now Topcliffe began to question him, and as he answered, he was often interrupted so that he could seldom or never end one sentence when he did begin. Then said he, 'I am decayed in memory with long and close imprisonment, and I have been tortured ten times. I had rather have endured ten executions. I speak not this for myself but for others; that they may not be handled so inhumanely, to drive men to desperation if it were possible.'

To this Topcliffe answered, 'If he were racked, let me die for it.'

'No,' quoth Southwell, 'but it was as evil a torture, of late device.'

'I did but set him against a wall,' quoth Topcliffe.

To which Southwell answered, 'Thou art a bad man.'

'I would blow you all to dust, if I could,' said Topcliffe.

'What, all?' asked Southwell.

'Ay, all,' said Topcliffe.

'What, soul and body too?' said Southwell.

Hereupon Topcliffe exclaimed that he found him in a corner treading upon books, and also having letters directed to him from Parsons the Jesuit; which letters Topcliffe showed, but nothing was read of them, nor of other papers nor books which he poured out of a bag.

The jury staying not above a quarter of an hour, returned saying 'Guilty'; so he is condemned to death.

22nd February. THE EXECUTION OF SOUTHWELL.[10] This day Southwell was haled upon a draw from Newgate, laid upon straw, to the place of execution by Tyburn, with a cord fastened about his wrists. All the way he prayed, with his countenance and eyes lifted towards Heaven, and used not any speech. When he was come to the place, as they were taking him off the draw, the minister of the Tower came to him and used these words: 'You hold the decrees of the Council of Trent for authentical?' 'I do,' said Southwell. 'Therein,' said he, 'is decreed that no man shall presume to believe that he is sure to be saved, but is to doubt. If you believe to be saved, you contradict the Council; if you doubt, being about to die, your case is hard; and you doubting, we must needs doubt.' Southwell replied, 'I hope to be saved by the merits of my Saviour; but I pray you trouble me not.'

So he was lifted into the cart, at which time his countenance appeared very modest, yet cheerful, like the sun when it breaketh out after that it hath dispersed the clouds. The minister began to speak to him again, to whom he answered, 'I pray you Master Minister, give me leave.' So turning himself to the under-sheriff, he asked him whether he might speak; who answered that he might, so that he would confess his fault. 'I will,' said he, 'speak nothing against the State.'

His beginning to pray had entrance with this place of the apostle, '*Siue viuimus Domino viuimus, siue morimur Domino morimur; siue viuimus siue morimur, Domini sumus*'; at which

[10] As for *20th Feb.*

words the sheriff interrupted him, so where it seemed he would have made some speech, being cut off, he desired all Catholics to join with him in prayer to Almighty God, that it would please Him to forgive him all his sins which he had committed in this miserable life; miserable not for that he died a reproachful death, ignominious in the sight of the world, but honourable before God, for that it was for the testimony of His cause; but miserable for that he had sinned so often against so merciful and gracious a God. He then prayed for the Queen, that she might enjoy all gifts of nature and grace, all helps of friends and faithful councillors, whereby she might reign to God's glory, and after this life be inheritor of the Kingdom of Heaven, and wished that she would pardon him for that he had come into her kingdom without licence. He prayed that God would be merciful to the whole land and vouchsafe to convert them which were out of the way of truth.

And so protesting that he died a Catholic priest and in the Roman faith, standing in his shirt, often repeating these words, '*In manus tuas, Domine,*' the cart was removed. When he had hanged a while, the sheriff made a sign to the sergeants to cut the rope, at which there was a great confused cry in the company that he prayed for the Queen; 'And therefore let him hang till he be dead,' said they. So he was not cut down till he was senseless. A man might perceive by the countenances of the beholders that there was almost a general commiseration; none railed against him. The Lord Mountjoy was present, who is said, having beheld the mild and godly end of this man, to have uttered these words: 'I cannot judge of his religion; but pray God, whensoever I die, that my soul may be in no worse case than his.'

26th February.   THE FORT AT BLACKWATER TAKEN.[11] Ten days ago the rebels in Ireland assaulted and took the fort and castle of Blackwater. Some 40 or 50 of Tyrone's men, having passed through the town and within the stone castle, made sudden assault against the door of the inner castle which was made of wood; there being within only Henry Marche, the warder, and 4 others, whereof 2 were straightway sore wounded. These killed and galled 13 of the rebels. When the assault had continued for a quarter of an hour, the warder and 3 others came out of the castle and drave them away with their swords. But afterward learning from

11 SP IRELAND 178:53.

the other Englishmen in the place that their munition was gone, and that the rebels would burn the castle, they were forced to yield.

6th March. LOPEZ'S WIDOW.[1] The Queen hath granted to the widow and children of Lopez, that was executed for his treasonable practices in June last year, the leases that he held in London, and of his goods, forfeit by his attainder, not exceeding £100, but excepting a jewel set with a diamond and a ruby that was sent to Lopez by some minister of the King of Spain.

15th March. THE EARL OF CUMBERLAND'S SHIP.[2] My Lord of Cumberland, not liking his ill partage with the Great Carrack in '92 nor the unhappier loss of two carracks last year for want of sufficient strength to take them, now buildeth a ship of his own of 900 tons at Deptford; which the Queen at her launching named the *Scourge of Malice,* the best ship ever built by any subject.

26th March. MR. CHAMPERNOUN'S CHOIRBOYS.[3] It hath been reported about the Court that Mr. Richard Champernoun, the music master, to satisfy his own humour doth use boys otherwise than were fit for one that professeth Christianity, gelding them to preserve their voices; which report he vehemently denieth.

1st April. NEWS OF SIR W. RALEGH.[1] A ship of Portugal is lately come into Plymouth, of 80 tons burden, laden with fish, a prize that was taken near Cape St. Vincent. The Portugals of this ship declare that they with five others were taken by Ralegh on the 28th February; and that he had some of the principal men aboard him for two days, and finding their lading to be but fish, took some small quantity out of every ship, also a pipe of wine and a pipe of water, and thus let them pass. They say that he was merry and in good health.

2nd April. THE BEGUILED TRIPE-WIFE.[2] There is a pamphlet written by one calling himself 'Oliver Oatmeal' concern-

[1] SP DOM 251:50.
[2] PURCHAS 16:25.
[3] SALISBURY PAPERS 5:155, 436.
[1] SALISBURY PAPERS 5:161; SP DOM 256:100 (misdated 1596).

[2] STC 18758: *A Quest of Enquiry by women to know, whether the Tripe-wife were trimmed by Doll yea or no,* by Oliver Oatmeal; see *10th Jan.*

ing the knaveries of Judith or Doll Phillips and the beguiling
of Mrs. Mascall, the tripe-wife. This old woman, being
much sought after in marriage for her goods, was at last
beguiled to the house of one of her sisters, where the wine
walking lustily about and many merry matters familiarly dis-
puted on, it was set down that the tripe-wife must dine next
day at her suitor's house. Thither she comes, where the time
being wasted in conference, home he would not let her go
that night, and then they so whittled her with wine that he
drew a promise of marriage from her. Shortly after, the widow
sitting asleep by the fire, he valiantly coming behind her
pulled the stool from her, when down fell she, and he by
(or upon) her, with that learned and witty adverb in his
mouth, 'Keep the widow waking.' Small rest had she that
night, for before it was daylight, they made her pass through
his cellar, enter a boat lying ready for her, and to sail so far
as Pepper Alley and thence to St. George's Church, where
she is married at two o'clock in the morning. But now the
wooer, being a grocer by trade, made such a brag of his
tricking the tripe-wife, and she such lamentations and complaints, that the matter is not only come to the law but also
is sung abroad by the ballad makers.

5th April. SOUTHWELL'S 'ST. PETER'S COMPLAINT.'[3] A
poetical book by Southwell, the Jesuit, is entered for the press,
entitled *St. Peter's Complaint,* wherein he saith, 'Poets by
abusing their talent, and making the follies and feignings of
love the customary subject of their base endeavours, have
so discredited this faculty, that a poet, a lover and a liar are
by many reckoned but three words of one signification.' In
his complaint Saint Peter mourneth his betraying of Christ,
and the griefs arising therefrom, together with loss of sleep.
There is added *Mary Magdalene's Blush* with her *Complaint at Christ's death, 'Look home,' Fortune's Falsehood, At
home in Heaven, Lewd Love is loss,* and other short poems.

12th April. DRAYTON'S 'ENDIMION AND PHOEBE.'[4] Michael
Drayton hath written a poem of *Endimion and Phoebe:
Idea's Latmus,* wherein is told that fable of the love of the
goddess Phoebe for the shepherd Endimion whom she found
upon Latmus; and when he had declared his love for her
she revealed herself to him, and transported him from earth
to heaven.

[3] SR 2:295; STC 22956.   [4] SR 2:296; STC 7192.

SIR PHILIP SIDNEY'S 'DEFENCE OF POESY.'[5] Last November Mr. Ponsonby entered his copy of that treatise of poetry written by Sir Philip Sidney, but without printing it; now Mr. Olney, ignorant of the former entry, hath entered another copy and published the same. Hereupon Ponsonby claimeth his prior entry, and agreement is made between them that he shall have it. In this treatise, entitled *The Defence of Poesy*, Sir Philip went about to defend poetry against those that speak against it, saying that it is not only a divine art, but greater than either history or philosophy. 'The poet,' quoth he, 'beginneth not with obscure definitions, which must blur the margent with interpretations and load the memory with doubtfulness; but he cometh to you with words set in delightful proportion, either accompanied with, or prepared for, the well inchanting skill of music; and with a tale forsooth he cometh unto you, with a tale which holdeth children from play and old men from the chimney corner.'

THE BENEFITS OF FISH DAYS.[6] There is set forth in print by the Lord Mayor a brief note of the benefits that grow by fish days, to be placed in the houses of all men and especially common victuallers. Firstly, forasmuch as our country is for the most part compassed with the seas, so by a certain expense of fish fishermen are the better maintained and men at all times held in readiness for her Majesty's navy. Secondly, because of the decay of many towns and villages upon the sea coast that in times past were not only replenished with fishermen, but also with shipwrights, ropemakers, sailmakers and divers other trades. Furthermore the trade of grazing cattle, through unlawful expense of flesh, is so much increased that many farm houses and villages are entirely decayed. Showeth also that by one day's abstinence in a week 13,500 beeves might be saved yearly in this City of London.

15th April. DR. FLETCHER'S DISGRACE.[7] The Bishop of London that was to have had the place of the Queen's

[5] SR 2:666 and 2:295; STC 22534–35. The *Defence* was first entered on 29th Nov 1594, by Ponsonby, presumably as a blocking entry; *Astrophel and Stella* had been published in 1591, against the wishes of the Sidney family, with a preface by Nashe. Olney entered a copy (called *The Apology for Poetry*) on 12th April and proceeded to print, but Ponsonby complained. Olney's entry was therefore cancelled, and it was agreed that Ponsonby should enjoy the copy. Olney's copy is usually preferred by editors, but Ponsonby's is the authorised edition; *The Defence of Poesy* would therefore appear to be the true title.

[6] SR 2:296; STC 9977. A reprint of the proclamation of 1593.

[7] SALISBURY PAPERS 5:171.

Almoner at the Maundy is now commanded not to deal it. It is said that both he himself and his wife have used insolent speeches and words to be wondered at concerning her Majesty.

16th April. 'THE OLD WIVES' TALE.'[8] There is entered for printing that play written by George Peele entitled *The Old Wives' Tale* which was played by the Queen's Players about 5 years since.

17th April. SPANISH PREPARATIONS IN BRITTANY.[9] It is reported that there are many men of war of the Spaniards come to the coast of Brittany. Of late the Spaniards took a bark of Guernsey, and sent all the men home saving 4 ancient men and good pilots for that coast, which putteth the people of that place in great fear of some attempt of the Spaniard. At Blavet are seventeen flyboats and three galleys.

23rd April. THE FEAST OF ST. GEORGE.[10] This year at the feast there were present thirteen of the Knights of the Garter. The Communion in the Chapel being ended, the Knights of the Order proceeded into the castle yard before her Majesty, who walked beneath a canopy of cloth of gold, lined with red, and held up by four. There were present many noblemen and ladies and gentlemen of the Court; who passed three times round the yard that all might take a good view of them. At the feast my Lord Cobham represented the Queen, being honoured as if she herself had been present, the guards serving him on the knee, and the Earls (who handed the water to him before and after) on both knees. The feast began at one o'clock and continued for over three hours, many foreign gentlemen being present, among them the envoy of the Duke of Wirtenberg who would remind her Majesty of her pretended promise to bestow the Order on his master.

26th April. THE DUKE OF WIRTENBERG'S ENVOY.[11] To-day the Queen gave audience to the envoy of the Duke of Wirtenberg that would importune her of a promise that he should be admitted to the Order of St. George; to whom the Queen returned answer that no such promise had been made nor could be, seeing that the Garter is not yet despatched to cer-

[8] SR 2:296; STC 19545.
[9] SALISBURY PAPERS 5:171.
[10] *Queen Elizabeth and some foreigners,* by V. von Klarwill, 1928, p. 375.
[11] As for *23rd April.*

tain Kings that were a long time past elected by the Order.
She added that the Duke should suffer our merchants to
carry on their trade in his realms with all security, and put
down those that slander her person.

30th April. TROOPS IN THE LOW COUNTRIES.[12] The Queen
hath now in her pay in the Low Countries 50 foot companies,
being 4 of 200 men, 44 of 150, and 2 of 100 each, making in
all 7,600, which men with their winter and summer apparel,
victuals, pay and others expenses cost annually £109,600.

6th May. 'A FIG FOR MOMUS.'[1] There is a new book of
Mr. Thomas Lodge entitled *A Fig for Momus,* dedicated to
my Lord of Derby, being sundry satires, eclogues, and
epistles. Of these, the satires are here published to prepare
the ear of the reader; because if they pass well, the whole
centon of them, already written, shall suddenly be published.
Treateth in this book of the necessity for parents to set good
examples in their lives before their children; of dreams; of
covetousness and the folly of ambition; of saving and spending. Concludeth with an Anatomy of Alchemy, very invectively condemning the professors of that science, yet, saith
he, unto artists there is a certain quality that can be perceived:

> It feeds the ear, it amplifies the thought,
> Except to those that know it, it is nought.

There is also an epistle to a lady that wrote to him asking
both the cause and the remedy of pursiness and fat. Nevertheless he is of an opinion that fatness is no deformity, for

> fat, slick, fair and full
> Is better lik'd than lean, lank, spare and dull.

8th May. A CATALOGUE OF ENGLISH PRINTED BOOKS.[2] A
catalogue of English printed books is to be printed by Mr.
Andrew Maunsell, bookseller, whereof the first part treateth
of such matters of divinity as have been either written in
our own tongue or translated out of other languages; the
second of books concerning the sciences mathematical, arithmetic, geometry, astronomy, astrology, music, the art of war,
navigation, physic, and surgery.

[12] SP Dom 251:126.
[1] SR 2:297; STC 16658. Entered 2nd
April; dated 6th May in Epistle to
the Gentlemen Readers.
[2] SR 2:297; STC 17669.

9th May. THE EARL OF CUMBERLAND'S COMMISSION.[3] The Earl of Cumberland is granted special commission to attack the powers of the King of Spain or any of his subjects and adherents with his ships, which shall not exceed the number of six. He shall also have full power to distribute all merchandises and prizes taken as he will, saving the usual customs and duties due upon all goods brought into the realm.

15th May. BANKS' HORSE.[4] There is one Banks hath a bay gelding, called Morocco, of wondrous quality, that can fight, and dance and lie; and find your purse and tell you what money you have.

22nd May. 'CERTAIN VERY PROPER SIMILES.'[5] Mr. Anthony Fletcher, a minister, hath collected more than two hundred and thirty godly similes and set them forth in a book with this title: *Certain very proper and most profitable similes, wherein sundry, and very many, most foul vices, and dangerous sins of all sorts are so plainly laid open, and displayed in their kinds, and so pointed at with the finger of God, in his sacred and holy Scriptures, to signify his wrath and indignation belonging unto them, that the Christian Reader, being seasoned with the spirit of grace, and having God before his eyes, will be very fearful, even in love that he beareth to God, to pollute and to defile his heart, his mind, his mouth or hands, with any such forbidden things. And also many very notable virtues, with their due commendations, so lively and truly expressed, according to the holy word, that the godly Reader, being of a Christian inclination, will be mightily inflamed with a love unto them.* Addeth thereto the cut of an idle tree.

25th May. THE NEGOTIATIONS WITH THE STATES.[6] These past weeks Mr. Thomas Bodley, her Majesty's Agent, hath urged her demands to the States that they ease her of the great charge of maintaining garrisons and repay some part of her expenses, appointing commissioners to settle a course how the whole sum disbursed upon their account and due to Sir Horatio Palavicino, to whom she payeth great sums in inter-

---

[3] RYMER 16:274.
[4] This date of the first appearance of Banks and Morocco is a guess, but the horse was certainly known before the end of the year (see *17th Dec*). There are many references to the performance collected by S. H. Atkins in *Notes and Queries*, 21st July 1934.
[5] SR 2:296; STC 11053. Entered 12th April; dated 22nd May in Epistle Dedicatory.
[6] SALISBURY PAPERS 5:179; CAMDEN'S ELIZABETH; BIRCH'S MEMOIRS 1:244.

est. Mr. Bodley is now come over with the answer of the States, which is that they acknowledge themselves infinitely bound to the Queen, and would pay according to their ability; but as for the demand made by the Lord Treasurer for £100,000 they are destitute of means to satisfy it, or even a far lesser sum. These proposals have greatly moved the Queen, who was even heard to say in Court that she wished Mr. Bodley had been hanged; whereat he stirs not abroad these ten days.

27th May. DR. JOHN DEE PROMOTED.[7] The Queen hath granted to Dr. John Dee the wardenship of Christ's College in Manchester.

'THE WORLD'S HYDROGRAPHICAL DESCRIPTION.'[8] To-day is published a little book entitled *The World's Hydrographical Description,* written by Captain John Davis, wherein is shown, not only by authority of writers, but also by late experience of travellers, and reasons of substantial probability, that the world in all his zones, climates and places is habitable and inhabited; and the seas likewise universally navigable, whereby it appears that from England there is a short and speedy passage by northerly navigation into the South Seas to China, Molucca, Philippine and India. Captain Davis writeth much of his own travels into the frozen parts of the north. Noteth that, being deserted of his consort, in one small bark of thirty tons without further comfort or consort he proceeded northward until he came to a great strait which he followed for eighty leagues until he came to many islands, whence he concludeth the north part of America to be all islands.

28th May. THE IRISH REBELLION.[9] The rebels, led in those parts by a notable traitor called Feogh MacHugh, have taken the fort at Enniskillen, that was held by some thirteen or fourteen with the constable. The rebels allowed them to come out of the castle with bag and baggage and promise of life, and then put them to the sword. Thirty-six heads of Mac-Hugh's men have been brought to Dublin where Tyrone shall shortly be proclaimed traitor.

[7] SP DOM 252:35. This is Dee the famous alchemist.
[8] SR 2:299; STC 6372. On the title-page is the uncommon inscription 'Published by I. Dauis of Sandrug by Dartmouth in the *Countie of Deuon.*

Gentleman. Anno 1595. May 27.' The Epistle Dedicatory to the Lords of Council bears the same date. It was entered on 1st June 1595.
[9] SP IRELAND 279:82.

THE CRUELTY OF THE TURK.[10] The Turk hath lately caused
to be executed his brother-in-law for having discovered some
matter of state. He caused a butcher to be quartered on his
own stool, and a baker to be burnt in his own oven for false
weights.

30th May.   MR. ROBERT DUDLEY'S RETURN.[11] Mr. Robert
Dudley is returned to England, having set out last November in the *Bear* as admiral, with the *Bear's Whelp,* vice-admiral, and two small pinnaces, the *Frisking* and the *Earwig.*
The vice-admiral and one of the pinnaces being separated
from him in a storm at their starting, he went on alone with
the other, sailing along the coast of Spain, and thence to the
Canaries. Thereafter shaping his course to Trinidad in the
West Indies, he came at length to Waliame, the first kingdom of the Empire of Guiana.

Here he was told by an Indian, his interpreter, of a golden
mine in a town called Orocoa in the river of Owrinoicke, but
his men being utterly unwilling that he should go himself,
Mr. Dudley sent forward a company of his discreetest men.
These went forward up the river, and there they were met by
the Captain of the town of Orocoa and of the mine, who told
them that by force they should have nothing but blows, yet
if they would bring him hatchets, knives and jews-harps he
would trade in gold with Mr. Dudley. Also he told them of
another rich nation that sprinkle their bodies with powder of
gold and seem to be gilt, and far beyond them a great town
called El Dorado.

The men being satisfied returned, having been absent sixteen days, but in pitiful case, almost dead with thirst, for they
had not drunk in three days before they recovered the ship,
so long were they out of the fresh rivers. Hereupon Mr. Dudley attempted his company to go with them again but they
flat refused.

On his return he came to the Isles of Flores and Cuervo,
hoping to meet with some great fleet from England, but finding none and his victuals being almost spent, he directed his
course alone for England. Soon after he met with a great
armada of 600 tons (the *Bear* being but of 200 tons), and
fought with her for two days, till his powder being all spent,

[10] SALISBURY PAPERS 5:189. This is
the Emperor Amurath. Cf. 'Not
Amurath an Amurath succeeds, But

Harry Harry' (*II Hen IV,* V. ii. 48–
49).
[11] HAKLUYT 6:164.

he left her 300 leagues from land and in miserable state so that in short space she sank.

In this voyage have been taken, sunk or burnt nine Spanish ships, which is a great loss to the enemy, though Mr. Dudley himself hath gained nothing.

5th June. A RIOT IN LONDON.[1] To-day a certain silkweaver came to the Lord Mayor's house, using some hard speeches concerning him and in dispraise of his government. The Lord Mayor said he was mad and so committed him to Bedlam as a madman, but not having his officers about him sent him thither by some of his own servants; but without Bishopsgate he was rescued by prentices and divers other to the number of two or three hundred persons.

9th June. NEWS FROM LISBON.[2] One lately come from Lisbon reporteth that eight ships of the Indian fleet have come in, bringing two English Captains, Captain John Middleton, and Captain Goddard, the Earl of Cumberland's man, and nine or ten mariners, who report that in the South Seas the *Dainty* is captured with Captain Hawkins who had taken great treasure. In March and April on a report that Sir Francis Drake was coming with a fleet of English, French and Hollanders' ships, about 8,000 fled; and now the coast is replenished with soldiers. The Canaries and the Azores are also being fortified.

10th June. A SKIRMISH WITH TYRONE.[3] On 27th May our soldiers set out from Newry, under Sir Henry Bagnal, being 1500 foot and 250 horse to revictual the garrison in Monaghan. On the way 1500 horse of the enemy appeared on a hill and would have drawn our horse after them, but the General would not. Next morning Tyrone brought all his forces to a straight which our men were to pass and turned off seven or eight companies to skirmish which annoyed them much, the passage being between a bog and a wood. They passed through this straight and reached Monaghan, having lost twelve slain and thirty hurt, the enemy's loss being 100 slain and many hurt. Having put victual into Monaghan and changed the ward, our men dislodged and marched back, being harassed by the rebels in the straights and passages, but at length they reached Newry, where our losses were found

[1] SALISBURY PAPERS 5:249.
[2] SP DOM 252:58. Richard Hawkins was son of Sir John Hawkins.
[3] CAREW MSS 154; SP IRELAND 179:95; 180:5, 6.

to be thirty-one slain, 109 hurt, but none hurt of account except Sir Henry Duke, Captain Cunye, five lieutenants, an ensign and a sergeant.

In this fight Tyrone had 14,000 foot, and 300 shot in red coats, like our English soldiers.

MacHugh is reported to be shot in the thigh and hurt with a skeyne in the body, flying from our men so fast that he threw away his helmet, target and sword, which are brought in.

13th June. DISORDERS IN THE CITY.[4] Divers prentices this day being pinched in their victuals took butter from the market people in Southwark, paying them but 3d. the pound, though they demanded 5d. Certain of these prentices are apprehended.

15th June. FURTHER RIOTING IN THE CITY.[5] Some prentices being to-day committed to the Counter by the constable for certain misdemeanours, others congregating themselves came to the Counter, and said they would have them forth again, using very hard speeches against the Lord Mayor; but as the gates were shut against them, they tarried not long but departed away.

Not long after a serving man, whose brother, being a prentice, had complained of his master's hard dealing, came to the master, and quarrelled with him; and in the multiplying of words the master's head was broken. By this brawl the people gathered together and much hurly-burly followed so that Sir Richard Martin hearing thereof came into the street, apprehended the serving man and sent him to the Counter by the constable. As they were going, the prentices that had already resorted to the Counter met them, rescued the serving man from the Counter, and brought him back to Cheapside. Whereupon Sir Richard Martin came forth suddenly with such company as he had of his own servants and forthwith he apprehended the serving man again, reprehended the prentices for their so great disorder, took six of the principal offenders, and so by the constable sent them all to the Counter, causing irons to be laid upon them.

About an hour afterwards, when all was quiet, the Lord Mayor cometh into Cheapside and commandeth Sir Richard Martin and Sir John Hart to take order for the safe keeping of these prentices. On his return, about London Wall, a prentice meeting him will not put off his cap; whereupon he also is sent to the Counter, which is done quietly and without opposition of any.

16th June. THE RIOTOUS PRENTICES.[6] Certain prentices and soldiers or masterless men are said to have met together in Paul's, and there had conferences, wherein the soldiers said to the prentices, 'You know not your strength.' Then the prentices asked the soldiers if they would assist them; and the soldiers answered that they would within an hour after be ready to aid them and be their leader; and that they would play an Irish trick with the Lord Mayor, who should not have his head upon his shoulders within an hour after.

The causes of these present inconveniences are said to be the great number of loose and masterless men about the City, pretending to be soldiers; the great dearth of victual; and the remiss care of the magistrates in time to have remedied the same. The Lord Mayor also is blamed for his insatiable avarice; for his selling and converting of offices to his own gain and then suffering those officers to be negligent; and for his refusing to bear or join with his brethren.

17th June. SLIGO TAKEN BY THE REBELS.[7] In Ireland, as Captain George Bingham sat writing in his chamber in Sligo Castle, his ensign, one Burke, and twenty of his men, all Clanricarde men, fell upon him suddenly and slew him.

20th June. 'THE TRUMPET OF FAME.'[8] One H. R. hath written a poem of encouragement to all sailors and soldiers that are minded to go with Sir Francis Drake and Sir John Hawkins, wherein are related the names of the ships and their former actions against the enemy.

23rd June. DISORDERS IN SOUTHWARK.[9] About 4 o'clock this afternoon some prentices and other servants, being sent to Billingsgate by their masters to buy mackerels and finding none there, were informed that divers fishwives a little before had gone on board the fisherboats and bought up the whole share and carried it with them to Southwark. Hereupon the prentices, in number sixty or eighty, pursued after them

[6] SALISBURY PAPERS 5:249-50.
[7] SP IRELAND 180:16.
[8] STC 21088, where the poem is attributed to Henry Roberts.
[9] *Remembrancia* 2:97.

without any weapons, having only baskets under their arms; and coming to the fishwives they took their mackerels from some of them, giving them money 4 for the groat (which is the rate formerly set by the Lord Mayor). Then one of the fishwives began to lay about her, and offered to strike some of the prentices with her fish basket; but when the constable, seeing the disorder, commanded these rude and unruly persons to surcease their strife then without any further unkindness or breach of the peace they departed.

27th June. RIOTOUS PRENTICES WHIPPED.[10] The riotous prentices that took from the market people at Southwark their butter were this day punished with whipping, setting in the pillory, and long imprisonment.

29th June. UNRULY YOUTHS ON TOWER HILL.[11] This Sunday afternoon a number of unruly youths on Tower Hill being blamed by the warders of Tower Street ward, drave them back with stones, being heartened thereunto by the sound of a trumpet. The trumpeter, one that formerly was a soldier, and many of the company are taken by the Sheriffs and in prison. About 7 o'clock this evening, Sir John Spencer, the Lord Mayor, with his officers rode to Tower Hill to see the hill cleared of tumultuous persons; and here some warders of the Tower and men of the Lieutenant told the Lord Mayor that the Sword ought not to be borne up in that place; and thereupon two or three of them catching hold of the Sword, there was some bickering and the sword-bearer hurt. But the Lord Mayor by his discretion and by proclamation in the Queen's name in short time cleared the hill of all trouble and rode back, the sword-bearer bearing up the Sword before him.

SIR JOHN HAWKINS' AGREEMENT WITH THE QUEEN.[12] It is agreed between the Queen and Sir John Hawkins concerning the voyage that he purposeth to the southward, that she shall at her own charges put in order and furnish six ships, for which she shall have a third part of any booty taken from the enemy; and Sir John at his own charge shall victual the same ships for four months, for which he shall have another third; the remaining third shall be to the sailors and servitors in those ships. If she shall stay the journey, the charges disbursed by Sir John shall be refunded.

[10] STOW'S ANNALS; see *13th June.*   [12] SP DOM 252:107.
[11] STOW'S ANNALS.

A SEDITIOUS PAMPHLET.[13] The Lord Mayor, being required to advertise the Council concerning the printing of a certain pamphlet by the Company of Weavers, hath discovered that 15 of them were privy to it. The pamphlet was printed by one Gabriel Simpson, and the proof of the first print was then read in the house of a certain Muggins in the hearing of the whole number. Twelve of them showed their dislike to have the pamphlet proceed into print, but the other three continued in their purpose and required the printer to print for them some 40 copies, which they would have delivered to the French Church, the Dutch Church, and one apiece to the Lord Mayor and Aldermen; but only 22 were printed, whereof 19 are taken. The principal doers in this business are one Millington, Muggins and Deloney, who with the printer are committed to Newgate.

2nd July. A CASE IN THE STAR CHAMBER.[1] This day was begun the hearing of the suit for slander brought against one Wood by Mr. Edward Talbot, brother to my Lord of Shrewsbury. This Wood had charged Mr. Talbot that he secretly intended the poisoning of the Earl by means of himself, and to this end gave him an annuity of £100 per annum. Mr. Talbot's counsel enforced the impeachment of Wood's credit by sundry deceitful practices in physic (he practising physic, being neither licensed nor graduate in any University), of ministering oil of stag's blood to the Countess of Shrewsbury for the gout, and divers other sophisticated oils, receipts and compositions, as oil of wax, butter, antimony, liquor of pearl and such like. Moreover he would show that this Wood had treacherously concealed this practice from my Lord for two years and a half, and had manifestly forged the deed of annuity. For the credit of the defendant, it was argued that things done in his youth should not be brought forward; gentlemen of Inns of Court and others have done many worse practices, and as for sophisticated drugs, many apothecaries in the town are in like fault. But the case is left unfinished.

4th July. UNLAWFUL ASSEMBLIES RESTRAINED.[2] Because of the late disorders in the City there is now issued a proclamation straitly charging all officers more diligently to punish offenders, and especially to suppress all unlawful assemblies, upon pain to be not only removed from their offices but to be

[13] *Remembrancia* 2:98.   [2] PROCLAMATIONS 330.
[1] HAWARDE, p. 13.

also punished as persons maintaining or rather comforting the offenders. And because the late riots are compounded of sundry sorts of base people, some known prentices, such as are of base manual occupation, some others rogues and vagabonds, and some colouring their wandering by the name of soldiers returned from the wars, therefore certain special orders are to be prescribed and published in and about the City. These her Majesty will have strictly observed, and for that purpose meaneth to have a Provost Marshal, with sufficient authority to apprehend all such as shall not readily be reformed and corrected by the ordinary Officers of Justice, and without delay to execute them upon the gallows by order of martial law.

ORDERS OF THE COUNCIL IN THIS TIME OF TUMULT.[3] No persons but such as be officers for preservation of peace or such as be of known honest conversation shall walk up and down the streets or fields after sunset or 9 o'clock at night; nor assemble themselves in a company at any time or in any place, other than in churches for prayers or sermons, or for appearances before Officers of Justice or by their commandment, or in common Halls of Companies. No householder nor any that keepeth inns or lodging for strangers do suffer his servants or guests (not being gentlemen) to go out into the streets in the evening; and if they cannot be restrained then to inform the officers speedily. No person to write or be privy to any seditious bills to be dispersed or set up, upon pain to be executed by martial law. And any person who shall reveal an offender, the information being found true and the party taken, the revealer shall have £20 or a better reward. All persons arrested by any officer shall obey him, and if any make resistance, every other person there present if required by the Officers shall assist to the best of his power. If any shall attempt to rescue the party arrested, he and all those accompanying him shall be apprehended and executed by the Provost Marshal by martial law.

TALBOT'S CASE CONCLUDED.[4] Mr. Talbot's case against Wood is concluded, the Lords condemning Wood for a most palpable machiavellian, but deferring their sentence till they had

---

[3] PROCLAMATIONS 331.
[4] HAWARDE, p. 16. Hawarde notes that Essex and the Archbishop were afterwards checked by the Queen. Wood after long imprisonment confessed that he was 'the only deviser, procurer, acter & plotter in all this action, for the which he loste both his eares in the pillorye, was slitte in the nose, sealled in the foreheade, and censured to perpetual imprisonment.' Hawarde's own spelling of 'process' is 'proces.' See 6th Dec.

heard the next suit, of the Earl of Shrewsbury against his brother, Mr. Edward Talbot, for that by practice of Wood he should have poisoned the Earl, first by gloves, and then by potion or plaster. This charge my Lord essayed to prove by no direct witnesses save Wood (who was not allowed but taken as infamous), and by circumstances that at the first seemed somewhat probable. My Lord's Counsel endeavoured to discredit the defendant for his haughtiness of mind, his prodigality and the like, showing that he had spent 10,000 marks in three years since the death of his father: and for his religion, for defending one John Baldwin who questioned whether there was a God; if there were, how He should be known; if by His Word, who wrote the same; and if the prophets and the apostles, they were but men, and *humanum est errare;* and such like most damnable doubts, which were not suffered to be read in the hearing of the court. Then the plaintiff argued that Mr. Talbot practised and agreed with Sir Edward Stapleton for effecting of the poisoning, and Sir Edward had suborned a man of his, of his own name, to buy the gloves.

At this the Court seemed dubious for a long time. The milliner therefore was summoned, and his man that sold the gloves, who denied upon the sight of Stapleton that he could be the man. So after long hearing (for this day the Lords sat from 9 in the morning until 6), Wood is herein condemned as a palpable ass, a very villain, and of Satan's brood, being called *Diabolos* for that he is an accuser.

After the Counsel had argued very learnedly, the Queen's Attorney craved that his silence might not prejudice the defendant's cause, for whom he spake in the former action wherein he was plaintiff, but could not now speak for him seeing that he was defendant. Whereupon he proved Wood to be no scholar for he used false orthography, for 'process' writing 'prossus,' whereas every scholar knoweth 'process' to come of *procedendo*.

The sentence of the whole court, excepting only my Lord of Essex and the Archbishop of Canterbury, is that Wood shall ride from the Fleet to Westminster with his face to the horse's tail, and there stand upon the pillory, and so ride to the Fleet again; and another day from thence to Cheapside to the pillory there; and be fined to the Queen £500 and to be imprisoned at her pleasure. But the Lord Treasurer moved that if Wood should confess his fault and submit himself to Mr. Talbot at the next assizes, then the £500 should be released.

16th July. THE EXPEDITION FROM PLYMOUTH.[5] Sir Thomas
Gorges that hath been sent down to Plymouth to join with Sir
John Hawkins and Sir Francis Drake reporteth that the ships
are in very good sort, for that Sir John is an excellent man in
those things and sees all things done properly. Sir Thomas's
coming at first greatly amazed them, they fearing that he had
been sent to stay them; but when they knew the contrary they
were very joyful that the Queen had sent down someone to
see their bravery. Their expedition cannot depart for 14 days
at least as some pinnaces are not yet ready.

17th July. A NOTABLE OUTRAGE.[6] One William Randolph, a
grazier dwelling about Cardiff who had much dealing about
London being very open with a certain Dernley, a man of
the same profession, told him that he was to ride through
Aylesbury to Wales with above £300. Hereupon Dernley
acquainted two men, called Parry and Richardson, of the
matter, who fell in company with Randolph and very courteously bare him company to Aylesbury. By the way one
Tayler of Aylesbury chanced among them, and noting by
Randolph's talk that he concealed not his charge of money,
besides observing how Parry and Richardson were horsed and
weaponed, warned Randolph against them; but the good old
man refused to believe him. These speeches came to the ears
of Parry and Richardson. Whereupon making show of displeasure, in the morning they went before him out of town.
Randolph hearing they were gone greatly blamed the chamberlain of the inn, and posted after, overtaking them near a
wood side where the way was hollow.

Then these hollow hearted companions, under colour of
kind salutation, turned their horses' heads to bid him welcome,
and Parry first with a Judas-like welcome discharged his pistol
in his bosom, while Richardson with the second bullet shot
him through hand and belly. So he fell down and they dou-
bling in his death wound upon wound mangled his face with
inhuman cruelty. Then drew they him into a thicket and rifled
his dead body, where Richardson yet unsatisfied with cruelty
stabbed him into the neck with such violence that in pulling
back his hand, the pummel and handle of his dagger came
off, but the blade he left sticking in his neck; which blade was
one witness against him.

This done they turned his horse into the wood and hovered

about the country some two days and more after, for it was the second day before the body was found by a fellow that sought cattle. When the hue-and-cry came to Aylesbury, Tayler among others went to see the body, and by the apparel better than the face knew it was the wretched man that refused his counsel at Aylesbury. He described the murderers' apparel, proportions, horses and all such marks as he advisedly had taken while he rid in their company. To London, toward Wales, and every way the hue-and-cry went. Parry was taken in Wales, and confessed the fact; Richardson at his own house in London. A while he denied the deed, but long he stood not on it, both of them accused Dernley; and to Aylesbury are they all gone to suffer deserved death.

18th July. THE PROVOST MARSHAL APPOINTED.[7] Sir Thomas Wyllford is appointed a provost marshal for these times of tumult, with power to attach notable and incorrigible offenders upon signification of the justices of peace and by justice of martial law to execute them openly. Likewise he shall repair with a convenient company to all common highways near London to apprehend all vagrant and suspected persons.

23rd July. AN ENGLISHMAN BURNT IN ROME.[8] About five weeks ago during a procession in Rome a young Englishman smote the Sacrament out of the hands of an archbishop that was carrying it in procession with such force that it fell to the ground, the crystal of the monstrance being broken and his hand cut withal. Whereon a crowd collected and thrusting burning torches in his face would have killed him had not the archbishop restrained them. The Englishman was then thrown into prison and tried by the Inquisition. A week afterwards he was handed over to magistrates; and the next day he was bound to a cart and his right hand cut off. Then he was taken through the City, being frequently smitten by the executioner with burning brands, and at last burnt alive in the Piazza del Capitolio.

24th July. THE UNRULY YOUTHS CONDEMNED.[9] Five of the unruly youths apprehended for the disorder on Tower Hill on 29th June were arraigned in the Guildhall and condemned of high treason two days since, and to-day were drawn from

[7] RYMER 16:279. [9] STOW'S ANNALS.
[8] FUGGER NEWS-LETTERS, pp. 527, 529.

Newgate to Tower Hill, where they were hanged and bowelled as traitors.

25th July. EXCESSIVE PRICES.[10] This year by reason of the transportation of grain into foreign countries, the same is grown into an excessive price, as in some places from 14s. to 4 marks the quarter, and more. In London, such is the scarcity of victual, that an hen's egg is sold for a penny, or three eggs at the most for 2d., a pound of sweet butter for 7d., and the like of flesh and fish, exceeding measure in price, such are our sins in deserving it.

26th July. THE SPANIARDS LAND IN CORNWALL.[11] From Cornwall it is reported that four hundred Spanish soldiers were landed from four galleys who burnt Moldsey, a small village, and Newlin, with Penzance, a very good town. The town of Penzance had been saved if the people had stood with Sir Francis Godolphin, but the common sort utterly forsook him, saving for some four or five gentlemen.

This landing of the Spaniards hath bred in the Court diversity of passions; but the most part take courage against them in such sort as they that have heretofore seemed abated in spirit do now lift up the crest. This night Sir Roger Williams hath, in presence of all the Court, received of her Majesty a friendly public welcome. This afternoon the Lord Admiral rode to Chatham to put order to the navy; and in effect it is a stirring world.

27th July. THE IRISH REBELLION.[12] This past month the army in Ireland under Sir William Russell, the Lord Deputy, and Sir John Norris, have made a journey through the rebels' country, setting forth from Dundalk on the 18th June and returning on the 17th July.

28th July. THE SPANISH LANDING.[13] Certain Englishmen that were landed by the Spaniards in Mount Bay say that after they had burned Penzance and other villages they had Mass the next day on the Western Hill by a friar, and there they vow to build a friary when they shall have conquered England.

[10] STOW'S ANNALS.
[11] SALISBURY PAPERS 5:290; BIRCH'S MEMOIRS 1:269; SP DOM 253:30; STC 4615.
[12] CAREW MSS 158.
[13] SP DOM 253:33.

7th August.   A NEW SPANISH ARMADA.[1] It is reported that a new armada is preparing by the King of Spain at Lisbon. There are ten Biscayan ships and thirty others, and some not yet come in; and enough biscuit prepared for 10,000 men.

11th August.   THE SPANISH SHIPS.[2] From Portsmouth comes news that fifteen or sixteen Spanish sail, whereof six are very great ships, were sighted off Scilly, and as many ride the other side of the Scillys.

13th August.   IRISH NEWS.[3] The Council in Ireland meeting to consider the measures to be taken to bring the rebels into obedience, it was concluded to send 1600 men under Sir John Norris through the Pale, and to this end pioneers, masons, carpenters, boats and carriages are being prepared. From the borders daily come the complaints of the soldiers, who have neither money, victuals, nor clothes, so that they grow into desperate terms and spare not to say to their officers that they will run away and steal rather than famish. There is considerable sickness, as much as twenty in every band, amongst the men from Brittany who, though they made no good impression on the Lord Deputy when they first came, are in proof found very good, though they like so ill of the country that they run away as fast as they can by any means escape; which to prevent some have been hanged for an example to the rest. Sir John Norris himself declareth that if there were good order and good provision made, not only these rebels might be in short time extirpated, but the country reduced into such terms as they should never be able to lift up their heads; but no success can be looked for so long as those that have the chiefest disposition of things there care not how long the war last so they may make their profit, whilst in England the chiefest hope of the good event is reposed upon accidents, whereby timely provisions are neglected and time lost. In Ardes 4000 Scots are landed to succour Tyrone, who offereth to give in marriage to the bachelors of them the daughters of his gentlemen and freeholders, every one a wife of degree proportionable to the man that is to marry her.

17th August. DEATH OF DON ANTONIO.[4] Don Antonio, that
is called King of Portugal, is dead in Paris five days since.
He died in great poverty, and frequent collections were made
for him at the French Court. The King appointed for him
certain revenues yet these were not paid regularly, wherefore
Don Antonio had to throw himself on the charity of others.

22nd August. RUMOURS.[5] There is a most certain expectation of the enemy attempting us next year, either directly
here at home or by the way of Scotland; and these fears are
grounded not on apprehension only but upon the sure knowledge that the preparations in Spain be far greater than in
'88. Whereupon there is great diversity of opinions of the
proceeding of this sea voyage; some would have it stayed,
alleging the impossibility of their return in small time, should
need require; the hazard of loss of so many mariners going
into hot countries; the absence of ships and ordnance. The
other party alleging the loss of the Queen and the adventurers
if it break off; the dishonour, and the probability that the
return might be timely enough, besides the hope of treasure,
which is our greatest desire and want. Some would convert
this fleet to an offensive course upon the ports of Spain; but
this is checked above, or crossed under hand, not without
great distemperature of humours on both sides for a few
days; yet in most men's judgments this is likeliest to succeed.

23rd August. THE LANDING IN CORNWALL.[6] From Fowey
in Cornwall comes news that the four Spanish galleys which
made spoil of the west parts about four weeks ago encountered
a fleet of hulks of seventy sail and gave chase to fourteen
of them that were severed from the company. In that fight
they lost 140 of their men and had one of the galleys so torn
that they could not carry her to Blavet; one of the hulks laden
with salt was sunk.

26th August. 'ORPHEUS HIS JOURNEY TO HELL.'[7] There
is entered a poem of *Orpheus his journey to Hell* written by
one R. B., telling the story of Orpheus, how his bride Eurydice
being slain by a serpent on her wedding day, he went down to
Hades with his harp to charm Pluto into giving her back again;
but on his return looking back on his beloved, she was
snatched away from him, and thereafter Orpheus would sit

4 *Calendar of State Papers Venetian*   6 SALISBURY PAPERS 5:322.
9:365, 373.   7 SR 3:48; STC 1060.
5 SIDNEY PAPERS 1:343.

complaining in invective ditties of the uncertain pleasures of unconstant love, until the women fell upon him in their rage and slew him.

A BOOK OF MERRY TALES.[8] A book of merry tales from the Spanish entitled *Wits, Fits and Fancies,* by Antony Copley, being a general collection of sententious speeches, answers, jests and behaviours of all sorts of estates, from the throne to the cottage, is to be printed.

MR. BARNES' 'DIVINE CENTURY OF SPIRITUAL SONNETS.'[9] Mr. Barnabe Barnes hath published *A Divine Century of Spiritual Sonnets,* which he dedicateth to Dr. Toby Matthew, Bishop of Durham.

TWO TALES OF BARNES.[10] Of this Barnabe Barnes, Nashe hath these two tales. The first of his French service four years ago, when, having followed the camp for a week or two, and seeing there was no care had of keeping the Queen's peace, but a man might have his brains knocked out, and no justice or constable near at hand to make hue-and-cry after the murderers, he went to the General and told him he did not like of this quarrelling kind of life and common occupation of murdering, wherein, without any jury or trial or giving them so much leave as to say their prayers, men were run through and had their throats cut, both against God's laws, her Majesty's laws, and the laws of all nations; wherefore he desired leave to depart, for he stood every hour in fear and dread of his person. Upon this motion there were divers warlike knights and principal captains who offered to pick out a strong guard amongst them for the safe engarrisoning and better shielding him from peril. Two stepped forth and presented themselves as musketeers before him, a third and fourth as targeteers behind him, a fifth and sixth vowed to try it out at the push of the pike before the malicious foe should invade him. But home he would and nothing could stay him.

The second of how he got him a strange pair of Babylonian breeches, with a codpiece as large as a Bolognian sausage, and so went up and down town and showed himself in the Presence at Court where he was generally laughed out by the noblemen and ladies.

[8] SR 3:47; STC 5748.
[9] SR 3:47; STC 1467. Barnes' skill as a sonneteer has not been fully recognised.
[10] T. Nashe, *Have with you to Saffron Walden* (ed. R. B. McKerrow 3:104, 109). See *23rd Oct* 1596.

31st August. DRAKE AND HAWKINS SAIL.[11] The fleet of
Sir Francis Drake and Sir John Hawkins are sailed from
Plymouth, being the *Defiance, Garland, Hope, Bonaventure,
Foresight* and *Adventure,* the Queen's ships, together with
twenty other ships and barks, and containing 2500 men and
boys. With them is gone Sir Thomas Baskerville as commander by land.

5th September. ESSEX'S ADVICE ON TRAVEL.[1] The Earl of
Rutland having a purpose to travel, my Lord of Essex hath
composed for him sundry letters of advice for his guidance.
In the first, setteth down the purposes of travel; to see the
beauty of many cities, to know the manners of the people
of many countries, and to learn the language of many nations. Some of these may serve for ornaments and all of
them for delights. By travel men reach of study, conference,
and observation which is knowledge; and the true end of
knowledge is clearness and strength of judgment, and not
ostentation or ability to discourse. The second letter giveth
more exact particularities for the traveller. He shall restrain his affection and participation of his own countrymen
and seek the acquaintance of the best sort of strangers, who
will instruct him in their abilities, dispositions and humours.
Nor should his aim be, like an intelligencer, to fish after
the present news, humours, graces or disgraces of the Court,
which may haply change before he come home, but to know
the consanguinities and alliance of Princes, the proportion between the nobility and the magistracy, the constitution of the
courts of justice, the state of their laws; how the sovereignty
of the King infuseth itself into all acts and ordinances; how
many ways they lay down impositions and taxes, and
gather revenues to the Crown; what be the liberties and
servitudes of all degrees; what discipline and preparation for
wars; what inventions for increase of traffic at home, for
multiplying their commodities, encouraging arts or manufactures of worth of any kind: also what good establishments
to prevent the necessities and discontents of the people, to
cut off suits at law and quarrels, to suppress thieves and all
disorders. In the last letter noteth other matters worthy of

---

[11] HAKLUYT 8:183.

[1] SPEDDING 2:1–20, who points out
that Bacon had a considerable share
in the compilation of these letters,
which were intended rather to display the wisdom of Essex than to
benefit Rutland. They were well circulated; there are three copies in
the Harleian Collection alone. The
letters are dated Jan 1596, but they
were presumably earlier, as Rutland
set out at the end of Sept 1595 (SID-
NEY PAPERS 1:353), and was at the
Hague on 5th Nov (MURDIN'S STATE
PAPERS, p. 697).

observation, concluding that if they be too many to remember then should he rather trust his notebook than his memory.

13th September. A PETITION AGAINST PLAYS.[2] Since the commission of the provost marshal was revoked masterless and vagabond persons that retired out of his precinct return to their old haunt and frequent the plays at the Theatre and Bankside. Wherefore the Lord Mayor petitioneth the Council for the suppressing of stage plays, declaring that they contain nothing but profane fables, lascivious matters, cozening devices, and other unseemly and scurrilous behaviours which are so set forth that they move wholly to imitation. Moreover he verily thinketh them to be the chief cause of the late stir and mutinous attempt of those few apprentices and other servants, who no doubt drew their infection from these and like places, and also of many other disorders and lewd demeanours which appear of late in young people of all degrees.

14th September. ABUSES IN THE CITY.[3] Mr. Richard Carmarden that was lately appointed to be Surveyor of the port of London seeketh to reform the abuses caused through the blindness and impotency of the late surveyor. Whereupon the better sort of the merchants yield, but some four or five most frowardly resist him. When by his command some packs belonging to one Leveson were stayed, this man on Wednesday last, with wild words despising the Queen's authority, beat Mr. Carmarden's substitutes and arrested one of them in an action of £200. The sheriffs' sergeants carried Leveson violently to prison, and the Clerks of the Court refused bail, Leveson saying that the Queen's letters patents, the order of the Exchequer and the Lord Treasurer's letters were all without the law.

CAPTAIN AMYAS PRESTON'S VOYAGE.[4] Captain Amyas Preston that set forth in the *Ascension* six months since is returned, being arrived in safety at Milford Haven in Wales. On his outward passage he surprised the Isle of Porto Santo to the northward of Madeira which is inhabited by old soldiers of the Kings of Portugal. Here after some skirmishes, our men possessed themselves of the town, though the inhabitants had conveyed their wives and children and the rest of their goods into a high hill. Nor would Captain Preston allow them

---

[2] *Remembrancia* 2:103; ELIZ. STAGE 4:318.

[3] SALISBURY PAPERS 5:376.

[4] HAKLUYT 7:172.

to redeem their town, because of their cruelty and treachery offered beforetime to some of ours, but caused the town and villages to be utterly burned.

Thence having joined with Captain Somers and his ship the *Gift* and three other ships they sailed westward to the Island of Dominica and from there to Margarita where the Indians fish for pearls. In the end of May they took the city of S. Iago de Leon, a very strong place, surrounded by high mountains, which they reached by a path used by the Indians. And here they had conference with the Spaniards for the ransoming of the town, Captain Preston demanding 30,000 ducats but the Spaniard refusing more than 4000, so the town was set on fire and consumed.

In July, off Cape St. Anthony, they met with Sir Walter Ralegh returning from his discovery of Guiana, with his fleet of three ships, but lost them in the night.

15th September. A GREAT FIRE AT WOBURN.[5] Last Saturday (13th) there was a great fire at Woburn in the County of Bedford, whereby houses and buildings to the number of one hundred and thirty are consumed, as well as barns, stables and the rest, with the goods and provisions therein, besides what was carried out into the streets and there purloined and embezzled. This fire started in a poor cottage at the further end of the town towards Brookhill where dwelt a single old woman, slow in speech, deaf in hearing, and very dull of understanding. She had shifted her bed straw and put new therein, laying the old in the chimney, supposing that there had been no fire therein, and afterwards going abroad upon her business. In the meanwhile the cinders in the chimney took hold of the straw and so set on fire this thatched house and others adjoining, which by the wind was soon driven from place to place. And so fierce did it wax that it made as it were a glade from the end of the town to the church; where by the violence of the wind a flake of burning thatch, as broad as it were a sheet, was carried clean over the chancel of the church, the school house and other buildings, and fell on the east side of the town. Moreover the confusion was much increased by those that came in to help from the country, many of them leaving their own labours, and freeing their hired workmen from their tasks (and paying them notwithstanding their day's wages), who in their hurly-burly increased rather than lessened the desolation and waste.

19th September. NEWS FROM IRELAND.[6] This morning comes advertisement from Ireland that Tyrone hath drawn our force to fight of necessity; that Sir John Norris is shot in the belly, Sir Thomas Norris shot in the thigh, and Capt. Richard Wingfield in the elbow with a musket and likely to lose life or arm, but the others not in danger of life. The hope of a peace is now turned to an assured war for 'twere much dishonour to dally longer.

20th September. FRENCH NEWS.[7] Because of the constant rumours concerning affairs in France, Sir Roger Williams was sent over to the French King some days since and arrived at Paris, all unexpected, on the 9th. The next day the King himself came to Paris, preparing to depart immediately to the succour of Cambray; but on the 14th he received advertisement that the enemy were in the town, and the soldiers forced to retire to the Castle. At Paris news is received that the Pope in public, with great solemnity, hath given absolution to the King in the person of the Bishop of Evreux, and that the greatest ceremony of joy was performed there in applause of it.

BRETON'S 'SOLEMN PASSION.'[8] Mr. Nicholas Breton hath written a poem in a high strain called *A Solemn Passion of the Soul's Love*, setting forth the great love of God for man.

MARKHAM'S 'MOST HONOURABLE TRAGEDY OF SIR RICHARD GRENVILLE.'[9] There is also Mr. Gervase Markham's poem of *The Tragedy of Sir Richard Grenville* that was slain in her Majesty's ship *Revenge* off the Azores in '91.

22nd September. LYLY'S 'WOMAN IN THE MOON.'[10] Mr. John Lyly's comedy of *The Woman in the Moon*, that was formerly presented before the Queen, is to be printed.

23rd September. THE EARL OF SOUTHAMPTON.[11] It is said at Court that my Lord of Southampton doth with too much familiarity court the fair Mistress Vernon, while his friends

6 SIDNEY PAPERS 1:347.
7 BIRCH'S MEMOIRS 1:296, 298, 300.
8 STC 3696.
9 STC 17385. See *20th Oct 1591.*
10 STC 17090.
11 SIDNEY PAPERS 1:348.

observing the Queen's humours to my Lord of Essex do
what they can to bring her to favour him, but it is yet in vain.

27th September.   THE FIGHT IN IRELAND.[12] The conflict between Sir John Norris and the Earl of Tyrone happened on
the return of Sir John to Newry from victualling the fort by
Blackwater, wherein he was assailed by 500 horse and 2000
foot of the enemy, Sir John having only 1000 foot and 120
horse. In this encounter Sir John was hurt with two musket
shots, the one through the left arm, the other athwart the
belly, but neither of them dangerous. Few of ours were slain
but 400 of the enemy left dead in the field. Notwithstanding there is an expectation of the Earl of Tyrone coming in
upon pardon for himself, O'Donnell and Macguire; and to
that end authority is given to the Lord Deputy.

RALEGH'S RETURN.[13] Now that Sir Walter Ralegh is come
back to England from his voyage to Guiana, many traduce
him, saying that his going to sea was but a bravado or even
that he went not to sea but lay hidden in Cornwall or elsewhere. Others, at his setting out, prejudged that he would
rather become a servant of the King of Spain than return to
England, and that he was too easeful and sensual to undertake a journey of so great travail. Nor hath he returned with
riches, for, saith he, it became not his former fortune to go
journeys of picory, to run from cape to cape and place to
place for pillage of ordinary prizes. But Sir Walter's friends
do tell her Majesty what great service he hath done unto her
in discovering the way to bring home the wealth of India
and in making known to that nation her virtues and her justice.
He hath brought hither a supposed prince and left hostages
in his place. The Queen gives good ear unto them.

30th September.   'A CONFERENCE ABOUT THE NEXT SUCCES-
SION.'[14] There are being circulated in England some copies
of a book called *A Conference about the next Succession
to the Crown of England,* dedicated to the Earl of Essex,
which was published abroad and written by one N. Dole-
man, who is believed to be Parsons the Jesuit.

The alleged occasion of the treatise was a meeting in
Amsterdam after the late Parliament of certain gentlemen of
divers nations qualities and affections, who, hearing that the

question of the succession had not been settled by the Parliament in England, began to debate the matter, and especially two lawyers, who agreed that each should deliver his opinion on the case, the one considering the principles of succession, the other the claims of those who pretend to the succession in England.

The first argueth that government by nearness of blood is not the law of nature nor is it divine law; and being only by human law, might upon just causes be altered, and the King deposed. The second, enumerating those who have claim by birth and family, noteth the King of Scots, whose favourers (of whom there are but few in England) believe him the first and chiefest pretender. In this line also is the Lady Arabella Stuart, whom the Lord Treasurer is supposed to favour.

The Puritans at home are thought to be the most vigorous of the parties in religion, having a great part of the best captains and soldiers on their side; but the Catholics by reason of the persecution of seminarists are also strong. The Earl of Beauchamp and the Earl of Derby have some voices, as also the Earl of Huntingdon. But whoever shall succeed it is likely that the affair cannot be ended without war at the first. As for the future, if a foreign Prince be admitted, the Infanta of Spain is likest to bear away the prize; if, on the other side, one of the domestical competitors, the second son of the Earl of Hertford, or the issue of the Countess of Derby.

6th October. THE SOLDIERS FURNISHED BY THE CLERGY.[1] Her Majesty being desirous to be truly informed of the state of the whole forces of the realm, the Lords Lieutenant have been directed to have the enrolled soldiers viewed, mustered, and trained. The clergy also who in '88 found certain able men as well of horse as of foot are now to review and supply the like number; and where there is defect in their armour, horse or furniture, to cause the same to be amended or supplied, and perfect rolls to be made of the names and surnames of the soldiers and of those that set them forth which shall be sent to the Council.

TROUBLE OVER THE STARCH MONOPOLY.[2] Of late certain apprentices of London violently took away a 1000 lbs. weight of

---

[1] APC 25:15. The volume of APC covering 26th Aug to Oct 1595 is missing.   [2] APC 25:16.

starch that had been seized on for her Majesty's use by Mr.
James Anton, her patentee, and not only carried the same
to a warehouse but grievously beat and wound Mr. Anton's
deputies.

9th October.   M. LOMENIE'S STOUT SPEECHES.[3] Sir Roger
Williams is returned from the French King, and with him
one M. de Lomenie, a secretary of the King's Chamber, who
both by the King's letters and his own speech hath dealt
so roundly with the Queen and the Council that there is great
offence at Court; for, not concealing that Cambray is lost
to the Spaniard, yet he would urge that some auxiliary forces
might forthwith be sent over into Picardy; and that afterwards commissioners appointed to treat about the managing
of the war. These things appearing preposterous to the Queen
and the Council, he grew impatient, imputing the loss of
Cambray to the Queen, saying that she rejoiceth in the King's
misery. Moreover the King declareth that he hath his absolution from the Pope and that there are deputed four cardinals
to give him the solemnity thereof; but that their chief er-
rand is to draw him to a peace with Spain and to unite against
all that are divided from the Church. He saith that the King
is assured to receive for himself honourable conditions, but
knowing that he shall be sought to be divided from the Queen
and the Low Countries, desireth by her to be enabled by a
common concurrency of both their forces that he be not
compelled to such a peace as willingly he would not make,
but such as may comprehend them all in such terms, as holding always together, they might be a balance against Spanish
greatness. That if she refuse him in it, he must provide for
himself as he may. These letters delivered with very stout
speeches have greatly offended the Queen who loveth not
to be terrified, so the gentleman is despatched without any
hope of obtaining relief from hence.

14th October.   WHEAT SPENT WEEKLY.[4] The Lord Mayor
complaineth to the Lord Treasurer how hard is this restraint
on the City from buying wheat from Kent and Essex, for
great quantities of wheat are required in the City, and by
reason of the restraint the prices are enhanced in more remote counties. There is consumed weekly in the City, brown

[3] SIDNEY PAPERS 1:354; CAMDEN'S   [4] *Remembrancia* 2:109.
ELIZABETH.

bread, 535 qrs.; white bread, 1317 qrs.; in markets, 600 qrs.; in houses providing for themselves, 40 qrs.; in all 2492 qrs.; besides Hackney and Stepney.

15th October. PLATT'S INVENTIONS.[5] Mr. Hugh Platt that last year put forth a book of inventions called the *Jewel House of Art and Nature* hath caused to be printed a little pamphlet, being *A Discovery of certain English wants,* wherein he complaineth that in his own experience it is an easier matter to devise many and very profitable inventions than to dispose of one of them to the good of the author himself; and because there are many gentlemen that be always ready and willing to entertain good suits, he giveth them to understand that he is still well furnished with inventions for them if they come in time, and whilst his small store lasteth, *videlicet;*—a means to prepare flesh without any salt, and fit to be laid up in storehouses for many years or to furnish ships withal; a defensative in the highest kind of all armour and artillery whatsoever from rusting in seven years after one preparation; some English secrets whereby we may be less beholding either unto France or Spain in some of their best commodities; an excellent oily composition defending all iron works from rust wherewith Sir Francis Drake is furnished in this last voyage; a pump not weighing 20 pounds in weight and yet sufficient to deliver five tuns of water in one hour, being an excellent engine to water all houses that are near the river Thames or any river, also for ships of war; a liquor to keep either boot, shoe or buskin made of dry leather both black in wearing and defensible against all rain, dew or moisture, to be had of the author in several kinds.

All those that are desirous to have any conference with the author may be advertised of his abode by William Ponsonby, stationer in Paul's Churchyard.

SIR WALTER RALEGH.[6] Sir Walter Ralegh is now in London and goes daily to hear sermons, because he hath seen the wonders of the Lord in the deep; 'tis much commended and spoken of.

27th October. HIGH PRICES.[7] Notwithstanding the seasonable harvest this summer, the price of corn and of white meat is of late greatly risen in many counties, which is thought

5 STC 19988. See *8th Aug* 1594.   7 APC 25:25, 31.
6 PENSHURST PAPERS 2:173.

due to the want of care of the Justices to seek reformation, and to the covetous dispositions of farmers, seek immoderate gain by enhancing the price of corn to the great oppression of the poor.

In London the price of sea coals standeth at a very high rate to the great oppression of the poor that are not able to furnish themselves with wood; the occasion whereof is that some of the richer sort of the town of Newcastle, having a lease of the Bishop of Durham of twelve coal pits, forbear to work the same but work in certain coal pits of their own which yield a worse sort of coal and less quantity. Moreover these owners outbid and hire from the rest all the coal wains that bring coals to the waterside.

29th October. AN ATTACK ON IRELAND FEARED.[8] A Spanish pilot, taken by a captain of the Earl of Cumberland's upon the south coast of Spain, confesseth that there are a number of Levant ships of war of great burden come to Lisbon this month, where there are also eight or nine great ships of war and others expected: of these the Adelantado is to take charge and to come with them upon some parts in the West of Ireland. If the Lord Deputy shall find the Spaniard to attempt any landing in any place of the South as Waterford or Cork, he shall leave the prosecution of the rebellion in Ireland and march against them, leaving the forts of Armagh and Monaghan well guarded; and to encourage the great towns to stand fast, 1000 footmen are to be put in readiness to be sent thither from Chester upon a day's warning.

1st November. RALEGH'S VOYAGE.[1] Sir Walter Ralegh hath now brought to completion and sent the account of his voyage to Guiana to the Lord Admiral.

After leaving Plymouth last February, he reached the island of Trinidad on 22nd March, where there is an abundance of stone pitch at a point called Tierra de Brea or Piche, wherewith he made trial in trimming the ships, for this pitch melteth not with the heat of the sun as the pitch of Norway. Thence by night he attacked a Spanish city called St. Joseph which they took, together with a Spanish gentleman called Berreo who was the governor there and hath travelled in Guiana,

---

[8] APC 25:37, 47.
[1] STC 20634–36; HAKLUYT 7:272. Ralegh's admiration of the scenery is noteworthy, as such appreciation of natural beauties is not very commonly expressed in Elizabethan literature.

whom Sir Walter used very courteously as his prisoner. When this Berreo learned that Sir Walter would make his way up the river to see Guiana he was stricken with great melancholy and sadness, using all the arguments he could to dissuade him, and saying that they could not enter any of the rivers with their barks or pinnaces, it was so low and sandy. Further, none of the country would come to speak with them, but would all fly, and if followed would burn their dwellings; and besides, that winter was at hand when the rivers begin to swell, and that the kings and lords of all the borders of Guiana had decreed that none of them should trade with any Christians for gold, because the same would be their overthrow.

When Sir Walter had by experiment found Berreo's words to be true he resolved to go on with the boats, and a galego boat, cut down and fitted with banks to row on. Into the galego were thrust sixty men, in three other boats and in Sir Walter's own barge ten a piece, making 100 in all. With this company, having passed over some twenty miles of rough sea, they entered one of the rivers which their guide declared would take them into the great river of Orenoque; and there might they have been lost in the labyrinth of rivers but by chance they met with a canoe with three Indians, one of them an old man; and him they took for guide. Up these rivers they sailed westward for many days often in great distress for lack of victuals.

At length they reached a port called Morequito where they were visited by the old King of that place called Topiawari, to whom Sir Walter made known the cause of his coming thither, of her Majesty's greatness, her justice, her charity to all oppressed nations, with many other of her beauties and virtues, and that her pleasure was to deliver them from the tyranny of the Spaniards; all which being attentively heard and marvellously admired, he began to sound the old man concerning Guiana.

The next day they sailed westward up to the river called Caroli, as well because it was marvellous of itself as also because it led to the strongest nations of all the frontiers; these are enemies of the Epuremi, that abound in gold, being subjects to Inga, Emperor of Guiana and Manoa. But when they came to this river, they could not row one stone's cast in an hour by reason of the force of the stream. Sir Walter therefore sent his guide to the people of those parts and there came down a lord or casique called Wanuretona, with

many people and much store of provision. Of them he learnt
that all who were either against the Spaniards or the Epuremi
would join with him, and that if he entered the land over
the mountains of Curaa he should satisfy himself with gold
and all other good things.

Here they landed to go by foot to view the great river,
and to see if they could find any mineral stone alongst the
river side; and when they came to the tops of the hills adjoining to the rivers they beheld that wonderful breach of waters
which ran down Caroli, and might from that mountain see
the river how it ran in three parts over twenty miles off; and
there appeared some ten or twelve overfalls in sight, every
one as high over the other as a church tower. For his own
part Sir Walter would have returned from thence, but the
rest were all so desirous to go near the strange thunder of
waters that they drew him on by little and little, till they
came into the next valley where they might better discern it.
'I never saw,' saith he, 'a more beautiful country, nor more
lively prospects, hills so raised here and there over the val-
leys, the river winding into divers branches, the plain adjoining without bush or stubble, all fair green grass, the
ground hard sand, easy to march on either for horse or foot,
the deer crossing in every path, the birds towards the evening
singing on every tree with a thousand several tunes, cranes
and herons of white, crimson, and carnation, perching in
the river's side, the air fresh with a gentle easterly wind, and
every stone that we stooped to take up promised either gold
or silver by his complexion.'

But now the fury of the river Orenoque began to rage and
overflow very fearfully, and the rains came down in terrible
showers, and gusts in great abundance. Having for well near
a month passed westward farther and farther from their
ships, at length they turned eastward. Returning therefore to
the country of Topiawari, Sir Walter again had conference
with the old man, who told him that four days' journey from
his town was Macureguarai, and that those were the next
and nearest subjects of Inga and of the Epuremi, and the
first town of apparelled and rich people, and that all those
plates of gold which were carried to other nations came
from the Macureguarai and were there made; but that
those of the land within were far finer, and fashioned after
the images of men, beasts, birds and fishes. The old King
would indeed have had Sir Walter stay and attempt this people, but he, knowing that Berreo did daily expect a succour

out of Spain and from Granada, was unwilling to attempt the enterprise at that season but promised to return next year.

Of marvels in those parts, noteth that in the parts south of the river there be a race of Amazons, and they accompany with men but for one month in the year, and at that time all the Kings of the borders assemble and the Queens of the Amazons, and, after the Queens have chosen, the rest cast lots for their valentines. If they conceive and be delivered of a son, they return him to the father; if of a daughter, they nourish it and retain it; and as many as have daughters send a present to the begetters. At the port of Morequito one gave him a beast called by the Spaniards 'armadilla,' which seemeth to be barred all over with small plates somewhat like to a rhinoceros, with a white horn growing in his hinder parts as big as a great hunting horn, which they use to wind instead of a trumpet. In those parts there be a people called Ewaipanoma; they are reported to have their eyes in their shoulders, and their mouths in the middle of their breasts, and a long train of hair groweth backward between their shoulders: these Sir Walter saw not, but so many of the inhabitants declare the truth of the matter that he is fain to believe. Moreover such a relation was written of by Mandeville whose reports were many years holden for fables, and yet since the Indies were discovered we find his relations true of such things as heretofore were held incredible. A Spaniard also, a man in all things else esteemed a man of his word, declareth that he hath seen many of them.

Sir Walter urgeth very vehemently the advantages of Guiana, a country that hath yet her maidenhead, never sacked, the face of the earth not torn, nor the virtue and salt of the soil spent by manurance, the graves not opened for gold, the mines not broken with sledges, nor the images pulled down out of the temples. It is besides so defensible that it could be held by two forts built on a channel by which all ships must pass; nor is there other way of entry.

5th November.   COURT NEWS.[2] On Monday last the Queen showed the Earl of Essex that printed book, called *A Conference about the Succession to the Crown of England*, written two years since (as is supposed) by Parsons the

---

[2] SIDNEY PAPERS 1:357. Essex's sickness were not entirely politic. He was apparently 'a bundle of nerves,' and when thwarted or rebuked he would quickly worry himself into a state of acute melancholy or actual illness; his nervous energy was another symptom of this lack of balance.

Jesuit and dedicated to my Lord; than whom, he saith, no man is in more high and eminent place at this day in the realm, whether we respect his nobility, or calling, or favour with the Queen, or high liking of the people; and consequently no man like to have a greater part or sway in deciding of this great affair, when the time shall come for determination.

At his coming from Court the Earl was observed to look wan and pale, and exceedingly troubled at this great piece of villainy done unto him. He is sick and continues very ill. Yesterday in the afternoon the Queen visited him; but the Earl is mightily crossed in all things, for Mr. Bacon is gone without the place of Solicitor. The Lord Treasurer is come to London and lies in bed so ill of the gout in his hands, arms, knees and toes that his pains make him pitifully groan.

6th November. MR. BACON AND MY LORD OF ESSEX.[3] Mr. Sergeant Fleming was yesterday made Solicitor, so my Lord of Essex and Mr. Bacon are finally disappointed. When the matter was concluded, my Lord came over from Richmond to Twickenham Park, where Mr. Bacon was, to break it with him, in these words: 'Master Bacon, the Queen hath denied me yon place for you, and hath placed another. I know you are the least part of your own matter, but you fare ill because you have chosen me for your mean and dependence. You have spent your time and your thoughts in my matters; I die if I do not somewhat towards your fortune; you shall not deny to accept a piece of land which I will bestow upon you.'

At first Mr. Bacon was somewhat unwilling to accept of the gift lest he should be too much bound to my Lord by this obligation. But my Lord bade him take no care for that, and pressed it. Whereupon Mr. Bacon saith, 'My Lord, I see I must be your homager and hold land of your gift: but do you know the manner of doing homage in law? Always it is with a saving of his faith to the King and his other Lords. And therefore, my Lord,' quoth he, 'I can be no more yours than I was, and it must be with the ancient savings, and if I grow to be a rich man, you will give me leave to give it back to some of your unrewarded followers.'

9th November. A TRUCE WITH TYRONE.[4] The Earl of Tyrone hath now made submission, complaining he was led

[3] SPEDDING 1:370–73, from Bacon's   [4] CAREW MSS 172, 173, 174.
Apology.

into these courses chiefly from the bad usage of him by Sir John Perrot. Now he would have pardon and declares that he will not join with any foreign prince. A truce is therefore made until the 1st January.

12*th November*. THE EARL OF HERTFORD COMMITTED.[5] The Earl of Hertford was committed to the Tower six days ago. The cause is said to be a record secretly put into the Court of Arches to prove his first marriage lawful and his children legitimate. 'Tis said he is one of the wealthiest subjects of England. It is since given out that by commandment his son shall no more be called Lord Beauchamp but Seymour; and it is credibly said that my Lady Hertford is become stark mad. Note that my Lord is the son of the Duke of Somerset that was Lord Protector to King Edward VI; his first wife was the Lady Catherine Grey (sister to the Lady Jane), whom he married after she had been divorced by the Earl of Pembroke; and for whose sake he was nine years in the Tower. This lady died in 1567.

My Lord of Essex hath put off the melancholy he fell unto by reason of the printed book delivered to the Queen, wherein by her gracious favour and wisdom the harm meant to him is turned to his good and strengthens her love towards him. Within these last days many letters sent to her from foreign countries are delivered to my Lord, and he to answer them.

EXTRAORDINARY MEASURES AGAINST INVASION.[6] The Lords Lieutenant of counties on the sea coast are specially warned to have all men that are apt for the wars in readiness to withstand any invasion of the enemy. These men shall be put into bands under principal leaders, and held in readiness with all necessary furniture to be sent to such landing places where the enemy hath a purpose to land. To every thousand men are appointed one hundred pioneers, with their necessary instruments, and provision made of carts and carriages with some small nags for the more speedy conveyance of the men, who shall take with them a convenient proportion of victual and some overplus of powder, lead and match to supply any want. All persons having habitations near the sea coast to attend with all their forces for the defence of the coast and of their land and habitations, as by the law of nature and of the land they are bound to do upon pain of forfeiture of their

[5] SIDNEY PAPERS 1:356, 358, 360. Collins' *Peerage*, ed. E. Brydges, 1812, 1:172.   [6] APC 25:64.

livelihoods and further punishment. The sum total of men to
be put in readiness by fifteen counties and the towns of
Southampton and London is 61,800.

17th November. ACCESSION DAY.[7] This day was held as a
day of great triumph at London for the Queen's long and
prosperous reign. The pulpit cross in Paul's Churchyard is
now newly repaired, painted and partly inclosed with a wall
of brick; here Dr. Fletcher, the Bishop of London, preached
in praise of the Queen before the Lord Mayor, Aldermen,
and citizens in their best liveries, and the sermon being ended,
upon the church leads the trumpets sounded, the cornets
winded, and the choristers sang an anthem. On the steeple
many lights were burned, the Tower shot off her ordnance,
and bonfires were made.

At the Tilt was a device of my Lord of Essex much commended. Some pretty while before he came in himself, he sent
his page with some speed to the Queen, who returned with
her glove. When my Lord himself came in, he was met with
an old hermit, a secretary of state, a brave soldier, and an
esquire. The first presented him with a book of meditations,
the second with political discourses, the third with orations of
brave fought battles, the fourth was but his own follower, to
whom the other three imparted much of their purpose before
his coming in. Each devised with him, persuading him to this
and that course of life, according to their inclinations. Then
comes there into the Tiltyard unthought on the ordinary
post boy of London, a ragged villain all bemired, upon a
poor lean jade, galloping and blowing for life, and delivered
the secretary a packet of letters which he straightway offered
to my Lord of Essex.

In the after-supper before the Queen they first delivered a
well-penned speech to move this worthy Knight to leave his
vain following of Love and to betake him to heavenly medi-
tation; the secretary's speech tending to have him follow
matters of state; the soldier's persuading him to the war; but
the esquire answered them all, and concluded with an excellent, but too plain English speech that his Knight would never
forsake his Mistress's love, whose virtue made all his thoughts
divine, whose wisdom taught him all true policy, whose beauty
and worth were at all times able to make him fit to command

---

[7] STOW'S ANNALS; SIDNEY PAPERS
1:362. SPEDDING, who prints the
speeches in full (1:377–92), showed

that Bacon was responsible for the
devices for which Essex received
credit.

armies. He showed all the defects and imperfections of all their times, and therefore thought his course of life to be best in serving his Mistress. Hereupon many constructions are made of these speeches, comparing the hermit and the secretary to two of the Lords, and the soldier to Sir Roger Williams; but the Queen said that if she had thought there would have been so much said of her, she would not have been there that night; and so went to bed.

20th November. SOUTHWELL'S 'TRIUMPH OVER DEATH.'[8] John Trussell hath sent to the press that consolatory epistle written by Southwell the Jesuit on the death of the Lady Margaret Sackville, Countess of Dorset. 'Our life,' saith he, 'is but lent, a good to make thereof during the loan our best commodity. It is a due debt to a more certain owner than ourselves, and therefore so long as we have it, we receive a benefit. When we are deprived of it, we have no wrong; we are tenants at will of this clayey farm, not for term of years. When we are warned out we must be ready to remove, having no other title but the owner's pleasure. It is but an inn, not a home; we came but to bait, not to dwell, and the condition of our entrance was in fine to depart.'

22nd November. COURT NEWS.[9] We wait to hear what the French King's countenance will be on the return of M. Lomenie, who went hence discontented and speaks lewdly of us wherever he goes. The King has not yet seen him, but the answers thence to our excuses of our usage of M. Lomenie are sour and savouring of an alienate mind. Sir Henry Unton is named as the man to be sent over but would stand upon terms. Then Sir Arthur Gorges had vogue one week; now it is Sir Henry again, who is warned on his allegiance and that Princes will not be capitulated with by their servants.

23rd November. IRISH NEWS.[10] Letters are come from Ireland with good news of Tyrone's submission which brought the Lord Treasurer to Court from his sick bed. The Council have been three days about this Irish peace, and a formal pardon, according to our Law, is now a drawing. Sir George Carew is presently to be sent over to take his oath and to be Commissioner in the business with the Lord Deputy, to

[8] SR 3:53; STC 22971. It is a sign of the great respect felt for Southwell that, so soon after his death, the printer should acknowledge the author's name and justify the publication in a poem 'To the Reader.'
[9] PENSHURST PAPERS 2:189.
[10] SIDNEY PAPERS 1:362, 363.

whom small countenance or trust is committed in this or anything else; and the credit of all things given to Sir John Norris.

26th November.   AN INQUISITION CONCERNING RECUSANTS.[11] Because of the increase of recusants at this time of danger; extraordinary care must be taken for their reformation. The Archbishops shall now cause the Bishops and ordinaries to make diligent inquisition into the number of recusants, their state, degree and value, and how many be vagrants and fugitives, and what means are used to reform them by instruction and teaching, and how many are indicted by form of law.

1st December.   FRENCH OPINIONS.[1] Mr. Edmondes, the English Resident in France, reporteth that M. de Lomenie (that came over with Sir Roger Williams about three weeks since) is returned to the King who is now besieging La Fere. The King by M. de Lomenie's relation is reduced from weak hope into strange despair of the English Court, so that he is resolved not to send M. de Sancy here as he had intended, for it would serve no other purpose than to give him more discontent, and to heap more indignity on him. The French say that they see clearly into our dispositions by our demand for Calais, which, they allege, doth much touch the heart of France: by our refusing to join in treaty with them; and this last proceeding with M. de Lomenie. They are in so hard condition that they know not how to subsist against the great forces wherewith the enemy doth threaten them; but that they see their apparent ruin before their eyes if they be abandoned by those who are interested in common fortune with them, they do not otherwise provide for themselves. These be their discourses; and to anything we can allege of former merit and future hope, they answer that past remedies do not cure present diseases; and that we pay them with words, and not with deeds, seeking nothing more than to keep them still miserable. The Spaniard so constantly seeking a truce in Brittany giveth great suspicion of further consequence, either of some attempt elsewhere, or else to extend it to a further treaty. Mr. Edmondes much lamenteth his own miserable estate and inability to serve longer by reason of his great debts, and earnestly petitioneth that her Majesty would have compassion on him and grant his revocation.

11 APC 25:85.   1 BIRCH'S MEMOIRS 1:328.

5th December. THE LIEUTENANT OF THE TOWER COMMITTED.[2] Sir Michael Blount, the Lieutenant of the Tower, is put out of his place. It is said that he grew very familiar with Mr. Neville, *alias* Latimer, and Captain Wainman, and in discourse with them, they began to talk of the dangers of the time; from that to argue of the town, how it might be made defensible, what provision, what men would serve the turn, what a brave command it was in a change. Then they grew madder as to talk of titles, and it is reported that the Lieutenant delivered his mind how he was affected; that he and his friends would keep the place till he saw great reason to yield it. But when they had waded so far, 'Masters,' said he, 'these matters we speak of are perilous, and therefore I will have nothing to do with them.' But the other two found means to discover it first to the Queen, whereupon the Lieutenant was examined by the Lords and is now committed to the Tower. Sir Drue Drury is sworn in his place.

6th December. WOOD IN THE PILLORY.[3] Wood that was condemned in the Star Chamber last July has now confessed. To-day on a pillory in Cheapside he had an ear cut off, and three letters burned in his forehead. He made an oration, declaring his confession is voluntary: in his examination he charges Lady Shrewsbury very deeply with the matter; but she denies it.

7th December. THE QUEEN'S LETTER TO THE KING.[4] On the 30th November Mr. Edmondes read before the French King a letter from the Queen answering those complaints of M. de Lomenie, and his demand for succours. He reminded the King of the great services which her Majesty had rendered him for a long space of time, and lastly at Brest when the Queen, though she had in hand several other designs both of honour and advantage, consented for the King's service to employ her forces by land and sea to drive the enemy from thence. As for the declaration that the King might be obliged to agree with the common enemy without comprehending her in the treaty, she would not suffer herself to be disturbed with the thought that the King's honour and so many vows on his part and so many services on hers could admit so odious and dangerous a resolution.

[2] SIDNEY PAPERS 1:372. See also STRYPE'S ANNALS 4:238.
[3] PENSHURST PAPERS 2:195. See *2nd* and *4th July*.
[4] BIRCH'S HISTORICAL VIEW, p. 28; CAMDEN'S ELIZABETH.

After the letter had been read, the King answered that he was not alone able to sustain the burden of the war for such reasons as are too true and too well known to all men; and that he would consult with the princes and officers of his crown, what he was to resolve on; wherein if necessity shall force him to change course, as the fault thereof shall not be his, so the Queen on her part, instead of excuses and justifications, shall have only cause afterwards of sorrow.

12th December. THE QUEEN DINES WITH THE LORD KEEPER.[5] The Queen in these days cometh much abroad. Yesterday she dined at Kew, at the Lord Keeper's house, where her entertainment was great and exceeding costly. At her first alighting she had a fine fan, with a handle garnished with diamonds. When she was in the middle way, between the garden gate and the house, one came running towards her with a nosegay in his hand, which he delivered with a short, well-penned speech; it had in it a very rich jewel, with many pendants of diamonds, valued at £400 at least. After dinner in her privy chamber, the Lord Keeper gave her a fine gown and juppin, which things were pleasing to her Highness; and to grace his Lordship the more, she of herself took from him a salt, a spoon, and a fork of fine agate.

13th December. DEATH OF SIR ROGER WILLIAMS.[6] Sir Roger Williams died of a surfeit in Baynard's Castle yesterday at 3 o'clock after midnight. He gave all he had to my Lord of Essex, who indeed saved his soul, for none but he could make him take a feeling of his end; but he died well, and very repentant. His jewels are valued at £1,000; 'tis said he had £1,200 out at interest; in ready gold £200; and £60 in silver. His plate is worth £60, his garments £30, his horses £60, and this is his end. He desired to be buried in Paul's, and my Lord of Essex means to have it done in very martial sort.

14th December. MR. DARCY'S GRANT.[7] Some days since three of the Company of the Leathersellers, having disobeyed her Majesty's grant made to Mr. Darcy for viewing and sealing of leather, were committed to the Marshalsea. To-day being at their own request admitted to make their excuse before the Council, relation was made of the whole proceedings since

[5] SIDNEY PAPERS 1:376.
[6] SIDNEY PAPERS 1:377. This genuinely religious strain in Essex is notable.

[7] APC 25:106. See 12th Mar 1593, 23rd Jan and 6th Nov 1595.

the grant was first made; but their Lordships, finding their obstinacy to proceed without due regard, return them to prison, there to remain until they shall submit themselves and permit Mr. Darcy to enjoy the benefit of his grant. Moreover the Lord Mayor shall inhibit the rest of the Leathersellers from putting on sale any leather until they have submitted themselves.

17th December. 'MAROCCUS EXTATICUS.'[8] There is a pamphlet called *Maroccus Extaticus, or Banks' Bay Horse in a trance,* set down in the form of a dialogue between Banks and his beast, anatomising some abuses and bad tricks of this age, and especially of those landlords who for raising of their rents will turn their houses into brothels.

19th December. THE LORD PRESIDENT OF THE NORTH DEAD.[9] The Lord Huntingdon, Lord President of the North, died on Sunday last past, the 14th of this month, having been sick for nine days. The Archbishop of York being with him desired two things of his hands; to prepare himself to die, which he did, not using many words but such as did give good assurance he died a good Christian; the second, to dispose of his estate, which by no means he would hearken unto, and said little to that, only that it was a wild world, which he would not think upon. This was at first kept from my Lady Huntingdon, but the Queen came to Whitehall very suddenly of purpose to break it to her herself.

When the news was brought on Wednesday morning, the Lord Keeper was sent to her from the Queen that my Lord was sick. In the afternoon he came again unto her to let her know the Queen was advertised he was in some danger and therefore besought her to consider what should be done about his estate. This morning my Lady Puckering came to see her, and finding her so disquieted, she told her by circumstances that his danger was great, and small hope of recovery. Being desired by my Lady to tell her the very truth, she then told her that indeed assured word was come he was dead. This evening, at 4 o'clock, the Queen herself came in a litter to visit her.

21st December. PRIVATE SHIPS FOR THE NAVY.[10] Letters are being sent to the principal officers of sundry port towns

8 SR 3:55; STC 6225.   10 APC 25:122.
9 SIDNEY PAPERS 1:380, 382.

that upon advertisement made of some attempt against this kingdom by way of invasion this next spring, the Queen hath given order to put the Navy Royal in readiness and to have the same assisted with some reasonable number of good ships of her subjects. Wherefore ships of good burden shall be prepared, manned and furnished, provided with munition and victual for five months, by the same that did contribute in '88; these ships to be ready by the end of March.

SIR HENRY UNTON SENT TO THE FRENCH KING.[11] Sir Henry Unton is sent ambassador to France to discover how the French King standeth affected, and hoping to divert him from a course with Spain which by his own answers and Mr. Edmondes and other conjectures, it seemeth he is like to enter into, the Pope working earnestly to bring it to pass, and almost all his Council discovering no good conceit of our amity.

THE INVASION IN CORNWALL.[12] After the sudden incursion of the enemy in Cornwall last summer, a collection was made both in Cornwall and some other counties for the relief of those that suffered spoil. Now it appeareth that this money was neither well ordered nor distributed, for the licence to gather was sold by the parties that undertook the collection, and the villages most spoiled like to be defrauded of it.

25th December. NEWS OF DRAKE.[13] At Plymouth an Irish captain new come from Lisbon declareth that Sir Francis Drake and Sir John Hawkins have taken great treasure at St. John de Porto Rico, besides other pillage of great value, and that the fleet will speedily return to England.

[11] SIDNEY PAPERS 1:378, 396. With Unton, Essex sent a secret memorandum on the way in which he should be received in France in order that the Queen might be forced to send reinforcements (BIRCH'S MEMOIRS, 1:353–54). Essex was not over-scrupulous in furthering his own schemes.
[12] APC 25:129.
[13] SP DOM 255:17.

Other Books Printed in 1595

i. A musical consort of heavenly harmony called *Churchyard's Charity,* by Thomas Churchyard, which he dedicateth to the Earl of Essex, noting that now, by reason of great age, his wits and inventions are almost wearied with writing of books, this being one of the last. In this poem, he lamenteth that great lack of charity in our days. Machievel, saith he, is now made an Englishman:

> Fine Machievel, is now from Florence flown
> To England where, his welcome is too great;
> His busy books, are here so read and known
> That charity, thereby hath lost her meat.
> Who doth for debt, in danger long remain
> Must fall down flat, and seldom rise again.

Also, he hath written *A Praise of Poetry,* some notes whereof are drawn out of the *Apology* made by Sir Philip Sidney that was published this last spring.

ii. A book of godly verses entitled *Hunnis' Recreations,* written by Mr. William Hunnis, the Master of the Children of the Queen's Chapel, being Adam's Banishment, Christ his Crib, The Lost Sheep, The Complaint of Old Age, published together with The Life and Death of Joseph.

iii. From Cambridge a book called *Polimanteia* showing the means lawful and unlawful to judge of the fall of a commonwealth by signs astronomical and the like, being put forward against frivolous and foolish conjectures. To this is added a letter of England to her three daughters, being the two Universities and the Inns of Court, exhorting their children to write of the worthies of our time; England to all her inhabitants exhorting them to stand together for that England can-

---

i. STC 5245. Churchyard was now aged about 75; he continued to write until his death in 1604. He comments in the margin of the stanza quoted:

'Want of charitie hath made me loose my pattent. My pattent shows that.'
ii. STC 13973.

not perish but by Englishmen; Religion's speech to England's children; and lastly Loyalty's speech.

iv. A new edition of that translation which Sir Thomas North published in 1579, made from the French of James Amyot out of the original Greek of *The Lives of the Noble Grecians and Romans, compared together* by that grave, learned philosopher and historiographer Plutarch of Chaeronea.

iii. STC 5883. Written by W. Covell. The book is apparently inspired by the genuine anxiety felt because on 5th Sept 1595, the Queen had entered on her Grand Climacteric (*i.e.,* the ninth of the fatal astrological periods of seven years). It is an important revelation of the anxious thoughts of intelligent minds in this year of alarm. See also *19th Jan* and *28th Mar 1596*.
iv. STC 20067.

3rd January. THE LADY HUNTINGDON.[1] My Lady of Huntingdon continues so ill of grief that many doubt she cannot live. She is so much weakened by sorrow that no officers of hers dare go to her sight to know her pleasure, either in her own private fortune or to know what shall be done with the dead body of my Lord.

8th January. 'THE BLACK DOG OF NEWGATE.'[2] There is entered a book called *The Black Dog of Newgate* by one Luke Hutton, dedicated to Sir John Popham, the Lord Chief Justice, and containing a poem of the Black Dog, being the jailor of Newgate, whom for his cruelty he likeneth to a dog; also a discourse between the author and one Zawny, a prisoner, discovering the ways of certain connycatchers, E. N. or N. S., that prey especially upon their fellows. Noteth that the rats be so many that they will take a candle from a man's hand, and when one dieth in the common ward they will prey upon his face ere he be fully dead.

18th January. VICTUALS FOR THE NAVY.[3] The Council having ordained the proportion of victuals of wheat, malt, pease, oxen, porks, bacon and cheese to be rendered by the several counties for the service of the navy, complaints are now being made by most of them that the charge is too heavy; so that in some cases the demand is abated.

19th January. 'A WATCHWORD FOR WAR.'[4] There is from

[1] SIDNEY PAPERS 1:386.
[2] STC 14029. See *20th Nov* 1598.
[3] APC 25:108, 138, 161, 164.
[4] SR 3:57; STC 11492. A valuable comment on the general alarm at the beginning of the year. Thomas Nun, in *A Comfort against the Spaniard*, 1596, begins his preface, 'Is it true that the Spaniards will come

this spring? And is it not true that we are ready to receive them? Hath this land at any time had either better provision or more soldiers?' See also *Polimanteia* (*Other Books . . . 1595*, iii, and note); and compare the closing words of Shakespeare's *King John*, written, I believe, a few months later.

Cambridge a godly book called *A Watchword for War*, by one C. G., published by reason of the dispersed rumours amongst us and the suspected coming of the Spaniard. Noteth and confuteth these fearful objections which make against us; as that the power of the enemy is great, and it may be he shall have the aid of the Indians, the assistance of the Pope, and perhaps the help of such as have greater cause to gratify us than be against us. Or some sinister civil practice; yet this is the common saying: 'If we be true within ourselves, we need not care or fear the enemy.' Many suspect the papists, yet, albeit they jar about matters of religion, when they see the Spaniard, they will join with us against him, if it were but to save their lives.

20th January.   'THE SECOND PART OF THE FAERY QUEEN.'[5] The second part of Mr. Edmund Spenser's *Faery Queen* is now entered for the press, containing the fourth, fifth and sixth books, being the Legend of Cambel and Telamond, or of Friendship; the Legend of Artegal, or of Justice; and the Legend of S. Calidore, or of Courtesy.

23rd January.   'A FIG FOR FORTUNE.'[6] There is a poem entered by Mr. Anthony Copley, dedicated to the Lord Viscount Montague and entitled *A Fig for Fortune*.

24th January.   UNTON AND THE FRENCH KING.[7] Sir Henry Unton reached La Fere, which the French King besiegeth, on the 7th, the King then being absent. On the 9th the King returned, and the next day gave audience to Sir Henry, who after due compliments delivered unto him the Queen's salutations and her letters; next he declared that he was come over according to the Queen's promise given to M. Lomenie to send one by whom she could more particularly express herself than by letters. Then, entering into particularities, he related why her Majesty was forced to withdraw her forces out of Brittany; why she could not assent to M. Lomenie's demands for succour for Picardy, and therewithal M. Lomenie's insolent carriage towards her Majesty; and lastly acquainted him with an Italian pamphlet wherein it was pretended that the King would make peace with Spain.

The King gave patient hearing, and after the ambassador's

[5] SR 3:57; STC 23082.
[6] SR 3:57; STC 5737.
[7] MURDIN'S STATE PAPERS, p. 701, which gives in full Unton's account of the negotiations.

speech was ended asked whether that was all the satisfaction he brought; for he was little favoured and the ambassador little honoured to be employed in so fruitless a message of words. Time no longer permitted him to trust words, for he looked daily to be assailed by a mighty enemy, as he had sufficiently and often made known to the Queen; seeing it will nothing prevail, he must, saith he, otherwise provide for his safety by such means as he may.

MR. DARCY'S PATENT IS ANNULLED.[8] The patent for searching and sealing of leather granted to Mr. Darcy is now revoked upon the leather sellers paying unto him the sum of £4,000.

25th January. CONDEMNED PRISONERS TO BE PARDONED.[9] The prisoners condemned to death at the late gaol delivery and meet to be favoured of their lives shall be pardoned and bestowed in the service of the wars with hope of their good demeanour hereafter.

26th January. NEWS FROM FRANCE.[10] Sir Henry Unton is much cast down at his ill success, which had been much worse but for the King's special favour, who took some pity on him for his former merit; the French term his message *'un discours du foin'* among themselves, and both the King and his Council take great scorn thereat. The King gave him private audience in his cabinet, saying that it was for Sir Henry's particular satisfaction, being loath to discontent one who had so well deserved of him, reputing him his soldier after the old manner howsoever he was now qualified with the title of the Queen's ambassador.

It is believed that this general truce between France and Spain is likely to ensue, whereof the grounds are these: the King's reconciliation with Rome; his being given to pleasures and desire of repose; the necessity of his estate, wanting treasure and forces to maintain the wars; his subjects being harried and wearied out with the former wars, which cry out for peace; the zeal of all his Catholics in their religion; the forwardness of his choice Councillors to sway the King to the amity of Spain; the threats of the King of Spain's intended invasion of Picardy upon the arrival of the Cardinal of Austria in the Low Countries, who bringeth war and peace with

[8] *Remembrancia* 2:142.
[9] APC 25:182.
[10] MURDIN'S STATE PAPERS, pp. 706, 707, 710.

him; and lastly the small comfort which the King expecteth from his confederates' association and aid.

30th January.   A SECOND VOYAGE TO GUIANA.[11] Four days since Laurence Keymis set forth from Portland in the *Darling* of London to make a further voyage of discovery at the charges of Sir Walter Ralegh.

31st January.   THE MILD WEATHER.[12] This month there hath been notable mild weather, and so like the spring time that the sparrows have been seen to build their nests.

1st February.   FLESH PROHIBITED DURING LENT.[1] The customary orders against killing and eating of flesh during Lent are published. This year 8 butchers are to be licensed within the City without paying anything for their licence, but bound in reasonable sums of money to observe the orders prescribed to them.

2nd February.   PROCEEDINGS WITH TYRONE.[2] Sir Henry Wallop and Sir Robert Gardiner, appointed commissioners to treat with Tyrone have met with the Earl, O'Donnell, and others. The commissioners at first would have him come to Dundalk but he refused, and on the 20th January they with three others met Tyrone and O'Donnell a mile out of the town, none of either side having any other weapons than swords. The forces of either side stood a quarter of a mile distant from them, and whilst they parleyed (which was on horseback) two horsemen of the commissioners stood firm in the midway between Tyrone's troops and them, likewise two horsemen of Tyrone's were placed between them and the English forces, to give warning of any treacherous attempt on either side. This treaty continued for 3 hours but without conclusion. The next day they met again, at which time the Irish behaved as men exceeding fearful, continually gazing about, their spies riding near, and themselves less attentive than at first. At the conclusion it was agreed that they should set down dividedly all the causes of their grievances, their demands and offers, and thereupon the commissioners would answer them so reasonably as they hoped would be to their satisfaction.

---

[11] HAKLUYT 7:362. See *25th July.*   [1] PROCLAMATIONS 352.
[12] T. Bastard, *Chrestoleros*, Bk. 2,   [2] CAREW MSS 184, 204.
Epig. 6.

3rd February. CONTRIBUTIONS TO THE FLEET.[3] The inhabitants of certain ports and coast towns in Essex having made complaint that the setting forth of 3 hoys laid upon them is too great, the Council give order that the inhabitants of the county in general being as much interested as the parts maritime shall confer and resolve of some good proportion to be given in this behalf.

4th February. FRENCH NEWS.[4] In the French King's camp it is said that the Cardinal of Austria hath power from the King of Spain to conclude a peace between France and Spain for certain years; but the Spanish King doth rather affect a long truce than a peace, whereby he might retain what he now possesseth in France. The Cardinal is now at Namur; he intendeth (as appeareth from certain letters taken) to draw out all the old soldiers into the field, to besiege Calais or Boulogne to divert thereby the siege of La Fere.

5th February. NEWS OF DRAKE.[5] A carvel from Havannah bringeth news that Sir Francis Drake has taken the castle there and landed 4000 men.

7th February. MR. THOMAS ARUNDEL'S RETURN.[6] Mr. Thomas Arundel that some months since went to take service under the Emperor against the Turk is now returned, having gotten an extreme cold by tumbling into the sea for safety of his life, when his ship was wrecked, and thereby his apparel, linen, horses, money, and whatsoever else all lost. So honourably hath he carried himself in the wars that the Emperor made him an Earl of the Empire. But when it was carried to the Queen that he hath presumed to a dignity from the Emperor without her privity he is to be committed to his lodging or to the Fleet until her pleasure be known.

11th February. FORGERS SENTENCED.[7] Five men called Nixen, Pepper, Ellis, Johnson and Anglesey, that had counterfeited the hands of the Lord Treasurer and others of the Council, were sentenced to-day in the Star Chamber. The first three are condemned to stand on the pillory and lose their

[3] APC 25:190.
[4] MURDIN'S STATE PAPERS, pp. 712, 715.
[5] SP DOM 256:37.
[6] SALISBURY PAPERS 6:43, 49. See *20th Mar, 15th April,* and *9th May, 2nd June 1597.* Acceptance of honours from foreign Princes was regarded by the Queen as an act of disloyalty; see *23rd April* and *8th May 1594.*
[7] HAWARDE, p. 37.

ears, and be branded on the forehead with an F, and condemned perpetually to the galleys. Johnson suffereth the same; but Anglesey, inasmuch as he wrote the names fearing lest Johnson would stab him, to the pillory and imprisonment only. The Lord Treasurer moved that since such burnings die out in a short time, they should be scarified on the cheeks with the letter F by a surgeon, and that some powder be put there to colour so it would never vanish; but the others made no reply to this.

12*th February*.   'THE BLIND BEGGAR OF ALEXANDRIA.'[8] Today there is a new play at the Rose by Chapman called *The Blind Beggar of Alexandria*. Herein one Irus, supposed a blind beggar, disguising himself as an humorous Count (one that maketh much of his pistol), an usurer, and a nobleman, marrieth several ladies to enjoy their love, and in the end, pretending that the Count and the usurer are suddenly slain, becometh King.

13*th February*.   FRENCH NEWS.[9] The Governors in Picardy take such alarm of the preparations of the Cardinal of Austria that upon the fear thereof they come to the French King to solicit him to furnish them with money and means, and especially the Governor of Calais; but they are all returned home only with good words. It is feared that Calais is ill furnished with means to endure a siege, and that the town is not so well fortified nor so strong for defence as it is in opinion.

COLSE'S 'PENELOPE'S COMPLAINT.'[10] There is entered a book called *Penelope's Complaint* or a mirror for wanton minions, by Peter Colse, dedicated to the Lady Edith, wife of Sir Ralph Horsey, Lord Lieutenant of the County of Dorset; which poem is committed to her Ladyship because an unknown author hath of late published a pamphlet called *Avisa*, overslipping so many praiseworthy matrons to praise the meanest. The book telleth of the complaint of Penelope at the departure of Ulysses, of the wooers' misrule, and of their slaughter at Ulysses' return.

[8] HENS. DIARY 1:28; 2:179; STC 4965; entered 15th Aug 1598. Count Hermes is the first of the important 'humorous' characters and much play is made with his black patch and pistol. *The Blind Beggar* was the most fantastic of all the Rose plays, the chief part presumably being written for Alleyn, who had a fine opportunity of showing the range of his skill as a quick-change artist in a succession of very different parts.
[9] MURDIN'S STATE PAPERS, p. 723.
[10] SR 3:59; STC 5582.

14th February. THE FRENCH KING AND THE QUEEN'S PIC-TURE.[11] The French King of late gave audience to Sir Henry Unton on the presenting to him of certain letters from the Queen. After which the King sent for Madame Gabrielle, and at her coming he drew near to her with great reverence, holding his hat at first in his hand, and declaring that the ambassador was so well known unto them both as he doubted not that she would welcome him; which she did, unmasking herself, and gracing the ambassador with her best favours. The King after these ceremonies passed took her on his left hand and the ambassador on his right hand, and so continued almost an hour walking together in the Park. Afterwards the King asked whether Sir Henry found his mistress anything changed, who answered sparingly in her praise and told him that, if without offence he might speak it, he had the picture of a far more excellent mistress and yet did her picture come far short of her perfection of beauty. 'As you love me,' said the King, 'show it me if you have it about you.' Sir Henry made some difficulties; yet upon his importunity offered it to his view very secretly, holding it in his hand. The King be-held it with passion and admiration, saying 'You are right; *je me rends*'; protesting he had never seen the like; so with great reverence he kissed it twice or thrice, the ambassador still retaining it in his hand. In the end, after some kind of contention, he took it away vowing that the ambassador might take leave of it, for he would not forgo it for any treas-ure; and that to possess the favour of the lively picture, he would forsake all the world and hold himself most happy, with many other most passionate words.

23rd February. THE SUBURBS.[12] Great abuses continue to grow by the multitude of base tenements and disorderly houses erected in the suburbs of London, and though the Council from time to time have given direction to stay or suppress such buildings, yet they have found little effect of their direc-tions. For there is an increase of dissolute and insolent people harboured in noisome and disorderly houses, such as be poor cottages and habitations of beggars and people without trade, stables, inns, alehouses, taverns, garden houses, bowling alleys

[11] MURDIN'S STATE PAPERS, p. 717. From a letter of Unton to the Queen dated 3rd February. Unton tactfully makes unfavourable comment on the King's mistress as 'attyred in a playne Sattayne Gowne, with a Vel-vet Hood all over her Head (to keape away the Weather from her) which became her verie ill; and, in my Opinion, she is altered verie much for the worse in her Complection and Favor, yeat verie grosselye painted.'
[12] APC 25:230. This problem was perennial; see *30th Nov 1594*.

and brothels; all pestering these parts of the City with disorder and uncleanness, apt to breed sickness and serve for the resort of masterless men, and the cause of cosenages, thefts and other dishonest conversations; and which may also be used to cover dangerous practices. The magistrates in the County of Middlesex are now ordered to suppress such places and the unlawful games or exercises used therein.

25th February. THE CONDEMNED PRISONERS.[13] The Lord Mayor, Recorder and Sheriff having now prepared a certificate of those condemned prisoners meet to be pardoned for service in the wars, the rest are to be executed, lest by overmuch toleration and evil example others be encouraged to like offences.

28th February. MASTERLESS MEN TO BE TAKEN UP.[14] For the defence of the new fort at Plymouth the Council require the Lord Mayor of London to take up 50 able men of such as are masterless and can best be spared, and to despatch them to Sir Ferdinando Gorges.

RELUCTANT SEAMEN.[15] Sundry mariners have conveyed themselves into remote parts of the shires away from the port towns that they may absent themselves from the press and stay at home till her Majesty's Navy be at sea, and then to go on merchant voyages. Proclamation is to be made in market towns that all mariners shall, on pain of death, repair to the port towns and there remain until the commissioners and presters shall take view of them and choose such as be fit for the service.

1st March. A HORRIBLE MURDER.[1] Two days since there was one Ralph Meaphon executed at Grinsted in Sussex for the murder of his wife at Mayfield. This man, whose trade was to dig in the iron mines and to make coals, coming home, his wife with her son of 5 years of age being abed, he knocked and was let in, whereon he fell to railing and chiding with her; and in the end, whether it were a matter pretended or otherwise, he drew out his knife and cut her throat, and so leaving her weltering in her own gore went again to his work. Soon after, the house was seen to be on fire, which the neighbours and the whole town came to quench, marvelling where the

13 APC 25:233; see *25 Jan.*   15 APC 25:253.
14 APC 25:250.   1 STC 17748.

good man and his wife was. The child was recovered from the fire and the body found, but they could not save the goods. Then was the child examined and required to tell when his father came home, and without any blushing fear (as commonly is seen in children) told them his father came home when his mother was in bed and first used some churlish speech unto her, then he drew out his knife, cut her throat and so left her; describing in good order the bigness of the knife and the colour of the haft, but wherefore his father did this wicked deed he could not say anything.

Hereupon they sent for the father from his work and strictly examined him of the same, who stoutly and most audaciously denied the fact. But his tale not agreeing with the words of his fellow workmen, he was for that night committed to the stocks. The next day being more thoroughly again examined in the cause, though the evidences were found too apparent, yet he still denied it. The coroner therefore committed him to the jail at Lewes, whence on the 24th February he was arraigned at Grinsted; where on the evidence of his son he was found guilty and on the 27th executed.

4th March.   SOLDIERS FOR IRELAND.[2] One thousand horsemen and 1500 footmen shall be sent over into Ireland at the beginning of next month, with another thousand to be held in readiness. Of these one half shall be shot, whereof a fourth part to be muskets, the other half to be armed with corselets and pikes saving some few halberts; all to be furnished with coats of good cloth well lined and of blue colour.

8th March.   THE SOLDIERS' COATS.[3] The men levied in the County of Kent for Ireland having been already provided with coats of marble colour, the Council allow the coats to serve at this time.

11th March.   TYRONE'S GRIEVANCES.[4] Sir Robert Gardiner, Lord Chief Justice of Ireland, is come over from Ireland with the grievances and demands of Tyrone and the rest, which were laid before the Queen, whereof for some part she findeth great cause of mislike that the commissioners should receive or give ear to any such presumptuous petitions. As for their petition for free liberty of conscience, this request is deemed disloyal, for the Queen will never grant to any subject of any

[2] APC 25:262, 264, 281.   [4] CAREW MSS 233, 234.
[3] APC 25:278.

degree the liberty to break laws, though heretofore she has acted mercifully.

ABUSES IN PLAY.[5] There is of late great abuse in play arising from false dice and dice of advantage to the undoing of many, and against which there is no statute law. The Lord Mayor is required to assist Mr. Cornwallis, her Majesty's Groom Porter, in his travail to suppress these abuses by providing some remedy against uttering false dice, and that neither haberdashers nor any other shall sell any but such as are square and good.

13th March.   THE QUEEN AND LORD BURLEIGH.[6] 'Tis said in Court that the Queen purposeth to make a progress of some fifteen days to consume the Lent, and to return to Greenwich eight days before the solemn feast which she will keep there; for she seemeth weary of Surrey and would go over into Middlesex, from thence to Osterley, Highgate and Hackney. The old Lord Treasurer, upon some pet, would needs away against her will on Thursday last, saying that her business was ended; and that he would for ten days go take physic. When the Queen saw it booted not to stay him, she said he was a froward old fool.

15th March.   THE LATE EARL OF HUNTINGDON.[7] The corpse of the late Lord President was embowelled, embalmed and closed in cerecloth and lead, but still lies unburied, attended nightly by four servants, for the Countess will neither accept administration nor give order for the funeral, to the great inconvenience of the Council in those parts.

17th March.   A SPANISH RAID NEAR PLYMOUTH.[8] Three nights since a Spanish pinnace came into Cawsand Bay with twenty-five men in her, who landed armed with muskets, and fixed barrels of powder and brimstone to the doors of five several houses and to two boats, and set them on fire, whereby the whole village would have been burned had not force arrived. A man having fired one shot at them, they all fled to their pinnace and put to sea.

20th March.   MR. ARUNDEL.[9] Mr. Arundel being still restrained because of his Earldom from the Emperor complain-

[5] APC 25:289.
[6] BIRCH'S MEMOIRS, 1:448.
[7] SALISBURY PAPERS 6:93. See 19th Dec 1595 and 3rd Jan 1596.
[8] SP DOM 256:89.
[9] SALISBURY PAPERS 6:105.

eth that he is more straitly treated than was Sir Anthony Shirley. Moreover, saith he, this will be a slender satisfaction to the Emperor and a certain breaking off of all well-hoped-for proceedings of amity with the Queen, for the princes of Germany cannot but take it very ill when they shall see the Queen attempt to infringe their privileges by taking on her the unmaking of an Earl Imperial; all Italy and Germany will think her not willing to offend the Turk. Besides, though a King can make an Earl, yet cannot an Earl be unmade but being tried and convicted by his peers.

21st March.   EVASION OF COMMON CHARGES.[10] Sundry persons of good ability in the county of Middlesex refuse to contribute the reasonable taxation at which they are assessed by their neighbours, some alleging that they are merchants and have their habitations in London, others pretending that they are mint men, moneyers, or have their living in other counties, or privileged by reason of her Majesty's service. The Council require that all manner of persons, under the degree of Lord of Parliament or of the Privy Council, that inhabit or hold any houses or land in the county shall henceforth pay these sums; wherein, if any refuse to contribute, then shall the commissioners for musters require them friendly to contribute as good and dutiful subjects ought to do with their neighbours in this public service. And if any of them persist, then to inform the Council, who will take such further order with them as may be convenient.

To the like effect complaints are being made by inhabitants of the liberties of Salisbury Court and Ely Rents, alleging that it may in after times be drawn in argument against their liberties; to the avoiding of which the Council have commanded an order to be entered in the register of Council, and also enregistered as an Act by the Lord Mayor of London. In the counties also many are unwilling to contribute to the charges of the Navy.

25th March.   SIR HENRY UNTON SICK.[11] Sir Henry Unton is reported to be very sick, with a violent burning fever for several days so that he hath no benefit of sleep, which redoubleth oftentimes with so extraordinary accidents (being as the physicians declare a malignant fever and accompanied with the purples) that he is in all opinion abandoned by them. The

10 APC 25:293, 296–301.   11 MURDIN'S STATE PAPERS, p. 730.

King hath visited him, although his own physicians would
have dissuaded him, to whom he answered that he had not
hitherto feared the harquebus shot and did not now apprehend the purples.

27th March. HAWKINS' DEATH REPORTED.[12] A certain mariner, one of the company of Sir Francis Drake and Sir John
Hawkins, that was taken by the Spanish and hath escaped to
Plymouth, reporteth that his ship having lost company was
taken by the Spaniards and the crew imprisoned in the Isle of
St. John de Porto Rico. The Spaniards sunk ships in the harbour to hinder the entrance, but Sir Francis summoned the
town, and when they refused to yield sent fifteen vessels to
burn the frigates. Two were fired, but by the light thus made
the Spaniards fired on the English ships and drove them away.
The English attacked the fort and Sir John Hawkins was killed.
Sir Francis then went to the south of the island to get provisions and thence sailed to Carthagena, but meanwhile the
treasure ships in Porto Rico sailed and are come safe to St.
Lucar.

28th March. THE BISHOP OF ST. DAVID'S UNHAPPY SERMON
BEFORE THE QUEEN.[13] Today the Bishop of St. David's
preached before the Court at Richmond, taking his text out
of Psalm xc., verse 12, 'O teach us to number our days, that
we incline our hearts unto wisdom,' and therein began to speak
of some sacred and mystical numbers as 3 for the Trinity, 3
times 3 for the Heavenly Hierarchy, 7 for the Sabbath, 7 times
7 for a Jubilee, and lastly 7 times 9 for the Grand Climacterical. The Queen perceiving whereto it tended began to be troubled with it. The Bishop discovering all was not well (for the
pulpit standeth *vis-à-vis* to her closet), he fell to treat of some
more plausible numbers as of the number 666, making 'Lat-
inus,' with which, said he, he could prove the Pope to be
Antichrist; also of that fatal number 88, which being so long
before spoken of for a dangerous year, yet it had pleased God
not only to preserve her but to give her a famous victory
against the united forces of Rome and Spain. He ended with
an excellent prayer, as if in her Majesty's person, in which
there occurred these words:

[12] SP DOM 256:111. See *1st May*.
[13] NUGAE ANTIQUAE 2:215; SALISBURY
PAPERS 6:139. According to Fuller
(*Church History*, Bk. x.) the Bishop
had previously made so favourable
an impression on the Queen by honest plain speaking in his sermons
that she promised him the reversion
of the Archbishopric of Canterbury;
hereafter the offer was withdrawn.
The sermon was published after the
Queen's death in 1603 (STC 21432).

'Oh Lord, I am now entered a good way into the climacterical year of mine age, which mine enemies wish and hope to be fatal unto me. But thou, Lord, which by Thy prophet Jeremy commanded the House of Israel not to learn the way of the heathen, nor to be afraid of the signs of heaven, and who by Thy Almighty hand and outstretched arm, madest the year of the greatest expectation, even '88, marvellous by the overthrow of Thine and mine enemies, now, for Thy Gospel's sake, which hath long had sanctuary in this land, make likewise '96 as prosperous unto me and my loyal subjects.' And again: 'Lord, I have now put foot within the doors of that age in the which the almond tree flourisheth, wherein men begin to carry a calendar in their bones, the senses begin to fail, the strength to diminish, yea all the powers of the body daily to decay. Now therefore grant me grace that though mine outward man thus perish, yet my inner man may be renewed daily. So direct me with Thy Holy Spirit that I may daily wax elder in godliness, wisdom being my grey hairs and undefiled life mine old age.'

The sermon being ended, the Queen, as is her manner, opened the window of her closet, but she was so far from giving him thanks or good countenance that she said plainly he should have kept his arithmetic for himself; 'but I see,' said she, 'the greatest clerks are not the wisest men.' With that the Queen went away discontented, and since by the Lord Keeper's command he has kept to his house.

COUNTERFEITING OF PASSPORTS.[14] Certain vagrants, that have been taken with counterfeit licences and passports, being strictly examined have confessed the names of divers lewd persons about the City of London that not only counterfeit the names of the Generals of her Majesty's forces beyond the seas but affix seals of arms to the same.

A SCARCITY OF GAME.[15] The purveyors of poultry for her Majesty's household complain of the scarcity of rabbits and conies, also of partridges and pheasants wherewith the Queen is served daily throughout the year; wherefore it is required by the Council that bonds shall be taken of all victuallers and poulterers that no rabbits be bought or uttered before the first of June or any partridges or pheasants sold hereafter.

29th March. CALVIN'S 'APHORISMS.'[16] Mr. Henry Holland hath translated Calvin's *Aphorisms of Christian Religion,* a

14 APC 25:320.   16 SR 3:62; STC 4374.
15 APC 25:322.

very compendious abridgment of his *Institutions* that were set
forth in short sentences methodically by M. Piscator. Herein
are handled twenty-eight commonplaces, as, Of knowledge of
God, Of Faith, Of Christian liberty, Of Predestination, Of the
Civil Magistrate, and the like. Noteth of predestination that
it is the eternal decree of God, wherein He determined with
Himself what He would have done with every man, as concerning their eternal salvation or damnation. Which doctrine
hath two notable fruits; the one, that we may with humble
adoration acknowledge how much we are bound unto God
that hath vouchsafed to choose us, so unworthy, out of the
company of the damned and to advance us to the state of
heavenly glory; the other, that we may with good assurance
rest ourselves on the unchangeable purpose of God touching
our salvation, and therefore be fully persuaded and assured
thereof in Jesus Christ.

30th March.   A BOOK OF SURGERY.[17] Mr. William Clowes,
one of the Queen's surgeons, hath written a profitable and
necessary *Book of Observations,* for all those that are burned
with the flame of gunpowder or wounded by musket or caliver
shot, and such like accidents, relating the cases and cures of
many of his own patients; also added thereto a treatise of *lues
venerea.*

2nd April.   CALAIS ASSAULTED.[1] Sudden news is come that
the Cardinal Albert of Austria that was threatening the French
King's siege of La Fere hath suddenly turned his course and
is seated round Calais.

4th April.   THE ATTACK ON CALAIS.[2] The Earl of Essex is
now at Dover, whence he hath sent Sir Conyers Clifford to
see whether he can get into Calais and view the state of the
town, but the wind was so scant that he could not stem the
tide; and another gentleman to Boulogne to find out what is
become of the King and his army, and what means they propose on that side to succour Calais.

[17] SR 3:62; STC 5442. In Ch. 27 is
given the contents of the chest
which the young surgeon should take
with him to the wars by land or sea.
The surgeon's tools are also illus-
trated.
[1] STOW'S ANNALS.

[2] DEVEREUX 1:355; SP DOM 257:4. In
the preparations made at Dover, Essex showed the utmost energy, never
sparing himself, and writing sometimes three letters a day to the
Court to expedite succours from
London.

5th April.   CALAIS.[3] My Lord of Essex, on his way from Dover yesterday to Court, met the Lord Admiral's packet between Canterbury and Sittingbourne, and seeing that the Queen had resolved to save Calais, he is returned to Dover to have all things ready. The enemy is now battering a ravelin to the east of the haven, which if taken will impede the succours; but the garrison promise to hold out two days.

SIR HENRY UNTON DEAD.[4] Sir Henry Unton is dead in the French camp, having been ill more than three weeks, although tended by the King's physicians. When the purple spots appeared above his heart they gave him *Confectio Alcarmas* compounded of musk, amber, gold, pearl, and unicorn's horn, with pigeons applied to his side, and all other means that art could devise to expel the strongest poison if he were not bewitched withal; notwithstanding he died shortly afterwards.

'CHRISTIAN COMFORT.'[5] Mr. John Norden hath written *A Christian familiar comfort and encouragement unto all English subjects* not to dismay at the Spanish threats; to which is added an admonition to all English papists who openly or covertly desire a change, also to all inferior magistrates and loyal subjects to show themselves watchful in these dangers which may move sudden and indiscreet hurly burlies. Noteth especially the policy of the enemy that by sudden reports, dangerous bruits and open hoobubs would move indiscreet tumult, that factious people might draw the rest to violate their sworn obedience and under colour of some public good for them or of some imminent danger, working their own confusion, may yield the more ease to the enemies' purpose.

6th April.   CALAIS.[6] My Lord of Essex makes all preparation for transport of the troops at Dover, hoping to embark them to-day, and to-morrow to send word that they are entered. All yesterday forenoon the enemy's battery played.

7th April.   A MUTINY AT CHESTER.[7] From Chester mutiny is reported of the soldiers sent from North Wales for the Irish service, some of them running away from their conductors; and the conductors appointed by the counties themselves refusing to see the soldiers conducted beyond Chester to the ports.

[3] SP DOM 257:10.
[4] SALISBURY PAPERS 6:122.
[5] SR 3:62; STC 18604. Another example of the general alarm of this year. Of *King John,* IV. ii. 141, 185.
[6] SP DOM 257:12.
[7] APC 25:331.

9th April.   SUDDEN LEVIES CALLED FOR.[8] Because of the news from Calais, the commissioners of musters are ordered with all speed to levy out of the trained bands 6,000 men furnished with their armour to be sent to Dover with their captains, and to be at the port of Dover by Sunday night at the farthest. This afternoon the Lord Mayor and Aldermen being in Paul's Churchyard hearing the sermon at the Cross were suddenly called from thence and forthwith by a precept from her Majesty and Council are ordered to press 1,000. By eight of the clock the men are ready and their furnishing will be complete ere morning.

10th April.   THE LEVIES DISMISSED.[9] Further news having been received that the forces cannot reach Calais in time, those already imprested are now dismissed.

THE QUEEN AND THE BISHOP OF ST. DAVID'S.[10] The Queen being displeased at the restraint of the Bishop of St. David's hath caused him to be released. Moreover she rebuked one of her ladies that spake scornfully of him and his sermon. And to show that the Bishop is deceived in supposing her to be so decayed in her limbs and senses as he, perhaps, and others are wont to be, she said she thanked God that neither her stomach nor strength, nor her voice for singing, nor fingering for instruments, nor lastly her sight was any whit decayed. And to prove the last before the courtiers, she produced a little jewel that hath an inscription of very small letters. She offered it first to my Lord of Worcester and then to Sir James Crofts to read, and both protested *bona fide* they could not. Yet the Queen herself did find out the posy and made herself merry with the standers-by upon it.

11th April (Easter Sunday).   THE LEVIES AGAIN REQUIRED.[11] Fresh advertisement now being received from the French King that the citadel of Calais will hold out longer than was before reported, the soldiers are required with all speed to be sent to Dover by to-morrow night. Wherefore this morning, being Easter Sunday, about ten of the clock, comes there a new charge from the Council that the soldiers shall again be levied, so that, all men being in their parish churches ready to have received the Communion, the aldermen, their deputies and the constables are fain to close up the church doors till they have pressed so many men to be soldiers. By noon they have in the

City 1,000 men and these, being furnished forthwith of armour, weapons, and all things necessary, are for the most part sent towards Dover to-night; and the rest follow in the morning.

THE SERVICE OF POSTS.[12] All mayors, sheriffs and other officers are commanded at their uttermost peril by the Council to assist in the service of posts, providing ten or twenty able and sufficient horses with furniture convenient to be ready at the town or stage where the post abideth. The owners to have such rates as the post from time to time payeth for his own horses.

13th April. THE EARL OF ESSEX'S COMMISSION FOR CALAIS.[13] The commission for my Lord of Essex is now drawn, making him Lieutenant-General of an army of 6,000 men for the relief of the citadel of Calais. But withal he is instructed not to carry over the forces unless the King signify his compliance with the condition of delivering the town to her Majesty until she is assured of her great expenses, and he better able to defend it without driving her still to these unsupportable burdens; not to take over more than the 6,000, and not to embark them unless he is likely to arrive in time to save the town; not to employ them unless the French King has such strength of horse and foot that the burden may not fall upon the Queen's subjects, but they be used as auxiliaries; not to attempt anything of importance without consulting the principal officers, and especially Sir George Carew and Sir Thomas Wilkes; to take with him only such nobles as have leave to go, namely, my Lords Sussex, Rich, Herbert and Burgh, but not Derby, Southampton, Mountjoy, Compton, Windsor, nor Sheffield, who shall return.

14th April. THE QUEEN'S LETTER TO THE EARL OF ESSEX.[14] This day the Queen went on board the ship *Due Repulse* and there with her own hand she wrote these words to the Earl of Essex. 'As distant as I am from your abode, yet my ears serve me too well to hear that terrible battery that methinks sounds for relief at my hands; wherefore, rather than for lack of timely aid it should be wholly lost, go you, in God's Blessed Name, as far as that place where you may soonest relieve it, with as much caution as so great a trust requires. But I charge you, without the mere loss of it, do in no wise peril so fair an army for another Prince's town. God cover you under His safest wings, and let all peril go without your compass.'

CALAIS.[15] Yesterday hard shooting was heard about Calais, so the truce is broken. The French think that M. Vidazon will hold out to the uttermost, and the King has sent him word that he shall hang him if he gives it up by composition.

15th April. MR. ARUNDEL RELEASED.[16] Mr. Arundel is now released. To-day he was with the Lord Treasurer, from whom he received his discharge and leave to go into the country or anywhere else, the Court excepted. The Lord Treasurer said that it was the Queen's pleasure to forbid his honour, and gave two reasons why he should satisfy himself that he had no wrong; the one, *nemo potest duobus dominis inservire;* the other, that stranger Earls have by courtesy a place above the Earls of this land, which to be granted to one that was but a squire were a great inconvenience.

A MURDER AT OXFORD.[17] Of late Robert Lingard, servant to Dr. Colepepper, Warden of New College, was murdered by one Winckle (or Wrincle), a townsman. Whereupon the Mayor and Recorder of Oxford, by virtue of their commission of Oyer and Terminer, purposed to have brought the man before them for his trial; but the Council, knowing that partiality is not unknown to be used in such cases concerning a townsman, advise that this Winckle receive his trial before the Justices of Assize for the avoiding of suspicion and other inconveniences.

16th April. CALAIS TAKEN.[18] My Lord of Essex and the Lord Admiral were very passionate at the delays in setting forth, but yesterday the whole afternoon was spent in embarking the army troop by troop with all their necessaries. In the evening as my Lord and the other noblemen were at supper on board the *Rainbow* with Captain Monson news was brought that the citadel of Calais has fallen.

17th April. THE TROOPS FOR CALAIS DISMISSED.[19] Now that the intended expedition for Calais is countermanded, the soldiers are to be returned under their captains to their own

[15] SP DOM 257:27.   [18] SP DOM 257:30, 35.
[16] SALISBURY PAPERS 6:145. [19] APC 25:353.
[17] APC 25:350.

counties, and strict charge taken that the armour, weapons and furniture be well and truly delivered back. Notice also is to be given to the counties that her Majesty levied this force upon very special advertisement from the French King, which afterwards proving very variable and not agreeable to her intent hath been the cause of the alteration of her purpose. Howbeit the readiness of the country to do her service she very graciously accepteth and commandeth that knowledge be given thereof.

18th April. FRENCH TREACHERY.[20] Shortly before the Spaniards took the citadel of Calais the States sent 400 resolute old soldiers, who in despite of the Cardinal's forces attained the walls and parleyed with the French within to give them entertainment, but though these soldiers had come only to their aid they would not receive them within the walls, so that, not being able to make long resistance without the walls, they were all slain by the Spaniards. For the French were all in one mind, being willinger that the Spaniards shall possess Calais than to permit either the English or other their friends to relieve it, saying, 'If the Spaniards win it, yet there is good hope by mediation of the Church to regain it; but if the English repossess it, they will never restore it.'

22nd April. THE CAUSES OF THE PRESENT NAVY.[21] There is published a *Declaration* showing the causes why the Queen's Majesty of England is moved to send a navy to the seas. Herein is shown how the Spanish King hath purpose to invade Ireland, and this last winter having amassed a great number of ships and men many of these same were destroyed. Nevertheless, not being warned by this just punishment by God's ordinance, and forgetting how by the favour of Almighty God his proud navy in the year '88 was overthrown, and his loss at Cadiz, yet still he pursueth his former purpose to animate the rebels in Ireland. Wherefore she doth appeal to all the world whether she be not necessarily enforced to send out this army to the seas. This declaration is printed also in the Latin, French, Dutch, Italian, Spanish and German tongues.

24th April. INSTRUCTIONS FOR THE FLEET.[22] It is ordained

[20] STOW'S ANNALS.
[21] STC 9203. According to Stow, the *Declaration* was printed at this time.
[22] SP DOM 257:45.

by the two generals that certain articles for the discipline of the fleet shall be read openly at service twice a week. Prayers are to be had twice a day, except urgent cause enforce the contrary, and no man shall dispute of matters of religion, unless to be resolved of some doubts, when he shall confer with the minister of the army; as it is not fit that unlearned men should openly argue of such high and mystical matters. Swearing, brawling and dicing are forbidden as they breed contentions and discords; picking and stealing shall be severely punished. Great care to be taken to preserve victuals, and every captain shall receive an account once a week how his victuals are spent, and what remains. Special charges shall be given for the avoiding danger by fire, and no candle to be carried without a lantern. The powder to be carefully preserved from spoil and waste, as without it there cannot be any great service; and care also taken not to bear too high a sail when going by the wind, and especially in a high sea, lest the spoil of masts endanger the enterprise. No spoil is to be made of any prizes, and whoever goes on board one to give an account for anything taken. No person shall land in any country without orders until his return to England upon pain of death. No person to strike any superior officer upon pain of death, nor any inferior under other severe punishment, and no report to be made which touches the reputation of any officer without producing the author, who will also be severely punished.

25th April. SHIRLEY'S VOYAGE.[23] Sir Anthony Shirley departed from Southampton two days since with nine ships and a galley, being the *Bevice,* admiral, 300 tons; the *Galleon,* vice-admiral, 240 tons; the *George,* rear-admiral, 160 tons; the *Archangel,* 250 tons; the *Swan,* 200 tons; the *George Noble,* 140 tons; the *Wolf,* 70 tons; the *Mermaid,* 120 tons; the *Little John,* 40 tons; together with the galley and a pinnace; all of which ships are furnished for ten months, and manned with soldiers and sailors, exceedingly well appointed, to the full number of 900 men.

26th April. THE RETURN OF DRAKE'S FLEET.[24] It is daily expected that the fleet of Drake and Hawkins will return to Plymouth, which may cause confusion since the place is appointed as the *rendezvous* of the army about to set out. The Council order that a pinnace shall continually lie out to command any ships to forbear to come into Plymouth except in case of necessity, but to come directly to Portsmouth. A messenger of the Chamber is also to be despatched to the Mayors and Customers of all ports from Portsmouth to Penzance, St. Ives and Padstow that they suffer none to come to land until he has been diligently searched for Spanish money, pearls, jewels or any other thing of value, lest her Majesty or any of the adventurers in the voyage be defrauded of the benefit that ought to come to them. The messenger shall leave a copy of his warrant with every Mayor and receive from him a certificate.

27th April. THE DEATH OF DRAKE AND HAWKINS.[25] Several of Drake's fleet have now come in to Falmouth, but he and Sir John Hawkins, and many men of worth are dead. They have brought back some things but not enough to countervail the charge of the journey. They bring news that a very great fleet is preparing at Ferrol, by the Groyne.

29th April. ONE CONDEMNED FOR SPREADING FALSE RUMOURS.[26] One Smith, being a base fellow, a peasant and a boy, was this day sentenced in the Star Chamber to lose one of his ears upon the pillory at Westminster, the other at Windsor, to be whipped, and to have a paper on his head containing his slanderous words, to be imprisoned during pleasure, and fined £20. This fellow being recently one of the pressed men at Dover reported when he was dismissed that the news throughout the soldiers was that the Lord Admiral's ship being searched by the Earl of Essex, and he, opening divers barrels wherein he supposed to have been gunpowder, found ashes, dust and sand; and thereupon he called the Lord Admiral traitor. And so they came both to Court, and there the Earl of Essex and the Earl of Cumberland before the Queen took the Lord Admiral by the beard, saying, 'Ah, thou traitor.'

1st May. RECUSANTS IN SUSSEX.[1] At the outside of Battle Park, Mr. Edmund Pelham, the chiefest justice of peace in that part and chief of Lord Montague's Council, is reported to be a man very backward in religion, and his wife a professed recusant. Many recusants resort to his house. At the time of the siege of Calais one Dorel, a notable recusant, lay there hovering about toward the sea coast; and when the men

25 SP DOM 257:48, 50.   1 STRYPE'S ANNALS 4:289.
26 HAWARDE, p. 39.

were to be shipped from Rye and Dover to Calais, a servant of his, mounted upon a gelding and well appointed with a case of pistols, rid to Sussex and a great part of the Weald of Kent with an alarm that the Spaniards were landed at three places in Sussex and had burnt Bourne and Pevensey. He could not be stayed but fled, leaving his cloak in the constable's hand. Upon that false alarm there was the greatest hurly burly and woeful outcries of the people; the soldiers at Rye ready to march out of the town, and the Calais service greatly hindered.

At the same time the Lady Montague's people seeing the town of Battle in that uproar and miserable state, rejoiced and showed signs of joy; insomuch that the people fell into great exclamation and cursings of them openly in the streets. When news was brought that Calais was lost, they gave out these speeches: 'God be thanked, we shall have better neighbours.'

THE LAST VOYAGE OF DRAKE AND HAWKINS.[2] The remainder of the fleet that set sail with Sir Francis Drake and Sir John Hawkins are returned to Plymouth, the last to come in being the *Defiance,* the *Garland,* the *Adventure,* and the *Phoenix.*

The first intent of this voyage was to land at Nombre de Dios and thence to march to Panama to possess the treasure that comes from Pene, and, if they saw reason, to inhabit and keep it; but a few days before they left Plymouth they received letters from her Majesty of an advertisement had out of Spain that the Indian fleet was arrived and that one of them with loss of her mast was put into Porto Rico. She commanded them therefore, seeing the weakness of Porto Rico, to possess themselves of that treasure and the rather for that it was not much out of the way to Nombre de Dios.

On 27th September of last year by break of day the fleet reached the chief town of Grand Canaria and by nine were at anchor before the fort to the eastward of the town. At one o'clock they offered to land 1,400 men in the sandy bay betwixt the fort and the town, but by this time the Spaniards had made a bulwark and planted ordnance so that our men could not land without endangering the whole force, which the General would not do. Then they went to the west end of the island and there watered; and here Captain Grimston going up the hill with six or seven in his company was set upon by the herdsmen, who with their dogs and staves killed him and most of his company. Moreover the *Solomon's* surgeon was taken prisoner, who also disclosed the purpose of the voyage so that the Viceroy sent a carvel into the Indies to all places where our fleet had intended to go. Howbeit they had previously received intelligence from the King of all our voyages the 8th August, which was three weeks before the fleet set forth from England; as also by a Fleming that had seen all their provision in London.

Thence the fleet stood away S.W. and S.S.W. some two hundred leagues until they came in the height of the islands of Cape Verde and so to Dominica and Guadalupe, where Sir John Hawkins who had been separated came up to them again. Here they watered, washed the ships, set up the pinnaces and refreshed the soldiers on shore. On 30th October Captain Wignol in the *Francis,* a bark of 35 tons, was chased by five of the King of Spain's frigates or zabras, ships of 200 tons apiece, which came of purpose with three other zabras for the treasure of St. John de Porto Rico. The *Francis* going room with them, supposing they had been our own fleet, was taken; but they left her driving with four or five sick men in her, taking the rest into their ships, as was afterwards learnt of prisoners.

In November they reached certain broken islands called Las Virgines but could find no fresh water there, though much fish was to be taken with nets and hooks, and fowls on shore. Here Sir John Hawkins grew extreme sick, which began upon news of the taking of the *Francis.* The 12th they set sail in the morning and that night came up to the easternmost end of St. John de Porto Rico, where Sir John Hawkins departed this life; whereupon Sir Thomas Baskerville went into the *Garland.*

Thence in the following afternoon they came to anchor in a sandy bay at the easternmost end of the chief town called Porto Rico, where they received twenty-eight shot from the forts and ordnance, of the which the last struck the admiral's mizzen, and the last but one, passing through her quarter into the steerage, struck the stool from under the General who was at supper; the shot hurt him not but wounded several who were at the same table, of whom Sir Nicholas Clifford and Mr. Browne died. Next day, shifting their anchorage to the west, they rode till night, when twenty-five pinnaces and small boats, manned and furnished with fireworks and small shot, went into the road within the great castles, and in despite of them fired the five zabras, quite burning the rear-admiral to the water, which was the greatest ship of them all, and also mightily spoiling the admiral and vice-admiral. But the treasure which the zabras had come to fetch had been conveyed into the strongest and surest castle of defence, being, as one of the prisoners confessed, 3,000,000 ducats or thirty-five tons of silver. The fight on our side was resolute, hot and dangerous, wherein 40 or 50 men were lost and as many hurt. There was also great death of the Spaniards aboard the frigates with burning, drowning and killing, besides some taken prisoners.

Some days being spent there, the fleet weighed anchor and came to Cape de la Vela, and in the morning of 1st December all the soldiers were embarked for Rio de la Hacha, which town our men took by ten o'clock at night. The 6th December the Spaniards came in to talk about the ransom, but not to the General's liking; and that night Sir Thomas Baskerville marched up into the country to overrun those parts, and the General the same night with some hundred and fifty men went by water six leagues to the eastward and took the Rancheria, a fisher town where they drag for pearl. The people all fled except some sixteen or twenty soldiers which fought a little but were taken prisoners, besides many negroes, with some pearls and other pillage. Next day Mr. York, captain of the *Hope,* died, and then Mr. Thomas Drake, the General's brother, was made captain. On the 10th the Spaniards concluded for the ransom of the town for 24,000 ducats, and one prisoner promised to pay for his ransom 4,000 ducats, and four days afterward they brought in the town's ransom in pearls, but rated so dear that the General misliking it sent it back again, giving them four hours to clear. The 16th December the Governor came into the town about dinner and after conference with the General told him plainly that he cared not for the town, neither would he ransom it; that the pearl was brought in without his consent; and that his detracting of time so long was only to send the other towns word that they were not of force to withstand our men that they might convey all their goods, cattle, and wealth into the woods out of danger. So the General gave him leave to depart according to promise, having two hours to withdraw himself in safety.

On the next day Sir Thomas Baskerville with the *Elizabeth and Constance,* the *Phoenix,* the carvel and four or five pinnaces went some five leagues to the westward, and landing, marched four leagues up into the country to a place called Tapia, which he took, and burned certain villages and farm houses about it. The 18th the General caused the Rancheria

and the town of Rio de la Hacha to be burnt clean down to
the ground, the churches and the house of a lady, who had
written to the General, only excepted. On the day following
they weighed and took the town of Santa Martha, the people
all being fled except a few Spaniards, negroes and Indians
which in a bravado gave them forty shot at their landing and
so ran away. This town was burnt two days later, but that
night the *Phoenix,* Captain Austin, Mr. Peter Lemond, and
the *Garland's* pinnace which stood along the shore were
chased by galleys out of Carthagena, and Mr. Lemond and
nine men taken; the rest came back safe.

They took Nombre de Dios on the 27th, all the people being fled except some hundred Spaniards which kept the fort
and played upon them, but seeing the resolution of our men
in running upon them, they all fled and took to the woods.
The town was big but nothing left of value, though there was
a show in their shops of a great store of merchandise that had
been there. There was a mill above the town, and upon the
top of another hill in the woods stood a little watch house
where was taken twenty sows of silver, two bars of gold, some
money in coin and other pillage. The soil in this place is subject to much rain and very unhealthy, having great store of
oranges, plaintains, cassavy roots and other such fruits, but
very dangerous to be eaten for breeding of diseases.

On the 29th Sir Thomas Baskerville with 750 armed men,
besides surgeons and provand-boys, went for Panama, but returned four days later, with his soldiers weary and hungry,
having marched more than half way to the South Sea. This
march was so sore as never Englishman marched before, the
way being cut out of the woods and rocks, both very narrow
and full of mire and water; and the Spaniards played upon
them divers times from the woods. Having marched ten
leagues, upon the top of a hill they came on a fort which the
Spaniards had set up and kept with 80 or 90 men who played
upon our men as they came up before they were aware of it,
and so killed more than twenty, amongst them, Captain Mar-
chant, Quartermaster-General, Ensign Sampson, Maurice Williams, one of her Majesty's guard, besides divers others hurt.
When Sir Thomas learnt that he must pass two such forts
more, if he got that, and besides that Panama was very strong,
the enemy knowing of their coming, also that the soldiers had
no victuals left nor any means to get more, these considera-
tions caused him to return and give over his attempt.

In the meanwhile the General had burned Nombre de Dios,

half on the 31st December and the rest on 1st January, with all the frigates, barks and galliots which were in the harbour and on the beach. On the 5th they again set sail, and on the 15th, the fleet being anchored at an island called Esendo, Captain Platt died of sickness, and then the General began to keep his cabin and to complain of a scouring or flux. The 23rd they set sail for Puerto Bello.

On 28th January at 4 o'clock of the morning the General, Sir Francis Drake, departed this life, having been extremely sick of the flux which began the night before to stop on him. He used some speeches at or a little before his death, rising and apparelling himself, but being brought to bed again within an hour died. He made his brother, Mr. Thomas Drake, and Captain Jonas Bodenham executors, and Mr. Thomas Drake's son his heir to all his lands, except one manor which he gave to Captain Bodenham.

That same day they anchored at Puerto Bello, where after the solemn burial of Sir Francis Drake in the sea, Sir Thomas Baskerville being aboard the *Defiance,* Mr. Bride made a sermon, having to his audience all the captains in the fleet. Then Sir Thomas commanded all aboard the *Garland* where he held a council, and there, showing his commission, he was accepted as General, and Captain Bodenham made Captain of the *Defiance* and Mr. Saville Captain of the *Adventure.* At that time also died Captain Josias of the *Delight,* Captain Egerton, a gentleman of the *Foresight,* James Wood, chief surgeon out of the *Garland,* and Abraham Kendall out of the *Saker.* Here they watered, washed the ships and made new sails, it being by the General and all the Captains agreed that if they could by any means turn up again for Santa Martha, they should; but if not, to go directly for England. Then the *Elizabeth* of Mr. Watts, the *Delight* and Captain Eden's frigate were discharged and sunk; and being mustered, there were left, sick and whole, 2,000. Thence they set sail on the 8th February.

On the 26th being off Cuba they espied twenty sail about one in the afternoon. This was a third part of the fleet which the King sent for Carthagena, the rest being gone for Honduras; they were in all sixty sails sent only to meet the fleet, being commanded wheresoever they heard our fleet to be that they should come upon them with all their forces. As soon as they descried our fleet they kept close upon a tack, thinking to get the wind; and when the admiral with all the rest of our fleet were right in the wind's eye of them, Sir Thomas Baskerville, putting out the Queen's arms, and all the rest of the fleet their bravery, bare room with them, and commanded the *Defiance* not to shoot but to keep close by to second him. The vice-admiral of the Spaniards being a greater ship than any of ours and the best sailor in all their fleet luffed by and gave the *Concord* the two first great shot, which she repaid again, and thus the fight began. The *Bonaventure* bare full with her, ringing her such a peal of ordnance and small shot that he left her with torn sides. The admiral also made no spare of powder and shot. But the *Defiance* in the midst of the Spanish fleet, thundering of her ordnance and small shot continued the fight to the end, so that the vice-admiral with three or four of her consorts were forced to tack to the eastward, leaving their admiral and the rest of the fleet who came not so hotly into the fight as they did. The fight continued two hours and better. At sunset all their fleet tacked about to eastward, but ours continued the course to lie westward for Cape de los Corrientes. In this conflict in the *Defiance* were slain five men, three Englishmen, a Greek and a negro. That night, some half hour after, their fleet keeping upon their weather quarter, our men saw a mighty smoke rise out of one of their great ships which stayed behind, and presently after she was all on a light fire, and so was consumed and all burnt.

The next day the Spanish fleet kept still upon the weather quarter but dared not come room with ours, although the admiral stayed for them, and not long afterward began to fall away astern. Thereafter they met with none of the enemy and on 9th April came to anchor on the south side of Flores in the Azores, where the *Defiance* was watered. Here they bartered with the Portugals for some fresh victuals and set on shore their two Portugal pilots which Sir Francis Drake had carried out of England with him. And so are they come back to Plymouth.

2nd May. SHIRLEY'S VOYAGE.[3] The fleet which sailed from Southampton with Sir Anthony Shirley some days since is anchored at Plymouth. Three ships and 500 soldiers now go with the Earl of Essex.

3rd May. A PROCLAMATION AGAINST COUNTERFEIT MESSENGERS.[4] Divers dissolute and audacious persons take upon themselves to be messengers of her Majesty's chamber, and for that purpose wear boxes or escutcheons of arms as messengers are wont to do. These men go up and down the country with warrants wherein are counterfeited the names of the Lords of the Council or of the Ecclesiastical Commissioners, and by colour thereof they warn gentlemen, ministers of the church, women, yeomen and others to appear before the Council, and exact fees of them for their labour and travel. By this practice divers gentlemen and other honest persons have been caused to repair from counties far distant from the court. And although divers of these counterfeit persons have been apprehended and brought into the Star Chamber, where some of them have been condemned and set on the pillory, lost their ears, and some also marked in the face, yet these notable abuses continue more and more.

Proclamation is now made that if any person so warned have any suspicion of the messenger or of the warrant to be counterfeit, he may cause the constable or the officer of the place to bring the supposed messenger before the next Justice of Peace, where the warrant may be viewed and the party thoroughly examined.

11th May. SIR THOMAS EGERTON MADE LORD KEEPER.[5] Five days since Sir Thomas Egerton, Master of the Rolls, was made Lord Keeper and had delivered unto him the Great Seal. To-day accompanied of the nobility and great numbers, he rode to Westminster and there took his place.

18th May. A MISCHANCE AT LONDON BRIDGE.[6] M. de la Fontaine that is to be the Duke de Bouillon's agent in London hath suffered a mischance like to have been very dangerous, being carried by the violence of the stream into the water mill at London Bridge through the negligence of a young waterman. To save himself the better he leapt out of the boat before he came to the fall of the water, and was carried through under the wheel and divers lighters as far as Billingsgate before he was recovered; and here he was miraculously preserved. He is very sorely bruised upon the forehead, but without any danger of loss of life, the skull being sound.

23rd May. SIR ANTHONY SHIRLEY'S VOYAGE.[7] Sir Anthony Shirley hath again put to sea from Plymouth with five ships, a galley and a pinnace.

31st May. CERTAIN MAYORS COMMENDED.[8] The Council

[5] STOW'S ANNALS.
[6] BIRCH'S MEMOIRS 2:6.
[7] HAKLUYT 7:213.
[8] APC 25:421–24.

have written letters commending and thanking the Mayors of Chester, Beaumaris and Liverpool, and the Sheriffs of Chester, for their care and diligence shown in her Majesty's service, and especially in their well ordering of the passage of the horse and foot lately sent over to Ireland.

1st June. THE ARMY AT PLYMOUTH.[1] Matters at Plymouth now grow to a ripeness, and the Generals have begun to embark their regiments, and will be gone when the wind is favourable. There are three hundred green headed youths, covered with feathers, gold and silver lace, and at least 10,000 soldiers, as tall handsome men as can ever be seen; in the navy, at least 150 ships, besides hoys and flyboats, whereof 18 of her Majesty's own, and since her reign never so many before. The States have sent 18 large ships of war and six others for the carrying of munition, but to be subject to our generals; they land 1000 men.

There have been some differences among the principal leaders at Plymouth, for it hath pleased my Lord of Essex to give Sir Francis Vere much countenance and to have him always near at hand, which draweth upon him no small envy; insomuch as open jars have fallen out betwixt Sir Francis and Sir Walter Ralegh and Sir Conyers Clifford. These my Lord hath qualified for this time, ordering that at all meetings at land Sir Francis shall have the precedence of Sir Walter, and he to have precedence at sea. Wherefore by Sir Francis' proposition are set down in writing the several duties that properly belong to every office in the field.

3rd June. THE FLEET SAILS.[2] The great fleet sailed from Plymouth on the 1st. All the soldiers and mariners being embarked, and the wind coming round to the N.W. and by N., the Lord Admiral being aboard the *Ark* commanded his master-gunner to shoot off a piece to give warning to all the fleet, which they did incontinently. While they lay at Plymouth the Lords Generals governed their charge with very good justice and martial discipline. Two soldiers were hanged upon the Hoe with papers upon them showing their offences: upon the one was written, 'For drawing his sword and raising mutiny against his commander'; upon the other, 'For running away from his colours.' A lieutenant that had taken £60 to dis-

[1] BIRCH'S MEMOIRS 2:14, 15, 17; *The Commentaries of Sir Francis Vere* (m.e. in *Stuart Tracts, 1603-1693*, ed. Sir Charles Firth, 1903). Vere's minute of the duties of the several officers in an army survives in the *Harleian MSS* (168, f119).

[2] STOW'S ANNALS.

charge men pressed in Wales was disarmed by proclamation, adjudged to repay the money, and banished the army. A soldier also in a Dutch regiment that had killed one of his companions was, by order of martial law, tied to the party murdered and so thrown both into the sea.

5th June. THE FLEET.[3] After setting sail on the 1st, the fleet reached Dodman's Point in Cornwall, but the wind scanting they were fain return again, the greater ships into the Sound of Plymouth, and the lesser into Cawsand Bay, lest any of the mariners should return again into Plymouth; but on the 3rd they set sail again and are gone with a favourable wind.

6th June. SUPERFLUOUS ALEHOUSES.[4] Many of the alehouses in London and the county of Middlesex that were suppressed some months since are again restored so that the rogues and vagabonds, which the Provost Marshals by day drive from about the City, keep the fields and commit pilferies in the country in the night season, and then stealthily return to the alehouses. The Council again require the alehouses to be suppressed, and no strong drink to be used or made in them.

DEFENCE OF THE REALM.[5] Seeing that the army and ships under the Earl of Essex and the Lord Admiral are to pass out of the Narrow Seas from the coasts of England to the Spanish Seas, it may be doubted that the enemy may make some particular attempts upon the coasts. The Lords Lieutenant of the counties by the sea are commanded to warn the inhabitants to put themselves in readiness, with continuance of watchings of beacons. Certain bands both of horsemen and footmen under meet conductors are to be ready upon convenient warning to repair to places subject to the danger of sudden landings. Furthermore, because there are reports that in divers places near the sea coast some have shown a disposition to withdraw inland, they shall be straitly warned in no wise to depart or to diminish their families that may serve for defence. If any shall attempt to do so they shall be warned on their allegiance to return, otherwise they shall be not only severely punished but have their houses and lands seized. All captains and constables in forts shall be resident with their retinues upon pain of forfeiture of their places.

In Kent where there are many foreigners, especially in Can-

[3] STOW'S ANNALS.   [5] APC 25:239, 442.
[4] APC 25:430.

terbury, Sandwich and Maidstone, the Lord Cobham is to take order that the exact number may be known, and that as they are partakers of the benefits of the realm in like sort as her Majesty's natural subjects, so they shall be contributory to the charges of the places where they remain. Furthermore, that the enemy may find less booty if any attempt be made perchance for spoil, the inhabitants by the coasts shall be warned that upon any probable alarum the herdsmen and shepherds shall withdraw their cattle to the more inward parts.

7th June. A SCOTTISH LORD'S INVENTIONS.[6] One Lord Neper (or Napier), a Scottish lord, hath made some secret and profitable inventions for the defence of this island, being a burning mirror that receiveth the dispersed beams of the sun and doth reflect them, united and concurring, in one mathematical point where it must necessarily engender fire; a piece of artillery which being shot passeth not lineally through an army but rangeth abroad superficially within an appointed place. There is also a round chariot of metal made of proof of double musket, which motion shall be by those that be within more easy, light and speedy than so many armed men would otherwise be, and of use in moving to break the array of the enemy's battle and to making passage. By staying and abiding within the enemy's battle, it serveth to destroy the environed enemy by continual shot of harquebus through small holes, the enemy being thereby abased and altogether uncertain what defence or pursuit to use against a moving mouth of metal. Besides these inventions, divers of sailing under water and the like.

11th June. SIR JOHN SMYTHE'S MISDEMEANOUR.[7] Very traitorous words are reported of Sir John Smythe that he uttered at a mustering of the train bands in the Windmill Field at Colchester. He rode on horseback with Mr. Seymour, the second son to my Lord of Hertford, and two other gentlemen into the field where Sir Thomas Lucas was training his band; and, coming in front of the pikemen as they stood in square

[6] BIRCH'S MEMOIRS 2:28. This paper (dated 7th June) occurring among the *Bacon Papers* was presumably sent to the Earl of Essex. Lord Napier was thus one of the early projectors both of the submarine and the tank. Poison gas was among the inventions of the ingenious Mr. Platt; in Thomas Arundel's chamber was found a note of various military devices, including the words, 'Learn of Mr. Platt his way to poison air and so to infect a whole camp' (SALISBURY PAPERS 7:167). Lord Napier was also the inventor of logarithms; see DNB.

[7] SP DOM 259:16, 21.

with two wings of bowmen standing in flank, he said, 'My masters, if you will go with me, you shall not go out of the land, but I will spend my life with you.' The pikemen asked if they should go with him then, to which Sir John replied, 'You shall go with a better man than myself or Sir Thomas Lucas; here is a nobleman of the blood royal, brother to the Earl of Beauchamp, to whom I am assistant.' He said also that there was a press out for 1,000 men, but those who followed him should go no further than he went, that there were traitors about the Court, and that the Lord Treasurer was a traitor of traitors; the common people had been a long time oppressed and should have redress if they would go with him.

The two gentlemen held up their hands and said they would go with him; and some of the soldiers stepping out of their ranks would have followed him, but through the persuasion of those standing by, being gentlemen, constables and men of the wiser sort, who asked them if they would be hanged, they returned to their ranks and made a condition that if their captains would go, they would; whereupon Sir John and his company went away greatly discontented.

13*th June*.   SIR JOHN SMYTHE.[8] The Council, being informed of the matter concerning Sir John Smythe, upon this offensive and unexpected accident send Sir Henry Gray to command him upon his allegiance to appear before them at Court forthwith; and if he shall make any extraordinary delay or attempt to escape, Sir Henry hath full authority to call unto him any forces which he may think necessary.

15*th June*.   DEATH OF DR. FLETCHER.[9] Dr. Fletcher, the Bishop of London, is dead upon the sudden. He was in his chair taking tobacco (wherewith since his unfortunate marriage he hath sought to smother his cares), when he cried out to his man that stood by him, 'Oh boy, I die.' Hereat one hath written this epitaph upon him:

'Here lies the first prelate made Christendom see
A bishop a husband unto a lady;
The cause of his death was secret and hid,
He cried out, "I die"; and e'en so he did.'

Before he was made Bishop of London (coming hither by

8 APC 25:450.
9 NUGAE ANTIQUAE 2:45; Fuller's *Wor-*   *thies* (Kent); CAMDEN'S ELIZABETH.
See *11th Feb* and *15th April* 1595.

way of Bristol and Worcester) he was Dean of Peterborough when Mary, Queen of Scots, was beheaded at Fotheringhay; to whom he made a wordy oration of her past, present and future condition, wherein he took more pains than he received thanks from her who therein was most concerned.

Once when there were two Councillors sworn within compass of one year, and neither of them had a grey hair, he glanced at it in his sermon with a sentence of Seneca against *iuvenile consilium, priuatum commodum, inuestum odium.* The Queen found no fault with this liberal speech, but the friends of the Councillors taxing him for it, he had the pretty shift to tell the friends of either that he meant it by the other.

SIR JOHN SMYTHE BEFORE THE COUNCIL.[10] To-day Sir John Smythe made his appearance before the Council, and, being charged to answer what he did and said to the company of pikemen to follow him, he answered very unwillingly and uncertainly. Whereupon the Council charged him with his manner of coming to the field where his pikemen were standing in order and his lewd speeches then uttered. To these charges he answered very uncertainly, confessing part of the words, alleging that he meant no harm towards her Majesty; and in some parts he sought to excuse himself by forgetfulness of what he said, colouring also certain words that he used of the Lord Treasurer with oversight by reason of his drinking in the morning of a great deal of white wine and sack. And yet in the end, finding himself charged with a multitude of witnesses, he began to defend his speeches, pretending that by the laws of the realm no subject ought to be commanded to go out of the realm in her Majesty's service, and concluding that he might lawfully advise the people not to go in service out of the realm at this time, and therefore he had just cause to use those kind of speeches. Moreover, saith he, he had been so informed by two lawyers, named Ridgeley and Wiseman. The Council now require further examinations and in the meanwhile Sir John is committed to the Tower.

16*th June.* THE TREATMENT OF SPANISH PRISONERS.[11] Divers of our Englishmen that have been taken prisoners and carried into Spain are used there with great rigour and cruelty, some in Seville and other places condemned to death, others put into the galleys or afflicted with great extremities which is far otherwise than any of the Spanish prisoners are

[10] APC 25:459. See *3rd Jan* 1598.   [11] APC 25:468.

used here in England. Her Majesty, lest her favourable usage to her enemies may be taken for a neglect of her own subjects or a kind of awe of the King of Spain, now commandeth that such Spanish prisoners as yet remain in England shall be restrained from their gentle usage. Mr. Nicholas Owsley that hath heretofore brought prisoners from Spain and carried Spanish prisoners back is now appointed to search out all Spaniards that yet remain here and to carry them to Bridewell or some such prison of severe punishment; and all that have in their keeping any Spaniards shall deliver them to Mr. Owsley. Nevertheless any man that holdeth any prisoners for ransom is assured that no prisoner shall be sent out of the realm without the knowledge and satisfaction of the party whose lawful prisoner he is.

27th June. THE CASE OF SIR JOHN SMYTHE.[12] The Council suspecting Sir John Smythe's late misdemeanour to proceed not from mere rashness but some farther ground of practice and conspiracy have directed the High Sheriff of Essex to repair to all houses of Sir John and to make diligent search for all letters, writings, books and any other things appertaining to any disloyal purpose and to have the same sealed and kept in a place of safe custody. The Attorney General and Solicitor General are now to examine Sir John and the charges made against him with a view to his speedy trial.

4th July. SERVICE WITHOUT THE REALM.[1] Mr. Nicholas Ridgeley of the Inner Temple that was committed to the Fleet for his opinions to Sir John Smythe is now to be released on his humble submission. He protesteth that he had no evil intent but doth indeed hold that her Majesty both by the common law and statute laws of the realm may lawfully compel her subjects to serve her beyond the seas in any parts wheresoever it shall please her, and that the experience of all time hath been so.

5th July. SIR ROBERT CECIL MADE SECRETARY.[2] This day is Sir Robert Cecil, second son to the Lord Treasurer, sworn Principal Secretary to her Majesty; which being done in the absence of my Lord of Essex is like to cause him much dis-

---

[12] APC 25:501, 506. In the letter to the Attorney-General, Burleigh added this postscript: 'I praie you to forbeare to examine him of anie part of his false reportes of me.'
[1] APC 26:3.
[2] CAMDEN'S ELIZABETH; APC 26:7.

content. Before his going he recommended Mr. Thomas Bodley with extraordinary praise of him as the fittest man, detracting at the same time from Sir Robert Cecil with such odious comparisons that neither is the Queen pleased to admit Mr. Bodley for Secretary (for now she showeth less favour to those whom my Lord most commendeth); nor doth the Lord Treasurer think good to join as colleague and partner to his son (which they had determined to do) one that they now suspect to be drawn to my Lord of Essex's party by reason of the immoderate praises given him by my Lord.

11th July. BLACKAMOORS IN LONDON.[3] Divers blackamoors have lately been brought into the realm, of which kind of people there are already here too many, considering how God hath blessed this land with as great increase of people of our own nation as any country in the world; whereof many for want of service and means to set them on to work fall to idleness and great extremity. By order of the Council the ten blackamoors that were brought in by Sir Thomas Baskerville in his last voyage shall be transported out of the realm.

15th July. THE EARL OF NORTHUMBERLAND NAMED AS AMBASSADOR.[4] My Lord of Northumberland being named as ambassador to the French King craves dispensation from the embassage, alleging two reasons in especial; the imperfection of his hearing and the poorness of his estate. Imperfection of hearing, saith he, must of necessity beget absurdities, as of trouble to the King who shall be forced to speak with often repetitions and to strain his voice above the ordinary. Further, my Lord protesteth that seeing the scoffing and scornful humours of the French to all of other nations in whom they discover the least imperfections they will lay upon him the reputation of a fool and grace him with some such disgrace which would nothing fit with her Majesty's honour or his contentment. As for his state, his debts are so great and for want of payments his credit for money matters so shaken that he knoweth not which way or by what means he may satisfy his desire to do her service.

17th July. IRISH NEWS.[5] The rebels led by O'Donnell now overrun the whole of Connaught; in Roscommon more than forty strong castles, besides forts, are lost without striking one

blow, whereat Sir Richard Bingham the governor (whom
some name *Improvido*) is greatly blamed. Nor is it yet concluded whether there should be a continuance of war or a
pacification. A great occasion of the continuance of these
troubles is the difference between Sir William Russell and Sir
John Norris, Sir John blaming the Lord Deputy for hindering
the service, for he provideth insufficiency of victual and carriage.

18th July.   BLACKAMOORS IN ENGLAND.[6] Mr. Casper van
Sanden, a merchant of Lubec, that at his own charges brought
back 89 of the Queen's subjects that were detained as prisoners
in Spain and Portugal, hath desired licence to take up so many
blackamoors and to transport them into Spain and Portugal;
which her Majesty thinketh a very good exchange and that
those kind of people may well be spared in the realm. The
Lord Mayor of London and other mayors and public officers
are required to aid Mr. Sanden to take up the blackamoors
with the consent of their masters.

19th July.   GREAT GOOD NEWS FROM SPAIN.[7] News is come
that on 19th June, 8 of the Queen's ships entered the bay of
Cadiz and fought with 22 galleys and 8 armadoes, whereof
they took 18 galleys, sunk 4 and burnt the *St. Philip,* a great
ship of war, with 4 others; that the next day the army arrived
and took 40 sail richly laden; the 21st they took the town of
Cadiz, and it is thought that they have taken St. Mary Port as
the Flemings that bring the news saw a great fire which burnt
all night.

22nd July.   PLAYING INHIBITED.[8] The players are forbidden
to use any plays about the City of London for that by drawing
of much people together increase of sickness is to be feared.

25th July.   THE SECOND GUIANA VOYAGE.[9] Captain Lawrence
Keymis is returned from his voyage of discovery to Guiana
and reporteth much of the rivers, nations, towns and casiques
(or captains) of those parts. Of Berreo, that Spaniard whom
Sir Walter Ralegh took in his voyage, he reporteth that after
Sir Walter's departure he returned to Trinidad with but 15
men, but being attacked by the natives and two or three of his
men killed, fled away towards the River Caroli, where the
Spaniards have made a fort to defend the passage of the river.

6 APC 26:20.   8 APC 26:38.
7 SP DOM 259:71.   9 HAKLUYT 7:358.

Captain Keymis was told that the old King Topiawari is dead, and the boy Hugh Goldwin, that was left behind, eaten by a tiger. They returned therefore from Topiarimacko, that was Topiawari's port, by another branch of the main river to the port of Carapana. He himself came not, but sent one of his aged followers to say that he was sick, old and weak. This old man declared that Carapana had repented him of his ambition ever to have sought by the Spaniard's means to have enlarged his countries and people, for now that the plenty of gold in that country is known, there can be no greater misery than if the Spaniards prevail; who perforce do take all things from them, using them as their slaves, and (that which is worst of all) they must be content to leave their women if a Spaniard chance but set his eye on any of them to fancy her. On the other side they could hope for no better state and usage than her Majesty's gracious government; 'for,' said the old man, 'the other year when we fled into the mountains, and measured your doings by the Spaniards in like case, we made no other account but that your commander being able, as he was, would doubtless have persecuted us to the uttermost. We found it far otherwise, and that none of your well governed company durst offer any of us wrong and violence; no, not by stealth, when unknown they might have done it.' Wherefore Carapana doth crave of her Majesty for himself and his people that they may enjoy her protection.

Hereby Captain Keymis would give this caveat to our English (who to steal the first blessing of an untraded place will perhaps secretly hasten thither) that they may be assured that these people, as they no way sought to harm but rather used our men with all kindness, so are they impatient of such a wrong as to have any of their people perforce taken from them, and will doubtless seek revenge. He concludeth that it will be blindness and deafness in those that spend their days in serving the commonwealth to seek either to forslow so fit an occasion or to forsake so general a blessing. This country of Guiana doth not only propose some hope of gold mines, and certain pieces of made gold, but also in the trade of these rivers brasil-wood, honey, cotton, balsamum, and drugs to help to defray the charges. 'The case then so standing,' saith he, 'is it not mere wretchedness in us to spend our time, break our sleep, and waste our brains, in contriving a cavilling false title to defraud a neighbour of half an acre of ground; whereas here whole shires of fruitful rich grounds, lying now waste for want of people, do prostitute themselves unto us like a fair and beautiful woman, in the pride and flower of desired years.'

26th July. THE DUNKIRK PIRATES.[10] Of late divers Newcastle men have been taken on the coasts of Norfolk and Suffolk by the Dunkirkers for that those hoys of Newcastle go so slenderly armed that they give occasion to the enemy to set upon them. The Mayor and others of Newcastle are now to require these ships to be furnished with iron ordnance, powder and some calivers or muskets, and to see them properly manned. Moreover, they shall go together in consort.

A PRESUMPTUOUS BALLAD.[11] There is a certain ballad published, written by Deloney, containing a complaint of the great want and scarcity of corn within the realm; and thereby the poor may aggravate their grief and take occasion of some discontent, the Lord Mayor hath called before him the printer and the party by whom it was put to print, who pretended a licence; but finding it untrue the Lord Mayor hath committed him. In the matter complained of, the Queen is brought in to speak with her people in very fond and undecent sort, and prescribeth orders for the remedying of the dearth of corn, extracted (as it seemeth) out of the book published last year.

27th July. THE POSSESSION OF THOMAS DARLING.[12] At the late assizes held at Derby by Sir Edmund Anderson, the Lord Chief Justice, there is condemned a certain witch called Alse Gooderidge that very grievously bewitched a boy, one Thomas Darling.

This Darling at the end of February last went hunting the hare with his uncle, one Robert Toone, dwelling in Burton upon Trent; but his uncle being earnest in following his game was parted from the boy, who returned home alone, and afterward waxing heavy, and growing very sick, was got to bed. The next morning he had some fits with extreme vomitings, and would many times point with his hands, saying, 'Look where green angels stand in the window,' and complaining of a green cat that would trouble him. Moreover the use of his

[10] APC 26:61.
[11] Wright's *Queen Elizabeth and her Times* 2:462.
[12] SR 3:85; *The most wonderful . . . witch named Alse Gooderidge of Stapenhill*, 1597. The pamphlet gives a long and detailed account of the boy's sufferings, compiled from the notes of Jesse Bee. Both in this narrative, and that of the Warboys case (see *9th April* 1593), the significant details are most carefully recorded. The Elizabethan eyewitness receives too little credit for the skill and accuracy of his reports of observed phenomena.

legs was taken from him. Many and strange fits he had, which being ended, he would fall upon his knees suddenly to prayer and that so pithily that the standers-by wondered thereat; and between the fits he requested them to read the scriptures. Wherefore they sent for one Jesse Bee, who read the 9th chapter according to St. John till he came to the 4th verse, at which time the boy was overthrown into a fit like the former, which fits lasted commonly about a quarter of an hour. Jesse continued reading the 11th, 12th and 13th of St. John's Gospel, and the 1st and 2nd of Revelations; during which time the fits continued one in the neck of another; and ending with a vomit he used to say, 'The Lord's name be praised.' When Jesse either ceased to speak of any comfortable matter, or to read the scriptures, the boy was quiet; but when he was so religiously occupied the fits came thick upon him, which Jesse Bee observing told the boy's aunt that he suspected the boy was bewitched.

The next morning the boy said unto the maid that made him ready, 'I heard my aunt tell Jesse Bee that I was bewitched: the same Saturday that my sickness took me, I lost my uncle in the wood, and in a coppice I met a little old woman; she had a grey gown with a black fringe about the cape, a broad thrummed hat, and three warts on her face. I have seen her begging at our door; as for her name I know it not, but by sight I can know her again. As I passed by her in the coppice, I chanced against my will to let fall a scape; which she taking in anger said, "Gyp with a mischief, and fart with a bell: I will go to heaven and thou shalt go to hell"; and forthwith she stooped to the ground.' Hereupon a more vehement suspicion arising, some judged it to be the witch of Stapenhill; others, because she was old and went little abroad, rather thought it to be Alse Gooderidge, her daughter, who was had in great suspicion of many as a doer of devilish practices.

The fits continuing thus by the space of five weeks, at length the boy's grandmother sent for Alse Gooderidge, and when, with much ado, she was brought into the chamber where the boy was, he fell suddenly into a marvellous sore fit.

Some days later Alse Gooderidge, together with her mother, was again brought into the boy's presence by order of Sir Humphrey Ferrers, and seeing that the boy straightway had fits at their presence, Sir Humphrey ordered them to be searched for those marks which are usually found upon witches. Whereupon behind the right shoulder of the old woman they found a thing like the udder of an ewe that giveth suck with two teats. So they bade her say the Lord's Prayer, which she huddled up after her manner, always leaving out the words 'Lead us not into temptation.' Then they searched Alse Gooderidge and found upon her belly a hole of the bigness of two pence, fresh and bloody, as though some great wart had been cut out of the place, which she declared to have been caused by a knife recently on a time when her foot slipped; but a surgeon judged it to be an old wound, for it was not festered and seemed to be sucken. After further examination Alse Gooderidge was committed to Derby gaol, but her mother dismissed.

Next day the boy had very grievous fits, his eyes closed up, his legs lifted up as stiff as stakes, and all his senses taken from him, at which times he uttered very strange sayings. In the mean season others wishing to be eye witnesses of these strange reports, Jesse Bee would read the Bible, and when he came to the 4th verse of 1st chapter of St. John's Gospel, 'In him was life, and the life was the light of the world,' the boy was overthrown into a fit. Many and grievous torments did the boy suffer in the days following, and when the fits ended, Jesse Bee would say, 'Thomas, shall we take the sword with two edges and bid Satan the battle?' To whom the child answered, 'Yes, very willingly'; but as Jesse would read in the 1st chapter of St. John's Gospel, so the fits would come upon him again.

At length a cunning man declared that he would make the witch confess and within a sennight after cure the boy. So he sent for her from the Town Hall to the house of Mr. Robert Toone, where many worshipful persons were ready to see proof of his skill. Being brought, they laboured to make her confess; to which she answered that it was the first that ever she committed and if they would give her liberty she would confess all the truth freely; whereat her speech was interrupted so that she could not speak, but she prayed them to forgive her. The cunning man seeing this would not prevail fell to trial of his conclusion. He put a pair of new shoes on her feet, setting her close to the fire till the shoes being extreme hot might constrain her through pain to confess. She, being thoroughly heated, desired a release and she would disclose all; which granted she confessed nothing. Being therefore threatened more sharply, she confessed to reveal all privately to Mistress Dethick, but when she began to speak her breath was stopped, so that she could say nothing but 'I pray you forgive me.' The company continued threatening and persuading her but she would say nothing to the purpose, and so she was sent again to the Town Hall, and the company departed; after which the boy had eight fits.

These torments having endured for nearly ten weeks, very grievously, on the 6th May the boy had twelve fits in the forenoon and ten in the afternoon. After one of them taking the chamberpot, he started suddenly saying, 'Look, where a man cometh out of the chamberpot'; in another fit he cried out, 'Flames of fire, flames of fire'; in another he said, 'I see the heavens open.' In most of these fits he bleared out his tongue, having his face wry turned towards his back, groaning and shrieking lamentably.

At length, the fits having in the meanwhile increased, there came one Mr. John Darrell, a preacher, who seeing the boy in divers of his fits, assured his friends that he was possessed with an unclean spirit, and exhorted both the boy and his parents and friends to resist Satan and to prepare themselves against the next day to that holy exercise of prayer and fasting.

The next day therefore the family with some others being assembled, the holy exercise of prayer and fasting was taken in hand, in the midst whereof the boy was taken with his fits but after a while fell into a trance, and there came from him a small voice saying, 'Brother Glassap, we cannot prevail; his faith is so strong, and they fast and pray, and a preacher prayeth as fast as they'; and, 'Brother Radulphus, I will go unto my master Belzebub and he shall double their tongues'; and later, 'Radulphus, Belzebub can do no good, his head is stroken off with a word; but I will go fetch the flying eagle and his flock.' At this time the boy declared that he saw an angel in the window, like a milk white dove, sent from the Lord to be with him and assist him. Then the voice said, 'We cannot prevail, let us go out of him, and enter into some of these here.' This voice came twice, and it made the standers-by afraid. And after other sayings, 'We cannot prevail, we cannot prevail, their Church increaseth'; at which time there came in two to join in prayer with the company. Then the voice said, 'Here cometh one of my people'; with that they looked back, and were ware of a man of bad life coming into the parlour, and albeit the boy was in one of his trances, yet he made signs to the company to get him away, which one of them perceiving did so.

About two in the afternoon he had a marvellous strange fit, at which time, if he were possessed with two spirits (as it is

probable he was), one of them went out of him. All day the
fits continued, but decreasing in strength; and at last, being
laid upon his bed, he began to heave and lift vehemently at
his stomach; and getting up some phlegm and choler, pointing
with his finger and following with his eyes, he said, 'Look,
look, see you not the mouse that is gone out of my mouth?'
Then he fell into a quiet trance; which ended, he was well
until 7 o'clock, when he with two or three others went to
supper. And as he sat at the table he fell into a trance and was
thence carried to bed. As he lay there a voice was heard, saying, 'My son, arise up and walk, the evil spirit is gone from
thee; arise and walk.' Upon this his keeper said, 'Let us see if
he can go betwixt us'; for indeed he had lost the use of his
legs since the beginning of his sickness. But he answered, 'No,
I can go of myself, I thank God,' and so standing on his feet
straightway he went forward without any difficulty.

The next day Mr. Darrell came again to him, and counselled
him to be now most heedful, lest the unclean spirit returning,
and his heart empty of faith, bring seven worse than himself
with him. He did indeed again fall into his trances, but the
Lord being with him, he was soon well both in mind and
body, and so hath remained ever since.

28th July.   THE SPANISH PRISONERS.[13] The Spanish prisoners
that are in the City having had notice of the late order keep
themselves close in secret places so that they may not be taken
going abroad. The Lord Mayor is now to make diligent inquiry where any Spaniards or professed subjects of the King
of Spain are harboured and to cause them to be apprehended
and carried to Bridewell to receive at least some part of that
usage whereof our countrymen do taste in more extremity in
the King's dominions.

30th July.   THE QUEEN'S PICTURE.[14] All public officers shall
yield their assistance to the Queen's Sergeant Painter touching
the abuse committed by divers unskilled artisans in unseemly
and improper painting, graving and printing of her Majesty's
person and visage, to her great offence and disgrace of that
beautiful and magnanimous Majesty wherewith God hath
blessed her. All such to be defaced and none allowed but
such as the Sergeant Painter shall first have sight of.

31st July.   A PROCLAMATION FOR THE DEARTH OF CORN.[15]

[13] APC 26:64. See *16th June*.   [15] PROCLAMATIONS 338.
[14] APC 26:69.

In divers counties rich farmers and ingrossers pretending the unseasonableness of this summer are increasing the price of the old corn, of mere covetousness. The Justices are forthwith to peruse diligently the orders made last year and to consider such points as may tend to the reformation of those that by their disorder and covetousness cause the prices of grain to be increased in this lamentable sort beyond reason. Moreover the Sheriffs, Justices and principal officers shall certify monthly to the Council the names of those Justices of Peace who dutifully towards her Majesty and charitably towards their neighbours perform the charge committed to them that her Majesty may be informed, and contrariwise to mislike those that shall neglect the execution of this commandant.

It is also forbidden at this time of scarcity that starch be made of corn of the realm.

1st August. NEWS FROM THE FLEET.[1] To-day, being Sunday, Sir Anthony Ashley came to Court from the Fleet and made relation of all the action first at the Council table, and after dinner to the Queen.

2nd August. PREPARATIONS FOR THE RETURN OF THE FLEET.[2] Sir Ferdinando Gorges, Mr. William Killigrew, and Mr. Richard Carmarden, the surveyor of the custom-house in London, are appointed commissioners to Plymouth to view the prizes as the ships return from Spain. As formerly merchants of London or residents in the ports have bought from the soldiers and mariners goods of great value but small bulk and carried them away secretly, inquisition is to be made, and merchants suspected of any such intentions to be ordered to depart on pain of imprisonment.

4th August. 'THE METAMORPHOSIS OF AJAX.'[3] Mr. John Harington, that hath lain almost buried in the country these three or four years, thinking to give some occasion to be talked of hath written and caused to be printed a very foul book entitled *A New Discourse of a Stale Subject called the Metamorphosis of Ajax,* treating of a new way to make a jakes that shall be rid of stink; but intermixed with many other unsavoury matters. The device is this: You shall make a false bottom to that privy that you are annoyed with, either of lead

---

[1] BIRCH'S MEMOIRS 2:95.
[2] SP DOM 259:88.
[3] STC 12779. I have suggested (in an edition of John Marston's *Scourge* *of Villainy,* 1925) that Jaques in *As You Like It* owes his name to this book. See also E. I. Fripp's *Shakespeare Studies,* 1930, p. 154.

or stone, the which bottom shall have a sluice of brass to let out all the filth, which if it be close plastered all about it and rinsed with water as oft as occasion serves, but especially at noon and at night, will keep your privy as sweet as your parlour.

Mr. Harington hath also this jest of Mr. Jaques Wingfield: Mr. Jaques Wingfield coming one day either of business or kindness to visit a great Lady in the Court, the Lady bade her gentlewoman ask which of the Wingfields it was. He told her 'Jaques Wingfield.' The modest gentlewoman, that was not so well seen in the French to know that 'Jaques' was but 'James' in English, was so bashful that to mend the matter, as she thought, she brought her lady word, not without blushing, that it was 'Mr. Privy Wingfield.'

5th August. CHURCHYARD'S POEM ON SIR F. KNOLLYS.[4] Churchyard hath written *A sad and solemn funeral* of Sir Francis Knollys that died a few days since.

8th August. A DAY OF TRIUMPH.[5] To-day, being Sunday, great triumph is made at London for the good success of the two Generals and their company in Spain, the winning, sacking, and burning of the famous town of Cadiz, and the overthrow and burning of the Spanish Navy.

THE TAKING OF CADIZ.[5] On the 20th June, being Sunday, early in the morning the fleet came to anchor within half a league of St. Sebastian, a friary at the west end of Cadiz; and here the Generals attempted to land straightway. They filled many boats and barges with soldiers, but the weather was very foul and the water went so high that two boats with some eighty soldiers armed sank, whereof some were drowned, the others saved by the other boats and set on board their own ships. This mischance did not happen as any token that God was angry with the enterprise, but that they had mischosen the day for attempting so great a work upon the Day of Rest. It was also a mercy of Almighty God, for they could not have landed there without great difficulty and much loss.

The next day, early in the morning, the Spanish fleet, which had ridden before the town under the forts and bulwarks, shot with the tide within the point of the mainland, and immediately after the English fleet weighed and came to anchor near

---

[4] STC 5254.
[5] STOW'S ANNALS. There are several accounts of the Cadiz expedition, apart from the various collections of State Papers; see, e.g., Vere's *Commentaries* and *The Monson Tracts*, ed. M. Oppenheim, Navy Records Society, 1902.

the place where the Spanish fleet rode before; and there the fort St. Philip and the rest played upon our ships with their great ordnance, and the galleys were very busy. But, by the Generals' commandment Sir John Wingfield in the *Vaunt-guard*, having some lesser ships, took them to task, and so lamed them that they were glad to seek to save themselves. These crept by the shore, first to the Puntal, and from thence into the Bay, and so to a bridge called Puente de Suazo, where striking their masts and by help of certain engines upon the bridge, they went round about the Isle of Leon and came to Rota.

But the eye and care of the two Generals was chiefly fixed upon the galleons and other great ships. Whereupon they resolved to send the Lord Thomas Howard to encounter with them in the *Nonpareil,* adjoining with him some few ships of the Queen's, for the place was so narrow that hardly ten ships could come to fight. With the Lord Thomas went Sir Walter Ralegh, Sir Francis Vere, Captain Robert Cross (with whom was the Earl of Sussex) and others. And although it had been agreed in council that the Generals should not hazard their ships of greatest burden in those shoals, yet the Earl of Essex could not endure to be only a looker-on in so honourable an action, but he put in amongst the thickest of them and fought very gallantly; which the Lord Admiral seeing, and not being able to bring in his own ship, took his long boat and went aboard the *Miranore.* With him into the fight went his young son Lord William, being at these young years very desirous to seek and share honour with the oldest captains.

This fight lasted till noon, by which time the galleons were cruelly rent and torn, and so much slaughter in them that the blood gushed out at the scuppet holes. Whereupon some of the Spaniards resolved to fly to Porto Real, some to burn their ships, some to run them aground; and divers of them leapt into the water, whereof some swam ashore, some were drowned, some taken, some slain. The Lord Admiral, beholding this miserable spectacle, had compassion of them, and took his boat and rowed up and down amongst them, forbidding these cruelties and preventing the firing of the Spanish ships so much as was possible; but they first fired and burnt the *St. Philip,* a ship of 1,500 tons, the *St. Thomas,* and the *S. Juan.* The other two apostles, *St. Matthew* and *St. Andrew,* ships of 1,200 tons apiece, were saved and are now brought back to England.

The battle by sea being thus happily fought and victory ob-

tained, the Lords Generals straightway set in hand the landing
of the soldiers, and in very little space there was such diligence shown that the Earl of Essex was on land near Puntal,
about a league from Cadiz, with 8,000 shot and pikes; with
him was the Earl of Sussex, the Earl Lodowick of Nassau,
the Lord Burke of Ireland, and divers other gentlemen adventurers. So soon as he was landed, the Earl of Essex despatched the Sergeant Major, Sir Christopher Blount, and Sir
Thomas Gerrard with their regiments to the Puente de Suazo,
with charge to impeach the passage so that no succours might
come to the Spaniards into the Isle of Leon; to break down
that engine by help whereof the galleys might pass; and to
surprise or force the castle at the head of the bridge, called
by the Dutch 'Herod's house.'

Meanwhile the Earl of Essex, having for his guide Captain
William Morgan, marched apace with his army toward the
town, although in no hope to lodge therein that night. Upon
the way he was encountered with 400 or 500 cavalleros of
Xeres and 600 or 700 footmen, but without any great difficulty they were beaten back and ran into the town, offering
to shut the gates. But my Lord made such haste that he entered with his troops pell-mell with them; and some made
such shift to get into the town that they climbed over the
walls.

By this time the Lord Admiral had landed his battle of
some 1,200 or 1,500 men and followed the Earl with a very
round march, being accompanied with all the chief commanders of sea and captains of ships with their retinue, among
them the Lord Thomas Howard and Sir Walter Ralegh, who
was not able to march so fast as the rest by reason that he was
hurt in the leg with a splinter in the fight with the galleons.
When the Lord Admiral came into the town, he found the
Earl of Essex skirmishing and fighting with the Spaniards,
who fought and fled still before him. Others threw down
stones from the battlements of houses which annoyed much
our soldiers. But after the forces of both the Generals were
joined together, the fight and resistance of the Spaniards continued not long, for they fled into the Castle and into the
Town-house in the market place, and other strong places. And
here Sir John Wingfield riding upon a nag unarmed, having
been hurt before in the thigh, was shot in the head from a loop
in the Castle, whereof he instantly died. Before night the
Town-house was taken, and therein the Generals lodged, being now masters of the whole town, except for the Castle

and the fort St. Philip, both which were rendered in the morning.

The Corrigidor and the rest of the town yielded on condition that they should have their lives saved and only their wearing clothes permitted them; all the rest of their goods and wealth should be spoil and pillage to the soldiers, and besides for their ransom they should pay to the Generals 120,000 ducats, and for payment thereof 40 of the chief men are to be held in England as pledges till the money be paid.

And now proclamation was made that no Englishman should offer violence to any religious person, to any woman or child, or any other of the Spanish nation; and the Generals sent away boats, barges and pinnaces first with the ladies and religious, and then the men and all other of the inhabitants of Cadiz (except the pledges and certain prisoners of the captains) to Porto Santa Maria. The women were suffered by the Generals to wear so much apparel as they were able to bear upon them and all their jewels, and because none of them should be spoiled by our ruder soldiers and mariners, the Lords Generals themselves stood at the water gates and saw to their embarking.

In this interim the Lord Admiral appointed the Rear-admiral to take some of the lesser Queen's ships and merchant ships that drew but little water to go after the Spanish ships which were fled to Porto Real, and there either to take them or to sink or fire them if they would not yield. While this was determined, offer was made of two millions to the Earl of Essex for the ransoming of the ships and their merchandise. The Lord Admiral would by no means agree to the ransoming of the ships but only of the merchandise. But the Duke of Medina Sidonia, the Admiral of Spain, decided this controversy; for he, being at Porto Santa Maria and always ill affected to them of Cadiz, gave order that the next morning before day the whole fleet at Porto Real should be fired. This was put in execution; nevertheless our men made such haste thither that they recovered much merchandise and divers pieces of ordnance, but none of the ships could be saved.

Thus is the whole fleet of the Spaniards, valued by some of them at ten or twelve million ducats, all either taken, sunk or burned in a short space; together with much rich merchandise in Cadiz, and that which pincheth the King of Spain most (his ships excepted) are the 1,200 pieces of ordnance taken or sunk in his ships. The Spaniards' losses in all are reckoned to be worth 20,000,000 ducats at the least.

These things being happily achieved, Sir John Wingfield was very honourably buried in Santa Cruz, the chief church of Cadiz, with all the funeral solemnities of war; the drums and trumpets sounding dolefully, the shot bearing the noses of their pieces downward, the pikes trailed. His body was borne by six knights, and the Generals threw their handkerchiefs wet from their eyes into the grave; and at that instant the most part of all the shot, great and small, aboard and ashore, were discharged.

The 27th June being Sunday the Lords Generals, with all the chiefs and gentlemen of the army, heard a sermon at S. Francisco, where after dinner they made a great many knights, even all almost that did deserve it, or affect it, or not neglect it and refuse it, as some did. In this prodigality of honour fifty-seven Englishmen are knighted, and as well the Count Lodowick of Nassau, Don Christopher (son to Don Antonio that was called King of Portugal) and four Dutch gentlemen are knighted; but Sir Samuel Bagnal and Sir Arthur Savage had been knighted before the town was taken for their bravery in the field.

The next day being Monday the 28th the Lord Admiral went aboard to set things in order in the fleet and to make ready for a new enterprise; and by his example also to draw the seamen and mariners to their ships that were loath to come out of the town.

About this time the Lord Admiral received from the Duke of Medina Sidonia, his old acquaintance since '88, two very honourable answers to two letters which he had written about the exchange of prisoners, Spanish for English, in the galleys. The Duke's answer was that he liked well of the motion and would do it so much as lay in him, but the charge was more particularly in the Adelantado of the galleys. To whom he wrote so effectually that within a day the Adelantado sent a principal captain to the Lord Admiral, who made full agreement for the exchange.

Upon the 1st July about forty of our English prisoners were delivered aboard the *Ark* by the galley called *La Fama*, and promise made for the rest, which was afterwards performed. This galley *La Fama*, whereof Don Julian Hurtado was captain, came from Rota to the English Fleet with a white flag of safe conduct according to the order of war, but an ignorant sea captain made a shot at her as she passed by him and hurt and killed three men in her. Whereat the Lord Admiral was much grieved and greatly offended with the captain and threatened to have hanged him, but the Captain of the galley and Don Pavo Patin, one of the pledges, made earnest suit to the Lord Admiral, which they obtained.

The Earl of Essex stayed all this while in the town with the rest of the commanders and captains, and companies of the army by land, which he suffered not to be idle. On the 28th June the ordnance was taken from the walls, castles and forts. Upon the 30th he made a road into the Isle and burned, razed, and spoiled all that might serve the enemy to any strength or relief. The next day he set pioneers a work, to raze and deface the forts and castle in the town. The 1st July the tower of the Town-house was battered down, and lastly upon the 4th July, he set the whole town on fire (the churches excepted) and saw all his men embarked, himself coming on board last. The next day the whole fleet set sail.

After sailing from Cadiz the fleet sailed along the coasts of Spain until they came before Ferrol where the Generals resolved to land. First Sir Amyas Preston and Sir William Monson and Captain William Morgan were sent in the evening to discover the passage in their pinnaces, and to view the place, to espy the forces, and to seek for fresh water and victuals. They brought answer next morning that the people were fled and had carried away their goods, and that they could not yet find any fresh water or victuals. For all this in the afternoon the Lords Generals landed with all their forces; but the Lord Admiral being not well, and having little hope of any relief there for their wants, at the earnest desire of the Earl of Essex, returned aboard his ship taking Sir Edward Wingfield with him, who was lame of a hurt which he had received at Cadiz.

The Earl of Essex being landed marched some two leagues with his army that night to Ferrol. He took the town with ease for the inhabitants had abandoned it and carried away most of their goods, but there was in the Nunnery some stuff, and in the palace of Bishop Ossorius a library of books, valued at 1,000 marks. There was also in the town some fruits and wines and a few hens; and in the Fort four pieces of great ordnance whereof one was the fairest and longest culverin which the King of Spain hath. Here the Earl appointed Captain Brett to march into the country with 800 soldiers of the strongest, chosen out of divers bands. He marched some two or three leagues to a town called Lotha, which he took and burnt, without any resistance; but if any of his troops straggled or were left sick upon the way, as many were, he found them at his return pitifully mangled, some with their hands chopped off, some their nostrils slit, and others killed. In this journey he got above a hundred cows and oxen and some swine for victual, and so returned to the Lord General who, after he had sacked and fired the town, the third day returned to the fleet.

All being now come on board again the Generals with their council held a new consultation on what was else to be done and how victuals and fresh water might be supplied. Some had great desire to go for Lagos; but ere anything was done the fleet was past the Cape St. Vincent, where a strong northerly wind took them and forced them to haul off into the sea and towards the Isles of the Azores. Here they called a council again and resolved to go for those islands, assuring themselves to have plenty of fresh water and victuals, and there to lie for the carracks and West Indian fleet and to encounter with the twenty-five Spanish men-of-war which lay at the Islands, as the Generals were advertised. But neither did this purpose hold, for the winds coming contrary, they held a new consultation and that was to bear with the coast of Spain and Portugal, and to search what shipping was in the harbours as they passed. This course was thought best, and kept for the most part until they came before the Groin on the 1st August.

Now lastly the Lords Generals resolved to come for England, and the rather by reason of the general wants of victuals and fresh water, and for that there were many sick men in the *Warspite* and divers others of the fleet, and for a great leak that was sprung in the *Vauntguard*, and principally for her Majesty's straight command that they should stay forth but five months in this voyage. Whereupon the Lords Generals shaped their course for England.

THE SCARCITY OF CORN.[6] The price of grain is still increased, and it is most evident that the ingrossing of corn and forestalling of markets by covetous men in buying great quantities of corn out of the market at farmers' houses hath been the cause of the dearth lately grown. The high sheriffs and justices of peace are required, even for conscience' sake, to deal severely with owners of corn that have any plenty thereof; and not only by assessment to compel them upon pain of imprisonment to bring weekly to the markets some proportions, but to overrule them in their prices so as the same may not be

6 APC 26:78, 95–98.

sold at any dearer rates than, at the least, these last two months. And if any shall murmur and repine against these orders in such a time of necessity, he shall be committed to prison until he conform.

Moreover order shall be taken for the preachers in their sermons and exhortations to admonish farmers and owners of corn of this unchristian kind of seeking gain, recommending to the richer sort keeping of hospitality for relief of the poor and avoiding of excess. And therefore that housekeepers of wealth would be contented with a more sober diet and fewer dishes of meat in this time of dearth, and to forbear to have suppers in their houses on Wednesdays, Fridays and fasting days. Gentlemen and others of meaner sort might forbear the keeping of hounds. These and other charitable deeds would be earnestly commended by the preachers and ministers; and special order taken that beneficed clergy should reside upon their benefices to give good example to others in using hospitality.

LADY UNTON.[7] It is reported that Lady Unton abideth at Broad Histon, there beautifying her sorrow with all the ornaments of an honourable widow, her voice tuned with a mournful accent and her cupboard, instead of casting bottles, adorned with prayer books and epitaphs.

9th August. THE CADIZ FORCES.[8] The Council have written to the Generals that it is greatly to her Majesty's misliking that she should now be solicited to be put to further expense to defray the wages of the soldiers and mariners, remembering their earnest protestations that she should not only be eased of that burden but assured of great profit to defray these and all other incident charges and precedent expenses, whereby she was by their persuasions drawn, very hardly, to disburse aforehand the sum of above £50,000, apart from the great burden of charges to which the port towns and City of London were put unto in setting forth the ships.

As for the disposing of the soldiers, those drawn from the Low Countries to the number of 2,200 are to be sent back thither, as was promised through Sir Francis Vere. Of the rest, being about 3,000, 1,500 or 1,000 at the least are speedily to be sent to Ireland with their captains. All these soldiers shall be searched before they depart.

11th August. THE CADIZ VOYAGE.[9] Commissioners are appointed for the City of London to search the ships which are come up the Thames for all goods, money, jewels or other commodities taken in the spoil of Cadiz to be reserved towards defraying the charge of voyage; notwithstanding there may be allowed to the soldiers and mariners that which is fit for them.

12th August. ESSEX AT COURT.[10] The Earl of Essex came to Court to-day about twelve, being a little lame by reason of a fall in his posting journey. My Lord hath now a beard which he began to grow on this voyage. The fleet is at the Downs and the greatest part of the army dispersed, many with leave, the rest without license, moreover there is infection among them.

When Sir Anthony Ashley brought the account of the action to the Court it was the Earl's intention to have it printed, but when his friends made a motion to the printers, they answered that they had received an inhibition from the Council by the Archbishop of Canterbury not to print any discourse of that kind without their special allowance. Moreover, the next day Mr. Fulke Greville was charged by the Queen to command Mr. Cuffe, my Lord's Secretary, upon pain of death not to set forth any discourse of this service without her privity. Hereupon Mr. Anthony Bacon resolved to send copies of it abroad, and his Lordship's friends would do the like.

The Queen these last few days hath been wholly possessed with discontented humours, which my Lord's backward friends nourish by all means possible. One great man being asked news of the expedition answered that there were many knights made; and that the Queen should not hereafter be troubled with beggars, all were become so rich; but where is the £50,000 she hath bestowed in the setting forth her navy and army to perform that service?

14th August. AN ITALIAN GENTLEMAN PRESENTED AT COURT.[11] One Signor Francesco Gradenigo, the son of a great man in Venice, was of late presented to the Queen at Court with letters of commendation from the French King. No

[9] APC 26:109.
[10] BIRCH'S MEMOIRS 2:103, 95, 96; *Calendar of State Papers Venetian* 9:505.
[11] *Calendar of State Papers Venetian* 9:505. From Gradenigo's letter to the Venetian Ambassador in France;

a short and interesting account of England which impressed him as 'so opulent, fat and abounding with all things that it may with truth be said that poverty hath no place there.'

sooner had he kissed hands than she said to him in Italian: 'My brother, the King of France, writes to me that I am to show you the most beautiful things in this Kingdom, and the first thing you see is myself, the ugliest.' To which Signor Gradenigo replied that the splendour of her virtues was so great that the whole universe knew how excellent she must be, being their source; and now that he had satisfied his eyes and fed his soul with the sight of her person, he cared to see naught else, being right well aware that the rest could not compare with her. Whereat the Queen smiled and said, 'Once on a time when I was a princess, I was more esteemed by your Lords than now that I am a Queen; but you are afraid of that old fellow'—meaning the Pope.

16th August.   THE FALL OF A HOUSE.[12] Last night between the hours of eight and nine o'clock at night, near to St. Bride's Church in Fleet Street, a house of timber, lately set up very high and not fully finished, suddenly fell down and with it an old house adjoining; by the fall the goodman, his servant, and a child are killed.

18th August.   THE QUEEN'S TOUCH.[13] This year at the touching the Queen touched ten, and then washed her hands, being served by the Lord Treasurer, the Lord Chancellor and my Lord of Essex, all three on their knees; the Treasurer in the middle, opposite the Queen holding a basin, the Chancellor on his right with a ewer of water, and on the left the Earl of Essex with a napkin which the Queen used to wipe her hands.

19th August.   THE CADIZ PLUNDER.[14] It is reported that certain ships followed the fleet not to do service but only to make private gain by buying from captains and soldiers commodities which they had got by spoils. By this means a great quantity of merchandise was taken into these ships and great store bought at an undervalue. Moreover, notwithstanding the order to the contrary, there hath been sale of goods both in Plymouth and other places. Gentlemen of those parts are appointed to take strict examination of such as can give any notice of commodity thus brought to land by these ships, and upon view of the nature and quality of the goods, the parties, if they shall be thought things fit to be sold, may have them again paying half so much again as they first gave.

[12] STOW'S ANNALS.   [14] APC 26:120.
[13] As for *14th Aug.*

THE ADVANTAGES OF THE CADIZ EXPEDITION.[15] By these late voyages much honour and profit has accrued to her Majesty. Being threatened with an invasion, she like a mighty and magnanimous prince, sent her army and navy to offer her enemies battle at their own doors, defeated and destroyed the best fleet the King of Spain had, and carried home in triumph two of his principal galleons, whereof one called the *St. Matthew* is thought to be equal with the *St. Philip* which was burnt. She hath defeated his fleet of galleys with so few of her ships, and when his galleys had such advantage, that their captain confessed on board the *Due Repulse* that forty galleys were not able to encounter one of her ships. She hath forced the Spaniards to deliver her poor subjects who were captives in the galleys, and in mercy has given up thousands of Spaniards who were captives under her. She has taken the fairest and strongest town the King of Spain had in those parts, and carried it as soon as her army was brought to look upon it. Her army was thirteen days on land, and no army of the King's dared look upon it. She hath got two good ships to strengthen her navy, which were never built for £14,000 or £15,000, and her soldiers and mariners are made rich, and fit to go into any action or service, as well with more ability as greater courage.

As for the enemy, he hath lost thirteen of his best ships of war, two of which may serve to fight against himself. Of his Indian fleet he has lost forty merchantmen, all well appointed ships, as also four others that were in his harbour and bound for the Levant Seas. He has lost a town of greater importance than any especially for traffic with the West Indies; and therein his infinite sea provisions, the which will not be got together again for many years. His merchants have lost in the fleet that was burned twelve millions, and so much in the town that almost all the great traders in the Indies will be bankrupt. Above all, he has lost most in now being half disarmed at sea, and in being discovered so weak at home.

20th August.   DISORDER ON THE BORDERS.[16] Proclamation is made straitly charging the Wardens and those that live within the Marches towards Scotland in no wise to make any incursion into Scotland publicly or privately. Great disorders have been committed by Scottishmen on the Borders, sundry murders, taking of prisoners, burning of houses, and taking

[15] SP Dom 260:46.   [16] PROCLAMATIONS 339.

of goods and cattle. Wherefore for the maintenance of the common peace between the Queen and the King of Scots, commissioners of both sides are appointed, amicably and peaceably to hear the complaints both of our nation and of the Scots, and to give speedy redress and satisfaction according to the laws and customs of the Borders.

22nd August. CAPTIVES IN ALGIERS.[17] There are yet eight Englishmen captives in Algiers that were left there by Captain Glemham three or four years since, still detained in very miserable sort until their ransoms be paid, for which a great sum is demanded for some piracy committed by Captain Glemham, who is since dead with very poor estate. The Archbishop is now moved to recommend a collection for these men, not only to relieve them out of thraldom, but lest they follow the example of others and turn Turk.

23rd August. SUNDRY REMEDIES AGAINST THE FAMINE.[18] Hugh Platt hath written a little book of remedies against famine upon the occasion of this present dearth, compiled partly from his reading and partly from observation. Saith that an excellent bread can be made of the roots of aaron, called cuckoopit, or starch roots, also of pompions. If parsnip roots be sliced into thin slices, dried and beaten into a thin powder, of which one part be kneaded with two parts of fine flour and made into cakes, then you shall find them to taste very daintily. Travellers may make a speedy or present drink for themselves when they are distressed for want of beer or ale at their inn if they take a quart of fair water and put thereto five or six spoonfuls of good *aqua composita,* which is strong of annis seeds, and one ounce of sugar and a branch of rosemary, and brew them a pretty while out of one pot into another; and then is your drink prepared.

29th August. THE TREATY WITH FRANCE SWORN.[19] The league offensive and defensive against the Spaniards between her Majesty and the French King was this day solemnly sworn by the Queen in the Chapel at Greenwich, before the Duke of Bouillon, and Viscount Turenne, Marshal of France, the Bishop of Chichester holding to her the book of the Gospel, and a great multitude of noblemen standing round about.

[17] APC 26:126. For Glemham, see *31st Mar* 1591.   [18] SR 3:69; STC 19996.   [19] CAMDEN'S ELIZABETH.

The principal terms of this treaty are that an army shall be raised as soon as may be to invade the Spaniard. Neither the King nor the Queen shall treat of either peace or truce separately without the consent of the other. Because the Spaniard at present infesteth the dominions of France that lie next to the Netherlands the Queen shall send 4,000 foot to serve for six months, and likewise for the same space in the years following if the state of England permit it; touching which the King shall stand to the Queen's affirmation and conscience. If the Queen be invaded and shall demand the King's assistance, he shall within two months raise 4,000 foot, which shall be sent into England at the King's charges. Each shall supply the other with all sort of munition and provision for war so far as may be done without prejudice to their own state. They shall reciprocally defend the merchants that are subjects of either prince in both their Kingdoms.

30*th August.* NEW COUNCILLORS.[20] This day, Sir Roger North, Lord North, was by the Queen's express commandment sworn of the Privy Council as Treasurer of her Household; and at the same time Sir William Knollys as Controller of the Household.

THE QUEEN'S EXPENSES ON BEHALF OF THE FRENCH KING.[21]

For 8 ships employed 3 months in the succour of Brest	£ 14,173
Bonds of the Duke of Bouillon to M. Sancy for £ 6,000 payable in 12 months	6,000
Bonds, Sept. 1589 to Sept. 1590	50,233
Before he was King of France	50,000
In Normandy, 1589 and 1591	48,502
In Brittany, 1591 and 1594	195,404
	£ 364,312

Since the year '89 there have been sent out of England to foreign parts 17,800 pressed men, and to Ireland nearly 3,300.

1*st September.* SPENSER'S 'FOUR HYMNS.'[1] Mr. Spenser hath written four hymns, of love and beauty, and of heavenly love and heavenly beauty, which he dedicateth to the Countess of Cumberland and the Countess of Warwick. Noteth that he composed the two former hymns in the praise of love and

[20] APC 26:135.
[21] SP DOM 257:76 (dated 6th May); 259:127.

[1] STC 23086. Dated in Ep. Dedicatory 'Greenwich this first of September 1596.'

beauty in the greener times of his youth, and finding that they too much pleased those of like age and disposition, he was persuaded by one of these Ladies to call in the same; but being unable so to do by reason that many copies were scattered abroad, he resolved at least to amend and by way of retractation to reform them, making instead of those two hymns of earthly or natural love and beauty, two others of heavenly and celestial.

5th September. VOLUNTEERS FOR THE LOW COUNTRIES.[2] There are needed 400 or 500 men to fill up the companies in the Low Countries under Sir Francis Vere. The Lord Mayor is therefore required to take up and imprest such soldiers or other voluntary men as shall be willing to serve, but not to take any man by force.

10th September. SOLDIERS FOR IRELAND.[3] For Ireland a force of 1,000 men is to be levied out of eighteen counties, and special choice to be made of able men of good behaviour, and not vagrant nor of the baser sort, which commonly run away from their captains as soon as they can find the means. They shall be assembled at Chester by the last of the month.

12th September. COMPLAINTS AGAINST LORD CHIEF JUSTICE ANDERSON.[4] Many complaints are made of the Lord Chief Justice Anderson this last circuit that he carrieth himself with so much wrath, so many oaths and reproachful words, that there is offence taken at it by persons of principal credit and note. At Lincoln, Mr. Allen, sometime the preacher at Louth, a man well accepted, by occasion of a variance with a justice of the peace concerning a lease was indicted by this justice for not reading all the prayers at once. Mr. Allen was caused to go to the bar and commanded to hold up his hand there: and my Lord Anderson standing up, bent himself towards him with strange fierceness of countenance. After he had insinuated some grievous faults (but not named) against Mr. Allen, he called him 'one of the great distempers,' putting him out of countenance, and not suffering him to speak for himself. He called him 'knave' oftentimes, and 'rebellious knave' with manifold reproaches besides. The simple people rejoiced in their return homeward saying that a minister's cause could

2 APC 26:140.
3 APC 26:161.
4 STRYPE'S ANNALS 4:264. See also

for further harsh proceedings, *26th June* 1592, *27th Mar* 1593.

not be so much as heard at the assizes and gathered that all preaching was now cried down. At Northampton he showed himself greatly grieved at the preacher at the assizes; and at Leicester likewise, where he also fell out with the high sheriff and showed himself displeased with the grand jury. At Nottingham there was offensive variance between him and one of the justices about such matters.

16th September. THE DEPARTURE OF THE EARL OF SHREWS-BURY.[5] The Earl of Shrewsbury and his company, together with Sir Anthony Mildmay that is the new ambassador to the French King, is departed on his way to France to take the oath of the King for the confirmation of this new league, and also to invest him with the Order of the Garter.

22nd September. THE QUEEN AND LORD BURLEIGH.[6] The Queen is highly displeased with the Lord Treasurer, with words of indignity, reproach, and rejecting of him as a miscreant and a coward for that he would not assent to her opinion that the Earl of Essex should not have the profit of the Spanish prisoners. The Treasurer wished that the Earl should first be heard that, upon the conditions with which the Earl received them, so the Queen should direct the compt. But herewith she increased her ireful speeches that the Treasurer either for fear or favour regarded the Earl more than herself. Coming from the presence the Lord Treasurer received a letter from the Earl of Essex, misliking him for the contrary reason that he would offend my Lord for pleasing of the Queen. The Lord Treasurer is now gone to Theobalds.

M. DE REAULX'S UNFORTUNATE BREATH.[7] M. de Reaulx that was about the Court on the French King's business is returned into France, and, as he gave out, to be married: but he was much troubled with a speech the Queen used of him which came to his ears. 'Good God,' said she, 'what shall I do if this man stay here? for I smell him an hour after he is gone from me.' It is indeed confirmed by divers at Court that the gentleman hath a loathsome breath.

[5] STOW'S ANNALS.
[6] DEVEREUX 1:398; from a humble letter written by Burleigh to Essex, who answered politely next day. This letter evidently gave great elation to Essex's own circle. Anthony Bacon, writing to Dr. Hawkins, commented that the renewed favour of the Earl 'hath made the old fox to crouch and whine, and to insinuate himself by a very submiss letter to my Lord of Essex, subscribed in these terms, *Your lordship's, if you will, at commandment,* an indication that neither Essex nor his followers were discreet in dealing with confidential matters. See BIRCH'S MEMOIRS 2:153. Compare *I Henry IV,* I. iii. 29.
[7] PENSHURST PAPERS 2:217.

Sir Walter Ralegh is not pleased that the Queen doth not esteem his services worth thanks, and protests that he will go to the plough and never hearken after employments any more.

23rd September. AN AID TO THE FRENCH KING.[8] A force of 2,000, chosen from thirteen counties or towns, is to be sent to France to the port of St. Valery in Picardy for the defence of Boulogne and to be ready by the 8th October. The men chosen shall be able and sufficient who are not to be taken out of the select or trained companies. Of these soldiers half shall be pikes and of the remainder half muskets, and provided with good strong cloth of a russet colour and lined. Sir Thomas Baskerville is to be their commander.

28th September. SIR RICHARD BINGHAM'S FLIGHT.[9] Sir Richard Bingham, the Governor of Connaught, that was commanded to Athlone to stand his trial because of the many complaints against him, is fled away secretly to England; whereat his enemies in Ireland say that he hath sought to shun this trial, being either overcarried by the greatness of his stomach to answer before the commissioners or stricken with the guiltiness of his conscience that he could not justify. But Sir Richard himself declareth that he is constrained to avoid the hard measure of his adversaries against him who work to the utmost his overthrow by indirect proceedings contrary to the rules of law and justice. He complaineth also that Sir John Norris put his brother Sir Thomas in his charge before the Queen's pleasure that he should be sequestrated was known; and moreover when he was summoned to Athlone, Sir John gave orders that he should not come through to Athlone but be stayed some five miles short, and have none of his friends near him, being used as a man utterly disgraced in the eyes of those base traitors which he had governed twelve years, and be at the mercy of the Irish to be murdered; none of his own horsemen or footmen to be permitted to come to meet him for his safety in passing through the country or himself suffered to lodge in the castle.

29th September. THE SOLDIERS' PAY.[10] Those who serve in

---

[8] APC 26:191.
[9] SP IRELAND 193:28, 46, 51. Bingham's chief offence seems to have been honesty. See *26th Aug* 1598.
[10] APC 26:216. Compared with parsons and schoolmasters, soldiers were generously paid. The captain drew pay for the nominal strength of his company but he had only to account for 90%. The extra 10% was called 'dead pays' and was his perquisite. This system of paying to soldiers led to many abuses.

France receive for their pay by the day as followeth. The chief colonel for his ordinary wages 10s, and 30s for diet and extraordinary charges 30s. The second colonel 10s, with an augmentation of 10s. The paymaster 10s; and his two clerks 3s 4d. The commissary for musters 6s 8d. For a band of 200: the captain hath 8s, the lieutenant 4s, and the ensign and the sergeants 2s; 2 drums 2s; one chirugeon 12d; and 180 men, with 20 dead pays, 8d each man. In a band of 150, the captain hath 6s; the lieutenant 3s, and the ensign 18d and to each of them the like sum daily for their imprest for victuals.

30th September.   'ULYSSES UPON AJAX.'[11] One calling himself Misodiaboles hath written against *The Metamorphosis of Ajax* (that Mr. Harington wrote) a libel called *Ulysses upon Ajax,* roundly rebuking the author for his immodesty therein. 'It is an affectation of singularity,' saith he, 'a fruit of discontent, a superfluity of wanton wit, a madding with reason, a diligence without judgment, a work fit for Volumnius the jester not Misacmos the courtier. In form contrary to all rules of science; in matter undecent, filthy and immodest: and touching the authorities, they are so weak and so wrested, as no chaste or Christian ear may in reason endure them.' Declareth Misacmos hath no judgment to find a law of reason against the law of reverence, for many necessities, of nature to be done, are not plainly to be talked of; a circumlocution and a blush is sufficient to interpret a filthy necessity.

3rd October.   HIGHWAY ROBBERS.[1] At the Sessions Richard Weekes, alias Hartrow, gentleman, and Thomas Simpson, a yeoman, were found guilty of assaulting one Kidwell in the highway, when they robbed him of £46 9s. 9d. in money. Simpson is found guilty and to hang; but Weekes stood silent and is committed to the *peine dure*. On the same day at Hampstead in company with one Hurford, known also as Marvyn or Browne, Simpson shot a labourer in the head

---

[11] STC 12782; approximate date. The answer lacks the wit, but none of the scurrility, of the *Metamorphosis;* it entirely misses the serious purpose behind Harington's book. It does, however, illuminate Elizabethan sanitary arrangements.

[1] MIDDLESEX SESSIONS ROLLS 1:229. Cases where the accused refused to plead and were sentenced to *peine forte et dure* are not uncommon. Of this penalty William Harrison in his *Description of England* says, 'Such felons as stand mute and speak not at their arraignment, are pressed to death by huge weights laid upon a board, that lieth over their breast, and a sharp stone under their backs; these commonly held their peace, thereby to save their goods unto their wives and children, which, if they were condemned, should be confiscated to the Prince.'

with a dag. Hurford also is condemned for being present and encouraging Simpson to shoot the man.

4th October. ADVICE FOR MY LORD OF ESSEX.[2] One of his followers hath written to my Lord of Essex very familiarly warning him of the danger of his present courses and advising him how he should carry himself for the future. The Queen, saith he, will see in my Lord a man of a nature not to be ruled; that hath the advantage of her affection and knoweth it; of an estate not grounded to his greatness; of a popular reputation; of a military dependence; nor can there be presented a more dangerous image than this to any monarch living, much more to a lady, and of her Majesty's apprehension. So long as this impression continueth in her breast, my Lord will find no other condition than inventions to keep his estate bare and low; crossing and disgracing his actions; carping at his nature and fashions; repulses and scorns of his friends and dependants; thrusting him into odious employments and offices to supplant his reputation. As for my Lord's particular disposition, when he happeneth to speak with compliment to her Majesty, he doth it with formality and not as if he feeleth it, whereas he should do it familiarly.

To win the Queen's favour he ought never to be without some particulars afoot which he should seem to pursue with earnestness and affection, and then let them fall upon taking knowledge of her opposition and dislike; such as to favour for void places some whom the Queen is likely to oppose unto; or to pretend a journey to see his living and estate in Wales. Nor should he neglect, as he doth, the lightest particularities in his habits, apparel, wearings, gestures and the like.

But that which breedeth to my Lord greatest prejudice is that of a military dependence; he should keep his greatness in substance, yet abolish it in shows to the Queen; for she loveth peace; she loveth not charge; and that kind of dependence maketh a suspected greatness. He should not therefore at this time seek the Earl Marshal's place, or the place of Master of the Ordnance, because of their affinity with a martial greatness; but rather that of Lord Privy Seal, for it is the third

---

[2] SPEDDING 2:40–45. This entry is based on Bacon's famous letter of advice to Essex. It is not likely that the letter was circulated, but most probable that Essex's faults were discussed by his true friends, who realised as clearly as Bacon what should be done, and avoided. This letter shows Bacon's immense practical wisdom; it explains, and justifies, his desertion of Essex. But Essex would never listen to sober advice; as De Maisse observed, *'Il est tout son conseil luy mesmes.'* Compare *Richard II*, I. iv. 25, for Bolingbroke's 'popular courses'; also *I Henry IV*, III. i. 176.

person of the great officers of the Crown; hath a kind of superintendence over the Secretary; and it is a fine honour, quiet place, and with its fees worth £1,000 by year. And if my Lord shall pretend to be as bookish and contemplative as ever he was, it should serve his purposes also.

Another impression is of a popular reputation. It is a good thing being obtained as my Lord obtaineth it, that is, *bonis artibus;* but would be handled tenderly. Therefore he should take all occasions to the Queen to speak against popularity and popular courses vehemently; to tax it in others; but nevertheless to go on his commonwealth courses. There is also the inequality of his estate of means and his greatness of respects; for till the Queen find him careful of his estate, she will not only think him more like to continue chargeable to her but also to have a conceit that he hath higher imaginations; and nothing can make the Queen or the world think so much that he is come to a provident care of his estate as the altering of some of his officers; who though they may be as true to him as one hand to the other, yet *opinio veritate maior.*

6th October.   RYE FROM THE EAST COUNTRIES.[3] There is a ship of the East Countries come to Harwich having on board 800 quarters of rye for use in the present great scarcity of grain. This ship has been stayed, but the Council order it to be transported to London without any delay lest by keeping the rye on shipboard it become corrupt and unserviceable.

7th October.   MY LORD OF LINCOLN.[4] My Lord of Lincoln is returned from his embassage to the Landgrave of Hessen that he undertook to present her Majesty's gift for the baptizing of the Princess Elizabeth, where he was most princely entertained both at the time of the solemnity and in going and coming. Upon his parting, the Landgrave presented my Lord with princely gifts, as cups of ivory, amber and crystal, and to fit his humour with Turks and jennets. But 'tis said that my Lord hath left behind him dishonours, clamours, and curses for his base miserliness and insupportable fancies or rather furies.

9th October.   AN INTRODUCTION TO PRACTICAL MUSIC.[5] Mr. Thomas Morley hath written *A plain and easy introduction*

---

[3] APC 26:223.
[4] SR 3:73; STC 18013; BIRCH'S MEMOIRS 2:178. The Earl seems not to have been wholly sane; see Index. 'Turks' are horses.
[5] SR 3:72; STC 18133.

to practical music (which he dedicateth to Mr. William Byrd, another of the gentlemen of her Majesty's Chapel), set down in form of a dialogue; whereof the first part teacheth to sing, with all things necessary for the knowledge of pricksong; the second treateth of descant and to sing two parts in one upon a plainsong or ground, with other things necessary for a descanter; the third of composition of three, four, five or more parts, with many profitable rules to that effect. To the reader Mr. Morley writeth of the great travail and difficulty of this book, and if any in friendship shall make him acquainted with ought they mislike or understand not, he will think himself highly beholding to them. 'But,' saith he, 'if any man, either upon malice or for ostentation of his own knowledge, or for ignorance (as which is more bold than blind Bayerd) do either in huggermugger or openly calumniate that which either he understandeth not, or then maliciously wresteth to his own sense, he (as Augustus said by one who had spoken evil of him) shall find that I have a tongue also: and that *me remorsurum petit,* he snarleth at one who will bite again, because I have said nothing without reason, or at least confirmed by the authorities of the best, both scholars and practitioners.'

10th October. THE FRENCH KING'S ENTRY INTO ROUEN.[6] From Rouen comes news of the French King's royal entry on the 5th of this month. In the suburbs of the town on the further side of the river was erected a most stately room of plaster of Paris where the King stood to behold the companies, and to receive the townsmen's submissions as they passed. First the order of the Friars Capuchins followed their cross, their habit russet, all be-patched, girt with hempen cords, shirted with haircloth, wearing sandals only. This order may have but one habit for a man during his life; they feed standing and sleep sitting, they live by alms and are much esteemed of the people. Secondly came the Grey Friars; which order hath a library in their house containing six and fifty paces in length with three rows of desks all along, replenished with many excellent books both of philosophy and of the Fathers, the most part manuscript. Thirdly followed the Carmelites and Celestins, the Jacobins, the Augustines. Then proceeded the priests and chantries of the town in their surplices, singing, bearing forty-two crosses of silver, and every cross with the great banner of a Saint.

[6] STOW'S ANNALS.

Then followed the mint-masters of Normandy, the merchants, receivers, customers, treasurers, advocates, procurators, and other officers of the palace. Then came Bachelors and Masters of Art, Doctors of Physic, Civil Law and Divinity, clothed in very fair and reverent garments of damask, satin and black velvet, and for the most part riding upon mules.

Then followed the officers and chancellors of the Chamber of Normandy; Judges and officers of estate in scarlet, to the number of forty; and the four Presidents of Normandy in robes of scarlet furred, wearing on their heads great caps of maintenance.

Then proceeded the several bands of the town, containing four regiments of foot and three cornets of horse, suited in green, russet and carnation satin and velvet, garnished with silver lace; their hats, plumes, scarfs and shoes white. After upon great coursers rode forty *enfants d'honneur* or henchmen, the properest and choicest young men of the town. Then came all the gallants and young gentlemen of the French Court, corvetting and fetching up their great horse, accompanied with divers of the nobility, Barons, Viscounts, Earls; the Knights of the Holy Ghost, being known by their blue ribbons and white crosses hanging thereat.

Then marched the King's three guards after their drums and fifes; the Swissers with shot and pikes, the Scots and French with halberds, the King's trumpets in horsemen's coats of green velvet and very well mounted.

At last came the King himself, mounted on a white courser, his own apparel, plumes and horses white, wearing the order of the Holy Ghost at a broad blue ribbon about his neck, and so entered the Cathedral Church of Notre Dame with all the ecclesiastical pomp that might be, whence after certain ceremonies he returned more privately to his Court by coach.

13th October. BASKERVILLE'S INSTRUCTIONS.[7] Sir Thomas Baskerville, being appointed to command the two thousand English soldiers sent to France, hath received instructions to this effect: Of the 2,000 soldiers, 1,000 shall be under his rule, and 1,000 under Sir Arthur Savage who shall be at his commandment when he shall have cause to require their service. The English soldiers are to join with a like number of French, sufficiently armed, in the towns of Boulogne and Muttrell and

7 APC 26:144.

no otherwhere, except when the King shall be personally in Picardy. Further it is covenanted that the English soldiers shall enter into wages from the time they arrive at St. Valery until their return, which shall be at farthest at the end of six months; in which time they shall make their musters every month and give their oaths to the King's commissioners faithfully to serve the French King, saving all fidelity and allegiance due to her Majesty.

The soldiers shall for all faults against the order of their own colonels and their discipline be corrected by their own chief Colonel, and if any other offences shall be committed against the King's orders general then the offenders to be ordered by the King's army, so as the colonels and captains of the Englishmen be called thereto for the assistance of the King's officers in their judgments.

The Captain General shall take care that the soldiers be preserved in good estate and provided of victual, lodging and other furniture whereby they may be continued without danger, and specially to have great care how to avoid the repair of any soldiers to any houses infected with the plague. And if he shall be required to serve in places where he knoweth the plague to reign, he shall in all dutiful manner protest against the same, and shall utterly refuse to put her Majesty's people in such evident danger, affirming that her Majesty hath sent her people to aid the French King against their common enemies but not to endanger their lives wilfully by infection of the plague.

He shall take care not to be drawn to hazard himself farther than the French are ready to accompany him, neither shall he put the people in any manifest hazard nor direct them to assault where the places are not likely to be recovered without danger of life and expense of blood. Moreover he shall use the best means he may that the whole forces of 2,000 may serve together.

Also, considering that they are in a strange country, the captains and officers of bands shall be charged to keep their people severely in good order without suffering them to quarrel with the French, or to spoil any houses or persons of the French, or to take any goods without payment; and especially that none of her Majesty's subjects enter disorderedly into any church or religious house, or use violence to any monuments. In both regiments the usual prayers shall be made, as near as may be, according to the use of this realm of England.

For the martial discipline of the forces there shall be used the same orders as were established for the army in Spain, which shall be published by proclamation immediately upon landing.

14th October. A THIRD VOYAGE TO GUIANA.[8] Ralegh hath set out his pinnace called the *Wat* under Mr. William Dowle to make further exploration of Guiana; and to-day the company sail from Limehouse.

15th October. THE LEAGUE WITH FRANCE.[9] On the 9th of this month the oath of confederation between the King and the Queen's Majesty was very solemnly taken in the Church of St. Owen in Rouen, in the presence of the French nobility, who that day took the right of the choir.

On the next day the Order of the Garter was most royally performed in the same Church, where both Princes had their estates and arms erected. The Queen's Majesty being Sovereign of the Order had that day the right hand of the choir and so had the Earl of Shrewsbury (the Lord Ambassador) with his arms, style and stall accordingly. Before the Queen's estate sat Mr. William Dethick, Garter, Principal King of Arms, in his robe of the Order. Before the Earl stood Mr. William Segar, Somerset Herald. Next to the Earl, the Lord Ambassador Lieger; then the Lord Cromwell, the Lord Rich, and all other knights and gentlemen according to their quality. On the left side sat the King between the Bishops of Anjou and Evreux, and attended by his nobility.

All things being accomplished with much honour, the King's Majesty invested and sworn, the vespers ended, and the benediction given by a bishop in his *pontificalibus*, the King took the Earl by the hand and they returned as they came, attended upon by the nobility, who two and two preceded before them. That night the King and the Earl supped together under one estate in the house of the Duke of Montpensier, where also was a general feast for all the English.

17th October. THE FORCES FOR FRANCE STAYED.[10] The forces to be sent for France that await passage are to be stayed, the Queen having thought good to enter into deliberation again touching the sending or staying of them.

[8] HAKLUYT 8:1; see *2nd July* 1597.   [10] APC 26:255.
[9] STOW'S ANNALS.

18th October. THE FORCES TO BE SENT TO FRANCE.[11] The Queen being again resolved that the forces for France shall be despatched and sent away with speed, the officers at London, Harwich, Gravesend and Southampton are forthwith to proceed to their embarking with as much expedition as may be.

20th October. CONTRIBUTIONS TOWARDS SHIPPING.[12] Although the Council have written several letters concerning the contributions to the charge of shipping in the voyage to Cadiz in some counties the money is still unpaid. In Somerset it is alleged that there is dearth of corn and victual and loss of cattle. Likewise in Dorset, Poole and Lyme Regis the contribution is unpaid.

23rd October. 'HAVE WITH YOU TO SAFFRON WALDEN.'[13] Nashe hath now published an answer to that book of Dr. Harvey written three years since and called *Pierce's Supererogation*, to which he giveth this title: *Have with you to Saffron Walden, or Gabriel Harvey's Hunt is up; Containing a full answer to the eldest son of the haltermaker: Or, Nashe his confutation of the sinful Doctor*. Speaketh very invectively of Harvey and of his family, saying that it is bruited up and down that Harvey pissed ink as soon as he was born, and haply some would conclude that he was begotten of an incubus in the shape of an ink bottle that had carnal intercourse with his mother. Harvey he declareth to be so enamoured of his own beauty, that he useth every night to walk on the Market Hill in Cambridge, holding his gown up to his middle to show himself, that the wenches may see what a fine leg and a dainty foot he hath in pump and pantofles; and if they give him never so little an amorous regard, he boards them with a set speech of the first gathering together of societies, and the distinction of *amor* and *amicitia* out of Tully's *Offices*. During the late plague the doctor lived upon Wolfe the printer, and thence passed into the country with Wolfe's boy as his servant, still owing £36; till at last Wolfe, perceiving himself to be palpably flouted, went and fee'd bailiffs who arrested him in the Queen's name, and without more

[11] APC 26:257.
[12] APC 26:260, 263, 265, 266. The Council found great difficulty in persuading neighbouring towns to contribute to the port towns for the expenses of the Cadiz expedition.
[13] STC 18369. For an account of the Harvey-Nashe quarrel see *The Works of Thomas Nashe*, ed. R. B. McKerrow, 5:65. This is one of the best pieces of abuse in the English language, full of scurrilous tales of Harvey's friends.

pause hurried him away, making believe that they were taking him into the City. But when they came to Newgate,
they thrust him in there, bidding the keeper take charge of
him. Here after fuming for some time, at length the keeper's
wife (the keeper himself being absent) came up to him.
Whereupon he runs and swaps to the door, and draws his
dagger upon her, with 'O, I will kill thee too: what could I
do to thee now?' and so extremely terrified her that she
screeched out to her servants, who burst in in heaps thinking
he would have ravished her. From this Castle Dolorous he
was at length relieved by the charity of the minister of St.
Alban's, then living in Wood Street, who entered bond for
him: and many like stories.

To Harvey's objecting to his beardless state, answereth that
the doctor hath a beard like a crow with two or three dirty
straws in her mouth, going to build her nest. In the latter
part of the book refuteth some of Harvey's former sayings.

28th October.   A GREAT ALARM.[14] Three pinnaces or carvels
are to be despatched with all speed from Plymouth to discover the intentions of the Spaniard, for there is some very
credible intelligence that there are great and speedy preparations making in Spain.

31st October.   GREAT PREPARATIONS FOR DEFENCE.[15] Because of this news out of Spain many preparations are being
made for the defence of the realm. Certain knights and
gentlemen residing about London are by the Queen's special
command to return for the defence of their counties. Three
or four ships with all diligence to be put in readiness and
sent towards Tilbury hope to give intelligence. From Hampshire and Wiltshire 900 men are to be sent to the Isle of
Wight. At Plymouth and other ports along the south coasts
the fireworks to be in readiness. In the counties the men
formerly held in readiness are to be mustered in bands, and
for every 100 footmen shall be provided 10 pioneers with
instruments to entrench and fortify, and carts and small nags
to carry their armour and weapons, with good supply of
powder, lead and match, weapons for store and victuals. The
watching of beacons to be continued or renewed with all
diligence. The numbers to be put in readiness are 69,000;
from the maritime counties 41,000 men and from the inland 28,000.

CORN SHIPS IN LONDON.[16] There are come into the Thames twenty sail of ships laden with corn from the East Countries. The Lord Mayor is required to take special order that this corn may be sold in such sort as the poor may be relieved thereby, and not ingrossed by such as use to buy great quantities to sell the same after at excessive prices.

2nd November. THE EARL OF SHREWSBURY RETURNS.[1] My Lord of Shrewsbury and those that accompanied him to Rouen are returned.

A PROCLAMATION CONCERNING THE DEARTH.[2] Because of the great dearth of corn this year proclamation is made against those ingrossers, forestallers and ingraters of corn that increase the price of corn by spreading a false report that much quantity of corn is being carried out of the realm by sea and thereby occasion given of want. Likewise it is straitly forbidden to carry any corn by sea out of the realm. Moreover sundry persons of ability that had intended to save their charges by living privately in London or towns corporate, thereby leaving their hospitality and the relief of their poor neighbours, are charged not to break up their households; and all others that have of late time broken up their households to return to their houses again without delay. Likewise those that have charge of any castle or forts upon the sea coasts shall presently repair to their charges and there reside in their own person during all this winter season, and to have care how the forts are furnished, and to make petition for their defects.

4th November. OPINIONS CONCERNING THE SPANISH DANGER.[3] There are many advertisements from Spain of these great preparations and a purpose to come for England. It is said that every fifth man in Spain is taken for service, and that 40,000 soldiers are appointed, but most of them simple ill-apparelled boys. Mariners of all nations are constrained to serve, but there are great stirs among them for want of pay and victuals, and a great dearth both in Portugal and Spain. Wherefor some hold that an invasion is meant, others only some spoiling on the sea coast in revenge for Cadiz. Many think that they will invade the Isle of Wight, Portsmouth and Southampton or attack London from the Thames;

[16] APC 26:281.
[1] STOW'S ANNALS.
[2] PROCLAMATIONS 340.
[3] SP DOM 260:82, 87, 93.

but all that this attack will be in winter when unlooked for and the Queen's navy not ready.

5th November. 'WITS' MISERY.'[4] Mr. Thomas Lodge hath written a book called *Wits' Misery, and the World's Madness, discovering the devils incarnate of this age.* As of Vainglory: he walketh in Paul's like a gallant courtier, where if he meet some rich choughs worth the gulling, at every word he speaketh, he makes a mouse of an elephant; he telleth them of wonders done in Spain by his ancestors, where if the matter were well examined, his father was but a swabber in the ship where Seville oranges were the best merchandise.

Or of Scandal and Detraction; that is a right malcontent devil. He weareth his hat without a band, his hose ungartered, his rapier *punto reverso,* his looks suspicious and heavy, his left hand continually on his dagger; if he walk in Paul's, he skulks in the back aisles. Well spoken he is, and hath some languages, and hath read over the conjuration of Machiavel; in belief he is an Atheist or a counterfeit Catholic; hath been long a traveller and seen many countries, but bringeth home nothing but corruptions to disturb the peace of his own country.

Another devil is Adulation, who generally goes jetting in noblemen's cast apparel: he hath all the sonnets and wanton rhymes the world of our wanton wit can afford him; he can dance, leap, sing, drink upsee freeze, attend his friend to a bawdy house, court a harlot for him, take him up commodities, feed him in humours. If he meet with a wealthy young heir worth the clawing, 'Oh rare,' cries he, do he never so filthily. He pulls feathers from his cloak if he walk in the street, kisseth his hand with a courtesy at every nod of the younker. If he be with a martial man, or employed in some courtly tilt or tourney, 'Mark my Lord,' quoth he, 'with how good a grace he sat his horse, how bravely he brake his lance.'

The devil Arrogancy is one that never speaks but he first wags his head twice or thrice like a wanton mare over her bit, and after he hath twinkled with his eyes, and chewed the words between his lips, to his servant he saith, 'My deminitive and defective slave, give me the coverture of my

[4] STC 16677; dated 5th Nov in the Epistle. The book is best known for its reference to 'the Visard of ye ghost, which cried so miserably at ye Theater like an oister wife, *Hamlet, revenge.*'

corpse to ensconce my person from frigidity'; and all this while he calls but for his cloak.

And Sedition, the trouble-world: this devil, detected for some notable villainy in his country, or flying under colour of Religion beyond seas, is lately come over with seditious books, false intelligences, and defamatory libels to disgrace his Prince, detract her honourable Council, and seduce the common sort. This fellow in Paul's takes up all the malcontents, telling them wonders of the entertainment of good wits in other countries. In the country he storms and rails against inclosures, telling the husbandmen that the pleasure of their Lords eats the fat from their fingers, and these racked rents (which in good sooth authority might wisely look into) are the utter ruin of the yeomanry of England.

7th November. PREPARATIONS FOR DEFENCE.[5] Musters of the horse and foot are now commanded in all counties, so that there may be a view of the whole forces of the realm; armour and horses shall be taken from recusants and put into the hands of those of better trust. Such as spread false rumours of malicious purpose to stir up the minds of the people, which oftentimes happeneth in these troublous times, are to be committed to the common gaol. In the City 10,000 are to be furnished and had in readiness.

8th November. A DOUBLE WEDDING.[6] To-day there was celebrated at Essex House the double marriage of the Lady Elizabeth and the Lady Katherine Somerset, the daughters of my Lord of Worcester, to Mr. Henry Gifford and Mr. William Petre; in honour whereof Mr. Spenser hath written a spousal verse entitled *Prothalamion*.

9th November. DEATH OF GEORGE PEELE.[7] George Peele that wrote *The Arraignment of Paris* after long illness is dead, 'tis said by the pox; and this day is buried in Clerkenwell.

14th November. A LAMENTATION FOR DRAKE.[8] There is a long poem called *Sir Francis Drake; His honourable life's commendation and his tragical death's lamentation,* published at Oxford, and written by Mr. Charles Fitzgeffrey. Herein

[5] APC 26:292–302.
[6] STC 23088.
[7] ELIZ. STAGE 3:459.
[8] STC 10943; a most interesting poem. The author's theology is classical throughout and he writes with catching enthusiasm; to many of the poets (as to Milton later) the gods of Rome were quite as real as the persons of Christian theology.

is the fame of Drake extolled and commended to gods and men, his exploits related, and the great loss of his countrymen set forth.

18th November. A SPANISH STRATAGEM IN SCOTLAND.[9] The Spaniards in Scotland have a stratagem to make the Queen odious there. They have made a great number of ensigns with the picture of a headless lady, with an axe all bloody, and a shamble likewise bloody, with an inscription that the horror of this fact requireth a revenge from heaven and earth.

21st November. RECUSANTS TO BE COMMITTED.[10] About two years since divers recusant gentlemen of good hability and livelihood were restrained and committed, some to the palace of Ely, some to Banbury; but after bonds had been taken they were released. Now that the King of Spain is encouraged by the English fugitives beyond the sea that in his intended purposes he shall have the assistance of those that are backward in religion, it is thought meet that such recusants should again be restrained.

A POEM OF DANCING.[11] There is in the press that poem of dancing by Mr. John Davies entitled *Orchestra,* wherein Antinous wooeth Penelope, Ulysses' Queen, with a discourse of dancing, which, saith he, is a wondrous miracle devised by Love, and his proper exercise. Love shaped the world and the planets to dance, and the Moon to make her thirteen pavins in the year; and the winds also and the sea; only the Earth doth stand still for ever, for her rocks remove not. All things are ordered in dancing, as speech with grammar, rhetoric and poetry. To this the Queen maketh answer that Love's child must therefore be evil, but Antinous declareth that true Love danceth in all human actions.

DRAYTON'S POEMS.[12] There are entered three poetical fables by Michael Drayton, being the *Tragical Legend of Robert, Duke of Normandy,* the *Legend of Matilda the Chaste,* and the *Legend of Piers Gaveston;* of these the first being in the form of a dream seen by the poet, the last two related of themselves by the ghosts of the dead.

[9] BIRCH'S MEMOIRS 2:196.
[10] APC 26:322.
[11] SR 3:74; STC 6360. First entered 5th June 1594, and again on 21st Nov 1596.

[12] SR 3:74; STC 7232. Another example of the autobiographical lament, originally popularised by *The Mirror for Magistrates;* see *19th Oct* 1593.

25th November. A THEATRE IN BLACKFRIARS.[13] James Burbage lately bought some rooms in the precinct of Blackfriars, near to the dwelling house of the Lord Chamberlain and the Lord Hunsdon, which he would convert into a common playhouse. But the noblemen and gentlemen petition the Council that the rooms be converted to some other use, showing the annoyance and trouble that will be caused by the great resort of all manner of vagrant and lewd persons that under colour of resorting to the plays will come thither and work all manner of mischief; also to the pestering of the precinct, if it should please God to send any visitation of sickness, for the precinct is already grown very populous. Besides, the playhouse is so near the church that the noise of the drums and trumpets will greatly disturb and hinder the ministers and parishioners in time of divine service and sermons. It is alleged moreover that the players think now to plant themselves in the liberties since the Lord Mayor hath banished them from playing in the City because of the great inconveniences and ill rule that followeth them.

27th November. 'A THEATRE OF GOD'S JUDGMENTS.'[14] Mr. Thomas Beard hath compiled a collection of histories out of sacred, ecclesiastical and profane authors concerning the admirable judgments of God upon the transgressors of His commandments, translated out of the French and augmented with more than three hundred examples. This book is dedicated to Sir Edward Wingfield and named *A Theatre of God's Judgments,* being composed in two books, the first of thirty-five chapters, the second of fifty-one.

Of Atheists giveth notable examples. Holdeth that for the same sin our poet Marlowe was notably punished, his death being not only a manifest sign of God's judgment but also a horrible and fearful terror to all that beheld him.

28th November. THE FORCE SENT TO THE ISLE OF WIGHT.[15] In the late alarm the 900 men sent to the Isle of Wight were

---

[13] SP DOM 260:116; ELIZ. STAGE 4:319, 320. This enterprise, though unfortunate, was another of James Burbage's strokes of genius. As he had been the first to realise the possibilities of the permanent theatre twenty years before, so now he first saw that the gentleman spectator was taking a serious interest in the drama of the professional companies, and would pay a high price for the privacy and comfort of the indoor theatre: but it was nearly twelve years before his son's company were able to occupy the Blackfriars building; see also note on Chapman's *Humorous Day's Mirth, 11th May* 1597.
[14] SR 3:75; STC 1659. As Beard prints very few contemporary examples, it is clear that Marlowe's death was notorious. See *1st June* 1593.
[15] APC 26:336, 337.

very ill chosen, being unable in their persons, apparelled very raggedly, and the furniture unmeet for service; which is a great marvel that so small regard should be used in the choice of men in a manner naked and without any provision at all for the defence of a place of that importance. Moreover the men arrived not at the Isle of Wight within 19 days after the Council had given order for them to be sent.

1st December.   ESSEX DEFAMED.[1] It is noted of many that since his safe return the Earl of Essex, that was beforetimes given to carnal dalliance, hath sithence changed his former ways. But of late there are bruits that he infameth a nobleman's wife, and one near to her Majesty; whereat his friends marvel at a course so dishonourable and dangerous to himself. Being taxed therewith the Earl protesteth that the charge is false and unjust.

8th December.   A DREADFUL SUDDEN TEMPEST AT WELLS.[2] At Wells last Sunday Dr. Rogers, being newly made priest by the Bishop of Wells, preached his first sermon in the Cathedral Church there before a very goodly auditory. In his sermon, according to a text which he had chosen, and having made no prayer, he began to discourse of spirits and their properties; and within a while after there entered in at the west window of the church a dark and unproportionable thing of the bigness of a football, and went along the wall on the pulpit side; and suddenly it seemed to break but with no less sound and terror than if an hundred cannons had been discharged at once; and therewithal came a most violent storm and tempest of lightning and thunder as if the church had been full of fire.

In this strange tempest all the people were sore amazed, many of them being stricken down to the ground, and the preacher himself being struck down in his pulpit. Many in the body of the church were marked in their garments, arms and bodies with the figures of stars and crosses, but there was no manner of mark upon any that was in the choir. This tempest brought with it a most terrible stench, and suddenly as it ceased, it brake down some stone work, melted the wires and irons of the clock but burned no timber. The storm being ended and the people beginning to come to themselves, the Bishop, being in the choir, spake cheerfully

---

[1] BIRCH'S MEMOIRS 2:218, 220.   [2] STOW'S ANNALS.

to them, inviting them to a sermon there in the afternoon, wherewith he recomforted them all.

10th December. THE SCOTTISH PRINCESS BAPTISED.[3] On Sunday, 28th November, the infant daughter of the Scottish King was baptised at Holyrood House, being carried and presented to the baptism by Mr. Robert Bowes, the English ambassador, supplying that office for her Majesty the only godmother. The child is named Elizabeth, the whole honour in the solemnisation of all the ceremonies being given alone to her Majesty, with good observation of all due compliments. It was very generally thought that the child should have been presented with some gift from her Majesty, but as Mr. Bowes had neither gift to deliver nor knowledge of the Queen's pleasure, he thought good to pass it over in the fairest and most indifferent terms he could for the best satisfaction of the King and Queen. The Bailiffs and chief of Edinburgh have in the name of the whole town given to the Princess 10,000 marks; to be paid at her marriage. The grant and assurance for payment is written in golden letters, enclosed in a golden coffer, and delivered to the Queen for her daughter.

14th December. SEDITION IN OXFORDSHIRE.[4] In Oxfordshire there was lately a rising planned at Enslow Hill of 200 or 300 seditious people from various towns of the shire that met with design of raising a rebellion when most of the gentlemen of the shire were to appear in a law suit at the King's Bench. They would spoil the gentlemen's houses of arms and horses and go towards London where they expected that they should be joined by the apprentices. These men are chiefly young and unmarried, and not poor; three are now in safe keeping.

18th December. 'THE ENGLISH SCHOOLMASTER.'[5] There is entered a book called *The English Schoolmaster,* written by Mr. Edward Coote, schoolmaster, of teaching the reading of the English tongue by syllables; setteth down an order how the teacher shall direct the scholars to oppose one another, a short catechism, with sundry prayers and psalms in verse, concluding with a table of words difficult to be understood. Hath also a poem of the schoolmaster to his scholars, beginning:

[3] RYMER 16:304.
[4] SP DOM 26:10.

[5] SR 3:77; STC 5711. The book reached a 42nd edition in 1684.

My child and scholar, take good heed
   Unto the words which here are set;
And see you do accordingly,
   Or else be sure you shall be beat.

19th December. A LOYAL RECUSANT.[6] Sir Thomas Cornwallis, who notwithstanding his difference of religion hath never been touched with any suspicion of disloyalty or ill affection towards her Majesty, is dispensed from the measures taken against recusants at this time.

A STRANGE EARTH MOVING.[7] In East Kent, at a place called Oakham Hill, there have been strange movings of the earth in divers places; the ground of two water pits, the one six foot deep, the other twelve at least, having sundry tusses of alders and ashes growing in the bottoms with a great rock of stone under them, was not only removed out of its place, but withal is mounted aloft and become hills, with the sedge, flags and black mud upon the tops of them, higher than the face of the water by nine foot. There were sundry other movings of the earth, the whole measure of the breaking ground being at least nine acres.

23rd December. TYRONE'S TREACHERY.[8] Tyrone now giveth many apparent proofs of his bad meaning; he hath made public restraint of all victuals to be carried to Armagh, stopping the convoy and cutting off some of the soldiers that went with the victuals. Of late an attempt was made to surprise the place, wherein thirty-five of the garrison were slain, himself countenancing the matter in person. His kinsmen and followers make violent incursions into the Pale with open force up to the River of Boyne. He hath treacherously attempted to surprise the castle at Carlingford, where, missing his main purpose, there were carried away as prisoners in lamentable manner two gentlewomen.

25th December. THE DEARTH.[9] The Council have written to the Lord Mayor putting him in mind of their orders last summer that all excess of fare might be avoided in public and private diet. And now because the greatest disorders are kept in tabling houses, taverns and inns, most strict order shall be taken that no persons have meat dressed in their houses at night on Wednesdays, Fridays or fast days; any

[6] APC 26:375.
[7] STOW'S ANNALS.
[8] CAREW MSS 257.
[9] APC 26:380, 383. See *8th Aug* 1596.

that offend therein shall be committed to prison and their names certified to the Council. Moreover, in spite of her Majesty's proclamation, there are more gentlemen come out of the country and at this present about the City than in other years, for they come hither in this time of dearth to avoid housekeeping.

The preachers shall exhort men especially at this time to abstinence and prayer, using all charitable devotion towards the relief of their poor neighbours, setting them on work, giving of alms and other charitable works. Further that especially at this time all persons be admonished not to give over housekeeping as many do, to live in good fellowship and discharge their servants to shift for themselves. Also the people shall be taught to endure this scarcity with patience and to beware how they give ear to any persuasions or practices of discontented and idle brains to move them to repine or swerve from the humble duties of good subjects, to the offence of God and displeasing of the Queen that hath so tender a care of their welfare.

26th December. CORN SHIPS TO BE STOPPED.[10] Owing to the great scarcity of corn, especially in Ireland, Sir Henry Palmer, Vice-admiral of the Narrow Seas, is expressly commanded to stay all shipping from the East Countries that shall pass by the Narrow Seas freighted with corn. This corn is to be sent to Waterford and Dublin, and for corn so seized Sir Henry shall give his bill and bind himself that, upon certificate from the place where the corn shall be unladen, there shall be good payment made to the owners or their assigns in London according to such prices as be thought reasonably worth, considering the place where it should be delivered. But if it manifestly appear that the corn was provided for Spain, it shall be seized as lawful prize. And for more assurance that these vessels with their corn sail immediately, to each of the ships shall be appointed one special man of trust and sufficient number of men to overcome the strangers if they should bend themselves to go to any other place. To waft these ships over to Ireland, the *Crane* is being sent out; and if the Vice-admiral think fit, the masters, factors and merchants of the strangers' ships shall be kept on board the *Crane* to prevent any practice against the Englishmen put on board, either of violence or carrying them to Spain against their wills.

[10] APC 26:393–97.

Other Books Printed in 1596

i. The Brownists that are in exile beyond the seas have caused to be printed a little book called a 'true confession' of the faith that they hold; being led, as they declare, to publish this testimony by the 'rueful estate of our poor countrymen who remain yet fast locked in Egypt, that house of servants, in slavish subjection to strange Lords and laws, enforced to bear the burdens and intolerable yoke of their popish canons and decrees, being subject every day they rise to thirty-eight antichristian ecclesiastical offices, and many more Romish statutes and traditions almost without number: besides their high transgression daily in their vain will-worship of God by reading over a few prescribed prayers and collects which they have translated verbatim out of the Mass-book and which are yet tainted with many popish heretical errors and superstitions instead of true spiritual invocation upon the name of the Lord.' In this book are set down 45 articles concerning the faith and duties of Christians, and very bitterly inveighing against the present state civil and ecclesiastical; as that Antichrist corrupted the offices and administrations of the Church and erected a strange, new forged ministry whereby all nations of the earth were forced to receive the Beast's mark and be brought into confusion and Babylonish bondage; that the Archbishops, deans, prebendaries and all others with the whole rabble of ecclesiastical courts are a strange and antichristian ministry and offices, and are not the ministry instituted in Christ's Testament, or allowed in or over his Church; that by God's commandment all that will be saved must with speed come forth of this Anti-Christian estate, leaving the suppression of it unto the magistrate to whom it belongeth.

ii. A book by Dr. Peter Lowe, chirurgeon in ordinary to the French King, entitled *An easy, certain and perfect method*

i. STC 237. Printed, apparently, in Amsterdam. This book largely confirms the opinion of the authorities of the seditious nature of Brownism (see *1st Mar 1593*).

to cure and prevent the Spanish sickness, being dedicated to the Earl of Essex, and treating of the causes, signs and cures of this disease. This disease was brought among Christians in the year 1492 by a Spaniard called Christopher Columbus with many Spaniards and some women who came from the new found Isles Occidental; afterward in 1493 when King Charles VIII. of France was besieging Naples with a puissant army, some of the Spaniards came to him, of which Columbus was chief, and spread this pernicious seed, terming it the 'Indian sickness,' which since hath its course not only among the Spaniards, who call it the 'Italian sickness,' but also among the Italians, who call it the 'malady of Naples,' for it began first to flourish in Naples. Amongst Frenchmen it is called the 'Spanish sickness'; in England the 'great pox'; in Scotland the 'Spanish fleas'; some call it the 'underfoot' because the infection often cometh by treading with the bare foot upon the spittle of the diseased. Some ignorant malicious people, saith he, call it the 'French disease,' without any cause or reason.

iii. A new edition of the *Perambulation of Kent,* containing the description, history, and customs of that county. This book was first written in 1570 by Mr. William Lambarde, published in 1576, and now increased and altered after the author's own copy. There is added a new card of the beacons in Kent that was made by the direction of the late Lord Cobham, Lieutenant of the Shire, so that upon firing of the beacons a man with little labour might learn from the directory lines where the danger lies, and so confusions be avoided.

ii. STC 16872.   iii. STC 15176.

1597

1st January. BAD WEATHER.[1] There has been such great rain day and night that no one can travel on the roads either by coach or on horseback.

8th January. THE LATE INTENDED RISING.[2] Some of those charged with the late intended rising in Oxford reveal that the matter arose about enclosures, for many in those parts have enclosed the common fields. One of them complaining to his fellow how hardly he maintained his wife and seven children with bread and water this hard year, the other made answer, 'Care not for work, for we shall have a merrier world shortly: there be lusty fellows abroad and I will get more, and I will work one day and play the other.' Saying also that there was once a rising at Enslow Hill when they were entreated to go down, and after hanged like dogs, but now would they never yield but go through with it. Servants were so held in and kept like dogs that they would be ready to cut their masters' throats. There was a mason in those parts who could make balls of wildfire and had a sling to fling the same whereby he could fire houses as occasion served. When they had risen they would go to my Lord Norris's in Ricott and get wine and beer, and take two of his brass ordnance and set them upon coach wheels and so proceed.

11th January. THE VICTUALS OF THE SOLDIERS IN IRELAND.[3] The soldier in Ireland when he is victualled from her Majesty's store hath in each week four flesh days and three fish days. On the former receiveth *per diem* loaf bread, 1½ lb.; beer, one pottle; beef, salt, 2 lb., or if it be fresh, 2½ lb., be-

[1] FUGGER NEWS-LETTERS 585.   [3] CAREW MSS 259.
[2] SP DOM 262:4.

ing without legs and necks. On fish days, loaf bread, 1½ lb.; beer, one pottle; butter, ½ lb., or instead thereof cheese, 1 lb., or 8 herrings *per diem*.

17th January. 'THE MIRROR OF HONOUR.'[4] Mr. Norden hath written a godly book entitled *The Mirror of Honour*, dedicated to the Earl of Essex; wherein every professor of arms, from the general, chieftains and high commanders to the private officer and inferior soldier, may see the necessity of the fear of God, and the use of all divine virtues, both in commanding and obeying, practising and proceeding in the most honourable affairs of war. Noteth the wicked assertion of a military man who affirmed that it is enough for the ministry to be masters of sin, and that it beseemeth soldiers to live like soldiers, to swear like soldiers, and to sin like soldiers.

23rd January. AN ARGOSY STAYED.[5] An Italian argosy of great burden, laden with grain and other provisions, that put into Portsmouth, is there stayed by the Lord Mountjoy. That the master and others of the ship may not conceive amiss, as though any wrong was intended unto them, they shall be assured that the corn, being taken only for the Queen's service, will be paid for in good sort at reasonable prices.

24th January. A GREAT VICTORY AT TURNHOUT.[6] From Sir Francis Vere comes news of a great victory of the Count Maurice over the Spaniards at Turnhout in Brabant on the 14th. The *rendezvous* being appointed for the 12th of the month at Gertrudenberg there arrived from all parts to the number of 5,000 foot and 800 horse. Next morning, by break of day, they began to march, drawing with them two demi-cannon and two large field pieces, and by the evening reached Ravel, one league from Turnhout. That night was spent in consultation, and in the end it was resolved to show themselves on the passage to Herentaulx, being the way of the enemy's retreat, with purpose if they left their quarter to be in the head of them; if they abode it to plant the cannon and dislodge them.

At dawn they marched, and the vanguard hastened to get the passage of a narrow bridge half way betwixt the quarters; which being gotten, and the troops put in order, some horse

4 SR 3:78; STC 18614. 6 SALISBURY PAPERS 7:24–5, 26, 30.
5 APC 26:445.

were sent into the enemy's quarter to know what they did; who presently returned word that the enemy was marched to Herentaulx and that his rearguard was in sight. Hereupon all the horse advanced and they followed with the most speed they could. A musket shot from their quarter their rearguard stood to countenance some few of their men appointed to break down a bridge by which they had passed, and by which only they could be followed. With some few shot these were beaten back and the bridge taken, there remaining no more than to carry a man abreast.

When one hundred musketeers were passed the bridge, our horse began to follow the enemy, and continued for near three hours with a very small number, the speed of the enemy and the badness of the passage making it impossible for our troops of foot to overtake the horse.

During all this time by many messengers the Count Maurice was advertised that, if he would send forward his horse, he might have a fair victory; if not, the enemy would soon be in safety. At length he gave a good part of the horse to the Count Hollocke to go before, and himself followed with the rest. The enemy by this time were gotten into a heath and making great haste towards the entry of a strait at the end of it, which gotten they would be safe, being now not far from Herentaulx; but now our horse began to appear on the heath. The enemy kept near the edge of the heath with their horse on the outside, marching in their battalions, not ranged in one front but in length, the Almains marching in front of the column, in the middle the Walloons, and last the Neapolitans who were the rearguard.

The Count Hollocke made the flank of them, and charged towards their horse, which fled. He pursued them not far but turned towards the flank of the Almains, at which time Sir Robert Sidney and Sir Francis Vere charging the Neapolitans, at one instant their vanguard and rearward were assailed and put in rout, and the mid battle kept them company. The Neapolitans keeping together were in a manner all slain on the place. Of the rest there are escaped very few, for of 4,000 foot, by their own confession they acknowledge that 2,400 were left dead in the field, and 600 taken prisoners, amongst which are sixteen captains. Their commander, the Count of Varras (or La Verall), was killed in the charge, and all their ensigns taken to the number of thirty-nine. On our side twenty men were slain and less hurt.

That same night the troops returned to Turnhout, and the next day, after some few cannon shot, the castle was yielded by composition. From thence the army returned to Gertrudenberg, and every troop was sent to its garrison. This blow will touch the Cardinal shrewdly, and, he being disappointed of those forces he kept of purpose in Brabant to make incursions, our men will be the safer, even though it should chance to freeze.

26th January. THE DEATH OF LADY CECIL.[7] On the death of Sir Robert Cecil's Lady many do write to console him in his great grief, and among them Sir Walter Ralegh to this effect:

'There is no man sorry for death itself but only for the time of death; everyone knowing that it is a bond ever forfeited to God. If then we know the same to be certain and inevitable, we ought withal to take the time of his arrival in as good part as the knowledge; and not to lament at the instant of every seeming adversity, which, we are assured, have been on their way towards us from the beginning. It appertaineth to every man of a wise and worthy spirit to draw together into suffrance the unknown future to the known present; looking no less with the eyes of the mind than those of the body (the one beholding afar off, the other at hand) that those things of this world in which we live be not strange unto us when they approach, as to feebleness which is moved with novelties. But that like true men participating immortality and knowing our destinies to be of God, we do then make our estates and our wishes, our fortunes and our desires, all one.'

30th January. BACON'S 'ESSAYS.'[8] Mr. Francis Bacon hath written a little book of *Essays,* being ten in number, *viz.:* of study; of discourse; of ceremonies and respects; of followers and friends; suitors; of expense; of regiment of health; of honour and reputation; of faction; of negotiating. There are added twelve Sacred Meditations in Latin, and a fragment 'Of the Colours of good and evil.'

---

[7] EDWARDS' RALEGH 2:161.

[8] SR 3:79; STC 1137. Dated 30 Jan 1597 in the Ep. Dedicatory to Anthony Bacon; entered 5th Feb. This is the first edition of the *Essays* which reached their final form in 1624; other editions were published in 1598, 1606, 1612 (2), 1613 (3), 1614, 1624, 1625 (2), 1629, 1632, 1639. The essay 'Of Studies' is here reproduced complete in its original form; at this time the essay is rather a collection of *sententiae* than a formal composition; see also *14th Oct* on *Politeuphuia.*

AN ESSAY OF STUDIES

'Studies serve for pastimes, for ornaments and abilities. Their chief use for pastimes, is in privateness and retiring; for ornament is in discourse, and for ability is in judgment. For expert men can execute, but learned ones are fittest to judge or censure.

¶ To spend too much time in them is sloth; to use them too much for ornament is affectation: to make judgment wholly by their rules is the humour of a scholar. ¶ They perfect Nature, and are perfected by experience. ¶ Crafty men contemn them, simple men admire them, wise men use them; for they teach not their own use, but that is a wisdom without them: and above them won by observation. ¶ Read not to contradict, nor to believe, but to weigh and consider. Some books are to be tasted, others to be swallowed, and some few to be chewed and digested: That is, some books are to be read only in parts; others to be read, but cursorily; and some few to be read wholly and with diligence and attention. ¶ Reading maketh a full man, conference a ready man, and writing an exact man. And therefore if a man write little, he had need have a great memory; if he confer little, he had need have a present wit; and if he read little, he had need have much cunning, to seem to know that he doth not. ¶ Histories make men wise, Poets witty: the Mathematics subtle, natural Philosophy deep: Moral grave, Logic and Rhetoric able to contend.'

2nd February. A DANGEROUS PERSON TAKEN.[1] There is lately apprehended one William Tomson, a very lewd and dangerous person, that is charged to have a purpose to burn her Majesty's ships or do some notable villainy. This man is to be examined concerning his devilish intents, and earnestly dealt with to declare by whom he hath been moved thereunto; wherein if by fair means and persuasions he be not moved to reveal the truth, then to be put to the manacles or the torture of the rack as in like cases is used.

5th February. A QUARREL AT COURT.[2] The Earl of Northumberland hath had a quarrel with the Earl of Southampton that was like to have proceeded to a combat, insomuch that my Lord of Southampton sent a gentleman with his rapier. Where-

[1] APC 26:457.   [2] BIRCH'S MEMOIRS 2:274.

upon my Lord of Northumberland asked whether he brought a challenge; if so, he accepted it beforehand. The gentleman answered that he did not, only he brought his rapier. My Lord of Northumberland answered that he had not a novice in hand; he knew well when he was before or behind in points of honour, and therefore had nothing to say further unless he were challenged. But the affair came to nought, for by order of the Queen they were summoned to Court on bond of their allegiance and called before the Lords of the Council, who assured him, on their honours, that my Lord of Southampton had not spoken the words complained of, which afterward he affirmed himself. My Lord of Northumberland answered that he would rather believe their Lordships than any other; and the lie he had given was nothing. So my Lord Southampton hath revoked his challenge and they are made friends.

6th February. IRISH TRADE WITH SPAIN.[3] No ships either of traffic or of war from the ports of Waterford or Wexford in Ireland are to go forth to the sea for the next six months unless very good bonds be given that they will not pass to any of the coasts of Spain or unto any of the King of Spain's dominions. This order is made because of the extraordinary preparations of the King of Spain, that in all likelihood are intended for Ireland, for which cause he stayeth and engageth in his service such serviceable mariners of other nations as do arrive there.

8th February. SPANISH DISASTERS.[4] An English pilot lately come from Ferrol declareth that he was pilot in the fleet of 90 ships, whereof 20 were men-of-war, that went out of Lisbon. Of these 45 were cast away between Lisbon and the Groin, one a great ship of 1,400 tons called the *Santiago,* with all the battery for the army; another the Admiral of the Levantiscos, with 1,200 men; 3 ships of 300 tons each, built by an Englishman called Lambart, with divers others all full of soldiers and provisions. In an Irish ship there were also cast away 14 Irishmen of name, capital rebels, and 200 common Irish soldiers. There now remain 70 ships of all sorts. They have great famine and sickness and daily look for provisions by sea from other parts of Spain. Their purpose was to go for Ireland, and they pretend so still.

THE BATTLE AT TURNHOUT.[5] Since the battle little hath been

3 APC 26:467. 5 STC 22993; SALISBURY PAPERS 7:43.
4 SP DOM 262:37.

done on either side. The Count Maurice sent the corpse of the Count of Varras to the Cardinal, who accepted it well, and yet was he buried without ceremony as one unworthy of any honour in that he had not better looked to his charge.

9th February. A NEW LOAN FOR THE QUEEN.[6] Her Majesty finding the charges sustained for preservation of the realm and subjects against their enemies so to increase thinketh it a reasonable purpose to require some present loan for the space of one year. The Lords Lieutenant are required to send for the collector of the last loan in their counties and by him and his books to understand the numbers and names of those that did lend sums of money to her Majesty in these later years; and if any be dead or departed out of the country to inquire who hath his lands and goods.

13th February. COMPLAINTS FROM WILTSHIRE.[7] In Wiltshire it is declared that the soldiers despatched to the defence of the Isle of Wight last November were not sent back orderly so that their arms might be restored to the inhabitants that did set them forth; but very many of the soldiers being loosely dispersed ran away, and a great quantity of their arms and furniture (even to the number of 200) is either utterly lost or so broken and mangled as to be unserviceable. Moreover great abuses have been committed in the discharge of divers soldiers for sums of money. The Lord Chief Justice shall examine this matter very diligently, especially because, when like abuses have been committed before, the matter hath been so shifted from the county to those that had the government of the soldiers and from these again to the county, that it could hardly be found where the fault lay.

TROUBLES IN OXFORD.[8] The new Dean of Christchurch is much misliked of the students there who complain that like a new lord he maketh new laws, endeavouring an innovation that will enrich himself and undo the society. The cause of their complaint is that he seeketh to take away the allowance of commons enjoyed since the foundation of the college and to exchange for it an allowance of 2s. a week.

17th February. TROUBLES OF THE KEEPER AT WISBEACH.[9] The Keeper of the Jesuits at Wisbeach very earnestly craveth

6 APC 26:468.   8 SP DOM 262:40.
7 APC 26:487.   9 SP DOM 262:42.

favour of Mr. Secretary because that two of his prisoners, both priests, are escaped from the castle by beating out the iron bars of their windows and letting themselves down by the bed cord. He would therefore have favour for three reasons; firstly, the prisoners escaped during his absence in London on a *subpoena,* wherefore his servants are to blame; secondly, because it was done in the night, when quiet rest is due to every man; thirdly, for that he is about to be married to a lady of sufficient ability, and if she should hear that he is in trouble, it might procure in her such an aversion that all his friends would hardly settle her again in any good affection.

21st February. COURT NEWS.[10] My Lord of Essex still keepeth his chamber, yet is he not believed to be sick. There is not a day passes that the Queen sends not often to see him, and himself goeth privately unto her. He giveth out very confidently that he will go into Wales, where his own land lies, to view it and see his friends. Sir Robert Cecil is now in greatest credit, the Queen passing the most part of the day in private and secret conference with him.

24th February. SIR THOMAS BASKERVILLE'S SOLDIERS.[11] The soldiers with Sir Thomas Baskerville are now at St. Valeries, their bands weakened with the number fallen sick so that of late at a mustering there were found to be sick 300 and odd, but only fifty-seven missing. All their apparel is worn out, the bareness whereof in this wild, cold, and wasted country is a principal cause of their sickness.

25th February. THE LORD MAYOR REBUKED.[12] The Lord Mayor is rebuked for the great slackness in the execution of the orders for the restraint of killing and eating of flesh in Lent, and especially during this dearth; which abuse is made known to the Council not only by the information of some few but almost every man in the City is an eyewitness to it.

4th March. COURT NEWS.[1] The Lord Treasurer is not well, and in this sharp weather keeps in. Sir Walter Ralegh hath been very often private with the Earl of Essex and is said to be a mediator of peace between him and Sir Robert Cecil, who likewise hath been private with him. Sir Walter allegeth that much good may grow by it; the Queen's continual unquietness

will turn to contentment; despatches for all matters of war
and peace for the safety of the land will go forward to the
hurt of the common enemies. The Earl, wearied with not
knowing how to please, is not unwilling to hearken to these
motions made to him for the public good. He purposeth in
three days' time, by her Majesty's leave, for some twenty days
to go towards Wigmore Castle and so to Raglan.

9th March.   A NOTABLE STRATAGEM AT THE CAPTURE OF
AMIENS.[2] The Spaniards suddenly took Amiens by a stratagem on the 1st of the month, which is a shrewd loss to the
King, for whole magazines of provisions for war are there
with forty pieces of battery.

The capture was on this wise. The whole affair was under
the conduct of the Governor of Dorlans, who had often been
inside Amiens disguised, as the Bishop of Amiens confesseth.
Hereby he perceived that the gate of the city which lieth on
the further side of the Somme towards Dorlans was very care-
lessly guarded, especially at the hour of the sermon, to which
all the good citizens went, leaving the gate in charge of mer-
cenaries and common troops. He therefore chose out 700
picked men, sending on ahead fifteen or twenty of them,
armed and with cuirasses, and carrying pistols and daggers,
but disguised as peasants. Behind them came a waggon covered with straw, and conducted by the Governor himself, also
disguised. The rest of the troops marched through the night
and in such excellent order that by the hour appointed they
were within a very short distance of the city.

About 8 o'clock in the morning, five or six of those in advance entered the gate, carrying sacks of nuts and apples as
though they were peasants from the neighbouring villages going to market. These sat down within the gate, feigning to be
weary, and waited until the waggon and the other men came
up. Then the waggon, having come on to the bridge, stopped
in such a way that half was under the arch of the gate where
the portcullis would fall, and the other half still upon the
bridge. Hereupon the men with the sacks, as though by mischance, spilt their nuts and apples, and the guard rushed after
them; whereat the Governor cut the traces of the horses in
the waggon so that it could not be moved, whilst his men with
their harquebusses fired upon the guard and slew them. The
men behind the waggon sprang in, and though the portcullis

was lowered, it came down upon the waggon, leaving space enough for the soldiers to pass in and out. By this the main body came up, and having raised the portcullis and drawn out the waggon, they made themselves masters of the gate, and (which is more to be wondered at) they marched right through the city with their drums beating and flags flying.

At first they were in doubt what to do, as these few men had intended only to seize the gate, but seeing that no opposition was offered, they placed guards at the cross streets and in the square without anyone raising a finger. Then the commander sent the Spanish by companies of fifteen and twenty to traverse the streets, and when they saw any of the townsfolk on the roads or at the windows they fired on them so that not a man had the courage to stir.

And in this wise a great city of 50,000 persons, amongst whom were 10,000 soldiers, is taken by 700, with the loss of less than ten on both sides.

10th March. THE WARDENSHIP OF THE CINQUE PORTS.[3] Owing to the death of Lord Cobham, there is competition for the post of the Cinque Ports, the Earl of Essex very earnestly moving the Queen for Sir Robert Sidney, that is governor of Flushing. But she said he was too young for the office and Mr. Harry Brooke, the now Lord Cobham, should have it. Whereupon the Earl was resolved to leave the Court, and this morning, himself, his followers and horse being ready, about ten o'clock he went to speak with my Lord Treasurer; and being by Somerset House, Mr. Killigrew met him and willed him to come to the Queen. After some speech had privately with her, she hath made him Master of the Ordnance, which place he accepteth and is contented thereby.

11th March. THE OFFICE OF LORD PRESIDENT.[4] There is still no one appointed as Lord President in the north, and again the Archbishop of York hath written to the Lord Treasurer that someone be appointed. The cause of this delay is said to be the want of fit men, but is rather that the race of nobles whom the Queen found at the beginning of the reign having passed away, she by her wisdom and experience knoweth all the defects and infirmities of the nobility now growing up. Yet if the Queen could resolve on a man, her commission and instructions and the ordinary proceedings of the Court

[3] SIDNEY PAPERS 2:27.
[4] SP DOM 262:64. The Earl of Huntingdon died 14th Dec 1595.

would sufficiently enable him. My Lord Huntingdon was very raw when he first came down, but having a resolute will to serve God and her Majesty grew to great experience.

12th March.   THE LORD TREASURER'S GRIEF.[5] This morning died Sir William Hatton in Holborn, and the Lady Kildare, it is said, hath begged the wardenship of his daughters. The Lord Treasurer takes it very heavily and weeps pitifully, calling to remembrance the many late crosses he hath been afflicted withal by the death of his friends. Sir John Fortescue, going to Court, lighted at his house, but word was brought that his Lordship was not to be spoken with, and all are turned back that have any business with him by this accident of Sir William Hatton's death.

14th March.   A WITCH HANGED AT LANCASTER.[6] At the Assizes holden at Lancaster on the 6th there was condemned and afterwards hanged one Edmond Hartley that had bewitched seven persons in the house of Mr. Nicholas Starkie, a gentleman dwelling at Cleworth.

About three years since the two children of this gentleman being taken ill very strangely he was at great charges of £200 for their cures; seeking remedy without due regard, first of a seminary priest, and then of this Hartley, that at first wrought some cure on the children, who remained well for almost a year and a half. During this time he would come to visit them; but at length feigned that he would go away into another county. Mr. Starkie therefore besought him to stay, and offered him a pension of 40s. a year; but after a time he would have more.

After this Mr. Starkie on a time going to his father's house, Hartley went with him. And being tormented all night long in bed, next morning he went into a little wood, not far off the house, where he made a circle, the compass of a yard and a half, with many crosses and partitions; which being finished he came back to call Mr. Starkie desiring him to tread it out, for he said he might not do it himself. This also being despatched,

[5] SIDNEY PAPERS 2:27.
[6] STC 18070. In 1598 Darrell and More were committed to the Clink, where this book was written to confute the Jesuits who declared that the Lancashire exorcisms were frauds perpetrated by the preachers; though the Jesuits themselves made capital out of one of the possessed women (see *15th June* 1598). The assizes, according to More, were held on 6th March; Hartley was probably executed about two days later; he was dead some days before the 16th. The law did not condemn a man to death for witchcraft but for murder by witchcraft; conjuration of evil spirits was however a capital offence. Lancashire was a hotbed of witchcraft at this time.

'Well,' quoth he, 'now I shall trouble him that troubled me, and be meet with him that sought my death.'

When he perceived this and other bad qualities in him, Mr. Starkie began to be weary of the fellow, especially as his children grew no better but rather worse. He then sought, though secretly, for help of the physicians; after that to Dr. John Dee at Manchester, who wished him to crave the help and assistance of some godly preachers, with whom he should join in prayer and fasting for the help of his children. He procured also this Hartley to come before him, whom he so sharply reproved that the children had better rest for some three weeks after. But then they began to have their accustomed fits; first John Starkie, Mr. Starkie's son, then his daughter, and five other women of his household, three being children of 14, 12 and 10 years, and two women of 30 years and more.

It was noticed that when this Hartley meant them a mischief he would kiss them if he could, and therewith breathe the Devil into their bodies. Amongst those afflicted was one Margaret Byrom, a kinswoman of Mistress Starkie, who would fall into fits when this Hartley came to see her. Hereupon some preachers, finding Hartley with her, asked him what he did with the maid. He said that he came to pray with her. 'Pray,' quoth one, 'why, man, thou canst not pray.' 'Yes, but I can,' quoth he. 'Say then the Lord's Prayer,' said the preacher; and he began to fumble about it very ill favouredly, but could not for his life say it to the end. They then thought him to be a witch, and caused him to be apprehended and brought before two Justices of the peace, by whom he was further examined and sent to Lancaster gaol.

When the assizes came, he was brought up, arraigned and convicted, Mr. Starkie having charged him with bewitching his children, which he proved sufficiently and made evident to the whole Bench. Howbeit for that they could find no law to hang him; whereupon Mr. Starkie called to mind the making of the circle, which being delivered on oath was received. Nevertheless Hartley stiffly denied it and stood out against him, and told him to his face that he should not hang him (for the Devil had promised him no halter should hang him); yet the jury cast him and the judge condemned him. When Hartley was hanged, the halter brake; whereupon he penitently confessed that he had deserved that punishment, and that all which Mr. Starkie had charged him with was true. And so he was hanged out the second time.

16th March. THE PRICE OF BEER.[7] These few days past divers brewers have appeared before the Council, some of them committed to prison and the rest bound to answer their contempt next term for selling beer at 10s. to 16s. the barrel, whereas no beer should be sold above 5s. the barrel for small beer, and 8s. the better sort. Nevertheless in answer to their petition that the price of malt is excessive, the Council will allow beer to be sold at 5s. for small beer and 10s. for the strongest.

THE EARL OF ESSEX'S PATENT.[8] The Earl of Essex cannot yet get his patent signed as Master of the Ordnance. Sir John Fortescue offered it twice to the Queen but she found some exceptions, and this afternoon the Earl took his Bill and presented it himself; but for all that it is not done, which moveth him greatly, especially as it is believed that the Lord Cobham's patent will be signed before or as soon as his. The Lord Cobham who, it is said, shall marry my Lord of Oxford's daughter, hearing how disdainfully my Lord of Essex speaks of him in public, doth likewise protest to hate the Earl as much.

20th March. FRENCH PIRATES.[9] Some short time since the Bonham of Poole being driven into Dartmouth by contrary winds met there with two ships of Dieppe, which continued in the port the space of two months; and they making forth to the seas a few days before the English ship and meeting with her shortly after, these two ships of Dieppe set upon the Englishmen, robbed and spoiled them of all their lading, goods and merchandise, with apparel, victuals, and other furniture, in most treacherous and barbarous sort, leaving them so destitute that they were like to perish.

27th March. AN EXPLOSION IN DUBLIN.[10] From Dublin Sir John Norris reporteth a lamentable accident of the burning of six lasts of powder on the quay. The ruin of the town is exceeding great and by estimation twenty houses near adjoining are thrown to the ground, nor any house or church within the walls but is marvellously damaged in the tilings, glass and small timbers. Six score persons of all ages and sexes are known to be slain, but few English, besides sundry headless bodies and heads without bodies that were found. There is little appearance of this having happened by treachery, but it is guessed that some nail in the bark struck fire.

[7] APC 26:543.
[8] SIDNEY PAPERS 2:30.
[9] APC 26:561.
[10] SP IRELAND 198:21.

28*th March*. THE POSSESSED PERSONS IN LANCASHIRE.[11] The children of Mr. Starkie continuing in their fits since the execution of the witch Edmond Hartley, the gentleman sent for Mr. Darrell, that wrought with the boy of Burton. At first Mr. Darrell was unwilling to come, but at the third sending he came on the 16th March to Cleworth, with Mr. George More, another preacher, and soon after their coming the children were thrown into their fits, and scorned the two preachers. For when they called for a Bible, the children fell a laughing at it and said, 'Reach them the bibble babble, bibble babble,' and continued with many other scornings and filthy speeches. The preachers determined therefore to fast and pray with the family. Having the whole family together, and divers honest neighbours for the holding and tending of the possessed, they made entrance into the preparation, which was by way of exhortation, intreating the Lord to put the Devil to silence and that He would charge and command the spirits to hold their peace so that they might have good audience in praying and speaking the Word; which indeed came to pass at that time.

Morning being come, great preparation was made in the family to set all things in good order, and having a fair large parlour already trimmed, they brought in thither beds upon which they laid the seven sick possessed persons, all of them greatly vexed by their torments. At 7 o'clock they began the exercise of humbling their souls unto God, and continued with the exercise till 3 o'clock in the afternoon without much interruption; but then, as if Satan was much heated by fasting and prayer, they all brake out into exceeding loud cries, all seven roaring and belling in extreme and fearful manner. Then was there such struggling and striving between those praying and the devils, crying out so loud with such violence and extension of voice, labouring who should be loudest, till the preachers' voices were spent and no strength almost left in them. This battle continued very near the space of two hours, till they were exceedingly weakened; but at last it pleased God to weaken Satan's power, for the possessed were cast down suddenly and lay all along, stretched out as they had been dead; and every one of them afterwards declared that the spirit had passed out in the likeness of some ugly crea-

[11] As for *14th*. The 'madness' and 'exorcism' of the Puritan Malvolio would be highly appreciated in 1600-1 when the pamphlet war, engendered by the efforts of Messrs. Darrell and More, was at its hottest. Malvolio's 'vain bibble-babble' and his fashionable yellow stockings show that he too was suffering from possession by the evil spirit of pride.

ture, as a crow's head, or an urchin (or hedgehog), or a foul ugly man with a bunch on his back.

In these possessions the children of Mr. Starkie have been very strangely afflicted, one of them, a girl of the age of thirteen years, being possessed, as it seemeth, with a spirit of pride that did most lively express both by words and gestures the proud women of our times, that cannot content themselves with any sober or modest attire. Whereupon she said, 'Come on, my lad,' (for so she called the spirit), 'come on and set my partlet on the one side as I do on the other.' And as she was setting of it, she said unto him, 'Thus, my lad, I will have a fine smock of silk, it shall be finer than thine. I will have a petticoat of silk, not red, but of the best silk that is; it shall be guarded and a foot high: it shall be laid on with gold lace; it shall have a French body, not of whalebone for that is not stiff enough, but of horn for that will hold it out; it shall come low before to keep in my belly. My lad, I will have a French fardingale, it shall be finer than thine; I will have it low before and high behind, and broad on either side, that I may lay my arms upon it. My lad, thy gown is crimson satin, but mine shall be of black wrought velvet, it shall be finer than thine. I will have my sleeves set out with wire, for sticks will break and are not stiff enough. I will have my periwinkle so fine, finer than thine. I will have my cap of black velvet with a feather in it, with flews of gold, and my hairs shall be set with pearls, finer than thine. I will have my partlet set with a rebater, and starched with blue starch; and pinned with a row or two of pins. My lad, I will have a busk of whalebone, it shall be tied with two silk points, and I will have a drawn wrought stomacher embossed with gold, finer than thine. I will have my hose of orange colour, this is in request, and my cork shoes of red Spanish leather, finer than thine. I will have a scarf of red silk, with a gold lace about the edge. I will have a fan with a silver steel and a glass set in it, finer than thine. My lad, thou must bring me a pair of gloves of the finest leather that may be, with two gold laces about the thumb, and a fringe on the top with flews and red silk underneath, that I may draw them through a gold ring, or else I will none of them.'

29th March.   ENGLISH PRISONERS IN SPAIN.[12] A poor mariner is lately returned to England escaped from St. Lucar. This

[12] SP Dom 262:86.

man was one of the company of the *Little Exchange* whereof Captain John Cross was captain, that was taken by the Spaniards. Captain Cross and others were brought to Seville, where they had no allowances in their imprisonment but lived by the good help of the under-jailor who is an Englishman. There the English priests, Parsons, Thorne, and Walpole, that is head of the English college, came daily to persuade them to change their religion, and in the end so prevailed with the Cardinal of Seville that Cross, Duffield, and Boyser, and eleven others were released and brought to the College, where all means were used to reconcile them to the Church of Rome, insomuch that they all reformed and received the sacrament; all but Captain Cross who was sent back to prison. While he was at Seville, seven persons were sent to England to be dispersed.

31st March. MENDOZA'S 'THEORIQUE AND PRACTISE OF WAR.'[13] The book of the *Theorique and practise of War*, written by Don Bernardino de Mendoza (that was Spanish ambassador here before '88) and published at Antwerp last year is now translated into English by Sir Edward Hoby. He counselleth that provisions or levies of men which are to be made for any manner of war, by sea or land, should be coloured with some different motive whereby no time may be given to the enemy to perceive it by preventing designs with the contrary. By no better means may this be effected than in sending upon such occasions ambassadors to those Kings who are most suspected oppose, plotting with them treaties of new friendships and good correspondency according to the humour and disposition in which they shall find them, lulling them asleep with such offers as may hold in suspense and at the gaze the more part of the potentates.

'VIRGIDEMIARUM.'[14] There is entered a book called *Virgidemiarum*, to be in six books; the first three books being toothless satires of matters poetical, academical and moral; the other three not yet ready. Quoth the author:

> 'I first adventure with foolhardy might,
> To tread the steps of perilous despite:
> I first adventure; follow me who list,
> And be the second English Satirist.'

---

[13] STC 17819; the book is commended at the end by a 'Censure' written by Don Francisco Arias de Bobadilla, who is apparently immortalised in Jonson's *Every Man in his Humour* (*16th Sept* 1598); Bobadil in the first version of the play appears as Bobadilla.

[14] SR 2:82; STC 12716.

2nd April. THE SOLDIERS IN FRANCE.[1] The great extremity that our troops endure by reason of the want of money hath caused Sir Thomas Baskerville to lay in pawn all his plate and all the other means that he hath to relieve them. Of late an enterprise was made to surprise Arras upon a vain hope and an uncertain French plot to blow open a port with a petard, assuring themselves by that to have entrance. But at their arrival there the strength of the place with little assistance from the town did frustrate their expectation. Our men had no loss but their toilsome march, though the French lost some few. In the camp the King is taxed for lechery, and Madame Gabrielle accounted cause of all ill-fortune, although every man seeth many nearer causes which cannot be remedied in that broken commonwealth.

5th April. 'CLITOPHON AND LEUCIPPE.'[2] A book called *The most delectable and pleasant history of Clitophon and Leucippe* is entered, written in Greek by Achilles Stacius an Alexandrian, and now newly translated into English by William Burton, and dedicated to the Earl of Southampton. Herein is related how Clitophon fell in love with Leucippe of Tyre, and how they fled from Tyre towards Alexandria, but being shipwrecked and separated both lovers endured many chances until they were strangely united in the Temple of Diana at Ephesus.

7th April. SEMINARIES TO BE BANISHED.[3] There is an intention to banish the seminary priests that are in divers prisons in the realm, and to this end the Attorney and Solicitor General and Mr. Francis Bacon are required to inform themselves what priests are in the prisons within and about the city of London and how far they are to be charged with any matter against the Queen or the State.

8th April. FORCES FOR IRELAND.[4] The forces levied for service in Ireland last October but afterward dismissed to their several counties are again to be viewed and mustered, and sent to the ports of embarkation by the last of this month, being in all 1,900 men, and in addition 560 men levied from the Midland Counties.

[1] SALISBURY PAPERS 7:125, 129, 130.
[2] SR 3:82; STC 90. The translator was brother to Burton the Melancholick. Southampton had a taste for this kind of book.
[3] APC 27:21.
[4] APC 27:21–6, 25–8.

10th April. AN ENGLISH PIRACY.[5] One William Holliday hath behaved in very contemptuous manner towards Mr. Michael Leeman and certain merchant strangers of Holland and Zealand. Some four years since great spoil was made on the seas by a ship called the *Tiger,* whereof this Holliday was owner, and two or three others upon certain ships belonging to merchants of Holland. These spoilers going to the seas without commission carried the goods to Barbary and then sold them; they sank one of the ships, and threw divers of the mariners overboard. Upon complaint whereof to the States of the United Provinces there had arisen some tumult in such sort that, if special care had not been taken, the English merchants there had been in danger of the loss of their goods and lives. Whereupon for satisfaction of the merchants, order was given that such other prize goods as should be brought in by the malefactors and their ships should be stayed and the monies made thereof converted to the satisfaction of the damnified merchants. After this the *Tiger* brought into Plymouth a Spanish carvel laden with ginger, sugar, hides, and some pearl, which by order of the Lord Admiral was seized and Mr. Leeman appointed to repair to Plymouth with a sergeant-at-arms and letters of assistance from the Council. This was done, but the merchants that were spoiled received not above 2s. in the pound towards their losses. Since which time Holliday, in contempt of these proceedings, hath commenced an action of *trouver* against Mr. Leeman for the same goods, and by the deposition of some of the mariners, that then stood indicted for piracy and since are condemned to die, a verdict was passed against Leeman for most part of the goods. The Council have now written to the Lord Chief Justice to take order in this matter.

13th April. TWO LADIES-IN-WAITING PUNISHED.[6] The Queen hath of late used the fair Mistress Bridges with words and blows of anger, and she with Mistress Russell were put out of the Coffer Chambers. They lay three nights at the Lady Stafford's, but are now returned again to their wonted waiting. The cause of their displeasure is said to be their taking of physic, and one day going privately through the Privy Galleries to see the playing at *ballon.* Some days since the Earl of Essex kept his chamber three days with a great heat in the mouth which happened by overmuch exercise at *ballon.*

[5] APC 27:31. There are several cases of piracy by English mariners during this year.

[6] SIDNEY PAPERS 2:38, 34.

THE MARINERS TO BE STAYED.[7] The mariners appointed to be at Chatham by the 25th of this month are now to be stayed till the midst of May.

HOUNDS FOR THE FRENCH KING.[8] The servants of the Earl of Shrewsbury carry over to France fourteen or fifteen couple of hounds and certain greyhounds for the French King.

16th April.   COURT NEWS.[9] There is news come out of Ireland that Tyrone hath yet put off the parley for fifteen days more. The two thousand foot are gone, and the Lord Burgh follows. This day he met Sir Oliver Lambart by the garden door within the Court; and asked him if he did not know him, and bid him put off his hat. The other said he owed him not that duty in respect of his usage of him. My Lord offered to pluck off his hat, which the other resisted and willed him to call to mind the place where he was. 'I do,' said my Lord, 'else would I have thrust a rapier through thee ere this'; and so they parted. About dinner time they met again at my Lord of Essex's, where my Lord Burgh secretly told him that he saw he braved him and bid him look to himself, for he would disgrace him. 'So I will,' said the other.

17th April.   THE CLOTH TRADE.[10] The Merchants Adventurers complain that divers disordered persons, not free of the Company of Merchants Adventurers, trade with English cloths and other woollen goods to Hamburgh in Germany as well as to Flushing and Amsterdam in the Low Countries, contrary to the special privilege. Hereby in the markets of Stade and Middleburgh, being the established mart towns, there is great loss to the Merchants Adventurers and the abating and pulling down of price of cloths, a thing much prejudicial to the woolgrowers and clothmakers of the realm. The customers are now required to take bonds of every person shipping woollen commodity in other than the Adventurers' ships that they shall land the same at Stade or Middleburgh and not elsewhere.

THE NEW LORD CHAMBERLAIN.[11] This afternoon the Lord Hunsdon had the White Staff given him and thereby made

7 APC 27:37.
8 APC 27:38.
9 SIDNEY PAPERS 2:40.

10 APC 27:5.
11 SIDNEY PAPERS 2:41.

Lord Chamberlain; and the Lords being in Council, her Majesty sent him to them, where he was sworn Councillor and signed many letters thereupon.

A DECEITFUL PRACTICE.[12] One Ross, pretending himself to be servant to the Earl of Essex, with a counterfeit warrant in the names of the Council apprehended a certain Francis Barker in the county of Kent and brought him up to London, where he kept him some days, shifting him up and down from place to place, and taking from him £47 in money and a gelding.

18th April. THE LORD BURGH TO BE DEPUTY IN IRELAND.[13] The Lord Burgh, that was Governor in the Brille, is now to be Lord Deputy in Ireland to reform the many great abuses in that country. He shall inquire of the state of religion, for notorious negligence is reported, and even in the English Pale multitudes of parishes are destitute of incumbents and teachers, and in the great towns of assembly numbers not only forbear to come to the church but are willingly winked at to use all manner of Popish ceremonies. Many captains in remote parts have untruly informed the Muster Master of their full numbers. To reform this abuse he shall consult with such of the Council as have no interest in these abuses, and appoint commissioners to take monthly musters in all remote places; which will be a hard matter seeing the great corruption used herein.

19th April. THE EARL OF ESSEX AND SIR R. CECIL.[14] Yesterday Sir Robert Cecil went in a coach with the Earl of Essex to his house, where Sir Walter Ralegh came and they dined together. After dinner they were very private, all three for two hours, where a treaty of peace was confirmed. Sir Walter hath taken upon him to provide victuals for three months for 6,000 men at an allowance of 9d. a man per diem. There is imprested unto him £3,000 a week for six weeks; he shall have Bridewell, Winchester House, and Durham House to be magazines for the victuals. He protesteth that he shall be loser by it, but few are of that opinion besides himself.

21st April. ALL SHIPS STAYED.[15] There is an order going forth for a general restraint throughout all the ports that no

12 APC 27:54.
13 CAREW MSS 267.
14 SIDNEY PAPERS 2:42.
15 APC 27:60.

ship, hulk, or other vessel of what burden soever shall be suffered to depart until further notice.

23rd April. ST. GEORGE'S DAY.[16] This day, the Court being at Whitehall, great solemnity for the Order of the Garter was observed. First, morning service in the chapel, with solemn music and voices, Dr. Bull playing; the Lords of the Order were present, who both in coming and retiring made three congées to the seat royal and so departed. Some hour after, they came again before her Majesty with all the officers of arms; and then came the Queen, with three ladies carrying her train, which were the Countess of Warwick, the Countess of Northumberland, and the Countess of Shrewsbury; the Earl of Bedford carrying the Sword before her, six pensioners carrying a rich canopy over her head. Then, after several congées there was short service, the clergy all being in their rich copes, with princely music of voices, organs, cornets, and sackbuts, with other ceremonies and music. Five new knights of the Order are made, being the Duke of Wirtenberg (that was formerly the Count Mompelgard), the Lord Hunsdon, the Lord Mountjoy, the Lord Thomas Howard and Sir Henry Lee. The Earl of Essex was exceeding earnest with his companions for Sir Henry, which he obtained. Then had he much ado to bring the Queen to give her consent to him.

28th April. THE STAYED SHIPS.[17] The Merchant Adventurers have made humble suit that the ten ships ready laden might be permitted to go on their voyage, and will enter bond for their return by the end of May, unless hindered by contrariety of wind. This is allowed, seeing that there are ten ships with corn daily expected; also the five ships for Middleburg.

DESERTERS FROM THE IRISH FORCES.[18] Of 47 men that were levied in Staffordshire for service in Ireland 10 are run away, and of the 47 men of Derbyshire 18, who are returned to their counties.

29th April. DANGERS FROM FRANCE.[19] The Cardinal of Austria is now reported to have drawn great numbers of the forces out of the Low Countries towards the seaside and coast of Boulogne, a matter greatly to be regarded, which may breed

[16] HAWARDE, p. 74; SIDNEY PAPERS   [18] APC 27:75; 26:64.
2:45.   [19] APC 27:80, 93.
[17] APC 27:74.

great danger to the realm because it is uncertain what attempt he may make with this great preparation. In Essex, therefore, Kent and Sussex, 600 are being mustered and trained to be ready on any occasion.

6th May. DISCONTENTS IN THE COUNTIES.[1] In the counties are many discontents by reason of this present scarcity. In the confines of Kent and Sussex divers have carried themselves in very tumultuous sort, inciting others with lewd words to commit outrage; wherefore it is purposed to renew the office of Marshal in the counties. In Norfolk, under pretence of need, some have entered into conspiracy to raise tumults and have begun with taking grain from the right owners by force and violence. In Sussex, Sir Thomas Palmer that was commanded a short while since to put in readiness 600 men was so slack and backward that the service was not executed; he is very sternly rebuked by the Council. At Hadley in Suffolk the Council have caused the Sheriffs to prohibit the officers of the town from making stage plays at the Whitsun holidays, for they doubt what inconveniences may follow thereon, especially at this time of scarcity when disordered people of the common sort are apt to misdemean themselves. Moreover the stage prepared is to be plucked down, and the officers informed that they are to obey this order as they will answer it at their perils.

9th May. MR. ARUNDEL.[2] Mr. Thomas Arundel (that was made Count of the Empire) is again in close imprisonment for that of late he would have sent one Smallman, a soldier, to the Emperor's court that he might show his pedigree, whereby the Emperor should see that he had not bestowed that title of honour upon any base man. This Smallman is reported to be a dangerous man, one that hath been in Rome.

MUSTERS AGAINST INVASION.[3] The Commissioners for musters are ordered to have in readiness from the counties able men to the number of 6,000 to have special training to defend the realm and withstand the enemy that are now prepared to attempt some dangerous enterprise on the realm.

11th May. THE MAYOR OF CHESTER COMMENDED.[4] The Mayor of Chester is very highly commended by the Council

[1] APC 27:56, 88, 92, 96, 97.   [3] APC 27:101-7.
[2] SALISBURY PAPERS 7:193, 195. See   [4] APC 27:215.
7th Feb and 15th April 1596.

for his diligence and discretion used in the transporting of
soldiers to Ireland, for he so governed the matter of payment
that he not only gave good satisfaction to all parties but yet
saved some good part of her Majesty's charge. If others upon
such occasions would use the like care, the Council would be
less troubled in giving directions, and the Queen's service much
better ordered than it is.

A PLAY OF HUMOURS.[5] To-day there is a new play of humours
at the Rose, called *An Humorous Day's Mirth*, and written
by Chapman. This play is of an old Count that hath a young
Puritan to wife, who by a certain gallant is tempted to the
Court and there mocked, so that she goeth back to her husband who would have hanged himself in jealous humour.
There is a young gull who hath this humour in his manner of
taking acquaintance, that he will speak to the very word of
compliment after him of whom he takes acquaintance.

20*th May*.   THE QUEEN ANGRY.[6] There hath been much ado
between the Queen and the Lords of the Council about the
preparation for sea; some of them urging the necessity of
setting it forward for her safety, but she opposing it by no
danger appearing towards her anywhere, and that she will not
make wars but arm for defence, understanding how much of
her treasure is spent already in victual only for ships and soldiers at land. She is extremely angry with them that make such
haste in it, and at the Lord Treasurer for suffering it, seeing
no greater occasion. Nor reason nor persuasion by some of
the Lords could prevail but that she hath commanded order

[5] HENS. DIARY 1:52; 2:184; STC 4987.
This is the first surviving play in
the new mode, of which Jonson's
Every Man in his Humour is the
most successful and famous example. The play is significant of several
changes in the playgoing public: it
is a society comedy of special interest to the gentlemen spectators
now beginning to invade the theatre; it substitutes society wit for the
usual clowning and romance which
had hitherto been served up as comedy; and, in an elementary form, it
presents a problem proper to comedy—whether Florilla is more Puritan than woman. Although the 'humours' of the characters are not
labelled in big letters, the *Humorous
Day's Mirth* certainly belongs to
the type, for the essential of a Humour play is a practical joke (usually in bad taste), designed to place
the 'humorous' person in a ridiculous
situation where his particular humour can be displayed at its most
foolish. Jonson was notably skilful
in managing such plots because he
could balance so many of these situ-
ations in one play. From this time
onward the younger generation begins to be noticeable. Young people
of independent means who belonged
neither to immediate Court circles
nor to the professions had not been
much in evidence for some years;
henceforward actors depend for support more on gentlemen of leisure
and culture than on the old-fash-
ioned patron or the crowd. Moreover, the gentlemen themselves not
only write poetry, but a few months
later begin to write plays, to pro-
duce them in private theatres, and
to print them.
[6] SIDNEY PAPERS 2:52.

to be given to stay all proceeding, and sent Lord Thomas Howard word that he should not go to sea.

23rd May. MACHUGH SLAIN.[7] In Ireland the traitor MacHugh is slain at Glynnes on the 8th, for our foot falling into that quarter where he lay, and coming several ways on him, he was so hardly followed that he was run out of breath and forced to take a cave where a sergeant to Captain Lee first lighted on him; and the fury of the soldiers was so great that he could not be brought away alive. Thereupon the sergeant cut off MacHugh's head with his sword and presented it to the Deputy. His head and carcase are now brought in to Dublin, to the great comfort and joy of all that are in that province. Many of his followers have been slain. If this blow be as well followed as it is well given, the storm in Leinster will be calmed for a long time and the Ulster rebels, having lost so capital a confederate, will grow to better feeling of their own condition. Sir Calisthenes Brooke, Sir Thomas Maria Wingfield and Sir Richard Trevor are knighted for their services in this action.

THE QUEEN AND THE LADY MARY HOWARD.[8] The Queen hath of late much annoyance from the Lady Mary Howard, one of her ladies-in-waiting, for as much as she refused to bear her mantle at the hour when her Highness is wont to air in the garden, and on small rebuke did vent such unseemly answer as bred much choler in her Mistress. On other occasion she was not ready to carry the cup of grace during dinner in the Privy Chamber, nor was she attending at the hour of her Majesty's going to prayer. All which doth so much disquiet her Highness that she swore she would no more show her any countenance but out with all such ungracious, flouting wenches; because forsooth she hath much favour and marks of love from the Earl of Essex, which is not so pleasing to the Queen, who doth still much exhort all her women to remain in virgin state, as much as may be. Moreover since the Irish affairs she seemeth more froward toward her women, nor doth she hold them in discourse with such familiar matter, but often chides for small neglects in such wise as to make these fair maids often cry and bewail in piteous sort.

The Lady Howard hath offended also in attiring her own person overfinely, which is rather to win my Lord of Essex than of good will to her Mistress. The lady is possessed with

---

[7] CAREW MSS (*Russell's Journal*), p. 259; SP IRELAND 199:25, 28.   [8] NUGAE ANTIQUAE 1:232–34, 361.

a rich border powdered with gold and pearl, and a velvet suit belonging thereto which hath moved many to envy; nor hath it pleased the Queen who thought it exceeded her own. Wherefore the Queen sent privately and got the lady's rich vesture, which she put on herself and came among the ladies. The kirtle and border were far too short for her Majesty's height and she asked everyone how they liked her new fancied suit. At length she asked the Lady Mary herself if it was not made too short, and ill-becoming; to which the poor lady did consent. 'Why then,' quoth the Queen, 'if it become not me as being too short, I am minded it shall never become thee as being too fine; so it fitteth neither well.' By this sharp rebuke the Lady Howard is abashed and hath not adorned her herewith sithence.

27th May.   A DEBTOR'S CASE.[9] One Francis Metcalfe for a debt of £7 hath been detained in the Fleet prison for the space of 5 years.

30th May.   PREPARATION FOR AN EXPEDITION.[10] Of those men ordered to be specially trained for the Queen's service 4,000 are now to be set in readiness and shortly to be despatched to London, there being discovered a very urgent cause and fit opportunity to employ them.

2nd June.   MR. ARUNDEL RELEASED.[1] Mr. Arundel is now released, since upon exact and careful examination he is not found guilty of any disloyalty, though this practising to contrive the justification of his vain title, contrary to his duty, is an act of great contempt. Nevertheless, the Queen, out of favour to Sir Matthew his father, hath remitted his punishment; but since his own house is haunted by massing priests he is committed to the care of Sir Matthew. It is not without cause for the State to be jealous of him, seeing by how strait an obligation he hath bound himself to a Prince so nearly allied to the Queen's chiefest enemy, and his own precious valuation of his title, which all other men do hold to be of little worth, doth give cause to believe that his own heart's love must be divided between the Queen and the Emperor.

SIR WALTER RALEGH RESTORED TO HIS PLACE.[2] Yesterday, the Earl of Essex being absent, Sir Walter Ralegh was brought

[9] APC 27:143.
[10] APC 27:160-64.

[1] SALISBURY PAPERS 7:229; see *9th May*.
[2] SIDNEY PAPERS 2:54.

to the Queen by Sir Robert Cecil. She used him very graciously and gave him authority to execute his place as Captain of the Guard, which he immediately undertook, and swore many men into the places void. In the evening he rode abroad with the Queen and had private conference with her; and now he comes boldly to the Privy Chamber as he was wont. Though this is done in the absence of the Earl yet is it known to be with his liking and furtherance. There is now love and kindness in all things between the Earl and the Lord Treasurer, and all furtherance given to his desires. About twelve days since the Lord Treasurer allowed the passing of a lease that by him was delayed these three years.

3rd June. LANGHAM'S 'GARDEN OF HEALTH.'[3] Mr. William Langham, practitioner in physic, hath by his long experience gathered together the sundry rare and hidden virtues of all kinds of herbs and plants into a book entitled *The Garden of Health;* all which simples, being plainly described in the book, can be gotten without any cost or labour, the most of them being such as grow in most places and are common among us. And for the better direction of the reader, the simples are set down in the order of the alphabet, with two general tables added, the one containing all the simples in order, the other setting down the names of the diseases and other operations needing these simples for any remedy for the same.

Noteth among many others, these remedies. A fig tied to a bull will make him tame though he be never so wild. The flowers of the bugloss comfort the brain, heart, memory and wit, ingender good blood, and void melancholy, madness and frenzy, and purge also the choler that cometh from heat. For chastity, commendeth *agnus castus,* docks, hemlocks, vervine, woodbine; but to provoke lust, anise, artichoke, carrots, garlick, ginger, mints, mustard, parsnips, radish and others. Briony is good for the rising or suffocating mother. For the hair; black and white helebore is good for worms in the head and falling hair, as also aloes, garlic, leeks, mustard, nettle, oak, walnuts, and others; milsoil maketh it to curl; box, ivy, marigold, walnuts will cause it to be yellow. Barley, hemp and nettle cause hens to lay. These and many hundreds of others hath Mr. Langham set down.

[3] SR 3:85; STC 15195. Title page misdated 1579. An important book for the understanding of Elizabethan homely medicine, and well worth the attention of Shakespearean students.

8th June. MACHUGH'S HEAD.[4] The Council have written to
the Lord Deputy of Ireland commending the service of Captain Lee in taking away that rebel Feogh MacHugh; but as for
the sending over hither of the rebel's head (to make, as it is
supposed, the fact of greater note or more acceptable to her
Majesty), it would have pleased the Queen better that it should
have been kept over there and bestowed among the fragments
of heads and carcases of like rebels, for she would not have
such ragged Robin Hoods to be regarded so honourably.
Nevertheless because the meaning was good the error was
less, and therefore the Council will send the head back again
by the same messenger.

ESSEX'S CLEMENCY.[5] One Chapman of Cunstall in Stafford
was this day brought before the Council touching certain un-
reverend, lewd, scandalous speeches uttered of the Earl of
Essex. Which words being proved, it was their Lordships' intention to have ordered him to be punished and to have appointed him to the pillory and to open whipping with loss of
his ears had not the Earl prevented their resolution, who would
not willingly have suffered the man to have been brought up
had he known him to be so base and contemptible as he is. The
Earl also signified his desire that the offence might pass for
this time without the deserved punishment; and to this the
Council assented seeing that Chapman made very humble submission, protesting that he uttered the speeches in great weakness and distemperature of mind after long sickness.

10th June. CALAIS.[6] One newly come from Calais reporteth
the place to be much fortified, a wall of earth and faggots
made outside the ditch to the height of fifteen feet, but the old
wall allowed to decay. There are 12,000 soldiers of all nations
in twelve companies, but scarcity of victuals and mariners.
The soldiers having only received a third of a month's pay
since October are like to mutiny.

11th June. SIR THOMAS BASKERVILLE DEAD.[7] Sir Thomas
Baskerville is dead in France. He lay sick not past five or six
days and died raving; a man that loved not many to show
them any extraordinary kindness, and is much taxed for covetousness; he is said to have detained a groat a week from every

[4] SP IRELAND 199:80; APC 27:185. See
24th Sept.
[5] APC 27:181.

[6] SP DOM 263:97.
[7] SALISBURY PAPERS 7:252, 242, 256,
200, 286.

soldier upon pretence to have money to relieve them when they were sick.

Our troops are now before Amiens which the King besiegeth and in as great a lack of treasure as ever, some captains being five weeks unpaid, all four. The King hearing of their wants hath lent the companies now in the field 2,000 crowns and makes show to esteem better of them than at any time since their coming.

RUMOURS.[8] There is now great talk of these preparations for a sea voyage but it is not known where or how it shall be employed. The common sort talk of Calais, others of the Isles of the Azores, others that it is to set upon the King of Spain's navy wheresoever they can find it, or to meet with the Indian fleet. The whole number consists of fifteen of the Queen's ships, besides the two Spanish ships taken last year and now new fashioned after the English manner, twenty-two men-of-war of Holland, and twenty-four fly boats and hoys that serve for carriage of men and victuals. They have with them 4,000 pressed men, and 1,200 musketeers that come with Sir Francis Vere out of the Low Countries. The Earl of Essex is General both at sea and land, the Lord Thomas Howard Vice-Admiral and Sir Walter Ralegh Rear-Admiral. The Earl of Southampton, the Lord Mountjoy, and the Lord Rich go as adventurers; other noblemen pretend to go but it is thought they shall not get leave.

12th June. SIR ARTHUR SAVAGE TO COMMAND IN FRANCE.[9] Now that Sir Thomas Baskerville is dead, Sir Arthur Savage hath the principal charge of the 2,000 soldiers sent into France to aid the French King. He is to take order that as few Irish as possible be retained in his company, and those cassed as soon as may be, though those officers and others that have deserved well may be continued. The sick men shall be sent back forthwith, for it is a mere abuse that her Majesty should pay so many and have the service of so few. He shall not allow strangers to be passed in the musters, except it be two Frenchmen in a company that may be necessary to make any provision or otherwise to be employed on messages.

14th June. ABUSES OVER MUSTERS.[10] From the counties of Devon, Norfolk, Suffolk, Sussex, Somerset and Oxfordshire complaints of great abuses are reported, as of exacting or taking sums of money or other compositions of divers persons to keep them from being impressed, and in changing or dismissing others for bribes that were levied, also in defrauding the county of arms and furniture.

25th June. THE STATE OF IRELAND.[11] Ulster is now universally revolted; no part of it is free from hostility and adherence to the capital traitors of Tyrone. In Connaught not one of the six shires is free from revolt; Sir Conyers Clifford with $21\frac{1}{2}$ companies of foot is not strong enough to reduce the rebels to obedience, for his companies are weak and O'Donnell tyrannizeth over most of the people at his pleasure. In Munster two rebels followed by a rabble of loose people stand out, and several murders of English undertakers have been committed, but many of the murderers are cut off. Leinster by the late cutting off of Feogh MacHugh will grow to better terms of settling and conformity, though many of his followers remain.

2nd July. THE 'WAT' RETURNS.[1] Ralegh's pinnace the *Wat* is come back safe to the Lizard. The company report well of the climate of Guiana, for though it standeth within the Tropic yet is it temperate enough, insomuch that they lost not a man upon the coast, and one that was sick before he came there was nothing sicker for being there but is come home safe. Of commodities there is great store; whereof they bring examples, as a kind of long hemp, fine cotton wool wherewith the women make a fine thread that will make excellent good fustians or stockings; great store of pitch, sweet gums, West Indian pepper, balsamum, parrots and monkeys. On their return divers whales playing about the pinnace, one of them crossed the stern and going under rubbed her back against the keel, but they sustained no loss thereby.

5th July. SHIRLEY'S RETURN.[2] Sir Anthony Shirley, that left Plymouth at the end of May 1596 with five ships, is returned. Not long after starting, being off Cape Verde, the General fell exceeding sick, and being hopeless of life and his company all dismayed and comfortless, he called his captains, masters and officers to him, and having his memory perfect made

---

[11] CAREW MSS 268. Calendared April 1597, but must be later than the death of MacHugh.

[1] HAKLUYT 8:1. See *14th Oct* 1596.
[2] HAKLUYT 7:213. See *25th April* and *23rd May* 1596.

a very pithy and brief speech to them. He said that as they were Christians and all baptized and bred up under one and the true faith, so they should live together like Christians in the fear and service of God; and as they were subjects of our most excellent Sovereign and had vowed obedience unto her, so they should tend all their courses to the advancement of her dignity and the good of their country, and not to enter into any base or unfit actions. And because they came for his love into this action that for his sake they would so love together, as if he himself were still living with them, and that they would follow as their chief commander him whom under his own hand he would give commission to succeed him. All which with solemn protestation they granted to obey.

From this contagious filthy place they directed their course for S. Tome, but being by no means able to double the shoals of Madrabomba they were enforced to bear up and chose another course, for the men fell sick, and the water falling from heaven did stink and in six hours turned to maggots where it fell, either among their clothes or in wads of oakum. They departed therefore for the Isles of Cape Verde and landed upon the Isle of St. Iago, and here the General happily began to recover. And there they entered upon and captured the city of St. Iago, a very strong place, but being within they were so powerfully assaulted by the Portugals that they lost in the first assault eighty men; so that after two days they were forced to depart the town and make for the ships, having lost many men.

Thence they sailed to an isle called Fuego where there is a very high hill which continually burneth. Arriving at Dominica the 17th October with all the men sick and feeble they found two hot baths wherein the weak were greatly comforted, and in a month all made well again. From here they coasted until they came to the town of St. Martha where the Spaniards yielded to them, but could afford no ransom, only they took thence their ordnance and a prisoner lost there by Sir Francis Drake. Thence to Jamaica, a marvellous fertile island. After other ill chances and in want of victuals, at last they shaped their course for Newfoundland, arriving there the 15th June, not having one hour's victuals to spare; and so after nine days they returned to England.

MR. WILLIAM PARKER'S VOYAGE.[3] With Sir Anthony is also come in Mr. William Parker, who at his own charges sailed

3 HAKLUYT 7:222.

from England in November last in the *Prudence,* a tall ship of 120 tons, and a bark called the *Adventure,* with Captain Henn, having one hundred men in his company. In March he met with Sir Anthony Shirley at the Isle of Jamaica and went in his company till they reached Truxillo where they parted.

Mr. Parker then set his course for Cape de Cotoche on the East part of Yucatan, until he came to Cape Desconoscido. Here he put fifty-six of his men into a *periago* or Indian canoe, and leaving his ship six leagues from the town of Campeche, at 3 o'clock in the morning he landed hard by the monastery of San Francisco and took the town of Campeche, with the Captain and the *alcade,* finding therein 500 Spaniards; and in two towns close adjoining 8,000 Indians. The multitude of the Spaniards which had fled in the first assault by ten o'clock in the morning assembling together, renewed their strength and set furiously upon Mr. Parker and his men, insomuch that six were slain, and Mr. Parker himself was shot under the left breast with a bullet that yet lieth in the chine of his back.

Being thus put into shifts, they devised on a sudden a new stratagem; for having divers of the townsmen prisoners, they tied them arm in arm together and placed them instead of a barricado to defend them from the fury of the enemies' shot. And so with ensign displayed, taking with them their six dead men, they retired with more safety to the haven, where they took a frigate which rode ready fraught with the King's tribute in silver and other commodities, and brought it and the cannon to the *Prudence.* They took also a town of 300 or 400 Indians called Sebo, where they found champeche wood (good to dye withal), wax and honey. This done they left the coast and turned up to Cape de Cotoche again, but the *Adventure* with Captain Henn and thirteen of the men was taken by two frigates of war, whom the Spaniards afterward executed. After they had stayed five weeks upon that coast they shaped course for Havannah, and returning by the Isle of Bermuda, crossed over to the bank near Cape Race, and thence sailing for England fell in with Sir Anthony and reached Plymouth on the 3rd of this month.

6th July. A PROCLAMATION AGAINST INORDINATE APPAREL.[4] The great inconveniences that grow and daily increase in the realm by the ordinate excess in apparel have again caused her

[4] PROCLAMATIONS 343. The detailed list of the stuffs permitted to the several ranks occupies 3½ large pages.

Majesty to make strait proclamation that the laws be duly executed. In this present time of difficulty the decay and lack of hospitality appears in the better sort in all counties, principally occasioned by the immeasurable charges and expenses which they are put to in superfluous apparelling their wives, children, and families; the confusion also of degrees in all places being great where the meanest are as richly apparelled as their betters, and the pride such inferior persons take in their garments, driving many for their maintenance to robbing and stealing by the highway. It is now laid down very exactly what stuffs may be worn by gentlemen and ladies in their several degrees.

SOLDIERS FOR PICARDY.[5] Seven hundred soldiers are to be sent as a supply for the forces in Picardy, to be gathered from the soldiers that were levied to serve in the voyage of the Earl of Essex but are now to be returned because that so many offer themselves voluntarily. The Lord Mayor is to make a privy search and to prest so many of the soldiers as he shall find new returned and such like vagrant persons of able body.

7th July. DELONEY'S 'JACK OF NEWBURY.'[6] There is a book called *The pleasant history of John Winchcomb in his younger years called Jack of Newbury*, the famous and worthy clothier of England that lived in the days of King Henry VIII, written by Deloney and dedicated to all famous cloth-workers of England. Herein is shown how Jack of Newbury was married to the widow of his master, and how she served him; how having become a man of great wealth after his dame's death he married one of his own servants; how he served King Henry; and how a draper in London that owed him money became bankrout, whom Jack found carrying a porter's basket, and set him up again so that he afterwards became an alderman of London.

8th July. THE COMPLAINTS OF THE COUNCIL OF WAR.[7] The Council of War of the fleet make great complaint that the ships are ill manned because of the monstrous abuse of the press-masters, who have furnished men of all occupations, of

[5] APC 27:283.
[6] SR 3:87; STC 6559. The book was first entered to Millington on 7th March, who assigned it to Lowndes on 25th May. Both entries include the condition that it be lawfully authorised—a reasonable precaution after the previous trouble with Deloney and Millington (see *29th June* 1595). A ballad, entered 8th July, gives the probable date of publication.
[7] SP DOM 264:12.

whom some did not know a rope and were never out at sea, while they let all the good men go at 20s. a piece. When they looked for a supply in the west, those of Dorsetshire sent not a man but all were either discharged underhand by the press-master or made a jest of the press.

10th July.   THE FLEET ENTER PLYMOUTH.[8] The fleet are all come together safe to Plymouth, though as they were athwart the Bolt, three leagues short of Plymouth, a sudden storm overtook them with infinite lightning and thunder, and great wind, with the night exceeding dark save when the flashes of lightning came. Nevertheless God so blessed them that not so much as a boat miscarried.

12th July.   VAGRANTS TO BE IMPRESTED.[9] The sheriffs and justices of Middlesex, Surrey and Kent are now bidden to aid the Lord Mayor to levy the 700 men for Picardy of the masterless men and such as have served in the wars, which will be a great ease and good to the country to be rid of those kind of people. Moreover standing watches shall be kept for the apprehending of masterless men, soldiers and vagrant persons, and as many as are taken to be bestowed in Bridewell.

18th July.   THE LORD MAYOR REBUKED.[10] The Lord Mayor is rebuked by the Council because, when he received direction to take up masterless men, he, as it seems, would only apportion to the City to the number of 100, and so that there might be fewer of this kind of people found in the City, he published abroad the directions given him by the Council in order to drive them out of the City into the counties adjoining. These proceedings are misliked, and the Council again require him to make up the number of 250 or else he shall be required to answer his backwardness before them.

20th July.   THE FLEET DRIVEN BACK.[11] News is come that the fleet having been buffeted for four days continuously is driven back to port by the great and contrary tempests, but safe. My Lord of Essex is at Falmouth, Sir Walter Ralegh at Plymouth. So great was the storm that the beams, knees and stanching of Sir Walter's ship were shaken well nigh asunder, and on Saturday night they thought to yield themselves up to God, having no way to work that offered any hope, the men wasted with labour and watching, and the ship so open, her bulkhead rent, and her brick cook-room shaken to powder. Many of the gentlemen and the knights are returned extreme weak and dangerously sick, among them being Sir Ferdinando Gorges, the Sergeant Major, and Sir Carew Reynolds, captain of the *Foresight*. The ships are now repairing, but much of the victual is spoiled, and water lost by leaking of the casks; moreover the beer carried aboard the victual ships is found to be very unsavoury by the great abuse of the victuallers and London brewers, as well for their careless brewing as for the unseasonable stinking casks.

22nd July.   ESSEX AT PLYMOUTH.[12] The Lord General with his ships is now come to Plymouth and joined with Sir Walter Ralegh, being dismayed even to death by their mischances. My Lord was much aided in these distresses by the Admiral of the Low Countries.

23rd July.   THE POLISH AMBASSADOR.[13] There lately arrived an ambassador from Poland, a gentleman of excellent fashion, wit, discourse, language and person, and the Queen was possessed that his negotiation tended to a proposition of peace. Her Majesty in respect that his father, the Duke of Finland, had so much honoured her, besides the liking she had of the gentleman's comeliness and qualities brought to her by report, resolved to receive him publicly in the Presence Chamber, where most of the Earls and noblemen about the Court attended, and made it a great day. He was brought in attired in a long robe of black velvet, well jewelled, and came to kiss her Majesty's hands where she stood under the state, whence he straight retired ten yards off her, and then with a strange countenance began his oration aloud in Latin.

The effect of his speech was that the King had sent him to put her Majesty in mind of the ancient confederacies between the Kings of Poland and England; that never a monarch in Europe did willingly neglect their friendship; that he had ever friendly received her merchants and subjects of all quality; that she had suffered his to be spoiled without restitution, not for lack of knowledge of the violence but out of mere injustice, not caring to minister remedy, notwithstanding many particu-

[12] SP DOM 264:40, 41.
[13] SP DOM 264:57. From a letter written by Sir R. Cecil to Essex on the 26th; the full text of both speeches is given in STOW'S ANNALS.

lar petitions and letters received. To confirm her disposition
to avow these courses (violating both the law of nature and
nations), because there were quarrels between her and the
King of Spain, she took upon her by mandate to prohibit him
and his countries, assuming to herself thereby a superiority
not tolerable over other princes; which he was determined not
to endure, but rather wished her to know that, if there were
no more than the ancient amity between Spain and him, it was
no reason why his subjects should be impeded, much less now
when straight obligations of blood had so conjoined him with
the illustrious house of Austria; and concluding that if her
Majesty would not reform it, he would.

The Queen being much moved to be so challenged in public,
especially so much against her expectation, after a short pause,
answered him extempore in Latin. The words of her beginning
were these: *'Expectavi Legationem, mihi vero querelam ad-
duxisti'*; and continuing to this effect: 'Is this the business the
King has sent you about? Surely I can hardly believe that if
the King himself were present, he would have used such language; for if he should, I must have thought that being a King
not of many years, and that *non de iure sanguinis sed iure
electionis, immo noviter electus,* he may haply be uninformed
of that course which his father and ancestors have taken with
us, and which peradventure shall be observed by those that
shall live to come after us. And as for you, although I perceive you have read many books to fortify your arguments
in this case, yet I am apt to believe that you have not lighted
upon the chapter that prescribes the form to be used between
kings and princes; but were it not for the place you hold, to
have so publicly an imputation thrown upon our justice, which
as yet never failed, we would answer this audacity of yours
in another style. And for the particulars of your negotiations,
we will appoint some of our Council to confer with you, to
see upon what ground this clamour of yours hath his foundation.'

24*th July*.   THE POLISH AMBASSADOR.[14] The merchants that
trade to Danzic or other parts in the East Countries forbear
all offices of ceremony towards the Polish ambassador, as of
visitation, sending presents or whatsoever of the like gratifica-
tion, until it is resolved on the answer to be given him.

[14] APC 27:307.

28th July. PLAYHOUSES TO BE PLUCKED DOWN.[15] The Lord Mayor and Aldermen again petition for the present stay and final suppression of stage plays at the Theatre, Curtain, Bankside and all other places, alleging four reasons in particular.

Firstly, they corrupt youth, containing nothing but unchaste matters and ungodly practices which impress the very quality and corruption of manners which they represent, contrary to the rules and art prescribed for them even among the heathen, who used them seldom and at set times and not all the year long.

Secondly, they are the ordinary places for vagrant persons, masterless men, thieves, horse-stealers, whoremongers, coseners, connycatchers, contrivers of treason and other dangerous persons to meet together and to make their matches, which cannot be prevented when discovered by the governors of the City, for that they are out of the City's jurisdiction.

Thirdly, they maintain idleness in persons with no vocation and draw prentices and other servants from their ordinary work, and all sorts from resort to sermons and other Christian exercises, to the great hindrance of trades and profanation of religion.

Fourthly, in time of sickness many having sores and yet not heartsick take occasion to walk abroad and hear a play, whereby others are infected and themselves also many times miscarry.

In answer to this petition the Council direct that not only shall no plays be used in London during this summer, but that the Curtain and Theatre in Shoreditch and the playhouses on the Bankside shall be plucked down, and present order taken that no plays be used in any public place within three miles of the City till Allhallow tide. Likewise the magistrates shall send for the owners of the playhouses and enjoin them to pluck down quite the stages, galleries and rooms and so to deface them that they may not again be employed to such use.

A LEWD PLAY.[15] Much offence also is caused by a play called *The Isle of Dogs,* full of seditious and slanderous matter, written by Nashe and Jonson, and played by my Lord of Pembroke's men at the Swan. Nashe is fled away, but Spencer,

---

[15] *Remembrancia* 2:171; APC 27:313, 338; HENS. DIARY 1:54; ELIZ. STAGE 4:321, 454; McKerrow's *Nashe* 5:29. Apparently the Lord Mayor had been reading Sidney's *Defence of Poesy,* but his immediate desire to reform the stage was more probably due to the quite real danger that the players might incite the mob at this uneasy time. Playing ceased until October (see *9th* and *11th Oct*), but the playhouses, as usual, survived intact.

Shaa and Jonson (who also acted in the play) are apprehended and committed to prison. Playing is now stayed.

29th July.   TROUBLES ON THE BORDER AND IN IRELAND.[16]
There is almost hourly complaint of devastation upon the Scottish Border, wherefore the Queen hath commanded that those
principal gentlemen of the Border, as the Witheringtons, the
Selbys and others, that are with the fleet at Plymouth shall be
sent back. In Ireland my Lord Burgh hath taken the fort at
Blackwater on the 14th in a skirmish between some of the
traitors' horse and foot; but his horse, led by Captain Turner,
the Sergeant Major, engaged themselves too far into a wood
so that he and nine others were slain. My Lord recovered the
bodies, made good the place and killed 200 hard upon Tyrone's own camp, who hath 5,000 men near Duncannon. The
place was well defended, as they had cast up sundry trenches
and laid pikes in the ford, but my Lord led the vanguard himself and was the second man inside the fort.

2nd August.   LORD HOWARD'S SHIPS RETURN.[1] The ships of
Lord Thomas Howard are now returned safe to Plymouth,
having been separated in the storm that drove back my Lord
of Essex.

7th August.   THE PICARDY FORCES DELAYED.[2] The two hoys
that were to transport 400 men under command of Captain
Henry Poore have for some days been delayed by contrariety
of winds.

13th August.   A PROCLAMATION CONCERNING THE SCOTTISH
BORDER.[3] A proclamation is published commanding those that
live on the Border to live in peace and quietness and to offer
no manner of incursion, stealth or injury, since the King of
Scots is desirous to yield satisfaction for the injuries committed by his subjects. Nevertheless if any offence shall be
offered by the opposites which shall not presently be satisfied
according to the laws of the frontier, the Queen will not only
leave her subjects to their liberty of just revenge, but will further enable them with extraordinary powers. The King of
Scots proposeth likewise to inform his subjects of this determination of the Queen.

19th August.   THE FLEET AGAIN SAILS.[4] Two days since the

[16] SP IRELAND 200:24, 25, 27; SP DOM
264:61.
[1] SP DOM 264:64.
[2] APC 27:324.
[3] PROCLAMATIONS 349.
[4] PURCHAS 20:44.

fleet again set forth from Plymouth, but much abated from the first assembly; for the former violent tempests much cooled and battered the courage of many of our young gentlemen, who, seeing that the winds and sea have affinity neither with London delicacy nor Court bravery, secretly retire themselves home, forgetting either to bid their friends farewell or to take leave of their General.

21st August. INGROSSERS.[5] Although the universal scarcity is now abated yet are there seen a number of wicked people, more like to wolves and cormorants than natural men, that most covetously seek to hold up the late great prices of corn and all other victuals by ingrossing the same into their private hands, bargaining beforehand for corn and in some part for grain growing, and for butter and cheese before it be brought to ordinary markets. The sheriffs shall therefore send up to the Council the names of all such; and for that men of good livelihood and in estimation of worship enrich themselves by such ingrossings, the sheriffs shall seek to reform them, not only with sharp reprehensions but also certify their names, and thereby avoid the just offence of the inferior sort which cannot but be grieved to see such corruption of the better sort suffered without restraint.

22nd August. A BOOK ON CHEATING.[6] There is a book called *Mihil Mumchance, His discovery of the art of Cheating in false dice play and other unlawful games,* showing also divers new devices of cosenage practised at fairs and markets, with many deceitful practices used by bad and lewd women. At fairs and markets there are some who, attiring themselves in mean attire, will buy a piece of very fine lawn or holland, worth £5 or £6, bound up very handsomely, with another bundle bound up after the same manner but within stuffed with nothing but old rags and such trash. These bundles the cheater will carry till he meeteth with some simple countryman that seemeth to have store of crowns, to whom very secretly, as if he had gotten the lawn by stealth, he will proffer it at half its worth. The simple countryman being covetous of a good pennyworth bargains with him, and gives all the money in his purse, which is not above 40s. or 50s. Then the cheater having got the money pockets it up and bobs the poor man with the counterfeit bundle of rags, reserving the other bundle still to himself.

5 APC 27:359.   6 SR 3:89; STC 17916.

These cheaters have a treasurer, a very trusty secret friend, that whensoever there cometh any jewels or treasure to their share the present sale whereof might discover the matter, then he will take it in pawn and make out a bill of sale as if things were done in good order and dealing; so that whensoever the cheater shall seek to make money of the pawn, if any question arise, he showeth a fair bill of sale for his discharge. Another help they have that of every purse which is cleanly conveyed, a rateable portion is duly delivered to the treasurer's hands, that whensoever by some misadventure any of them happen to be laid in prison this common stock may serve to satisfy the party grieved, thereby to save them from the gallows.

29th August. 'RICHARD THE SECOND.'[7] Mr. William Shakespeare's play of *The Tragedy of Richard the Second* that was publicly acted by the Lord Chamberlain's men is being printed, but without that scene of the deposing of King Richard.

6th September. AN AMBASSADOR FROM DENMARK.[1] To-day Mr. Arnold Whitfield, Chancellor of the realm of Denmark, with his assistant, the Court being at Theobalds, had audience before the Queen, to whom they made certain requests which her Majesty answered without pause. The first, that the league and amity between the Queen and the late King should be continued to the new King, now newly adopted and crowned. The second was that it would please the Queen that the King his master might make a motion of peace between her Majesty and the King of Spain, and if he found the parties thereto addicted, to proceed further for the effecting thereof. To which her Majesty replied that she thought the King his master was too young to know the cause of the breach of the league between her and Spain, and as it was not broken by her consent, so it should not be sued nor sought by her, nor any in her behalf. 'For,' said she, 'know now, and be it known to the King your master, and all Kings, Christian or heathen, that the Queen of England hath no need to crave peace, for I assure you that I never endured one hour of fear since my first coming to my Kingdom and subjects.'

This being her Majesty's birthday the ambassador took occasion to say that sith it had pleased God on this day to glorify

[7] SR 3:89; STC 22307. A popular book which went quickly into three editions; the first is anonymous, but Shakespeare's name appears on both editions of 1598. There was no further edition until 1608 which first included the Deposition Scene; presumably after the troubles of John Hayward it was thought inadvisable to continue publication.
[1] STOW'S ANNALS.

the world with so gracious a creature, he doubted not that the King should have an happy answer of his requests. 'I blame you not,' answered her Majesty, 'to expect a reasonable answer, and a sufficient; but you may think it a great miracle that a child born at four o'clock this morning should be able to answer so wise and learned a man as you are, sent from so great a Prince as you be, about so great and weighty affairs you speak of, and in an unknown tongue, by three o'clock in the afternoon.'

15th September. SLANDERS AGAINST THE LORD MAYOR.[2] A slanderous report is of late raised that the Lord Mayor hath caused the price of corn, that began to fall, to be enhanced to a higher rate, and that having brought into the Thames certain corn he kept up the market that he might sell his corn at a higher rate. The Queen being much offended at these reports now causeth a proclamation to be published, not only clearing the good name of the Lord Mayor, but showing that the grain was brought hither by his providence, whereof great numbers of poor people have been sustained in this time of dearth.

16th September. NEWS OF THE FLEET.[3] There is a gentleman come from my Lord of Essex with news that meeting with a stormy northerly wind as soon as they had doubled the South Cape, they were put off sixty or eighty leagues towards the Azores, and the wind so continuing, and fresh water lacking, they go for the Islands, to lie for the carracks and West Indian ships.

20th September. SIR JOHN NORRIS DEAD.[4] News is come that Sir John Norris is dead in Ireland, to the Queen's grief. He is succeeded as President of Munster by his brother Sir Thomas.

CONDEMNED PRISONERS.[5] There are at this time 28 persons lying in prisons condemned to be executed, 19 being men and 9 women; of these the Queen is pleased to pardon 8 men and 8 women.

22nd September. THE QUEEN'S LETTER TO THE LADY NORRIS.[6] Upon the news of Sir John Norris's death, the Queen wrote to the Lady Norris, his mother, in these terms: 'If it be true that society in sorrow works diminution, we do assure

2 PROCLAMATIONS 350.
3 SP DOM 264:110.
4 SP IRELAND 200:130.

5 APC 28:8.
6 Nicoll's *Progresses*, vol. iii.

you, by this true messenger of our mind, that nature can have stirred no more dolorous affection in you as a mother for a dear son, than gratefulness and memory of his services past hath wrought in us his Sovereign apprehension of our miss of so worthy a servant. But now that nature's common work is done, and he that was born to die hath paid his tribute, let that Christian discretion stay the flux of your immoderate grieving, which hath instructed you both by example and knowledge that nothing of this kind hath happened but by God's divine Providence.' And at the top of the letter in her own hand she wrote these words: 'Mine own Crow, harm not thyself for bootless help; but show a good example to comfort your dolorous yokefellow.'

23rd September.   THE GOVERNOR OF DUNKIRK TAKEN.[7] Some of the garrison of Ostend have taken the Governor of Dunkirk and brought him prisoner to Sir Edward Norris. Sir Henry Palmer is now sent in person to bring the Governor over to England in all haste and to lodge him in Dover Castle.

24th September.   MACHUGH'S HEAD.[8] Some days since two boys going to fetch their cattle from Enfield Chase found there a man's head. Hereupon, enquiry being made, Mr. John Dewrance, whose field it was, declareth that about a month since one John Lane brought this head to his house in Enfield, saying that it was the head of MacHugh, that arch traitor of Ireland, who was slain by Captain Thomas Lee and his company. Lane brought the head into England to the Earl of Essex, who referred him to Mr. Secretary for payment, but seeing that the head money had already been paid in Ireland Lane was told that he might bestow the head where he would; and having it with him he made proffer to leave it with Mr. Dewrance, who would no wise permit it nor suffer it be buried in his garden. Lane therefore gave the head to his boy to bury in Enfield Chase, but the boy set it upon a tree.

29th September.   THE SPANISH DANGER CEASES.[9] Now that the season is so far advanced there would appear to be no danger of an attempt of the enemy against the realm; wherefore to save the charges the soldiers entertained for the defence of Guernsey and Jersey are to be withdrawn.

[7] APC 28:10.   [9] APC 28:27.
[8] SALISBURY PAPERS 8:395. See *8th June.*

5th October. AN ESCAPE FROM THE TOWER.[1] Last night John Gerard, a Jesuit priest, who hath been a prisoner more than three years and John Arden, a recusant, escaped from the Tower. They tied a rope to one of the cannon on the roof of the small tower, and thence they slid down across the moat to the wall where their friends were in waiting, who conveyed them away by boat from Tower Wharf. Gerard left behind him letters justifying his escape and to the Lords of the Council declaring his innocence from meddling in affairs of state. The warder also in fear of his life lest he be charged with their escape is fled away. The Lieutenant of the Tower has sent hue and cry to Gravesend and to the Lord Mayor, but as yet nothing is heard of them.

8th October. THE PLAYERS RELEASED.[2] Spencer, Shaa and Jonson, the players committed because of the play of *The Isle of Dogs*, are now to be released, from the Marshalsea.

9th October. A DISORDERLY ELECTION.[3] There hath been no small disorder in the election of those to serve in this forthcoming Parliament as Knights of the Shire for the county of York. On the 3rd October, about 8 o'clock, at the Castle at York the writ of summons for the election was duly read, also a letter sent from the Privy Council for the better direction of the election; proclamation was also made by order of the Archbishop and the Council that no person thither assembled, except he were a freeholder of 40s. per annum above all charges and reprises, should presume to give voice in the election. Which things being done, first were nominated Sir John Stanhope, Sir Thomas Hoby, and Sir John Savile; whereat Sir John Savile caused the sheriff to read out to the freeholders certain statutes to the effect that none should be chosen to that place but such as were resident in the county at the head of the writ. Then Sir John cried out to the people, 'Will you have a Maleverer or a Fairfax?' meaning, as some said, to make knights at his own will or otherwise to distract the voices of the freeholders from the other two nominated.

Hereupon for the space of two hours and more the cries and voices of the people continued confused and diverse for Sir John Stanhope, Sir Thomas Hoby, Sir John Savile and

---

[1] *John Gerard: The Autobiography of an Elizabethan.* Tr. and ed. by Philip Caraman, 1951, pp. 128–39.
[2] APC 28:33. See *28th July.*

[3] SALISBURY PAPERS 7:411–15. Reported to the Council by the Archbishop of York who blamed Sir John Savile.

Sir William Fairfax; but for some good space after the first cries, the number for Sir John Stanhope and Sir Thomas Hoby seemed to be more in show by some 600. Afterwards the greater number seemed doubtful, and it was agreed that some indifferent gentleman should be assigned to discern the companies and voices of each part, first by view, and then by trial of the polls for their freehold or residency. Whereupon the companies on each part being severed and divided, the undersheriff with the gentlemen went up into a chamber where they might see the companies and reasonably esteem of the great number of persons; with result that they did esteem those that stood on the hillside for Sir William Fairfax and Sir John Savile (being next the gate) to be more in number than the side for Sir John Stanhope and Sir Thomas Hoby by about 200 persons. But then some of the gentlemen did think that there were on that side citizens and inhabitants of York, women and children and other strangers, not having lawful voices, to the number of 500 or 600. It was therefore agreed that the companies should be further examined by pools upon their corporal oaths.

The undersheriff and the gentlemen triers then proceeded to the gate, whither the sheriff went also and took paper with him, the gentlemen having sticks to take the number of them by scotches or marks. It was further concluded that the company of Sir John Savile, being nearest the gate, should first be tried. The gentlemen and the undersheriff being thus come to the gate, it was agreed to shut the gate and no more to let any in on any side; then that two of the gentlemen triers on either side should nick every score, and that all should be sworn and examined against whom any exceptions should be taken, and that the undersheriff and his man were there for the purpose. So Mr. Wortley (who was of the part of Sir John Stanhope and Sir Thomas Hoby) took a knife and a stick to nick on the scores on his side.

Thereupon the undersheriff commanded the people back from out of the gatestead. Whereat came Sir John Savile on horseback, and called the undersheriff and demanded what he was about; who answered, to proceed to trial by poll according to agreement and law.

Sir John replied, 'Though they would make you an ass, they shall not make me a fool.' He would have no such trial; he would hold what he had; and, after other words, commanded the gate to be opened. The undersheriff replied that it might not be so, for he must do as the law required; to which Sir John answered, 'Open the door or break it open,' and himself pressed forward, so that the gentlemen triers shifted themselves away as well as they could, and two were in danger of their lives. Then also the undersheriff went out with Sir John without staying to proceed, whereby those who stayed behind knew not whether any election had been made or not.

After this, by the space of two hours or more, the knights, gentlemen and freeholders on the part of Sir John Stanhope continued in the castle hall and yard expecting the return of the sheriff; but he would not be found, being with Sir John Savile at dinner. Then Sir John Savile and Sir William Fairfax returned together with the undersheriff, who, first making proclamation of silence, immediately and without any further proceeding did pronounce Sir John Savile and Sir William Fairfax to be the knights lawfully elected; which thing was denied by the other part of Sir John Stanhope and Sir Thomas Hoby.

10th October.   THE ART OF BRACHYGRAPHY.[4] There is a new edition published of *The Art of Brachygraphy,* that is to write as fast as a man speaketh treatably, writing but one letter for a word, including also the order of orthography, for the speedy writing of true English, and the key of caligraphy opening the ready way to write fair, invented by Mr. Peter Bales. This art serveth for an infinite number of uses; the memory is strengthened and as much can be written in one day as in a whole week by other writing; by it you may with speed write out any excellent written book or copy, never yet imprinted, to your private use and benefit; moreover the sermons, lectures and orations of excellent learned men shall hereby be kept, recorded and registered. The method of this brachygraphy is to denote words by single letters, to each letter being added a prick or tittle.

11th October.   'THE TRIMMING OF THOMAS NASHE.'[5] There

[4] STC 1311; dated on title pages. The work of an Oxford man, with a number of dedicatory verses. Bales's system is very general and could not be used for anything more elaborate than note taking. Entered 10th Nov 1599 (SR 3:150).
[5] SR 3:92; STC 12906. McKerrow (*Nashe* 5:107) points out that as the *Trimming* is concerned only with Nashe's Epistle to the barber and not with his quarrel with Harvey, it is not likely to be Harvey's work, nor does it resemble Harvey's style. I suspect that it was written by some Cambridge man, possibly with the approval of the barber, who may well have resented Nashe's unsolicited advertisement. With this book the Harvey-Nashe 'flyting' ceased.

is an answer to Nashe's Epistle to Richard Lichfield, the barber of Trinity College in Cambridge (that he wrote in *Have with you to Saffron Walden*), entitled *The Trimming of Thomas Nashe*. Herein Nashe is very straitly trimmed for his many ribaldries and lewd courses of life. Saith that there was a time when Nashe and his fellow Lusher lay in Coldharbour together when they had but one pair of breeches between them both, but not one penny to bless them with; so that by course Lusher wore the breeches one day and went conny-catching for victuals whilst Nashe lay in bed; and the next day Nashe wore the breeches to go and beg, for all the world like two buckets in one well. Taunteth him also with his *Isle of Dogs* for which he was proclaimed by the crier, and deserved the cropping of his ears. Saith that Nashe hath been cast into many prisons and hath polluted them all.

PLAYING RESUMED.[6] To-day began my Lord Admiral's and my Lord Pembroke's men to play at the Rose after the restraint, the play being *The Spanish Tragedy*.

THE ELECTION AT YORK.[7] The Council being informed of the contemptuous behaviour of Sir John Savile have required the Archbishop of York to commit him to prison, thereby to notify to the world, not that her Majesty's meaning nor the Council's is to mislike any man to use that freedom for his election which the law doth warrant and discretion requireth, yet, where authority is established as in such a nature the Archbishop and his Council hath, she will not suffer any precedency of contempt to go unpunished for warning to others.

12th October. A PROCLAMATION AGAINST ENGLISH MERCHANTS.[8] News is come out of Germany that the Emperor by proclamation hath commanded all English merchants to depart the Empire within three months, they and their goods, on pain of confiscation and imprisonment, so that the Merchant Adventurers must needs leave Stade.

[6] HENS. DIARY 1:54; 2:186.   7:429; F. Peck's *Desideria Curiosa*,
[7] SALISBURY PAPERS 7:426.   Bk. 5, p. 21.
[8] SP DOM 264:143; SALISBURY PAPERS

14th October. 'POLITEUPHUIA, WIT'S COMMONWEALTH.'[9]
Mr. N. Ling hath completed the book called *Politeuphuia:
Wit's Commonwealth* which was compiled by Mr. John
Bodenham. Herein are to be found many definitions beginning
with that 'Of God' and ending 'Of Hell' and beneath each
certain pithy sentences expanding the same; as 'Of Generals
in War,' defined thus: 'Generals are the heads and leaders
of armies, and they ought to be great, magnanimous and
constant in all their doings; free from the defects of rashness and cowardice.' There are eight conditions that a general
ought to have; to avoid unjust wrongs, to correct blasphemers,
to succour innocents, to chastise quarrellers, to pay his soldiers, to defend his people, to provide things necessary, and
to observe faith with his enemies.

19th October. INGROSSERS AND BUILDERS PUNISHED.[10] To-
day in the Star Chamber, one Francis Parker that hath been
an ingrosser these sixteen years and every year carried corn
to London in a boat without a licence is fined £500 to the
Queen, imprisonment, £20 to the poor, to go to Westminster
Hall with papers and to confess his fault. Others are fined
£40 with imprisonment. At the same time one Negoose
and others for building cottages in London contrary to the
proclamation are fined; one £100, one £40 and another
£20; the houses to be destroyed for their base condition
and the timber sold for the poor. If any be brothel houses,
to burn them standing if it can be done without peril, otherwise to burn them in the fields; and those that are beautiful
and spacious edifices to be converted into garners and storehouses.

DELONEY'S 'GENTLE CRAFT.'[11] Deloney hath written a book
in praise of shoemakers called *The Gentle Craft*, showing
what famous men have been shoemakers in time past in this
land, with their worthy deeds and great hospitality. Relateth
the pleasant history of St. Hugh (from whom cometh it
that the shoemakers' tools are called St. Hugh's bones); the
tale of Crispin and Crispianus; and lastly how Sir Simon
Eyre, being first a shoemaker, became in the end Lord Mayor

[9] SR 3:93; STC 15685. A most popular book; a 17th edition appeared in
1655, and at least six further editions came out before 1700. One of
the many commonplace books so
popular at the time.

[10] HAWARDE, p. 78.
[11] SR 3:93; STC 6555. Dekker dram-
atised the last section in *The Shoemaker's Holiday*.

of London through the counsel of his wife, and how he
builded Leadenhall.

20th October. 'RICHARD THE THIRD.'[12] There is to be printed
that play acted by the Lord Chamberlain's men called *The
Tragedy of King Richard the Third*, written by Shakespeare,
wherein Burbage played the King with great applause.

22nd October. THE LORD ADMIRAL TO BE ADVANCED.[13] It
is said in Court that to-morrow the Lord Admiral shall be
created Earl of Nottingham. The heralds have been with
him; he hath borrowed my Lord of Pembroke's robes; his
coronet is made and his patent is a drawing.

23rd October. THE LORD ADMIRAL ADVANCED.[14] As the
Queen came from the Chapel this day, being Sunday, she
created the Lord Admiral Earl of Nottingham. The Earl
of Cumberland carried his sword, the Earl of Sussex his
cap and coronet. He was brought in by the Earls of Shrewsbury and Worcester. The Queen made a speech unto him
in acknowledgment of his services, and Mr. Secretary read
the Letters Patent aloud, which are very honourable; all
his great services *anno* '88 recited, and those lately at Cadiz.
He is to take his place *vt Comes de Nottingham,* for so are
the words in the patent. Hereby shall he take precedence
over the Earl of Essex.

OSTEND THREATENED.[15] News is lately come of the approach
of the enemy unto the town of Ostend, whereby it is supposed that some enterprise is intended. Four companies with
Sir Arthur Savage are now to be sent from Picardy for
the better security of the town.

24th October. THE PARLIAMENT ASSEMBLES.[16] This day
the Parliament, being her Majesty's ninth Parliament, assembled at Westminster, where many of the knights of the
shires, citizens of cities, burgesses of boroughs, and Barons
of ports, having made their appearance before the Earl of
Nottingham, Lord Steward of the Household, took the Oath
of Supremacy seven or eight at a time before him and Sir
William Knollys, Sir John Fortescue and Sir Robert Cecil.
This done they passed into their own House to await her
Majesty's pleasure.

[12] SR 3:93; STC 22314. Very popular,
being reprinted 1598, 1602, 1605, 1612,
1622, 1629, 1634.
[13] SIDNEY PAPERS 2:69.

[14] SIDNEY PAPERS 2:70.
[15] APC 28:48.
[16] D'EWES' JOURNALS, pp. 548, 524;
STOW'S ANNALS.

The Queen being then come into the Upper House and set in her chair of estate, the Commons were summoned, and as many as conveniently could admitted. Then Sir Thomas Egerton, the Lord Keeper, by her Majesty's command, declared the cause of the summoning of this present Parliament, and having expressed his insufficiency for that task, spake to this effect:

'You are to enter into a due consideration of the laws, and where you find superfluity to prune and cut off; where defect to supply, and where ambiguity to explain; that they be not burdensome but profitable to the commonwealth. Yet as nothing is to be regarded if due mean be not taken to withstand the professed enemies which seek the destruction of the whole State, this before and above all is to be thought of; for in vain are laws if such prevail as go about to make a conquest of the Kingdom. Wars heretofore were wont to be made either of ambition to enlarge dominions or of revenge to quit injuries; but this against us is not so. In this the Holy Religion of God is sought to be rooted out, the whole realm to be subdued, and the precious life of her Majesty to be taken away, which hitherto hath been preserved, maugre the Devil, the Pope and the Spanish Tyrant. Her Majesty hath not spared to disburse a mass of treasure and to sell her land for maintenance of her armies by sea and land, whereby, with such small helps as her subjects have yielded, she hath defended and kept safe her dominions from all such forcible attempts as have been made. Which though performed at infinite charge, her Majesty doth notwithstanding hear of nothing more unwillingly than of aids and subsidies from her people. The taxations at this day, howsoever they seem, are nothing so great as heretofore. In the time of Edward the Third, and of those before and after him, the payments of the Commons did far exceed any that have been made since her Majesty's reign; but never cause so great to employ great sums of money as now. To spare now is to spare for those which seek to devour all; and to give is to give to ourselves, her Majesty's part only being carefully to bestow what is delivered into her hands. This war is just; it is in defence of the Religion of God, of our most Gracious Sovereign, and of our natural country, of our wives, our children, our liberties, lands, lives, and whatsoever we have.'

Whereupon the Commons were dismissed to choose the Speaker, who shall be presented on Thursday next. The Commons therefore straightway repaired to their own House, and there being assembled and sitting some space of time very silent, at last Sir William Knollys, the Controller, stood up and spake:

'Necessity constraineth me to break off this silence and to give others cause for speech. According to the usual custom we are to choose our Speaker, and though I am least able and therefore unfit to speak in this place, yet better I deem it to discover my own imperfections than that her most Sacred Majesty's commandment to me delivered should not be fulfilled, or your expectation of this day's work by all our silences be frustrate.'

Having then spoken a little on the necessity for a Speaker, he saith, 'Now because that knowledge doth rest in certainty, I will with the more speed set afoot this motion, deliver my opinion unto you who is most fit for this place, being a member of this House, and those good abilities which I know to be in him'—here he made a little pause, and the House hawked and spat, and after silence made, he proceeded—'unto this place of dignity and calling in my opinion'—here he stayed a little—'Mr. Sergeant Yelverton'—looking upon him—'is the fittest man to be preferred'—at which words Mr. Yelverton blushed, put off his hat and sat bareheaded—'for I am assured that he is, yea, and I dare avow it, I know him to be, a man wise and learned, secret and circumspect, religious and faithful, no way disable but in every way able to supply this place. Wherefore in my judgment I deem him, though I will not say best worthy among us, yet sufficient enough to supply this place; and herein if any man think I err, I wish him to deliver his mind as freely as I have done; if not, that we all join together in giving general consent and approbation to this motion.'

So the whole House cried, 'Ay, ay, ay, let him be.' Then Sir William made a low reverence and sat down. After a little pause and silence Mr. Sergeant Yelverton rose up, and, after very humble reverence made, thus spake:

'Whence your unexpected choice of me to be your mouth or Speaker should proceed, I am utterly ignorant. If from my merits, strange it were that so few deserts should purchase suddenly so great an honour. Nor from my ability doth this your choice proceed; for well known is it to a great number in this place that my estate is nothing correspondent for the maintenance of this dignity; for my father dying left me a younger brother and nothing to me but my bare annuity. Then growing to man's estate and some small practice of the law, I took a wife by whom I have had many children, the keeping of us all being a great impoverishing to my estate, and the daily living of us all nothing but my daily industry. Neither from my person or nature doth this choice arise; for he that supplieth this place ought to be a man big and comely, stately and well spoken, his voice great, his carriage majestical, his nature haughty, and his purse plentiful and heavy; but contrarily, the stature of my body is small, myself not so well spoken, my voice low, my carriage lawyer-like and of the common fashion, my nature soft and bashful, my purse thin, light, and never plentiful. Where I now see the only cause of this choice is a gracious and favourable censure of your good and undeserved opinions of me. But I most humbly beseech you recall this your sudden election; and therefore, because the more sudden, the sooner to be recalled.' For such good reasons he begged then to proceed to a new election.

After this speech, Sir John Fortescue, the Chancellor of the Exchequer, stood up, affirming all the former commendations and also nominated Mr. Yelverton to be their Speaker, and moved the House for their liking and resolution therein, who all with one accord and consent yield unto this election.

Whereupon Mr. Controller and Mr. Chancellor rose up and placed Mr. Sergeant Yelverton in the Chair. Which done, Mr. Yelverton after some small pause stood up, and giving the whole House most hearty thanks for their good opinions and conceit of him, signified unto them nevertheless that by their good favours he will endeavour when he shall come before her Majesty, to be a humble suitor unto Her Highness to be discharged of this place, if so he can.

After this the House immediately rose.

Divers people to-day pressing between Whitehall and the College Church to see the Queen and the nobility riding to the Parliament, Sir Thomas Gerrard the Knight Marshal and his men making way before them, were smothered and crushed to death.

26th October. A SUDDEN VERY GREAT ALARM.[17] To-day is come to Court a gentleman with news that he discovered the Spanish fleet, and finding one ship lagging took prisoner her captain, master and purser. The ship was rescued, but some letters taken in her show that they will make their rendezvous at Falmouth. Mayors and chief officers in the ports on the south shall now, as they regard the Queen's

[17] SIDNEY PAPERS 2:71; APC 28:50–56.

service and upon peril of their lives, send out as espials some of the best fisher boats to gain early intelligence of the designs of the enemy. The Picardy soldiers are to be landed in England with all possible expedition. Victuals and all kinds of provision are being collected in the West parts to replenish the fleet of the Earl of Essex which is looked for within a few days.

27th October. THE FORCES MUSTERING.[18] In Devon, Cornwall, Dorset, Hampshire, Berkshire, Kent, Sussex, Surrey, Wiltshire and Somerset the whole forces, both horsemen and footmen, are being put in readiness. All men that dwell anywhere near the sea are forbidden to leave their houses; and gentlemen of every county for the most part are commanded to go home for the defence of the sea coast. The Lord Chamberlain departeth at once for the western coast to command such forces as shall be fit for the resistance of the enemy if they land, and captains are appointed to attend him.

THE LORD BURGH DEAD.[19] The Lord Deputy, Lord Burgh, is dead in Ireland. Being on a journey to revictual the fort of Blackwater, he fell dangerously sick of an Irish ague at Armagh on the 6th, and being taken back in a litter to Newry died there on the 13th. His death comes very untimely, for there is not another fit man able to second the course already begun, all the money spent is lost, and besides there hangeth an imminent danger of a present and general revolt throughout that Kingdom.

THE SPEAKER PRESENTED.[20] To-day in Parliament, the House being set, Mr. Chancellor of the Exchequer moved and admonished that none of the House shall hereafter enter into the House with their spurs on for offending of others, and that none shall come in before they have paid the Sergeant's fees due to him according to the accustomed usage of the House.

This afternoon the Queen going by water repaired to the Upper House, accompanied with divers Lords spiritual and temporal, and the Commons having notice, Mr. Sergeant Yelverton was brought into the Upper House, and by the hands of Sir William Knollys and Sir John Fortescue, Chancellor of the Exchequer, presented.

Mr. Speaker in a speech full of gravity and moderation

18 SIDNEY PAPERS 2:72; APC 28:57–61.   20 D'EWES' JOURNALS, pp. 550, 526.
19 SP IRELAND 201:17, 14.

signified the election of the House of Commons, but, excusing himself by pretence of many disabilities and imperfections, and wishing earnestly he were of sufficiency to perform the duty of that place, made humble suit to her Majesty that he might be discharged and that the House of Commons might proceed to a new election. This excuse was not allowed by her Majesty, as the Lord Keeper delivered answer, who very well approved the choice of Mr. Yelverton and commended his sufficiency.

Mr. Speaker then proceeded in another speech, according to custom, to undertake this charge and to present her Majesty, in the behalf of the Commons, certain humble petitions, for access upon needful occasions, and for the using and enjoying of such liberties and privileges as in former times have been granted by her Majesty and her progenitors. Whereunto her Majesty, by the mouth of the Lord Keeper, yielded gracious assent, with admonition that these liberties should be discreetly and wisely used, as is meet.

The Parliament is adjourned until the 5th November.

PLAYING RESUMED.[21] To-day the Lord Admiral's players that have been absent for the last three months are now returned from the country and again begin to play at the Rose.

28th October. THE EARL OF ESSEX RETURNS.[22] This morning came letters to Court of the Earl of Essex's safe landing in Plymouth, that he hath unfortunately missed the King's own fleet with the treasure but fell upon the merchants' fleet. Four of them he hath taken and brought home safe, and sunk many more. The Earl of Southampton fought with one of the King's great men-of-war and sunk her. The Spanish fleet commanded by the Adelantado still hovers up and down upon the coast but as yet is not landed. The Earl of Essex put in to victual and to have fresh men, and with all possible speed to go to sea again; my Lord Mountjoy sailing to Plymouth was by three of the Spanish fleet chased in.

The King of Spain is said to be dead, who made his son swear by the Sacrament that he should never make peace with England till he revenged these disgraces. The Adelantado, by the young Prince's threatening to hang him if he put not to sea, is upon our coast and vows to land though he never return.

A mass of money is being sent down to the Earl of Essex for all wants and supplies needed to refurnish the fleet. My Lord's offers and ready disposition to adventure his life in this service are very graciously accepted by the Queen. The Earl of Pembroke also is bidden to furnish such further aid as shall be required of him both in men and supplies.

30th October. PREPARATIONS IN THE WEST.[23] A sum of £3,000 has been sent into the West for provisions to revictual the fleet, of which sum the Lord Thomas Howard, Lord Mountjoy and Sir Walter Ralegh may draw up to £2,000, and more will be sent if need require. The loans of money hitherto respited are to be brought in with all speed for the service.

31st October. OSTEND BESIEGED.[24] The Cardinal hath now besieged Ostend, lying on the west side of it, but 'tis not yet known whether for a bravado or whether he will remain there for some design. Meanwhile the Lord Cobham stayeth all the hoys at Dover and Sandwich so that, if there be cause, they may carry over men and victuals. The forces of the shire are mustered and the castles being viewed.

2nd November. THE ISLANDS VOYAGE.[1] The accounts of the late voyage are now to hand. Soon after the fleet had set sail, it was again caught by another great tempest on St. Bartholomew's Day, and many of the ships scattered, thirty ships with Sir Walter Ralegh the Vice-admiral being separated from the rest; but most of the remainder staying with the Earl of Essex. It had been ordained that if any separation should happen, there should be three places of rendezvous, the first at the North Cape, the second at the Rock, and the third at the South Cape. To the Rock therefore came Sir Walter Ralegh, who had been delayed by the breaking of his main mast, and there joined him some thirty sail; and here they

[23] APC 28:67.
[24] SP DOM 264:163, 164.
[1] PURCHAS, vol. 20. This account is based on the narrative of Sir Arthur Gorges, who was an enemy of the Essex faction and therefore not impartial, but other writers are even more condemnatory. Monson, who was Essex's own captain, wrote: 'No man can receive blame hereby; all is to be attributed to the want of experience in my Lord, and his flexible nature to be overruled.' With the return of the expedition Essex's reputation amongst the intelligent observers began to wane as it was more generally realised that he was not only an incompetent commander but acutely jealous of other and abler leaders than himself; he was, moreover, attracting the devotion of the more desperate and reckless adventurers. From this time onward Essex begins to be a definite menace to the commonwealth. For the best modern commentary on the expedition see *The Naval Tracts of Sir William Monson*, ed. by M. Oppenheim, 1902, for *The Navy Records Society* (vols. 22–23).

met with a small bark of England by whom they were told that the Adelantado was gone to the Islands to waft home the Indian fleet; which news was afterwards found to be false. Sir Walter therefore thinking it very requisite that the Admiral should be informed of this advertisement, sent one of his small ships to seek the fleet, which by good hap it found the next day, so that within two days after Sir Walter received two letters from the Earl of Essex requiring him to follow him to the Islands forthwith. Which was accordingly done and the Isle of Tercera reached on the 8th September; and on the 14th they met with the rest of the fleet at Flores to the great joy of the General, especially as many had buzzed doubts and jealousies in his ear concerning Sir Walter. Then a council was held whereat it was determined to take in some of the islands and an orderly course was set down, which was for the Admiral and Rear-admiral to undertake Fayal; the Lord Thomas Howard and Sir Francis Vere to undertake Gratiosa; the Lord Mountjoy and Sir Christopher Blount to St. Michael's; and the Netherland squadron was quartered to Pyke where is the greatest store of wines, and therefore, it was presumed, would not be taken in ill part of them.

Here the ships of Sir Walter purposed to water whilst the rest of the fleet plied up and down, looking for the Adelantado. But whilst the casks were being prepared, about midnight, being the 16th September, a message was brought that my Lord General was borne up for Fayal, and meant to take it straightway, and therefore willed Sir Walter to follow with all speed instantly; further that all wants of water and fresh victuals should be supplied at Fayal. The ships with Sir Walter accordingly weighed anchor and next morning making Fayal entered the road but found not the Lord General; whereat they greatly marvelled, because when he had sent for them, he was six leagues nearer to it than they. As soon as the fleet was seen, the inhabitants of the town began to pack away with bag and baggage all they could. The town, which is some four miles from the place where they were, was defended by two forts, one at the end, the other on the top of a high mountain near adjoining, very inaccessible by nature, and artificially fenced with flankers, rampiers, and a ditch, and with six pieces of great artillery, and 200 Spaniards for a garrison. There were also sent six companies to intrench themselves on the shore side to impeach the landing of our men.

Hereupon Sir Walter in his barge rode close aboard the high fort and all along the shore side towards the town to see what fit place there was to make a descent against the Lord General's coming. So Sir Walter held a council of many captains and officers to consult of taking the town if still the Lord General came not. Moreover the soldiers and mariners began to mutiny and rail on the Rear-admiral and all the commanders as not daring the taking of the town; and besides they were more eagerly set upon the spoil because they saw no great likelihood of any other benefit to be gotten from this voyage. At this council, some would by no means consent to the landing without the Lord General's knowledge, and especially Sir Gelly Merrick, but those of Sir Walter's own squadron were of the contrary opinion. They stayed therefore two days, and then a third, but on the fourth Sir Walter determined to land.

They made ready therefore a barge, a long boat, and a pinnace with sixty muskets and forty pike rather to guard the landing than to attempt any encounter. But no sooner were the men in the boats, than many companies of foot began to hasten down to possess themselves of the trenches where our men were to land. Sir Walter therefore rowed to Sir William Brooke's ship and Sir William Harvey's, and desired them to accompany him; to which they willingly assented, and there were made ready in addition with shot and pike 160 more men in the boats. Then the men from the Low Countries that belonged to my Lord of Essex's squadron cried out to be taken too, but Sir Walter durst not, not knowing for what service my Lord had intended them: but promised to send back his boats for them.

So the pinnaces hasted forward toward the landing place, but as the shot began to play thick upon them, the mariners would scarce come forwards, having the lesser liking to the business the nearer they came to it; and some of the leaders themselves stood blank so that Sir Walter did not spare to call upon them openly and rebuke aloud with disgraceful words. Sir Walter, seeing that it was both more disgrace and more dangerous for the mariners to make stay, with a loud voice commanded his watermen to row in full upon the rocks and bad as many as were not afraid to follow him. Hereupon some boats ran in, and so clambering over the rocks, and wading through the water they passed pell-mell with swords, shot and pikes upon the narrow entrance. Whereupon those that were at the defence, after some little resistance, began to shrink, and then suddenly retiring cast down their weapons, and fled away to the hills. The landing being thus gained with some few men lost, the boats were sent back for the men from the Low Countries, who, when they were come ashore, made up a force of 460 men, well armed and appointed, and of these thirty or forty were captains and gentlemen.

They therefore resolved to pass by the two forts and enter the town, and the next morning to attack these forts; which could not then be done, the day being far spent and the men overwearied with the last work, together with a long march and extreme hot weather, besides lack of victuals. So they set forward, the Rear-admiral with divers of the gentlemen going before the rest some twelve score paces in the manner of a vauntguard in a slow steady march, being shrewdly pelted by the muskets and great ordnance of the fort; but the main body that for a while marched in good order so soon as they began to find themselves within the mercy of the musket shot began to break their ranks, and from marching fell to flat running in straggling manner so that they were upon the heels of the vauntguard. Whereupon Sir Walter cried out on them for this shameful disorder and asked their captains if this was the manner of their old Low Country troops to show such base cowardice at the first sight of the enemy. To which they answered that these companies were men taken out of Flushing and Brille, and raw soldiers that ever lived in a safe garrison and seldom or never had seen the enemy. And indeed such as only serve to take pay, to walk rounds and guard ports in garrison towns, in the field will commonly be missing, or, if present, do little hurt for conscience' sake.

Then Sir Walter called for some to go out to survey the passage by the high fort, but the lieutenants and sergeants were very unwilling, so he said that he would go himself; 'notwithstanding,' quoth he, 'though I could enforce others to do it, they shall well perceive that I myself will do that which they dare not perform.' So with some few with him he went to discover the passage and to search out the strengths and ascents of the hill, being shrewdly troubled by the great artillery which beat upon the old walls as they passed, insomuch that two had their heads stricken clean from their bodies and divers others were hurt, and the Rear-admiral himself was shot through breeches and doublet. The passage being discovered, the rest of the troops were summoned to come on towards the town. But as they drew near the town, those in the other fort withdrew and fled up into the country; so that they entered the town peaceably, having lost some seven or eight slain and twenty-five hurt. Barricadoes were immediately made, good guards placed in divers places and a strong court of guard in the market place, and straggling forbidden on pain of death. That night they rested without further trouble than two false alarms.

Next morning, being 22nd September, the Lord General himself with his fleet bore into the road of Fayal, having all this while been looking about for the Adelantado and other adventures; and hereupon the intent to attempt the high fort was frustrated. Meanwhile the proceedings in Fayal were by Sir Gelly Merrick related at large to the Lord General, and so aggravated and wrested into an evil sense by him, Sir Christopher Blount, Sir Anthony Shirley and others, by putting into my Lord of Essex's head that these parts were played by Sir Walter Ralegh only to steal honour and reputation from him, and to set his own frowardness to the view of the world. Which intimation of theirs was an exception that they knew my Lord of Essex is very apt of his own disposition to take hold of, being a man that affecteth nothing in the world so much as fame, and to be reputed matchless for magnanimity and undertaking, and can hardly endure any that shall obscure his glory in this kind, though otherwise he favour them never so much. It was besides alleged that the presumption and scorn to land such forces without my Lord's leave was not to be passed over without severe punishment, and a martial court fit to be called, to censure the offence and breach of order and discipline. These and such other bitter arguments were used to aggravate the General's wrath against all that were in this action, and especially against the Rear-admiral; against whom they spared not so far to inveigh as that he was well worthy to lose his head for his labour. So well did they persuade the General that all the forenoon was spent in reprehending and displacing the land officers that went in the action.

Sir Walter was then sent for to answer before the Lord General in his ship, but before the messenger came for him was already gone in his barge to see my Lord, looking for great thanks at the General's hands. But when he was entered my Lord's cabin, after a faint welcome, my Lord began to challenge him of breach of order and articles, in that he had landed troops without the General's presence or his order. To which Sir Walter answered that there was an article that no captain should land anywhere without direction of the General or other principal commander; but that he himself was a principal commander and therefore not subject to that article, nor under the power of the law martial, because a successive commander of the fleet under her Majesty's letters patent.

This dispute lasted some half hour and then the Lord General went ashore and rested himself in the Rear-admiral's lodging, being well enough satisfied at that time, this dispute having been brought to a quiet conclusion by the friendly mediation of Lord Thomas Howard. Thus the whole day was spent in reprehending and disciplining those with the Rear-admiral for their pains. That night the Spaniards in the high fort abandoned the place with all their baggage and fled into the country; and next morning, when it was too late, direction was given to guard the high fort. So when news was brought that they had abandoned the fort and carried all away, there was much murmuring, for if there had not been bestowed more labour in disciplining pretended faults than discretion in prosecuting the enemy who was at a disadvantage, then had not been lost the benefit of the prisoners' ransoms and the spoil which they had carried out of the town to that place for safety.

On the 26th September the whole fleet made towards Gratiosa, where the chief men of the Island submitted themselves to the Lord General, being required to yield some provisions of wine, fruits, and fresh victuals. Here the Lord General and some of the commanders would have stayed, but the Master of his ship, one Grove, was against that counsel, protesting that it would be dangerous for the whole fleet to anchor there. Wherefore they weighed anchor and made for St. Michael's Island, but as they came near two of the sternmost of the fleet shot off twice or thrice and bare up with all the sails they could pack on to the General's ship. These brought news of the Indian fleet, coming directly from the road of Gratiosa.

Upon this intelligence they cast about, and, within some three hours afterwards, they encountered and took three Spanish ships coming from Havannah, the greatest being of about 400 tons, and esteemed to be a very rich ship. To this Spaniard the *Wastspite*, being nearest, gave chase and caused her to strike and yield; but the Lord General, hasting after, would suffer none but his own boat to go aboard her, being full of good prisoners and pillage besides her lading, which was cochinella and other rich wares. This ship made relation of forty sail of Indiamen, whereof eight were freighted with the King's treasure, bound for Spain. Of these ships, some of ours fell in with sixteen, whereof they foundered one, and whilst they were busy seeking to take the spoil off her, the rest escaped and recovered Tercera. With all speed therefore our fleet followed them to Tercera, where they had entered some six hours before and had moored their ships under the town and fort.

Now there was a general council called aboard the Admiral what course to take herein, some of the colonels and captains offering with 1,500 men to take both island and forts but the sea commanders utterly against it, so that in the end it was deemed inconvenient and impossible to be effected as the forces then stood, and the time of year so far spent, with the winds and seas grown so tempestuous for landing in boats. The fleet therefore returned to St. Michael's and there anchored.

There it was consulted about landing and the taking of this good town, promising so many rewards to the victors. The General appointed that all companies should be made ready to land forthwith, but the Rear-admiral asked that he might first be permitted to view the place and to find out where the army might best make a descent. To this the Lord General at first yielded, but as Sir Walter was putting off, and scarce gone from the ship's side, my Lord, standing in his gallery with Sir Charles Blount, called him back again in great haste, and said that he would go himself and view it. Whereupon the Rear-admiral returned again, and my Lord went out of the ship into his barge, unarmed altogether but with his collar and sword, and without either shot or pike to wait on him. Sir Walter therefore called aloud to him, desiring him to take his casque and targetproof with him if he purposed to go near the shore, seeing there lay so many muskets on the rest there to receive him. Whereunto my Lord answered that he would none, because he disdained to take any advantage of the watermen that rowed with him.

The landing places being viewed afar off were not so well liked, so that upon another consultation being held it was agreed that the Rear-admiral, with all the strength of the fleet, should lie as near before the town of St. Michael as conveniently they could to hold them in expectation whilst my Lord and the rest with 2,000 men should embark into the small barks and pinnaces and secretly in the night convey themselves about the point to land at a town called Villa Franca.

So the troops were shipped, and the Lord General also, and made haste to Villa Franca, where they arrived safe and were all landed by the next morning without any manner of resistance, while the ships under the command of the Rear-admiral all the night gave the enemy perpetual alarums with shot, drums and trumpets in such boats as were left, sometimes in one place, sometimes in another alongst the shore.

Next morning those with the Rear-admiral looked to see our troops marching over the hills and plains; but this good town of Villa Franca had so welcomed and entertained our men that the army was content there to ingarrison without any further pursuit of St. Michael's town; and there for six days they lay feasting, and carrying on board of oade, wheat, salt and other merchandise into certain private men's ships that followed the fleet for such a purpose.

While the fleet lay gaping for the coming of the army, which in all this time never sent word of their determination, there came a little Brazil man and let fall his anchor in the midst of our fleet, and a little after him a mighty huge carrack was discerned which made towards our fleet supposing it to be the Spanish armada, for indeed the King of Spain's men-of-war, when he makes fleets, are compounded of the shipping of divers nations, and besides with ours were not only Hollanders but the great Spanish galleon, the *St. Andrew*. Then by general commandment of the Rear-admiral, our ships took in all their flags, and directions were given that no man should weigh an anchor or shoot off a piece or put off a boat, but with leave and order. All this while she still bare in with all sails to the boat's end, when suddenly one of the Holland squadron weighed his anchors, hoisted his top sail and made towards the carrack. Whereupon discovering our ships to be enemy, she changed her course, and with the gale changing ran herself aground hard under the town and fort. Immediately there came out multitudes of boats, fetching away their men and best wares, and, that done, she was instantly set on fire in many places at once, so that though our men hasted all they could in all the boats that were left, they came all too late, for the broth was too hot for their supping. This vessel was judged to be of 1,800 tons, of infinite wealth, fraughted with the riches and wares both of the

East and West, which was a loss as lamentable as inexcusable, for if the General and his troops had not lingered in Villa Franca, she had either fallen in their hands on shore or been taken at sea by the fleet.

After some days the fleet was summoned to Villa Franca, to the great joy of the inhabitants of St. Michael's. The wind and seas now beginning to rise and the opportunity being past of doing any damage to the enemy, preparations were now made for a return, and with all haste the soldiers were conveyed back to the boats with the help of the small pinnaces and boats, wherein my Lord twice was in very great danger of tumbling into the sea in overcharging his own boat with soldiers, amongst whom at such times it is very hard to keep any order or moderation. At this embarking the Spaniards and Portuguese made a brave skirmish, which being thoroughly answered, the General did make certain knights. At length on 9th October the fleet set sail for England.

5th November. OSTEND.[2] News is come from Sir Edward Norris, governor of Ostend, that there is no present danger. The enemy lie about the town and have divers times presented themselves before it; forces from the Low Countries have now been sent there.

THE QUEEN'S LETTER TO THE EMPEROR OF ETHIOPIA.[3] One Mr. Lawrence Aldersey, after many travels in foreign countries, being yet inflamed with a desire more thoroughly to survey and contemplate the world, now undertaketh a long and dangerous journey into the kingdom of the Emperor of Ethiopia. He beareth with him a letter from the Queen that he may enter that kingdom under the safeguard and protection of the Emperor's favour, and there remain safe and free from danger.

A MOTION IN PARLIAMENT AGAINST INCLOSURES.[4] To-day in the Parliament a Bill was read for the first time against forestallers, regrators and ingrossers. Whereupon Mr. Francis Bacon spake first and made a motion against inclosures and depopulation of towns and houses of husbandry. He had perused, said he, the preambles of former statutes and by them did see the inconveniences of the matter, being then scarce out of the shell, to be now full ripened. It might be thought ill and very prejudicial to Lords that have inclosed great grounds, and pulled down even whole towns, and converted them to sheep pastures; yet considering the increase of people and benefit of the commonwealth, every man would deem the revival of former moth-eaten laws in this point a praiseworthy thing. 'I would be sorry,' quoth he, 'to see within this Kingdom that piece of Ovid's verse prove true, *iam seges ubi Troia fuit*, so in England, instead of a town full of people, nought but green fields, but a shepherd and a dog.'

After Mr. Bacon, Sir John Fortescue, the Chancellor of the Exchequer, in like manner showed his opinion, and so moving for a committee to consider of this motion, the House nominate all members of the Privy Council, being members of this House, all knights of the counties and all citizens of the cities returned to this present Parliament, together with Sir Edward Hoby, Mr. Francis Bacon, Mr. Nathaniel Bacon, Mr. Finch, Mr. Solicitor and divers others.

This concluded, Mr. Finch showing sundry great and horrible abuses of idle and vagrant persons, greatly offensive both to God and the world, and further the extreme and miserable estate of the godly and honest sort of the poor subjects of this realm, the matter is also referred to the same committee.

6th November. SPANISH PRISONERS AT LARGE.[5] Divers Spaniards that have of late been taken on the seas are allowed ordinarily to go up and down at their own liberty: but now the Lord Mayor shall inform himself of those that are within and without the City and see them committed to Bridewell, there to be safely kept with the diet of the house and set to work if they be not able to pay for their diet, and especially those lately taken by Newport; for it is against reason that any of the King of Spain's subjects should be suffered to enjoy their liberty here seeing the hard usage that is offered to our countrymen.

7th November. 'THE THEORICK AND PRACTICK OF MODERN WARS.'[6] Mr. Robert Barret hath written a book called *The Theorick and practick of modern wars*, discoursed dialogue-wise. Herein is declared the neglect of martial discipline and

[5] APC 20:102.
[6] SR 3:95; STC 1500. One of the most interesting and best written of the military text books. Michael Cassio, in Iago's estimation, was another of your reading captains, a bookish theoric.

the inconvenience thereof; the imperfection of many training companies and its redress; the fittest weapons for our modern war, and their use; the part of a perfect soldier in general and in particular; the officers in degrees with their several duties; the embattling of men in forms now most in use, with figures and tables to the same; with sundry other martial points, comprehended in six books. Yet he would have captains trained by experience and not by book; for your reading captain when he is come into the field with an hundred men will rank them three and three, but at every third rank he must call to his boy, 'Holla sirrha, where is my book?' And having them all ranked, then marcheth he on fair, and far wider from his soldiers. Then cometh he to cast them into a ring, about, about, about, till he hath inclosed himself in the centre; now there is he puzzled—'Holla master, stand still until I have looked in my book.' Addeth to his book a table of the foreign words used by soldiers.

9th November. THE EARL OF ESSEX ABSENT FROM COURT.[7] To-day the Queen told my Lord Hunsdon that she much wondered at the absence of the Earl of Essex. He pleaded my Lord's want of health, the shooting in his temples upon cold or long speech, and yet his readiness to attend if she should be pleased to command his service. She accounted his duty and place sufficient to command him, and said that a prince was not to be contested withal by a subject. Nevertheless there is nothing but kindness and comfort to my Lord, if he will but turn about and take it.

PRIVILEGES OF THE HOUSE.[8] Two days since Sir Thomas Knivett showing that since being a member of this Parliament he had been served with a *subpoena* to attend in the Chancery, the matter was referred to the committee for examination of such matters. Yesterday Mr. Brograve, Attorney of the Duchy, declared that the committee had met together and are of opinion that the serving of a *subpoena* is a manifest contempt committed against the whole House; for by reason of such process, a member so served must needs be withdrawn from the service of the House, both in his mind and person, by the mere necessity of following his own private business elsewhere. It was resolved therefore that two members should be sent to the Lord Keeper in the name of the whole House to require him to revoke the *subpoena*. Where-

upon Sir Edward Hoby and Mr. Brograve went to the Lord
Keeper and delivered the message of the House, to which the
Lord Keeper asked whether they were appointed by any advised consideration of the House to deliver their message unto
him with the word 'require.' They answered his Lordship,
'Yea.' Then his Lordship said that as he thought very rever-
ently and honourably of the House and the liberties and privileges of the same, but so to revoke the *subpoena* in that sort
is to restrain her Majesty in her greatest power, which is justice in the place wherein he serveth her. He saith that he will
be advised further before giving his answer to the House.

ABUSES IN BRISTOL.[9] When Captain Docura, upon the recent
alarm of the Spanish fleet, was sent into Bristol to see the
trained bands which should have been in readiness and to train
them to serve, the men were presented to him after many delays and altogether unarmed. Moreover he found very small
care or feeling in the Mayor in these occasions, for he trusted
to the situation of his town, being a great indraught in the
land. This slender regard in these times of danger deserveth
much to be blamed.

10*th November*. THE PARLIAMENT.[10] This day in the Parliament a Bill for taking away clergy from certain offenders was
sent up to the Lords; committees were appointed touching the
sundry enormities growing by patents of privilege and monopolies and the abuses of them; and a motion was made touching
the abuses of licences for marriages granted by ecclesiastical
persons.

14*th November*. KNIGHTS OF THE POST.[11] There is a book
entered called *The discovery of the Knights of the Post*, written by one E. S. The knights of the post are those who will
pretend themselves to be citizens of substance and so bail a
man out of arrest for a reward. In term time they are most
commonly to be found in Fleet Street, about St. John, or about
Chancery Lane or in some of the pudding-pie houses in Westminster; but out of the term, then in Duke Humphrey's alley
in Paul's, or at the Lion on the backside of St. Nicholas
Shambles, or at the Rose in Pannier Alley, or the Dolphin at
the end of Carter Lane, or the Woolsack.

9 APC 28:111.
10 D'EWES' JOURNALS, p. 555.
11 SR 3:46; STC 21489. A lively book, in the form of conversations on the Plymouth road.

INCESTUOUS MARRIAGES.[12] In the Parliament Sir John Fortescue declared that yesterday her Majesty called Mr. Secretary and himself unto her, and telling them that she had been informed of the horrible and great incestuous marriages discovered in the House, commanded them to take information of the grievances in particular of the members of the House that she might have certain notice thereof and thereupon give order for their due punishment and redress.

15th November.   THE SUBSIDIES.[13] Mr. Chancellor, putting the House in remembrance of the Lord Keeper's speech on the first day of the Parliament touching the causes of the summoning of this Parliament, declared how great and excessive have been her Majesty's charges for the defence of her realm, amounting to more than treble the value of the last three subsidies and six fifteenths and tenths granted by the last Parliament. Then Mr. Secretary Cecil showed at large the purposes, practices and attempts of the King of Spain against her Majesty at sundry times, together with his great overthrows in the same by the mighty hand of God and of her Highness's forces, to his perpetual ignomy and great dishonour throughout the world. And so, after a large discourse most excellently delivered by him, concluded with a motion for proceeding to a committee; which is agreed by the House.

16th November.   MY LORD OF ESSEX'S ABSENCE.[14] There are many different censures about my Lord of Essex's absence from the Parliament, some earnestly expecting his advancement, others that daily make use of his absence confess his worth but wish him well only in words. Yet is my Lord for all his good parts least perfect in working his own good, for his patience continually giveth way to his crosses, and upon every discontentment he will absent himself from Court. Some there be that would say to him 'Let nothing draw thee from the Court; sit in every Council, yet so that there may be nothing concluded but with thy good liking and privity. Thou hast 100,000 true hearts in this small isle that daily expect and wish thy settled content, and the fall of them that love thee not. What dignity is done to them, or indignity to thee, but in thy absence? Thy enemies are thereby made strong and thou weak. And whereas thou retainest many in thy favour as true and

[12] D'EWES' JOURNALS, p. 556.
[13] D'EWES' JOURNALS, p. 557.
[14] SP DOM 265:10. From a long letter to Essex from 'thy true servant not daring to subscribe.' Compare Bacon's advice noted on 4th Oct 1596. The register of attendances in APC shows that Essex was absent from Council meetings from 3rd Nov to 22nd Dec.

secret friends, remember that Christ had but twelve and one proved a devil.'

18th November. THE EARL OF ESSEX ABSENT FROM PARLIAMENT.[15] Report was made by the Lord Keeper in the House of Lords that the Earl of Essex received not the writ of his summons till yesterday, through the negligence of the messenger, and now wanting health to give his attendance desireth to be excused of his absence, the Earls of Worcester and Southampton testifying his sickness.

19th November. THE SUBSIDIES.[16] Sir John Fortescue, Chancellor of the Exchequer, showed that at the committee of Parliament yesterday it was agreed to grant unto her Majesty three entire subsidies and six fifteenths and tenths. Whereupon, some members of the House being for delay in the payments of these subsidies, Sir Robert Cecil gave very many forcible reasons and causes of great importance for the speedy performance of the subsidies; which done, it was upon question resolved that the last payment of the subsidies shall be made in one year and at one entire payment in like sort as the two first of the same three subsidies are to be paid.

Then Mr. Davies, showing many corruptions in the Masters of Colleges in the Universities of Oxford and Cambridge in their abusing the possessions of Colleges contrary to the intents of founders, converting the same to their own private commodities, prayed the advice and assistance of the House for the better digesting of a Bill which he had drawn to the purpose. Herein Mr. Speaker referreth him to such members of the House as are of the Temple. Whereupon Sir Edward Hoby, liking very well of Mr. Davies' motion, moveth that the like consideration be had of Deans and Chapters.

Yesterday one Mr. Thomas Layton, one of the knights for the county of Salop, having been much visited with sickness since his coming up to this session of Parliament, is for better recovery of his health licensed by Mr. Speaker to depart home.

20th November. DISORDERS IN WALES.[17] During the late attempt of the Spaniards two of their ships were driven ashore in Wales; whereof one was forced into a creek in a place

[15] D'EWES' JOURNALS, p. 529.   [17] APC 28:119, 121.
[16] D'EWES' JOURNALS, p. 559.

called Galtop. Hereupon Mr. Hugh Butler, that was in command of the trained bands in those parts, prepared six fisher boats to board the ship; but the Spaniards set out a play of truce and offered to send their cockboat ashore. This being perceived by one John Wogan, a gentleman of those parts, he with his brother and other associates to the number of twenty entered the ship before Mr. Butler, and not only withstood him by force but wounded him in three places, while his company rifled the ship of all her goods, money and things of value. At Caldey, the other Spanish ship in which there was treasure for Dunkirk is escaped through the disorderly behaviour of others.

THE SPANISH LOSSES.[18] There is news from Spain that forty-nine ships are arrived back on the coast, whereof twenty-nine are the King's galleons; fifty of the fleet are missing. The *St. Peter* is leaky, the *St. Lucas* ran aground; they had to cast most of their horses and mules overboard. The fleet was within two days' sail of Land's End. One of the galleons with Don Pedro de Guevara, General of artillery, in her took fire and hath not since been seen; another ship, wherein were the materials for fortification and for firing our ships in harbour, attempting to aid her, took fire and was blown up, and a French ship with her, full of soldiers. There is now nothing but confusion, stories of misfortunes, yet brags of what they will do next spring; yet the defeat of an army so long in preparing hath been very sudden. Their plan was to have landed 8,000 in long-boats westward of Plymouth by peep of day while the ships occupied our forces west of Falmouth till the whole army was landed.

The Spanish King hath been very sick, and there are bonfires and processions for his recovery. He had a palsy and for two days was fed with liquor blown into his throat by the Infanta.

21st November. PRIVILEGE OF THE HOUSE.[19] Sir Edward Hoby moved the House for privilege for Sir John Tracy, being a member of the House and at that time at the Common Pleas to be put on a jury. Whereupon the Sergeant of the House was sent straightway with the Mace to call Sir John to his attendance in the House, and Sir John then returned to his place.

22nd November. A PETITION OF THE UNIVERSITIES.[20] Because of the speeches lately uttered by Mr. Davies in the Lower House of Parliament greatly tending to the utter discredit of the Governors and Heads of Colleges generally, the Vice-Chancellors both of Cambridge and Oxford have petitioned their Chancellors that Mr. Davies may be compelled to make such proof as he can of those scandalous matters, lest by colour of these scandalous defamations uttered in so public a place some new statute may pass to the general prejudice of both Universities.

23rd November. THE PARLIAMENT.[21] Mr. Walgrave delivering a Bill to the Speaker declareth that the transportation of a great number of herrings to Leghorn both occasioneth a very great scarcity of herrings in the realm, and is, saith he, a great means of spending much butter and cheese to the enhancing of the price thereof.

Mr. Attorney General and Mr. Dr. Stanhop having brought from the Lords an Act passed with their Lordships concerning the deprivation of divers bishops at the beginning of the reign, after their departure it was shortly found by Sir Edward Hoby that the Act was not duly and rightly endorsed by their Lordships; the endorsement being made above the Contents of the Act which ought to have been made under it. Whereupon the House being made privy thereto by the Speaker, Mr. Comptroller, with divers members, was sent to the Lords with the Act to signify the error and to pray amendment. Later Mr. Attorney and Dr. Stanhop came from the Lords with the Act endorsed according to the ancient former usage of Parliament, signifying to the House that the faulty endorsement of the Act in such manner before did grow only by an error in the Clerk of the Upper House, who had never exercised the place before the present Parliament; moreover their Lordships, liking very well of what the House had done touching this error, withal wish the House to continue all former good order and courses in all Parliament proceedings.

28th November. THE FRENCH AMBASSADOR RECEIVED.[22] To-day M. de Maisse, who is sent over by the French King, was received in audience by her Majesty. When he was conducted to the door of the Privy Chamber he made reverence to the

[20] British Museum, *MSS Addit.* 5843: f.449.

[21] D'EWES' JOURNALS, pp. 562–63.

[22] DE MAISSE, p. 22.

Queen who was sitting by herself, and at some distance from the Lords and Ladies. As he entered she rose and came forward to the middle of the Chamber. M. de Maisse kissed the border of her garment, and she raised him with both hands and with a favourable countenance began to excuse herself that she had not given him audience sooner, saying that the day before she had been sick of an affliction on the right side of her face, and he would believe it if he looked at her eyes and countenance, for she did not remember when she had been so ill before. At this meeting the Ambassador spoke but in general terms, noting that as he spoke the Queen ofttimes raised herself from her chair and seemed to be impatient at his words. She complained of the fire that it hurt her eyes, although there was a great screen before it, and called for water to put it out.

30th November.   A PRISONER RELEASED.[23] One Gilbert Layton that hath lain a prisoner in the Tower these six years is now to be released with condition that he shall at all times be forthcoming upon warning given him to be at a certain place in London, and also to behave himself as a good subject, and when her Majesty shall be at any of her houses in London not to repair to the Court. This man formerly confessed that he would kill the Queen.

1st December.   GERARD'S 'HERBAL.'[1] Mr. John Gerard, Master in Chirurgery, hath written a great work called *The Herbal or general history of plants,* being dedicated to the Lord Burleigh. This work is in three books, whereof the first treateth of grasses, rushes, corn, bulbous or onion-rooted plants in 106 chapters. The second containeth the description, place, time, names, nature, and virtues of all sorts of herbs for meat, medicine or sweet smelling use, etc., and hath 511 chapters. The third of trees, shrubs, bushes, fruit-bearing plants, rosins, gums, roses, heath, mosses, some Indian and other rare plants, also mushrooms, coral and their several kinds, which book hath 167 chapters; and to all the chapters are there one or more cuts of the things described therein. Concludeth with a description of the goose-tree or barnacle, found in the north parts of Scotland.

On this tree do grow certain shellfishes of a white colour tending to russet wherein are contained little living creatures;

which shells in time of maturity do open and of them grow those little living things, which falling into the water become the fowls which we call 'barnacles,' in the north of England brant geese, and in Lancashire tree geese. Mr. Gerard hath himself found similar between Dover and Romney, for causing the trunk of an old rotten tree to be drawn out of the water, there were growing on it many thousands of long crimson bladders, in shape like unto puddings newly filled before they be sodden, very clear and shining. At the nether end did grow a shellfish, fashioned somewhat like a small mussel, but whiter. In these shells were found living things without form or shape; in others things that were very naked in shape like a bird; in others the birds covered with soft down, the shell half open and the bird ready to fall out.

3rd December. THE VENETIAN CORN SHIP.[2] There is still dispute concerning that Venetian ship the *St. Agatha Morisini* which was driven into Portsmouth last January laden with corn that was sold because of the then scarcity. Martin Frederico, a merchant of Venice, hath procuration from the Signiory to follow a cause, complaining that the corn was undervalued, sold at low prices, and a great part missing. Dr. Julius Caesar and others are appointed to examine the matter and to certify to the Council what fault they find in the dealing of the Commissioners, for her Majesty hath care that the Signiory should have all the satisfaction in these causes which in equity ought to be afforded them.

4th December. THE SERMON AT PAUL'S CROSS.[3] Mr. John Howson to-day preached the sermon at Paul's Cross on Matthew xxi., 12 and 13, showing how unlawful is the buying and selling of spiritual promotion. Saith that this buying and selling in the Church will make barren the two Universities; for those that be bred up in learning having in childhood suffered great and grievous affliction in the grammar schools, when they be come to the Universities live either of the College's allowance, needy of all things but hunger and fear, or being maintained by their own or their parents' cost, do expend in necessary maintenance, books, and degrees £500 or 1,000 marks before they be come to perfection. If they then cannot purchase a poor parsonage or vicarage of £40 or £50 a year unless they pay to the patron for the lease of their life either in annual

[2] APC 28:167. See *23rd Jan.*
[3] SR 3:100; STC 13881. There were two editions. A second part of the sermon was preached 28th May 1598.

pension or above the rate of a copyhold, what father will be so improvident to bring his son up at great charge? Concludeth that this buying and selling is indeed the sin of simony, an heresy intolerable, and one that will cause the Universities to be decayed, the Church supplied with ignorant pastors, hospitality removed from the clergy and the sign and forerunner of some evil to ensue to the Commonwealth.

8th December.   A BOY POSSESSED AT NOTTINGHAM.[4] Some weeks since a boy called William Sommers of Nottingham began to be strangely tormented in body and gave great tokens that he was possessed by a wicked spirit; whereupon the Mayor and some of the Aldermen of Nottingham sent instantly for Mr. Darrell (who by prayer and fasting hath already restored eight or nine persons that have been vexed in like sort). At first Mr. Darrell was unwilling to come, but by their importunate letters and messengers at length he condescended to their desires, and came to Nottingham on the 5th November. The 7th was appointed for the exercise of prayer and fasting to the end that Sommers might be dispossessed; which at the prayers of Mr. Darrell and others to the number of a hundred and fifty is brought to pass. Hereupon Mr. Darrell is retained as preacher in Nottingham.

Sommers being dispossessed discovered certain witches, one whereof was called Doll Freeman, allied to one Freeman an Alderman of Nottingham. This Freeman offended that his kinswoman should be called in question threatened Sommers that he was himself a witch, and caused him to be committed to prison, where the Devil appeared unto him in the likeness of a mouse, threatening that if he would not let him re-enter and would not say that all he had done concerning his tormenting during his possession was but counterfeit, then he should be hanged; but if he would yield, the Devil would save him.

Thus a new stipulation being made between them, the Devil entered; and afterwards Sommers constantly declared that all which he had done before was only counterfeit. A general opinion being now conceived that Sommers hath counterfeited all his former proceeding, Mr. Darrell preacheth very bitterly against that conceit, persuading his auditory that Satan will lurk sometimes about one out of whom he hath been cast, suffering the party to be well for a good space, but will not give him over until in the end he have repossessed him.

[4] See note on *25th July* 1598.

11th December. THE SUBSIDY.[5] The Bill for the granting of six fifteenths and tenths and three entire subsidies had a second reading to-day and was ordered to be ingrossed.

14th December. THE LORDS' PRIVILEGE ABUSED.[6] Six days since one William Cole, one of the Knight Marshal's men, that had arrested John York, the Archbishop's servant, was brought before the Lords by the Sergeant at Arms; and being found upon examination to have wilfully offended therein against the privilege of the House was committed to the Fleet; but to-day he is enlarged on paying only his fees.

THE ABUSE OF MONOPOLIES.[7] Mr. Francis Moore, one of the committees for consideration of the method and substance of the humble thanks to be yielded by Mr. Speaker unto her Majesty on behalf of the House for her care and favour in repressing sundry inconveniences and abuses practised by monopolies and patents of privilege, delivered a note of the meeting and travail of the committee therein. This being read by the Clerk was well liked of. Whereupon the Speaker moved the House that, albeit he was ready to perform their commandment according to the substance and effect of the note, yet they would not tie him to the strict and precise form of the words and terms; which is yielded unto accordingly.

MONSIEUR DE MAISSE.[8] M. de Maisse was again received by the Queen to-day, and saith that when he entered the Chamber one was playing the virginals, and she seemed to be so attentive to the music and as it were surprised by his entrance that he excused himself for interrupting her pastime. The Queen replied that she loveth music and every day playeth a pavan. She spoke several times of the King of Spain, his wishing to kill her. Whilst they conversed she would ofttimes make digression, as if she would gain time and not appear to be pressed by the ambassador's demands; which she would excuse saying, 'You will say, Master Ambassador, the tale I told you is mere trifling; see what it is to conduct affairs with old women such as I am.' She said also to him that she had long hands, both by nature and by power, for, quoth she, *'anne fas longas regibus esse manus?'* whereat she took off her gloves, showing her hands, longer than the ambassador's by three thick fingers.

---

[5] D'EWES' JOURNALS, p. 571.   [7] D'EWES' JOURNALS, p. 573.
[6] D'EWES' JOURNALS, pp. 532, 533. [8] DE MAISSE, p. 55.

17th December. TWO LONDON CRIMES.[9] The body of Mr.
Richard Anger, a double reader of Gray's Inn, that hath been
missed almost a month, was lately found floating in the
Thames; and being viewed by certain skilful surgeons it is
thought he was not drowned in the water but stifled or murthered, and after thrown into the Thames, which by other
conjectures is greatly to be suspected. There are great pre-
sumptions against one of his sons, Richard Anger, and Edward Ingram, the porter of Gray's Inn. Forasmuch as the fact
is so horrible that an ancient gentleman should be murdered
in his chamber, these two are to be examined very strictly, and
if they cannot be brought to confess the truth, then shall they
be put to the manacles in Bridewell.

There is also one Richard Remchin, a gentleman, that hath
long used the clipping of coin, and upon search there is found
in a house of his in Fetter Lane a great quantity of clippings
and coin clipped, to the sum of £20 in gold. This man's goods
are to be seized and kept in the Tower until he hath been convicted, when they shall be converted to the Queen's use.

20th December. A DISPUTE CONCERNING PROCEDURE.[10] The
Parliament stands adjourned over Christmas until the 11th
January at 8 o'clock in the morning.

Some days since a Bill was sent up to the Lords and by
them passed with amendment of one word and so sent down
to the Lower House, where it was found that the amendment
had been affiled to the Bill and ingrossed in parchment with
the words '*soit baille aux Communes*' contrary to precedent.
Wherefore the House caused the Bill to be returned to the
Lords for amendment, saying that they had no warrant to take
notice of that amendment because it was in parchment and
not in paper. To-day the Lords answer that they do not expect
an exception of such levity from the gravity of the House, taking it to be immaterial whether such amendments be written
in parchment or in paper, either white paper, black paper or
brown paper. Thereupon some members of the House charged
the Clerk that by his default and error the House was charged
with levity; to which he himself prayed that some of the ancient Parliament men of the House might examine the matter.
After the Clerk had been heard and the matter blamed on the
inexperience of the Clerk of the Upper House, it is determined

⁹ APC 28:187, 188–219.
¹⁰ D'EWES' JOURNALS, pp. 573–74, 575–
77.

by these ancientest Parliament men that all the members of the House, being Privy Councillors, together with the best sort of the rest of the members, accompanied with the Sergeants of the Law, shall straightway be sent to the Lords to signify in the name of the whole House that the House has not in any manner of sort erred in returning that Bill and amendments in parchment to have the same done in paper according to the ancient order of Parliament; and that the House doth take itself to be very hardly dealt with to be taxed by their Lordships with imputation of levity, and reproached by other unusual and unnecessary terms.

21st December.   ESSEX'S INDIGNATION.[11] 'Tis said in Court that the Queen hath advanced the Earl of Essex to be Lord Marshal, whereby his precedency over the Lord Admiral is restored. My lord doth now show himself in more public sort and is purposed to have the patent of the new Earl of Nottingham altered. But he will have none of it, and yesterday in the afternoon he gave over his White Staff as Lord Steward, and to-day is gone to Chelsea where he purposeth, as 'tis said, to be sick, for the Queen by this long patience and suffering of his is grown to consider the wrong done unto him, which now she lays upon the Lord Treasurer and Sir Robert Cecil, though with infinite protestations they deny it. The Earl of Essex desires right to be done him, either by a commission to examine it, or by combat, either against the Earl of Nottingham himself or any of his sons or name that shall defend it; or that it will please her Majesty to see the wrongs done to him, and so will suffer himself to be commanded by her. There is such ado about it as troubles the place and all proceedings. Sir Walter Ralegh is employed to end this quarrel and make atonement between them. But the resolution of Lord Essex is not to yield but with altering the patent, which cannot be done by persuasion to bring the Earl of Nottingham to it.

THE QUEEN AND M. DE MAISSE.[12] The Queen gave audience to M. de Maisse to-day, and in their conference together she declared that she would do naught without her Council, for there is naught so dangerous in affairs of State as self-opinion; but no longer hath she such a Council as formerly, for she hath lost twenty or twenty-two of them. The Ambassador replied that she could always make others; but the Queen answered that they were young and not yet experienced in matters of State. The Queen spake also of the love of her people, saying that it is incredible, and she loveth them no less for it, and would die rather than lose any of it, to which the Ambassador answered that they are indeed happy to live under so good a Princess. The Queen said also that she was now come almost to the edge of her grave, and ought to bethink her of death; whereat suddenly she checked herself in her speech saying, 'I think not to die so soon, Master Ambassador; nor am I so old as they think.'

Nevertheless M. de Maisse complaineth that nothing is resolved, for the Queen cannot assemble the Council because of the discontents of my Lord of Essex who will not sit with the rest, and she will resolve nothing without him. Twice my Lord hath left the Court not to return again, but each time he has been sent for the same day and come back again. Since the ambassador's coming there has been nothing spoken of in Court but this brabble.

24th December.   THE PRICE OF PEPPER.[13] This Christmas-tide pepper is being sold in London at 8s. the pound, which is much noted because of the former restraint of the bringing in of pepper till all that captured in the Great Carrack, four years since, should be sold. Raisins this year are being sold at 6d. the pound, Gascon wines at 2s. 8d. the gallon, and sweet wines at 4s.

[13] STOW'S ANNALS; for the Great Carrack, see *12th Feb* and *22nd Dec* 1593.

Other Books Printed in 1597

i. A little book called *God's Arithmetic* by Mr. Francis Meres, Master of Arts of both Universities, and student of Divinity. 'There be four parts of Arithmetic,' saith he, 'Addition, Multiplication, Substraction and Division, whereof the first two take their beginning from the right hand, and do multiply and increase: and these be God's numbers. The other two begin from the left and do substract and divide, and these be the Devil's.' Treateth of the advantage of marriage, and especially of ministers of religion. Saith that in old time Jacob served seven years for Rachel and bought his wife by his service, but now men must be hired to take wives, as if to take a wife were to take up a cross, and hence it ofttimes comes to pass that marriage is not good because the end of it is for goods and not for love.

ii. A witty book by Mr. Nicholas Breton entitled *Wits' Trenchmour* in form of a pleasant conference between an angler and a scholar.

iii. The tragedy of *Romeo and Juliet,* written by William Shakespeare, that hath been often played publicly with great applause by the servants of the Lord Hunsdon.

i. STC 17833.
ii. STC 3713. The kind of book read by Beatrice and Benedick.

iii. STC 22322. This is the pirated First Quarto.

A Table of Ages

It may be an aid to the reader's imagination in visualising the Elizabethan age to note the ages of some of the more interesting men. The dates of birth are taken for the most part from the *Dictionary of National Biography;* dates marked with an asterisk are approximate.

1520 William Cecil, Lord Burleigh
1520* Thomas Churchyard
1525* John Stow
1527* Sir John Perrot
1530 Sir John Anderson, Lord Chief Justice
1530 John Whitgift, Archbishop of Canterbury
1532 William Cardinal Allen
1532 Sir John Hawkins
1533 QUEEN ELIZABETH
1535 Christopher Yelverton, Speaker
1536 Lord Charles Howard, Lord Admiral
1536 Thomas Sackville, Lord Buckhurst
1538* William Byrd
1540 Sir Thomas Egerton
1540 Sir Christopher Hatton
1540* Sir Francis Drake
1540* Hugh O'Neale, Earl of Tyrone
1540* Sir Roger Williams
1543* Thomas Deloney
1544 Richard Bancroft, Bishop of London
1545* Nicholas Breton
1545* Sir Thomas Bodley
1546 Father Robert Parsons
1547 George Carey, Lord Hunsdon
1547* Sir John Norris
1552 Sir Walter Ralegh
1552* Richard Hakluyt
1552 Sir Edward Coke
1552 Edmund Spenser

1554   Richard Hooker
1554*   John Lyly
1555   Lancelot Andrewes
1557   Sir Henry Unton
1557*   Thomas Lodge
1557*   George Peele
1558   George Clifford, Earl of Cumberland
1558   Robert Greene
1559*   George Chapman
1560   Sir Francis Vere
1561   Francis Bacon
1561   Lord Thomas Howard
1561   Sir John Harington
1561*   Father Robert Southwell
1562   Samuel Daniel
1563   Sir Robert Cecil
1563   Charles Blount, Lord Mountjoy
1564   Henry Percy, Earl of Northumberland
1564   Christopher Marlowe
1564   William Shakespeare
1565   Sir Anthony Shirley
1566   KING JAMES VI of Scotland
1566   Edward Alleyne
1567*   Robert Devereux, Earl of Essex
1567*   Thomas Nashe
1567*   Richard Burbage
1569*   Barnabe Barnes
1569   John Davies
1572*   Thomas Dekker
1573   Henry Wriothesley, Earl of Southampton
1573   John Donne
1573*   Ben Jonson
1574   Joseph Hall
1574   John Marston
1576   Roger Manners, Earl of Rutland
1577   Robert Burton
1579   John Fletcher
1582   John Webster
1584   Francis Beaumont
1591   Robert Herrick
1593   George Herbert
1594   Prince Henry of Scotland

ANCHOR BOOKS

DRAMA

ANCHOR BOOKS ON DRAMA

THE ANCHOR SEVENTEENTH-CENTURY SERIES

The Anchor Anthology of
Short Fiction of the Seventeenth Century

SELECTED AND EDITED BY CHARLES C. MISH   AC–1

The Complete English Poetry of John Milton

ARRANGED IN CHRONOLOGICAL ORDER WITH AN
INTRODUCTION, NOTES, AND VARIANTS BY JOHN T. SHAW-
CROSS   AC–2

The Complete Poetry of Robert Herrick

EDITED WITH AN INTRODUCTION AND NOTES
BY J. MAX PATRICK   AC–3

The Complete Poetry of Ben Jonson

EDITED WITH AN INTRODUCTION, NOTES, AND VARIANTS
BY WILLIAM B. HUNTER, JR.   AC–4

The Anchor Anthology of Jacobean Drama, VOLUME I

EDITED WITH AN INTRODUCTION, NOTES, AND VARIANTS
BY RICHARD C. HARRIER   AC–5a

The Anchor Anthology of Jacobean Drama, VOLUME II

EDITED WITH AN INTRODUCTION, NOTES, AND VARIANTS
BY RICHARD C. HARRIER   AC–5b

The Meditative Poem

EDITED BY LOUIS L. MARTZ   AC–6